D0406353

PRAISE FOR JAMES BOVARD'S

"feeling your pain"

"James Bovard is Washington's most hated truth-teller . . . His newest book—*feeling your pain*'—is another grand achievement."

—Steven Greenhut, *Orange County Register*

"A devastating indictment . . . *feeling your pain*' is even better than *Lost Rights*."

—Neal Boortz, *WSB Atlanta*

"I suspect *feeling your pain*' may well survive as the best political obituary of the Clinton era—earning Jim Bovard an honor he might just as soon have forgone as our modern Cassandra."

—Vin Suprynowicz, *Las Vegas Review Journal*

"Bovard is a prodigious researcher and clear writer . . . Ranging from the IRS, to HUD, from the Superfund to the Americans with Disabilities Act, from trade policy to drug enforcement, from Waco to Ruby Ridge, he delivers a compendium of examples of the way a powerful, arrogant, hyperactive government tramples the rights of ordinary citizens."

—*Baltimore Sun*

"James Bovard has carved out a niche, if not a swatch of destruction, by policing the presumptions of power and hypocrisies of government . . . The reader soon finds himself on an entertaining and engaging journey that highlights the cunning, incompetence, and dangers of unchecked government."

—Matthew Robinson, *Human Events*

"James Bovard has been America's muckraker par excellence during the last decade . . . Bovard has recorded every facet of government's corruption of freedom."

—Richard Ebeling, *Freedom Daily*

"The best book on the Clinton/Gore police state."

—Financial Privacy Report

"Invaluable . . . Jim Bovard is one of the few journalists in Washington (or elsewhere) to show much interest in government abuse of power beyond the occasional sexy scandal."

—Alan Bock, *World Net Daily*

"Encyclopedic . . . Bovard seemed determined to let nothing get by him . . . No anti Clintonian, no libertarian, should be without this book. In fact, we need such a book about every presidency."

—Lew Rockwell, *LewRockwell.com*

"Superb . . . If you buy and read only one book this year or the next, *'feeling your pain'* should be it."

—Tina Terry, *Sierra Times*

"*'feeling your pain'* is a magnificent reference work. Buy yourself an epiphany."
—Brian Wilson, *KSFO/San Francisco*

"Bovard is one of the best journalists out there . . . *'feeling your pain'* establishes what Clinton's legacy will be in the history books: the incredible explosion of government abuse and power. Everybody should read this."

—Kirby Wilbur, *KVI Seattle*

"I love the book because it doesn't just point out this one man is the root of the problem—the root of the problem is big government. It's a wonderful book—check it out."

—Jim Sharpe, *KFYI Phoenix*

"This is a fabulous book. You cannot arm yourself with better ammunition than *'feeling your pain.'*"

—Lucianne Goldberg, national radio talk show host

"This is an excellent book. The only reason this book does not have its binding ripped off is because it landed in a chair, not against the wall, when I threw it."
—Greg Garrison, *WIBC-AM Indianapolis*

"Bovard portrays the President's terms in office as a nightmarish progression of unconstitutional federal intrusion into the individual rights of citizens . . . He documents in exacting detail numerous examples of government gone mad. This controversial work gives the reader much to ponder."

—*Library Journal*

"Americans, Bovard says, must stop being subjects and become the self-reliant citizens the Founding Fathers envisioned. Replete with quotable lines . . ."

—*Kirkus Reviews*

"Bovard's aggressive antigoverment sentiments will not be universally accepted."
—*The Bookman*

"*'feeling your pain'* is brilliant. If any one book can help turn the tide against Clinton-style Big Government, this is it."

—Bill Winter, *LP News*

" . . . powerful . . . "

—*Insight Magazine*

"feeling your pain"

THE EXPLOSION
AND ABUSE OF
GOVERNMENT POWER
IN THE
CLINTON-GORE
YEARS

JAMES BOVARD

palgrave

for St. Martin's Griffin

"FEELING YOUR PAIN"
© James Bovard, 2000, 2001
All rights reserved. No part of this book may be used or reproduced in any manner whatsoever without written permission except in the case of brief quotations embodied in critical articles or reviews.

First published 2000 by
PALGRAVE™
175 Fifth Avenue, New York, N.Y.10010.
Companies and representatives throughout the world

PALGRAVE is the new global publishing imprint of St. Martin 's Press LLC Scholarly and Reference Division and Palgrave Publishers Ltd (formerly Macmillan Press Ltd).

ISBN 0-312-23082-6 hardback
ISBN 0-312-24052-X paperback

Library of Congress Cataloging-in-Publication Data
is available from the Library of Congress

Design by planettheo.com.

First paperback edition: October 2001
10 9 8 7 6 5 4 3 2 1

Printed in the United States of America.

CONTENTS

FOREWORD

CLINTON'S FINAL FRAUDS

"We have a new sense of optimism in America . . . America has come back under his regime," declared White House press spokesman Jake Siewert at the final White House briefing of Clinton's presidency on January 19, 2001. Siewert recognized his gaffe and quickly repeated himself, substituting the word "administration" for "regime." But actually, the word "regime" is far more accurate—as far as how Clinton and his flacks wish Americans to view Clinton's rule.[1]

A few days before the end of Clinton's presidency, the White House released a 110-page report, *Eight Years of Peace, Progress and Prosperity.*[2] Reading a Clinton White House document requires the same skepticism that statisticians used when analyzing Soviet economic data—always looking for the absurd baselines.

The *Eight Years* report contains many surprises, such as the assertion that "In 1992, home computers were rare."[3] Actually, home computers were about as rare in 1992 as white picket fences were in 1952. But claiming that computers were rare in 1992 allows Clinton to take credit for scores of millions of home computer purchases since then.

Readers will also be stunned to learn that "In 1992, the technology revolution was just about to hit."[4] Silicon Valley was a hotbed long before 1992—and the United States had led the world in computer production for years before Clinton took office. But the White House wanted to make Americans think that Clinton's inauguration somehow unleashed the modern age. The report asserts: "President Clinton and Vice President Gore have fostered the tremendous growth in technology in the past eight years and helped to ensure that the New Economy has flourished, turning around the stagnant economic growth of the 1980s."[5] The report was one last effort to make Americans view Clinton as the Sun King—he from whom all benefits flowed. The "New Economy" had hit the skids before Clinton left office; the NASDAQ stock index fell more than 50 percent in Clinton's last year in office.

Some of the assertions in the report look like the tripe a person expects to encounter in a Sociology 101 course. The report declares: "Through the 1980s,

America's sense of community and shared purpose began to disintegrate."[6] The report declares that, prior to 1993, there had been "no significant new investment in community service in a decade. Previous generations of Americans had answered the call to service of their country through programs such as the Civilian Conservation Corps, the Peace Corps and VISTA. However, it had been more than a decade since the federal government challenged the energy of Americans by putting significant resources behind a meaningful effort to expand community service opportunities."

At the time that Clinton took office, roughly 90 million Americans were volunteering their time each year to aid some charitable activity. But for Clinton, the only efforts that are "meaningful" are ones that are politically controlled and managed from the top down. Since politicians could not claim credit for the efforts Americans made to help their neighbors, townsfolk, and others, those efforts did not exist—at least by Washington's calculation.

The report continues the Clinton campaign to convince Americans they are undertaxed, asserting: "Federal income taxes as a percentage of income for the typical American family have dropped to their lowest level in 35 years."[7] Yet, federal taxes as a percent of the gross national product were higher in 2000 than at any time since World War II. Because Congress and Clinton effectively exempted tens of millions of people from paying federal taxes (extending a policy begun under Reagan), the "typical" family often pays no taxes and actually receives a federal handout from the IRS (the so-called Earned Income Tax Credit). And almost every "tax cut" that Clinton supported increased politicians' power over citizens by creating new levers to reward or punish specific behavior.

Some of Clinton's achievements are admirable only to people who believe citizens should be beasts of burden for their rulers. The report brags that the Clinton administration produced "the Largest [budget] Surplus Ever: The surplus in FY 2000 is $237 billion—the third consecutive surplus."[8] Why is it a good thing if government overcharges people by a few hundred billion dollars for the services which it deigns to render in any given year? Is there any reason to expect that politicians will honorably use the surplus? And if the president and Congress have the right to overtax Americans by $200+ billion, why shouldn't they have the right to run up a $500 billion "surplus"? Or a trillion dollar "surplus"? Or why not just let them lay claim to the entire output of all Americans so Washington can brag that the mega-surplus proves that government is serving people better than ever before?

Eight Years of Peace, Progress and Prosperity and Clinton's other victory lap festivities were quickly overshadowed by the controversy arising from Clinton's cavalcade of last-minute pardons. Among the people who qualified for a presidential pardon award were Marc Rich, two former cabinet members, his brother Roger, fellow tight-lipped Whitewater visionary Susan McDougal, and child sex offender and former congressman Mel Reynolds. Clinton also sparked controversy with a deluge of midnight regulations—the *Federal Register* on one of his last days amounted to almost a thousand pages of new regulations, rulings, etc. [9] (Some of the last-minute rules have been blocked by the Bush administration.)

$$\approx \quad \approx \quad \approx$$

In a farewell speech to the nation on January 18, 2001, Clinton declared: "I have sought to give America a new kind of government, smaller, more modern, more effective, full of ideas and policies appropriate to this new time, always putting people first, always focusing on the future."[10]

These specific benefits were often difficult to detect in many of the agencies under Clinton's jurisdiction. In the year since the galleys closed for the hardcover edition of *Feeling Your Pain*, numerous developments have occurred that highlight the problematic nature of public service in the Clinton era:

AMERICORPS. After I visited Mississippi to investigate AmeriCorps programs in the summer of 1999, I met with AmeriCorps Inspector General Luise Jordan and Assistant Inspector General Robert Shadowens to pass on some of my observations on the Mississippi Action for Community Education (MACE). The Inspector General launched an investigation of MACE. In federal district court in Greenville, Mississippi, on May 8, 2001, Ruby Buck, the chief executive office of MACE, was indicted on 16 counts of misappropriating AmeriCorps funds. While she denies the charges, sixteen AmeriCorps members (including the mayor of Metcalfe, Mississippi) allegedly received living stipends for work they did not perform.[11] If Buck is convicted on all charges, she could receive 17 years in prison and a quarter-million-dollar fine. The case is expected to go to trial later this year.

HUD. After Secretary Andrew Cuomo's perennial denunciations of Congress for failing to appropriate more money for his department, the department of Housing and Urban Development spent more than a quarter million dollars for the printing and distribution of two books glorifying his rule. A 104-page book, *Exposing Injustice: A Chronicle of HUD's Mission in the Forgotten America, 1997-2001,* included ten photos of Cuomo—including pictures showing him "on stage with Jesse L. Jackson and NAACP President Kweisi Mfume . . . with Israeli Prime Minister Ehud Barak and with South African President Thabo Mbeki," *Washington Post* columnist Al Kamen reported.[12] The glossy book presumably lifted the spirits of everyone living in squalid public housing projects across the land. Some cynics suspected that the book aimed to buttress Cuomo's campaign for the Democratic nomination for the New York gubernatorial race in 2002.

KOSOVO. President Clinton declared in his farewell address: "If the wars of the 20th century, especially the recent ones in Kosovo and Bosnia, have taught us anything, it is that we achieve our aims by defending our values and leading the forces of freedom and peace."[13] The U.S. support of the Kosovo Liberation Army greatly increased the KLA's military clout. After the war with Serbia ended, the KLA proceeded to invade Macedonia. As of this press time, another civil war in the Balkans is imminent. But NATO has already pledged its determination to provide as much help as possible to improve the situation.

RUBY RIDGE. The developments in the Ruby Ridge case over the past year further illustrate why this is a landmark case that will define how much deadly, arbitrary power federal agents shall possess over private citizens.

The cover-up of the killing of Vicki Weaver at Ruby Ridge, Idaho, in the last months of the Bush administration continued past the last days of the Clinton administration. After a federal judge in Idaho ruled that FBI sniper Lon Horiuchi could not be prosecuted for the killing of Vicki Weaver, prosecutors working for Boundary County, Idaho, took the case to the Ninth Circuit Federal Court of Appeals. On June 14, 2000, a 2 to 1 ruling by the appellate court sought to create a new license for federal agents to kill private citizens.

Federal judges Ferdinand Fernandez and William Shubb ruled that Horiuchi's actions were "objectively reasonable" and protected under the "Supremacy Clause" of the Constitution.[14] Judge Shubb wrote, "Horiuchi does not have to show that his action was in fact necessary or in retrospect justifiable, only that he reasonably thought it to be"; he stressed that the prosecution "has presented no evidence of evil or malicious intent" by Horiuchi.[15] Since prosecutors could not produce convincing evidence of what Horiuchi was thinking when he gunned down Vicki Weaver, federal judges must presume that he had no bad intent—and thus that neither he nor the federal government has any liability for the wrongful killing.

Federal judge Kozinski harshly dissented, declaring that, "Law enforcement officials may not kill suspects who do not pose an immediate threat to their safety or to the safety of others simply because they are armed."[16] Kozinski warned that the decision gives "officers a license to kill even when there is no immediate threat to human life, so long as the suspect is retreating to 'take up a defensive position.'" Kozinski declared that the decision created a new James Bond "007 standard for the use of deadly force" against American citizens. Kozinski warned that the new lax standard for lawmen's shootings "now applies to all law enforcement agencies in our circuit—federal, state and local."

Boundary County, Idaho, appealed the decision to the entire Ninth Circuit; the judges voted to re-hear the case en banc (with all the judges of the circuit in attendance). Preserving federal agents' license to kill was a top priority for the Clinton Administration; Seth Waxman, solicitor general of the United States, personally argued the case before the judges, appearing as a friend of the court on behalf of Horiuchi. Waxman sought to put the issue to rest by informing judges that "Federal law-enforcement officials are privileged to do what would otherwise be unlawful if done by a private citizen. It's a fundamental function of our government."[17] (Waxman's devotion to principle was rewarded when, shortly after leaving office, he was made an honorary agent of the Federal Bureau of Investigation.[18])

On June 5, 2001, by a vote of 6 to 5, the Ninth Circuit reversed the original appellate ruling and remanded the case back to federal district court for further proceedings. Kozinski, writing for the majority, declared: "A group of FBI agents formulated rules of engagement that permitted their colleagues to hide in the bushes and gun down men who posed no immediate threat. Such wartime rules are patently unconstitutional for a police action."[19] Kozinski ruled that "Horiuchi's criminal responsibility, if any, for killing Mrs. Weaver is a matter of state law, to be determined by a jury after a trial."[20]

The dissent, written by Judge Michael Daly Hawkins, proclaimed: "Every day in this country, federal agents place their lives in the line of fire to secure the liberties that we all hold dear. There will be times when those agents make mistakes, sudden judgment calls that turn out to be horribly wrong. We seriously delude ourselves if we think we serve the cause of liberty by throwing shackles on those agents and hauling them to the dock of a state criminal court when they make such mistakes, especially when the prosecuting state concedes they acted without malice. None of us on this court, thankfully, knows what it is like to be engaged in an altercation with armed and dangerous criminals. Special Agent Lon Horiuchi does, as do the thousands of other federal officers who daily risk their lives to protect ours."[21] The dissent invoked humanitarian concerns to justify dropping all charges: "The majority's insistence on sending this case back for still more proceedings frustrates the clear intent of the law that Horiuchi and other federal officers be free from the harassing threat of state criminal prosecution for honest mistakes of judgment they make when carrying out their federal duties."[22] The dissenting judges fretted more about federal agents being subjected to legal procedures than about private citizens being slain by federal bullets.

According to the five dissenting federal judges, the key to preserving liberty is to give federal agents life-and-death power over every citizen. Kozinski criticized the dissent: "An officer may not raise a Nuremberg Defense and claim that he shot a suspect who posed no threat because he believed his duty required him to follow orders."[23]

Former U.S. attorney general Ramsey Clark, who argued the case as an unpaid volunteer for Boundary County, Idaho, observed: "We won because a courageous court carefully considered a difficult case and stood up for the rule of law and the individual's right to freedom. You've got a right not to be shot for nothing, you know. And Mr. Horiuchi can have his day in court like anybody else."[24] Steven Yagman, a Los Angeles lawyer who also volunteered his time to serve as prosecutor for Boundary County, said after the verdict: "This is a significant victory for individual rights and for states against an often evil federal government. I think it's time the federal government put the FBI out of business and built from the ground up a competent federal law enforcement agency."[25] FBI Director Louis Freeh said "we are very disappointed . . . and will continue to support Agent Horiuchi and his family as this litigation continues."[26]

Kozinski's opinions on Ruby Ridge exemplified a principled approach to law enforcement—one that recognizes that blind deference to government badges is the route to tyranny. Unfortunately, Boundary County, Idaho, prosecutor Brett Benson wasted no time after the federal appellate decision to request a federal judge in Idaho to dismiss the manslaughter charge against Horiuchi. (Benson was elected as county prosecutor in 2000, defeating incumbent prosecutor Denise Woodbury, who had courageously stood up to the federal government in earlier Horiuchi proceedings. Federal judges cannot force state officials to prosecute a wayward federal agent. Justice Department rulings in 1994 and 1997 guaranteed that Horiuchi had nothing to fear from federal prosecutors.) Benson issued a Clintonesque explanation of his decision: "The Ruby Ridge incident was a tragedy that deeply affected and divided many citizens of this county and country. It is our hope that this decision will begin the healing process that is so long overdue and so much deserved."[27] Apparently, justice is not part of the healing process.

WACO. The continuing investigations and cover-up of federal action at Waco, Texas, in 1993 provides perhaps the starkest statement of how the Washington establishment perceives the rights of government and the duties of citizens. And the conclusion of the last Waco investigation of the Clinton administration also provides perhaps the best epithet for Clinton's presidency.

In late 1999, Janet Reno hand-picked former U.S. Senator John Danforth to conduct another investigation of federal action at Waco. In late July, 2000, after word spread that Danforth was a finalist for the Bush campaign's vice-presidential slot, he rushed out his report even though his investigation was not finished. Danforth, aided by a crack team of 20 postal inspectors and other federal officials, spent $17 million and ten months investigating Waco. On releasing his report, Danforth—known in Senate days as Saint Jack—summarized his findings: "I think when people are intent on burning themselves up, there's not much you can do about it."[28]

The powers that be immediately hailed Danforth's report as the final word on Waco. "Seven years of absorbing unproven allegations and unfounded criticisms has levied a heavy burden on the agents who were at Waco and their families as well," FBI Director Louis Freeh declared.[29] "This report brings great solace to them in that its findings reaffirm that which we have always believed—they did their best and for all the right reasons." PBS NewsHour host Jim Lehrer congratulated Danforth on national television: "You did tremendous investigating."[30]

But even by the standard of recent Washington whitewashes, the report was a disgrace. Danforth performed contortions to justify dismissing stark bureaucratic guilty pleas. Danforth's was perhaps the first investigation into a cover-up that justified the cover-up. Danforth masterfully dredged up any possible exculpatory material for the feds and ignored key issues on which the government has no defense.

Danforth repeatedly minimized or absurdly misrepresented the amount of force the feds used against the Davidians. Confidential FBI documents made public in 1999 reveal that during the 51-day siege, FBI agents repeatedly threw flash-bang grenades at Davidians who tried to leave the residence. When Sen. Charles Grassley asked Danforth about this at a post-report hearing (attended by only three senators), Danforth replied that flash-bangs are "in the nature, as I understand it, of, you know, firecrackers. They make a flash and they make a bang. And they don't cause injury, as a general rule . . ."[31]

In Vancouver, Washington, two years ago a flash-bang blew the hand off of a 13-year-old girl, and two apartment residents in Minneapolis were killed by a flash-bang in 1989.[32] Flash-bangs also have a history of starting fires. A flash-bang started an apartment fire in Minneapolis in March 2000 and set a house on fire in Allentown, Pennsylvania, in 1997.[33] According to Mike McNulty, one of the masterminds of the 1998 Academy Award–nominated documentary

Waco: Rules of Engagement, six flash-bang devices were found in the rubble after the fire—including three found at or near the locations where the fire started.[34]

The FBI's 1999 reversal and admission that it used pyrotechnic devices to inject tear gas on the final day was the key factor in reviving the Waco controversy. Yet Danforth told the Senate that "the use of the pyrotechnics, itself, under these circumstances was not a big thing." Danforth also assured the senators: "I don't think that there's been anybody that I know of connected with the government who has ever believed that the use of pyrotechnics, in this case, had anything to do with the fire."[35]

Nowhere did Danforth distort reality more than in discussing whether the FBI intentionally destroyed much of the Davidians' home while the women and children were still inside, possibly incapacitated by potentially lethal CS gas. After the FBI had gassed the Davidians for more than four hours and exhausted almost its entire gas supply, FBI tank drivers were ordered to demolish the building. In the next hour, tanks smashed into the residence eight times and collapsed at least one-quarter of the Davidians' home. Yet Danforth laments in the report's preface: "Sensational films construct dark theories out of little evidence and gain ready audiences for their message."[36] Later in the report, Danforth asserts: "The FLIR [Forward Looking Infrared] video does not show a 'deliberate and surgical . . . dismantling of the gymnasium,' and the agents in (the tank) were fully credible in stating that they were not given the mission to dismantle the gymnasium."[37] It's unlikely that anyone not on the federal payroll would reach that conclusion from watching the tape.

Danforth insisted that the tanks just wanted "to make a path to the base of the tower," to make it easier to gas the Davidians. The report later claims that the tanks were also trying to create "exit routes" to allow the Davidians to leave their residence peacefully.[38] But as noted by former federal attorney David Hardy, author of a new book, *"This is Not An Assault,"* the Davidians' residence had roughly "seven doors, 69 windows, and an underground tunnel."[39] Was the FBI assuming that, instead of jumping out of a window, people gasping from tear gas would prefer to claw through jagged rubble and debris—and perhaps be crushed by a tank's next intrusion?

Danforth had been instructed to determine the following: "Did any employee of the United States make or allow others to make false or misleading statements, or withhold evidence or information from any individual or entity entitled to receive it, or destroy, alter, or suppress evidence or information relative to the events occurring at the Branch Davidian complex on April 19, 1993?" Danforth found that plenty of federal employees either withheld information or made false statements—but only with the best of intentions. A

St. Louis Post-Dispatch headline perfectly summarized his report: "Officials Had Nothing to Hide—But Hid Some Things Anyway."[40]

The Danforth report examined why information about the FBI's use of pyrotechnic devices—which, according to *Newsweek,* was known by "as many as 100 FBI agents and officials"—hadn't been disclosed in previous investigations. Danforth finds the culprit: An FBI lawyer had it on her "to do" list in 1996 to inform higher-ups about the pyrotechnics but, for some reason or other, never got around to it. As Danforth explained to the Senate: "What happened in this case was that this fairly young lawyer simply goofed, simply failed to do an adequate job . . . The fact that she blundered in not turning over the information was a little thing; it was a human thing."[41] Danforth vehemently opposed prosecuting the FBI lawyer for her alleged obstruction of justice.

In the report's preface, while calling the actions "reprehensible," Danforth goes to great lengths to defend dissembling federal officials: "In today's world, it is perhaps understandable that government officials are reluctant to make full disclosures of information for fear that the result of candor will be personal or professional ruin. Any misstep yields howls of indignation, calls for resignations, and still more investigations. Several Department of Justice personnel told Office of Special Counsel investigators that they viewed the 1995 Congressional hearings as a partisan effort to attack Attorney General Reno. An FBI official complained about the 'us against them' atmosphere."[42] In his comments on the 1995 hearings, Danforth says nothing about the Clinton administration's orchestrated efforts to smear congressional critics as enemies of law enforcement and dangers to the republic. Nor does Danforth ever criticize the FBI or the Justice Department for ignoring subpoenas and withholding vital evidence from those hearings.

While Danforth purportedly received marching orders from Janet Reno to discover the truth, he devoted more energy and enthusiasm to understanding "How can it happen that when there is really no evidence that government agents did these terrible things, how can it happen that people would come to believe that? How or why is it that we as a people are so ready to believe such dark things?"[43] Danforth bewailed, "Ample forums exist to nurture our need to place blame on government."[44] To talk about "our need to place blame" makes it sound like he is diagnosing a mental illness. And naturally, his cure consists of little more than increased public credulity.

Readers of Danforth's report are left with the revelation that all the federal agents had the best of intentions—including those who lied to get military aid, those who led an unnecessary military-style no-knock assault on the Davidians' home, those who gassed the children, those who accidentally crushed much of the building after many Davidians most likely had been semi-paralyzed from the gassing, and those who subsequently lied and obstructed justice.

With hate crimes, federal prosecutors claim that an act deserves a far harsher sentence because the government somehow knows that the perpetrator had evil motives toward the victims. But, as the Danforth report made clear, when the government abuses people, there can be no crime because public servants by definition could never wish to abuse the public.

Danforth proclaimed: "All of us should be more skeptical of those who make sensational accusations of evil acts by government."[45] According to Danforth, not only are citizens obliged to trust the government—but regardless of how often government changes its story, citizens must heartily accept the latest version as the Absolute Truth—at least until government changes the story again.

Danforth concluded the preface to his report by declaring his hope that his investigation will "begin the process of restoring the faith of the people in their government and the faith of the government in the people." This last phrase is more revealing than anything else in the entire report. From Danforth's view, federal officials have been wrongfully victimized by the distrust of the American people. From Danforth's view, federal officials have been wrongfully victimized by the distrust of the American people. Few statements more starkly exemplify the Clinton administration's attitude toward the abuse of power.

At the time that Danforth issued his reports, some cynics questioned his objectivity. Danforth resolved that question with a personal note he sent to Janet Reno in early 2001: "I've heard you talk about the decision you made in Waco. I have had the chance as your special counsel to review that decision. I did not pass judgement on it in my report but I want you to know that I think you did exactly the right thing."[46]

Perhaps Danforth gives Reno credit for the fact that, despite the final assault Reno authorized on April 19, 1993, most of the children in the state of Texas did not die that day. Danforth apparently considers it no blemish that Reno initially justified the final assault because of ongoing child abuse. After that charge collapsed, Reno in October 1993 shrugged off her error: "I now understand that nobody in the [FBI] told me that it was ongoing. We were briefed, and I misunderstood."[47] It was a harmless error, except for the kids who were gassed or burned to death after Reno misunderstood.

In May 2001, speculation arose that Danforth was seeking to curry prominence and favor in order to snare a nomination to the Supreme Court. Danforth got a big splash in the *Washington Post* on June 1, 2001, when he declared that some FBI officials initially sought to stonewall his Special Counsel investigation on Waco. Danforth stated his belief that the FBI may not have turned over all the evidence to his investigators. But he reassured the *Post* that, regardless of whatever evidence the FBI withheld, "there is no chance that it would have any effect on our findings."[48]

It is unusual for a prosecutor to absolve his target after publicly admitting that he may have failed to gather all the necessary information. Danforth's latest comments highlight how he continues to view Waco primarily as an opportunity to offer personal absolution to the federal government and high-ranking government officials.

At the time of Danforth's interview with the *Post*, his credibility was taking a drubbing. A key issue for Danforth's investigation was whether FBI agents fired on Davidians during their final attack. Rhythmic patterns on FLIR tapes made by an FBI plane strongly suggested automatic weapons fire came from positions near the FBI tanks. Danforth persuaded federal Judge Walter Smith to conduct a reenactment last year of the final day's action. Danforth then proclaimed that the film from the reenactment proved beyond a doubt that federal agents did not shoot at Davidians—in large part because the muzzle flashes on the reenactment were much shorter than the shots from the April 19, 1993, tape.

A 2001 film, *The F.L.I.R. Project*, produced by Mike McNulty, revealed fatal flaws in Danforth's reenactment.[49] On April 19, 1993, FBI agents relied on a commercial, off-the-shelf ammo—the type that would be used by any hunter or shooter. For the March 19, 2000, Danforth-FBI reenactment, the FBI used military-issue ammunition that had a special chemical coating on the gunpowder to reduce muzzle flash (helpful in preventing soldiers from being detected in combat). The military ammo thus had a built-in flash suppressant.

The Danforth-FBI reenactment further biased the test results by having the FBI agents use weapons with a 20-inch barrel—instead of weapons with 14-inch barrels that agents carried on April 19, 1993. The longer a weapon's barrel, the less muzzle flash will be shown from each shot.[50]

This is a tricky way to do an accurate reenactment. But the reenactment produced the politically correct result and Danforth proceeded to denounce the American people for thinking bad things about their federal masters. Democratic pollster and strategist Stuart Rothenberg predicted on July 9, 2001, that if Vice President Dick Cheney is forced to resign for health reasons, Danforth is the most likely choice for a replacement.[51]

If President Bush and Attorney General John Ashcroft want to restore the faith of the American people in the federal government, they must open the vaults on Waco. Neither Bush nor Ashcroft should have any incentive to cover-up the abuses of Reno and other Clinton administration officials. On the other hand, if Bush and Ashcroft do not have the will or gumption to force the FBI, the ATF, and the Justice Department to come clean about Clinton-era abuses, what hope can we have of their honesty regarding any abuses occurring after January 20, 2001?

વ   વ   વ

It remains to be seen how much lasting damage the Clinton administration did to American political culture, constitutional traditions, and liberty. Much of the long-term impact of Clinton's policies depends on whether his successors exploit or scorn the precedents he set for untrammeled government power. President George W. Bush is, at a minimum, often hitting different rhetorical themes from Clinton. In a July 4, 2001, speech in Philadelphia, Bush declared that, 225 years earlier, thanks to the Declaration of Independence, "A wonderful country was born, and a revolutionary idea sent forth to all mankind: Freedom, not by the good graces of government but as the birthright of every individual . . ."[52]

But how much elbow grease will Bush devote to curbing federal policies that destroy Americans' birthright of freedom? Bush, like many other Republicans, at least claims to recognize the danger of excessive regulation. Will he exert himself to end the bombardment of new regulatory edicts? Will he and his appointees rein in and fire wayward enforcement agents—or continue the same cover-ups and blanket immunity for bureaucratic hooligans that disgraced the previous administration? How many federal agencies and programs will he seek to abolish? Or will he do little more than perpetuate and sanctify Leviathan? How will Bush mesh his belief in freedom with his passion to escalate the war on drugs? His father hailed DEA agents in 1992 as "the greatest freedom fighters any nation could have, people who provide freedom from violence and freedom from drugs and freedom from fear."[53] Will his son's vision of freedom prove to be another bonanza for the prison-building industry? Will George W. Bush have the wisdom and self-control to recognize, as George Washington did, that his own power is a grave threat to Americans' birthright of freedom?

NOTES

1. "White House Regular Briefing; Jake Siewert, White House Spokesman," *Federal News Service*, January 19, 2001.
2. Document at http://clinton6.nara.gov/2001/01/2001-01-09-fact-sheet-on-eight-years-of-peace-progress-and-prosperity.html
3. Ibid.
4. Ibid.
5. Ibid.
6. Ibid.
7. Ibid.
8. Ibid.
9. Cindy Skrzycki, "'Midnight Regulations' Swell Register," *Washington Post*, January 23, 2001.
10. "President Clinton's Farewell Address," *Federal News Service*, January 18, 2001.
11. Ronald Adderton, "MACE Official Charged," *Delta Democrat Times*, May 9, 2001.
12. Al Kamen, "Cuomo's HUD Tenure One for the Books," *Washington Post*, February 5, 2001.
13. "President Clinton's Farewell Address," *Federal News Service*, January 18, 2001.
14. *Idaho v. Horiuchi*, No. 98-30149, 215 F.3d 986 (June 14, 2000).
15. Ibid.
16. Ibid.
17. David Kravets, "Appeals Panel Unsure Whether Idaho Can Charge FBI Sharpshooter," *Associated Press*, December 20, 2000.
18. John McCaslin, "Inside the Beltway," *Washington Times*, July 9, 2001.
19. *Idaho v. Horiuchi*, No. 98-30149, 2001 U.S. App. LEXIS 11743, June 5, 2001.
20. Ibid.
21. Ibid.
22. Ibid.
23. Ibid.
24. Betsy Z. Russell and Susan Drumheller, "Idaho can prosecute FBI sniper," *Spokesman-Review* (Spokane, Wa.), June 6, 2001.
25. "Sharpshooter Faces Trial," *The Recorder* (California), June 6, 2001.
26. George Lardner, "Ruby Ridge Charge Is Reinstated On Appeal," *Washington Post*, June 6, 2001.
27. Thomas Clouse and Susan Drumheller, "No Last Shot at Ruby Ridge; Benson Drops Charges against FBI Sniper," *Spokesman-Review* (Spokane, WA), June 15, 2001.
28. "Hearing of the Administrative Oversight and Court Subcommittee of the Senate Judiciary Committee; Subject: Interim Report on the Waco Incident," *Federal News Service*, July 26, 2000.
29. "Statement of FBI Director Louis J. Freeh Regarding the Recent Waco Findings by Special Counsel/Senator John Danforth," FBI National Press Office, July 21, 2000.
30. Transcript #6815, The NewsHour with Jim Lehrer, Public Broadcasting Service, July 21, 2000.
31. "Hearing of the Administrative Oversight and Court Subcommittee of the Senate Judiciary Committee; Subject: Interim Report on the Waco Incident," *Federal News Service*, July 26, 2000.
32. James Bovard, "The Latest, Greatest Waco Whitewash," *American Spectator*, October 2000.
33. Ibid.

34. Author interview with Mike McNulty, August 5, 2000.
35. "Hearing of the Administrative Oversight and Court Subcommittee of the Senate Judiciary Committee; Subject: Interim Report on the Waco Incident," Federal News Service, July 26, 2000.
36. "Interim Report to the Deputy Attorney General Concerning the 1993 Confrontation at the Mt. Carmel Complex, Waco, Texas," July 21, 2000. Available at http://www.netar-rant.com/specials/00wacoreport/waco report.htm.
37. Ibid.
38. Ibid.
39. Author interview with David Hardy, August 14, 2000.
40. William Freivogel and Terry Ganey, "Waco Secrecy Fed Public Mistrust, Danforth Says; Officials Had Nothing to Hide—But Hid Some Things Anyway," St. Louis Post-Dispatch, July 23, 2000.
41. "Hearing of the Administrative Oversight and Court Subcommittee of the Senate Judiciary Committee; Subject: Interim Report on the Waco Incident," Federal News Service, July 26, 2000.
42. "Interim Report to the Deputy Attorney General Concerning the 1993 Confrontation at the Mt. Carmel Complex, Waco, Texas," July 21, 2000. Available at http://www.netar-rant.com/specials/00wacoreport/waco report.htm.
43. From Danforth's PBS interview with Jim Lehrer, available at http://www.pbs.org/newshour/bb/fedagencies/july-dec00/danforth_7-21.html.
44. "Interim Report to the Deputy Attorney General Concerning the 1993 Confrontation at the Mt. Carmel Complex, Waco, Texas," July 21, 2000. Available at http://www.netar-rant.com/specials/00wacoreport/waco report.htm.
45. "Special Counsel John C. Danforth Issues Interim Report on Waco Investigation," PR Newswire, July 21, 2000.
46. Transcript # 052000CN.V47, CNN Late Edition with Wolf Blitzer, Cable News Network, May 20, 2001.
47. Michael Isikoff, "FBI Clashed Over Waco, Report Says; Attack on Davidians Draws No Criticism," Washington Post, October 9, 1993.
48. Dan Eggen, "FBI Termed Uncooperative in Waco Probe," Washington Post, June 1, 2001.
49. For further information on the film, see www.flirproject.com.
50. Matt Kelley, "Official Questions FBI Simulation," Associated Press, June 1, 2001
51. "Bush's VP Options If Cheney Bows Out Examined," Bulletin's Frontrunner, July 9, 2001.
52. "Remarks at an Independence Day Celebration in Philadelphia, Pennsylvania," Public Papers of the President, July 4, 2001.
53. "Remarks by President Bush at the Dedication of the DEA New York Headquarters," Federal News Service, June 29, 1992.

"feeling your pain"

ONE

INTRODUCTION

THE VICTORY OF WILLIAM JEFFERSON CLINTON in the 1992 presidential election was supposed to launch a new era in American politics. The Clinton-Gore team promised a "New Covenant" between government and the people that would propel government beyond its past failings. Clinton sought to make government strong enough to hoist and harangue the citizenry to higher ground, once and for all. And there was little to fear from expanding government power because, as Clinton promised, his would be "the most ethical administration in history."[1]

Yet, after nearly eight years of his rule, America is bedeviled by independent counsels crowding Washington streets, cynicism as far as the eye can see, and more hostility to government agencies across the board, from the Census Bureau to the National Highway Traffic Safety Administration. The attempt to forcibly lift people left government in the gutter—at least in the minds of tens of millions of Americans.

From concocting new prerogatives to confiscate private property, to championing FBI agents' right to shoot innocent Americans, to bankrolling the militarization of local police forces, the Clinton administration stretched the power of government on all fronts. From the soaring number of wiretaps, to converting cell phones into homing devices for law enforcement, to turning bankers into spies against their customers, free speech and privacy were undermined again and again. From dictating how many pairs of Chinese silk panties Americans could buy, to President Clinton's heroic efforts to require trigger locks for all handguns in crack houses, no aspect of Americans' lives was too arcane for federal intervention.

The Clinton administration built its "bridge to the twenty-first century" by filling every sinkhole along the way with taxpayer dollars. From AmeriCorps projects that beat the bushes to recruit new food stamp recipients, to a flood insurance program that multiplied flood damage, to programs to give the keys to lavish new single-family homes to public housing residents, the Clinton administration's record domestic spending produced record fiascoes. For Clinton, the only wasted tax dollar was one that did not buy a vote, garner a campaign contribution, or provide a chance to bite his lip on national television.

In the same way that the success of NATO's attack on Serbia was measured largely by continual proclamations of "record numbers" of sorties flown and "record numbers" of bombs dropped, so the Clinton administration gauged its domestic policy successes by the number of new laws passed, new programs enacted, and new activities prohibited—by record fines levied and record prison sentences imposed. Federal agencies issued more than 25,000 new regulations—criminalizing everything from reliable toilets to snuff advertisements on race cars.

While the media focused primarily on the new benefits that Clinton promised, little attention was paid to the swelling tax burden on working Americans. Federal income tax revenue doubled between 1992 and 2000.[2] The total tax burden on the average family with two earners rose three times faster than inflation.[3] Though the IRS wrongfully seized hundreds of thousands of Americans' paychecks and bank accounts during Clinton's reign, almost all of the agency's power survived unscathed.[4]

Faith in the coercive power of the best and brightest permeated Clinton administration policymaking. More commands, more penalties, and more handouts were the recipe for progress. The Clinton administration consistently acted as if nothing is as dangerous as insufficient government power.

The history of the Clinton administration cannot be understood apart from the president's personal view of government. Clinton portrayed government as the Lone Ranger—or, more accurately, millions of Lone Rangers, each with a sacred mission to rescue people whether they want to be rescued or not. For Clinton, government was never merely a bunch of clerks in some drab office vegetating toward a pension. Instead, government was "a champion of national purpose,"[5] "the instrument of our national community,"[6] and "a progressive instrument of the common good."[7] Clinton urged Americans in 1998 to commit themselves "to a new kind of government . . . to give all our people the tools to make the most of their own lives."[8] Clinton's invocation of "government as toolmeister" ignored the abysmal record of federal job training, literacy, and other programs purportedly created to help people help themselves.

Many of Clinton's policies can be explained only by his belief in his own moral superiority. For Clinton, the officially proclaimed intent of a specific government policy or action far transcended whatever force government agents use against citizens. And any protests about excessive force were met by appeals to "the rule of law"—regardless of whether the law was on the side of federal agents. The more people government brings to its knees, the fairer society becomes—simply because government power is the personification of fairness.

And the loftier the goal Clinton proclaimed, the more irrelevant private collateral damage became. One visionary foreign policy speech was more important than a thousand cluster bombs dropped on foreign civilians. Vigorous denunciations of international terrorism were more important than the cruise missiles that destroyed Sudan's only pharmaceutical factory. Continual invocations of "the children" at every political whistle-stop mattered more than the deaths of dozens of children after an FBI gas attack at Waco.

The Clinton recipe for public safety was: if politicians frighten enough of the people enough of the time, then everyone will be safe. Because Clinton felt government must constantly intervene in people's lives, people had to be convinced that they are doomed unless politicians save them on a daily basis. The result: constant efforts to alarm the citizenry on everything from health care to speed limits, to secondhand smoke, to global warming, to garbage dumps, to radon, to guns.

Clinton owes much of his popularity to his "stealth statism." Clinton was the master of intellectual shell games. In his 1996 State of the Union address, he announced "the era of Big Government is over."[9] Yet, once he had won reelection by campaigning as a moderate (or, in the words of presidential adviser Dick Morris, "campaigning as Pope"),[10] he opened the floodgates. In his 1997 State of the Union address, Clinton called for a "national crusade for education standards" and federal standards and national credentials for all new teachers; announced plans "to build a citizen army of one million volunteer tutors to make sure every child can read independently by the end of the third grade"; called for $5 billion in federal aid to build and repair local schools, a new scholarship program to subsidize anyone going to college, a $10,000 tax deduction for all tuition payments after high school, and federal subsidies for private health insurance; demanded a new law entitling women who have had mastectomies to stay in the hospital 48 hours afterwards; advocated a constitutional amendment for "victims' rights"; urged Congress to enact a law criminalizing any parent who crossed a state line allegedly to avoid paying child support; and proposed enacting juvenile crime legislation that "declares war on gangs," hiring new prosecutors, and increasing federal spending on the war on drugs. Clinton also announced plans to expand NATO and declare "10 American Heritage Rivers" (thereby effectively prohibiting thousands of landowners from using their property along those rivers). Clinton, deeply concerned about American ethics, also demanded that "character education must be taught in our schools." (This demand was not repeated in later State of the Union addresses.)

In his 1999 State of the Union address, Clinton proposed more than 40 new laws and programs. Citizens applauded proposals for more government regardless of how poorly existing government programs functioned and despite the fact that most Americans personally distrusted Clinton at the time he sought more power over them. In his 2000 State of the Union address, Clinton talked for almost an hour and a half and, according to one estimate, proposed the equivalent of $4 billion of new federal spending per minute.[11]

This book focuses primarily on the Clinton administration's domestic policies and programs. A chapter on the war against Serbia is included because that adventure vividly illustrates the Clinton administration's moralism and arrogance. The Clinton presidency must not be judged solely on whether the Senate convicted him on impeachment charges, or whether he and his wife were shown to have obstructed justice during the Whitewater investigation, or whether a federal judge fined him for perjury, or whether a clear link is discovered between Chinese military front companies and Clinton's 1996 reelection campaign. The danger of focusing narrowly on the best-known scandals is that people may forget or fail to realize how much misgovernment occurred during the 1990s. Far more Americans have been affected by IRS depredations, HUD-ruined neighborhoods, and FDA-denied drugs than by Clinton's personal misbehavior. Many of the worst abuses of the Clinton administration never appeared on the media's radar screen. Instead, they were buried in Inspector General reports, General Accounting Office studies, or the proceedings of court cases followed by few.

The Clinton administration changed the political fabric of this nation and the political expectations of the American people and the American media. Clinton's policies and rhetoric helped infantilize the American populace. The entire political system was subtely transformed year by year, crisis by crisis, hoax by hoax.

Clinton's administration was far from unique in its contempt for constitu-tional or taxpayer rights. Most of the pernicious trends in federal policy started long before Clinton's arrival in Washington. President Franklin Roosevelt was as voracious for power as was Clinton. Lyndon Johnson was more successful in passing sweeping laws to swell the federal government. The Bush administration was as feckless in its resolution to terminate failed government programs—and even President Ronald Reagan was far more tolerant of wasteful government spending than many of his fans recall.

The fact that the Clinton administration championed so many flawed programs and policies does not mean that good government would have resulted if the Republican Party held the White House. The Republicans controlled both houses of Congress for six of the eight years of Clinton's administration. Most congressmen of both parties showed little understanding of, or curiosity about, how federal programs were functioning.

This is not an attempt to pass final judgment on the Clinton administration. Such an effort must await the unraveling of numerous cover-ups and the surfacing of further flaws in new programs and policies. Instead, it is an effort to present many details and key issues that must be part of a broad assessment of the impact of the Clinton administration on America.

Once a president leaves office, his record usually quickly blurs. All that is recalled are a few high points, a few catch phrases, and a few indictments. The rest is swept under the rug of failing memories and the spin-doctoring of supporters and detractors. Americans cannot understand the nation's political course without recognizing the follies and fiascoes of the recent past, the constant expansion of government programs and power, and the resulting momentum for ever more coercion.

TWO

AMERICORPS: SALVATION THROUGH HANDHOLDING

PRESIDENT CLINTON, in an August 9, 1999, speech to AmeriCorps members, declared, "AmeriCorps is living, daily, practical, flesh-and-blood proof that there's a better way to live . . . that if we . . . hold hands and believe we're going into the future together, we can change anything we want to change. You are the modern manifestation of the dream of America's founders."[1]

In reality, AmeriCorps looks more like a federal relief program for nightclub comics:

- In Buffalo, New York, AmeriCorps members helped run a program that gave children $5 for each toy gun they brought in—as well as a certificate praising their decision not to play with toy guns.[2]
- In Lone Pine, California, AmeriCorps members put on a puppet show to warn four-year-olds of the dangers of earthquakes.[3]
- In Fort Collins, Colorado, AmeriCorps recruits poured out large piles of mud from which they sculpted imitations of ovens once used by Indians. AmeriCorps offered the mud monuments as its gift to local residents.[4]
- In San Diego, AmeriCorps recruits carried out an "Undergarment Drive" to collect used bras, panties, and pantyhose for a local women's center.[5]

- In Los Angeles, AmeriCorps recruits busied themselves sewing a quilt to send to victims of the Oklahoma City bombing—but never bothered to finish the project.[6]

AmeriCorps was supposed to provide an army of inspired labor to help re-energize the nonprofit sector of American life. AmeriCorps, created in 1993, may be President Clinton's proudest achievement. Clinton said in 1994 that AmeriCorps "may have the most lasting legacy of anything I am able to do as your President, because it has the chance to embody all the things I ran for President to do."[7] Later that year, Clinton declared: "AmeriCorps is the most important commitment your President ever tried to make to the American people, to give us a chance to come together, to move forward together."[8] In his 1995 State of the Union address, Clinton saluted AmeriCorps as "citizenship at its best" and called the program "the essence of the New Covenant."[9] In February 1999, at an AmeriCorps recruiting rally held during Clinton's Senate impeachment trial, Clinton declared: "America needs to think of itself as sort of a giant AmeriCorps, getting things done together . . . We cannot do good around the world unless we are good at home."[10] Clinton appealed for support for the expansion of AmeriCorps "to use this moment to prove that this generation of young people, far from being a generation of cynics and slackers, is instead a generation of doers and patriots." Clinton was greeted outside the University of Maryland speech site by a demonstrator holding a sign calling for "Jail to the Chief"—but inside he was a conquering hero and moral visionary.

AmeriCorps recruits almost anyone age 17 and older. Full-time members are supposed to put in 1,700 hours of "service" and receive a stipend of up to $8,750 (sometimes paid as a straight wage), health insurance, emergency dental care, free child care for their offspring, and an education award worth up to $4,750 for tuition or paying off college loans. Many AmeriCorps recruits are on the dole, and the money they collect from AmeriCorps (unlike money from a private job) does not affect how much they receive in food stamps or housing subsidies. AmeriCorps press spokeswoman Anne Bushman called AmeriCorps members "heroes"—in large part because they supposedly labored for sub-minimum wages.[11] Actually, many AmeriCorps recruits are unskilled, and their pay and benefit package is more than they could earn in the private sector. The average recruit costs AmeriCorps and AmeriCorps sponsors more than $23,000—the equivalent of almost $12 an hour.[12]

AmeriCorps started with 20,000 recruits a year in 1994 and had 50,000 on the payroll by 1999 (many of whom worked only half or quarter time). Almost half of AmeriCorps recruits quit the program before completing their term of service.[13] Clinton, in his final budget proposal in early 2000, proposed to boost AmeriCorps to 100,000 members by the year 2004 and to increase its budget from $433 million to $533 million.

SELF-RELIANCE, AMERICORPS-STYLE

According to AmeriCorps chief (and former U.S. Senator) Harris Wofford, "National service reduces our reliance on Government by mobilizing citizen action."[14] But AmeriCorps members routinely do little more than beat the bushes to boost the number of Americans on the dole:

- In Charleston, South Carolina, AmeriCorps members went door-to-door seeking to entice small businesses to apply for government-subsidized loans.[15]
- In Chicago, AmeriCorps members devoted themselves to creating a directory of welfare programs available for female Job Corps members, specifying addresses, contact numbers, and other pertinent information to help trainees get food stamps, subsidized day care, public housing, et cetera.[16]
- In New Jersey, AmeriCorps members are busy recruiting middle-class families to accept subsidized federal health insurance for their children under Clinton's new "Kiddie Care" program.[17]
- AmeriCorps is bankrolling the Welfare Rights Organizing Coalition in Washington state. According to the Coalition's director, Jean Colman, "People are poor because they don't have enough money. We don't seem to trust poor people enough to spend their money wisely, so we don't give them enough."[18]

The Mississippi Action for Community Education (MACE) program, which has been on the AmeriCorps gravy train since 1994, promised in its 1999 grant application that its AmeriCorps members would "conduct door-to-door canvassing to identify potential food stamp recipients"[19] and would also provide "assistance . . . in completing necessary applications for food stamps." The goal of the program was to enroll "75 percent of surveyed rural Mississippi residents who are eligible for food stamps, but are not receiving them." However, many people refuse to accept food stamps because of pride. Furthermore, some studies have shown that food stamps have little or no impact on the quality of a recipient's diet. (According to a study published in late 1999 in the *American*

Journal of Agricultural Economics, the primary effect of food stamp participation is increased consumption of meat, sugar, and fat—hardly a blessing considering the epidemic obesity and rising diabetes levels among low-income Americans.)[20]

MACE headquarters is in Greenville, Mississippi, the heart of the Mississippi Delta—one of the poorest regions in America. When I arrived there, I was surprised to discover that it was one of the fanciest-looking buildings in Greenville—the plush leather chairs in the waiting room were a stark contrast to the shabbiness of the neighborhood. Uncle Sam has been good to MACE, which has received money from many different federal programs in recent decades.

When I asked MACE director Fanny Woods what her AmeriCorps program was doing, she repeated the old saying that "if you give a man a fish, he will eat for a day, but if you teach him how to fish, he can feed himself for his entire life."[21] I asked about MACE's involvement with food stamps, and Woods indicated that the program did little or nothing with food stamps. I quoted to her a passage from the MACE website that mentioned food stamp recruitment. Woods admitted that MACE did inform some people about food stamps but emphatically stated that it would be illegal for AmeriCorps members to directly advocate that people go on food stamps. I then mentioned that I had read that AmeriCorps members were going door-to-door telling people about food stamps. Woods then conceded that AmeriCorps members drove people directly to the food stamp offices—but said that they did not go inside with them because that would be illegal. Woods said that some food stamp officials had "dogged" applicants, making the application process unpleasant for them. (At the same time that MACE is boosting food stamp enrollment, local governments in the Delta are bragging that new gambling casinos have created an economic mini-boom, enabling thousands of residents to find work and get off of food stamps.) Ms. Woods claimed to have no written information, brochures, or summaries of what her AmeriCorps program was doing.

MACE is one of four AmeriCorps' "Beyond Food" programs devoted to boosting food aid. (The other programs are in Vermont, Wisconsin, and Washington, D.C.) Beyond Food/DC set up a hotline that referred people to local food stamp offices; one of its goals is that "an additional 500 people will be referred to appropriate services to satisfy their food needs."

The Congressional Hunger Center (CHC), the lead grantee for the "Beyond Food" programs, exemplifies AmeriCorps' humility. In its 1999 grant applications, it stated: "Beyond Food/DC exists to fight hunger by developing leaders ... Our members ... learn in a 'Capital' environment where some of our nation's greatest humanitarian experts work."[22] CHC's website proclaims that "advocacy" is one of its key tasks and provides direct links to the congressional websites of Rep. Tony Hall (D-Ohio) and Rep. Frank Wolf (R-Va.), the CHC co-chairmen.[23](The MACE website also stated that "political advocacy" was one of its primary purposes.[24])

I asked AmeriCorps chief Wofford how food stamp recruiting meshed with his statements that AmeriCorps promoted self-reliance. Wofford replied, "A self-reliant citizen knows what their [sic] opportunities are and figures out how to make use of those opportunities."[25] Apparently, the key to self-reliance is knowing the address of the welfare office.

FEDERALLY PAID RABBLE-ROUSING

President Clinton declared in 1994 that he looked forward to AmeriCorps members "revolutionizing life at the grassroots level."[26]

Some AmeriCorps projects seem to be largely federally paid rabble-rousing. AmeriCorps is paying four members to work with the Political Asylum Project of Austin, Texas. Program director Nidia Salamanca declared: "There are a lot of immigrants who are in detention right now—we see how their rights are being violated by police officers and by detention officers—we document INS encounters with immigrants—if they are respecting their rights."[27] AmeriCorps support of the Whatcom [Washington State] Human Rights Task Force is paying for AmeriCorps members to "organize the Hispanic Population . . . to develop a program of monitoring, reporting and stopping INS [Immigration and Naturalization Service] abuses of the Hispanic population . . . " and to "write at least six press releases. Press releases should include the results of needs assessment and INS reports."[28] And, in case these actions are not sufficient to incite public opinion, an AmeriCorps member will also "organize rallies as needed," according to the organization's successful grant application.

Federal law prohibits AmeriCorps grantees from engaging in advocacy. But as long as an organization is not directly involved in a political campaign, advocating bigger government is fine and dandy with AmeriCorps headquarters.

AmeriCorps has poured millions of dollars into organizations fighting for rent control and more federal housing subsidies. An AmeriCorps grant to the National Association of HUD Tenants pays for AmeriCorps members to "door knock and organize general meetings in each selected [subsidized] development," as does a separate grant to the Gray Panthers of Rhode Island.[29] AmeriCorps members agitate residents to lobby Congress; as the grant application noted, "All tenants in Section 8 [federal rental subsidies] buildings will have to make sure that Congress provides funds each year."[30] The grant application also aims to help residents "increase tenant collective bargaining strength and access with HUD and other agencies." But by supporting continued rent control, Ameri-Corps-aided groups buttress government policies that have created artificial housing shortages that harm millions of Americans.

AmeriCorps has provided more than $60,000 to support Equality Colorado, an organization that describes itself as "dedicated to social change through education, advocacy and organizing to combat violence and negative attitudes towards GLBT [Gay/Lesbian/Bisexual/Transgender] people in our society."[31] According to the grant application AmeriCorps approved, the federal money will pay to "organize community building and empowering activities to the GLBT and allied communities," among other purposes.[32] The project appears designed in part to recruit young people; one objective is to "develop relation-ships with other area service providers who can help youth explore their sexual orientation effectively and build a referral network of people informed about sexual orientation issues." Equality Colorado lobbies for special legal protections for gays, for mandatory health benefits for the partners of gay and lesbian employees, and for equal legal status for homosexual marriages. Private citizens are entitled to lobby for what they please; but the AmeriCorps grant conveys a federal seal of approval for *all* the organization's activities.

The Los Angeles Gay and Lesbian Center, the nation's largest gay rights organization, has received over $200,000 in support from AmeriCorps. The center is a must-stop for Democratic presidential candidates; both Al Gore and Bill Bradley visited its headquarters within a three-day period in June 1999. Some AmeriCorps officials were concerned about LAGLC even before it was launched; AmeriCorps executive director Deb Jospin warned in a 1997 internal memo that "the LAGLC is a well-known advocacy organization."[33]

The official Memorandum of Agreement between the Corporation for National Service (CNS), the federal agency that includes AmeriCorps, and the LAGLC stated: "The Agreement between the Corporation for National Service and the Sponsor provides for the assignment of up to Four (4) [AmeriCorps] members to the Sponsor for the purpose of performing volunteer service to strengthen and supplement efforts to eliminate poverty and poverty-related human, social and environmental problems."[34] But internal files at AmeriCorps headquarters show that the project had nothing to do with poverty. A March 31, 1999, program update from LAGLC informed AmeriCorps headquarters that the AmeriCorps members and LAGLC staff were "focusing on society's last 'acceptable' prejudice: anti-gay bias."[35] The project was summarized by one AmeriCorps member as "working to reduce the problem of homophobia and hate violence in the LA schools and making schools safer for gay youth, and those who are perceived to be gay."[36]

Anti-gay violence, like violence against anyone, is deplorable. Americans are far more tolerant of gays now than they were a few decades ago. But is anti-gay violence in Los Angeles schools a proper concern for a federally funded, national program like AmeriCorps? Anti-gay violence comprises a nearly infinitesimal fraction of all the crimes committed in the Los Angeles Unified School District (a bureaucratic superstructure with more than 900,000 students and over 900 schools).

As part of the project, AmeriCorps members distributed a survey that clearly implied that students should report to school authorities any time they heard any student make a derogatory comment to any other student. (The survey classified graffiti as a hate crime.) Gwen Baldwin, executive director of LAGLC, stressed that the program "is really [about] tracking and monitoring the instances of both hate crimes or anti-gay activities."[37] An example of anti-gay bias that Baldwin offered was "one person not being invited to a lunch table." (Attorney General Janet Reno, on the Justice Department website section on hate crimes and kids, also used the lunch table example.)

MAXIMIZING FALSE ACCUSATIONS

AmeriCorps has provided more than $600,000 in aid for the Child Victim Rapid Response Program run by Florida's Attorney General's Office. This program sends 19 AmeriCorps recruits into schoolrooms to lecture about child abuse and domestic violence. The program's 1999 AmeriCorps grant application promised that, as a result of the program, "there will be an increase by 25 percent over last year in the number of incidents of child abuse reported . . . as well as the number of domestic violence incidents reported to police by the student population."[38] (The goal of a 25 percent increase in accusations was mentioned several places in the application.) The grant application also set a goal of a 25 percent increase—from 331 to 415—in the number of students and families "served" with emergency injunctions and child custody orders as a result of AmeriCorps activism. Once the accusations have been made and parents dragged into the dock, AmeriCorps helps pay for the accusers' court costs, including the costs of a court reporter.

I called program director Cynthia Rodgers and asked if there is any kind of safeguard in the system to avoid encouraging false accusations. Ms. Rodgers responded, "No. But if you look at reports out there, the number of false accusations are low—the criminal justice system, and the people who interview children, is very sophisticated, and certainly much more sophisticated than a child's mind."[39] However, Florida was the site of some of the worst child abuse witch hunts in recent decades—including the false child abuse accusations in a case spearheaded by State Attorney Janet Reno's office and based on a bevy of absurd accusations coerced by psychiatrists out of young children.[40] I asked how many of the charges of child abuse that resulted from AmeriCorps activism were "sustained"—i.e., how many of the parents were found guilty. Ms. Rodgers replied: "We would not even address that," and stated that she had no information on the results of the charges. This practically implies that increasing the number of child accusations is in the public interest, regardless of whether the charges are valid. (False child abuse accusations have become a national scandal in recent years.)[41]

FLUSH FOLLIES

In southern California, 37 AmeriCorps recruits busy themselves distributing "ultra-low-flush toilets" and low-flow shower devices.[42] The devices that AmeriCorps members foist on low-income people have spurred a tidal wave of protests on Capitol Hill. According to the National Association of Home Builders, three-quarters of their members complained that the new federally mandated low-flush toilets are more prone to clogging and other problems. Ben Lieberman, a lawyer and regulatory expert with the Competitive Enterprise Institute, observed, "People complain about having to flush the new toilets twice. The low-flow toilets do not work nearly as well. Some new models are unbelievably noisy."[43] The new federal toilet mandates created a black market for older toilets; AmeriCorps helped "solve" this problem by rounding up and crushing older, more reliable toilets. The new shower heads severely restrict the amount of water people can use—a "federal dribble mandate." AmeriCorps members are effectively carrying out new EPA regulations to forcibly reduce the amount of water each person uses.

LITERACY FRAUD

Patriotism may be the last refuge of a scoundrel, but promising to teach children to read is the last refuge of federal boondoggles.

AmeriCorps is a flag bearer in Clinton's literacy crusade; almost half of all AmeriCorps members are involved in teaching literacy or mentoring students.

In his August 9, 1999 speech, Clinton congratulated AmeriCorps members: "You have . . . taught millions of children to read."[44] One AmeriCorps official ridiculed Clinton's claim and expressed doubt that AmeriCorps members had taught even a dozen children to read.[45] Robert Sweet, the former director of the National Institute of Education, the premier federal education research agency, observed, "AmeriCorps is not working—and Clinton's program is still the fraud that it was in the beginning. The whole foundation of this approach towards teaching reading is faulty."[46]

AmeriCorps Chief Wofford bragged in 1998 congressional testimony that AmeriCorps had set a goal for itself of "effective education and literacy for every child."[47] The proclamation made for good public relations, regardless that the vast majority of AmeriCorps recruits had no experience or competence for this task.

Some AmeriCorps programs take welfare recipients off the streets and send them into classrooms to be reading tutors.[48] Yet, welfare recipients are among the least literate groups in American society. The largest single item that AmeriCorps spends for training its own members is for General Equivalency Degree (GED) preparation—helping AmeriCorps members get their high school degree. In many cases, AmeriCorps members receive literacy credit for teaching other AmeriCorps members how to pass the GED.[49] Derrick Max, the former chief investigator for the House Education and Workforce subcommittee on Investigations and Oversight, recalled: "We went through and looked at the background of people tutoring and mentoring. We found that a lot of them were still studying for their GED—it made no sense to me. If they haven't graduated from high school, don't send them back to mentor in the elementary school."[50] Robert Sweet observed, "If trained professional teachers who have spent four-plus years at a university cannot teach kids how to read, then why do we think that a week's training session for some college kid or welfare recipient is going to help kids learn how to read?"

I visited one of the premier AmeriCorps literacy programs, the Energy Express program that enrolls 600 college students to staff West Virginia classrooms during the summer. At the Ranson, West Virginia site, I asked several AmeriCorps members how much training they had received to teach children how to read. Each of the members that I asked looked at me as if I was off my rocker. AmeriCorps member Brian Farar observed: "We're not teaching them to read—we are just exposing them [to reading] and getting them to like it. You just want them to think they're doing a good job" when reading. (AmeriCorps members are careful not to correct children's grammar.) "We are trying to trick them into learning," Farar said.[51] Children sat in cardboard boxes or in indoor tents to do their reading. Puppet shows are also a big part of the summer, as is 15 to 20 minutes of "noncompetitive recreation" each day.

Some AmeriCorps literacy programs get the least bang for the buck. In late 1998, AmeriCorps awarded $1.2 million to the state of Mississippi to give AmeriCorps education awards of $4,750 to assistant teachers who are already on the state government payroll.[52] The Mississippi legislature created the assistant teacher program in 1982 to boost literacy in Mississippi's worst schools. However, Mississippi assistant teachers are only required to read at an eighth-grade level. The primary requirement that the assistant teacher–AmeriCorps members face is to provide an average of three hours of extra tutoring a week to school students. (The grant application the state of Mississippi submitted to AmeriCorps was chock full of grammar errors.) AmeriCorps is effectively paying nearly $50 an hour for tutoring by individuals with meager reading ability. This AmeriCorps program simply permits AmeriCorps headquarters to brag about the total number of AmeriCorps recruits. Besides, enrolling state government employees into AmeriCorps is a clear violation of federal law.

The Mississippi program was not the only one to successfully submit a quasi-illiterate literacy program grant application. The Rockin' Magicians Sports Association, a Harlem-based program, sent in an application that was full of the type of errors, such as sentence fragments, that should guarantee flunking a high school freshman English class.[53]

AmeriCorps suffers from literacy delusions. In testimony submitted in 1998 to the Senate Appropriations Committee, Wofford claimed of one summer program: "AmeriCorps members provided support to 3,544 students and improved testing scores in mathematics, language, arts, science, and literature in all sites, 16 cities, by 63 percent to 97 percent."[54] Sen. Kit Bond (R-Mo.) challenged the claim, asking, "Does that mean that school testing scores are so low that you can improve scores essentially by 100 percent?" Wofford admitted that his testimony was wrong but blamed the AmeriCorps grantee because its report to AmeriCorps "had been written in a way that was misunderstood" by AmeriCorps staffers. The 97 percent number actually referred to an increase in attendance at the program and had nothing to do with academic gains.

AmeriCorps is not a band-aid to cover the failure of government schools: instead, it is a photo opportunity of a facade of a band-aid. The AmeriCorps literacy program is based on perfect Clintonite logic: there is a need; there are people who care; Voila!—the problem is solved. AmeriCorps is, at best, similar to federally subsidized teacher aides provided by the Title I program for the nation's poorest school districts. The General Accounting Office concluded that Title I failed to boost student achievement.[55] Besides, any short-term benefit from AmeriCorps intensive reading–playing–back-slapping is probably lost in the dismal public schools to which most of the kids must return.

AUXILIARY GOVERNMENT BUREAUCRATS

Clinton claims that AmeriCorps "represents the best of our country."[56] Congress, in the legislation creating AmeriCorps, promised that the new program would "reinvent government to eliminate duplication."[57]

But, in many cases, AmeriCorps members are merely auxiliary government bureaucrats. From the first, AmeriCorps has often been more concerned about helping government than helping citizens.

- One New York City AmeriCorps project states that its top goal is to "set up and administer programs to mobilize private sector resources to lessen the burdens of government agencies."[58]
- In Cherryfield, Maine, an AmeriCorps recruit was put on the payroll as a grant writer for a local resource and development council. One of his first tasks was to solicit federal funding to pay for committee meetings on forestry issues.[59]
- An AmeriCorps member was detailed to the Central Oregon Intergovernmental Council in Redmon, Oregon, to "assist the city of La Pine to achieve incorporation and . . . assist in identifying appropriate economic development projects to receive lottery dollars."[60]

A small touch from an AmeriCorps member can redeeem the life of almost anyone the program chooses to save. There is no shortage of hot air in AmeriCorps' programs' promises. One project after another promises to "raise community awareness," "empower" low-income citizens, and "address human needs" of targeted groups. AmeriCorps members working for the YMCA in Everett, Washington, "facilitate two tracts of enrichment activities . . . to help the youth develop strong life skills that will assist them in becoming successful adults."[61] AmeriCorps justifies its New Hampshire Philharmonic Orchestra Music Education Program by claiming that "this unique program helps disadvantaged preschool children develop their spatial and logic skills through music education."[62] Even when AmeriCorps members do mundane tasks, program descriptions make it sound like they are on the verge of creating utopia: In Moab, Utah, 32 AmeriCorps members seek to help at-risk youth and low-income families "through a community gardening project in order to increase participant esteem, responsibility, healthy social skills and a service ethic."[63] A Pawtucket, Rhode Island AmeriCorps program promised that "80 percent of [children] enrolled in summer Enrichment programs will report improved attitudes."[64]

AmeriCorps members are supposed to develop personally and professionally during their time on the government payroll. Each grant application must contain specific, quantifiable standards to assess AmeriCorps members' progress. The result is a profusion of goals that look as if they were lifted from a Dilbert cartoon:

- The number one "Member Development Objective" for the Ohio Teen Bridges program, a driver's education program for young offenders, is that 21 AmeriCorps members "will participate in training sessions, resulting in a better understanding of 'inspiring a shared vision' thru service by 50 percent, as measured by pre- and post-tests and the Leadership Practices Inventory."[65]
- MACE AmeriCorps members were obliged to "Give a reflection and self-assessment." The result would be measured by "Self/diagnosis [sic] in an end-of-year survey." As a result, each member would achieve "a 75 percent increase on average in understanding about self."[66]
- The Milwaukee Community Service Corps (MCSC) concentrates on "Ethical Training": "Using well-established curriculum from the Institute for Global Ethics, the youth development dept at MCSC will implement a series of Ethical Fitness workshops for corps members that will increase awareness of ethics and develop a concept of what is ethical."[67] The report noted that "An increase of knowledge by at least 50 percent is mandatory." (The report did not specify what penalty would be imposed on any member whose ethical knowledge increased only 49 percent.)

The fact that AmeriCorps program directors believe that such things can be easily quantified raises severe doubts about their competence for any task more complex than picking up beer cans along a highway.

Many AmeriCorps activities seem primarily designed to suffuse its members with a feeling of virtue. In Greenville, California, AmeriCorps members busied themselves writing and presenting a mini-play about discrimination to schoolchildren.[68] In Largo, Florida, AmeriCorps recruits organized a Fun Fest that included a balloon toss, face painting, and prizes for every child.[69] EnviroCorps Indiana members dress up in a giant blue puffy suit to parade before children as "Kerplop the Rain Drop," when they are not organizing a recycled raft race, making and distributing pro-environmental beanie babies, and doing face painting.[70]

AMERICORPS AS POLITICAL PROP

USA Today noted that AmeriCorps' "T-shirted brigade is most well known nationally as the youthful backdrop for White House photo ops."[71] When President Clinton arrived in San Francisco to speak to the American Society of Newspaper Editors on April 15, 1999, a small army of AmeriCorps members was at the airport to hail his arrival. When Clinton arrived in Colorado Springs to give the commencement address at the Air Force Academy on June 3, 1999, a flock of AmeriCorps members were on hand to greet Air Force One.[72] AmeriCorps members get paid for the time they spend cheering the president.

Clinton has repeatedly violated federal law by conducting campaign-style rallies in which he urges AmeriCorps members to lobby Congress for more money for their program or to hype specific legislative goals. On June 3, 1998, Clinton gave a speech to AmeriCorps members in Cleveland, Ohio, in which he urged the recruits to "help me send back to Washington" the message "that AmeriCorps works and it should be extended by Congress into the twenty-first century." Clinton also appealed to the AmeriCorps members attending his speech to "help me send a loud message back to Washington, D.C., to act and act now" on his proposed tobacco legislation.[73] AmeriCorps members are prohibited by law from "participating in, or endorsing, events or activities which are likely to include advocacy for or against political parties, political platforms, political candidates, proposed legislation or elected officials." Rep. William Goodling and Rep. Pete Hoekstra wrote a letter to President Clinton on June 24, 1998, complaining of the illegal political content of the rally but received no response.[74] In his August 9, 1999 address to AmeriCorps members, Clinton harangued the audience about the grave danger of the pending Republican tax cut.[75]

AmeriCorps grantees have repeatedly been caught in scandals involving illegal advocacy. In San Francisco, AmeriCorps recruits devoted themselves to lobbying against anticrime provisions of 1994 congressional legislation.[76] Ameri-Corps bankrolled the Green Corps, an affiliate of the California Public Interest Research Group; AmeriCorps members were illegally used to train people to conduct petitioning drives intended to influence legislation.[77] In Denver,

AmeriCorps troops distributed election leaflets attacking Hiawatha Davis, a city council member who was blocking a government grant to the non-profit group where the AmeriCorps members worked.[78] AmeriCorps gave over a million dollars to ACORN (Association of Community Organizations for Reform Now), a radical group involved in political action and confrontations. Ameri-Corps canceled its involvement with ACORN after revelations that federal money had been directly used for advocacy—but AmeriCorps management made little or no effort to get ACORN to refund the ill-spent money.[79]

A RISING TIDE OF FRAUD

Clinton bragged in 1994 that AmeriCorps is "the least bureaucratic, least nationally directed program I have been associated with."[80] In practice, this means the feds shovel out the money and ask few, if any, questions about how recipients spend the windfall.

The moral smugness of many AmeriCorps officials has gone hand-in-hand with slip shod accounting—which produced a "target-rich environment" for fraud, according to Inspector General (IG) Luise Jordan. In 1995, 1996, and 1997, auditors concluded that the agency's books were "unauditable"—in such a mess that auditors could not even attempt to render a judgment on what happened to the billion dollars that Congress delivered to AmeriCorps in those years. While the agency has made some progress, auditors found that Ameri-Corps actually had more "significant material weaknesses" (i.e., gross failures of financial controls) in 1998 than in 1997.

A 1998 IG report found that AmeriCorps routinely used illegal contracting methods to award contracts to its friends and favorites. This was especially the case when AmeriCorps management gave contracts to minority-owned firms. In other cases, the IG found that AmeriCorps violated federal contracting law simply because doing so was "easier than competitive contracting."[81] The IG also reported in 1998: "Only 3 of 14 cooperative agreement files contained evidence of [AmeriCorps] monitoring and oversight of grantee activities."[82]

AmeriCorps negligence has opened the door to con artists around the country. Bruce Smith, director of the AmeriCorps Vision Youth Works program in Harrisburg, Pennsylvania, was convicted of defrauding AmeriCorps members in a federal court in December 1998. Smith required that every youth (most of whom were mentally handicapped) pay him an "activity fee" of $40 in cash each time they received their living allowance. Smith was sentenced to four months in prison and four months of home detention and fined $8,100; he was also required to perform 80 hours of community service—hopefully not in an AmeriCorps program.[83]

An Indiana AmeriCorps program was engulfed in scandal in June 1999 after the *Terre Haute Tribune-Star* revealed that various high school students were given credit toward the $4,750 AmeriCorps education award for time they spent baby-sitting, playing high school sports, going to band practice, working as a lifeguard, and attending Sunday School.[84] Brian Sullivan testified at a House hearing in September 1999 that he was told that "[i]f you work with kids, they will let you get credit for just about anything."[85] (Sullivan received AmeriCorps credit for time he spent as a paid camp counselor for the city of Terre Haute.) A state audit found that the program could provide no documentation of service for the vast majority of people who received AmeriCorps education awards, and also found "significant nepotism" in the program.[86] Inspector General Jordan observed that the Indiana scandal is "a microcosm of everything that we have reported as far as audit weaknesses and investigative findings—this is what we have been warning them against."[87]

Some AmeriCorps programs have liberal ideas on the meaning of service. The IG found AmeriCorps members "claiming and receiving certified service hours for inappropriate activities, such as working at McDonald's to 'novel' approaches to accruing service hours such as the 'team concept,' where everyone on a team earns the total accumulated hours of the team for any given day, and the 'inherited service hours,' where new AmeriCorps members 'inherit' the service hours of a departing member."[88] Some AmeriCorps members who did not complete their 1,700 hours received prorated education awards as bribes to keep them quiet after they threatened to publicly broadcast their dissatisfaction with AmeriCorps.[89]

When the Inspector General in 1998 informed AmeriCorps management of pervasive violations of federal law and regulations by AmeriCorps grantees, AmeriCorps headquarters denied responsibility for the problem. CEO Wofford replied that "the Corporation [for National Service] has no direct contractual relationship with operating or placement sites. Accordingly, the Corporation's efforts are focused on strengthening state commission and parent organizations so that they conduct proper training and oversight at the local level."[90] AmeriCorps headquarters seems more interested in "plausible deniability" than in accountability. Inspector General Jordan retorted: "The lack of a direct contractual relationship does not relieve the Corporation of its responsibility as the Federal agency providing AmeriCorps funding to establish effective controls over compliance with laws and regulations related to the program."[91]

DRIVE-BY SALVATION

If AmeriCorps helped at a barn-raising, AmeriCorps members would claim afterward not just to have helped someone build a barn—but swear that they also redeemed the person's self-esteem, gave him a purpose in life, and made him aware of the value of multiculturalism and diversity.

Most AmeriCorps success claims have no more credibility than a political campaign speech. The vast majority of AmeriCorps programs are "self-evalu-ated": the only evidence AmeriCorps possesses of what a program achieved is what the grant recipients claim. One of the corporation's technical assistance consultants formally encourages AmeriCorps programs to inflate the number of claimed beneficiaries: "If you feel your program affects a broad group of individuals who may not be receiving personal services from members . . . then list the whole community."[92] The southern Californian toilet distribution project claimed it benefited 30 million people—almost the entire population of California.

A February 2000 General Accounting Office report revealed that Ameri-Corps relies on Soviet-style accounting to gin up its achievement claims. GAO noted that AmeriCorps "generally reports the results of its programs and activities by *quantifying* the amount of services AmeriCorps participants perform . . . Although [AmeriCorps] has enumerated and characterized a number of positive program activities, *counting them* does not fully measure program results or outcomes as required by the Government Performance and Results Act of 1994."[93] The fact that X number of bodies appeared for X number of hours at X number of work sites does not prove that AmeriCorps has achieved anything more grandiose than boosting the number of government employees standing around with their hands in their pockets. GAO criticized AmeriCorps for failing to make any effort to measure the actual impact of its members' actions. One college graduate with the AmeriCorps National Conservation Corps program bitterly commented in his resignation letter: "There are no new projects. Teams are sent to the same state parks over and over again. Teams are told they are doing work that really doesn't need to be done. Do you think it goes over our heads that sometimes sponsors are just trying to keep us busy? I hope that they [management] can understand that part of the reason I am leaving is *because* I am so committed to education."[94]

AmeriCorps members often do little more than attempt to patch holes resulting from the failures of other government programs. Public school teachers dismally fail to teach reading; AmeriCorps members are sent in to do magic. National parks abysmally fail to maintain their trails and other facilities;

AmeriCorps members are sent in for photo opportunities with shovels and picks. Public housing projects continue deteriorating, in large part because residents have no incentive not to trash the surroundings; AmeriCorps members are sent in with paint brushes.

According to President Clinton, "every young AmeriCorps volunteer . . . typically will generate 12 more volunteers helping on whatever the service is."[95] Clinton and other defenders claim that AmeriCorps is a big success because recruits "leveraged" their efforts by persuading other people to volunteer more hours of charity work. This makes the entire program smell like a con: the feds paying certain people to hustle other people to work for free. At best, this is the Tom Sawyer model of virtue.

Besides, AmeriCorps' claims of being a miraculous generator of volunteers are false. A study by Independent Sector, a coalition of voluntary organizations, found that AmeriCorps members were actually responsible for only a "3.5 percent increase in hours volunteered by genuine volunteers."[96] AmeriCorps uses statistical bait-and-switches to inflate its claims. AmeriCorps reporting forms ask programs for both new volunteers and existing volunteers supervised by AmeriCorps members. Thus, if an AmeriCorps volunteer shows up at a Habitat for Humanity home-building project and pretends to supervise 30 people one afternoon, this counts as 30 new volunteers generated by AmeriCorps. If there is a single AmeriCorps recruit in a nonprofit organization, then politicians become entitled to claim credit for all the nonprofit's good deeds.

More than 93 million Americans work as unpaid volunteers each year.[97] At best, AmeriCorps' 40,000 members amount to less than one-twentieth of 1 percent of all the volunteers in America. Rep. Pete Hoekstra (R-Mich.), the program's most vigilant critic, observed: "What the president has done is create a national identity for AmeriCorps that in some ways competes with these other charitable organizations."[98]

Wofford bragged in 1999: "The evidence shows that [AmeriCorps] has instilled an ethic of continuing service in the members."[99] But it is difficult to distinguish the AmeriCorps Alumni Association from any other Washington lobby. The association recently announced: "Feedback over the past two years indicates that the most pressing issue on the minds of AmeriCorps alumni is the taxation of the education award."[100] The association is lobbying to convert the education award into a tax-free benefit. Vollie Melson, the association's executive director, observed, "A lot of people are frustrated with the tax because they feel they're serving their country."[101]

AmeriCorps recruits do auxiliary work with a number of upstanding, effective charities such as the United Cerebral Palsy, the Boy Scouts, and the

Red Cross. AmeriCorps members assisted in July 1999 when the World Special Olympics took place in Raleigh, North Carolina. But these are organizations and events that were established and widely respected before the first Ameri-Corps member appeared on their doorstep. The Independent Sector study found that posting AmeriCorps members at government and nonprofit agencies produce quantitative results "over and above what the agencies were mandated and ostensibly funded to provide."[102]

AmeriCorps defenders talk as if the program were a good thing in itself. But the more the federal government confiscates to spend for this bogus volunteer program, the less citizens will have to finance their own preferred voluntary and charitable activities.

CONCLUSION

Many of its supporters hope that AmeriCorps will be a stepping stone to laws compelling all young Americans to surrender their time to government-approved "service" activities. When he was in the Senate, Wofford championed legislation to give federal grants to high schools that imposed compulsory service on all students.[103] In an interview, Wofford talked about how AmeriCorps could provide its members with the "moral equivalent of war"—the supposed moral stimulus that occurs from subjugation to some higher collective goal. (Wofford mentions his own character-building experience in the Army Air Corps in World War II in almost every speech he makes—but never mentions publicly the fact that he never saw any combat.[104])

AmeriCorps is little more than social work tinged with messianic delusions. AmeriCorps is special because it is work that is "politically blessed"—work that has received the blessing of politicians—and thus is far more meaningful than mere private sector work—as if any work that is financed by coercion (tax payments) is more meaningful than work paid for voluntarily.

Politicians exploit AmeriCorps to brandish their own image. Maryland lieutenant governor, Kathleen Kennedy Townsend, the sponsor of a law that imposed compulsory service on Maryland high school students, praised Clinton at the February 10, 1999, AmeriCorps pep rally: "You call out the best in our citizens. You remind Americans of the good that politics and education can accomplish."[105]

At best, AmeriCorps allows politicians to claim credit for good deeds that citizens would have performed if AmeriCorps never existed. At worst, Ameri-Corps pulls nonprofit organizations into the government orbit and sows the seeds of bureaucratization and politicalization. According to Doug Bandow, former special assistant to President Ronald Reagan and a Cato Institute fellow, "By paying a handful of young kids and claiming they are 'volunteers,' AmeriCorps may be undermining and squeezing out real volunteers."[106]

AmeriCorps makes far more "difference" to politicians than to any other group. For every other group in society, Americorps' efforts are negligible compared to those of the legions of volunteers who don't need a federal handout to do a good deed.

PLUNDERING AND BLUNDERING: THE IRS

On July 30, 1996, while reluctantly signing a bill to provide meager additional protections to taxpayers, President Bill Clinton proclaimed: "We say to America's taxpayers, when you deal with the IRS, you also have privileges and we respect them. You have protection and we will help provide it. You have rights and we will shield them."[1]

There may have been a few Americans who actually believed the president's assertions. However, since Clinton took office, the IRS has seized over 12 million bank accounts and paychecks, put liens on over 3 million people's homes and land, directly confiscated more than 100,000 people's houses, cars, or property, and imposed over 100 million penalties on people for allegedly not paying sufficient taxes, paying taxes late, et cetera.[2] The IRS has also audited roughly 15 million American families and businesses—and the audit process (at least through 1998) was intentionally designed to pressure people to pay more taxes than they actually owed. The IRS has collected tens of billions of dollars in wrongful penalties and taxes not owed since 1993.[3]

The image of the IRS goes to the heart of Clinton's attempt to make people think of government as a warm, fuzzy abstraction—rather than as an entity that browbeats citizens and twists arms in the name of the Greater Good. Because Clinton sees government revenue as the source of all progress and all justice, his administration continually fought to minimize the rights of taxpayers and to stretch IRS discretionary power on every front.

In 1994, after the General Accounting Office (GAO) issued a report on taxpayer abuse, IRS Assistant Commissioner Michael Dolan publicly complained: "We believe that the use of the term 'taxpayer abuse' is misleading, inaccurate and inflammatory."[4] The IRS fiercely opposed any system to track the number of cases of taxpayer abuse. IRS Commissioner Margaret Richardson, appearing before a congressional committee in March 1995 to urge congressmen not to enact legislation to expand taxpayers rights, stated, "My hope is that the overwhelming number of taxpayers who come in contact with us will come to know us as a genteel, Gulliver-like giant."[5] But, as IRS agent Jennifer Long testified to Congress in 1997, revenue agents are encouraged by IRS management to use "tactics—which appear nowhere in the IRS manual . . . to extract unfairly assessed taxes from taxpayers, literally ruining families, lives, and businesses—all unnecessarily and sometimes illegally."[6]

The following cases provide a baseline by which Clinton's action and rhetoric must be measured. It is not simply that the IRS sent out a couple of wrong notices or accidentally raided a few wrong bank accounts. Clinton used all his prestige and all his chips on Capitol Hill to perpetuate the agency's power to use and abuse the American people.

DESTROYING A "CLASSIC DEADBEAT FREELOADER"

In 1993, Carole Ward, a 46-year-old Colorado Springs businesswoman, became incensed when, during a meeting between her son and IRS auditor Paula Dzierzanowski, Dzierzanowski began asking questions about her family's children clothing stores that Ms. Ward felt showed gross ignorance. Ms. Ward taunted the auditor: "Based on what I can see of your accounting skills, you'd be better off dishing up chicken-fried steak on an interstate somewhere in west Texas."[7]

The IRS responded by seeking to impose a financial death penalty on Ms. Ward. Three weeks later, IRS agents swarmed into Ms. Ward's three stores, proclaiming that Ms. Ward owed $324,889 in taxes. They froze her bank accounts, shut down and confiscated the stores and all their inventory, and allegedly informed some of her customers that Ward was suspected of drug smuggling. The IRS even sought to seize the house owned by Carole Ward's 74-year-old mother, claiming that it was somehow related to her daughter's tax dodging.

Prior to the seizure, the IRS had made no finding that either Ms. Ward or other family members who co-owned the stores owed any taxes. The IRS violated federal law by seizing the assets without first formally giving her a notice of deficiency of taxes—especially since the IRS had no reason to suspect that Ms. Ward would load up her clothing stores and flee to Rio de Janeiro.

Ms. Ward hotly denied that she owed any taxes and demanded that the IRS audit her. After the examination—which covered seven years of Ward's tax returns—the IRS concluded that she owed only $3,400 in additional taxes— barely 1 percent of the amount they had already confiscated. However, before the agency would accept her $3,400 check and return her confiscated assets, the agency insisted that she sign a statement promising not to sue the IRS for violating her rights. Ms. Ward's stores offered specialized children clothing, including white baptismal gowns. The seizure occurred shortly before Pope John Paul II came to Denver in 1993, and an IRS official told Ms. Ward that if she "played ball," the IRS would return her merchandise in time for the pope's visit.[8]

Ms. Ward refused to sign such an agreement, complaining that "you don't have to surrender your constitutional rights in order to pay your taxes." After Ward publicly protested the IRS's treatment of her, IRS District Director Gerald Swanson and an assistant spoke on a Colorado Springs talk show and disclosed information from her tax return. Ward called up during the talk show to dispute the officials' allegations that she still owed $324,000, despite the fact that the agency had determined her tax bill to be a tiny fraction of that amount. According to Ward, an IRS official called her lawyer after the program and shouted: "If that bitch wants to play hardball, we will show her what hardball is! She will never get her stuff back unless she signs the document" promising not to sue the agency.

Eventually, the IRS relented and took her check. After Ms. Ward continued publicly complaining about the IRS abuses, IRS officials sought to vilify her by repeating the same accusations against her that the IRS had originally made, and that had already been discredited by the IRS's audit of her returns. IRS agent James Scholan, who participated in the raids shutting down Ward's stores, wrote a letter to the *Colorado Springs Gazette* declaring that people like Ward and her son "are the biggest problem our society faces" and denounced her as a "classic deadbeat freeloader." IRS officials also erroneously disclosed information from Ward's tax return to the television program *Inside Edition*.

Five months later, the IRS returned about 75 percent of the merchandise it had seized. Ward complained: "They took almost $3,500 out of the stores' cash registers and they gave us receipts for it—and they have never applied it to taxes or given it back to us. They gave us back three stores full of summer clothing just in time for Christmas."[9] Thanks to the IRS's actions and allegations, Ward lost her lease at one store.

Ward wanted her day in court, but because her finances were exhausted by the initial seizure and struggle to get her business back on its feet, and because of statutory limitations on legal fees for winning parties, she could not afford to hire a lawyer until after the statute of limitations had expired for the wrongful seizure. Eventually, she sued the IRS for wrongful disclosure of her personal tax information.

On June 2, 1997, federal judge William Downes slammed IRS agent Scholan for acting with "reckless disregard" for the law. Downes concluded that evidence offered at trial showed that the IRS's "wrongful conduct" caused Ms. Ward's "personality to change. She became bitter and consumed by a battle with the IRS in an effort to establish that what IRS agents and employees had said and done was incorrect."[10] The judge awarded Ward $325,000 in compensatory and punitive damages and warned the IRS that "reprehensible abuse of authority by one of its employees cannot and will not be tolerated." Downes decreed: "The conduct of our Nation's affairs always demands that public servants discharge their duties under the Constitution . . . with fairness and a proper spirit of subservience to the people whom they are sworn to serve."[11]

The Justice Department filed a motion to deny attorneys' fees to Ward's lawyers and, as Denis Mark, Ward's lead trial counsel, observed, "If the government chooses to file an appeal, this case might be dragged out for many more months or years."[12] Of the three agents whom the judge found violated Ward's rights, one has retired, one is still on the payroll in the same position, and the third has been promoted to chief of IRS collections for the state of Colorado.

Bob Kammen, a Phoenix tax attorney and a National Taxpayers Union counsel, observed, "The unfortunate aspect of the Carole Ward case is that it gives people the mistaken impression that there is some actual recourse— you have to assume that for every case like that where there are damages awarded, there are 50 to 100 problem cases where the advice to the client is: you cannot afford to take on the federal government."[13] Even in the rare cases in which judges award damages to victims of an IRS abuse, the Justice Department is renowned for using every possible legal stratagem to see that the person never collects a dime.

Ward commented in 1998 that "the fact that I won in court does not remedy the fact that my entire family has been bankrupted and destroyed."[14] And she was contemptuous of congressmen who seem more concerned about having their picture taken with her than about curbing the IRS's power.

SAVAGING A FORMER FIREFIGHTER

Tom Savage, a retired fireman and businessman, was at home in Wilmington, Delaware on the morning of April 4, 1993, when an IRS agent knocked on his door.[15] When Savage came out, the agent pointed at the "For Sale" sign in front of his house and asked: "What are you doing, trying to get out of town before you pay your taxes?" The agent demanded to see Savage's personal tax documents and Savage obliged him, assuming that a quick examination would prove that he owed nothing to the government.

Savage's firm, Tom Savage Associates, was in the prison construction business. Unbeknownst to him, a subcontractor of his firm had failed to pay payroll taxes for its employees. This was the first time that Savage had ever done business with that particular firm, yet the IRS agent announced that Savage was personally liable for all the payroll taxes of his subcontractor. This demand was totally in violation of federal tax law. Savage hired a law firm, and within a week, the IRS abandoned its wrongful demand.

However, the IRS agent, on his own authority, created and registered a new partnership—purportedly consisting of Tom Savage Associates and the other firm—assigned them an Employer Identification Number, and then demanded that Savage personally pay $315,000 in taxes for the nonexistent partnership.[16] IRS agents have no legal authority to create new partnerships: the agent's audacity stunned Savage and his lawyers. Once again, the lawyers went back to the IRS to get the wrongful demand dropped.

Before Savage's lawyers could meet with IRS appeals officials, the IRS confiscated a $145,000 check from the state of Delaware to Tom Savage Associates. The IRS is prohibited by federal law from seizing taxpayers' money until a tax deficiency has been formally assessed. The IRS's action completely flouted the law—but once the agency had Savage's money, the law no longer mattered.

Savage's lawyers sued the agency on September 23, 1993, to get the money returned. On November 1, 1993, Acting Assistant Attorney General Michael Paup, head of the Tax Division of the Justice Department, sent a memo informing the IRS that "we believe that the levy in question was wrongful, even assuming the facts in their most favorable light . . . No assessment existed against TSA [Tom Savage Associates] or the alleged joint venture partnership . . . In fact, we read your defense letter to essentially concede that the levy was wrongful, and yet the levy was pursued, notwithstanding the fact that the U.S. Department of Justice Tax Division wrote that it was wrongful."[17]

Yet, Justice Department lawyers, manipulating legal tactics and court rules on behalf of the IRS, found one excuse after another to continue denying the agency's wrongdoing. Government lawyers also made it clear that even if Savage won in federal district court, the government would appeal the decision all the way to the Supreme Court—and run up his legal expenses as high as possible. As Savage's lawyer, Jerome Grossman, commented: "They had the money— they felt that they could wear us down" with delays, appeals, and other court tactics.

A year and a half later, Savage settled the case by allowing the IRS to keep $50,000 of his wrongfully confiscated money; the agency returned $95,000 to Savage. Savage did not want to settle, but his company faced destruction unless he could get some of the money back and move forward.

The IRS's abuse of Savage cost him $167,016.32 cash out of pocket and several hundred thousand dollars of lost business. It also forced him to delay his retirement for three years. Neither he nor his wife drew a salary from the corporation from 1994 through 1998, and he is still working to pay off the debts from the battle with the IRS. Savage observed: "The emotional damage done to my wife and me outstrips the financial damage we suffered. All this time and you are scared to death. They can come and take your home away and you have no say."[18] Savage commented bitterly that the IRS agents "didn't give a damn. They were acting illegally. They knew it. And they didn't care." Savage concluded that the lesson is "the old story that power corrupts." (The IRS officials and Justice Department lawyers who abused Savage were never reprimanded or sanctioned for their actions.)

SQUASHING A TAX PREPARER

On March 29, 1995, Richard Gardner arrived at the office of his tax preparation service in Tulsa, Oklahoma, to find 15 armed IRS agents and 5 U.S. marshals waiting for him. Gardner related to the Senate Finance Committee in 1998: "One of the IRS special agents directed me into one of my other offices, handed me a search warrant and said, 'We are seizing all of your clients' tax returns, computers, large printers, personal papers and other records.' He then said, 'I want you to make a phone call for us. I will tell you what to say. We will tape it. And if you do this for us, we will ask the judge to be lenient on your sentencing.' The agent was using me to set up the accountant to deliberately get him into trouble."[19] Gardner refused to backstab his colleague. At the time of the IRS raid, the agency had no complaints against Gardner, who ran one of the largest independent tax preparation services in Oklahoma. One IRS agent was angry that Gardner had filed for bankruptcy a few months earlier, after being told to pay overdue employee taxes. Two days later, Gardner paid all the taxes and canceled the bankruptcy filing.

Two years after cleaning out all the records in his office and attempting to put him out of business, the IRS and the Justice Department announced a 23-count indictment against Gardner. "It was the intent of the IRS to break me emotionally and financially, over what eventually would be a total of 33 months, so that I would plead guilty to at least one count each of bankruptcy and tax fraud," Gardner testified. "They tried to force some of my clients to wear a hidden microphone into my tax office to record me. And when they refused the special agent became angry and hinted, as a result of their refusal, that they too might experience some problems with the IRS. My employees were threatened with the loss of their jobs and were informed that they could buy out my tax business cheaply since I would soon be out of business."[20] Gardner noted, "The IRS lied to the grand jury on the indictment." Gardner summarized the agency's proceedings: "In the end, the IRS had put between three and five agents working on my case and had supposedly put between 6,000 and 8,000 tax returns on its computers in an attempt to show fraud, and failed. The IRS examined between 35,000 and 45,000 of my client tax returns for fraud, and failed. It had questioned hundreds of my clients, threatening them and spent hundreds of thousands of dollars to prove wrongdoing, and failed."

After getting Gardner indicted, the IRS became strangely reticent about presenting its evidence to a judge. At a pretrial hearing in December 1997, the IRS asked that its expert witness not be required to file an official expert report and informed the judge that the agent in charge would not be testifying. At a January 5, 1998, hearing on Gardner's motion to dismiss the case because of prosecutorial vindictiveness, the Justice Department and IRS announced the charges were being dropped.[21]

Gardner then sued the IRS and the federal government for his attorney fees, claiming that the prosecution had been in bad faith. The Justice Department fought this suit, claiming that "a defendant does not prevail in a criminal case unless he is acquitted on all or substantially all counts or he affirmatively succeeds in bringing the entire prosecution to an end in his favor."[22] The Justice Department also claimed that Gardner had not prevailed because the government still had the option to re-indict him on some of the same offenses. Thus, even though the feds dropped the charges to avoid an embarrassing court loss, the judge was still supposed to presume that the accused had been guilty.

When Judge Sven Erik Holmes issued his opinion on Gardner's suit, he was not impressed by the feds' attempt to weasel out of any liability: "Specifically, the Government argues that there is no 'criminal case' until a grand jury returns an indictment against a defendant and that the 'position of the United States' refers to the Government's litigating position after the defendant has been charged, and therefore only the litigating position of the Department of Justice, not the conduct of the IRS, is relevant."[23] Holmes ruled that IRS misconduct was relevant and ordered the government to compensate Gardner for its abusive prosecution.

The IRS never provided Gardner with any explanation for the raid—or why the indictment was dropped.[24] In January 1999, the Justice Department paid $75,000 to Gardner's lawyer, Thomas Seymour, for violating a 1997 law intended to curb prosecutions that are "vexatious, frivolous, or in bad faith."[25]

PURGATORY, IRS STYLE

Fifteen heavily armed IRS agents wearing bulletproof vests stormed into the office of SunValley Realty in Sunriver, Oregon, one day in 1995. Six more IRS agents raided the home of the owner of the company, James Montgomery. After three hours, the agents left the office, carting away 50 boxes of documents— "every scrap of paper in the office," according to Montgomery. The raid was apparently sparked by a government informant—a former employee of Montgomery's company who, after making sensational charges of cash skimming and tax dodging, subsequently pled guilty to manufacturing methamphetamine. Four years after the raid, the feds had still failed to get even a court indictment of Montgomery, but the case is still open and the feds have still refused to return any of the material they seized. The raid devastated Montgomery's image in the small town and the perpetual cloud of accusations over his head has devastated his business. The *Washington Post* reported in 1999 that, since the raid, Montgomery said "he has lost about 100 of his 150 rental properties. He said a national real estate franchise canceled its relationship with him, citing the raid, and he lost several agents and dozens of referrals of vacation homes to manage."[26]

James Bruton, former deputy assistant attorney general overseeing criminal tax prosecutions, observed of this case: "The assumption in the [IRS Criminal Investigations Division] is that virtually everybody cheats on their taxes, and if they squeeze hard enough, we'll get 'em . . . They will spend multiple years sifting through records to see if they can come up with anything."[27] The confidential history of the IRS's Criminal Investigations Division bluntly states that the division has "concentrated on investigating high impact, high visibility cases, to achieve greater media attention, maximize deterrent effect and generate support" for the Internal Revenue Service.[28]

Since Clinton took office, the amount that the IRS pays to informants has risen almost fivefold.[29] In 1997, the IRS raised its maximum allowable reward to informants 20-fold, from $100,000 to $2 million.[30] The new IRS regulations also made it much easier for someone who becomes an informant to receive part of the money the IRS collects from people they accuse.

PREYING ON THE WEAK

In recent years, the IRS has greatly increased its audit rate for low-income families at the same time that the audit rate for wealthy Americans has fallen. One IRS criminal investigator told the Senate in 1997 that the management of the Criminal Investigations Division "encourages and emphasizes opening and closing traditional tax cases, what they referred to as mom-and-pop cases, which are easy hits and can be opened and closed quickly . . . rather than investing time in the large cases which require more time and resources to prove."[31]

The IRS, like many stalkers, has a special affinity for unattached women. The vast majority of married couples sign joint returns. After a divorce, the agency often hounds both former spouses, demanding that each pay the full amount they allegedly owed as a couple. GAO estimated that the IRS wrongfully pursues 50,000 ex-spouses each year, demanding additional taxes they do not owe. Sen. William Roth (R-Del.) observed that "the agency is all too often electing to go after those who would be considered innocent spouses because they are easier to locate, as well as less inclined and able to fight."[32] The vast majority of innocent victims are women, according to tax experts. Yet the Clinton administration resisted fundamental changes in the law that would protect innocent ex-spouses. Instead, it claimed that the problem can be solved by "public education." (Congress modified the law in 1998 to give innocent spouses a better chance with the IRS.)

Former IRS District Chief David Patnoe observed in 1998: "More tax is collected by fear and intimidation than by the law. People are afraid of the IRS."[33] An IRS instructor in the Arkansas-Oklahoma district was caught on videotape lecturing collection agents in 1996 on how to treat taxpayers: "Make them cry. We don't give points around here for being good scouts. The word is enforced. If that's not tattooed on your forehead, or somewhere else, then you need to get it. Enforcement. Seizure and sales. That's our mind set . . . You're not out there to take any prisoners. Prisoners are like an installment agreement. They have to be fed and clothed and housed. All that stuff. They're expensive. We're not here to do that. If you've got an assessment, enforce collection until they come to their knees."[34] The instructor mocked the effort by Congress to rein in IRS power with so-called Taxpayer Bill of Rights legislation, insisting that "Nothing has changed in our operation in 134 years."[35] Despite the incriminating tape, the official still works for the IRS training collection agents.

In 1988, Congress prohibited the IRS from evaluating its employees based on statistics of additional taxes they collected. The IRS ignored the law and continued to use statistical evaluations that help turn IRS agents into public enemies. One confidential IRS document uncovered in 1997 revealed that IRS auditors in the San Francisco region were expected to assess at least $1,012 in additional taxes for each hour they spent auditing a taxpayer's return.[36] Any auditor who failed to achieve that quota of additional assessments could lose cash bonuses or promotions. Joseph Lane, president of the National Association of Enrolled Agents, declared: "Whenever an enforcement agency resorts to using production statistics for evaluative purposes, be they audit yields or traffic tickets, the first casualty is citizen rights."[37]

An audit released in December 1997 on the IRS's Arkansas-Oklahoma district found that a third of the property seizures carried out violated federal law or IRS regulations. The report concluded: "District management's goals and performance expectations are focused heavily on specific statistical targets, including dollar targets" per employee. IRS revenue officers ignored regulations and guidelines before seizing property; in one case, the only effort an IRS agent made before confiscating two cars "consisted of driving to the taxpayer's house, honking his car horn, and noting that no one came out of the house in response."[38] Another IRS audit report a month later found that, though the IRS is prohibited by law from the "setting of enforcement goals such as dollars collected at the group levels . . . group enforcement goals were set by upper management in 33 of 77 groups reviewed."[39]

There are few limits to the scams that the IRS can use to boost the amount of taxes citizens supposedly owe. IRS auditors sometimes simply make up income and then demand that the person pay additional taxes based on the IRS fantasy. IRS agents use Bureau of Labor Statistics data for the average income in a certain geographical area. If they are not satisfied with the additional taxes they have ginned up for someone they are auditing, they assume that the person actually has the average income, and thus owes thousands of dollars of additional taxes, penalties, and interest. Bruce Strauss, a private tax preparer who worked for IRS collections for over 30 years, observed that "the IRS now has the authority to assign additional income to a taxpayer at its discretion, without any basis in fact."[40] Any IRS assertion about a person's income—even if there is no evidence to support it—automatically receives a presumption of correctness in the Tax Court and in federal district courts. The IRS can impose crushing legal costs on someone merely by asserting that they owe an extra $10,000 in income—which the person then must fight and disprove in court.[41]

In 1996, taxpayers who challenged additional taxes assessed during audits obtained dismissals of more than $9 billion of the $13.6 billion assessed.[42] The great majority of taxpayers do not challenge additional taxes assessed during audits, in part because they may not know their legal rights.

IRS agents have been indoctrinated to see taxpayers as class enemies. This attitude is epitomized by "Culture Bingo," a game used to train IRS agents and auditors. The goal of the game was to make participants recognize "an IRS organizational culture regarding the audit process." The game encouraged IRS agents to recognize or practice the following:

- "I use summons to get third party records."
- "Fraud referrals help an examiner get promoted."
- "Most taxpayers deposit unreported receipts in their bank accounts."[43]

After an IRS agent got enough other agents in the class to sign onto his "bingo" card, he shouted out "I've got culture!" and the class launched into a discussion of the reasons why these beliefs and practices were true and necessary. One of the most damning "lessons" of the training was the doctrine: "Taxpayers seem to live better than I do." This game raised the resentment agents feel toward the taxpayers whom they audit. (The IRS claims the game is no longer being used in training.)

Such beliefs enable the IRS agents to disrupt taxpayers' lives so that IRS bureaucrats can win brownie points. In October 1999, a Treasury IG report revealed that the IRS had wrongfully sought to seize money from nearly 10,000 New Jersey taxpayers, many of whom owed little or no money to the feds. The report concluded: "New Jersey taxpayers were inappropriately issued levies without proper notice, in hardship situations, and when they were not liable for the tax in question. However, many of the personnel involved with this initiative were acknowledged by their managers for what was considered a successful project."[44] Many of those blindsided were experiencing medical or financial hardships.[45] The IRS justified seizing people's bank accounts and paychecks without proper notice or any warning because the taxpayers were classified as "uncooperative." But the IG found that in most cases, "there was no documented attempt to assess the taxpayer's willingness to cooperate and/or ability to pay prior to levy action."[46] The Dow Jones News Service reported, "The New Jersey District Office, which carried out a special computer income-matching project in 1996-97 to close cases quickly to meet certain statistical goals, subsequently lost all of the records associated with the effort even though the division nominated it as a 'best practice' within the IRS."[47] IRS commissioner Charles Rossotti tried to whitewash the situation by claiming that there was no evidence that people who did not owe money actually paid the taxes demanded. (This is a good defense to make after the IRS "loses" all the records associated with the seizures.) Rossotti declared that "it would have been an unusual situation" for someone to pay taxes they didn't owe, since he thought that taxpayers are generally quick to complain if their tax bill isn't correct.[48] (Many citizens prefer to write the government a check rather than risk a confrontation that could lead to a much wider audit or investigation—or simply risk having to deal with the bastards again for any reason.) Rossotti's comments implied that as long as no one could identify specific lives ruined by the IRS's action, the media was somehow obliged to presume "no harm, no foul"—as if potentially terrorizing thousands of innocent people was a mere paperwork snafu. The vanished IRS records effectively meant that the agency could not even track down and recompense those whom it had wronged. The 1999 report also noted that the abuses of procedure and lack of notice to victims of levies was continuing—after the Clinton administration claimed such abuses were banished from the IRS playbook.

Some of the most abusive IRS actions in recent years have involved people who actually paid their taxes but who were cast into purgatory by poor IRS record keeping. The GAO reported in 1998 that in 64 percent of cases "involving multiple individuals and companies, we found that payments were not accurately recorded to reflect the reduction in the tax liability of each responsible party. For example, in one case we reviewed, three individuals had multimillion dollar tax liability balances, as well as liens placed against their property, even though the tax had been fully paid by the company."[49]

The federal tax code creates far more pitfalls than most Americans realize. During Mark McGwire's rush to break Roger Maris's major league home run record, a reporter asked an IRS spokesman what would happen if someone caught the baseball that broke the record and returned it, gratis, to McGwire. IRS spokesman Steven Pyrek announced that "the giver is responsible for paying any applicable tax on any large gift."[50] If the record-breaking baseball was valued at $1 million, the person who returned it to McGwire could face an IRS bill of $140,000 or more. Sen. Kit Bond (R- Mo.) commented, "If the IRS wants to know why they are the most hated federal agency in America, they need look no further than this." After a hailstorm of criticism, the agency backed off of its interpretation.[51] However, if the case had been less publicized, the donor might well have been gouged.

SNOOP ONE, SNOOP ALL?

The IRS scorns safeguarding the confidentiality of taxpayers' financial secrets. The National Research Council reported in 1993 that an ongoing multibillion-dollar overhaul of IRS computers could "lead to a wide range of potentially disastrous privacy and security problems for the IRS unless the IRS develops effective, integrated privacy and security policies."[52]

In August 1993 the IRS revealed that 369 of its employees in one regional office had been investigated for browsing through the returns of friends, relatives, celebrities, and others. (Roughly half of the agency's employees had access to computer systems with private and corporate tax information.) Some IRS employees even altered the files of neighbors or created fraudulent returns. Most of the wrongdoers received only slaps on the wrist—or counseling—for their violations of federal law or IRS policy. Sen. Byron Dorgan (D-ND) went ballistic: "What on earth kind of counseling would be advisable for an employee that violates confidentiality of taxpayers' returns? Don't you, when you find people doing unauthorized things with taxpayers' records, fire them?"[53]

When IRS Commissioner Margaret Richardson was urged to notify taxpayers whose private information had been browsed illegally by IRS employees, Richardson replied, "I'm not sure there would be a serious value to that in terms of tax administration or in connection with what I see as protecting taxpayers' rights."[54] Richardson's concept of "taxpayer rights" did not include informing the taxpayer when an IRS agent has violated his or her rights and privacy. Richardson and other IRS executives promised Congress that they would institute a "no tolerance" policy for browsing. The following year, when additional cases of IRS employees wrongfully accessing citizens' computerized tax records became public, Richardson capitalized on the scandal to call for a larger congressional appropriation to buy new computers for the IRS. A GAO official testified to Congress in July 1994, "IRS internal auditors found that there were virtually no controls programmed into the Integrated Data Retrieval Systems to limit what employees can do once they are authorized . . . access."[55]

The IRS again promised to fix the problem and show "zero tolerance" to offenders.[56] In 1997, GAO revealed that since the 1993 scandal more than 1,500 IRS employees had wrongfully browsed through the tax returns of celebrities, acquaintances, relatives, and others. A third of the IRS employees caught wrongfully browsing in other people's tax records received no punishment whatsoever.[57]

Exasperated by IRS broken promises, Congress in 1997 enacted the Taxpayer Browsing Protection Act, which mandated a heavy fine and up to one year in prison for IRS employees caught wrongfully accessing citizens' confidential financial information. Despite the new law, IRS employees continued their illegal trolling. In the 14 months after the new law took effect, the IRS Office of Chief Inspector identified 5,468 potential cases of unauthorized access. Three hundred thirty-eight cases were determined to justify further investigation. Of the 37 cases completed by early 1999, 21 were found not to have been unauthorized access and the other 16 resulted in IRS employees resigning.[58] All 16 cases were referred to U.S. attorneys for prosecution but, in every case except 1, the charges were dismissed by the Clinton-appointed attorney. While Congress clearly intended that the IRS notify all taxpayers whose accounts had been wrongfully accessed, the IRS notified only the three taxpayers whose accounts had been accessed by the one IRS employee who was formally prosecuted. The 1997 law specified that taxpayers would have a right to sue IRS employees who violated their privacy for damages. The IRS's interpretation of the law effectively protected almost all of the agency's wrongdoers from civil suit. GAO concluded in early 1999 that "the new IRS system aimed at catching employees who illegally 'browse' through taxpayer files is working on only one of several computer systems, and it cannot detect which activities are legitimate and which are not."[59] And when privacy wasn't obliterated on purpose, the IRS accomplished it with sheer incompetence. A January 1999 GAO report found that six IRS facilities had lost a total of 397 computer tapes with confidential financial information on thousands of taxpayers.[60]

SENATE INVESTIGATION AND CLINTON COUNTERATTACK

The Senate Finance Committee, under the leadership of Sen. William Roth, held oversight hearings into IRS abuses in September 1997 and April 1998. The hearings smoked out the Democrats as unabashed champions of the tax collectors. A few days before the first hearings, Treasury Secretary Robert E. Rubin warned that hearings that did not take into account the millions of taxpayers treated fairly "will ultimately prove detrimental to customer service and revenue collection"[61]—as if the only thing worse than marauding IRS agents was a public exposé of such agents tyrannizing citizens.

The Clinton administration initially vehemently denied that any IRS problem existed. After Congress failed to buy that line, the White House announced that it had already solved the problem by itself. On March 18, 1998, Vice President Al Gore addressed a throng of cheering IRS employees and announced that the Clinton "reform" package "will help us ensure that we have an IRS that is not just taken off people's backs, but put on their side."[62] Gore praised the National Treasury Employees Union: "We need more of this kind of labor-management cooperation, and I would say it is the single greatest reason for our success thus far." (The union busied itself with such activities as fighting congressional legislation to remove solitaire and other games from government workers' computers.)[63]

Gore revealed to the awestruck crowd that "one of the first principles of reinvention is: 'Go to where the ideas are.'"[64] Gore announced a 200-step reform to make the IRS the friend of the American people—visionary changes such as "build a system that focuses on Customers," "develop a new Mission Statement," "measure performance on the Right Things," and "Create an Ideas Advocate." Reform Action #C103.6 inspired civil servants everywhere: "Ensure an adequate supply of forms and materials are available to allow employees to do their jobs."

The Clinton-Gore reinvention package sought to derail any reform that would actually decrease the IRS's power over American citizens. The Clinton administration sought to recast the controversy over the IRS as merely a question of providing better service. After the Senate finished its hearings on IRS abuses, Clinton bragged on May 2, 1998, that "now you can call the IRS and get telephone service six days a week, 18 hours a day. Soon it will be 24 hours a day."[65] Clinton also falsely declared that his new IRS commissioner had spent his entire career in the private sector. Actually, Rossotti was one of the so-called whiz kids of Defense Secretary Robert McNamara during the Pentagon's body-count glory days of the Vietnam War.

Congress eventually enacted IRS reform legislation, which Clinton signed on July 22, 1998.[66] As a result, taxpayers now have the option of making their tax payment checks out to the Treasury Department, instead of the IRS. Former IRS Commissioner Margaret Richardson said the change "could have a very positive psychological impact and help lessen the antagonism" between citizens and the IRS.[67] Perhaps if Congress had voted to allow citizens to make out their tax payments to "Uncle Sam," public approval of the IRS would reach 100 percent. The legislation also created a new oversight board—with a seat at the table guaranteed for the IRS employees union. (This is part of the reason why the union strongly supported the reform bill.)

The final bill required "the IRS to provide an accounting and receipt to the taxpayer (including the amount credited to the taxpayer's account) when the IRS seizes and sells the taxpayer's property."[68] A new law was apparently necessary to compel the IRS to provide better treatment to citizens than that provided by the average carjacker. The act also authorized hefty pay increases for top IRS officials and more power for the IRS unions. Several provisions of the new law provided additional procedural protection to citizens.

While Clinton and Rossotti both claimed speedy and profound turn-arounds in how the IRS treated people under its power, the 1998 law did not stop the abuse of taxpayers. An April 29, 1999, IG report found "no evidence" that almost half of audited taxpayers had been given a copy of IRS Publication 1 (*Your Rights As a Taxpayer*) at the start of the audit, despite federal law requiring that people receive this document. The report also noted, "IRS employees used discretionary enforcement powers in a way that appeared to create an unnecessary hardship for taxpayers. In two districts, 3,500 audits of low-income taxpayers claiming an Earned Income Tax Credit were started by sending a 6-page questionnaire requesting more than 80 items of information. The items requested included amounts spent on food, clothing, gifts, and cosmetics. Much of the information requested was intrusive and had little, if any, relevance to the issues being questioned."[69] The report also found that IRS employees may have been illegally browsing in taxpayers' files in order to selectively target certain people for audits.

A September 1999 IG report found that the IRS failed to give 26 percent of affected taxpayers 30 days' notice before levying their bank accounts or paychecks, or to inform them of their right to appeal a levy action before it happens.[70] Another report found that the agency failed to follow legal and internal guidelines in 36 percent of seizures of taxpayers' property.[71] Although the 1998 legislation prohibited the IRS from "evaluating individual work performance in a way that may violate or encourage employees to violate taxpayer rights," the Inspector General, in another September 1999 report, found many cases in which tax collection statistics were still being used for such evaluations.[72] GAO reported in October 1999 that the IRS continued to place a higher priority on raising revenue than on customer service in its evaluations of employee performance. GAO observed that there was little reason to expect the IRS to change how it treated taxpayers in part because of the agency's "poor track record for implementing reforms."[73] GAO concluded that "it could be years before a new performance management system is fully operational."

SMITING CLINTON'S ENEMIES

In the 1970s Congress responded to President Nixon's political abuse of the IRS by severely restricting political contacts between the White House and the IRS. But this law, like many other laws, did not apply to the Clinton administration.

In 1995, the White House and the Democratic National Committee produced a 331-page report entitled "Communication Stream of Conspiracy Commerce."[74] The report attacked magazines, think tanks, and others who had criticized President Clinton. In the subsequent years, many of the organizations mentioned in the White House report were targeted for IRS audits. Overall, more than 20 conservative organizations and almost a dozen high-profile Clinton critics were audited.

In 1996, responding to a letter sent over from the White House, the IRS launched an audit of the Western Journalism Center.[75] The center's director, Joseph Farah, wrote in 1998, "When our accountant questioned the direction of the audit, IRS field agent Thomas Cederquist responded: 'Look, this is a political case and the decision will be made at the national level.'" Farah noted, "The IRS showed little real concern with our bookkeeping procedures, our financial records or our fund-raising techniques. Instead, the tax collector questioned our journalistic standards and practices, our choice of investigative reporting projects and, most of all, our continuing probe of [Vince] Foster's death." The audit dragged on for nine months; as a result, half the center's staff was laid off and, according to Farah, the "strain on our time and resources nearly bankrupted the organization."[76]

The Landmark Legal Foundation was another conservative nonprofit hit by an IRS audit. After being cleared by the IRS, the foundation filed a Freedom of Information Act request to find out who initiated the charges that led to its audit and the audit of other conservative organizations. The foundation's lawsuit quoted IRS officer Terry Hallihan, who allegedly stated, according to an attendee at an IRS meeting, "that documents identifying the names of members of Congress and their staffers as the source of audit requests had been, or were being, shredded—and then went on to suggest ways to disguise future requests so that they did not appear to be coming from Congressmen."[77] After losing two separate lawsuits over its stonewalling, the IRS provided the Foundation with roughly 8,000 pages detailing who made the accusations that led to audits. But most of the information on the pages was blacked out. (Results of a congressional investigation are pending.) The IRS claimed that it could not find 114 key files relating to possible political manipulation of audits of tax-exempt organizations.[78] The Justice Department sought to block the Landmark Legal Foundation from even questioning the IRS official who allegedly suggested shredding, but federal judge Henry Kennedy overruled the government's ploy.[79] The Clinton administration bent over backwards to protect congressmen—and its own White House officials—who had tried to set the IRS on conservative tails. A *Wall Street Journal* editorial observed: "The IRS position is incredible. It says letters from politicians asking that someone be audited are confidential tax-return information."[80]

On November 15, 1999, the Associated Press revealed that "officials in the Democratic White House and members of both parties in Congress have prompted hundreds of audits of political opponents in the 1990s. The audit requests ranged from the forwarding of constituent letters and newspaper articles alleging wrongdoing to personal demands for audits from members of Congress."[81] The Associated Press noted, "Lawmakers' requests are stamped 'expedite' to remind IRS officials they must reply in writing within 15 days. A few requests reviewed by the AP were marked with notations such as 'hot politically' or 'sensitive.'. . . The IRS computer tracking system in Washington denotes the name of a politician who refers a matter. The original letter from the White House or lawmaker is forwarded to the case agent."[82] This exposé should have been a major bombshell, but most politicians of both parties showed no interest in discovering whether the IRS had been used to suppress criticism of the Clinton administration.

CONCLUSION

Clinton succeeded in preserving almost all the powers of the IRS. His IRS policy was based on the presumption that the federal government could almost always spend a dollar more wisely and productively than the person who earned it. Thus, preserving the IRS's vast power and procedural advantages over average citizens was deemed necessary for national progress.

The obituary of the Clinton administration's reinvention of the IRS was contained in a February 2000 GAO report that found that the IRS frequently continued to suffer "significant delays—in some instances in excess of 10 years— in recording payments made by taxpayers to related taxpayer accounts. We also found payments that were not recorded at all in related taxpayer accounts. Some of these delayed or unrecorded payments were made in the late 1980s."[83] Taxpayers continued to suffer because of IRS incompetence. GAO noted, "In one case, it took 18 months for the IRS to correct an input error that resulted in an erroneous assessment of over $160,000 against a taxpayer who was actually due a refund."[84] GAO warned that "we continued to find serious weaknesses with IRS' general controls designed to protect computing resources such as networks, computer equipment, software programs, data, and facilities from unauthorized use, modification, loss, and disclosure."[85] GAO groused that the IRS was still unable to balance its own books, that the agency could not produce trustworthy financial statements, and that the "IRS continues to be plagued by serious internal control and systems deficiencies that hinder its ability to achieve lasting financial management improvements."[86]

In early 2000, the Clinton administration proposed the biggest increase in the IRS budget since the 1980s.[87] IRS Chief Rossotti fretted that the IRS was auditing fewer people than in earlier years; Rossotti warned that the decline in IRS audit rates "poses the risk of increased unfairness in administration of the law, and ultimately, undermining our entire system of voluntary tax compliance."[88] As usual, the key to voluntary tax compliance was creating sufficient fear to keep people submissive. Treasury Secretary Lawrence Summers warned that "we need to begin increasing capacity" to enforce the tax laws "to maintain people's confidence that this is a tax system that works."[89] The Clinton administration continued to claim that more people lose faith in the tax system through insufficient enforcement than because of the IRS abusing millions of citizens every year.

FOUR

AFFIRMATIVE ACTION, NOW AND FOREVER

PRESIDENT BILL CLINTON PRIDED HIMSELF on his sensitivity on racial issues. In 1997, Clinton proclaimed that he wanted "to lead the American people in a great and unprecedented conversation about race . . . Honest dialogue will not be easy at first. We'll all have to get past defensiveness and fear and political correctness and other barriers to honesty."[1]

For Clinton to call for "honesty" on racial issues was ironic. Clinton appointees perfected the art of mugging businesses with bogus discrimination statistics. His administration openly defied Supreme Court and other federal court rulings on affirmative action. The "massive resistance" tactics of the 1950s were revived and used to defend federal (instead of state and local) racism. Clinton also liberally indulged in race-baiting and smearing the motives of his critics.

THE NEW "MASSIVE RESISTANCE"

In 1995, the Supreme Court ruled in the case of *Adarand v. Pena*. In that case, a Colorado construction company was denied a subcontract on a federal highway contract despite offering the lowest bid because the company's owner was white and the prime contractor was under a federal Transportation Department mandate to use black contractors, even though they charged more. After the white-owned company sued, the Clinton administration pulled out all the stops to defend the preferential contract system.

The Supreme Court, in one of the most eloquent decisions of the decade, struck down the racial quotas as unconstitutional: "Any person, of whatever race, has the right to demand that any governmental actor subject to the Constitution justify any racial classification subjecting that person to unequal treatment under the strictest judicial scrutiny."[2] Justice Clarence Thomas wrote, "Racial paternalism and its unintended consequences can be as poisonous and pernicious as any other form of discrimination. So-called 'benign' discrimination teaches many that because of chronic and apparently immutable handicaps, minorities cannot compete with them without their patronizing indulgence. Inevitably, such programs engender attitudes of superiority or, alternatively, provoke resentment among those who believe that they have been wronged by the government's use of race. These programs stamp minorities with a badge of inferiority . . . Under our constitution, there can be no such thing as either a creditor or a debtor race."[3] Justice Antonin Scalia wrote: "To pursue the concept of racial entitlement even for the most admirable and benign of purposes is to reinforce and preserve for future mischief the way of thinking that produced race slavery, race privilege and race hatred."[4]

A Congressional Research Service report a few months before the *Adarand* decision found that the federal government ran more than 160 racial preference programs, which steered more than $10 billion a year to minority firms.[5] Many of the programs contained explicit quotas and heavy penalties for incorrect color-coding.

Clinton responded to the *Adarand* decision by going through the pretense of promising to follow the Constitution. In a July 1995 speech, Clinton denounced the type of affirmative action that seeks to "impose change by leveling draconian penalties on employers who didn't meet certain imposed, ultimately arbitrary, and sometimes unachievable quotas. That was rejected out of a sense of fairness."[6] Yet that is exactly what federal agencies were doing. Clinton defended affirmative action by making one inaccurate statement after another and appearing "shocked, shocked" that anyone would think that the government was imposing racial preferences. Clinton declared, "I know some people are honestly concerned about the times affirmative action doesn't work, when it's done in the wrong way. And I know there are times when some employers don't use it in the right way. They may cut corners and treat a flexible goal as a quota. They may give opportunities to people who are unqualified instead of those who deserve it . . . When this happens, it is also wrong. But it isn't affirmative action, and it is not legal." Thus, "affirmative action" was only the imposition of good quotas—quotas that were not quotas—quotas that just happened after some government official held a regulatory gun to someone's head.[7]

Clinton announced that he directed all federal agencies to comply with *Adarand* and that he would tolerate "no quotas in theory or in practice." Clinton concluded, "We should reaffirm the principle of affirmative action and fix the practices. We should have a simple slogan: Mend it, but don't end it."[8]

Assistant Attorney General for Civil Rights Deval Patrick best captured the administration's response when he declared: "It is important that we are not intimidated by *Adarand*. We have to take *Adarand* on."[9] The Justice Department saw its role as actively combating any Supreme Court decision that limited arbitrary federal power on racial issues. And when a president ignores a Supreme Court ruling on civil rights, there is no higher power to send in the National Guard.

On April 22, 1996, a federal judge issued an injunction banning the Houston Metropolitan Transit Authority (MTA) from using racial preferences in its contract awards. Houston MTA had required that 21 percent of its contracts be given to certified minority "disadvantaged business enterprises." Four days later, Gordon Linton, administrator of the Federal Transit Administration (FTA), warned Houston that hundreds of millions of dollars of federal highway and mass transit money would be withheld unless the racial preferences were put back into the contract system.[10] If city officials resurrected the quotas, they could have been sent to prison for contempt of court. A *Houston Chronicle* editorial observed, "Linton, who took an oath to uphold the Constitution, stands on precarious ground when he insists that Metro behave in a manner that a federal judge has found unconstitutional."[11] Federal funds were frozen and the rebuilding of Houston downtown streets was delayed for over a year. The controversy was resolved with a disingenuous "compromise." The feds granted the Houston MTA a temporary exemption from having an affirmative action program—conditioned on a promise that the MTA "would continue to monitor the racial makeup of contractors." The FTA stressed that the MTA "will be expected to study the racial makeup of contracts . . . If after April 30 [1998] Metro has not been found by coincidence to be awarding at least 21 percent of its construction business to women and minorities in the previous six months, the FTA will again cut off funding," the Houston Chronicle reported on September 20, 1997.[12]

On March 19, 1996, a federal appeals court, applying *Adarand*, struck down as unconstitutional racial preference criteria used for admissions and financial aid at the University of Texas Law School.[13] The appeals court ruled that "the use of ethnic diversity simply to achieve racial heterogeneity, even as part of the consideration of a number of factors, is unconstitutional."[14] The Texas attorney general ruled that, in light of the court decision, all Texas colleges must cease using race as a consideration for admission and financial aid.

Norma Cantu, the assistant secretary for civil rights in the federal Education Department, responded by sending a letter threatening Texas education officials with a cutoff of $500 million in federal aid to higher education if they obeyed the court decision. Cantu warned Texas officials that universities "have a clear legal obligation" to continue using race as a factor for admissions.[15] Cantu backed down after receiving a letter from acting Solicitor General Walter Dellinger informing her that the appeals court decision "was the law in Texas."[16] When Clinton was asked, after making a speech to black journalists, about the fracas between the Education Department and Justice Department, he assured the audience that his appointees would "continue to use federal law to the maximum extent we can to promote an integrated educational environment." Clinton told the audience, in response to questions about anti-quota efforts, that "there may be some ways to get around it, and we're looking at it and working on it."[17]

In November 1996, California voters—thanks to the courageous leadership of Ward Connerly—passed Proposition 209, which banned all racial quotas and preferences by state and local governments. The Clinton administration was outraged. The Justice Department filed a brief with a federal appeals court charging that Proposition 209 violated the equal protection clause of the Fourteenth Amendment to the Constitution by placing a "special burden on the ability of women and minorities to obtain beneficial programs through the political process."[18] The Justice Department complained that Proposition 209 "does more than simply repeal existing affirmative action programs . . . It also effectively limits the access of minorities and women—the primary beneficiaries of affirmative action—to the levers of government." The Justice Department asserted: "States may not . . . single out racial and gender issues for unique treatment in the political process, where that treatment effectively places a special burden on minorities and women."[19] The logic was bizarre: because women and minorities had won special preferences through political processes, any attempt to restore equal rights would violate the equal protection clause. The Justice Department complained, "In such a case the majority has not merely won a political battle. It has altered the rules for all future political battles and thereby impermissibly entrenched its power." In fact, the Justice Department was not concerned about the "power" of the majority—but about any limitations on government officials to dictate racial winners and losers. Lawyer Michael Carvin noted that, according to the Justice Department, "the Fourteenth Amendment grants minorities and women . . . a constitutionally-guaranteed veto power over any state policy that does not 'inure to their benefit.'"[20] A federal appeals court demolished the Clinton position; after paraphrasing the Justice Department's legal theory, the court ridiculed it: "If merely stating this alleged equal protection violation does not suffice to refute it, the central tenet of the Equal Protection Clause teeters on the brink of incoherence."[21] After the federal appeals court trounced the Justice Department's position, Clinton announced that affirmative action supporters must "regroup and find new ways to achieve the same objective."[22] And since Clinton controlled the federal government and effectively ignored federal court decisions, preserving affirmative action was not difficult.

Because blacks and Hispanics tend to score significantly lower than whites and Asian Americans on standardized tests such as the SAT, they are often admitted in lower percentages to top universities. The Education Department came up with a simple solution: criminalize the SAT. Proposed federal rules, released in May 1999 and entitled "Nondiscrimination in High-Stakes Testing," declared: "The use of any educational test which has a significant disparate impact on members of any particular race, national origin, or sex is discriminatory."[23] Thus, reliance on SAT scores for admission decisions would be a near-automatic civil rights violation—and could cost an offending college all federal funds (including loans received by its students). Deputy Assistant Education Secretary for Civil Rights Arthur Coleman announced: "Excellence and equity must, as a matter of educational policy and legal standards, go hand and hand."[24] The proposal set off a firestorm in academia as university administrators recognized that the new policy could destroy their ability to select students without a federal veto. Colleges were initially given less than a week to respond to the proposal before it was finalized.[25] John Leo noted in *U.S. News and World Report:* "The department is in effect saying that colleges using standardized tests can expect to be called in for long and grueling interrogations that most of us would call harassment."[26] Terry Pell of the Center for Individual Rights called the proposal "an extralegal form of bureaucratic terrorism."[27] Former Justice Department Deputy Assistant Attorney General for Civil Rights Roger Clegg observed that it is typical for the Education Department's Office of Civil Rights "to coerce people through subregulatory guidance—in other words, without giving formal notice and opportunity for comment to the general public. The office instead proceeds by threats and intimidation tactics that it administers informally and, where possible, secretly. But this time, college officials were sufficiently perturbed by the guidance to leak it to the press."[28] (The Education Department may have felt emboldened by their 1996 success in browbeating the College Board and Educational Testing Service into making the PSAT easier for girls.[29])

The Clinton administration made little or no change to the vast majority of federal racial preference programs. In a few cases, formal quotas and set-asides were replaced by "aspirational goals"—sounding like mere friendly requests by federal overseers. But, as Roger Clegg observed, "You don't want to disappoint the 'aspirations' of an 800-pound gorilla, and that is what the federal government is."[30] Clegg said that even reformed programs were still de facto quotas.

The *Adarand* decision did not dim the Justice Department's enthusiasm for imposing hiring quotas. The Justice Department sought control over the personnel policies of police departments that did not hire enough blacks or women. As Clegg noted, the Justice Department "sued the Philadelphia area's regional transit police for discriminating against female applicants by requiring them to be able to run 1.5 miles in less than 12 minutes. The Department says this requirement is 'unrelated to job performance' and wants different standards for men and women.'"[31] (The Justice Department proffered no evidence that muggers run slower when chased by a female cop.)

Clinton's Justice Department strong-armed local governments to redefine what a good cop should be. The Justice Department's Civil Rights Division worked overtime to dumb down the Nassau County, New York, police department. The Justice Department effectively compelled the department to use a hiring test that was "validated" to insure the correct numbers of racial winners and losers. As Professor Linda Gottfredson reported in the *Wall Street Journal:*

> Many exceptionally well-qualified candidates received very low or failing scores. Some had years of experience as probation officers or as cops in other jurisdictions; others had or were pursuing graduate degrees in law or criminal justice. A look at those who passed the test is even more disturbing. According to close observers, a high proportion of top scorers not only have poor academic records, but also have outstanding arrest warrants, are unable to account for years of their work history or refuse to take a drug test.
>
> The final test battery . . . replaced scores on a reading test with a pass/fail grade: Candidates merely had to read as well as the worst readers—the bottom 1 percent—among incumbent police officers . . . [and excluded] from consideration all traditional cognitive tests, despite their superior value in predicting job performance.[32]

Washington lawyer Dennis Shea noted in a column on MSNBC, "Since testing for cognitive skills like reading comprehension, writing and memory has a 'disparate impact' on certain minority groups, the Justice Department know-it-alls have decided to pressure police departments across the country to emphasize non-cognitive 'skills' like personality traits and personal interests when devising their own entrance exams. The Justice Department has threatened legal action if the police departments don't go along with their 'suggestions.' The obvious purpose of the department's bullying tactics is not only to force police departments to hire by quota but to ensure that the police entrance exams are racially gerrymandered." Lowering hiring standards to boost minority hiring can also boost the crime rate. An April 2000 *Economic Inquiry* article by economist John Lott concluded that cities under Justice Department consent decrees to boost minority hiring suffered significant increases in crime: "Violent crime rises by 1.9 percent and property crime by 2.1 percent for each additional year the consent decree is in effect."[33] Lott noted that "it is the most heavily black communities that are the most at risk from the increased crime produced by affirmative-action policies."

The future of affirmative action was telegraphed by the policies that the Clinton White House imposed on the federal workforce:

- The Food and Drug Administration put out an "Equal Employment Opportunity Handbook" that provided guidelines for hiring, announcing that, as Stuart Taylor reported in *Legal Times*, "the common requirement for 'knowledge of rules of grammar' and 'ability to spell accurately' in clerical and secretarial job descriptions' should be shunned because it may impede courtship of 'underrepresented groups or individuals with disabilities.'" The handbook also warned managers that interviews should not be used "to judge highly subjective traits such as motivation, ambition, maturity, personality and neatness."[34]
- In 1995, the Pentagon sent out word that "special permission will be required for the promotion of all white men without disabilities."[35]
- Navy Secretary John Dalton issued a policy that henceforth naval officers will be commissioned "in a percentage approximately equal to the racial makeup of the populace."[36]
- The U.S. Forest Service was harshly criticized for failing to hire enough female firefighters (many applicants failed the strength test). The agency sought to solve the problem with a job announcement declaring: "Only unqualified applicants may apply." A second announcement specified, "Only applicants who do not meet [job requirement] standards will be considered." The *Washington Times* noted, "An internal Forest Service document indicates that, in some cases, critical firefighting positions were left vacant or filled with unqualified temporary workers because no women applied for the posts."[37]

VOLUNTARY NUKES

When does a goal for hiring become a racial quota?

When there is a federal agent sitting across the table with a nuclear bomb. The Office of Federal Contract Compliance Programs (OFCCP), a little known but extremely powerful branch of the U.S. Department of Labor, is America's premier racial racketeering agency. OFCCP Director Shirley Wilcher announced in 1995: "Enforcement of equality in the work place includes penalties to deter violations and to get results as quickly and efficiently as the law permits."[38] Not equality of opportunity, not equal chances for equal talent— but equality, plain and simple, by hook or by crook.

OFCCP gains much of its power from its ability to debar private companies from federal contracts. Assistant Secretary of Labor Bernard Anderson described this power as "kind of like a nuclear weapon."[39]

For many products, the federal government is a monopoly buyer: private companies that produce such products either satisfy government demands or perish. The OFCCP enforces affirmative action obligations on federal contractors. Over 200,000 companies and institutions with over 25 million employees are subject to the OFCCP's racial and gender dictates. The OFCCP, with over 500 compliance officers, conducts over 4,000 compliance reviews a year.

Wilcher described her agency's mission in 1994: "We see whether or not minorities or women are underutilized in an organization, based on a very elaborate formula. We look at the availability of our protected groups in the labor force . . . [and] argue that the . . . employer really needs to have a goal to achieve parity with the available work force."[40] If the employer does not achieve parity, the OFCCP condemns them for "bad faith" and demands exorbitant amounts of back pay for people not hired, as well as more federal control over hiring and promotion.

The agency routinely begins its investigation of a federal contractor by "discovering" the "underrepresentation" of women or certain racial or ethnic groups in particular jobs. It then requires the contractor to establish "goals and timetables" to increase its minority hiring. Wilcher lied to Congress in 1995, claiming that "the numerical goals approach . . . is not based on racial or gender preferences" and that, under OFCCP regulations, "selections for employment or promotion must be made without regard to race or gender."[41] But a September 1994 discussion paper on affirmative action requirements for construction contractors stated: "OFCCP's experience has demonstrated that utilization goals [for minorities and women] are the most concrete and effective system for implementing the affirmative action obligation contained in the Executive Order."[42]

OFCCP's passion for correct numbers far exceeds its devotion to the law. Peter Kirsanow, a black Cleveland labor lawyer, observed: "The OFCCP as it now operates is a racial spoils system. For a long time we just called them the Office of Racial, Sexual and Ethnic Engineering."[43] New Jersey human resources consultant Mary Jane Sinclair observed: "The government regs take the standing that you are out to screw the system so we are going to screw you first. It is like you are sitting down with a Mafia don . . . they put the fear of God into you— that is how they get the numbers."[44]

In 1995, an OFCCP compliance officer descended upon City Utilities of Springfield, Missouri, and spent almost an entire year going through its files. After he went through the company's 250-page affirmative action plan and found no violations, he ordered the utility to completely recalculate its personnel analyses, hoping that the revised version would produce grounds to condemn its hiring and promotion policies. The official demanded "documentation and reasons why virtually every minority and female considered for promotion and new hire was not selected for nearly every opening," Jennifer Taylor, the company's personnel director, testified to Congress.[45] Though the company had roughly the same percentage of minorities on its payroll as in the local labor market, the OFCCP demanded that the company in the future recruit from the Kansas City area—170 miles away. Taylor observed, "We must ignore a readily obtainable source of local labor, which is more motivated to remain with us because of our [location], simply because of their race."

An OFCCP compliance officer arrived at the offices of Carolina Steel in Greensboro, North Carolina, in 1993 to analyze its hiring and personnel practices. Carolina Steel had a significantly higher percentage of blacks on its payroll than were in the local labor force. However, the OFCCP capitalized on the company's location to find it guilty. Carolina Steel's main office is a block and a half from the local unemployment office. Because unemployment compensation recipients are required to submit a certain number of job applications each week, Carolina Steel was deluged with them. The OFCCP judged the company by its large number of black applicants who were not hired. At the time of the OFCCP audit, Carolina Steel was hiring for an isolated work site fifteen miles away from Greensboro; since there was no public transportation to the site, workers were required to provide their own transportation. Since a higher percentage of black applicants did not own cars, a higher percentage of them were not considered for jobs at that site. That was all that was necessary for the OFCCP to convict the company. Sadie Cox, the company's human resources director, observed, "The OFCCP was totally inflexible. They would not listen to anything that we had—they would not consider the statistics that showed we are in compliance."[46]

The OFCCP issued a settlement demand that would have destroyed the company and put Carolina Steel's 500 employees out of work—so that OFCCP would have a pot of money to distribute to people who had never worked a day at its mills. After two years of haggling, the OFCCP issued a press release announcing the company had agreed to pay $300,000 to 22 rejected job applicants. Even this claim was false. Carolina Steel had agreed to pay only about $120,000, and that was scattered among 264 applicants—many of whom were not hired subsequently because they failed drug tests. Carolina Steel CEO Len Wise said, "We don't think that we were fairly treated under the law, but we settled in order to get them off our back."[47] The workers didn't seem to think it was fair, either; a local television station interviewed the company's black employees, and not one of them said they thought Carolina Steel was racially biased.

On February 13, 1995, an OFCCP official conducted a "compliance" inspection of Konza Construction Company of Junction City, Kansas.[48] A month later, the OFCCP sent the company a "conciliation agreement" that condemned it for failing to have 6.9 percent females working as concrete finishers, truck drivers, and laborers—the national goal first proclaimed by OFCCP in the 1970s. The company had done everything it could to attract skilled female employees, including contacting the state employment service and women's employment groups in the area. The OFCCP dropped its demand after the company's chief, John Trygg, said that he was going to complain to his congressman about the agency imposing a mandatory hiring quota."[49] (The OFCCP may have been unusually sensitive to such a tactic, since Republicans had just captured Congress and were huffing about ending racial quotas.)

The OFCCP dumbs down the work force. The agency announced in 1995: "No distinction is made between minimum and other qualifications in an evaluation of the total selection process [hiring and promoting]" to detect racial or gender bias in hiring and promotion.[50] Former OFCCP Director Ellen Shong Bergman noted that one OFCCP district director penalizes contractors for "failure to select a woman, Black, or Hispanic who is as qualified as the least qualified incumbent, irrespective of superior qualifications of other non-minority applicants."[51] The OFCCP has sanctioned many companies for relying on written application tests that had a disparate impact on minorities.

The OFCCP is carrying out a jihad against the so-called glass ceiling—invisible "attitudinal" barriers to the advancement of women or minorities into the top ranks of corporate power. In 1996, the OFCCP sent a notice of violation to the University of Cincinnati instructing it to inform 157 faculty members that "they are part of a group of female and minority professors whose salary should be adjusted." James Wesner, the university's general counsel, explained the crackpot statistical method by which the agency supposedly proved the university's guilt: "It involves creating a hypothetical average faculty member—one male, one female [who] has an average salary of X. You then go through and compare females or minorities with different salaries. And there are certain percentages above and below that average salary—and the ones that are below are [assumedly illegally] underpaid."[52] Even in cases in which one professor had a doctorate from an Ivy League school and another had a master's from Ball State, or one had 20 years experience and another was a rookie, the OFCCP made no adjustment in comparing salaries. The agency's slipshod calculations were sufficient to seek to browbeat university officials into paying millions of dollars of back pay and raises to "protected groups." One of Washington's most experienced labor lawyers observed of the method used in this audit: "They do that all the time. They see this as a quick and dirty way to collect a lot of back pay from institutions that are very dependent on government contracts."[53] The OFCCP's glass ceiling methods are routinely characterized as blackmail by labor lawyers.

The OFCCP is legendary for the pretexts that it concocts to accuse private companies of violating the Equal Pay Act. One manager at a Washington, D.C. area company summarized the attitude of the OFCCP official who descended upon her firm: "We don't need no stinking statistical significance!"[54] As long as there are racial or gender disparities in salaries, the company can be proclaimed guilty. American Enterprise Institute economist Diana Furchtgott-Roth observed, "Measuring so-called discrimination by comparing women's wages to the median wage is like saying there's something wrong with oranges because they are smaller than grapefruits."[55]

A report by the Equal Employment Advisory Committee, an organization of large government contractors, noted that some OFCCP auditors considered compensation decisions based on "performance ratings history" and "promotion, demotion, or downgrades" as unacceptable "because these may be seen as 'subjective' factors over which the employer has some control."[56] The report notes, "The federal pay system with which compliance officers are most familiar is a very rigid one consisting of 15 grades and 10 steps within each grade. Over time, everyone progresses through the same series of within-grade step increases and/or promotion-related grade increases."[57] The fact that a private company does not treat its employees like government workers—that is, paying them largely according to how long they have hung around the office—appears to some compliance officers like foul play.

Some OFCCP agents are rewarded for abusing their power. Former Director Bergman told Congress in 1995: "There is an institutional tolerance for compliance officers who can cajole, defraud or bully contractors into behavior that goes beyond the agency's legitimate authority, and sometimes goes beyond that permitted by any law . . . Never, never have I seen or heard of such an employee being dismissed; sometimes they are promoted. There are not, and never have been, any meaningful consequences to individual employees of the OFCCP who engage in intimidating contractors or misrepresentation of law or policy." Bergman noted that some high-ranking officials routinely and openly lie about what federal law requires contractors to do. One district director in California achieved notoriety for his heavy-handed methods. According to one highly respected attorney, the director shows up at site visits and warns the contractor: "If you get a lawyer, I will make it more difficult for you." The director has proclaimed to harrowed employees during audits: "You won't have a job around here much longer unless you cooperate with us because you are in deep trouble."[58] Contractor employees have been left in tears by his bullying. His methods have been so successful at racking up settlement numbers that he has been invited to other OFCCP districts to lecture about his "enforcement model."

Many federal contractors presumed that the Supreme Court's 1995 sweeping rejection of affirmative action in the *Adarand* decision meant that the OFCCP could no longer dictate their hiring, promotion, pay, and firing policies. But high-ranking OFCCP officials bragged a few months after the decision that they had "come down hard" on contractors and lawyers who claimed that the Supreme Court decision eviscerated OFCCP's power.[59]

FEAR-MONGERING FOR EQUALITY

Gilbert Casellas, Clinton's first chairman of the Equal Employment Opportunity Commission, noted at his inaugural press conference in 1994 that some businessmen are frightened when they get a call from the IRS or the EPA. Casellas warned, "By the end of my term, I hope people worry when they get a call from the EEOC."[60]

Here was a laudatory public policy goal: maximization of fear and anxiety in the private sector. EEOC staff did its best to fulfill Casellas's aspirations.

The EEOC tried to fry Koch Poultry Co. in 1995 for hiring too many Hispanics and not enough blacks. Mark Kaminsky, the Chicago-based chicken company's chief financial officer, recounted the EEOC's demands: "They told us that we were supposed to take out newspaper ads that asked for people who might have applied for a job, or if they were thinking about applying, so they might be entitled to a financial settlement. They said they wanted $5.2 million. They never put that in writing, but the EEOC investigator spelled it out for us. Of course, the entire company isn't worth that much, so we told them no way, we can't afford it . . . Then they told us that they didn't know what we could afford unless they saw our financial records. So we gave them our records. And they said: 'OK, you can afford this.' And they made it $1.5 million. And then they dropped it to $800,000."[61] Kaminsky later commented that EEOC officials "really don't have any specific individuals" who the company supposedly discriminated against. Kaminsky summarized the EEOC's method: "It is like being guilty by association—since you have all these Hispanics, you must have discriminated."[62] The company spent a quarter-million dollars defending itself.

No evidence is required for the EEOC to launch an inquisition. Hans Morsbach, owner of several restaurants and pubs in Chicago, was pressured by an EEOC inspector in 1994 to sign a "conciliation agreement" and make large payments to people who had never worked for him and had never even applied for a job at his restaurants. The EEOC inspectors refused to even tell him what crime he had been accused of committing. After Morsbach refused the agency's initial demand, an EEOC employee sent him a letter informing him: "Although I cannot release your file to you at this time, I can advise you that the finding [of illegal discrimination] is based in large part on a notice placed with an employment agency, the Job Exchange, on September 16, 1993, seeking 'wts' described as 'young, bub.'"[63] The agency noted that none of the four people Morsbach hired since that date had been over the age 40. Therefore, he was guilty of violating the Age Discrimination Act. *Chicago Tribune* columnist Mike Royko summarized subsequent events:

> So Mr. Morsbach made what appears to be a reasonable suggestion: He asked the EEOC bureaucrats if they would show him the ad, tell him in what publication it appeared, who placed the ad, and he might be able to figure out what the heck is going on.
>
> No, say the bureaucrats. He has two options: He can mediate a settlement, which means hiring four people who are over 40 years old, giving them back pay, full benefits, seniority, etc. etc . . . If he doesn't do these things, then they will take him to court.[64]

Morsbach complained: "They gave me no particulars, none at all. They refused to even discuss the matter of guilt at all—it was a given."[65] The company that allegedly placed the ad for Morsbach denied that it had ever printed ads with such language, and stated that the EEOC had not been in touch with them to investigate the case. An analysis by *Crain's Small Business* magazine noted, "The absence of evidence that the restaurant had turned away any job applicant on account of age was apparently irrelevant to the EEOC."[66]

On March 29, 1994, Russell Vernon, the owner of West Point Market in Akron, Ohio, received a notice from the EEOC informing him that his firm had "failed and/or refused to hire Blacks for all positions because of their race."[67] The EEOC had received no complaints from frustrated job seekers; instead, the investigation was launched solely at the behest of an EEOC commissioner. (EEOC regs allow the agency to pursue a "Commissioners' Charge"—often high-profile cases designed to advance the agency's national agenda.) On January 21, 1995, the EEOC issued a "decision" that the agency had "reasonable cause" to believe that the market was guilty of racial bias in hiring. The EEOC then offered a settlement under which, as Vernon related, his company would "have to buy full-page ads aimed exclusively at blacks, impose a 33 percent minority hiring quota, and pay nearly $100,000 to 24 African-American applicants we hadn't hired. If we refused, we faced a long, costly court battle."[68] The EEOC backed down just after Congress passed legislation in 1996 to make it easier for small companies to sue the government for abusive prosecutions. The market and the EEOC reached a settlement under which the company paid no money and admitted no wrongdoing but did pledge to reach out more broadly in its hiring efforts. As part of the settlement the company encouraged the 24 job seekers to reapply and offered $1,000 scholarships if they stayed with the company for a year. None of the 24 people reapplied.[69]

The EEOC will sue a company over almost any procedure that results in an incorrect number of minority employees. *Crain's Small Business* concluded:

> Owners of businesses sued by the EEOC . . . told strikingly similar stories of investigators who seem to presume an employer is guilty, an investigative process that affords the employer scant opportunity to present a defense, and non-negotiable settlement demands invariably including large monetary penalties. Employers often are shocked to learn that long-standing personnel practices used for legitimate business purposes sometimes run afoul of employment discrimination laws . . . A company using word-of-mouth hiring courts trouble if the method yields a workforce that does not reflect the ethnic composition of the area deemed by the EEOC to represent its labor market.[70]

The EEOC measures its success by how many employers it finds guilty, and by how much money it takes them for. The EEOC routinely pressures employers to pay off complainants, even when the EEOC lacks clear evidence that the employer was guilty of discrimination. A December 27, 1999, EEOC press release bragged that, in the most recent fiscal year, the agency had increased "the rate of resolutions favorable to charging parties to 16.5 percent (up from 12 percent in FY 1998 and 9 percent in FY 1996)."[71] Filing unwarranted discrimination complaints has long been a tactic of retaliation or intimidation against employers or former employers. Apparently, the EEOC would consider itself doing a perfect job if it could conclude that 100 percent of discrimination complaints were justified. In the "EEOC Accomplishments Report for Fiscal Year 1999," the agency declared that the new chairwoman, Ida Castro, "has focused on . . . pursuing fair and vigorous enforcement against 'bad actors.'"[72] But many EEOC employees consider any accused employer a "bad actor." The report bragged that the agency had "obtained a record $307.2 million in monetary benefits for charging parties." The EEOC's internal newsletter, *Equal Times*, frequently lists victories achieved by regional offices that result in payments of $2,500 or $5,000 to employees or ex-employees who threatened to sue their employers for discrimination. While such achievements look good on a press release, the EEOC fails to mention that the average cost of defending against a discrimination lawsuit for an employer is far higher than such settlements. The more expensive discrimination lawsuits become, the more arbitrary the power the EEOC acquires over employers.

In late 1993, the EEOC proposed new rules to prohibit what the agency called religious harassment in the workplace. The agency stated in the *Federal Register* that "recent case law on this issue emphasizes the importance of considering the perspective of the victim of the harassment rather than adopting notions of acceptable behavior that may prevail in a particular workplace."[73] The agency's proposed restrictions were so broad that they evoked protests from across the political spectrum. Gary Bauer, president of the Family Research Council, complained, "Rather than rely on an unambiguous standard that requires a showing of significant and actual harm to an employee, the EEOC has set a legal standard that will make it of doubtful legality for any company employee to place a calendar with a religious theme on his bulletin board; share her faith with coworkers around the donut cart at break time; invite another employee to come to his church or for Bible study."[74] The ACLU observed that the proposal was so broad that it "could lead someone to the erroneous conclusion that a religion-free workplace is required." Congress was outraged; the House voted 366 to 37 to prohibit the EEOC from using any funds to enforce any policy "covering harassment based upon religion."[75] The agency tucked its tail between its legs and withdrew its regulations.

On October 26, 1999, the EEOC revealed that it might compel employers to rehire and provide back pay to fired employees who were illegal immigrants. This new policy reversed without warning a policy that the EEOC had promulgated ten years before: a 1986 law made it punishable by up to five years in prison to knowingly hire an illegal immigrant. EEOC Chairman Ida Castro announced: "This guidance makes clear that the anti-discrimination laws under the Commission's jurisdiction protect all employees across the country, regardless of their work status."[76] EEOC promised that it would keep complaints from illegal workers confidential—though the agency could use the threat to notify the INS as a lever to bring an employer to its knees. The EEOC had a legal obligation to notify the INS about illegal immigrant workers but effectively announced that its obligation to equal opportunity exempted it from the federal statute book. The EEOC's "full employment for illegal aliens" policy was a bone pitched to Hispanic voters at a time when the Gore campaign was struggling.

The EEOC does have a hard job, though, considering the mendacity of some employers involved in cases before the agency. Take the case of Sean Haddon, a French chef. After he married a black lady, his co-workers began harassing him and he believed he was wrongfully denied a promotion. Haddon filed a complaint with the EEOC. Haddon's employer was furious about the embarrassment generated by the complaint. Haddon's supervisor, Gary Walters, wrote a memo declaring: "Chef Haddon must go! He has slandered me . . . his frivolous EEOC complaint has wasted innumerable hours of otherwise productive time" of employees and supervisors.[77] After he was fired, his employer, in an attempt to block him from filing a discrimination suit, publicly announced that he had quit voluntarily.[78] It is illegal to fire someone for filing an EEOC complaint.

Unfortunately for Haddon, his employer was the Clinton White House. A Secret Service investigation found, as the *Washington Times* noted, "Mr. Walter's [the chief White House usher] memo and a Secret Service investigative report show that Mr. Haddon's fellow workers made false allegations about him following his EEOC complaint, with one co-worker even claiming he had threatened to poison the first family. After one of those allegations was made, the Secret Service on July 6, 1994, pulled Mr. Haddon's permanent White House pass, suspended his access to the White House and interrogated him and his colleagues. But the Secret Service quickly determined that the charges were false and ordered Mr. Haddon's access to the White House kitchen returned."[79] After it became clear that White House officials had lied in public statements about the details of the case, Haddon sought a hearing at the EEOC—a routine occurrence for federal employees seeking vindication. The Justice Department threw its weight into blocking Haddon's suit, arguing that such a public hearing should be prohibited because it would provide an improper look at the "inner workings of the executive residence and matters relating to the personnel who work there . . . Because the executive residence is not only part of the federal government but is the home of the first family, such matters historically have been treated with greater confidentiality than would be the case in a federal executive agency."[80] Haddon got a hearing, but the White House succeeded in preventing the transcript of the hearing from becoming public, in direct violation of the standard EEOC rules for such cases.

RACIALLY MOTIVATED BANK ROBBERIES

The Community Reinvestment Act (CRA), enacted in 1977, was supposed to prevent banks from taking deposits in one neighborhood and making loans only in other neighborhoods. But since President Clinton took office, the federal government has largely ignored the law and instead relied on threats against banks to force them to loan more to favored groups.

In 1993, Clinton proposed new legislation that would have slapped million-dollar-a-day fines on banks and bank officials who were decreed to be out of compliance with the CRA. While the 1993 expansions were blocked, federal banking agencies did add burdensome new CRA rules in 1995.[81]

To get government approval to open a new branch—or sometimes even to open a new ATM machine—or to merge with another bank, a bank must effectively get approval from community activist groups, thanks to the CRA. Some of these groups are explicit about their goal, Bruce Marks, executive director of Union Neighborhood Assistance Corporation in New York City, described himself as an "urban terrorist."[82]

Federal CRA regulations invite extortionate demands by community groups. Jonathan Macey, a Cornell University professor, observed, "You see really weird things when you look at the Code of Federal Regulations . . . like federal regulators are encouraged to leave the room and allowing community groups to negotiate *ex parte* with bankers in a community reinvestment context . . . Giving jobs to the top five officials of these communities or shake-down groups is generally high up on the list [of demands]. So, what we really have is a bit of old world Sicily brought into the U.S., but legitimized and given the patina of government support."[83] Most victims of these policies were afraid to complain. Harold F. Still, former president of the Pennsylvania Bankers

Association, wrote in early 1999: "The threat of action from the so-called community groups . . . caused all of us to keep our mouths shut."[84]

Activists can shaft bankers on almost any pretext. In 1995, GreenPoint Bank of New York sought to take over 60 branches of another bank. As *Crain's New York Business* reported, "Community activists sued to hold up the deal because GreenPoint was lending too much money in minority neighborhoods . . . In one of the most bizarre challenges to a bank deal under the [CRA], activists claimed that GreenPoint wasn't being judicious enough in its lending, and it should commit money to counseling programs for minority borrowers. Naturally, these counseling programs would be administered by the community groups."[85] The magazine concluded that the CRA had become "a tool for blackmailing banks in the name of social justice." Economics professor Tom DiLorenzo stated: "These groups use the CRA mainly to fund their war chests, and funnel mortgage and small-business loans to their friends."[86]

When Phil Gramm became chairman of the Senate Banking Committee in late 1998, he announced plans to reform the CRA. Gramm proclaimed that the CRA was resulting in banks being compelled to make "kickbacks and bribes" to activist groups.[87] Banks had pledged almost $10 billion to community groups protesting mergers, with no oversight of their use of the money, Gramm noted.[88] Senate Banking Committee staffers investigated the types of deals that were cut between banks and community groups; in one case, a group received money from the bank to make loans itself—and was allowed to pocket 2.75 percent of the value of each loan.[89] Bank loans made to fulfill CRA pledges have a default rate six times higher than other bank loans, according to Gramm.

Clinton spared no effort to block Gramm. Thirty-six federal bank examiners were summoned to the White House and instructed "to seek testimonials from bankers" about the CRA's benefits.[90] Using bank regulators to pressure bank officials to promote a political agenda is illegal. After Gramm's committee exposed Clinton's political machinations, Robert Garsson, the chief spokesman for the Office of Comptroller of the Currency, announced that the agency had "made a mistake, but one that was made for the best of intentions."[91] (Garsson did not explain why regulators kowtowing to a White House request should be assumed to have good intentions.) Naturally, there was no liability or threat of prosecution for any lawbreaking federal employee. Gramm said the White House interference showed "an incredible misuse of power. It shows once again that the Clinton Administration corrupts everything . . . They're like a sewer leak in the main water line."[92]

Major banking reform legislation was almost derailed in 1999 because of the Gramm-Clinton CRA impasse. At the last minute, Gramm agreed to allow the CRA to survive—with the proviso that henceforth the secret deals made between banks and CRA activist groups would be made public.[93] This may be the poison pill that leads to the law's repeal in the coming years.

MISCELLANEOUS RACE-BAITING

On Martin Luther King Day in 1998, Vice President Gore announced "the largest single increase in the enforcement of our civil rights laws in nearly two decades."[94] Gore was revealing a budget proposal—and, as usual, an increase in federal spending was equated with a triumph of justice. Gore explained that the White House was trying "to prevent discrimination before it occurs."[95] And the surest way to do that is to punish companies and individuals before they break the law.

In a speech to the National Association for the Advancement of Colored People on July 16, 1998, Vice President Gore declared: "I've heard the critics of affirmative action. I've heard those who say we have a color-blind society. They use their color-blind the way duck hunters use a duck blind: They hide behind it and hope that the ducks won't notice."[96] Gore implied that anyone who criticized affirmative action was the equivalent of a sniper waiting to gun down racial progress. In the same speech, Gore announced that he was declaring war on prejudice.

Former EEOC Director Clifford Alexander observed in 1998: "Manipulating issues of black and white in America to distract our attention has been a favorite pastime for this president."[97] Alexander noted that Clinton "gravely told the nation of his vivid memory of church burnings in Arkansas when he was growing up. Journalists' inquiries revealed that there were no church burnings in Arkansas during Mr. Clinton's early years."[98]

Clinton sought to turn the church fires into a symbol of racial oppression. In a June 8, 1996, radio address, Clinton declared: "In the end, we must all face up to the responsibility to end this violence."[99] Clinton's comments implied that the burning of a handful of churches somehow implicated every American who did not feel collective guilt over the fires. In a July 9, 1996, speech, Clinton declared: "We all know when someone burns a house of worship it must mean that the person committing the crime views the people who worship in that house as somehow fundamentally less human."[100] But if someone was burning a church to collect the insurance money, it probably did not reflect any disdain toward the humanity of the church members. There was no evidence of a statistically significant increase in the number of fires at churches—either black or white, as journalist Michael Fumento proved.[101] And, despite the best efforts of high-profile federal investigations, no evidence was ever brought forward to show that the church fires were the result of an anti-black conspiracy.

CONCLUSION

Clinton declared in 1995: "It is simply wrong to play politics with the issue of affirmative action and divide our country at a time when, if we're really going to change things, we have to be united."[102] Yet Clinton's demagoging over affirmative action and other issues was the most racially divisive political action of the 1990s. Clinton fought hard to preserve racial quotas not simply out of a concern about racial fairness—but out of a love of power, of rules that allow politicians to dictate winners and losers and win votes by sacrificing people's freedom.

FIVE

FEMA: CLINTON'S GREATEST SNOW JOB?

"FEMA is now a model disaster relief agency, and in some corners, thought to be by far the most successful part of the Federal Government today."
—President Bill Clinton, March 25, 1995[1]

SINCE TAKING OFFICE IN JANUARY 1993, President Clinton has declared a "major disaster" some place in the nation on average every week. Clinton has doled out more than $50 billion in disaster relief—far more than any previous president. Whether it is paying for snow plowing in West Virginia or bombarding California voters with unsolicited checks, the Federal Emergency Management Agency (FEMA) symbolizes the reinvention of government under the Clinton administration. FEMA won the 1996 Federal Public Service Excellence Award presented by Reinvention Man himself, Al Gore.

Clinton's presidency has been based on establishing the persona of a Great Leader who cares—the father figure that citizens are encouraged to run to with almost any problem. There are few better ways for Clinton to show that he "feels your pain" than by flying to a disaster area and having his lackeys throw federal checks at everyone they see. FEMA is a prime example of the Nanny State—a government agency determined to spend tax dollars to rescue citizens, regardless

of how irresponsible or negligent they have been and regardless of whether they
have requested help.

FEMA is also the Clinton agency par excellence. FEMA has roughly ten times
as many political appointees as other agencies its size—which might explain some
of its contempt for safeguarding taxpayers' money. FEMA symbolizes government
workers as knights on white horses, riding to the rescue with leaf blowers scattering
federal dollars in every direction. While the agency's motto, "People Helping
People," is plastered on its publications and headquarters, a more accurate slogan
would be, "People Helping People to Other People's Money."

DISASTERS, DISASTERS EVERYWHERE

Until the early 1900s, disaster response was handled almost entirely by state and
local governments and by private charities. Then the federal government began
doling out flood relief, which proved to be a popular pork barrel. As a result, federal
disaster aid was slowly expanded over the decades. FEMA was created in 1979
largely to help civilians in case of a nuclear attack. However, under Clinton, this
agency function was almost completely disregarded. As one career FEMA employee
observed, "These people don't give a hoot in hell about national security."[2]

In 1988, Congress enacted the Stafford Disaster Relief and Emergency
Assistance Act, which declared that requests for declarations (and therefore
federal assistance) shall be based on a finding that the incident "is of such severity
and magnitude that effective response is beyond the capabilities of the State and
the affected local governments and that federal assistance is necessary." But,
neither federal law nor FEMA regulations provide any clear guidance for what
a disaster is. Instead, a disaster is whatever an incumbent politician says it is.
FEMA's Inspector General reported in 1994 that "neither a governor's findings
nor FEMA's analysis of capability is supported by standard factual data or related
to published criteria."[3]

CALIFORNIA MANNA FROM HEAVEN

The biggest natural disaster on Clinton's watch was the 1994 Northridge
earthquake. Clinton and cabinet descended upon California as if God had
personally sent Clinton manna from heaven. California was a key state for
Clinton's reelection campaign, and FEMA surpassed all its previous records
of generosity.

After the quake, FEMA swung into action by sending thousands of homeowners unsolicited checks of up to $3,450 out of the blue, simply because they lived in zip codes that reportedly had been hard hit. FEMA issued over 47,000 checks—totaling $142 million—to individuals under "fast-track" procedures involving no inspection before a check was delivered.[4] After FEMA's "generosity" was exposed by the *Los Angeles Times,* FEMA chief spokesman Morrie Goodman denied that any mistakes were made in the big giveaway: "Anyone who says an error was made doesn't know what they are talking about. We receive very, very few calls from people who felt they didn't need the aid."[5] Goodman explained the agency's rationale: "We felt, as an agency, it was better to send the checks than to wait until we had inspectors out there." Such policies explain why, when a local paper sponsored a contest for the "Top Ten Reasons Why David Letterman Should Move his Late Show to Los Angeles," a top submission was: "Two words: FEMA money!"[6] (Over 400,000 southern Californians received FEMA grants, with $2,800 being the average benefit.[7])

FEMA also permitted many homeowners to double dip by collecting insurance payments for home damage as well as a hefty federal grant for the same costs. *Investor's Business Daily* reported in May 1994: "FEMA shelter checks, which subsidize rent for alternative housing and cover up to $10,000 for minor household repairs, have been cut with no questions asked about residents' property insurance or income."[8] An audit later found that FEMA made no attempt to recover payments to individuals that exceeded the cost of renting alternative housing or repairing their homes.

FEMA worked mightily to suppress suspicions that it had fizzled away hundreds of millions of dollars on unworthy aid recipients. FEMA media chief Vallee Bunting declared in 1998 that only 10 percent of the 48,000 Californians the agency bombarded with "fast-track assistance" (based largely on their zip code, instead of any evidence of damage) were ineligible for handouts.[9] Yet, the General Accounting Office discovered that there were almost 100,000 more applicants for FEMA aid than there were housing units damaged—and most of the applicants were approved.[10] FEMA, according to GAO, greatly understated the amount of its handouts that it should have recovered.

FEMA created a golden opportunity for "code racketeering" by local and state governments—raising their standards after a disaster and sending the bill to Washington for the upgrades. FEMA now routinely bankrolls lavish new upgraded buildings to replace buildings that received trivial amounts of damage. FEMA's Inspector General noted, "Based on damage repair costs in recent years, FEMA program officials now estimate upgrading costs to be between 50 and 1,000 percent (the majority being at the higher end) of the cost of repairing *actual disaster damage.*"[11]

The *Los Angeles Times* reported, "If a single ceiling tile fell from a classroom, or a single light fixture was jarred loose, the entire [school or college] campus could qualify for more quake-proof ceilings or lights, courtesy of FEMA's mitigation fund. In L.A., many schools fit that bill."[12] The Inspector General noted: "We identified numerous facilities where replacement was authorized in spite of minimal disaster damage because of the high cost of code upgrades."[13] It would have cost FEMA $1.1 million to repair the earthquake damage to the University of Southern California Psychiatric Pavilion. However, because of code upgrade costs of $44 million, the costs of the "repairs" exceeded half the cost of the structure, so FEMA generously paid out $64 million to construct a new pavilion. FEMA's policy of paying for new buildings when repair costs exceed 50 perfect is the sort of harebrained edict that would make private insurance executives call for an ambulance and straitjackets. (A year after the 1994 quake, during a local earthquake preparedness drill, one comedian quipped that, as part of the exercise, "The FEMA office even practiced processing bogus claims.")[14]

FEMA also pays lavishly for repairs of profit-making sports ventures and upper-class golf courses. After the Northridge quake, FEMA gave $5.5 million to fix the scoreboard at Anaheim Stadium, home of the Anaheim Angels, and $88 million for repairs and upgrades at the Los Angeles Coliseum, former home of the Los Angeles Raiders.[15] Perhaps most surprisingly—or perhaps simply an example of Clinton's compassion for his big Democratic donors out West— FEMA gave over $870,000 for repairs to cart paths and sprinklers at the Indian Wells Golf Resort in California and $246,102 to "fix the fairways, greens and cart paths at the Palm Springs Golf Course" after 1993 flash floods.[16]

SNOWBALLING TAXPAYERS

The Clinton administration has stretched the concept of "major disaster" to cover routine events rarely covered before—such as snow. Snow accounted for a large portion of the skyrocketing number of federal emergency proclamations. FEMA implicitly assumed that any local or state government was incapable of plowing the snow on any main highway after a big storm.

FEMA now routinely covers 75 percent of the overtime costs of labor, equipment, and supplies during any 48-hour period of a snowstorm that is subsequently designated a "major disaster." After a snowstorm hit western New

York in early 1999, FEMA announced that any school district whose snow-removal costs exceeded $1,000 was eligible to apply for aid.[17] After his town received a check for $86,000 from FEMA in 1999, Hamburg, New York Highway Superintendent James Connolly observed, "That's the money we are getting to be reimbursed for expenses that occurred during that January storm that everybody has probably forgotten about . . . A great deal of what we have spent was for outside contractors who we needed to bring in to remove the snow from our lake shore area."[18] Calling in outside contractors proved the town suffered a "major disaster." After FEMA certified three New York counties eligible for snow-removal assistance, Senator Charles Schumer (D-N.Y.) proclaimed: "This is great news for those areas hardest hit by last week's blizzard. It would have been unfair to make local taxpayers bear the entire burden of this extraordinary act of nature."[19] Apparently, no one living in the Snowbelt should be held liable for the cost of plowing snow.

When snowstorms hit Illinois in early 1999, FEMA paid out $30 million for snow plowing. After Mundelein, Illinois, received a FEMA check for $31,368, the village's public works director, Kenneth Miller, explained, "We had to pay time-and-a-half since (the blizzard) happened on the weekend"—another clear national emergency. As the *Chicago Herald* noted, "Because the remainder of the winter was mild in Lake County, the village did not take a financial hit that the FEMA funds will not cover. Miller concluded, 'We ended up quite well. I look at it as a positive.'"[20] One local transit provider received a $10,000 FEMA check to cover the costs of shoveling out bus garages and park-and-ride lots.[21] Sometimes a full-court press by local politicians helped persuade FEMA officials to reconsider initial data and send out a check to cover the cost of snowplow drivers. Illinois state representative Jack Franks observed, "When I saw a chance to get free money for McHenry County, I just jumped on it."[22]

FEMA's snow bonuses can undermine sound local government policies. Consider the experience of the town of Vernon, Connecticut. This town of 30,000 received a FEMA emergency relief grant of $40,023 in 1996 to help cope with the cost of the preceding winter's storms. The total local government cost for snow removal in the winter of 1995-96 amounted to $258,000, or only $8.60 per person—probably less than the average householder would pay a 12-year-old to shovel out his driveway after a good snowfall. But the town had budgeted only $104,516 for snow removal—and thus claimed to be overwhelmed by the heavy costs. What lesson did the town managers deduce from FEMA's generosity? As the *Hartford Courant* reported, an "optimistic town council has already set the proposed 1996-97 snow-removal budget at $69,383, the lowest level in 15 years."[23] Some local officials may believe that having a low budget for snow removal will make it easier for them to rattle their tin cup in FEMA's direction when it is exceeded.

FEMA officials were very sensitive about their snow-blowing bankrolling. After I wrote a piece in *Playboy* mocking such relief, FEMA media chief Bunting wrote to the magazine that Americans depend on FEMA "to recover from the most devastating event in their lives."[24] Perhaps FEMA employees are more prone to hysteria than are average Americans. Only in FEMA's imagination does the average American look out his window and exclaim, "Mabel! It snowed 15 inches last night. How are we going to walk the dog? Our lives are ruined!"

Disaster declarations are also now routinely made for occurrences that would have never popped up on the federal radar screen a decade or two ago. Local flash floods can qualify as national "major disasters." On July 15, 1997, the river town of Montgomery, Vermont—population 623—was hit by a flash flood. (Heavy rains also caused some damage in nearby areas.) Only nine people in town had flood insurance, and damage for a handful of families was substantial—though no one was injured and no pets were washed away. The scant impact did not deter the White House from issuing a proclamation on July 28: "The President today declared a major disaster exists in the State of Vermont, saying, 'Our thoughts go out to the people of Vermont who have been hit very hard over the past couple of weeks by severe storms and flooding.' The President ordered Federal aid to supplement state and local recovery efforts in the area struck by excessive rainfall, high winds, and flooding on July 15-17, 1997."[25] John McLaughry, director of the Ethan Allen Institute in Concord, Vermont, observed, "From a local standpoint it was a disaster. From a state standpoint it was a blip."[26] McLaughry said that some FEMA officials "made the flood sound like Pearl Harbor." The highlight of Associated Press accounts of the "major disaster" was the fact that a Boy scout camp had to be temporarily evacuated; scoutmaster Steve Kerr declared that "this has been a great adventure for" the boys.[27]

PAYING BY THE WORD

Looking at a list of FEMA grant recipients, one suspects that a disaster can lead to temporary insanity among federal employees. How else to explain the fact that, after the 1994 Northridge quake, FEMA gave $152,137 to the Los Angeles Alliance for a Drug Free Community and $365,354 to the Asian American Drug Abuse Program?[28] The money was intended for "crisis counseling," though FEMA exercised scant oversight of how the money was spent. Perhaps FEMA believed that many drug addicts lost contact with their traditional suppliers after the earthquake and needed federally subsidized relief until supply lines could be restored.

In an agency flier entitled "FEMA: Significant Accomplishments, April 1993–September 1995," the first achievement listed is: "Increased the comfort level of citizens around the country that there is an effective disaster management agency that can help them in a disaster." FEMA apparently sees itself as national therapist. The agency now routinely makes major cash injections to boost hot air circulation after a disaster. For instance, after North Dakota was hit by floods in early 1997, FEMA gave $712,000 to fund 200 "paraprofessionals" to go door-to-door around the state and offer to listen to people talk. A FEMA tabloid bragged that the "crisis counselors" visited some elderly women at a North Dakota nursing hospital and "let the women reminisce for hours about earlier, more peaceful years in Grand Forks."[29] Perhaps next will be a FEMA program to help rural people exchange fudge recipes in the wake of tornadoes.

WELFARE RECRUITING

FEMA at times looks like a contemporary version of 1960s Great Society federal welfare recruiting crusades. After California floods in 1997, FEMA coordinating officer Ronald Bearse announced: "We want to get as many flood victims as possible registered so that they can get the help they need to get back on their feet."[30] After a one-day flood in the Milwaukee area, FEMA regional director Michelle Burkett "urged residents who had damage to call the FEMA number, even if they thought they didn't qualify for help," the *Milwaukee Journal Sentinel* reported in 1997.[31] A few months after floods in North Dakota had subsided in 1997, Keith Bjerke, the state coordinating officer for flood relief, fretted in a FEMA tabloid published for his state: "We are particularly concerned that senior citizens whose homes were flooded may not register for assistance because they do not feel the damage is serious."[32] (FEMA officials stressed that federal aid was available for people with flooded basements.) After a flood in northern Colorado, FEMA spokeswoman Buffy Gilfoil declared that anyone who had any flood damage could apply for a federal handout—even college students who merely suffered damage to their school materials. Buffy said of the college students: "They're just as enfranchised as somebody who is out of school."[33] Apparently, being "enfranchised" nowadays means getting a federal handout—as if anyone denied a FEMA check to cover the cost of their waterlogged *Penthouse* magazines somehow has their rights violated.

Governor John Engler (R-Mich.) requested a federal disaster declaration for Michigan after a wave of storms swept through the Detroit area in 1997. Charles Seehase, director of Macomb County Emergency Management, warned: "If the President doesn't approve the relief, we're stuck with whatever the costs of cleanup turn out to be."[34] After the president blessed Michigan with a disaster declaration, FEMA published a tabloid newspaper, *Disaster Times,* with prominent pictures of Clinton and Engler under a headline: "President, Governor Pledge Fast, Caring Aid."

Regrettably, the squall was not the last emergency Detroit faced that summer. A month after the storms, Detroit Mayor Dennis Archer and U.S. Senator Carl Levin issued an emergency appeal pleading with Detroiters to file more requests for federal aid. Levin bemoaned that the vast majority of people who he believed should be getting a federal handout had not yet submitted their applications: "We've had a very slow return of applications and that worries us." Mayor Archer jumped forward to do his bit to uplift the American character: "It is not an embarrassment to need, and it is not an embarrassment to apply for those grants or loans."[35] In response to the politically catastrophic low level of aid requests, the deadline for applying for FEMA aid was extended by two weeks.[36]

Jonathan Ellis, an intern with the South Dakota state government who was assigned to a FEMA detail after a 1998 flood emergency, later observed: "FEMA's community relations teams have one cardinal rule: promote FEMA's telephone registration number . . . The more people registering for aid, the more success a community relations team is having. And this means getting people to register for aid who shouldn't . . . More copies of *Disaster Times* were printed than South Dakota's entire population."[37]

FEMA allows politicians to use tax dollars to buy a reputation for generosity. President Clinton, in a 1996 conference call to a meeting of disaster workers, reminisced about how he had gone to a disaster site in Washington state a few days earlier and a geezer who had lost everything came up to him and told him: "Well, I'm 70 years old and I've never had a president shake hands with me before. It was nearly worth losing my home to do that at my age." Clinton observed: "I thought to myself I wished that spirit could kind of somehow capture America."[38] Naturally, politicians enjoy watching people grovel and treat them like a deity—in politicians' eyes, the highest spirit the American people can achieve.

PRO-FLOOD FLOOD RELIEF

When NASA's *Pathfinder* spacecraft landed on Mars in 1997 and sent back pictures showing that Mars was once flooded, comic Alan Ray quipped: "Of course, Mars lacks the one factor that makes high waters on Earth so much more devastating. Mars has no FEMA."[39]

The National Flood Insurance Program (NFIP) is FEMA's crown jewel. Unfortunately, the heavily subsidized flood insurance bribes people to scorn common sense, damage the environment, and create staggering liabilities for taxpayers. Federal flood insurance illustrates how selling at a loss can be politically profitable.

The federal flood insurance program was created in 1969 to lower the costs of federal disaster assistance. Politicians at that time claimed that selling federal insurance for flood damage would help cover the cost of repairing and rebuilding after floods.[40] Instead, Uncle Sam's subsidized insurance provided a green light for far more building in river flood plains and coastal areas long favored by hurricanes.

A March 19, 1997, report in the *Idaho Statesman* on a Boise river flood concluded that the NFIP "has backfired—bringing more people into harm's way" and has made risky development "look not only possible, but attractive."[41] Doug Hardman, Boise-Ada County emergency services coordinator, observed that subsidized flood insurance "did exactly the opposite of what it was designed to do. It has encouraged people to move there and encouraged developers to develop there."[42]

Scott Faber of American Rivers, a conservation organization, observed, "Prior to the 1960s, you didn't have much development in flood-prone areas because you couldn't find any insurer crazy enough to underwrite it. But the federal government came along and said it is okay—we are going to make it financially possible for you to live in a flood plain. The effect of this has been much more dramatic in coastal areas, where we have seen a huge boom in coastal development in the last 30 years."[43]

The primary effect of federal flood insurance is that far more property is now damaged by floods than would have occurred if the insurance had not made it possible to build in flood-prone areas. The Long Island Regional Planning Board in 1989 complained that federal flood insurance "in effect encourages a cycle of repeated flood losses and policy claims."[44] And, especially in places like Long Island, the program underwrites the vacation homes of the wealthy.

Consider the experience of Topsail Island, a 26-mile island off the North Carolina coast, right in the middle of "hurricane alley." At a time when North

Carolina Governor Jim Hunt was trying to discourage rebuilding on the island, FEMA came in and deluged the area with more than $100 million to rebuild private and public facilities after two hurricanes hit the island in 1996. In 1998, the island was hit by another hurricane—and FEMA rushed in to spend another $10 million to repair things. The 1998 damage was greater than it otherwise would have been because FEMA had extended the sewer system after the previous hurricane, thus opening the door to new development.[45] Federal relief spending over a three-year period amounted to more than $10,000 for each permanent resident on the island.[46] "The original development wasn't sound, and now for the third time in three years, we're going to have to come in and provide assistance. There's very little common sense," observed Kevin Moody of the U.S. Fish and Wildlife Service.[47] FEMA paid almost the entire cost of rebuilding local government buildings and infrastructure and federal flood insurance paid the large majority of the cost of rebuilding private homes. The *Charlotte News and Observer* observed in 1997 that "the taxpayer-financed [FEMA] bailout [after the preceding hurricane] has reimbursed resort towns for just about any piece of public property that blew away in the storm . . . [it] has undermined years of efforts to discourage unwise development."[48]

FEMA pretends that merely shifting the cost of flood damage from a homeowner to taxpayers in general is almost as good as preventing a flood. FEMA is running a national television advertising campaign (entitled "Cover America") urging Americans to buy into the NFIP. FEMA Director James Lee Witt declared in 1996: "The greater the coverage we can achieve, the healthier the flood insurance program will be, and there will be less of a burden on the disaster program."[49]

However, it is scant consolation for taxpayers whether they get mulcted for disaster relief directly or for payouts under an insurance program designed to reward risky behavior. According to one agency analyst, "The way they advertise the flood insurance is disgusting. It is a Ponzi scheme—and they have to replenish that sucker because it is running dry. The NFIP is amazingly generous: you are talking of up to $250,000 for property damage coverage for only a few hundreds a year . . . that is absurd."[50] Private insurance companies in some cases would charge a $10,000 annual premium for many of the insurance policies that FEMA gives away for chickenfeed.

American taxpayers currently face almost $500 billion of exposure from NFIP policies written on over 4 million properties. Witt adamantly insisted in 1997: "The NFIP is a self-supporting program; claims and operating expenses are paid from policyholder premiums, not taxpayer dollars."[51] Yet, the NFIP is currently almost a billion dollars in debt to the U.S. Treasury because of heavy borrowings to cover its massive losses in recent years. In 1985, the NFIP received a billion dollar "loan" from the U.S. Treasury to cover its losses; two years later, Congress quietly "forgave" the loan, thereby maintaining the fiction that the program is not an actuarial rathole.

Witt told Congress in 1996: "If flooding incidents drop to a more normal level, we expect that we will pay [back the money borrowed from the Treasury] within five years."[52] Despite the surging levels of red ink, Witt hailed the NFIP in congressional testimony in 1998 as "another governmental success story." A deluge of floods followed Witt's testimony, showing that it was naive to expect the NFIP to "get healthy" any time soon. Since FEMA is subsidizing many, if not most, of the people who buy the policies, the more policies FEMA sells, the greater the financial crash-and-burn will be when Mother Nature catches up with the agency.

Witt claimed that communities are required to "enforce sound flood plain management in exchange for the availability of affordable flood insurance."[53] But since FEMA is anxious to sign up as many people as possible for the NFIP, the agency is grossly negligent at requiring sound policies in return. Beth Milleman of Coastal Alliance, an environmental activist group, scorned FEMA's campaign to get more flood insurance enrollees: "They are merrily skipping around the country tossing subsidized insurance policies at anyone who has a damn bathtub." Milleman observed that the flood insurance "encourages people to rebuild in harm's way, which is also bad for the coastal environment. What disaster relief and flood insurance wind up doing is giving people the financial means to build or rebuild in exactly the same spot that we know is disaster prone. And it is no strings attached nine times out of ten."[54]

FEMA claims that the flood insurance program encourages responsible behavior because, unless a person gets the flood insurance contract, the agency will only give him one bailout of up to $10,000 to cover his losses from a flood— next time, he is out of luck. However, even this wiffle-ball penalty provision is a mirage. The agency's Inspector General reported, "FEMA regional staff generally were not effective in identifying ineligible applicants who received grants during previous disasters but did not comply with flood insurance purchase and maintenance requirements." The report also noted, "Neither FEMA nor most states maintain records of who purchased insurance and if they maintained it for the required time. Without such records, it is not possible to monitor compliance."[55]

"Forget and forgive" is FEMA's attitude toward repeat claimants. A National Wildlife Federation study estimated that 2 percent of properties covered by federal flood insurance had "multiple losses accounting for 60 percent of the program's total claims, and more than 5,600 properties had collected claims exceeding the total value of the property."[56] Almost $3 billion has been spent in the last two decades "repairing and rebuilding the same structures two, three and four times."[57] One Houston home suffered 16 floods; its owner collected more than $800,000 in compensation for repair costs.[58] The flood insurance program paid $200,000 for repairing and rebuilding a Louisiana home worth only $30,000, which was hit by 15 floods. The *Houston Chronicle* reported the case of "a modest $49,300 home in Canton, Miss., which was flooded 25 times and brought $161,279 in insurance payments."[59]

While the federal government heavily subsidizes flood insurance, it also has dozens of programs to prevent a shortage of floods. As *Sierra Magazine* noted in 1999, "More than 40 separate federal programs and agencies, governing everything from highway construction to farm export policy, encourage building and farming on flood plains and wetlands. In 1996 alone . . . over $7 billion was poured into ten programs that aggravate flooding."[60]

FEMA discovered a new way to justify higher budget demands to Congress: going around the country and buying the homes of people in areas with the highest risk for floods. A skeptic may consider this program simply an entitlement program for people with pumpkins for brains—people whose homes have been flooded so often that federal bureaucrats simply cannot resist writing them another big check. It is ironic that FEMA is spending millions of dollars for such buyouts at the same time that President Clinton fiercely resists legislation requiring the federal government to compensate landowners prohibited from using their land in order to protect watering holes for migrating birds or endangered flies. However, from another perspective, the two policies are consistent: both FEMA buyouts of homes and federal prohibitions on private land use maximize politicians' power.

"THE KING OF CHAOS"

The response to Hurricane Floyd in September 1999 exemplified how disasters have become Clintonized. Hurricane Floyd was quickly labeled "the King of Chaos" by southerners. Unfortunately, foolish evacuation orders and snafus disrupted the lives of far more people than were seriously hassled by the hurricane itself.

The hurricane did serious damage, especially in North Carolina and in parts of Virginia and New Jersey, but largely missed Florida and South Carolina. Clinton preemptively declared federal emergencies in several states even before the hurricane touched the continental United States. With FEMA encouragement, southern states issued mandatory evacuation orders to nearly three million residents of coastal areas.

Those orders produced some of the worst traffic jams in the history of the South. Florida drivers were trapped in 30-mile-long backups; some Floridians were caught in jams with no movement for 12 hours.[61] It took some South Carolinians 16 hours to drive from Charleston to Columbia—normally a 2 hour drive.

Being in an auto is among the most unsafe places to weather a hurricane. If Floyd had sped up and caught the jammed motorists, the result could have been the worst hurricane disaster since Galveston in 1900. Charleston Mayor Joseph Riley was outraged and denounced fellow Democratic Governor Jim Hughes: "What you're doing is running the risk of killing my people."[62] The *Charleston Post and Courier* editorialized: "The state was unconscionably inefficient in its evacuation effort . . . Though the traffic was bound to be bad, the state's inept strategy made it much worse than it had to be."[63] The mayor of Isle of Palms, South Carolina, told the Associated Press that "one woman vowed never to leave [in response to future evacuation orders] after she had to stop by the road to relieve herself in front of a long line of traffic."[64]

Clinton administration officials wasted no time spinning the fiasco. Vice President Al Gore proclaimed on September 15: "All things considered, it's gone very smoothly."[65] FEMA Chief Witt praised state officials for their rapid and thorough response.

The evacuation cost more than $2 billion, according to state emergency experts. However, assuming that the 2.5 million evacuees lost an average of two days each, the total time lost from the evacuation was equivalent to the normal life span of almost 250 people. Since 95 percent of the cost of the evacuation was borne by the evacuees, the government can proclaim it was a great success—simply because politicians and bureaucrats don't have to foot the bill.

Clinton declared on September 16: "There may be some people who question . . . whether we did the right thing to recommend all the evacuations. But now that we have this technology at the National Weather Center, we have to act on it."[66] Apparently, pre-landfall federal panic-mongering will be mandatory for all future hurricanes. Once Clinton issued his preemptive emergency declaration, state and local officials were free to rev up spending and send the bill to Washington. Florida, which suffered little damage, was promised that the feds would cover 75 percent of overtime for police, firefighters, and other government workers and other related costs in response to the proclaimed emergency. FEMA paid for everything except extra rolls of toilet paper in the bathrooms of government buildings.

The hurricane presented the usual opportunities for presidential tear-jerking. After visiting North Carolina on September 20, Clinton fretted that his benevolence might be impeded by people's pride. He urged North Carolina residents to "take advantage" of federal aid: "The American people know that no individual can handle this alone."[67] Clinton did not specify exactly what "no individual can handle alone"—though many residents had to do little more than sweep the debris off of their walkways and wait a few days for fresh water. Clinton announced a special distribution of federal food stamps to people who would not normally qualify for such handouts.

Clinton also recited a long list of federal benefits available to flood victims and urged the audience: "So you all need to take advantage of these things." A White House press release trumpeted the opportunity for folks to collect disaster housing assistance, grants to low- and moderate-income individuals, Small Business Administration (SBA) loans for business and personal property disaster, Agriculture Department (USDA) emergency loans to farmers who suffered crop or chicken losses, reimbursement for paying the cost of clearing roads and carrying away downed trees, et cetera.[68] Clinton did not mention that SBA and USDA disaster loans have stratospheric default rates, roughly 10 to 15 times higher than the average default rate for private loans. Federal disaster loans have lured many people to bankruptcy, compounding Mother Nature's harm.

As always, Clinton relished his role as savior. When he released the first $528 million in disaster aid for Floyd, he declared, "You probably can't imagine how many times over the last 6½ years an American citizen has come up to me . . . and thanked me for the emergency work that we do."[69] Perhaps for the best, Clinton did not go into details of how grateful citizens sought to thank him.

SLOWING DOWN RECOVERY
AND BROWBEATING CRITICS

By raising the prospect of a windfall of federal cash, FEMA can slow down recovery operations. Jeffrey Tucker, vice president at the Mises Institute in Auburn, Alabama, described FEMA's effect in the days after Hurricane Opal hit Auburn, Alabama, in 1995:

> Everything was being cleaned up—the city government going crazy—then it turned out that we might be eligible for disaster assistance. And everything came to a halt. The city stopped doing anything—everything froze— this went on for weeks. Trees were still in the streets. Why? Because FEMA people were

coming through to determine whether we needed aid. And in order to get aid, we had to leave the place looking trashed. Then—FEMA decided that it was a disaster. But, instead of starting to cleanup then, the city delayed further clean up until it received FEMA money. The first half of the cleanup occurred in the first 24 hours—and the aid from FEMA simply made local government bigger.[70]

Tucker's boss, Lew Rockwell, wrote an op-ed piece in the *Los Angeles Times* criticizing the adverse effects of FEMA's intervention after the hurricane. Morrie Goodman, FEMA's director of public communications, went ballistic after seeing the article. Goodman called up Tucker and declaimed that "I gave you a $100,000 grant" to study emergency warning systems in Alabama last year. But the grant went to Auburn University, not the Mises Institute. The institute receives no government subsidies and was not blackmailed into silence. After Tucker wrote an article about Goodman's threat, Goodman called back and left a phone message on an answering machine calling Tucker "a very sick and dangerous human being."[71]

FOMENTING IRRESPONSIBILITY

State and local governments are at the top of FEMA's welfare list. California has been by far the largest beneficiary of FEMA largesse since Clinton took office. California local and state governments and universities hit the jackpot when FEMA paid to repair and upgrade their facilities after earthquakes, floods, et cetera. Yet, in 1999, when FEMA proposed a rule requiring government buildings to have insurance coverage in order to be eligible for FEMA rebuilding aid, Californian politicians became indignant. Though FEMA had provided more than $3 billion to repair and upgrade government buildings after the Northridge quake, Los Angeles city officials claimed to be overwhelmed by the potentially "tens of millions of dollars" cost of the insurance. The *Los Angeles Times* noted, "Instead of holding commercial insurance, the city considers its buildings to be self-insured because it can dip into its $30 million reserve fund for repairs in an emergency."[72] Los Angeles Mayor Richard Riordan publicly complained that the FEMA insurance mandate "does nothing for public safety and is unrealistic from both a practical and a political standpoint."[73]

FEMA spending soared in the 1990s in part because members of Congress were either asleep on the job or lobbying to expand the gravy train. When FEMA Director Witt appeared at congressional hearings, congressmen competed in heaping praise on his head and imploring him to spend more money in their districts. Witt testified to a Senate Appropriations Committee in 1996: "As we are all aware, disasters are very political events as well."[74]

WASTE NOT, VOTE NOT

While politicians and much of the news media lavishly praise FEMA for speedily delivering checks after a disaster, little attention is paid to the agency's underlying financial chaos. A 1995 FEMA IG report concluded: "Disaster Relief Fund financial data are often unreliable . . . Financial audits of the Fund have not been performed because the systems, records, and lack of controls made the Fund unauditable."[75] The report noted ruefully: "Many accountants and analysts did not know what their jobs entailed, and questioned their own value to the operation."[76] The IG report noted, "Few financial staff had any training, experience, or preparation for financial management of disasters."

GAO reported in 1996 that FEMA policies provide windfalls to local governments. FEMA Director Witt rejected GAO's suggestion that his agency tighten its spending guidelines: "The more FEMA attempts to tighten eligibility by closely prescribing every possibility, the more we will appear bureaucratic and inflexible."[77] And what are a few billion dollars among friends to avoid appearing bureaucratic?

Clinton continually pushed to expand FEMA's salvation mission. After the 1996 crash of TWA Flight 800 off Long Island, Clinton sent FEMA Director Witt to New York to be Clinton's "eyes and ears." Then, after Clinton visited with relatives of the deceased passengers, he announced plans to push Congress to allow FEMA to respond to "airplane crashes."[78] It is only a matter of time until some president proposes that FEMA be allowed to respond to car accidents and bicycle wrecks. Perhaps the logical conclusion is to automatically entitle any American who views a Weather Channel prediction of local bad weather to a FEMA grant for "crisis counseling."

FEMA under Clinton sought to maximize the number of people who hold out their hands for more benefits from Washington. Politicians have trained citizens to come running to the nearest federal agency even for routine problems like snow or flooded basements. And after FEMA publicity campaigns generate more calls to the agency's 800 numbers, politicians and bureaucrats proclaim that the record-setting aid requests prove that FEMA is needed more than ever before.

The political windfalls that follow a natural disaster epitomize how politicians' and citizens' interests are antithetical. The more citizens suffer, the more politicians profit by throwing money and promises in all directions. The only concept of "disaster" guiding federal policy now is the horror that politicians may miss a chance to use tax dollars to buy themselves more votes.

Rather than a triumph of good management, FEMA has simply been converted into a political cotton-candy machine. FEMA's expansion symbolizes the proliferation of acceptable political pretexts for one citizen to stick his hand in another citizen's pocket. FEMA's popularity is one more sign of the decline of individual responsibility—or even a semblance of respect for such responsibility—in American political culture.

THE CONTINUING FAILURE OF THE WAR ON DRUGS

PRESIDENT CLINTON did not start the war on drugs—but he made it worse.

- Since 1993, almost four million Americans have been arrested for marijuana violations, the vast majority for simple possession.
- The number of people arrested for drug offenses rose by 73 percent between 1992 and 1997, according to the American Bar Association.[1]
- The Clinton administration bankrolled the militarization of local police, sowing the seeds of a scourge of no-knock raids at wrong addresses and a massive increase in efforts to intimidate average citizens in big cities around the country.
- "Zero tolerance" became the fount of one absurdity after another, from import bans on bird seeds to expulsion orders against school children munching breath mints.
- Clinton championed ineffective drug education programs that provided nothing except bragging rights for politicians.
- The United States fumigated foreign nations with toxic sprays that devastated their farmers and poisoned their water. American policies and aid helped equip governments to militarily suppress their own people.

Clinton bragged in early 1999 that, since he took office, "In every successive year, I have proposed a larger anti-drug budget. In 1999—we had a 30-percent increase just between then and 1996 . . . Under [drug czar] General McCaffrey's leadership, we have put these resources to good use: unprecedented new tools for domestic enforcement; unprecedented new campaigns to convince young people to stay off drugs . . . unprecedented new efforts to stem the flow of drugs across our borders . . ."[2] Regrettably, Clinton's political grandstanding perennially subverted public health.

PUTTING CHEMO PATIENTS IN THEIR PLACE

In 1997, the CBS situation comedy *Murphy Brown* featured star Candice Bergen suffering from the aftereffects of chemotherapy. A friend provided her with some marijuana. DEA chief Thomas Constantine denounced CBS for "doing a great disservice" by "trivializing drug abuse" and "pandering to the libertarian supporters of an 'open society' and to the myths of legalization." Constantine barked: "I am extremely troubled that at a time when teenage drug abuse is doubling . . . a television show of the caliber of *Murphy Brown* would portray marijuana as medicine. It is not medicine . . . More dangerously, the show sends the message to our children that marijuana must be OK because it's medicine."[3] Constantine promised to investigate "if any laws were broken."[4]

Clinton's drug policy was haunted by the specter of emaciated chemotherapy patients desperately needing something to stop their vomiting and fire their appetites. And nothing works better for this than smoking marijuana. (The feds approved pills with THC, the active ingredient in marijuana; however, pills are scant help to someone heaving their guts.)

The scientific evidence on the medicinal benefits of marijuana cascaded in throughout the 1990s:

- A 1997 study performed on animals at the University of California at San Francisco found that cannabinoids (the active ingredient in marijuana) can be an effective reliever of pain without the adverse side effects of opiates.[5]
- The British medical journal *Lancet* reported in 1998 that marijuana is safer than alcohol or tobacco. *Lancet* editorialized in 1995 that "the smoking of cannabis, even long term, is not harmful to health."[6]
- The *American Journal of Psychiatry* reported in 1999 that German researchers successfully used the major psychoactive ingredient in mari-

juana to treat Tourette's syndrome (a complex neuropsychiatric disorder characterized by sudden spasms).[7]

- The *Proceedings of the National Academy of Sciences* reported in 1998 that marijuana may protect brain cells during a stroke.[8]
- British researchers revealed in early 2000 that a marijuana compound was very effective in controlling the muscle spasms that afflict people with multiple sclerosis.[9]

These reports followed in the path of more than a hundred medical studies on the pharmacological benefits of marijuana conducted since the mid-1800s. The National Academy of Science's Institute of Medicine concluded in 1982: "Cannabis and its derivatives have shown promise in the treatment of a variety of disorders, [including] glaucoma, . . . asthma, . . . and in the nausea and vomiting of cancer chemotherapy."[10]

Despite all of this evidence, marijuana is classified by the federal government as a Schedule 1 drug, which means it has "no currently accepted medical use in treatment." As a result, the government effectively prohibits research on the pharmacological benefits of marijuana. Researchers would have to provide subjects with marijuana—and if they did not have federal approval, they could be sent to prison as drug traffickers. The California Medical Association, in a 1998 resolution, condemned "the virtual standstill in research on [marijuana's] medical benefits" resulting from a de facto federal prohibition on research.[11]

A 1999 Gallup poll found that almost three-quarters of Americans favored permitting the use of marijuana as medicine.[12] Starting in 1996, the issue of whether marijuana should be legal for medical purposes was a hot issue in state referendums.

Luckily for Americans, Clinton's drug czar General Barry McCaffrey was a wiser scientist than all the "experts" who researched marijuana's effects. On August 15, 1996, while campaigning in California against Proposition 215, which would have legalized the medical use of marijuana, McCaffrey declared: "There is not a shred of scientific evidence that shows that smoked marijuana is useful or needed. This is not science. This is not medicine. This is a cruel hoax."[13] On December 30, 1996, when asked by a CNN reporter "is there any evidence . . . that marijuana is useful in a medical situation?" McCaffrey responded: "No, none at all. There are hundreds of studies that indicate that it isn't."[14] McCaffrey ridiculed claims of marijuana's benefit as "Cheech 'n' Chong medicine."[15]

After voters passed the proposition, the drug czar's office put out a press release warning: "The passage of [Proposition 215] creates a significant threat to the drug control system that protects our children . . . The decision to bring appropriate criminal or administrative enforcement action will be, as always, decided on a case-by-case basis." McCaffrey's warning sparked a vision of a DEA agent lurking underneath the desk of every doctor.

Federal judge Fern Smith issued a preliminary injunction on April 30, 1997 prohibiting the feds from punishing doctors: "The government's fear that frank dialogue between physicians and patients about medical marijuana might foster drug use . . . does not justify infringing the First Amendment . . . [T]his case is about the ability of doctors, on an individualized basis, to give advice and recommendations to bona fide patients suffering from serious, debilitating illnesses regarding the possible benefits of personal, medical use of small quantities of marijuana."[16]

Clinton administration officials sneered at marijuana referendum results. Attorney General Janet Reno declared in October 1998: "I don't think that the determination as to whether there is a medical, a scientific medical use of marijuana, should be made at the ballot box. I think it should be made in an informed way after appropriate scientific evaluation."[17] And if government officials chose to ignore all the scientific evidence, then that was merely political science. (Even an administrative law judge at the DEA had recognized and ruled that marijuana does have medical benefits; his decision was denounced and overturned by the chief of the agency.)[18]

The federal government in 1978 began a program providing marijuana directly to a small number of people with illnesses that undeniably benefited from consuming marijuana, such as glaucoma and epilepsy. But the Bush administration closed the program to any new entrants in 1992 after only eight people were certified—even though hundreds of thousands of people suffered from the same illnesses. The Clinton administration refused to reopen the program to new sufferers. The Justice Department, in a 1999 brief, declared: "It became clear that the potential widespread use of marijuana for 'medical' purposes under the program . . . was bad public policy." According to the Justice Department, the first requisite of good public policy is to pretend that individual citizens do not exist.

Most people who smoke marijuana do not do so for medicinal purposes—unless one considers alleviation of tension or boredom or unhappiness as medicinal. Marijuana may have fewer side effects than Prozac, Zolaft, or other widely used antidepressants. It is also debatable whether moderate marijuana use is more mind-numbing than an addiction to television. Recent studies showed that marijuana's danger has often been exaggerated:

- A 1997 long-term study released by Kaiser Permanente found that marijuana smokers had no higher rate of mortality than nonsmokers of marijuana: "Relatively few adverse clinical health effects from the chronic use of marijuana have been documented in humans. [However] the criminalization of marijuana use may itself be a health hazard, since it may expose the consumer to violence and criminal activity."[19]

- A 1998 study by the New Zealand Health Ministry concluded "the current public health risks of cannabis use are small to moderate in size, and are less than the public health risk of tobacco or alcohol use."[20]
- A 1999 study by the University of Toronto found that marijuana has far less adverse effect on drivers than does alcohol.[21]
- A 1999 study by the National Academy of Science's Institute of Medicine concluded: "Except for the harms associated with smoking, the adverse effects of marijuana use are within the range of effects tolerated for other medications."[22]

Clinton administration officials suppressed research results of United Nations affiliates that embarrassed the U.S. drug war. The World Health Organization (WHO) completed a major study of marijuana's effects in 1997. The draft of the final report included a comparison of the adverse effects of cannabis with alcohol and tobacco. However, the WHO, bowing to pressure from the U.S. government and other drug warriors, suppressed that chapter. *New Scientist*, a British magazine, acquired a copy of the study and reported that, in five out of seven categories of long term health damage, alcohol was judged more harmful than marijuana. The report also observed that "in developed societies, cannabis appears to play little role in injuries caused by violence, as does alcohol."[23]

The National Organization for the Reform of Marijuana Laws (NORML) complained in 1997, "The Clinton administration is waging a more intensive war on marijuana smokers than any other presidency in history. Marijuana arrests are up 60 percent since Clinton took office."[24] Nearly 700,000 people were busted for marijuana violations in both 1997 and 1998. More people were arrested for marijuana offenses in 1998 than were arrested for murder, rape, robbery, and aggravated assault combined.[25]

In 1998, Congress provided $23 million to the Agriculture Department to concoct new funguses that would wipe out coca and marijuana plants. Rep. Bill McCollum, chairman of the House Subcommittee on Crime, claimed that the new fungi might be the "silver bullet in the war on drugs."[26] Environmentalists were horrified, fearing that any new fungi released to kill one or two species could devastate vast numbers of other crops and species. The Florida "drug czar" moved in the late 1999 to begin testing a "marijuana-eating fungus"—

much to the horror of environmentalists who recalled other government species-introduction fiascos, such as kudzu.[27]

SHOWBOATS FOR POLITICIANS

Despite a sharp increase in federal antidrug spending and in arrests, drug use by teenagers soared during Clinton's administration. The percentage of eighth-graders who used marijuana, cocaine, and LSD tripled between 1991 and 1997.[28] Clinton responded by embracing the Drug Abuse Resistance Education (DARE) program. During his 1996 State of the Union address, the president pointed to his special guests seated in the balcony and declared, "People like these DARE officers are making a real impression on grade school children that will give them the strength to say no when the time comes."[29] In a July 23, 1996, campaign speech, Clinton declared, "We can give more funds to more communities so everybody can have a DARE program like you do, because they work and they really make a difference in children's lives."[30] Drug czar McCaffrey declared in July 1999: " DARE shows the important role [police] officers can play in educating youth to help prevent them from turning to drugs and engaging in criminal activity."[31]

According to Clinton, DARE "reaches more than 26 million students each day in nearly 75 percent of our Nation's school districts, encouraging young Americans to resist peer pressure and to lead lives free from the shadows of drugs and violence."[32] Federal, state, and local governments and private donors are spending roughly $700 million a year on DARE. America is deluged with DARE paraphernalia—including bears, bumper stickers, buttons, Frisbees, hats, jeeps, and, in Woodford County, Kentucky, a four-foot-tall robot squirrel—to spread DARE's message.

DARE was the brainchild of Los Angeles Police Department Chief Daryl Gates, who launched the program in the early 1980s. A few years later, Gates, testifying to Congress, proposed the following solution to the drug problem: "The casual drug user ought to be taken out and shot."[33] Gates's moderation continues to permeate the program's literature—and to destroy its credibility with many young people.

The DARE curriculum is taught by police primarily to fifth and sixth graders one hour a week for seventeen weeks, though children as young as those in kindergarten and as old as those in senior high school also receive DARE instruction. The police are supposed to serve as role models, trusted confidants, and wise men and women.

The federal Bureau of Justice Assistance, the research branch of the U.S. Justice Department, paid $300,000 to the Research Triangle Institute (RTI), a North Carolina research firm, to analyze DARE's effectiveness. The RTI study found that DARE failed to significantly reduce drug use. Researchers concluded that "DARE's limited influence on adolescent drug behavior contrasts with the program's popularity and prevalence. An important implication is that DARE could be taking the place of other, more beneficial drug-use curricula."[34] The Justice Department, unhappy with the report's politically incorrect conclusions, refused to publish it.

Other studies documented DARE's failure:

- The police department in Austin, Texas, in 1996 dismantled the DARE program after a city audit found "the percentage of DARE students with drug-related offenses who ended up in Travis County Juvenile Court was 4.9 percent, compared with 3.1 percent of the study group that did not attend DARE," as the *Austin American-Statesman* reported.[35]
- Dennis Rosenbaum, professor of criminal justice studies at the University of Illinois at Chicago, surveyed and tracked 1,800 kids who had DARE training and concluded in 1998 that "suburban students who participated in DARE reported significantly higher rates of drug use . . . than suburban students who did not participate in the program."[36]
- A 1999 study by the California legislative analyst's office "concluded that DARE didn't keep children from using drugs. In fact, it found that suburban kids who took DARE were more likely than others to drink, smoke and take drugs," the *Los Angeles Times* reported.[37] California legislators responded to the study by increasing the amount of money the state provides for DARE programs.
- A 1999 University of Kentucky study, funded by the National Institutes of Health, examined the effect of DARE on students' behavior over the subsequent ten years. The report concluded: "Our results are consistent in documenting the absence of beneficial effects associated with the DARE program. This was true whether the outcome consisted of actual drug use or merely attitudes toward drug use."[38]

DARE can have dire side effects. Some DARE-trained children have phoned police and gotten their parents arrested for drug violations.[39]

The perception from DARE photo opportunities—that politicians both hate drugs and love cops—means that the federal cash spigot stays open regardless of DARE's harm to kids and families. Politicians become addicted to "feel good" programs, incapable of recognizing or caring about the long-term adverse impact. And the longer the politicians bankroll programs like DARE, the more muddled their minds become.

Though DARE is the nation's most heavily funded antidrug program, the Education Department also bankrolls other anti-drug programs under the federal Safe and Drug-Free Schools and Communities Act. Clinton perennially hyped the Safe and Drug-Free Schools program as the flagship of his war on drugs. In his 1996 reelection campaign, Clinton continually portrayed Republican attempts to cut the program's budget as proof that only Clinton was stalwart in fighting drugs. In a radio address on October 26, 1996, Clinton bragged: "We've greatly expanded the Safe and Drug-Free Schools program, so that in every classroom we can have good role models telling our young people constantly, drugs are dangerous, illegal, and wrong."[40] In Minneapolis on October 28, 1996, Clinton declared: "I don't think it is conservative to want to cut the Safe and Drug-Free Schools program in half."[41] Clinton kept up the drumbeat after the election: in a December 20, 1997, radio address surveying his achievements in office, he declared, "Most importantly, we fought to protect the Safe and Drug-Free Schools program that helps to keep drugs out of classrooms and away from children."[42]

But the Safe and Drug-Free Schools program was a farce. A September 1998 Los Angeles Times exposé showed that the $6 billion spent since 1992 had little or no positive impact. Federal antidrug education money "paid for motivational speakers, puppet shows, tickets to Disneyland, resort weekends and a $6,500 toy police car. Federal funds also are routinely spent on dunking booths, lifeguards and entertainers, including magicians, clowns and a Southern beauty queen, who serenades students with pop hits," the Times reported.[43] In Virginia, "state education officials spent $16,000 to publish a drug-free party guide that recommends staging activities such as Jell-O wrestling and pageants 'where guys dress up in women's wear,'" as well as providing instruction on how to "conduct cow chip bingo." In Michigan, $18,500 in federal antidrug money was spent for recordings of the "Hokey Pokey." In Los Angeles, federal drug-free school money paid for four Glock handguns, a $22,000 Pontiac Grand Prix for police use, and over $10,000 in Dodger tickets.[44]

A 1997 federal Department of Education audit concluded that "few schools employed program approaches that have been found effective in previous research." Rep. George Miller (D-Cal.) explained the failure of the programs:

"Every elected official wants these programs in their district. Once you succumb to that pressure, you're just dealing with a political program. You're not dealing with drug prevention or violence prevention."[45]

After years of smearing congressmen who criticized the Safe and Drug-Free Schools program, Clinton in 1999 effectively admitted that the program was a failure. In a May 1999 message to Congress, Clinton declared: "We would strengthen the Safe and Drug-Free Schools and Communities Act by concentrating funds on districts with the greatest need for drug-and-violence-prevention programs, and by emphasizing the use of research-based programs of proven effectiveness."[46] Clinton's top drug warriors unloaded on the program in July 1999. McCaffrey complained in Senate testimony: "There is no statutory requirement that [schools] use drug prevention programs that are proven to work . . . Few schools adopt research-based, proven programs."[47] McCaffrey had groused earlier that the program just "mails out checks . . . There are almost no constraints on it."[48] McCaffrey's deputy, Rob Housman, whined: "We've got tons of schools that are receiving low amounts of funds. We are not helping anyone by trying to help everyone."[49]

Yet, in a September 11, 1999, radio address touting his administration's drug war successes, Clinton talked as if the unreformed program was still the greatest thing since sliced bread: "We've strengthened and expanded our Safe and Drug-Free Schools program, which helps school districts provide counseling, after-school activities, and violence mediation among other things."[50]

Although thousands of schools nationwide proudly post "Drug-Free School Zone" signs outside their buildings, this hasn't kept them from simultaneously arranging to have kids drugged for teachers' benefit. Across the country, children line up outside their principal's or nurse's offices at lunchtime to get another dose of Ritalin, an amphetamine-related stimulant that calms some children down. Schools sometimes pressure parents to administer Ritalin to hyperactive and allegedly hyperactive kids to make the children more docile in the classroom.

Ritalin is being prescribed largely in response to an alleged epidemic of Attention Deficit Disorder (ADD). Potential side effects of Ritalin use include "stunted growth, facial tics, agitation and aggression, insomnia, appetite loss, headaches, stomach pain and seizures." The DEA estimated in 1999 that Ritalin use had increased 500 percent in the previous five years.[51]

Columnist George Will noted that "American youngsters [are] consuming 90 percent of the world's Ritalin. In 1996, 10 to 12 percent of all American school boys were taking the addictive Ritalin."[52] In early 1999, the United Nations International Narcotics Control Board warned of excessive Ritalin consumption in the United States.[53]

Not surprisingly, Ritalin is abused by students who do not have a prescription. If the drug is crushed and snorted, it provides a quick high. Schools have cracked down on unapproved users, who could also face federal drug trafficking charges for passing around or selling their siblings' Ritalin prescriptions. Ritalin is apparently wonderful if taken with government sanction and terrible if taken without sanction.

ZERO TOLERANCE FOR COMMON SENSE

"Zero tolerance" was the Clinton administration motto on drug policy. The "zero tolerance" spirit emanated from Washington and inflamed the minds of law enforcement, school officials, and others at all levels of government.

In September 1999, the DEA ordered the seizure of a 53,000-pound shipment of birdseed coming in from Canada. The birdseed was made with sterilized seeds from the hemp plant. As the *New York Times* noted, "Hemp and marijuana are different varieties of the same plant species, *Cannabis sativa,* though the Government rarely distinguishes between them."[54] The birdseed contained less than 10 parts per million of THC, the active ingredient in marijuana.[55] The DEA may have been seeking to strangle in the crib the rising surge of imports of hemp for a variety of products ranging from horse bedding to granola bars. Don Wirtshafter, a lawyer for the importing company, complained: "The DEA's action reverses over 60 years of precedent. The sterilized seeds of the Cannabis plant are specifically exempted from the Controlled Substances Act. Until now, the DEA has never claimed they are prohibited by the act."

School officials made headlines with their vigilant application of "zero tolerance": 13-year-old Brooke Olson was suspended from Riverwood Middle School in Kingwood, Texas, after a drug-sniffing dog found Advil that she had forgotten in her backpack. She violated the strict school district policy that all medications must be taken to the school nurse for safekeeping.[56] *USA Today* noted in 1999 that "kids have been kicked out of school for possession of Midol, Tylenol, Alka Seltzer, cough drops and Scope mouthwash—contraband that violates zero-tolerance antidrug policies."[57]

Some law enforcement agents let their enthusiasm get the best of them. Federal judge Lawrence Karlton denounced California Bureau of Narcotics Enforcement agents in 1998 for a botched methamphetamine sting that helped "poison the public." Drug agents gave two recently released convicts the raw chemicals to produce more than 100,000 doses of meth. The agents intended to stop them before they sold the finished product, but postponed the bust so they could build up their case. Karlton declared that "if they did not have badges," the narcs might have gotten life in prison for what they did. Karlton asked: "How many people got started on meth who wouldn't have if not for the conduct of these agents? There may be some child out there who's dead because of what went on." A spokesman for the California Department of Justice announced: "We hope the judge holds the criminals in as much disdain as he apparently does these fine agents."[58]

The drug war encouraged federal agencies to be broad-minded about their choices of associates. The DEA was embarrassed in late 1999 by revelations that it had paid more than $2 million to informant Andrew Chambers, whose testimony had helped the agency send scores of people to prison. Chambers worked on more DEA cases over a 15-year period than any other informant, specializing in "reverse sting" operations where he sold people illicit drugs. The DEA continued to use Chambers after it became aware that he frequently committed perjury in court testimony; federal public defender Dean Steward complained that Chambers "has lied under oath virtually every time he has been put on the witness stand."[59] Chambers routinely denied in court that he had a criminal record—despite his six arrests on charges of forgery, theft, domestic assault, soliciting prostitution, and impersonating a police officer. DEA officials violated the law when they did not inform defense attorneys of Chambers's criminal history. The DEA sought to stonewall a California public defender's Freedom of Information Act requests on the agency's use of Chambers. Federal judge Gladys Kessler slammed the agency in 1999 for "extensive government misconduct," ruling that "it is clear from the far-reaching and serious conse-quences of the activities and collaboration of Chambers and DEA that there is a substantial public interest in exposing any wrongdoing in which these two parties may have engaged."[60] After scandal erupted over Chambers's criminal background, a DEA spokesman defended the agency's actions by labeling Chambers "an invaluable asset in the war against drugs."[61] Defense attorney David Chesnoff charged that Chambers is "just the tip of the iceberg of abuse by informants of the federal government."[62] The *Los Angeles Times* noted that, as a result of the Chambers controversy, "The DEA is now instituting a rule forbidding an informant who has lied on the stand from being used again without special exemption."[63] The new policy should reassure Americans that federal agencies will act responsibly in the future when they use perjurers to send them to prison.

The Drug Czar's office was embarrassed in February 2000 when news broke that his operatives had been giving payola to television networks to include antidrug messages in television shows. Congress had appropriated a billion dollars for paid anti-drug ads in 1997; the drug czar's deputies and television networks cut a deal in 1998 that allowed the networks to get paid for programs with federally approved anti-drug themes and messages. In some cases, White House drug officials reviewed scripts ahead and time and suggested changes.[64] *New York Times* columnist Max Frankel noted, "Not even during the Cold War, with our faith in democracy at stake, did federal authorities dare so to subsidize and subvert our media . . . Everyone understood that the government's heavy hand on the scale of public opinion could distort the weight of any argument and diminish the public's freedom."[65]

MILITARIZATION
OF LAW ENFORCEMENT

Since 1995, the Pentagon has deluged local law enforcement with thousands of machine guns, over a hundred armored personnel carriers, scores of grenade launchers, and over a million other pieces of military hardware.[66] Instead of relying on street smarts, police departments are resorting to high-tech weaponry, courtesy of Uncle Sam.

Thanks in large part to federal aid, SWAT teams have proliferated across the country. The SWAT acronym originally stood for "Special Weapons Attack Team" but was later sanitized to "Special Weapons and Tactics." SWAT teams are most often used for no-knock raids in drug cases—increasingly with deadly results:

- On December 16, 1996, the Secret Service, the Customs Service, and a swarm of local police launched a predawn raid on a house in a quiet residential neighborhood in Albuquerque.[67] Because the cops thought that the people inside were engaged in meth trafficking—as well as making counterfeit drivers' licenses, birth certificates, and checks—they came in wearing camouflage, black ski masks, and toting automatic weapons. Sixty-nine-year-old Ralph Garrison, who lived next to and owned the house that was being raided, awoke to smashing and breaking noises. Garrison stuck his head outside, then raced to dial 911: "They're breaking in with, uh, axes and all kinds of stuff." Police claimed they identified themselves, but with a Customs Service helicopter hovering overhead, it is unclear whether the elderly man understood. Garrison complained to the 911 operator that "they've got flashlights on my face and everything. There's a whole bunch." Garrison repeatedly pleaded with the 911 operator to "hurry up" and send police to the scene to stop the destruction of his rental house. Garrison finally declared "I'm gonna get my gun." Garrison showed up in the back doorway with a .22 pistol. Three cops responded by machine-gunning him with automatic rifles. At least a dozen shots were fired by the cops (police later refused to disclose the total ammo consumption that morning). After downing the suspect, police handcuffed him and called for an ambulance. Garrison still had his cell phone in his hand when he was cut down—the 911 tape ends with a volley of gunfire. He died a few minutes later. For good measure, police also shot Garrison's 14-year-old chow dog. The raid at the rental property was a failure: no arrests were made. An internal police investigation concluded that the officers who killed Garrison followed official procedures.

- At 11 P.M. on the night of August 9, 1999, 20 SWAT officers from the El Monte, California, police force attacked a home occupied by a half dozen sleeping Hispanics in Compton, 20 miles from El Monte. Police made themselves welcome by shotgunning off the locks on both the front and rear doors and exploding a flash-bang grenade inside. El Monte Assistant Police Chief Bill Ankeny later explained: "We throw flash-bang grenades. We bust open the doors. You've seen it on TV. We do bang on the door and make an announcement—'It's the police'—but it kind of runs together. If you're sitting on the couch, it would be difficult to get to the door before they knock it down." Two SWAT team members wearing masks rushed into the bedroom occupied by 63-year-old Mario Paz, a father of 6 and grandfather of 14, and his wife, Maria Argueta, who screamed, "My husband is sick! He's an old man!" One cop (whom the police refused to identify) shot Paz twice in the back at near-point-blank range. Police later claimed that Paz was shot because police thought he was armed (as he lay in bed); later, police said Paz was shot because they thought he was reaching for a gun; still later, police declared that Paz was shot because they saw him reaching for a drawer where a gun might have been kept. Whatever. Paz's son, who was in the house at the time of the raid, later said that the family thought they were being robbed. Paz was reaching under the bed to get the $10,000 he had withdrawn from a Tijuana bank earlier that day (survivors said he got the money out because of fears that Y2K problems would shut down the bank).[68] Police seized the money and briefly considered confiscating it as ill-gotten gains. Police targeted the Arguetas' house because a narcotics suspect they had arrested and released earlier that day had occasionally used the Arguetas' mailing address. Police made no effort to determine if the house was occupied—or by whom—before attacking.[69]

- In Osawatomie, Kansas, at 1:25 A.M. on February 13, 1999, police from three different jurisdictions smashed into the home of Willie Heard, 46-years-old, setting off a flash-bang grenade. Heard's 16-year-old daughter, Ashley, was frightened and screamed "Daddy!" Heard apparently thought his daughter was in danger and picked up an unloaded .22 bolt-action rifle—not the weapon of choice of major drug terrorists. An officer kicked open the door to Heard's bedroom, saw him with the rifle, and shot him in the chest, killing him almost instantly.[70] Police records showed that a mere 11 seconds elapsed from the moment of forced entry to when Heard was gunned down. The raid was a success: police found a small amount of marijuana.[71]

- On September 29, 1999, Denver police carried out a no-knock raid at a small house in a Hispanic neighborhood. Six heavily armed police shot Ismael Mena, a 45-year old Mexican and father of nine, eight times. Police later realized that they had the wrong address; no drugs were found in Mena's home; the officer who wrote the affidavit for the search warrant was subsequently charged with perjury. A veteran police officer on the raid team later told investigators that he had been pressured, after the fatal shooting, "to make it appear as though there had been earlier reports of trouble at Mena's home when there had not."[72] The *Denver Rocky Mountain News* analyzed police reports and found that Denver police carried out 146 no-knock drug raids in 1999; however, no felony arrests occurred in two-thirds of the raids and only two suspects were sent to prison. Arrests from no-knock drug raids were "far less likely to result in prison sentences" than were other felony arrests. The *News* reported, "Often, information given by confidential sources goes unsubstantiated. In many of last year's raids . . . no drugs or much less than expected were found."[73]

No-knock raids at wrong addresses have become a national scandal. Naturally, some police departments have responded to the problem by seeking to define it out of existence. New York City Police Commissioner Howard Safir insists that his officers have not wrongfully raided someone's house unless they go to a different address than that typed on the search warrant—regardless of whether they have any justification for busting down doors.[74]

Once local governments militarize the police, they find more and more pretexts to send in the troops, if for nothing else than to keep people in place. How else to explain the practice of St. Petersburg, Florida, in deploying SWAT teams to keep order along a parade route? Or of the Greenwich, Connecticut, SWAT deployment for crowd control any time lottery jackpots exceed $1 million?[75] Palm Beach County in Florida has 12 separate such teams; weapons were found in fewer than 20 percent of the locations they raided in 1996.[76]

U.S. military forces have been heavily used for antidrug patrols along the Mexican border, purportedly to stop drug runners. On May 20, 1997, Esequiel Hernandez, an 18-year-old high school sophomore, was killed by U.S. Marines who were lurking outside of Redmond, Texas, waiting for drug traffickers. Hernandez was herding his 40 goats at the time he was killed; the Marines claimed that he had fired at them with his old .22 rifle. The heavily camouflaged Marines pursued him for 20 minutes before taking him down with an M-16. The killing sparked an uproar. A Pentagon investigation concluded that after the teenager was shot, the medical care the Marines provided was "substandard as measured by any humanitarian standard."[77] According to Rep. Lamar Smith (R-Tex.), the Justice and Defense Departments undermined the criminal investigation and prevented the truth from coming out about how Hernandez was killed.[78] Texas Rangers Sergeant David Duncan complained: "The federal government came in and stifled the investigation. It's really depressing. The system we hoped would work failed at the federal level."[79] The federal government paid $1.9 million to settle the Hernandez family's wrongful death suit, but denied that the Marines had done anything wrong in killing the goatherder.[80]

The Coast Guard used to be known as rescuers of wayward boaters. But, beginning in 1999, Coast Guard sharpshooters on helicopters began firing on boats of suspected smugglers. The Coast Guard engages in such target shoots—aiming at engines—in international waters in the Caribbean. At the September 1999 press conference unveiling "Operation New Frontier," Czar McCaffrey bragged: "We have made the drug smugglers afraid. We will now make them disappear."[81] Coast Guard helicopters sometimes fire machine guns across the bows of boats to make them surrender. But Coast Guard sharpshooter Charlie Hopkins insisted, "We're still humanitarian," noting that the helicopters carry life rafts for survivors in case the Coast Guard sinks a targeted vessel.[82]

CORRUPTING LAW ENFORCEMENT

In Tucson in November 1998, a Customs Service guard team wandered off while a huge shipment of illicit drugs was being burned. Someone snuck into the trash-burning plant and absconded with 500 pounds of marijuana. In recent years, up to 60 tons of illicit drugs may have been stolen at this burn site and put back on the streets of America.[83] (The Customs Service was prohibited from counting the heists toward fulfillment of mandatory recycling goals for federal agencies.)

The Customs Service warned Congress in 1999 that drug trafficking was "the undisputed greatest corruption hazard confronting all federal, state and local law enforcement agencies today."[84] The pervasive corruption mocks politicians' efforts to strictly control what every citizen carries in his pocket.

The reputation of the Los Angeles Police Department went down in flames in late 1999 after one officer—seeking leniency after pleading guilty to stealing eight pounds of cocaine from police evidence lockers—detailed how an anti-gang police unit formally known as CRASH (Community Resources Against Street Hoodlums) became a major terrorist organization. Police routinely carried illicit drugs with them in order to plant them on people they decided to frame. In several cases, police shot unarmed men and then planted weapons on them to make the shootings look justified.[85] Police shot an unarmed, handcuffed man in the head and then lied in court and got the victim sent to prison.[86] Perjury was pervasive, as was theft and drug-dealing by police. The Immigration and Naturalization Service (INS) worked in cahoots with the corrupt cops, recommending deportation of Hispanic suspects who could not be charged with any crime[87]—or whose primary offense was being a witness to police brutality.[88] One senior INS agent complained that LAPD was "targeting a whole race of people. That's not a gang anymore, that's a culture. The LAPD only wanted to do one thing: sweep the street and turn the bodies over to the INS."[89] The unjustified arrest of young Hispanics led to some of them being denied U.S. citizenship. An official report by the LAPD concluded: "This scandal has devastated our relationship with the public we serve and threatened the integrity of our entire criminal justice system."[90] Hundreds of convictions could be overturned as a result of the scandal.

Joseph McNamara, former police chief of Kansas City, Missouri, and a fellow at the Hoover Institution at Stanford University, observed that "the pattern of small gangs of cops committing predatory crimes has occurred in almost every large city in the nation and in a great many less populated areas as well. The lure of fortunes to be made in illegal drugs has led to thousands of police felonies: armed robbery, kidnapping, stealing drugs, selling drugs, perjury, framing people and even some murders. These police crimes were committed on duty, often while the cop gangsters were wearing their uniforms, the symbol of safety to the people they were supposed to be protecting."[91] This kind of police corruption is a cost of the war on drugs that politicians like Clinton never deign to notice.

HOSING DOWN THE HEMISPHERE

Carlos Ball, the publisher of one of Venezuela's largest newspapers before being driven into exile over criticisms of his government, recently observed: "The War on Drugs has done more harm to democratic institutions in Latin America than all the Communist guerrillas of the past 35 years ever managed to inflict."[92] Ball noted, "Washington politicians always end every discussion of drug trafficking by deciding how many more helicopters should be sent to Colombia, how much more money to spend spreading herbicides that may ruin agricultural lands for generations, and how to promote the substitution of crops."

The federal government has been heavily bankrolling the war on drugs around the Western Hemisphere since the early 1980s. Under Clinton, such "aid" skyrocketed. President Clinton bragged in January 1999 that "we have witnessed a decline in cocaine production by 325 metric tons in Bolivia and Peru over the last 4 years. Coca cultivation in Peru plunged 56 percent since 1995."[93] But, as fast as output fell in one nation, it soared in other nations. GAO reported in 1998: "Despite long-standing efforts and expenditures of billions of dollars, illegal drugs still flood the United States. Although U.S. counternarcotics efforts have resulted in the arrest of major drug traffickers, the seizure of large amounts of drugs, and the eradication of illicit drug crops, they have not materially reduced the availability of drugs in the United States."[94]

Colombia has received almost a billion dollars of anti-narcotics aid since 1990. The result: Colombian coca production is skyrocketing—doubling since 1996 and forecasted by GAO to increase another 50 percent in the next two years. Colombia now supplies roughly three-quarters of the heroin and almost all the cocaine consumed in the United States.

For the Clinton administration, the obvious answer to this problem is more U.S. tax dollars. On July 16, 1999, drug czar Barry McCaffrey proposed an emergency billion-dollar antidrug package for the Andean nations, including $600 million for Colombia.[95] McCaffrey sought to give Colombia—already the third largest recipient of foreign aid, just after Israel and Egypt—even more money than the Colombian government asked for. (In early 2000, the Clinton administration upped the ante, demanding that Congress appropriate an additional $1.6 billion in aid for Colombia.)

But, while Clinton sought to throw more money at Colombia, U.S. policy was hit by one embarrassment after another. On July 23, 1999, five American military officers died when their high-tech spy plane went down in southern Colombia. The Pentagon trotted out the usual explanation: out-of-date maps. (The Andes Mountains grow much faster than other mountains.) Other observers speculated that the plane was shot or forced down by Marxist guerrillas. The Clinton administration succeeded in sweeping the deaths under the rug; there was no television coverage or presidential lip biting when the bodies were returned, in the middle of the night, to Dover Air Force Base in Delaware.[96] A few weeks later, the wife of Col. James Hiett, the commander of U.S. military antidrug operations in Colombia, was indicted for shipping kilos of cocaine via embassy mail to contacts in New York— a clear violation of postal regulations. At the same time that the United States demanded that Colombia end drug-related corruption, its own embassy was being used for smuggling. Col. Hiett pled guilty in April 2000 to helping his wife launder the money from her cocaine sales; the Justice Department cut a deal under which he received probation and was allowed to stay in the military another seven months in order to qualify for a larger pension.[97]

The United States is foisting itself deeper into a civil war that has raged in Colombia for decades. There are approximately 200 U.S. military advisers already on site, and U.S. personnel are now actively training the Colombia military. The *Dallas Morning News* noted in 1999 that "tens of millions of taxpayer dollars are going into covert operations across southern Colombia employing, among others, U.S. Special Forces, former Green Berets, Gulf War veterans and even a few figures from covert CIA-backed operations in Central America during the 1980's."[98] The United States is providing key intelligence to the Colombian military from U.S. intercepts of guerrilla radio messages.

Congress in 1996 prohibited any U.S. foreign aid to military organizations with a penchant for atrocities. The Colombian army has a poor human rights record, but few in Congress seem to care about the administration's open flouting of the law.

Most U.S. antidrug aid has gone to pay for chemical warfare: blanketing coca-growing areas with herbicides from crop-duster planes and helicopter gunships. (Three U.S. civilian pilots of crop-dusters have died in recent years, shot down by guerrillas, farmers, or paramilitary forces.) Yet after continual escalation in the amount of spraying, the amount of land in coca production is four times greater than what it was in 1994, and now exceeds 300 square miles. CIA analysts estimate that only about a quarter of the aerial fumigation actually kills the coca bushes.[99]

Much of the herbicide dumped from the planes misses the target acreage, according to experts. Many farmers raising non-coca crops have been devastated by herbicides dropped indiscriminately on their fields. The Colombian minister of health strongly opposed the initiation of spraying in 1992. Coca farmers have responded in part by going deeper into the jungles and hacking out new land for planting; environmentalists complain that the herbicide attacks are a major cause of deforestation. Colombian Environmental Minister Juan Mayr publicly declared in 1998 that the crop-spraying program has been a failure and warned, "We can't permanently fumigate the country."[100]

The Clinton administration intensely pressured the Colombian government to allow a much more toxic chemical to be dumped across the land. The Colombian government briefly agreed in 1998 to allow tebuthiuron (known as SPIKE 20) to be used on a test basis on coca.[101] Dow Chemical, the product's inventor, protested that the product was not safe for use in mountain terrain. Environmentalists warned that dumping the product over the Colombian landscape could poison ground water and permanently ruin the land for agriculture. The U.S. ambassador to Colombia, Curtis Kamman, derided such concerns: "For a net environmental positive effect, getting rid of coca is the best course for Colombia."[102] Even as the Clinton administration decreed clean-air standards severely limiting Americans' exposure to chemicals that pose little or no health threat, it sought to deluge a foreign land with a toxic chemical in a way that would be forbidden in the United States.

It is doubtful that increased U.S. aid would allow the Colombian government to win a decisive victory over the guerrillas any time soon. The Colombian military is renowned for losing almost all the major engagements it fights with the guerrillas. Many farmers see the war on drugs as a war on farmers, and the herbicide spraying further undercuts the legitimacy of a government that already has miserably served its people.

And even if the guerrillas were defeated, Colombians would still have an incentive to grow coca—as long as U.S. laws make that crop 20 times more profitable than any other. American-funded drug suppression efforts result in a "push down, pop up" effect: the harder the United States tries to repress coca production in one area, the more likely production is to start up in another.

POLITICALLY EXEMPT

Presidents and congressmen have perennially demanded that Americans be forced to pay any price and bear any burden so that politicians can proclaim victory in the war against drugs. But, as many well-connected Washingtonians suddenly remember, sometimes the highest element of justice is mercy.[103]

- In June 1993 Richard Riley Jr., son of Education Secretary Richard Riley, received a sentence of six months' house arrest for conspiring to sell up to 25 grams of cocaine and 100 grams of marijuana. Seven months earlier

Riley had been indicted by a federal grand jury in Greenville, South Carolina, and charged, along with 18 others, with distributing cocaine and marijuana, conspiring to possess cocaine and marijuana, and conspiring to possess those drugs with the intent to distribute them. The initial charges carried a penalty of ten years to life in prison. Riley Sr. became one of the most prominent antidrug spokesmen of the Clinton administration.

- Gayle Rosten, the daughter of House Ways and Means Committee Chairman Dan Rostenkowski (D-Ill.), was busted in 1993 after police found her in possession of a gram of cocaine in her car. Three years earlier, Rosten had been charged with possession of 29 grams of coke with intent to deliver. She avoided up to 15 years in prison by pleading guilty to a lesser charge, paying a fine, and going on probation. The 1993 cocaine charge would have been a stark violation of her probation, but a kindly Cook County judge dismissed the charge, ruling that the search of Rosten's car was illegal. (Strangely, he upheld the search of two other people in Rosten's car who were busted at the same time.)

- Cindy McCain, the wife of Senator John McCain (R-Ariz.), admitted stealing Percocet and Vicodin from the American Voluntary Medical Team, an organization that aids Third World countries. Percocet and Vicodin are Schedule 2 drugs, in the same legal category as opium. Each pill theft carries a penalty of one year in prison and a heavy fine. McCain stole the pills over several years; she became addicted to the drugs after undergoing back surgery. Rather than face prosecution, McCain was allowed to enter a pretrial diversion program and escaped with no blemish on her record. McCain did suffer from the incident, though: shortly after the scandal broke, a Variety Club of Arizona ceremony at which she was to receive a "humanitarian of the year award" for her work with the medical team was canceled because of poor ticket sales.

- Dan Burton II, the 18-year-old son of Representative Dan Burton (R-Ind.), was busted in January 1994 in Louisiana on charges of possession of marijuana with intent to distribute while allegedly transporting seven pounds of pot in a car from Texas to Indiana. According to the *Baton Rouge Advocate*, Burton and a friend "[allegedly] told agents that they heard marijuana was cheap in Houston, where they allegedly purchased the pot. The pair were coming from Houston, where they paid $6,000 for the drugs." Even though Burton was involved in an interstate crime, his case was handled solely by officials in Louisiana. Burton pleaded guilty to felony charges of possession of marijuana with intent to distribute;

instead of facing 10 to 16 months in federal prison, he was sentenced to five years' probation, 2,000 hours of community service, three years of house arrest and random drug screening. After the arrest was made public, Congressman Burton declared: "Any time one of your children gets into this kind of trouble, it's horrible for the parents and for the whole family." Five months later young Burton was busted again after police found 30 marijuana plants in his apartment in Indianapolis. They also found a shotgun. Under federal mandatory-minimum rules, that could have guaranteed him at least five years in federal prison, as well as a year or more for his arrest while on probation for a previous drug charge. However, the case was again processed in the state system, where the charge was reduced to a misdemeanor. An Indiana prosecutor threw out all charges against him, saying, "I didn't see any sense in putting him on probation a second time."

- In 1993 Josef Hinchey, the 26-year-old son of Congressman Maurice Hinchey (D-N.Y.), was busted along with more than a score of accomplices for allegedly running a drug ring in upstate New York. Hinchey was accused of possession with intent to distribute individual cocaine doses, a crime punishable by up to 20 years in prison. Hinchey pleaded guilty to one count of conspiracy to distribute cocaine and was sentenced to 13 months in prison, with the term suspended until he completed a drug-treatment program.

- Perhaps the most special treatment was granted to the son of Vice President Al Gore. It was reported in the foreign press that 13-year-old Al Gore III was caught smoking what appeared to be marijuana by school authorities at the exclusive St. Alban's School. Al III was suspended as a result of the offense while his father managed to suppress the story. The *Daily Telegraph* of London noted: "The crusading American media and Washington's political elite have closed ranks to protect Vice President Gore from embarrassment over his teenage son's indiscretion." If young Gore had been busted for possession, that could have resulted in fingerprinting, mug shots, and a drug-possession conviction on his juvenile record.

PUNISHMENT AS AN END IN ITSELF

Drug czar-general McCaffrey assured a congressional committee in early 2000: "For those who say this is a war, we are winning."[104] A year earlier, McCaffrey asserted that the fact that federal anti-drug spending was increasing proved that the "national anti-drug policy is working."[105]

But by any reasonable measure, federal drug policy is a disaster. More Americans died from drug overdoses[106] and more Americans went to hospital emergency rooms for drug-related problems in 1998 than ever before.[107] More high school students (90 percent) reported that marijuana was "fairly easy" or "very easy" to get than ever before.[108] The federal government estimated that cocaine imports jumped almost 15 percent between 1998 and 1999.[109] The price of heroin and cocaine were near all-time lows at the end of the 1990s—signaling the total failure of U.S. interdiction policies.[110] And, while Clinton and Congress competed to concoct draconian drug policies, the drug czar's 2000 National Anti-Drug Strategy report conceded: "A significant treatment gap . . . exists. Approximately five million drug users needed immediate treatment, while 2.1 million received it."[111]

Vice President Al Gore revealed on February 8, 1999, when announcing the Clinton administration's budget request for more antidrug spending, that "I've always believed that, along with all the other dimensions of [the drug] problem, this is a spiritual problem. And if young people have emptiness in their lives . . . if they feel there's phoniness and hypocrisy and corruption and immorality, then they are much more vulnerable to the drug dealers."[112] (Gore made this comment during the middle of the Senate impeachment trial for his boss.) Unfortunately, the effort to scourge people to higher spirituality through draconian drug penalties has failed.

Despite all the government's valiant efforts, some Americans still consumed illicit drugs. More than 14 million Americans admitted to government-funded pollsters that they used illicit drugs during the Clinton administration.[113] Thus, wonderful opportunities remain for further victories in the war against drug users.

With our current moral-judicial system, talking about drugs disapproved of by politicians is a worse crime than killing citizens. The average murderer serves eight years in prison. According to Julie Stewart of Families Against Mandatory Minimums, many people have been sentenced to ten years or longer merely for "conspiracy" via indiscreet discussions with federal informants—"dry cases," in which no illicit drugs are directly linked to the defendant.[114] The number of people in federal and state prisons on drug charges has increased tenfold since 1980; since 1987, drug defendants have accounted for nearly three-quarters of all new federal prisoners.[115] The *Boston Globe* reported in 1998 that 84 percent of the people sentenced under state mandatory minimum laws were first-time offenders sentenced to an average of five years—one year longer than the average sentence received by robbers, rapists, and other violent offenders.[116]

Despite the failure of prohibition, the Clinton administration refused to consider any approach to the drug problem that reduced politicians' power to punish wayward citizens. Drug czar McCaffrey was haunted by a foreign menace: the Netherlands, where marijuana is legal for adults. Just before visiting Holland in 1998, McCaffrey announced that the Dutch drug policy was "an unmitigated disaster." McCaffrey crowed: "The murder rate in Holland is double that in the United States. That's drugs."[117] Actually, the Dutch murder rate is barely one-fourth that of the United States. McCaffrey relied on a source that added together homicides and attempted homicides in the Netherlands, which McCaffrey then compared only to homicides in the United States. One of his underlings defended his gaffe: "What you are left with is that [the Dutch] are a much more violent society and more inept [at murder], and that's not much to brag about." The percentage of Americans who have used marijuana during their lifetime, or in the last month, is more than double the percentage of Dutch who have used marijuana. Similarly, Americans are more than three times as likely to have used cocaine than Dutch citizens.[118]

Drug warriors blamed everybody but themselves for their debacles. DEA chief Constantine whined in February 1999: "The use of drugs is really a prevention issue, and the long-term solution for this nation is when our own citizens, families, teachers and employers take this as seriously as they do the Y2K (Year 2000 computer) problem."[119] Constantine said, "I just don't think that we've paid enough attention" to the issue of illicit drugs. Similarly, drug czar McCaffrey complained in March 1999 that Americans "haven't begun to get serious about the problem" of drug abuse—as if all the overfilled prisons were simply a sign of light-hearted mirth.[120]

"Keeping up appearances" was the heart and soul of Clinton's drug policy. Regardless of how many million people were fined or arrested or jailed—as long as the president preserved his "tough on crime" image and as long as Republicans were deterred from razzing either Clinton or Gore about their alleged pot smoking, it was all worthwhile.

SEVEN

SEARCHING EVERYWHERE

THE CLINTON ADMINISTRATION consistently championed the right of government employees to stick their noses almost anywhere—in people's e-mail, car, house, or pants. Clintonites set off one false alarm after another to justify extending government's right to intrude. The administration sacrificed technological progress in order to maximize government's control over the citizenry.

AN ANCIENT BASELINE

The Fourth Amendment of the Bill of Rights states, "The right of the people to be secure in their persons, houses, papers, and effects, against unreasonable searches and seizures, shall not be violated, and no Warrants shall issue, but upon probable cause, supported by Oath or affirmation, and particularly describing the place to be searched, and the persons or things to be seized." The purpose of the Fourth Amendment was to prevent government officials from having dictatorial power over citizens.

Limiting government officials' power to stop, search, and seize private citizens was long a guiding principle of American jurisprudence. The Supreme Court ruled in a 1886 Fourth Amendment case: "The principles laid down in this opinion affect the very essence of constitutional liberty and security . . . they apply to all invasions on the part of the government and its employees of the sanctity of a man's home and the privacies of life. It is not the breaking of his doors, and the rummaging of his drawers, that constitutes the essence of the offense; but it is the invasion of his indefeasible right of personal security, personal liberty, and private property, where that right has never been forfeited by his conviction of some public offense."[1]

The prohibition of unreasonable searches is the key to the Fourth Amendment. Unfortunately, each extension of government power makes further extensions "reasonable"—since "reasonable" is defined on a sliding scale, by however much intrusion people will tolerate from the government.[2] The Clinton administration often sounded as if the only searches that were unreasonable were the ones that government officials did not care to do.

LOOKING GUILTY

President Clinton was shocked to discover in 1999 that law enforcement agencies targeted suspects based on their race or ethnicity. In a June 9, 1999, "Memorandum on Fairness in Law Enforcement" for federal agencies, Clinton declared: "Stopping or searching individuals on the basis of race is not effective law enforcement policy, and is not consistent with our democratic ideals, especially our commitment to equal protection under the law for all persons. It is neither legitimate nor defensible as a strategy for public protection. It is simply wrong."[3] On the same day, at a discussion devoted to "increasing trust between communities and law enforcement," Clinton orated: "We also must stop the morally indefensible, deeply corrosive practice of racial profiling . . . Racial profiling is, in fact, the opposite of good police work, where actions are based on hard facts, not stereotypes. It is wrong; it is destructive; and it must stop."[4]

Clinton's comments received glowing press coverage. However, some critics always find reasons to nit-pick. The Hispanic Business Roundtable was especially surprised by Clinton's sudden awakening to the dangers of drug courier profiles based on race or ethnicity. In a press release issued the day after Clinton's comments, the Roundtable noted, "As Governor of Arkansas, Mr. Clinton publicly defended a police program that used racial profiling against Hispanics."[5] The state of Arkansas was sued over the program and a federal judge settled the case in 1998 when Arkansas signed a consent decree ending the illegal practice. The *Arkansas Democrat-Gazette* summarized an October 1989 speech to a joint session of the Arkansas legislature: "Clinton was critical of a federal consent decree that prohibited state police troopers from stopping drivers on interstate highways just because they match a certain profile which usually meant they were Hispanic and from Texas, according to a lawsuit filed to stop it."[6]

Clinton also ignored his own administration's use of race-based profiles. Georgetown University law professor David Cole noted, "The White House Office of National Drug Control Policy's Website engages in racial profiling. It states, for example, that 'minorities' sell heroin in Denver and that in Trenton, N.J., 'crack dealers are predominantly African-American males and powdered-cocaine dealers are predominantly Latino.'"[7] Cole also noted that "a computer search of all federal court decisions [involving prosecutions by federal agencies] from Jan. 1, 1990, to Aug. 2, 1995, in which drug courier profiles were used and the race of the suspect was discernible revealed that 95 percent of those stopped were minorities."[8] The Drug Enforcement Administration, through its "Operation Pipeline" training program for state law enforcement agencies, is a fount of enforcement methods targeting blacks and Hispanics.[9]

The sharpest controversies occurred over searches conducted by the Customs Service, the nation's leading employer of amateur proctologists. Some drug smugglers swallow condoms full of cocaine or heroin. Because of such ruses, Customs agents insist on the right to detain some suspects until they have a bowel movement. African Americans and Africans have frequently been targeted for such "searches"—which can include putting a person in leg irons next to a toilet for up to 48 hours, incommunicado until they have a bowel movement, which Customs agents can properly inspect. In Chicago, Customs agents strip-searched far more women than men, even though they are much less successful in finding drugs on females.[10] According to Rep. John Lewis (D-Ga.), "Ninety percent of the individuals [detained at Atlanta's international airport] sent to hospitals to be x-rayed for drugs being transported internally were African Americans. These individuals usually were strip-searched before being hand-cuffed and hauled off to the hospital. Meanwhile, only 20 percent of African Americans detained by customs officers were found to be carrying illegal drugs."[11] The Customs Service vehemently denied that any racial targeting was occurring. However, a March 2000 GAO report noted that black women who were U.S. citizens were 900 percent more likely to be x-rayed for drugs than were white women who were U.S. citizens—even though the black women were less than half as likely to be caught with contraband.[12]

Very little "evidence" is required for Customs agents to target someone. A federal court ruled in 1997 that Customs inspectors were justified in forcing an African American woman to undergo a "stool search" in part because inspectors found a small container of Vaseline in her suitcase—which they claimed could have been used to help insert drugs into her body. A Customs handbook suggests that people can be targeted for invasive searches based on factors such as appearing nervous, wearing baggy clothes, appearing sick, or being unusually polite or argumentative.[13]

In 1999, the Customs Service deployed new BodySearch equipment that uses x-rays to see through the clothes of designated lucky travelers. The ACLU's Gregory Nojeim warned that the new body scanners could show "underneath clothing and with clarity, breasts or a penis, and the relative dimensions of each. The system has a joystick-driven zoom option that allows the operator to enlarge portions of the image."[14] Customs spokesman Dennis Murphy explained: "What (the BodySearch) does is alleviate the need for us to touch people, because people don't like to be touched, and we don't blame them, because our inspectors also feel uncomfortable touching people."[15] Assuming that Customs inspectors don't enjoy touching people is as plausible as assuming that traffic police don't enjoy writing tickets: this is the kind of people those jobs attract. The BodySearch system has the capacity to save images of what it views—so travelers may now look forward to a new kind of trip souvenir: a picture of their privates on file at some government agency.

Even though the Customs Service admits that it fails to stop the vast majority of illicit drugs from coming in at the border, Customs agents now have time on their hands to conduct sweep searches with drug dogs in high schools. In early 1999, Customs agents used canines to sweep a high school in Sierra Vista, Arizona, for drugs.[16] Customs Service spokeswoman Layne Lathram stressed that Customs dogs are only used to search in schools when Customs is invited in by school officials or by local law enforcement.[17]

PAWING IS NOT SEARCHING

The Clinton administration claimed that few, if any, government searches were blocked by the Fourth Amendment. In early 2000, the Supreme Court heard the case of *U.S. v. Bond.* A Greyhound bus was stopped at an internal Border Patrol checkpoint in Texas. After agents checked all the passengers' identification, one agent went through and pawed, squeezed, and manipulated each piece of luggage in the overhead bins. He detected a suspicious object in one canvas bag—and Steven Bond was shortly thereafter charged with possession of a brick of meth. Bond's lawyer argued that groping the luggage was an unconstitutional search. Bond got 57 months in prison.

The Clinton administration argued that no constitutional rights were violated because Bond and other passengers had no "legitimate expectation of privacy." The Clinton administration brief asserted: "The fact that tactile inspection of a bag's exterior may reveal information about its contents no more establishes a search than when officers standing on a public sidewalk or in open fields make observations of the contents of a car or a house. Passengers handling bags in a manner similar to the manner of Agent Cantu may not pay attention to what they sense, or know how to interpret it. But nothing bars government officers from using specialized knowledge to keep themselves alert to, and to help them interpret, that which any other member of the public might have sensed."[18]

To take this reasoning to its logical conclusion, since people in rush hour subway trains are occasionally most uncomfortably pressed against each other— a cop should be allowed to enter a train and press his body against that of any passenger. The police could justify such deviant behavior by invoking the old Mae West line—just checking to see whether other passengers were happy to see them or whether they had guns in their pockets.

Some of the Clinton administration's antidrug policies were highly egalitarian, striving to violate everyone's privacy. During the 1996 presidential campaign, Clinton proposed mandatory drug tests for all teenage applicants for drivers' licenses.[19] This followed the Clinton administration's endorsement of mandatory drug tests for school students in a 1995 Supreme Court case. Clinton administration Solicitor General Drew Days argued that a school district "could not effectively educate its students unless it undertook suspicionless drug testing as part of a broader drug-prevention program."[20]

FEDERALLY FUNDED HASSLING OF AMERICA

Seatbelt crackdowns proved how much Bill Clinton cared about America's children. On September 2, 1999, Clinton declared, "Today I'm pleased to announce the Departments of Transportation and Justice will release a total of over $47 million in grants to help communities combat drunk driving and underage drinking and increases [sic] seatbelt use."[21]

Under Clinton, the U.S. Department of Transportation (DOT) awarded tens of millions of dollars annually to local and state police departments and highway patrols to set up roadblocks and fine all violators of mandatory seatbelt laws.[22] DOT's website warned that the feds have "zero tolerance for unbuckled children." DOT gave bonus awards to local and state agencies that inflict the most tickets on citizens. The agency also suggested offering free hats, T-shirts, and coffee mugs to "enthusiastic officers who are personally committed to increasing seat belt and child safety seat use"—that is, who write the most tickets.[23]

George Black of the National Transportation Safety Board huffed about the seatbelt crackdown: "This is such a societal public health problem. If it were anything else in the world we would have declared an emergency—we would declare war on it."[24] The names of the federally-financed crackdowns illustrate the goal of military-style intimidation of recalcitrant drivers. The New Mexico intensive enforcement effort during Thanksgiving 1998 was named "Super-blitz." Elsewhere, seatbelt crackdowns have been carried out by "Operation Wolfpack"—roving groups of police cars sporting the same moniker used by German submarine groups in World War II.[25] The Georgia seatbelt crackdown is named "Operation Strap and Snap"[26]—which may help explain why that state has become a popular destination for S-M tour groups.

Federal subsidies for seatbelt crackdowns encourage local law enforcement agencies to mulct citizens rather than protect them. After Washington, D.C., resident Gary Kettler got hit in 1998 with two $50 tickets for his and his wife's seatbelt violations, he complained to the *Washington Post*: "My wife saw a young man with a gun beating up an old man, and we had to walk through a gang of people dealing drugs to report the assault to the 10 police officers who were standing on another corner handing out tickets for not wearing seat belts. It may be zero tolerance for minor offenses, but it's business as usual for the serious stuff."[27] Kettler grumped about the seatbelt roadblock: "You find yourself surrounded by all of these police officers who are armed and geared up to hassle you. You are presumed guilty as they search to find anything to justify making the stop."[28]

State police in Colorado ignored the Colorado legislature's refusal to allow them to stop and ticket people solely for seatbelt violations. Instead, the police—with the benefit of a half-million-dollar federal grant—searched for pretexts to stop cars and slap on a seatbelt fine. Capt. Steve Powell of the Colorado State Patrol told the *Denver Post*: "Ninety percent of the cars out there are doing something that you can pull them over for. There are a jillion reasons people can be stopped—taillights, windshields cracked, any number of things."[29]

As usual, the children were invoked to justify this expansion of government power. A press release from the 1998 crackdown on seatbelt violators proclaimed that the campaign "represents the largest coordinated effort by law enforcement to protect children in America's history."[30] Apparently, nothing government has done in the last two centuries is as benevolent as making parents pay $50 for unbuckled kids. Yet, while children are ritually invoked, the vast majority of tickets are written to nail adults not wearing seatbelts.

Some people may assume that a check for seatbelt compliance is the least intrusive of police stops. However, once a car is stopped, police have a blank check to demand insurance papers and licenses, closely surveil the auto and its occupants, interrogate the driver and passengers at length, and have a drug-sniffing dog circle the car to provide an excuse to forcibly search the entire vehicle. Law professor Nadine Strossen, writing about drunk driving checkpoints, observed, the "searches are intensely personal in nature, involving a police officer's close-range examination of the driver's face, breath, voice, clothing, hands, and movements."[31] Supreme Court decisions have given police authority to forcibly search vehicles based on the flimsiest "probable cause" assertion.

A 1998 DOT report to Congress proclaimed that "highly visible enforcement . . . is more effective because the perceived risk of receiving a seat belt citation is increased, even if the actual risk is only slightly higher."[32] Thus, the federally funded roadblock campaign is an exercise in mass deceit. People are presumed to be fools who must be continually frightened by government agents or else they will all go plunging over a cliff to their death.

"No warnings, no excuses" is the mantra of the seatbelt enforcement campaign—yet this standard does not apply to the U.S. Department of Transportation. There have been no prosecutions of federal bureaucrats who lied or misrepresented the danger of air bags, the federal mandate of which resulted in the deaths of more than 90 children.[33] A 1991 National Highway Traffic Safety Administration memorandum discussed the agency's concern that "bad press [on air bag deaths] could cause a lot of harm to the public's positive perception."[34] After scandal erupted about killer air bags in 1997, federal safety officials blamed parents—since the children had not been sitting in the back seats. Yet, federal officials long claimed that the bags posed no threat to children in the front seat. The Transportation Department also wrongfully claimed that raising the interstate speed limit would sharply increase traffic fatalities; in reality, higher speed limits resulted in less speed variance, concentration of police resources on real problems, and lower death rates.[35] Now, because citizens are skeptical of federal safety claims, the government needs more power to punish them.

CRIMINALIZING FINANCIAL PRIVACY

The Clinton administration greatly extended the federal government's long-term assault on financial privacy.

In 1970, Congress enacted the Bank Secrecy Act, which made it a federal crime for banks to keep secrets from the government. Subsequent laws created new crimes and reporting requirements. Congress in 1978 passed the Right to Financial Privacy Act—but created an exemption for any confidential information sent by banks to federal regulators.

Banks and other financial institutions are required to submit a Currency Transaction Report (CTR) to the federal government for each cash transaction involving more than $10,000. Between 1987 and 1995, banks and other institutions delivered 62 tons of CTRs to the feds—over 77 million separate reports. But only 580 people were convicted of money laundering during that period, according to former Federal Reserve Governor Lawrence Lindsey.[36] The feds harvested 12 million CTRs in 1997 alone. Home buyers are routinely reported to the IRS as potential criminals when they go to a closing with a cashier's check larger than $10,000.[37]

Money laundering laws are popular with law enforcement because they make it easy to entrap average citizens suffering from normal greed and stupidity. The U.S. Sentencing Commission estimated that almost 90 percent of money laundering convictions not involving drug money have been achieved via government sting operations.[38]

Clinton's Justice Department was adamant that criminal intent was unnecessary for a citizen to be a criminal under banking laws. Waldemar and Loretta Ratzlaf, an elderly couple, paid off their Nevada gambling debts in large cash payments. The couple did not know that it was a federal crime to pay off debts in chunks of less than $10,000 each—prosecutors call it "structuring," a new crime created in 1986 to apply to actions people took to avoid triggering the $10,000 reporting requirement. A federal appeals court overturned their money laundering conviction because the couple had no intent to break the law. When the case went to the Supreme Court, the Justice Department warned the justices: "When a defendant employs an artifice for the specific purpose of depriving the government of information to which it is entitled, there is no basis for concluding that he is in some sense engaged in 'innocent conduct.'"[39] The Supreme Court rejected the Clinton administration's attempt to create new cadres of illicit, unlucky geezer gamblers. Justice Ruth Ginsburg, writing for the majority in the early 1994 decision, harshly criticized lower federal judges for treating the "willfulness" requirement as "mere surplusage—words of no consequences." Ginsburg concluded that the Court was "unpersuaded by the argument that structuring is so obviously 'evil' or inherently 'bad' that the 'willfulness' requirement is satisfied irrespective of the defendant's knowledge of the illegality of structuring."[40]

Obviously, a federal money laundering law that generated prosecutions of hapless citizens had problems. So Congress, in August 1994, at the Clinton administration's behest, enacted the Money Laundering Suppression Act. This law "improved" the existing statute by removing the "willfulness" requirement from the law, thus making it easier to convict citizens who have no idea they are violating the law. Treasury Undersecretary Ron Noble proclaimed that the new law would "further the growing partnership between the banking industry and law enforcement."[41]

In 1996, Clinton administration bureaucrats issued new regulations requiring banks to file Suspicious Activity Reports (SARs) on any transaction that "has no business or apparent lawful purpose or is not the sort in which the particular customer would normally be expected to engage, and [the bank] knows of no reasonable explanation for the transaction after examining the available facts, including the background and possible purpose of the transaction." This reg would make sense only if bankers were omniscient—or if the feds sought to intimidate bankers into turning in large numbers of customers on dubious pretexts. The feds now receive almost 100,000 SARs a year. A federal appeals court ruled in 1999 that banks do not need a "good faith belief" of criminal activity before filing an SAR on someone.[42] The "safe harbor provisions" provided by federal regulators allow defamatory statements by anonymous informants against innocent citizens. As Greg Nojeim of the American Civil Liberties Union observed, "Congress barred financial institutions from telling their customers that their bank had spied on them by reporting their transactions to the federal government."[43]

Pressuring banks to turn in their customers can have devastating results; as the *Los Angeles Times* reported in December 1999, "In Florida, BankAtlantic became suspicious about some third-party checks moving from its offices in Miami to Colombia. The Fort Lauderdale–based bank reported the activity to law enforcement agents, who promptly seized 1,100 bank accounts—containing $22 million—that had some activity connected with Colombia. In the end, no criminal case was brought and a judge ruled the bank overreacted by turning over information about so many accounts. But it was eight months before the customers—including many immigrants—got their money back, causing hardship for cash-strapped families and the collapse of some small businesses . . ."[44]

The Clinton administration's biggest salvo against financial privacy came on December 7, 1998, when four federal agencies proposed Know Your Customer (KYC) regulations, which would have compelled banks to report far more information about their customers than they were required to before.

The FDIC alone was hit with more than 250,000 comments opposing the KYC regulations, and only 105 comments in favor of them. The proposed KYC regs ignited a firestorm because people perceived them as an overt attempt to convert banks into conspirators against their depositors. The American Banking Association, which had helped draft the regs, turned against them and publicly denounced the proposal.

The proposed regs required banks to "determine its customers' sources of funds, determine, understand and monitor the normal and expected transactions of its customers, and report appropriately any transactions of its customers that are determined to be unusual or inconsistent."[45] Banks would have been obliged to create "profiles" of each customer—dossiers that law enforcement could use if it decided to target that person. Banks would also have been obliged to perform "a risk assessment of the customer and the intended transactions of the customer."[46] The standards for violations were so vague that anyone who had a one-time surge in income—such as selling a car or receiving a bonus at work—could have been reportable as a suspected drug dealer.

Under the KYC regs, banks would have been required to surrender any financial information on customers within 48 hours after receiving a request from law enforcement—no search warrant required. And much of the information the banks gathered on their customers could have been transferred to a database maintained by the Treasury Department's Financial Crimes Enforcement Network (FinCEN) and could therefore be accessible by any law enforcement agency in the nation, and also by all those with whom lawmen share information.

The purpose of the rules, as announced in the *Federal Register,* was to empower government to better "combat illicit activities."[47] But the feds have criminalized so many financial transactions over the years that combating "illicit activities" could justify providing the government information on the transactions of tens of millions of innocent citizens.

Any bank failing to report "unusual or inconsistent" behavior by its depositors would have faced major investigations and an array of sanctions. A regulatory sword of Damocles would have hung over the head of any bank official who hesitated to "drop a dime" on any customer. *Money Laundering Alert* newsletter reported that the "big winners" from the "revolutionary" proposed rules would be "U.S. law enforcement agencies."[48]

The Know Your Customers regulations were largely a response to the failure of federal money laundering statutes to curb the flow of drugs. As usual, the feds responded to drug war failures by creating broad new classes of criminals who have nothing to do with narcotics trafficking.

Sen. Phil Gramm (R-Tex.), the chairman of the Senate Banking Committee, impaled the regulators: "If you ever wondered whatever happened to the people in the former Soviet Union who used to run things there and now are permanently out of work, the answer is they're all in the Clinton administration, and they're running the banking authorities of this country."[49] Gramm denounced the regs as "an unconstitutional, unjustified, and unwarranted search and seizure." A Senate resolution objecting to the proposed regs passed 88-0.

On March 23, 1999, the proposed regulations were withdrawn—though administration officials made it clear that they might issue a new proposed regulation or simply announce "guidelines" or a "policy statement," which could still bind banks but would not stir a public furor.[50]

The withdrawal of the KYC regs may have been an illusory victory for privacy. Federal banking regulators are already arm-twisting banks to implement "know your customer" programs. The Federal Reserve issued a Bank Secrecy Act Examination Manual in September 1997 that advised banks to check out people who open new accounts by making "follow up calls to the customer's residence or place of employment to thank the customer for opening the account. Disconnected phone service warrants further investigation."[51] The FDIC issued a revised Manual of Examination Policies in February 1999 that warned banks that "it is imperative that financial institutions adopt 'know your customer' guidelines or procedures to enable the immediate detection and identification of suspicious activity at the institution."[52]

The feds had chutzpah demanding more personal financial information, considering their abysmal record of safeguarding the information they already collect. The Comptroller of the Currency issued a rule in November 1998 authorizing the release of Suspicious Activity Reports to "any supervised entity and to other persons, without a request for records or testimony."[53] GAO reported in 1998 that 13 state agencies had violated federal rules for the use of confidential SAR information they receive.[54] According to *Money Laundering Alert,* "in two major U.S. cities local police departments have made SAR filings available to private investigators."[55]

Other threats to financial privacy are on the horizon. In September 1999, Marvin Goodfriend, a senior vice president at the Federal Reserve Bank of Richmond, proposed that the government use new technology to penalize citizens who do not spend their cash as fast as the government wants. Goodfriend suggested: "The magnetic strip [in new U.S. currency] could visibly record when a bill was last withdrawn from the banking system. A carry tax could be deducted from each bill upon deposit according to how long the bill was in circulation."[56] As Wired News noted, the feds could effectively impose a "carry tax" to "discourage 'hoarding' currency, deter black market and criminal activities, and boost economic stability during deflationary periods when interest rates hover near zero."[57] Rep. Ron Paul (R-Tex.), a member of the House Banking

Committee, denounced the proposal: "The whole idea is preposterous. The notion that we're going to tax somebody because they decide to be frugal and hold a couple of dollars is economic planning at its worst."[58]

A POSTAL WHACK AGAINST PRIVACY

Throughout American history, the federal government has often shown more enthusiasm for surveillance than for mail delivery.[59]

In 1999, the Postal Service launched a campaign to torpedo its competitors in the private mail box industry. Up to two million Americans rely on private mail box services provided by Mail Boxes Etc., Pak Mail, and similar companies. This is an industry spawned by government incompetence and contempt for customers. Private mail box services first arose during the 1970s, when the Postal Service was telling people that they had to wait two or more years for a post office box.

Private mail box services have been lifesavers for many small business owners. Private services provide longer hours and far more services than the government deigns to offer. For instance, private mail box companies accept deliveries from UPS and Federal Express, which the Postal Service refuses to do for its box holders. And the Postal Service makes windfall profits out of the private mail box services. Delivering a carton of mail to a private post office is far cheaper than having postal carriers take individual letters to dozens of different homes and businesses.

But the Postal Service was embarrassed by the success of the private mail box industry. Rather than offering better service to attract more customers, the Postal Service announced in 1997 that it was considering imposing new burdens and restrictions on people using private mail box services. The Postal Service received 8,097 comments opposed and 10 comments in favor of the new regs.[60] The Postal Service recognized the 10 positive comments as a mandate to regulate. (The Postal Service is exempt from the Administrative Procedures Act. The Postal Service can use its monopoly over first-class mail like a tourniquet to punish competitors.)

In early 1999, the Postal Service announced that it would soon cease delivering mail to any private mail box not identified as a "PMB" (Private Mail Box) in the address. Thus, even though the Postal Service knew that an address was correct, it would spitefully return the letter to the sender. Many box owners now simply use the street address of the Mail Boxes Etc. outlet; customers sometimes add a suite number to the address. The mandatory "PMB" designation was the equivalent of a scarlet A—an attempt to make an entire industry appear a little bit shabby and shady.

The Postal Service also mandated that private mail box companies require anyone who has a box or picks up mail to show two types of identification, including a photo ID, and provide their home address. The Postal Service initially said that they would keep a registry of this personal information and provide it to anyone who asked. Juley Fulcher of the National Coalition Against Domestic Violence complained that the proposed regulation "could be particularly dangerous for battered women who are trying to conceal their location from someone who is stalking them."[61] After getting its own battering in the press, the Postal Service announced that it would modify its disclosure policy but some women's advocates were still doubtful. The *Los Angeles Times* noted that the new rules could also hurt "police officers who don't want criminals to get their home addresses . . . and residents of rough neighborhoods where mail routinely gets rifled."[62]

The Postal Service justified the new burden by warning of the danger of fraud. However, the Postal Service could provide no information as to the number of fraud convictions related to private post boxes compared to Postal Service mail boxes. Postal officials, at a briefing for skeptical congressional aides, were asked how many criminal cases had arisen from the abuse of private mail boxes. The bureaucrats responded by playing a videotape on fraud on *Dateline NBC.* The congressional aides were dumfounded that that appeared to be the only evidence the Postal Service had.[63] A few anecdotes flourished by government officials were sufficient to sanction new restrictions on millions of citizens.

The Postal Service claimed the crackdown was necessary to deter scam artists. But what about scam artists in the Postal Service and the Clinton administration? The Postal Service intentionally slowed down first-class mail delivery in the early 1990s—and "compensated" with a deluge of expensive advertisements bragging about what marvelous mail service Americans receive.[64] The Clinton administration, in its initial "Reinventing Government" campaign, promised that no American would have to wait in line at a post office for more than five minutes. The clock is still ticking on that one.

THE RISE OF THE SURVEILLANCE STATE

Should every new computer and telephone have a welcome mat for the FBI and other wiretappers? The Clinton administration thought so. A 1998 ACLU report observed that the Clinton administration had "engaged in surreptitious surveillance, such as wiretapping, on a far greater scale than ever before . . . The Administration is using scare tactics to acquire vast new powers to spy on all Americans."[65]

FBI Director Louis Freeh told a Senate committee in March 1994 that Americans "want to have a cop" on the digital information highway.[66] Unfortunately, what Freeh demanded and Congress enacted was the equivalent of not just having a cop on the digital information highway, but having a cop potentially listening to every phone call and reading every e-mail.

On April 16, 1993, the Clinton administration revealed that the National Security Agency had secretly developed a new microchip known as the Clipper Chip. A White House press release announced "a new initiative that will bring the Federal Government together with industry in a *voluntary* program to improve the security and privacy of telephone communications while meeting the legitimate needs of law enforcement."[67] This was practically the last time that the word "voluntary" was mentioned.

Such initiatives targeted encryption software, programs that allow individuals to send messages between computers that cannot be read by third parties. Encryption is vital to prevent fraud or abuse of financial transactions and is widely used in the United States and in other countries. Encryption has a long history in this country: Thomas Jefferson used secret codes in his correspondence to avoid detection by the British.

Clipper Chip advocates presumed that it should be a crime for anyone to use technology that frustrates curious government agents. The ACLU noted, "The Clipper Chip proposal would have required every encryption user (that is, every individual or business using a digital telephone system, fax machine, the Internet, etc.) to hand over their decryption keys to the government, giving it access to both stored data and real-time communications. This is the equivalent of the government requiring all homebuilders to embed microphones in the walls of homes and apartments."[68] Marc Rotenberg, director of the Electronic Privacy Information Center, observed, "You don't want to buy a set of car keys from a guy who specializes in stealing cars."[69] When the federal National Institute for Standards and Technology formally published the proposal for the new surveillance chip, fewer than 1 percent of the comments supported the Clipper Chip plan.

The Clinton administration eventually abandoned its Clipper campaign but stepped up its attacks on purveyors of encryption software. The administration spent three years hounding Phil Zimmerman, the inventor of Pretty Good Privacy, an encryption program that Zimmerman distributed for free. Someone placed Zimmerman's software on an Internet site, thus making it available to anyone in the world who chooses to download it. The feds threatened Zimmerman with a five-year prison sentence and a million-dollar fine for exporting "munitions."[70] Zimmerman noted in a 1999 interview that "in a number of countries with oppressive regimes, PGP is the only weapon that humanitarian aid workers have to prevent hostile dictatorships from monitoring their communications."[71]

In 1995 congressional testimony, FBI Director Freeh warned: "Unless the issue of encryption is resolved soon, criminal conversations over the telephone and other communications devices will become indecipherable by law enforcement. As much as any issue, this jeopardizes the public safety and national security of this country. Terrorists . . . will use telephones and other communications media with impunity knowing that their conversations are immune from *our most valued investigative technique*."[72] But, according to the government's records, fewer than one-half of 1 percent of all wiretapping requests are cases involving bombs, guns, or potential terrorist activity.[73]

The Clinton administration's wiretap bill was named the "Digital Telephony and Communications Privacy Improvement Act of 1994." Naturally, the key to improving privacy was to allow government agents to stomp it out whenever necessary. In the final cut-and-paste on Capitol Hill, the bill was renamed the Communications Assistance for Law Enforcement Act.

On October 16, 1995, the telecommunications industry was stunned when a *Federal Register* notice appeared announcing that the FBI demanded that, as a result of the new law, phone companies provide the capability for simultaneous wiretaps of one out of every hundred phone calls in urban areas.[74] As the ACLU noted, the FBI notice represented "a 1,000-fold increase over previous levels of surveillance."[75] FBI Director Freeh denied that any expansion of wiretapping was planned.[76]

The 1994 law led to five years of clashes between the FBI and the communications industry over the new standards. The Federal Communications Commission (FCC) was designated in the act as the arbiter of such clashes; in August 1999, the FCC caved and gave the FBI almost everything it wanted. Thanks to the Clinton administration, people will soon be forced to pay higher phone bills for the privilege of letting the FBI listen in. Telephone companies were required to modify their equipment to make it easier for the government to conduct wiretaps. The U.S. Telephone Association estimated that complying with the new rules would cost its members up to $3 billion.[77] The FBI estimated in 1992 that the cost of making all phone lines easily accessible to government wiretaps would add "less than 20 cents per month" to the average monthly phone bill.[78] If a 15-cent-a-month fee was added as a separate line on phone bills and was called the Federal Wiretap Surcharge, a few malcontents might become suspicious.

The FCC also bowed to FBI demands and required that all new cellular telephones be de facto homing devices. Cell phones must now include components that allow law enforcement to determine the precise location of any caller using the device. As *Electronic Design* magazine noted, "Unlike the location feature being created for 911 emergency services, this capability will apply to all calls and users won't be able to turn it off."[79] The *New York Times* noted, "Law-enforcement officials have asserted that since the location of wired telephones is already public information, there is no intrusion of privacy in determining the location of wireless phones."[80] This is like saying that since police can determine a person's home address by checking the phone book, it is not a violation of privacy to let police follow the person around every place he goes. Jim Dempsey of the Center for Democracy observed, "The FCC order threatens the privacy of all Americans, whether they use cellular phones, traditional wireline phones, or advanced digital voice and data systems."[81]

The 1994 law also gave the attorney general authority to approve or disapprove new technology used by phone companies and other telecommunications vendors. David Sobel of the Electronic Privacy Information Center complained: "We have reached the point where law enforcement is dictating our nation's telecommunications standards."[82] FBI wiretap demands were criticized for "dumbing down" the nation's communications systems.

In the final years of Clinton's second term, scandals over federal agencies' intrusions erupted on a regular basis:

- In February 1999, the *Washington Post* revealed that the U.S. Secret Service had a contract with a New Hampshire company to build a national identity database of photographs of all drivers' license applicants in the nation.[83]
- In August 1999, the Justice Department submitted proposed legislation, the "Cyberspace Electronic Security Act," to Congress to allow law enforcement to obtain search warrants "to secretly enter suspects' homes or offices and disable security on personal computers as a prelude to a wiretap or further search."[84] The bill would make government secure by making it easier to intrude on private communications. The legislation would permit G-men to carry out the kind of "black bag jobs" on average Americans that had previously been used in espionage or national security cases. Attorney General Janet Reno, in a letter to Congress, justified the new powers: "When criminals like drug dealers and terrorists use

encryption to conceal their communications, law enforcement must be able to respond in a manner that will not thwart an investigation or tip off a suspect."[85] The ACLU's Barry Steinhardt observed "that people who are the subject of searches should have notice and the opportunity to challenge the search. This is particularly dangerous since it will be difficult to guarantee that evidence hasn't been tampered with. What they are proposing to do is alter computer files."[86]

- In October 1999, members of the international Internet Engineering Task Force revealed that the federal government was pressuring them to create a "surveillance-friendly" architecture for Internet communications. The FBI urged the task force to build "trapdoors" into e-mail communications programs that would allow law enforcement easy access to supposedly confidential messages.[87] Several of the nation's top high-tech experts publicly warned: "We believe that such a development would harm network security, result in more illegal activities, diminish users' privacy, stifle innovation, and impose significant costs on developers of communications."[88] The ACLU's Steinhardt wrote: "What law enforcement is asking . . . is the equivalent of requiring the home building industry to place a 'secret' door in all new homes to which only it would have the key."[89] The Task force rebuffed the FBI pressure. But the fact that the FBI even attempted to pressure software engineers to sacrifice e-mail reliability to allow government intrusions is a warning of how audacious and manipulative the feds have become.

THE BIGGEST INTRUSION?

Beginning in late 1999, the existence of Echelon, a spy satellite system run by the National Security Agency along with the United Kingdom, Australia, New Zealand, and Canada became a major scandal. Echelon reportedly scans millions of phone calls, e-mails, and faxes each hour, searching for key words. The European Union and the governments of Italy and Russia loudly protested Echelon's intrusions into their sovereign domains. One Portuguese paper complained that Echelon is "like a technological nightmare extracted from the crazy conspiracy theories of the X-Files."[90]

Rep. Bob Barr, a former CIA employee and the most vigilant congressman against G-men high-tech threats, observed, "By all appearances, what we have is a massive government program that scoops up unbelievably huge numbers of private communications, indiscriminately, without any oversight or court involvement. There's a very important, but fine, line between legitimate foreign intelligence gathering and unconstitutional eavesdropping on American citizens, and it appears that line has been crossed."[91] Barr attached a rider to an appropriations bill in late 1999 that required NSA and the CIA to report to Congress on the standards Echelon used to tap Americans' communications. NSA sent members of Congress a letter in February 2000, stating, "We want to assure you that the NSA's activities are conducted in accordance with the highest constitutional, legal and ethical standards, and in compliance with statutes and regulations designed to protect the privacy rights of U.S. persons."[92] NSA reminded congressmen that "the Fourth Amendment protects U.S. persons from unreasonable searches and seizures by the U.S. Government or any person or agency acting on behalf of the U.S. Government"[93] Thus, since excessive intrusions or vacuum searches without a warrant would be unconstitutional, congressmen had no reason to worry that NSA would do anything wrong—since it was inconceivable that the agency would break the law. But NSA sought to block House inquiries into Echelon's operations.

A February 2000 report by the European Union charged that Echelon is used for economic espionage. Former CIA Director James Woolsey told a German newspaper a few weeks later that Echelon collects "economic intelligence." In a *Wall Street Journal* editorial page piece on March 17, 2000, Woolsey justified Echelon's spying on foreign companies because some foreigners do not obey the U.S. Foreign Corrupt Practices Act (which prohibits paying bribes to snare foreign contracts).[94] In the view of Clinton's first CIA director, Americans have an unlimited right to spy on Europeans because Europeans are morally inferior. Europeans are obliged to accept that the United States will only use the information it steals for good purposes, not for its own self-interest. Woolsey sneered at the idea that the United States would be stealing advanced technology since Europeans are supposedly so backward compared to Americans. (One wonders if Mr. Woolsey has been to Stuttgart lately.)

CONCLUSION

Clintonites were far too dedicated to rescuing the masses to permit the Constitution to impede their benevolence. Perhaps at some point the Clinton administration will explain how its anti-encryption, anti-privacy policies differed from those of Communist China. Intrusive Clinton administration policies should alarm any American who thinks the government is not entitled to read their e-mail, squeeze their packages, tap their calls, or know precisely where they are.

FORFEITURE FOLLIES

Seizure fever has permeated the Clinton administration since its first months in office. Clinton's Justice Department fought tooth and nail to maximize the government's prerogative to confiscate private property based on mere gossip or rumor—hearsay evidence. The Justice Department continually hustled the Supreme Court to uphold the most abusive forfeitures and to preserve law enforcement's prerogative to plunder whom they please. And the Clinton administration repeatedly derailed bipartisan efforts in Congress to curb the worst forfeiture abuses.

The Justice Department confiscated 42,454 cars, boats, houses, stacks of cash, and other items of private property in 1998—booty valued at $604,514,733.[1] Federal agents can seize a person's house, car, boat, or other property by invoking more than two hundred different federal statutes involving everything from wildlife to carrying cash out of the country to playing poker for cash with friends and relatives. The vast majority of people whose property is seized by federal agents are never formally charged with a crime.

Asset forfeiture became a national scandal even before Clinton took office. The *Orlando Sentinel* won a Pulitzer Prize for its 1992 series of articles on abusive seizures by a local sheriff's department. In 1992 a federal appeals court questioned whether "we are seeing fair and effective law enforcement or an insatiable appetite for a source of increased agency revenue."[2]

Forfeiture actions are based on medieval legal doctrines that permit government to sue a physical item, not the item's owner. Since cars, boats, and houses have no constitutional rights, the government exploits the stacked procedural deck. The titles of forfeiture cases such as *United States v. 1994 Mercedes-Benz* or *United States vs. Twelve Thousand Three Hundred Ninety Dollars* capture this anachronistic legal doctrine. In most forfeiture court proceedings, the owner must prove that his house, car, or the cash in his wallet is innocent—the government has no obligation to prove that the property is guilty.

Forfeitures are often based on the word of confidential informants (sometimes ex-convicts), who are given up to 25 percent of the value of any property the government seizes based on their accusations. One informant in a Customs Service entrapment operation against Mexican bankers collected $2 million in 1998 for his work.[3] The Justice Department paid out over $17 million to informants in fiscal year 1996—more than triple the amount paid prior to Clinton's ascension into office.

MONTY PYTHON JUSTICE

In the movie *Monty Python and the Holy Grail,* one of King Arthur's knights stumbles upon a mob of peasants wrangling over whether a suspect is actually a witch. The leader of the mob proposes using the most scientifically advanced test available—checking to see if the alleged witch weighs more than a duck. After the suspect fails the duck test, the joyful peasants drag him off to be burnt.

Justice has made great progress in the subsequent 1000-plus years. Nowadays, law enforcement is not allowed to seize a person's life savings unless a dog wags his tail, barks, paws the ground, or otherwise shows a positive alert.

In California, police seized $30,060 from a motorist based solely on a police dog's alert after it sniffed the money. The dog's reaction indicated that the money was tainted with illicit drug residue—thus supposedly proving that the money was the fruit of narcotics trafficking. The motorist, Albert Alexander, filed suit. At the trial, toxicologists presented evidence that most of the currency in the nation has acquired some micro-trace of cocaine or other illicit drugs—enough to alert a trained dog. A federal appeals court concluded, "If greater than 75 percent of all circulated currency in L.A. is contaminated with drug residue, it is extremely likely a narcotics detection dog will positively alert when presented with a large sum of currency."[4]

Though prosecutors know that most American currency is unclean, they continue to invoke the "tainted currency" claim to grab as much as they can.[5] On September 1, 1994, Leo and Antoinette Muhammed and their infant son went to the St. Louis airport to catch a flight back to their home in Los Angeles. Muhammed had paid for his plane tickets in cash at a travel agency, and the agency had alerted the DEA as to his travel schedule. Inside the airport, DEA agents separated the Muhammeds; they were not advised that they had any right to avoid interrogation. Muhammed had $70,990 on him; he said he worked for the Nation of Islam collecting cash from chapter activities. A drug dog alerted to the money, so it was seized. His wife was carrying $22,000 in her girdle; her money was also confiscated. A 1996 federal appeals court decision noted, "Criminal charges have never been brought against the Muhammeds. The facts alleged by the government to discredit the Muhammeds are spare indeed. The government points out that Mr. and Mrs. Muhammed had been married only three months but already had a two-month-old son. This information may be of prurient interest, perhaps, but is wholly immaterial."[6] The panel of judges concluded that "We are faced with a seemingly baseless government seizure of its citizens' cash currency." The judges condemned the DEA's "knowing capitalization on the Muhammeds' confusion to avoid being put to its proof in a court of law." The judges noted that "the war on drugs has brought us to the point where the government may seize up to $500,000 of a citizen's property, without any initial showing of cause, and put the onus on the citizen to perfectly navigate the bureaucratic labyrinth in order to liberate what is presumptively his or hers in the first place. Should the citizen prove inept, the government may keep the property, without ever having to justify or explain its actions." Nine months after the federal appeals court decision, the DEA and the U.S. attorney's office withdrew their seizure notice. However, four days earlier, the IRS had filed a jeopardy assessment against Leo Muhammed and snared the money before it was returned. Leo Muhammed then sued the IRS and the DEA but his suit was dismissed in November 1998, in large part due to the sovereign immunity of the federal government.[7]

On November 7, 1996, Manuel Espinola and his brother were stopped as they passed through a security checkpoint in Boston's Logan Airport to catch a flight to Las Vegas. A security guard noticed a "dark block" in the x-ray of his briefcase. After Espinola opened the suitcase for her, she noticed two packets of cash and summoned state police troopers. (Airport employees routinely receive kickbacks from law enforcement when their tip-offs and accusations lead to a seizure.) Espinola told Officer Stephen Lynch that the money was for a down payment for a house in Las Vegas, where he was moving. Espinola said he had earned the money doing door-to-door sales for Equinox International. Because he did not have one of the company's business cards with him, Lynch assumed he was lying and notified him that his money would be seized and given to the

Drug Enforcement Agency. After they went to the police barracks, Lynch counted out the money and gave Espinola a receipt for $14,665. Lynch then put the money into a manila envelope and brought out a drug dog named Alf, who showed a positive alert. Law enforcement officials apparently made little or no effort to verify any of the information that Espinola provided; instead, they simply assumed he was lying and kept his money. Federal judge Nancy Gertner summed up the case: "The government presents a slightly nervous young man, carrying $14,665 in cash, en route to Las Vegas to find a new home. The man accurately reported his identity and prior to the initiation of forfeiture proceedings, largely confirmed his employment. No criminal charges were brought; indeed, the young man had no criminal record of any kind."[8] Judge Gertner, in her July 1998 ruling, nullified the seizure and denounced the government for "overreaching" and offering a case "based on a troubling mix of baseless generalizations, leaps of logic, or worse, blatant ethnic stereotyping."

On April 7, 1995, an airline ticket agent at Chicago's O'Hare Airport called DEA agent William Grant to alert him that Manuel Sanchez had just paid in cash for a round-trip ticket to Houston. Grant and another DEA agent proceeded to the gate and asked Sanchez to leave the plane for questioning. Grant asked Sanchez if he was carrying any money and Sanchez replied that he had about $9,000 in cash. Grant asked how he had earned it and Sanchez said that he had earned it working at a jewelry store. Grant asked the name of the store and Sanchez hesitated and said he could not remember. Grant informed Sanchez that he was confiscating the money because he believed it was related to narcotics trafficking. The money was put before a drug dog who dutifully alerted. Federal judge James Moran struck down the forfeiture in December 1996, ruling that "the government must come forward with more than a 'drug-courier profile' and a positive dog sniff in order to link the defendant funds to illicit drug transactions . . . It is not reasonable for this court to infer from the mere fact that [the] claimant was in possession of an envelope with a considerable sum of money that he was involved in activities proscribed by the Drug Act."[9] The judge was offended that the government apparently did nothing to justify its accusations against Sanchez; Moran observed that "there must be some independent objective factual basis for determining the validity of the government's assertions beyond their mere recitation by a drug agent clothed with official authority."

On October 13, 1996, Carlos Maldonado was traveling through a Puerto Rican airport, en route from Colombia to Miami. A security guard noticed that he had bundles of currency in his carry-on luggage and alerted a DEA task force. A DEA agent came to the security checkpoint and questioned him. Maldonado provided his correct name and address and stated that he had earned the money selling gold in South America. After Maldonado accompanied the agent to the narcotics group office at the airport, a drug dog named Tonto alerted to the cash. Maldonado was informed that his money was being seized because of a suspected link to narcotics trafficking. Federal judge Moran overturned the seizure in 1998, ruling that "there are absolutely no allegations in this complaint that claimant can be linked, directly or indirectly, with any drug trafficking organization."[10] Moran concluded by noting that, if this seizure had been upheld, "the property of virtually any person traveling with a substantial amount of cash would be subject to forfeiture."

In December 1998, the Drug Enforcement Agency confiscated $19,000 from Corie Blount, a Los Angeles Laker basketball player who was stopped while driving in Ohio; a highway patrolman pulled him over because his car windows were allegedly too darkly tinted. Luckily, the patrolman had a drug-sniffing dog in his car, who dutifully alerted to the bag holding Blount's money. (The DEA was brought in because state law did not allow the highway patrol to directly confiscate the money; forfeiture routinely involves collusion between multiple law enforcement agencies to evade restrictions on their power.) As the *Columbus Dispatch* reported, the money amounted to less than a week's salary for Blount (who stated that the money was from a car he sold).[11]

Sen. Max Cleland (D-Ga.), responding to dog-disparaging judges, proposed the "Drug Currency Forfeitures Act" in 1998 to allow federal agents to confiscate the cash of anyone who possessed more than $10,000, who was traveling on a highway, and whose money generated a positive alert from a government canine. Because the dogs are trustworthy, "legitimate owners of untainted money will be protected," Cleland declared.[12] Cleland explained: "This does not set up a situation that justifies willy-nilly seizures. It sets up a presumption that if it walks like a duck and talks like a duck, it's a duck—and is therefore subject to drug forfeiture statutes." (Ducks are not automatically forfeitable under current federal law.) Cleland's bill was written in large part by Justice Department lawyers.

GUILTY, GUILTY EVERYWHERE

On February 17, 1998, federal attorneys in Houston confiscated the Red Carpet Motel because the owners had, among other crimes, refused a demand by police to raise their room rates. (The feds claimed that higher rates would have discouraged drug dealers from using their premises.) Drug dealing was rampant in the rough neighborhood where the motel was located. Though the motel owners did everything that they could feasibly do to stem the wave of drug crime—including calling police to their premises dozens of times—federal attorneys seized their business anyway, claiming that they were guilty of "tacit consent" to drug dealing. The *Houston Chronicle* editorialized that the crime problem "appears to be the result of ineffective police work and of . . . prosecutors' inability to build cases against scofflaws operating in an open drug market. Good people should not have to fear property seizure because they operate businesses in high-crime areas. Nor should they forfeit their property because they have failed to do the work of law enforcement."[13] On July 17, 1998, after getting its nose bloodied by the news media, the local U.S. attorney's office announced that the seizure was being dropped after the hotel owners agreed to increase security on the premises. But the only changes the owners had to make were to put up two lights, put up a sign announcing that there was security on the premises, and lock one of the hotel doors after sunset.[14]

Federal prosecutors in Pittsburgh nearly destroyed Anna Ward in 1994 after she had fully cooperated with them in their efforts to solve the murder of her husband, Darryl Ward. Prosecutors decided that Darryl Ward had been a drug dealer and that all of his previous income was drug related. They confiscated almost all of Anna Ward's assets (she had her own legitimate business), including the family's furniture and the children's toys. Prosecutors even sought to confiscate the proceeds of her husband's life insurance. Anna Ward and her three children were forced to go on welfare.[15]

In situations like these, if a citizen wants to get his property back after it has been seized by federal agents, he must post a bond equal to 10 percent of the property's value (to cover the government's costs in defending itself against his lawsuit) and file a notice within 20 days of the seizure.[16] Legal costs for suing the government to recover property can easily exceed $5,000. Thus, if the government seizes only a small wad of cash or an old car, a citizen cannot possibly break even by suing to recover his property. And even if he wins in court and recovers his property, there is no provision for reimbursement of his attorney costs.

According to Justice Department forfeiture point man Stefan Cassellas, asset forfeiture is justified because 85 percent of the victims fail to dispute the seizures.[17] However, this is evidence of the bias in the process rather than proof of the guilt of the owners. In fiscal year 1995, the most recent year for which statistics are available, the Justice Department made roughly 35,000 seizures. Most owners chose not to fight the feds in court. In 5,250 cases, the owners challenged the seizure. U.S. attorneys chose to drop almost 60 percent of these cases—3,057. Of the 2,193 complaints that were litigated, the federal government lost 48 cases.[18] The fact that over half of all cases were dropped when the owner challenged the government action raises doubts about the other 30,000 unchallenged seizures. The more expensive the government makes it to challenge a forfeiture, the more justified forfeitures appear to be.

ROBBERY AT THE BORDER

Most travelers do not realize they have a legal duty to notify the federal government whenever they take a large wad of their own cash out of the country. The 1970 Bank Secrecy Act made it a federal crime for anyone to exit or enter the United States with more than $10,000 in cash without filing a report with the U.S. Customs Service.

The Customs Service's modus operandi is for agents to pick out individuals heading for international flights or bus trips and ask them if they are carrying more than $10,000 in cash. If the person does not answer honestly, the Customs Service can seize the person's money and the person faces several years in federal prison for lying to a federal agent. Customs officials use the threat of prison to persuade many people to surrender their right to their cash.

In February 1996, a Customs agent dressed in blue jeans approached Cambodian refugee Malis Chum as she was waiting to catch a flight back to her homeland from New York's Kennedy Airport. Chum later explained: "I don't know the person. He looked kind of weird, make me suspect. I didn't know whether I should tell the truth." Chum denied carrying excessive cash; a subsequent search turned up $77,452—her money and that of other refugees that she was taking back to "rebuild a Buddhist temple and assist relatives in their ravaged homeland."[19] Though Customs had no reason to suspect that Chum had acquired the money illegally, the agency stalled the efforts of a New York Legal Aid lawyer to recover Chum's money. Finally, after the *New York Law Journal* contacted Customs about the seizure almost three years later, the agency returned the cash to Chum. As the *Journal* noted, "For Ms. Chum, the settlement is bittersweet. She said an aunt of hers died of uterine cancer in Cambodia awaiting money she was bringing her for surgery in Vietnam."[20]

In 1997, 14 employees of Bob's Space Racers, of Daytona Beach, Florida, crossed the U.S. border into Canada. The employees had been paid in cash— the usual practice for traveling circuses. As lawyer David Smith subsequently noted in a 1999 statement to a congressional committee, "Customs agents at the North Dakota border seized all their money on the theory that, when the Customs agents aggregated all the money carried by each of the 14 employees, the total came to just over $10,000—the amount of money triggering the regulations about 'declaring' and filing Customs' 'cash reporting' forms.

Customs had no basis for 'aggregating' the money of the employees."[21] Customs eventually gave the company's employees 75 percent of their money back—after they promised not to sue the government over the original seizure or for keeping the other 25 percent. Smith observed, "Customs does not have a helluva lot to do on the North Dakota border."[22]

One of Customs Service's currency seizures led to the biggest forfeiture defeat in the Supreme Court. Customs in 1994 seized $357,144 in cash from a Syrian immigrant, Hosep Bajakajian, who was searched at Los Angeles International Airport prior to heading back to Syria. The money consisted of profits from his two gas stations and loan repayments for Syrian relatives. He and his wife had hidden the money deep in their luggage because they feared that overseas customs agents would steal it.

Both a federal district court and an appeals court concluded that the money had been honestly acquired and ordered most of it returned to Bajakajian. The Clinton administration was adamant that the fact that the money was untainted was irrelevant, and further insisted that Customs' confiscation was justified solely because Bajakajian failed to fill out the federal form disclosing that he was taking more than $10,000 in cash out of the country.

At oral arguments before the Supreme Court in late 1997, the Clinton administration's Irving Gornstein declared that money that is not reported "and is more than $10,000, this is dangerous money. We have a dangerous situation on our hands . . ."[23] One wonders, if currency is so inherently dangerous, then why does the government print up so much of it? Gornstein, when asked whether the government was entitled to confiscate any property involved in a crime, declared: "I would except that one small category of cases where perhaps the property is involved in what might be a minor infraction such as a parking offense."[24]

The Justice Department warned: "The essence of the offense is therefore smuggling money out of the country, not simply failing to file a report."[25] Apparently, the issue of who owned the money was completely irrelevant. The Clinton administration's brief to the Supreme Court declared: "The government has an overriding sovereign interest in controlling what property leaves and enters this country." The Justice Department seemed to believe that all cash and all property have the legal status of a serf and cannot be moved without government permission. This was not a legal doctrine that the Founding Fathers remembered to include in the Constitution.

Immigrants are among the people most susceptible to such penalties: since they often come from nations with corrupt customs services, they can be leery of making any declaration of cash on hand.[26] According to the administration's view, because someone does not trust the government, the government somehow thereby acquires the right to rob the person.

The Justice Department also claimed that seizing undeclared currency prevents crime: "Forfeiture encourages persons to inform the government they are transporting more than $10,000 outside the country and prevents such money from being used in circumvention of requirements in the future."[27] Using the same reasoning, Uncle Sam could confiscate the contents of anyone's bank account to prevent them from making any illicit purchases.

The Supreme Court rejected this absolutist view. Justice Clarence Thomas, writing for the majority in a 5-4 split, declared that "a punitive forfeiture violates the Excessive Fines Clause if it is grossly disproportional to the gravity of a defendant's offense."[28] Thomas noted that the crime in question "was solely a reporting offense." The maximum fine Bajakajian faced under federal sentencing guidelines was $5,000, and the government suffered no harm from his failure to fill out the form. This was the first time the Supreme Court rejected a fine as a violation of the excessive fines clause of the Eighth Amendment. Thomas also noted that the forfeiture of Bajakajian's cash "bears no correlation to any injury suffered by the government."

The dissent, written by Justice Anthony Kennedy and joined by Chief Justice William Rehnquist and Justices Antonin Scalia and Sandra Day O'Connor, repeatedly invoked a 1381 English statute that authorized the confiscation of all gold and silver exported without a license from the king. "Forfeiture of the money involved in the offense would compensate for the investigative and enforcement expenses of the Customs Service," wrote Kennedy. (If the government decides to spy on you, it becomes entitled to seize your possessions to cover the cost of spying.) Kennedy lamented that in this case, "the majority in effect approves a meager $15,000 forfeiture." Kennedy and the other dissenters apparently never considered whether the government deserved a cent of the man's money.

Customs responded to the Supreme Court defeat by sharply escalating its efforts to confiscate travelers' cash. In April 1999, testimony to a Senate Appropriations subcommittee, Customs Chief Ray Kelly declared, "Outbound currency seizures experienced a 59 percent increase in the amount of currency seized compared to the same time period in FY 1997."[29] A month later, Kelly bragged: "Customs officers have dedicated innumerable hours to uncovering outbound currency being smuggled in a variety of sophisticated concealment methods."[30] Perhaps the "innumerable hours" that Customs agents spend searching for money helps explain why Customs fails to intercept the vast majority of incoming narcotics. At Houston International Airport, 100,813 passengers were searched in 1998, but Customs inspectors were able to find pretexts to strip only 8 people of their cash, including a Mexican mother with a baby and $18,924. Customs's crackdown is known as Operation Buckstop. The *Wall Street Journal* reported in December 1999 that "each passenger [must] walk past a checkpoint of agents empowered to search bags, open mail and, sometimes, remove a suspect from a flight."[31] Los Angeles immigration attorney Andres Bustamante observed that it is "common" for Customs agents to "approach Mexicans at the airport" during the holiday season "and take their money. They get a receipt and go on their way."[32] The National Council of La Raza denounced Operation Buckstop as "racial profiling."[33]

In response to the Supreme Court's ruling in the Bajakajian case, the Clinton administration also sought a legislative remedy, proposing a bill in November 1999 to criminalize the action of anyone who "conceals more than $10,000 in currency in any vehicle . . . and transports, attempts to transport, or conspires to transport such currency in interstate commerce . . . knowing that the currency was derived from some form of unlawful activity, or knowing that the currency was intended to be used to promote some form of unlawful activity."[34] Deputy Assistant Attorney General Mary Lee Warren testified to Congress before the new bill was submitted that the administration favored creation of a "new bulk cash smuggling offense" that would allow the feds to confiscate currency even when a person was not leaving the country and even when they had not failed to file a Customs Service disclosure form.[35] Naturally, it would be up to the accused individual to prove that the currency would not be used in the future in some type of unlawful activity.

CIRCLING THE WAGONS AT THE SUPREME COURT

Other recent Supreme Court forfeiture cases highlight the Clinton administration's affection for boundless government power.

THE NUISANCE OF INNOCENT OWNERS

In 1996, the Supreme Court ruled on a case involving John Bennis, a steelworker who picked up a prostitute on a Detroit street on his way home from work. Police swooped down upon the two of them as she was, in the words of the *Baltimore Sun*, "performing a sex act on him."[36] (Such delicate phrasing was common in the days before Monicagate.) Because he was caught in the act, the police seized his car. It was business as usual in Detroit, where nearly 3,000 cars were confiscated in 1995 in an effort to crack down on men who patronize hookers.

The co-owner of the 1977 Pontiac was one Tina Bennis, John's wife. She was outraged that the city government confiscated her car even though she had no guilt or complicity in her husband's illicit escapade.

During preliminary arguments at the Supreme Court, the Justice Department blamed Tina Bennis for her husband's illicit use of their auto. The Clinton administration's brief declared that Tina Bennis "did not allege or prove that she took all reasonable steps to prevent illegal use of the car . . . [Bennis] claimed only that she lacked actual knowledge that her husband would use the car illegally." The brief asserted that because a security guard testified at the trial that he had seen John Bennis soliciting prostitutes in the neighborhood on two prior occasions, Tina Bennis "should have known" that John Bennis was "likely to use the car" illegally.[37] Because Tina Bennis did not hire a detective to tail her husband, she condoned his use of the car for adultery.

The court gave its blessing to the seizure. Chief Justice Rehnquist, who wrote the majority opinion, based his decision heavily on an 1827 case involving the seizure of a Spanish pirate ship that had attacked U.S. ships. Rehnquist did not deign to explain the legal equivalence of piracy in the 1820s and oral sex in the 1990s.

Rehnquist ruled that since the property had been involved in breaking the law, there was no violation of due process in its seizure. "The government," Rehnquist decreed, "may not be required to compensate an owner for property which it has already lawfully acquired under the exercise of governmental authority other than the power of eminent domain."[38] By asserting that the government had already "lawfully acquired" the Bennises' car simply because it had a law authorizing seizure of the car, Justice Rehnquist basically granted government unlimited power to steal: if it wants to "lawfully acquire" private property without compensation, all it needs to do is write more confiscatory laws.

FREEING GOVERNMENT FROM THE TYRANNY OF PAPERWORK

The Supreme Court, at the Clinton administration's behest, ruled in January 1999 that innocent owners have no right to information on how to recover property wrongfully seized by government agents. This decision ensured that more Americans will be caught in Kafkaesque nightmares.

In 1993, police searched the modest home of Lawrence and Clara Perkins of West Covina, California. The Perkinses had previously rented a room to a person who was a murder suspect but who no longer resided there. As part of the search, police broke into the Perkinses' locked bedroom, damaged doors, rummaged through their closet, and found $2,467 in cash. (The money had been saved so that

Clara Perkins could take her children to visit her mother in Alabama.) The police confiscated the money and some other personal items found in the house.[39]

The police left a "To Whom It May Concern" notice listing the property seized and stating that "for further information, call . . ." When Lawrence Perkins called the number at the police station to get his money, he was given bureaucratic runarounds. Perkins went to the police department twice and to the local court, but each time his efforts were blocked.

Perkins finally became exasperated and sued in federal court to get his property returned. On the eve of the start of the trial, the government returned his property. Perkins sued anyhow, claiming that his right to due process had been violated. A federal appeals court agreed, ruling that government agencies must provide owners with sufficient information on procedures to recover their property.

The Clinton administration urged the Supreme Court to overturn the appeals court decision. The administration declared in its brief that due process is satisfied as long as property owners receive an "individualized notice that government officers have seized property under authority of a court-issued warrant."[40]

The Supreme Court agreed, decreeing that "the Constitution does not demand that the owners be given help on retrieving their money or property." Justice Anthony Kennedy, writing for a unanimous Court, stressed that the Perkinses' cash had been "lawfully seized" during the search.[41] But all that means is that the cops saw the money, they took it, and since they were law enforcement, the seizure was practically automatically lawful. According to the Supreme Court, a list of what is confiscated is all that the victim is entitled to. Any citizen who does not have the skills and diligence of a legal researcher apparently does not really deserve to retain his own property.

HASSLE-FREE SEIZURES

The Supreme Court in May 1999, again at the Clinton administration's behest, generously reduced the paperwork burden on lawmen itching to seize someone's car. When Tyvessel White was arrested in October 1993 in Bay County, Florida, at his job on unrelated charges, police claimed that White had used his car to deliver drugs several months earlier and seized his car as "contraband" of the drug trade. Simply accusing him of having used his car to transport drugs was sufficient to strip him of his vehicle. Police found $10 worth of cocaine in the ashtray of the car—for which White was convicted— but that was completely separate from and subsequent to the confiscation of his auto.

The Florida Supreme Court overturned the car seizure, ruling that "we simply cannot accept the government's position that it may act at any time, anywhere . . . . to seize a citizen's property once believed to have been used in illegal activity . . . Indeed, the entire focus of the seizure here was to seize the vehicle itself as a prize because of its alleged prior use in illegal activities."[42]

When the case went to the Supreme Court, the Clinton administration's brief noted, "A similar federal statute provides for forfeiture of any vehicle that is used or intended for use in transporting or in any manner facilitating the transportation, sale, receipt, possession, or concealment of various described property, including controlled substances."[43] Thus, if a federal wiretap overhears a phone conversation between two people planning to get together and smoke a joint, the DEA can seize the car they assume will be used to transport the nickel bag.

The Clinton administration also argued, curiously, that seizing someone's property is less intrusive than searching their vehicle. The administration's brief asserted that the "standard of reasonableness" that governs "seizure of property that affects the owner's possessory interest" should be more lenient than the standard that governs a search "which intrudes upon expectations of privacy." The brief noted, "Because the car was located in a public place, its seizure did not involve an official intrusion into any area protected by the Fourth Amendment." Apparently, as long as government officials "respect" privacy, they should be able to seize as much private property as their hearts desire.

The Supreme Court blessed the seizure, declaring that "although . . . the police lacked probable cause to believe that . . . [White's] car contained contraband . . . they certainly had probable cause to believe that the vehicle itself was contraband under Florida law." Justice Stevens dissented, noting that the seizure was motivated largely by the desire to avoid the "hassle" of getting a warrant; Stevens concluded: "I would not permit bare convenience to overcome our established preference for the warrant process." After this Supreme Court decision, police officers need to do little more than pronounce the magic word "contraband" in order to nullify citizens' rights.

STONEWALLING ON CAPITOL HILL

Forfeiture abuses became so blatant that, in June 1993, even members of Congress claimed to be concerned about the injustices. When Rep. Jack Brooks (D-Tex.), the chairman of the Judiciary Committee, announced plans to hold hearings on forfeiture abuses, Attorney General Janet Reno interceded and asked that the Justice Department have a chance to examine the law and propose reforms to "insure fairness and due process to all innocent owners" before Congress took action. Brooks bowed to the new attorney general's request.[44]

In early 1994, the Justice Department released a report revealing that the real problem with forfeiture law was insufficient forfeiture power. The Justice Department proposed a new law to empower its lawyers to issue "civil investigative demands" to compel citizens to answer an unlimited number of questions regarding their property or themselves. Any property owner who invoked the Fifth Amendment to avoid self-incrimination in response to Justice Department lawyers' questions would be presumed guilty, and his property would almost automatically be confiscated. This "reform" would have played nicely into the "seize now, prove later" tactics beloved by law enforcement. The Justice Department's counterproposal, along with lobbying by law enforcement officials, successfully blocked any movement on congressional forfeiture reform.[45]

In 1997, Rep. Henry Hyde, the chairman of the Judiciary Committee, and Rep. John Conyers, the ranking Democrat on the committee, cosponsored legislation to reform forfeiture. The Justice Department strongly objected to the bill and heavily lobbied Hyde. In June 1997, on the day before a subcommittee was scheduled to mark up his bill, Hyde sidetracked his own 15-page reform bill and pledged himself to a new 64-page bill—with almost all the new material written by Justice Department lawyers. This was like letting burglars write the laws on breaking and entering. The new bill greatly expanded prosecutors' power to seize people's assets before a trial (thereby potentially crippling a person's ability to hire defense counsel), made it much more difficult for citizens to get summary judgments against wrongful seizures, and greatly increased the number of crimes that could trigger seizure of a person's or a corporation's assets. The Justice Department's Stefan Cassella characterized most of the new provisions as "non-controversial good-government additions."[46]

Hyde pushed the new bill through the Judiciary Committee on June 21, 1997, by a 26-1 vote. The lone dissenter, Rep. Bob Barr (R-Ga.), a cosponsor of Hyde's original bill, said the new bill "seems to be precisely what the Department of Justice wanted. The problem is that it has a good title [the "Civil Asset Forfeiture Reform Act"] and with the reputation of Chairman Hyde behind it, that carries a lot of weight."[47] In 1998, Hyde reversed himself again, abandoned the Justice Department bill, and re-embraced his original bill. But, by that time, there was not sufficient time left on the legislative calendar to move the original bill forward.

LACKEYS FOR LEVIATHAN

Many congressmen of both parties were eager accomplices of some of the worst policies of the Clinton administration. Few examples better illustrate this than the 1999 congressional debate over forfeiture reform.

Hyde finally got a forfeiture reform bill through his committee and to the House floor in 1999. Hyde's bill would have shifted the burden of proof to the government in forfeiture cases, abolished the requirement that people must post cash bonds before being permitted to sue to get their property back, and made other procedural changes to level the playing field. Hyde's bill was no panacea but it would have curbed some of the worst abuses.

The House debated Hyde's bill on June 24. Hyde made a passionate, eloquent case for the need for reform. And then the caterwauling began.

Rep. Asa Hutchinson (R-Ark.) introduced a substitute "reform" bill that would have greatly increased federal power to confiscate property. (Most of Hutchinson's substitute bill was written by the Justice Department.) Hutchinson demanded to know: "How does disarming law enforcement fit into the war on drugs?"[48] Thus, decreasing a DEA agent's power to seize someone's car is the equivalent of taking away his sidearm. Apparently, the main "armament" in the war on drugs is the sweeping power of law enforcement over nonviolent, private citizens

Several congressmen recited cases of forfeiture abuses. Rep. Benjamin Gilman (R-N.Y.) brushed off such concerns by introducing into the record a letter he received from the superintendent of the New York State Police that assured him: "We are aware of no instance, since the inception of the federal equitable forfeiture sharing program, of any case involving this agency whereby a hardship was endured by a truly innocent owner. It is not the intention of this agency, nor, in my opinion, the intention of law enforcement in general, to deprive truly innocent owners of property due to the illegal use of the property by criminals."[49] Thus, the fact that a police chief asserted that he was not aware of any specific injustice should have allayed all concerns about any abuses.

Rep. Anthony Weiner (D-N.Y.) raised the caliber of the debate with a perfect gem of logic: "The abuses that exist, and they do, they represent the straw man in this debate because indeed we all want to do away with the abuses."[50] Thus, because all members of Congress presumably wished that abuses did not occur, it was unfair to actually consider seizure abuses when seeking to reform the law.

Rep. Ed Bryant (R-Tenn.) debunked other congressmen's comments about the number of people whose money was seized though they had no drugs on them: "The way the system works in this is when there are couriers . . . they either have the money or they have the drugs, but they do not have them both

. . . So we either find drugs on the person or money on the person, depending which way they are going."[51] Thus, the fact that someone is caught with lots of money but no drugs proves that they are a drug courier.

Hyde's bill would have allowed judges the option to appoint counsel for indigent citizens challenging forfeiture actions. This was denounced by opponents as guaranteeing that taxpayers would be forced to bankroll attorneys for every drug cartel chieftain in the hemisphere. Rep. Jim Ramstad (R-Minn.) fretted that "frivolous claims would be encouraged by this legislation."[52] The problem occurs not from the government seizing people's property—but from providing a mechanism to allow owners to get their goods back.

Rep. John Sweeney (R-N.Y.) warned that limiting forfeiture power would mean "removing the teeth from the most valuable tool in what seems to be a losing war against drugs." Sweeney pleaded with his colleagues: "Can we not strike a balance between free enterprise and criminal enterprise?"[53] Sweeney did not specify whether he believed wrongful seizures by government agents should be considered "criminal enterprise."

The Hutchinson "substitute" to expand government confiscatory power was defeated by a vote of 268-155. Afterwards, Hyde's bill passed by a vote of 375-48. The bill then went to the Senate.

On July 21, 1999, the Senate Subcommittee on Criminal Justice oversight held a hearing dominated by law enforcement lobbies who sounded the alarm—as if the nation was only one less forfeiture away from capitulation to barbarian hordes. Sen. Strom Thurmond (R-S.C.) mumbled that the House bill "may undermine the use of forfeiture law in the war against drugs, child pornography, money laundering, telemarketing fraud, terrorism and a host of other crimes."[54] The "Chicken Little" syndrome worked overtime.

Richard Fiano, DEA chief of operations, assured the senators that "DEA's asset forfeiture actions all take place within a legal framework with built-in protections for the innocent."[55] Fiano also declared, "Law enforcement must be able to take the profit out of drug trafficking." According to most estimates, the illicit drug trade in the United States generates more than $60 billion in revenues per year. At most, forfeitures are taking a few percent out of the illicit drug cash flow per year. Currently, forfeiture imposes less burden on the drug trade than the federal corporate income tax imposes on the Fortune 500.

Deputy Attorney General Eric Holder wailed at the Senate hearing that "elevation of the standard of proof [for forfeiture] to 'clear and convincing evidence' would have a devastating effect on the government's ability to establish the forfeitability of the property in complex money laundering and drug cases."[56] Holder portrayed the Justice Department as a helpless giant at the mercy of any forfeiture victim who casts aspersions on the government's credibility. Forfeiture funds have turned law enforcement agencies into independent fiefdoms, able to spend millions on whatever they please with no legislative oversight. And any threat to this off-budget cash flow is treated as a great betrayal.

Holder also told the senators that "we are eager to see civil asset forfeiture reform that includes provisions needed to make the asset forfeiture laws more effective as law enforcement tools," and he urged Congress "to expand forfeiture into new areas . . . From telemarketing to terrorism to counterfeiting to violations of the food and drug laws, the remedy of asset forfeiture should be applied." Holder's statement was mystifying, since the Food and Drug Administration already has sweeping power to confiscate property based on the slightest alleged violation of its edicts.[57]

The Clinton administration strove to cast forfeiture as a motherhood-and-apple-pie issue. Treasury Undersecretary James Johnson told senators that the Treasury forfeiture fund had paid for the explosive detection canine teams that swept Columbine High School in Colorado and also paid for a program in 27 cities to target illegal sources of guns used by young people.[58] Clinton administration officials implied that, unless government officials are allowed to continue seizing private property on the merest whim, all public safety programs could end.

At the same time that the Clinton administration was making tactical concessions on the reform bill, it was also pushing new legislation that would have broadly expanded federal forfeiture powers. Attorney David Smith noted that some of the administration's proposals "reflect an unseemly desire to overrule Supreme Court decisions that have correctly rejected the government's position on issues like fugitive disentitlement and excessive fines under the Eighth Amendment."[59]

Congress finally passed and Clinton signed a largely hollow forfeiture reform measure in April 2000. Citizens received some new procedural advantages in forfeiture cases, but the playing field remains heavily tilted in the government's favor. The Justice Department was not crucified on a requirement of "clear and convincing evidence" for property grabs; instead, federal agencies merely have to show "probable cause"—i.e., rumor or hearsay evidence—before confiscating property. If some citizen challenges the seizure, the government must show by a "preponderance of evidence" that the seizure was justified. (Since the vast majority of seizures are not challenged, the new standard of evidence will mean little or nothing to most forfeiture victims.) And "preponderance of evidence" means simply that there is a 51 percent chance that property was wrongfully used—according to the assertions of law enforcement. The right to free counsel for forfeiture victims was effectively gutted. The new law does nothing to curb law enforcement profiteering from forfeitures: the basic conflict-of-interest is perpetuated untouched. The law imposes a new ludicrous requirement that citizens who file suit to recover their property must swear that their claim is not "frivolous." Any citizen who allegedly lies and files a frivolous suit can face three years in prison simply for filing the suit. E. E. Edwards, the co-chairman of the forfeiture task force of the National Association of Criminal Defense Lawyers, said that the perjury threat is "a thinly veiled attempt to intimidate people from making a claim."[60] On the other hand, there are no penalties for frivolous seizures of private property by federal agents; the punishment for such behavior will continue to be outstanding performance evaluations.

BLOCKADING HARBORS FOR FREE TRADE

IN HIS 1998 STATE OF THE UNION ADDRESS, Clinton bragged, "In the last five years, we have led the way in opening new markets, with 240 trade agreements that remove foreign barriers to products bearing the proud stamp 'Made in the USA.'"[1]

In reality, at least a third of those agreements were actually one-sided edicts compelling foreign governments to restrict the amount of clothing and textiles they sold to American consumers.[2] Such agreements did nothing to open foreign markets to American-made goods. Yet Clinton perennially paraded the total number of "agreements" as victories for free trade.

American consumers and businesses have been forced to pay more than $600 billion in higher prices due to U.S. trade barriers since 1993.[3] Clinton fought doggedly to perpetuate almost all the trade barriers that existed at the time he took office and to minimize the benefits American consumers reaped from international trade agreements.

Mickey Kantor, Clinton's first Trade Representative, declared shortly after Clinton took office: "We hope to avoid getting bogged down in long, drawn-out theological debates about free trade versus protectionism. This is a senseless exercise and ultimately futile."[4] Administration officials began by disavowing a principled approach. Clinton's trade policy quickly degenerated into one protectionist measure after another to accommodate politically connected industries.

Clinton's Commerce Department found pretexts to condemn foreigners for unfair trade in almost all of the dumping cases filed against foreign companies, ranging from Chilean salmon, to Chinese pencils and paper clips, to Romanian steel pipes, to Italian pasta, to Taiwanese roofing nails, to German printing presses, to Indonesian mushrooms. These rulings effectively locked hundreds of foreign companies out of the American market and damaged the competitiveness of American manufacturers who needed foreign inputs and raw materials.

"Fairer than thou" was the Clinton administration's mantra in trade conflicts. And since, to the Clintonites, no one else was playing fair and the United States was always being victimized, the United States was entitled to retaliate against any country it chose. Clinton's appointees repeatedly went to the brink of major trade wars with Canada, Japan, China, and the European Union. The United States demanded that foreign nations provide American companies with guaranteed sales levels in future years at the same time that Clinton denounced foreign nations for not having open economies.

FASHION CZAR FROM ARKANSAS

No one told voters in November 1992 that they were choosing a fashion czar.

In 1791, Treasury Secretary Alexander Hamilton said the clothing industry was a prime example of a struggling industry that deserved a few years of protection. After almost 200 years of high tariff walls, textiles are now America's oldest infant industry. In addition to tariffs, the government imposes import quotas on 3,000 textile products, including tampons, typing ribbons, tarps, twine, towels, tapestries, and ties.[5]

Overall, the combination of high tariffs and import quotas adds the equivalent of a 50 percent tariff surcharge to the price of imported clothing.[6] Poor Americans are hurt much more than are the rich. The United States has no import quotas for fancy dresses from Paris, but has strict controls on imports from Pakistan, Bangladesh, and Nepal. The products from Third World countries tend to be lower quality and lower priced—and those are the products that the U.S. government is most anxious to keep out.

Because protectionism is addictive, Clinton's textile policy consisted of an unending series of alarms over incursions by perfidious foreigners. After each panic over trace amounts of imported clothing, the Clinton administration dutifully erected new blockades around American harbors.

President Clinton announced in May 1993 that the United States might send troops to aid and protect the Macedonians. But, while Macedonia was struggling with a flood of refugees from Bosnia and threats of a Serbian invasion, the U.S. Commerce Department launched a preemptive attack on a trickle of Macedonian clothes exports.

In early 1993, Macedonia was exporting men's and boy's wool suits to the United States at an annual rate of 240,000. But the Commerce Department prohibited Macedonia from exporting more than 80,000 wool suits a year to the United States—a 66 percent slash in export levels.[7] A Commerce Department spokesman asserted that the action was taken in response to "rampantly rising imports." But Macedonian exports amounted to less than 3 percent of the total number of men's and boys' wool suits bought in the United States. The Commerce Department throttled Macedonia's most important export to the United States. The tariff on wool suits is 21 percent—levying a $63 tax on a $300 suit. But it was not enough to severely tilt the playing field in American industry's favor; the U.S. government was also obliged to lock foreign teams out of the stadium.

The quota undermined Macedonians' ability to raise sufficient funds both to feed and defend themselves. Shortly before the announcement of the quota, the Clinton administration harshly criticized the European Community for supporting the arms embargo against Bosnian Muslims. But the Clinton administration slapped a partial economic embargo on Macedonia. The U.S. action was ill-timed since Macedonia was struggling to shed its socialist legacy and enter the capitalist world. U.S. troops went to Macedonia shortly after the quota was announced—but it was unclear whether their mission was to defend the country or serve as an advance guard for the U.S. Customs Service.

KENYAN CAPERS

On May 18, 1994, the Commerce Department announced that Americans would be prohibited from purchasing more than 1,565,616 Kenyan pillowcases in the following year. At that time, Kenyan pillowcases accounted for less than 1 percent of the pillowcases Americans bought. Yet, Commerce lamented in a *Federal Register* notice, "The sharp and substantial increase in [pillowcase] imports from Kenya is disrupting the U.S. market for cotton pillowcases."[8]

Despite the proclamation of a trade emergency, there had been no news reports of chaos in the pillowcase sections of major department stores, nor had foreign pillowcases sparked panic in the streets. There was no evidence that any American worker had lost his job as the result of the Kenyan imports. When asked about the impact of the imports on U.S. employment, Commerce International Trade Specialist Helen LeGrande replied, "I have no idea." Nor did Commerce have any evidence that Kenyan imports had caused the price of U.S. pillowcases to fall. Kenyan pillowcase imports had increased; *ergo,* according to the U.S. government, the U.S. market was disrupted.

The official notice, signed by Rita Hayes, Commerce's deputy assistant secretary for textiles, solemnly declared, "The United States remains committed to finding a solution concerning [Kenyan pillowcases]."[9] The only solution acceptable to the U.S. government was new trade restrictions. One textile trade expert summarized the U.S. government's attitude toward the Kenyans: "Let them eat pillowcases. There is a lot of fiber there—it is good for them." Both Portugal and Spain export far more pillowcases to the United States than does Kenya, but the United States dared not impose quotas on members of the European Union. The United States had provided over $2 billion in foreign aid to Kenya since 1980. Much of this aid was targeted to helping Kenya develop its own private sector. When the Kenyan apparel industry finally starting exporting, the U.S. Commerce Department seemed intent on strangling the infant industry in its crib.

Other African nations also felt the wrath of American bureaucrats. Commerce Secretary Ron Brown visited Egypt in January 1994 and publicly criticized the government for its slowness in pursuing market-oriented economic reforms. A few days after Brown left Egypt, the Commerce Department announced plans to slap import quotas on Egyptian shirts. (Since 1993, the United States has provided over $10 billion in economic aid to Egypt.) Commerce's announcement sparked a furor in Cairo and threatened to disrupt the delicate Middle East peace talks process. James Pringle of the American Chamber of Commerce in Egypt observed, "The Egyptians were shocked. This has disrupted an industry that had a bright future and showed all the private-sector initiative that the U.S. has been trying to encourage in Egypt."[10]

BLOCKING RED ARMY REMNANTS

On January 9, 1994, Clinton announced: "One of our priorities should be to reduce trade barriers to the former Communist states."[11] The United States was lavish in its aid to former East Bloc nations; for example, it pledged $700 million in economic aid to Ukraine during 1994.[12]

But, after $18 million worth of Ukrainian wool coats penetrated the American mainland that year, the Commerce Department slapped on import quotas. Ukrainian factories that formerly made coats for the Red Army had, as a result of defense conversion, begun making coats for American consumers. Ukrainian coats proved a blessing for moderate-income Americans. Prior to the arrival of the imports, good wool coats routinely cost over $200. The Ukrainian coats were available for under $100. Matthew Burns, chief executive of the Eastland Woolen Mills of Corinna, Maine, fretted that a Ukrainian coat was "an excellent garment. It's well-tailored. It's well-manufactured. It's stylish."[13]

Many experts feared that the economic chaos in the Ukraine could result in a nuclear civil war. Clothing was one of the few competitive Ukrainian exports. The U.S. quotas effectively restricted future exports to 1994 levels. One of the leading Ukranian clothing factories laid off 300 workers as a result of the quotas. The *New York Times* noted, "For Ukraine's government, the curbs on coat shipments is a setback for the reformers who are just beginning to win a battle for liberalization of their economy . . . Importers said that while they would still be able to buy Ukrainian coats, though not in the quantities they would like, the mere presence of the quotas made the business less attractive and more bureaucratic."[14]

President Leonid Kuchma, elected a few months before the quotas were announced, was struggling at the time to end the country's addiction to communist economic policies. The U.S. import quota forced the Ukrainian government to exercise much more control over clothing factories, dictating which factories were permitted to export how many coats to the United States. This was a partial revival of Soviet-style central planning. In 1996, the United States imposed new quotas on Ukraine, restricting their exports of men's and boys' cotton shirts.[15]

JUMP-STARTING HAITI

On September 19, 1994, the United States effectively invaded Haiti, landing troops on the island only hours after its military junta agreed to resign and allow the Clinton-backed politician, Jean-Bertrand Aristide, to take over the government.

A few weeks after the troops landed, the Clinton administration announced that the United States was reimposing quotas on imports of Haitian clothing and textiles.[16] (The quotas had lapsed because of the Bush-Clinton economic embargo against Haiti.) The action hit Haiti's most important industry, its largest employer, and its largest earner of U.S. dollars. While Clinton was willing to risk the lives of 20,000 American soldiers in Haiti, he was not willing to risk the profits of a single American textile manufacturer.

The United States reimposed the same quota levels on Haitian exports that it previously imposed on the Haitian dictators who ruled before Aristide's election in 1990. Haiti was treated worse than other countries subject to U.S. textile quotas. Though Haiti's population was more than double that of El Salvador, Haiti was allowed to export to the United States only one-third as many woven shirts.

In lieu of open access to American markets, the Clinton administration deluged Haiti with foreign aid to "jump start" its economy. The Clinton administration gave Haiti $45 million to help protect the Haitian currency against instability caused by trade deficits and $25 million to help Haiti pay its foreign debts.[17] Clinton forced U.S. taxpayers to underwrite Haitian trade deficits at the same time that his administration refused to let Americans buy Haitian-made clothes.

POOR FOLK NEED NOT APPLY

Silk clothing was the fastest growing segment of the American clothing business in the early 1990s. For the first time in history, silk clothing became affordable to working-class Americans, appearing in such mass-market outlets as JCPenney. The Clinton administration responded by carrying off the largest panty raid in history.[18]

Almost all the silk clothing was coming from China. Though silk clothing imports had been doubling each year since the early 1990s, the Clinton administration in 1994 forced the Chinese to slash import growth to 1 percent a year. Silk imports have never faced high trade barriers because the United States has no silkworms and produces not a single article of silk clothing. But the Clinton administration feared the sale of silk blouses might undercut the sale of American-made cotton and polyester blouses. Martin Trust, president of the company that owns Victoria's Secret stores, observed, "We have been able to produce silk at relatively moderate prices and make it available even for lower-income people. With the new quotas, lower-income people will have to give up silk clothing and buy something else."[19]

CAMBODIAN CUT-UPS

Commerce Department employees were vigilant to threats from the world's poorest nations. In early 1999, the United States forced Cambodia to restrict how many pairs of underwear its factories sold to Americans.[20] The United States also restricted Cambodian exports of sweaters, trousers, and coats.[21] At that time, Cambodia was desperately struggling to overcome the effects of Khmer Rouge genocide and a long-term civil war. (The United States has given hundreds of millions of dollars in foreign aid to Cambodia since 1993.) In 1999, the United States announced that it might permit a special 14 percent increase in the amount of clothes Cambodia was permitted to export—as long as Cambodia satisfied U.S. demands to have pro-union policies that pleased the Clinton administration.[22]

THE MIRACLE OF THE TOWELS

More than 40 nations are assigned quotas that specify how much of each type of textile and apparel product each restricted nation may sell to American consumers. Some factories occasionally evade the restraints by "transshipping" clothing to a third country (where labels are attached stating "Made in . . .") before being exported to the United States. Transshipments provide American consumers with greater selection and lower prices and provide a windfall to the U.S. Treasury, since importers pay the high U.S. clothing tariffs in full. But the U.S. textile industry demanded that the federal government take any and all steps to block transshippers.

In early 1994, the United States accused China of transshipping $2 billion worth of textile products to the United States each year.[23] The $2 billion figure, repeated ad infinitum by U.S. officials, quickly reached the status of divine revelation in American trade policy. The U.S. government provided no evidence to support its claim of multibillion-dollar transshipments.[24] At a "background" briefing, a senior Clinton administration official (probably Trade Representative Mickey Kantor or one of his top aides) was pressed by a journalist to explain how the $2 billion figure was reached; the official replied, "Look, it's a real difficult thing to do. There's no scientific procedure to it . . . It is merely an estimate. That's all it is."[25]

At a January 6, 1994, press conference, Kantor announced that China was guilty of illegally transshipping 625 million kilograms of shop towels through Honduras to the United States. (Shop towels are small cotton towels used to wipe grease and oil off of machinery.) Kantor repeatedly used the 625-million kilogram figure, as it was by far the largest case of alleged Chinese cheating. Kantor declared, "What we're dealing with here is massive fraud."[26]

Total U.S. imports of shop towels from all nations are less than 6 million kilograms; thus, China was accused of transshipping more than a hundred times more shop towels than the total amount the United States imports each year. Six hundred twenty-five million kilograms works out to roughly 19 billion shop towels. The average U.S. consumption of shop towels is less than 400 million a year. Thus, according to Kantor, the Chinese had nefariously snuck in enough shop towels to satisfy U.S. shop towel consumption for almost the next half century.[27]

After I phoned the Customs Service, the Office of the U.S. Trade Representative (USTR), the Commerce Department, and private trade experts checking out this accusation, a senior U.S. trade official conceded that Kantor "had been given the wrong number."[28] The actual alleged shop towel transshipment was 626,000 kilograms; Kantor exaggerated the Chinese alleged violations by almost a thousandfold. Kantor made no public admission that his accusations against the Chinese were ludicrously exaggerated.

Kantor also demanded that U.S. Customs Service inspection squads be permitted to descend unannounced on Chinese clothing factories. The Customs Service established "jump teams" to jump on foreign textile factories to check whether they had the capacity to produce the amount of clothes those nations shipped to the United States. These teams have visited 34 nations searching for violators of U.S. textile import regulations. (The jump teams were trained in part by the American Textile Manufacturers Institute.) Ten nations, including China, refused to sign agreements with the United States. No U.S. agency has the right to conduct surprise visits on American factories to count their underwear inventory; yet, this is what the U.S. government demanded of China and other countries.

FAILING THE QUACK TEST

Textile import regimes spawn disputes over product tariff classifications. Consider the case of TV Ducks—cotton products made to sit on the arm of a couch and hold a TV remote control. Robert Capps, who owned a small company in Skyland, North Carolina, ordered a large shipment of the products from China, but the Customs Service prohibited their entry in 1995. Customs claimed that the little novelty items belonged in the same tariff category as bedspreads—and thus that Capps needed a textile import quota before he could import them. No U.S. company was making TV Ducks, but Customs officials were hell-bent on protecting American consumers from the product.[29] Capps hired a lawyer, who quickly convinced a federal judge to overturn Customs' edict. However, the Justice Department appealed the decision and dragged the case out for a year and a half, costing Capps millions of dollars in lost sales, before a higher panel of federal judges again trounced the agency.[30]

Import quotas rarely inconvenience high-ranking government officials. The *Rushford Report* newsletter, the best source of information on U.S. trade follies, revealed in 1998 that Commerce Secretary Bill Daley bought three suits and eight shirts at Sam's Tailor Shop in Hong Kong during a 1997 visit.[31] Daley paid no tariffs on his purchase; instead, some of the goods were mailed to him and some were carried back to America by a Daley aide. Chief U.S. textiles negotiator Donald Johnson bought a suit and two shirts at Sam's. The more U.S. textile negotiators traveled to restrict other Americans' clothing choices, the more lavish their own wardrobes became.

Clinton was president when the Uruguay Round of the General Agreement on Tariffs and Trade (GATT) negotiations was completed. The core of the agreement to liberalize trade rules was largely completed by the Bush administration but signed by Clinton. The agreement required all textile import quotas to be phased out over a ten-year period. Textile import quotas were one of the most important GATT issues for Third World nations, who have long felt like beggars of market share. But the expected phaseout largely vanished in the bowels of the Commerce Department and the Office of the U.S. Trade Representative. Clinton administration policymakers finagled numbers and shifted almost all of the liberalization in textile trade to 2004. This bureaucratic sleight of hand meant that American consumers paid tens of billions of dollars in higher clothing costs than they would have paid if Clinton had honored the spirit of the GATT agreement he signed.[32] Scheduling almost all of the phaseout to occur at the end of the ten-year period also maximized the likelihood of a successful backlash by protectionist congressmen.

DUMPING DUE PROCESS

In 1999, U.S. antidumping laws became a major source of international conflict. Many foreign nations protested that the U.S. government perennially shafted imports based on the flimsiest of pretexts. Clinton, in an interview on the eve of the Seattle World Trade Organization (WTO) meetings, declared, "We can't give up our dumping laws as long as we have the most open markets in the world, and we keep them open to help these countries keep going, and other countries don't do the same. They shouldn't be able to take advantage of temporary economic developments to do something that otherwise the free market economy wouldn't support."[33] (Actually, several other nations, including Hong Kong, New Zealand, and Singapore, have more open markets than does the United States.) Clinton justified refusing to change U.S. antidumping laws because "there has to be some sense of fairness and balance here."[34] According to Clinton, because the U.S. market was open for most products, the U.S. government should have a blank check to treat other imports as it damn well chose.

Dumping penalties are the epitome of the New Protectionism—arcane trade barriers often concocted behind closed doors by government bureaucrats accountable to no one. Instead of openly raising tariffs, governments create convoluted trade laws that allow them to convict almost all foreign companies while pretending that they are not subverting free trade. The antidumping law is a sword of Damocles hanging over every foreign company exporting to the United States.

Antidumping laws treat low prices as federal crimes. Dumping occurs when a company sells a product for a lower price ("less than fair value") in an export market than in its home market, or when a foreign company sells a product for less than its cost of production plus a large profit. When the Commerce Department finds a foreign company guilty of dumping, and the U.S. International Trade Commission (ITC) also concludes that the dumped product injured competing American companies, the United States imposes penalty tariffs on the imports equal to the alleged dumping margin.

The U.S. government has imposed more dumping penalties against low-priced imports in recent years than has any other government in the world. During the Clinton administration, the Commerce Department found foreign companies guilty in 98 percent of dumping investigations.[35] (The ITC had a lower conviction rate, in part because there was sometimes no evidence that the imports were adversely affecting the profits of American competitors.)

Protectionists perennially assert that dumping is a predatory activity, intended to destroy American industries. But the actual U.S. definition of dumping mocks this claim. A foreign company is guilty of dumping if it earns less than an 8 percent profit on its U.S. sales. The higher the profit the company allegedly made in its home market, the easier it becomes to label their U.S. prices unfairly low. The Commerce Department is extremely arbitrary in how it convicts foreign companies for selling at unfairly low prices.

The steel industry is the most frequent beneficiary of the dumping law. Clinton routinely invoked the suffering of the U.S. steel industry to justify perpetuating U.S. dumping laws. The steel industry—which has been massively protected by either import quotas or Byzantine dumping laws for more than 30 years—effectively has veto power over U.S. trade policy. The Commerce Department bends over backwards to create pretexts to block steel imports.

On June 22, 1993, the Clinton administration took hundreds of American manufacturers hostage.[36] The Commerce Department announced that day that it was imposing dumping duties of up to 109 percent on steel imports from 19 nations. The ruling effectively excluded almost all flat-rolled steel imports from Argentina, Australia, Brazil, Finland, France, Japan, Italy, Mexico, Poland, Romania, Spain, Sweden, and the United Kingdom. Once dumping duties greater than 15 percent are imposed on a foreign company, experts estimate that its steel is effectively barred from the U.S. market. Because many of the types and qualities of imported steel are not produced in the United States, this was a harsh blow to many American manufacturers.

Most of Commerce's rulings were based on a disregard of the actual prices of foreign steel. Since foreign steel companies' prices were not as high as Commerce's make-believe prices, Commerce pronounced all the foreign companies guilty and sought to bar most of them from the U.S. market.

Commerce used two types of make-believe prices. The first was based on Commerce analysts recalculating foreign companies' cost of production (often arbitrarily increasing the cost of components and other factors), then adding 8 percent for profit and 10 percent for administrative overhead.

The second "make-believe" method consisted of invoking the "best information available"—often simply the allegations made by U.S. steel producers in their complaints to Commerce. Even in cases in which Commerce had the chance to verify most of the information submitted by foreign companies, U.S. bureaucrats found pretexts to reject foreign submissions and instead christened the unsubstantiated accusations made by American companies as gospel truth. The decision as to whether an American manufacturer could buy the steel he needed hinged on whether a low-level Commerce bureaucrat could detect any errors in the tens of thousands of pages of documentation submitted by foreign steel producers.

Secretary of Commerce Ron Brown falsely declared when the rulings were announced that "information used in making our final determinations was verified."[37] But, for most of the "best information available" determinations, Commerce did little or no verification of the allegations made by U.S. companies.

Vice President Al Gore visited Warsaw in April 1993 and hailed the "green shoots of free enterprise springing up in cities and on the land" in Poland.[38] But the Commerce Department in the 1993 rulings judged and penalized Poland as if it were still a Communist country. Commerce has special rules for nonmarket economies (which Poland denied being, since it had thrown out Communist rule in 1989 and embarked on fundamental reforms), which allegedly lacked realistic price systems. Commerce officials randomly selected third countries and compared guesses about third-country production costs to the prices of nonmarket economies' exports. Commerce officials compared Poland's U.S. export prices with the alleged costs of production in Thailand, South Africa, and Malaysia. Commerce then revealed that Polish steel was guilty of a dumping margin of 62 percent.[39]

Steel-using industries employ 30 times more Americans than do domestic steel manufacturers—yet the Commerce Department cared only about steel producers. Throughout the investigation, the Commerce Department behaved like a wholly owned subsidiary of the U.S. steel industry. While Commerce Secretary Ron Brown met with chief executive officers from U.S. steel companies, he refused to meet with representatives of any of the foreign companies involved in this case.

The federal government currently imposes more than 500 company-specific dumping orders against steel imports, according to David Phelps of the American Institute for International Steel.[40] Because Commerce almost always finds foreign steel companies guilty of unfair trade, Commerce officials have been able to browbeat many foreign nations into accepting import quotas and price controls on their steel exports to the United States as part of a deal to cease dumping investigations. These "suspension agreements" would be a violation of WTO rules on trading if they were openly labeled as import quotas.

Commerce's formal agreements reeked of mendacity. For instance, the "Agreement Concerning Trade in Certain Steel Products from the Russian Federation," signed by the Commerce Department and the Russian Ministry of Trade on July 12, 1999, began, "For the purpose of encouraging free and fair trade in Certain Steel Products (as defined in this Agreement) to establish more normal market relations, and to allow continued market access . . ."[41] Yet, the agreement prohibited Russia from exporting any steel rails, any certain tin-mill products, any metallic-coated flat-rolled steel products, and any steel wire rod for part of 1999. The agreement gave the Russian Ministry of Trade de facto control over all Russian steel exports—another windfall benefit from the U.S. government to the old Communist planners.

A 1999 agreement between the Commerce Department and Brazilian exporters imposed price controls on Brazilian steel exports. The agreement stated, "The Reference Price for Category One steel (commercial quality, not pickled and oiled, not tempter-rolled, and not edge-trimmed) shall be fixed on the last day of that Quarter (and Quarterly, thereafter) at the higher of the average U.S. Market Price for that Quarter, less 6 percent, or $327. The prices for the other categories of Hot-Rolled Steel shall be adjusted accordingly."[42] The agreement prohibited the export of all types of steel not listed in the agreement. Brazil agreed to slash its exports of hot-rolled steel to the

United States by 28 percent under the agreement. The *New York Times* noted that "Brazil's steel industry agreed to 'voluntarily' reduce shipments to the United States, hours before a deadline that would have imposed tariffs of about 50 percent on its imports."[43]

Rather than resting on fairness, the dumping law in practice relies on government employees' ingenuity in making misleading comparisons. As Cato Institute trade analyst Brink Lindsey observed, "In the typical antidumping investigation, the Commerce Department compares home-market and U.S. prices of physically different goods, in different kinds of packaging, sold at different times, in different and fluctuating currencies, to different customers at different levels of trade, in different quantities, with different freight and other movement costs, different credit terms, and other differences in directly associated selling expenses (e.g., commissions, warranties, royalties, and advertising). Is it any wonder that the prices aren't identical?"[44] Lindsay examined 141 dumping calculations the Commerce Department made between 1995 and 1998. Commerce based the dumping margin strictly on comparisons of U.S. and foreign home-market prices in only four cases.[45]

A 1998 Congressional Budget Office (CBO) study noted, "The United States progressively and substantially increased the initial duty rates it imposed . . . The average initial rate imposed from 1993 through 1995 was almost triple the average from 1981 through 1983."[46] The average dumping margin imposed between 1995 and 1998 by the Commerce Department was 44.68 percent.[47] Few importers can afford to pay that type of surtax—especially since Commerce can retroactively increase the dumping penalties in subsequent rulings.

Dumping penalties tax the competitiveness of America's leading industries. The CBO study noted, "Most U.S. antidumping activity—approximately four-fifths of active measures and approximately two-thirds of the products covered by the active measures—is against upstream [i.e., inputs] goods."[48] Dumping cases have inflated the prices American businesses must pay for semiconductors, flat-panel computer screens, steel, railroad rails, and ball bearings. The dumping law effectively turns midlevel Commerce Department employees into the czars of American industrial policy. Government employees without the skill to get a job on the assembly line at Caterpillar's Peoria, Illinois, factory acquire the power to dictate whether Cat will be permitted to buy the foreign steel it needs. Bureaucrats who could not be hired as a data-entry clerk at Apple Computer gain the power to dictate whether Apple will be allowed to buy foreign semiconductors. CBO concluded that the antidumping law "has become a form of general trade protection, which harms the overall economy."[49]

Foreign nations are increasingly imitating U.S. dumping laws to bushwhack American exporters. Outside of the U.S. market, American companies are hit by dumping penalties more often than those of any other nation.[50] The Clinton administration has disregarded the needs and interests of U.S. exporters—even though the United States is the world's largest exporter.

The Commerce Department is effectively above the law in how it runs its dumping regime. It routinely takes a company three to five years of litigation and hundreds of thousands of dollars to successfully challenge an absurd dumping decision by the U.S. Commerce Department. Though the Commerce Department is often found by federal judges to have violated federal law, the agency routinely refuses to accept such court rulings as binding precedent. The United States has chosen to disregard numerous GATT rulings that found its dumping rulings violated its international obligations.

WHEAT WAR WITH CANADA

Clinton's trade policy was slave to almost any pressure group that caterwauled on the White House doorstep. And even if a problem had been caused by foolish government policy, the solution was always new government restrictions and more government power.

The Clinton administration came under intense pressure from congressmen from northern Plains states to stem the influx of durum wheat from Canada.[51] Durum wheat is used for pasta products, certain breads and pastries, cereals, and other basic food items. Canadian durum wheat is often higher quality than American durum because of Canada's cooler growing climate and superior grain-handling practices.[52]

Undersecretary of Agriculture Gene Moos told the Senate Agriculture Committee on September 21, 1993, that he had formally recommended that the president "consider an emergency proclamation establishing quotas on the imports of Canadian wheat," and Trade representative Mickey Kantor declared that "we're looking at moving very quickly on the [proposal for import quotas on] wheat."[53] Agriculture Secretary Mike Espy and Canadian Agriculture Minister Ralph Goodale met in Marrakesh (more fun than Buffalo) to try to work out a deal in what the Canadian press described as a "nasty, nasty meeting."[54]

At the same time that some congressmen were outraged at Canadian imports, the U.S. government was spending $700 million to dump American-grown durum and other types of wheat on world markets at fire-sale prices. The

United States subsidized the export of over 30 million bushels of durum wheat in 1993—roughly equal to the amount of Canadian imports. The combination of falling U.S. production of durum and artificially increased demand for durum caused by the export subsidies drove the U.S. durum price far above the world price. The high prices sent a signal to foreign producers that the U.S. market needed more durum.

U.S. wheat policy pummeled American pasta makers. Foreigners could buy U.S. wheat much cheaper than American food manufacturers could. American imports of pasta and pasta products more than doubled after the USDA began dumping U.S. wheat on the world market. The United States heavily subsidized durum exports to Turkey, where the wheat was processed into pasta products and exported back to the United States.

In September 1994, the United States imposed a one-year tariff-rate quota on Canadian wheat imports. The quotas, combined with a bad 1995 U.S. growing season, almost doubled durum wheat prices. Partly as a result, a pasta factory in Buffalo closed in February 1995, destroying 165 jobs.[55] When the quotas expired in September 1995, U.S. trade officials warned Canada that they would take new action if wheat imports exceeded the level of the "expired" quotas.[56] The United States continued to threaten Canada over imports into 1997, a year in which American durum wheat production was almost 40 million bushels less than the amount needed by the U.S. milling and food industry.[57]

AFFIRMATIVE ACTION FOR AMERICAN EXPORTS

While Clinton never tired of lecturing Americans about their need to worship diversity and adore multiculturalism, his trade policy often consisted of old-fashioned Japan bashing.

"Temporary quantitative indicators" was one of the mottos of Clinton trade policy. From 1993 to 1995, the Clinton administration was fixated on forcing Japan to agree to a compulsory affirmative action program to boost purchases of exported American autos, auto parts, and other products. Clinton announced in early 1993 that, regarding trade with Japan, "I would like to have a focus on specific sectors of the economy, and I would like to obviously have specific results."[58] Deputy Treasury Secretary Roger Altman declared in 1994, "What we will wait for, until hell freezes over, is an agreement that there will be measurements."[59] Yet, in July 1993, at a speech at Tokyo University, Clinton insisted that the United States was not seeking "so-called trade by the numbers."[60]

U.S. Trade Representative Kantor asserted on March 3, 1994, "Japan is unique among developed nations in maintaining closed markets."[61] But U.S. exports to Japan had more than doubled since 1985, and U.S. exports to Japan had increased much faster than Japanese exports to the United States over the previous half decade. While Clinton administration officials denounced Japanese protectionism, American personal computer makers—such as Dell, Compaq, and Apple—were taking the Japanese market by storm, with soaring sales and rising market share. Those companies offered better products at lower prices than did Japanese computer makers. Clinton's approach made some of America's premier manufacturers look like pathetic losers dependent on political fixes. And, as for autos, most American autos shipped to Japan at that time still had the steering wheel on the left side. (The Japanese, like the British, drive on the wrong side of the road.)

In May 1995, the Clinton administration announced plans to slap 100 percent penalty tariffs on 13 Japanese luxury cars to compel the Japanese to set specific quotas for the sales of U.S. autos and auto parts in Japan. Kantor declared: "Our market is open to Japanese products. Their market should be open to our products. It is a fundamental question of fairness."[62] But, as William Cline of the Institute for International Economics observed, the "guilt by pattern of results" charge by the U.S. government made little sense. Cline noted that "as an organizing principle for international trade, quantitative targets risk destroying market principles in order to save them."[63] The Clinton administration backed down from the threat at the last minute.

Clinton routinely portrayed competition from Japan as inherently unfair. In a November 1999 visit to a Harley-Davidson motorcycle plant in Pennsylvania, Clinton told the workers: "Several years ago you were subject to unfair competition in the American market, and it took some action to get that straightened out."[64] Harley had benefited from protection in the 1980s, but it was a temporary tariff imposed by President Reagan under a law that requires no evidence of foreign unfair competition. As the *Rushford Report* noted, "Harley ran into trouble partly because of its own management weaknesses and partly because of events that it could not control like the 1983 severe recession. Harley's Japanese competitors were vigorous competitors but they were not cheats."[65]

SABOTAGE IN SEATTLE

In late 1993, in the final days of the Uruguay Round of trade talks, U.S. Trade Representative Mickey Kantor had a brilliant idea: to change the name of a toothless international oversight body from the General Agreement on Tariffs and Trade to the World Trade Organization (WTO). Kantor, a former Hollywood lawyer, wanted an organization name that would befit Clinton's delusions of grandeur. (The Bush administration indulged in similar foolish labeling: if the North American Free Trade Agreement had been simply called a "limited tariff reduction agreement between three countries," it would not have become a lightning rod. However, Bush needed a campaign issue, so the NAFTA label stuck. NAFTA was not really a free-trade agreement: instead, it was an agreement to give preferential treatment to imports from two nations, thus disadvantaging imports from other nations.)[66]

Both GATT and the new WTO consisted largely of binding arbitration panels that heard and ruled on trade disputes between member nations. Neither GATT nor WTO could bomb Belgrade since they were simply a bunch of desk workers with no air force, navy, or nukes. Many critics feared that the WTO would turn the United States into a fiefdom. But the WTO cannot violate U.S. sovereignty because it possesses no tools to impose its decisions on the U.S. government. The WTO cannot force the United States to change any law (though it could authorize other nations to impose limited penalty tariffs on U.S. exports if the United States refused to comply with a WTO panel ruling).[67] If the WTO suddenly morphs into an organization that subverts U.S. national interests, the United States can exit at the drop of 51 senators' hats.

There was no consensus or broad demand in early 1999 for another round of international negotiations to reduce trade barriers. But the planners in Clinton Legacy Central were hungry for something to solidify Clinton's reputation as a world leader. Since the end of World War II, the United States had taken the lead in launching international negotiations to lower trade barriers. One hundred thirty-four nations responded to the Clinton administration's summons to gather in Seattle to launch "the Clinton round."

The name WTO proved, as should have been expected, a lightning rod for opponents of capitalism, trade, and modern civilization. A few weeks before the summit, Clinton declared, "I'm actually kind of glad all these demonstrators are coming to Seattle, even though it may be kind of messy, because we ought to have a big global debate on this. And the people who feel like they've been shut out ought to be brought in and listened to, not just the environmentalists but the others as well."[68] Clinton rolled out the red carpet to the anarchists and others that turned downtown Seattle into a tear-gas-streaked, rubble-strewn battleground.

Clinton detonated the meetings even before he arrived. In a telephone interview with the *Seattle Post-Intelligencer* published on the opening day of the talks, Clinton declared that a WTO working group "should develop these core labor standards, and then they ought to be a part of every trade agreement, and ultimately I would favor a system in which sanctions would come for violating any provision of a trade agreement."[69] Clinton thus made clear what U.S. Trade Representative Charlene Barshefsky had long denied: that he wanted a new agreement that authorized imposing penalty tariffs on imports from any nation that did not pay a global minimum wage. White House aides later tried to brush off the comment by claiming that Clinton was speaking merely "in an aspirational way." Clinton's comment stunned delegates. India's minister of commerce and industry later told his country's parliament that Clinton's remark was "the last straw . . . It made all the developing countries and least-developing countries harden their position. It created such a furor that they all felt the danger ahead."[70]

Clinton sacrificed the WTO talks for domestic political advantage. He sought to impress U.S. labor unions with his hostility to imports from low-wage countries and to assure environmentalists that he would allow them to disrupt trade whenever they raised sufficient hell in the streets. Clinton sought to turn the entire meeting into a photo opportunity for Vice President Gore's floundering presidential campaign.

Clinton continued to pander to the demonstrators even after they had hassled, assaulted, and denounced the delegates to the convention on the streets of Seattle. In his first speech in Seattle, Clinton declared, "They are knocking on the door here, saying, let us in and listen to us." Clinton declared that the delegates must "be prepared to give an answer" to the demonstrators.[71] Many of the leftist demonstrators foamed as if the WTO was the trade policy equivalent of "The Protocols of the Elders of Zion." Yet Clinton never challenged the demonstrators' key assertions and made no effort to refute them.[72]

Clinton's machinations were aided by trade-illiterate members of the press corps. The *New York Times* idiotically reported that Clinton sought to build a reputation as a "free trader with a social conscience"[73] and that he pushed for the Seattle meetings because he "was convinced that he had one free-trade victory left."[74] As long as White House aides kept telling journalists on background that Clinton, deep down, still wanted free trade, it did not matter how many lamebrained protectionist schemes he proposed.

Clinton's shenanigans in Seattle may have done permanent damage to the WTO. Clinton's Seattle fiasco greatly energized the enemies of free trade.

CONCLUSION

The high point of the Clinton administration's free-trade activism was a May 4, 1994, *Federal Register* announcement that soccer teams arriving for World Cup matches in this country would be permitted to bring foreign-made clothes for personal use with them. Surprisingly, the Clinton administration's decision did not generate protests from American jockstrap producers.

Clinton, as a result of the conclusions of negotiations on NAFTA and GATT, received credit for being less of a protectionist than he actually was. The final NAFTA agreement was significantly more protectionist and Statist than were the tentative NAFTA agreements and the bargaining positions of the United States during the Bush administration. Similarly, the Clinton administration took a number of arch-protectionist positions in the final months of the GATT negotiations. As Columbia University professor Jagdish Bhagwati observed, Clinton's "successes, principally with the Uruguay Round, reflect the completion of initiatives begun by his predecessors. His failures, dramatic indeed, have been his own."[75] The Clinton administration was not unique or novel in having a lousy trade record; the record of the Bush administration was also a national embarrassment.[76] And Clinton was not as protectionist as many members of Congress of both parties.

Clinton's trade policy was premised on politicians' right to use and abuse consumers as they saw fit. Trade Representative Kantor, when asked in 1994 about the impact on American consumers of slashing Chinese clothing imports, denied that it would have any impact, stating, "I think the American consumer will be fully able to buy quality products made in the U.S. made by U.S. workers."[77] Because the price of clothing did not matter to a millionaire lawyer such as Kantor—he could conceive of no reason why any American would be concerned about the price. "Protectionism-by-default" was the inevitable result of Clinton's unprincipled approach.

Clinton presumed, in trade as in other areas, that progress depends on maximizing politicians' pretexts to meddle. Clinton's trade policies illustrated how protectionism depends on continued deceit—on continual denial of any responsibility for domestic failures—and on the constant creation of new standards by which to denounce foreigners.

HUD:
THE ETERNAL
BOONDOGGLE

FEDERAL HOUSING EFFORTS IN THE 1990s degenerated into a multibillion-dollar crusade to give preferential treatment to welfare recipients, to allow politicians to shake down one housing-related industry after another, and to stretch HUD's influence as far as possible. The Department of Housing and Urban Development (HUD) is the archetypal Clinton agency—continually proclaiming to have reinvented itself and continually demanding more tax dollars to solve problems that it claimed were fixed long ago. And after each rearrangement of the deck chairs on the HUD *Titanic*, all observers are honor bound to accept the promises that the agency is finally upright and sailing smoothly.

HUD Secretary Henry Cisneros admitted to Congress in June 1993: "HUD has in many cases exacerbated the declining quality of life in America."[1] Vice President Al Gore denounced public housing projects in 1996: "These crime-infested monuments to a failed policy are killing the neighborhoods around them."[2] HUD Secretary Andrew Cuomo, appointed after Cisneros's indictment on perjury charges, conceded in 1998 that HUD used to be "the poster child for failed government."[3] As the *Washington Post* callously noted in 1999: "For three decades, HUD has been a notorious symbol of welfare-state government run amok, better known for sweetheart deals, wasteful programs and bad management than for improving the lives of the poor."[4] Luckily, all it took to transform a boondoggle into a blessing were pure hearts—plus lots more tax dollars.

Despite HUD's abysmal record, the agency received over $200 billion from Congress during Clinton's reign. HUD now directly bankrolls the mortgage bills or rents for 5 million residences—more than 12 million Americans. HUD also insures 6 million subsidized mortgages, exposing taxpayers to the risk of hundreds of billions of dollars in defaults.[5]

FAIR-HOUSING FLIMFLAMS

On January 18, 1999, Martin Luther King Day, President Bill Clinton declared that he was "pleased to announce the largest settlement in history in a lending discrimination [case], for home lending . . . the Columbia National Mortgage Company will offer—listen to this—$6.5 billion in home mortgages and extra effort to help 78,000 minority and low and moderate income families unlock the door to homeownership."[6] The announcement gave Clinton a photo opportunity and a triumphal newspeg to divert attention from his ongoing Senate trial.

The settlement was a hoax. The announcement epitomized Clinton moral methods: continual far-fetched accusations, continual record "settlements," and continual efforts to convince people that the federal government is the sole force preventing America from slipping into barbarism. The Clinton administration used explicitly racially biased standards to denounce and convict private companies—and then used the settlements with those companies to persuade everyone that America suffered from an epidemic of racism.

The Fort Worth Human Relations Commission received a $100,000 grant in 1996 from HUD to send pairs of testers to mortgage companies to investigate possible fair housing violations. The commission sent three pairs of testers to a local Columbia National loan office to see if the company discriminated in how people of different races or ethnicities were treated.

There was no problem with the first two pairs, but the third tester pair uncovered sufficient discrimination to electrify HUD headquarters. A white male tester spent an hour with a female loan officer, while a Hispanic male tester spent only 20 minutes with a male loan officer. The white male had to wait five minutes after arriving before seeing his loan officer, but that was irrelevant. However, the loan officer who saw the Hispanic male, after shaking his hand, "excused himself to use the restroom. Within approximately two minutes, he returned from the restroom and the interview began," according to the official report on the incident by the Fort Worth Human Relations Commission.[7] The report concluded that there were no "extenuating circumstances" to justify the bathroom break during the interview with the Hispanic male. The subsequent $6 billion "settlement" made this appear like the most expensive piss-stop in history.

HUD, in the official settlement statement on this case, stressed its grave concern about an alleged difference "in the level of encouragement given to apply for a loan" between the Hispanic and white applicant.[8] Yet, the Columbia National officer sought to pre-qualify the Hispanic for a mortgage and provided him with a loan application and his business card. However, HUD believed that the difference in the time the loan officers spent with the two applicants was conclusive proof of wrongdoing. (One wonders why anyone would encourage any citizen to endure more than the sheer minimum of time with a mortgage loan officer.) HUD later admitted that the two testers gave different information; the Hispanic tester, for instance, claimed to have less personal savings than did the white tester. Neither individual would provide their Social Security number or address, nor would they allow the loan officers to pull their credit reports. Columbia National CEO Dave Gallitano noted that such conduct "is very unusual. It would result in a good sales person spending time with them—being courteous—but they will not spend a huge amount of time because it is not an application yet."[9]

HUD routinely drops the entire weight of its enforcement machinery on a company for a single alleged violation of equal treatment. A HUD official involved in the case, who spoke on condition of anonymity, said "no formal investigation was ever completed; therefore, there was no formal finding one way or the other."[10] HUD could not even make an estimate of how many other HUD-subsidized testers had visited Columbia National offices around the country sniffing for discrimination.

Columbia National was blindsided by the president's announcement of the $6.5 billion settlement. The settlement agreement mocked Columbia National's supposed vast crimes. Columbia National made no admission of any crime and the Human Relations Commission waived the right to sue the company or take any further administrative or investigative action against the company regarding the charges in the case.[11] The only payout in the agreement consisted of a pledge by the company to, within 90 days of the agreement, "send the Fort Worth Human Relations Commission $5,000. The money will be used by the Commission to further fair housing initiatives through education, outreach, and testing." Columbia National did "commit annually" to make certain levels of loans to minorities during the following five years but the agreement specified that the "term 'commit' . . . shall be qualified . . . subject to the availability of sufficient qualified borrowers" and "the reasonable business discretion of Respondent."[12] In other words, if business continues to be good, the company would continue doing business as usual. While HUD trumped the agreement as a "settlement" of serious charges, the agreement contained no penalty clauses in case Columbia National did not fulfill the lending goals.

Regardless of whether the agreement generated any new loans to favored groups, "$6 billion" made the average television viewer believe the government had nabbed some heinous criminal. Gallitano observed, "Clinton gets on national TV and makes us sound like bigots. This is the kind of statement from a person in his position that could put us out of business. And it could cause a large number of our employees who are minorities to become very demoralized and begin to wonder whether we or the president are telling the truth."[13]

RACE-BAITING TO RACIAL HARMONY

The "record settlement" with Columbia National was officially part of President Clinton's "One America Initiative." Clinton announced the initiative in June 1997 as a means to ease racial tensions. However, Clinton had a different agenda: two months later, he announced that increased enforcement of the Fair Housing Act would become a major goal "as part of our initiative to create One America of equal opportunity."[14] The Clinton administration used the initiative to inflame the sense of persecution among minorities—and thereby tighten his lock on his most loyal constituency.

Abusive, heavy-handed prosecutions on doubtful evidence are HUD's specialty and HUD Secretary Cuomo used the Fair Housing Act to build up his national image. At a September 30, 1997, press conference, Cuomo announced, "We will double the number of enforcement actions against [fair housing violators] in the president's second term."[15] Cuomo stated that he had been ordered by Clinton to double the number of enforcement actions against fair housing violators to between 60 and 70 a month.[16]

The first to fall under HUD's renewed obsession was AccuBanc, a Texas-based mortgage lender, in April 1998. The Fort Worth Housing Human Relations Commission sent in several pairs of testers to an AccuBanc office. One pair consisted of a white couple with a good credit history and a black couple with severe credit problems in the past. The AccuBanc lenders spent an hour with the white couple and 20 minutes with the black couple. One high-ranking AccuBanc official later observed, "We did not deny credit to the black couple—but there was less we could do for them," considering their bad credit record.[17]

But the test was all that HUD needed to bring the roof down on the company. "HUD officials sat down with an agreement—they claimed that they just needed to finalize the paperwork. 'We just need to tie up the loose ends by the end of the year,' they said, and we agreed to sign it. The next day, we got blasted by Mr. Cuomo in one of his television statements," the AccuBanc official said. Company officials were shocked at the scapegoating: the reconciliation agreement between HUD and the company did not require the company to do anything that it had not already done for the previous three years. "If Mr. Cuomo was not trying his darndest to position himself for the vice presidency, he might not be quite as rabid," the corporate official observed.[18]

Cuomo announced the AccuBanc settlement in a press release "commemorating the 30th anniversary of Dr. Martin Luther King Jr.'s assassination and the passage of the Fair Housing Act" on April 3, 1998.[19] (The same press release announced a HUD lawsuit against four Missouri men accused of burning a cross to intimidate a Portuguese immigrant.) Cuomo boasted in an interview a month later: "Just a few weeks ago, we settled the largest Federal suit ever, with a *penalty* of $2.2 billion" against AccuBanc.[20] In the same interview, Cuomo wrongly stated that the testers claimed to have identical assets and liabilities.

The Fort Worth Human Relations Commission was one of Cuomo's favorite federally funded fair housing investigators. Cuomo bragged that $10 billion in settlements had been reached with mortgage companies solely as a result of the 100 pairs of testers sent out by this Fort Worth commission.[21] But Commission Chief Vanessa Ruiz Boling, who actually ran the testing survey, disagreed with Cuomo's characterization of the AccuBanc settlement: "There was no penalty imposed—it was a no-fault agreement. If Secretary Cuomo is using the term penalty that is an interesting word—we would not penalize anyone who we did not make any findings against or who was not subject to an investigation."[22] Boling rejected the official portrayal of the case: "There were no investigations—there was no determination of liability—there was no investigative process that resulted from the filings of the complaints. So we don't know whether or not they committed any discriminatory acts or practices. And any statements to that effect would be inaccurate."[23]

Clintonites stretched the Fair Housing Act to hammer banks. In 1994, the Justice Department announced that Chevy Chase Bank, based in Montgomery County, Maryland, was guilty of violating the Fair Housing Act because it did not pursue potential black borrowers in neighboring Washington, D.C., and Prince George's County, Maryland. At an August 22, 1994, press conference, Attorney General Reno declared, "To shun an entire community because of its racial makeup is just as wrong as to reject an applicant because they are African

American."[24] Reno bragged that the settlement was "unprecedented"—which it was, since the Justice Department chose to ignore established law and precedents in tarring Chevy Chase. Cornell law professor Jonathan Macey noted, "Under this bizarre view, restaurants, convenience stores and all other businesses that locate outside of black communities also could be said to be racist."[25] Former Assistant Treasury Secretary Paul Craig Roberts observed, "The Justice Department is simply trying to establish by consent decree a system of racial quotas in lending regardless of credit risks."[26]

The Justice Department announced that the Chevy Chase settlement should send a warning to banks and thrifts that ignore minorities "in or near their service area." The feds used the same arguments in 1997 to punish Albank Federal Savings Bank for not having branches or seeking business in minority areas in the northeast United States. As *Mortgage Banking* noted, after the Chevy Chase settlement, "fair lending laws are to be read as imposing an affirmative obligation to direct marketing efforts to all markets equally, with little or no guidance as to how one is to accomplish that as a practical matter."[27]

The federal fair housing law was first enacted in 1968 and primarily sought to ban overt prohibitions on blacks' freedom to rent or buy housing. The law mushroomed; amendments made to it in 1998 made far more types of private behavior federal crimes.[28] William Apgar, one of Cuomo's senior advisers, warned: "Fair-housing violations are now very subtle." Cuomo announced in late 1998: "Housing discrimination is much more insidious today than it was two to three decades ago."[29] Thus, since discrimination is so insidious, the government must become more devious to ferret out violators.

HUD sought new harvests of violators by plowing more money into local fair housing councils. Federal handouts to such groups tripled, rising to $40 million during the Clinton administration. In federal criminal cases, defense lawyers routinely argue that a citizen must have shown a predisposition to commit a crime before the government can target him. However, there is no such restraint on the actions of fair housing councils. Much of the activity of the councils amounts to institutionalized, federally funded entrapment—with a maximum incentive for the testers to vary their conduct sufficiently to generate "guilty" responses from lenders.

HUD does little or no policing of how fair housing groups use their federal grants. The Central Alabama Fair Housing Center (CAFHC) sent pairs of black and white testers to Lowder Realty Co. in Montgomery, Alabama. CAFHC then sued Lowder in federal court, claiming that the company violated Fair Housing law by "steering—directing black customers away from predominantly white neighborhoods and to black areas of town because of their race." CAFHC presented four cases; the judge threw out two on summary judgment because the evidence was so flimsy. After a two-year investigation and a nine-day trial, a multiracial jury took less than two hours to eat lunch, elect a jury foreman, and find Lowder not guilty. James Lowder, chief executive officer of the company, declared: "This lawsuit was never about fair housing or discrimination. From the outset, it was about money and recognition for the group that brought the lawsuit. It was a malicious, mercenary effort to extort money from an honest enterprise, and my companies will never yield to such tactics."[30]

CAFHC Director Faith Cooper stated that, even though her center lost the case, "We believe it will make a difference in raising the public's awareness of housing discrimination."[31] A disgraceful loss in federal court actually helped the CAFHC fulfill the conditions of its HUD grant. The grant agreement specified that CAFHC would "process at least 80 new complaints of housing discrimination during the term of this grant." The Council was also expected to "appear on at least 10 local television and radio programs to discuss fair housing laws, methods of recognizing housing discrimination and CAFHC's services."[32] The primary method of trumpeting the CAFHC's services was "through media coverage of enforcement activities we have already carried out." A vicious spiral results: a fair housing council must continually make heavily hyped charges in order to continue to get new cases in order to justify continued receipt of federal funds.

The unspoken premise of HUD's fair housing crackdowns is that one realtor's balk at showing one person one house means that that person will never get a house. Thus, any disparity in treatment of any minority customer does irreparable damage. Since everyone in "protected classes" is helpless, HUD needs draconian power to save them.

The onus of being prosecuted for racism by the federal government and repeatedly denounced over a long trial is sufficient to make most companies raise a white flag and open their checkbook. Because most realtors, mortgage companies, and other targets do not wish to spend a half-million dollars or more to fight the charges in federal court, they sign agreements with HUD and fair housing councils to cut their losses. The results are different when the cases go to final decision in an independent forum. The federal government has lost more than half of all the fair housing testing cases that went all the way to a court verdict since 1992.[33] (A 1998 IG report found that HUD was doing an abysmal job of overseeing fair housing grantees. HUD's operation was so disorganized that it could not even provide Congress with mandatory annual reports of the operations of the fair housing councils.[34])

HUD targets any industry related to housing. In 1995, HUD gave a $1.5 million grant to five housing groups to bankroll testers to dragoon insurance companies. HUD financed a lawsuit by Housing Opportunities Made Equal (HOME), a Richmond, Virginia, activist organization, to prove that Nationwide Insurance Co. violated the Fair Housing Act by quoting different insurance rates in black and in white neighborhoods. A jury, after hearing a surfeit of racist denunciations, quickly convicted Nationwide and ordered the company to pay $100 million in damages. This trial revealed the dubious methods of HUD testers. They asked for rate quotes on homes of differing sizes, values, and ages; the resulting disparities supposedly proved racial bias. Some testers destroyed most of their notes, making verification impossible. Robert Detlefsen noted in *National Review* that "inner-city homes tend to have substandard heating and wiring components (generally a function of age) and to be located in neighborhoods with much higher than average rates of burglary, vandalism, arson, and building abandonment—all of which are significant risk factors."[35] Regardless, Cuomo gloated: "I congratulate HOME for its outstanding work on this case, and I am proud of HUD's involvement as HOME's partner in the fight for housing equality." Cuomo also subtly noted: "This $100 million verdict tells companies loud and clear that it is now their turn to pay a terrible price if they continue to discriminate."[36] The jury verdict aided other shakedowns. The *Richmond Times-Dispatch* reported on May 7, 1999: "An insurance company [Liberty Mutual Group] that was facing a fair housing complaint filed by Housing Opportunities Made Equal has promised to give the organization $4.25 million over the next two years to promote home ownership in Richmond."[37] (The $100 million verdict was overturned by the Virginia Supreme Court in January 2000.[38])

HUD bankrolled the crackdown on insurance companies despite its possession of a $650,000 study entitled "Testing for Discrimination in Home Insurance" for which it contracted the Urban Institute. The Urban Institute conducted an exhaustive analysis, using testers, of insurance markets in Phoenix and New York. The study was largely completed in 1995 but HUD effectively suppressed the report. However, the Urban Institute finally published the study itself in November 1998. The study found that in Phoenix, "testers in white neighborhoods received quotes 98 percent of the time; testers in Hispanic neighborhoods, 97 percent." The study concluded that "white testers were not favored over minority testers in either Phoenix or New York."[39] George Galster, the project director, observed: "What was most surprising is the lack of discrimination on virtually all measures."[40]

Ignoring the Urban Institute's findings, Cuomo championed the idea that racism was the reason why fewer black families own their homes than white families do (45 percent and 72 percent, respectively). Cuomo declared in 1998:

"We will not tolerate a continued homeownership gap as wide as the Grand Canyon that divides Americans into two societies, separate and unequal."[41] In September 1999, Cuomo released a study on mortgage discrimination compiled by ACORN (Association of Community Organizations for Reform Now), a radical advocacy organization. Cuomo whined that in the face of "a great economy, a great Dow Jones, discrimination is getting worse, not just flourishing."[42] However, a 1995 Federal Reserve Board study examined over 200,000 mortgage loans and found that, as the *Wall Street Journal* reported, "blacks defaulted about twice as often as white borrowers . . . the finding undercuts arguments that lenders often hold minority applicants to higher standards than whites. If that were true, they said, their study should have found lower default rates—since minorities would presumably be exceptionally qualified given the alleged higher standards."[43] The study noted that "black borrowers exhibit significantly higher default rates in both urban and suburban locations," and that "losses occurring in the event of default tend to be greater on loans extended to black borrowers."

Cuomo's demonization of mortgage disparities was debunked by a 1999 federal study. A survey of 80,000 individuals by Freddie Mac (formerly the Federal National Mortgage Corporation, a government-sponsored corporation) found that blacks are almost twice as likely as whites to have bad credit ratings[44]—even among people of the same income class. (Asian Americans had far better credit ratings than either whites or blacks.) Among households with incomes between $45,000 and $65,000, 48 percent of blacks had bad credit, compared to only 21 percent of whites and 15 percent of Asians. Hugh Price, head of the Urban League, commented on the findings: "If people have bad credit, they'll be denied loans, end of story."[45] The Freddie Mac study noted that poor credit "is often cited as one of the leading factors in the rejection of mortgage applications."[46] The differences in bad credit ratings were roughly equivalent to the mortgage reject rates for different races. HUD ignored the report.

Fair Housing versus Free Speech

The more aggressive HUD becomes, the fewer free speech rights Americans have. Many words and phrases are now effectively forbidden in real estate ads. The *Bismarck Tribune* noted in September 1999, "In the last year, several newspapers in North Dakota have faced discrimination complaints for the wording of housing ads. You can't say your apartment is 'near the university,' because it implies you'll rent only to students. You can't say it's 'in the Cathedral

District,' even if that's what it's called, because it implies you'll rent only to religious folks. You can't advertise that your place is 'in a quiet neighborhood,' because it suggests children aren't welcome."[47] In 1994, two church-affiliated nursing homes in Minnesota announced that they had been required to expunge Christian crosses from their ads in the Yellow Pages as a result of HUD pressure on the Yellow Pages publishers. Several other Yellow Pages publishers were pressured by HUD to change their policy regarding religious symbols in nursing home ads.[48] (The same mentality begot other HUD buffooneries: residents of the Boston Housing Authority were told at diversity workshops that displaying the Irish shamrock was offensive to non-Irish residents; the shamrock was put in the same category as a Nazi swastika.[49])

HUD sought to financially destroy and intimidate critics. The Fair Housing Act Amendments of 1988 added drug addicts, alcoholics, and the mentally disabled to "protected groups" covered by the federal Fair Housing Act. As a result, HUD has claimed that criticizing group homes for housing such people could be a violation of federal law. Unfortunately, large numbers of recovering alcoholics and drug addicts revert to the bottle or needle.

In Berkeley, California, HUD officials in late 1993 subpoenaed three residents who had complained about plans to convert a ratty-looking motel next to a liquor store into a home for alcoholics and mentally disabled AIDS patients. (The neighborhood was already saturated with rehab centers.) A federally funded fair housing activist organization complained to HUD about the group's action, and HUD launched a full-scale investigation of the three. In November 1993, HUD demanded to see any letters they had written to public officials or newspapers and any petitions they had circulated, including the names, addresses, and phone numbers of anyone who had indicated support for the group's efforts. HUD's San Francisco office concluded that the three were guilty of illegal opposition to a federally subsidized housing project.[50] John Deringer, who lived next to the soon-to-be shelter complained: "We didn't feel we had done anything wrong, but we were very, very intimidated. The threat was we could be fined $100,000 and jailed if we didn't give them the information they wanted. It was chilling."[51] HUD Assistant Secretary for Fair Housing Roberta Achtenberg revealed: "In every case of this nature, HUD walks a tightrope between free speech and fair housing. We are ever mindful of the need to maintain the proper balance between these rights."[52] Apparently, there are two separate versions of the Bill of Rights—one for private citizens and the other for federal bureaucrats and politicians—since the word "balance" does not appear in the copies that normal citizens have access to.

After a tornado of bad publicity, HUD backed down. The three residents sued HUD. In December 1998, federal judge Marilyn Hall Patel declared that "the very act of informing the plaintiffs that they were under investigation and potentially subject to penalties up to $100,000 is sufficient to substantiate (their) claim that their First Amendment rights were chilled."[53] Patel stunned many government employees by declaring that the HUD officials responsible could be held personally liable for damages.[54]

CLINTON'S WRECKING BALL FOR THE SUBURBS

In September 1993, HUD Secretary Henry Cisneros warned, "All of the money that we might put into public housing . . . will not be successful as long . . . as America is a society divided spatially."[55] Cisneros called economic integration an "over-arching objective," and, as the *Washington Post* noted, he "ordered his agency to advance economic integration at every opportunity."[56]

Section 8 was the flagship of the Clinton administration's effort to impose subsidized housing on American suburbs. The Clinton administration used Section 8 rental subsidies for blockbusting suburban neighborhoods with welfare recipients. Through the Section 8 rental subsidy program, HUD gave poor people the keys to the best apartments in town—and sent the bill to the middle class. HUD spending for Section 8 has increased from $7 billion in 1993 to $18 billion in 1999.

Section 8 requires beneficiaries to pay 30 percent of their income toward rent. Once people initially qualify for Section 8, many housing authorities make little or no effort to check their incomes in subsequent years—thus encouraging people to stay permanently on the dole. HUD was losing $900 million a year because of the feeble controls it used to verify tenant incomes, according to the General Accounting Office.

In *Federal Register* notices, HUD rotely declares that Section 8 subsidy levels are set at levels needed to pay for "rental housing of a modest (non-luxury) nature."[57] In reality, Section 8 is often very generous. HUD will pay up to $1,680 a month for welfare recipients to live on the island of Maui, Hawaii; $1,689 a month in Fairfield, Connecticut; and $1,815 a month in San Francisco, California.[58] Any family or person with less than 80 percent of the median income for their area is eligible for Section 8.

HUD bends over backward to portray Section 8 as noncontroversial. Cisneros declared in 1994: "There are almost no cases in America where people resist Section 8."[59] This is news to the millions of unsubsidized people living in the vicinity of Section 8 projects and renters:

- 1993: A *Boston Globe* editorial on Section 8 rent recipients noted: "The majority occupy homes owned by absentee landlords who are reluctant to evict tenants, even for the most egregious lease violations. For landlords, the guaranteed subsidy payment proves a stronger incentive than the desire to maintain a safe building."[60]
- 1993: The *Bergen County (New Jersey) Record* reported of a public meeting on Section 8 in Haledon, New Jersey: "The meetings were as rancorous as any ever held in the borough. Residents denounced their neighbors in federally-subsidized housing, accusing them of ruining property values and bringing a bad element to the borough. The two meetings held to protest the 'problem' were standing-room only."[61]
- 1996: The *Washington Post* reported: "Dissatisfaction with the federal Section 8 housing subsidy program . . . has become so intense in affluent Fairfax that some officials want to impose a local moratorium on the program. Two county supervisors, both Democrats, have called on Congress to rewrite federal law so that Fairfax effectively could bar any more Section 8 beneficiaries from moving into several low-income neighborhoods along U.S. Route 1."[62]
- 1997: *The Kansas City Star* reported: "In some neighborhoods, a single Section 8 house can significantly drag down property values."[63]
- 1999: The *Pittsburgh Post-Gazette* reported: "Clustered together . . . Section 8 housing often leads to poverty pockets where juvenile delinquency, crime and other social problems fester. Out-of-town landlords often let the property deteriorate because they receive guaranteed rent from the federal government."[64]

The public housing residents that HUD dispersed through Section 8 came from areas with crime rates up to ten times the national average.[65] Capitalizing on the program's dubious image, a Washington, D.C., rap band named itself Section 8 Mob.

It was easy to understand why many politicians preferred Section 8 over housing projects: Section 8 created fewer photo opportunities to embarrass HUD. Dispersing the problem made it more difficult to hold government officials responsible for the havoc they sowed.

Section 8 is not a formal entitlement program that guarantees benefits to anyone below specified income limits: the number of vouchers and the level of spending is limited by congressional appropriations. Section 8 has been wracked by fraud for decades; the HUD Inspector General annually charges vanloads of local housing authority officials and others with accepting kickbacks to illegally distribute the vouchers.

The Clinton administration continually decked its Section 8 reforms in deceptive rhetoric. A 1994 program that gave Section 8 certificates to welfare recipients was labeled "Moving to Independence." In 1998, Secretary Cuomo launched a new program to allow recipients to use Section 8 to pay mortgages —which he said turned Section 8 into "empowerment vouchers."[66] The new Section 8 program was a slap in the face to the tens of millions of self-reliant Americans struggling to save money for a down payment for their own house.

On December 30, 1999, Clinton announced that his proposed budget for FY 2001 would include $690 million for 120,000 new housing vouchers to help low-income Americans "move closer to job opportunities. Housing vouchers are a critical part of my Administration's efforts to reform welfare, reward work, support working families, and provide affordable housing for low-income families."[67] Cuomo proclaimed: "It's not a building, it's a voucher; the voucher can move you to where the job is. People moving off welfare tend to be in urban areas; the jobs they need tend to be in suburban areas."[68] Cuomo also declared: "We have the greatest need for affordable housing in history."[69] The notion of using Section 8 to encourage people to find jobs is especially lame because Section 8's payment formula has the same impact as a 30 percent tax on all income. As for the supposed large, unmet demand for housing subsidies, the fact that people desire de facto free rent proves nothing except that people have heard that the government is giving away money. (Cuomo was embarrassed at a March 30, 2000 Senate hearing when it was revealed that, though Congress bankrolled an additional 110,000 Section 8 vouchers in the previous years, HUD had only gotten around to passing out 3,300 of the new rent subsidies.)[70]

HOPELESS HUD's BIGGEST FARCE?

In 1993, HUD launched HOPE VI. "HOPE" stands for Housing Opportunities for People Everywhere. Four previous HOPE programs had failed to achieve Valhalla but HUD is very hopeful about VI. (Congress skipped HOPE V for some mysterious reason.)

HUD awarded over $3 billion since 1993 to local public housing authorities to destroy existing housing projects and replace most of the units with top-notch new single-family homes or townhouses. HUD is seeking to attract more affluent residents to live amidst welfare recipients. Announcing a bevy of demolition grants in September 1999, Cuomo declared: "These developments represent the worst of the public-housing stock in the United States. By tearing them down, we're making room for neighborhood revitalization."[71] Cuomo sought to be hailed a great benefactor for announcing plans to remove some of the pestilence his agency had injected into cities across America. As *Engineering News-Record* noted, "Instead of awarding all 1999 grants at once, HUD has been making a series of announcements, sometimes with appearances by Secretary Andrew Cuomo and local House members, senators, or other officials."[72]

In Nashville, thanks to HOPE VI, many residents of the Preston Taylor project received keys to fancy new townhouses. They pay an average of only $112 a month in rent.[73] In Los Angeles, the Pico Aliso project is being replaced with townhouses with two bedrooms, two bathrooms, and all the latest appliances, including a built-in washer and dryer. Some of the townhouses will be sold for roughly $120,000—but lucky public housing tenants will be able to rent the new units for less than $200 a month.[74] Elinor Bacon, HUD's deputy assistant secretary for public housing investments, explained: "It's about transforming the lives of the people, not just the real estate. It's a whole new way of looking at public housing."[75] In Tulsa, Oklahoma, HUD spent roughly $100,000 for each replacement unit for the Osage Hills project; for the same price, someone could "buy almost three existing homes in the urban renewal area near the project, or almost any single home almost anywhere in Tulsa," according to Rep. Tom Coburn (R-Okla.).[76] A local HUD spokesman explained the reason for the relatively fancy homes: "We want you not to think that this is public housing."[77] A HOPE VI project on Capitol Hill in Washington will provide very cheap housing to low-income families—and will sell other townhouses for up to $260,000.[78] James Didden, a top executive of the National Capital Bank on Capitol Hill, observed, "What they're calling homeownership is really just public-housing rentals."[79] Didden was not optimistic: "My suspicion is that it will deteriorate into a ghetto. The developer has no ongoing responsibility for the project." In La Jolla, California, an very affluent suburb of San Diego, HUD financed apartments with market values of up to $500,000, each with lavish furnishings and panoramic 180-degree views of the Pacific Ocean. HUD selected 28 welfare recipient families—with incomes as high as $34,000—and gave them the keys to the kind of housing that most Americans can barely dream about.[80]

When Cuomo announced a $30 million grant to the D.C. Public Housing Authority to raze and replace ragtag public housing in Anacostia, he declared: "We are making public housing a launching pad to opportunity, jobs and self-sufficiency, instead of a warehouse trapping people in poverty and long-term dependence."[81] Apparently, the only reason that poor people are not self-sufficient is because government has not given them fancy enough housing. John Milchick, HUD's Kentucky coordinator, commenting on a Louisville HOPE VI project, declared that economic diversity "stabilizes an area and people are not afraid to invest in their community, to spend in their community, to keep their properties up. They have a stake in their neighborhood . . . they're not afraid to speak up if they see crime in the street. They have a sense of ownership."[82] Milchik implied that poor people could acquire a "sense of ownership" simply by having middle-class neighbors—not by having had to work and earn the money to buy a house. In the same way that forced busing presumed that black kids could not learn unless they were in the same classroom as white kids, HOPE VI and mixed-income projects assumed that welfare recipients won't act civilized unless they live next to middle-class folks.

Because HOPE VI funds targeted the most dilapidated public housing projects in the nation, local housing authorities have an incentive to let their projects degenerate into greater squalor. The HUD IG, in a July 1999 report on the Newport, Rhode Island, Housing Authority, observed:

> The Authority made a decision to limit expenditures for maintenance and vacant unit preparation at Tonomy Hill in anticipation that a portion of the units would be renovated or demolished at some time in the future . . . In May 1999, the Authority submitted an application for HOPE VI funds to demolish all of the Tonomy Hill units and replace them with 425 units of mixed-income housing. However, the Authority is in competition for limited HOPE VI funds, and there is no guarantee that their application will be approved.[83]

The IG recommended that if the Newport Housing Authority refused to fix the problems, HUD should cease paying it subsidies for its vacant units. (HUD awarded a $215,000 grant to demolish 43 public housing units in Weymouth, Massachusetts—the same units that it had spent $2 million renovating only a few years before.)[84]

The idea underlying HOPE VI is that quasi-gold plated public housing will transform the nature of people living in it. This is not the first time that the feds have sought to buy welfare recipients into the middle class. A 1966 GAO report condemned HUD for the inclusion of balconies and frills such as hardwood floors, marble interior window sills, costly kitchen cabinets, and ornamental walls in new public housing projects. As Harvard University's Howard Husock observed, "As a practical matter, the greater the amenities provided for public-housing residents, the less the likelihood that the private, lower-income housing market could match them. Thus the incentive to move up and out would be undermined. In effect, the goal of fixing up the projects works at cross purposes with the goal of encouraging residents to find private-housing alternatives."[85]

HUD has never examined the effect that receiving housing subsidies has on the incentive to take care of the property under one's feet. HOPE VI skirts that basic question—as if it would be politically incorrect to even consider whether the basic problem is housing subsidies per se, not the design of subsidized housing.

HUD also bankrolls the destruction of private housing—even when local housing authorities offer little or nothing to take its place. HUD gives billions of dollars in Community Development Block Grants (CDBG) to local governments each year. There are few constraints on how this money is used, and some locales use the money to pay for the confiscation and destruction of private housing. Baltimore is using HUD aid to aggressively raze the old row houses that helped make the city famous. The city bulldozed more than 4,000 row houses between 1996 and 1999. Thanks to high crime and lousy schools, Baltimore suffered a population exodus, leaving many homes vacant. The city government proclaimed a goal of destroying 20 percent of the 66,000 houses in the center city by the year 2004. In 1999, the Maryland legislature gave the city government the right to demolish all the houses on a block when 70 percent of the housing is vacant; elderly still living in the row houses receive only seven days' eviction notice and a pittance check for their old home. ACLU lawyer Barbara Samuels denounced the city's demolitions as "completely planless—the last slap in the face for the mostly elderly homeowners left."[86] The threat of imminent condemnation deters homeowners from keeping up their property— thus spreading the blight that the demolitions were supposed to remedy. Local politicians were convinced that destroying old houses will be sufficient to attract a new type of resident to Baltimore—as if the more dictatorial powers the local government received, the more attractive the city would become to potential new residents.

CUOMO'S PERSONAL ARMY

Cuomo is obsessed with changing HUD's image; he declared in 1999: "The PR is the most important thing I do. I'm trying to get out a message that people need to hear, and I'm fighting 30 years of negative stereotypes about this agency . . . Eighty percent of this battle is communications."[87] Cuomo's devotion to PR is evident in his championing of his Community Builders program, a new cadre of 800 HUD employees specially recruited and paid up to $100,000 a year to spread the word about HUD's achievements. A 1998 *National Journal* profile of the program noted that Community Builders will be "handed . . . state-of-the-art laptops, which HUD officials believe will move the agency 'light-years ahead,' in its ability to respond to communities effectively."[88] New laptops for a few hundred favored employees were supposed to counterweigh the thousands of collapsing public housing apartment buildings HUD was bankrolling around the nation. *National Journal* also noted that, in May 1998, HUD "unveiled the prototype for its new local field offices where Community Builders will set up shop. These offices, equipped with stylish furniture and workstations, will feature touch-screen electronic kiosks for information on home improvement loans and how to file housing complaint forms."[89] If only a few more people would accept subsidized loans and make accusations against landlords, all of HUD's problems would be solved.

Cuomo claimed that the Community Builders would allow HUD to apply the "brightest minds" to "the greatest needs in communities" and help "turn back decades of decline in urban America and bring a new prosperity to people and places in need."[90] In a June 16, 1999, speech to HUD employees, Cuomo made it clear that one purpose of the Community Builders was to mobilize opposition against HUD's abolition; Cuomo was bitter that recipients of HUD benefits had not rallied to protect the agency.[91] Cuomo created his "urban Peace Corps" with no authorization or appropriation from Congress; instead, he merely shuffled HUD's books and used money "saved" by laying off other HUD employees.

In August 1999, Community Builders were instructed to distribute a form letter to local community groups to spark opposition to a proposed Republican tax cut. As *Newsday* reported, "Local Community Builders were then expected to fill in blank spaces in the form letter, inserting the number of local jobs that would be lost and the number of housing units that would not be built in case of a tax cut. The letter cites Appalachia, the Mississippi Delta, Indian reservations 'and closer to home' as places that have not benefited from the economic boom . . . For Manchester, N.H.—that's in the big presidential primary state, by the way—builders were instructed to inform local groups that $1.437 million would be lost because of the tax cuts, there would be 50 fewer local jobs, 158 fewer housing units and five fewer homeless or AIDS persons served."[92]

Many congressmen were dubious about Cuomo's pet project. The HUD IG launched an audit, which HUD sought to derail. Michael Beard of the Inspector General's office testified to Congress in November 1999: "Senior management provided employees a list of "questions and answers" to be used if they were interviewed in the course of the audit . . . In many of our interviews, employees requested confidentiality for fear of reprisal."[93] A 1999 IG report concluded that "most of the Community Builders' goals are activities rather than actual accomplishments. HUD classifies 15 of the Community Builders' 19 goals as activities performed, rather than outcomes measured."[94] Most of the Community Builders the IG interviewed said they spent most of their time on "public relations activities." The new cadre made HUD even more wasteful: "As a result of the Community Builder interference, HUD spent more than $4.7 million in holding costs or lost sales proceeds. In one instance, HUD sold a property that it had invested $17 million to a nonprofit for $10."[95] The IG received many complaints about ethnical misconduct by Community Builders; the IG investigation found Community Builders repeatedly violating a federal law prohibiting "publicity or propaganda designed to support or defeat legislation pending before Congress."[96] The IG report concluded: "The one clear effect of the Community Builders is the dramatic increase in the number of people at HUD not part of a specific program, engaged in customer relations, and owing their jobs to the Department's political management."[97] Sen. Kit Bond derided the program as "Cuomo's personal army."[98] One HUD official declared that the Community Builders were seen as "Democratic ward-heelers who act as a pipeline between Democratic city officials, party leaders, and the administration and the Democratic National Committee."[99]

AN AGENCY IN SHAMBLES·

Cuomo acts as if the more money HUD spends on political fixes, the more indisputable it becomes the agency loves the poor—as if maximizing the number of slush funds was the secret of salvation for urban America. However, HUD management is in shambles. HUD Inspector General Susan Gaffney testified to Congress on February 17, 2000, that "there is evidence that the [HUD] downsizing that started in 1995 has increased costs as well as program abuse."[100] The IG concluded in a December 1999, report that Cuomo's constant reform initiatives have "had a crippling effect on many of HUD's ongoing operations."

Cuomo and his predecessor, Henry Cisneros, have been prodigious innovators. The number of HUD program activities has increased from 240 to 328 between 1994 and 1997—and is much higher now.[101] Cuomo, a master of "Reinventing Government" shticks, knows that it is far easier to start two new programs than to fix an existing one. (Cuomo's anti-gun escapades will be chronicled in chapter 14.)

HUD laid off many employees who handled defaulted FHA homes—hired an incompetent contractor to do the same thing—and the number of homes sitting vacant around the nation because of HUD rose sharply. The IG noted, "Vacant, boarded up HUD-owned homes have a negative effect on neighborhoods, and the negative effect magnifies the longer the properties remain in HUD's inventory."[102] Sen. Barbara Mikulski (D-Md.) complained that HUD's negligence in selling foreclosed homes in Baltimore was contributing to "the destabilization of neighborhoods . . . another form of old-fashioned block busting . . . FHA is contributing to this problem by its inability to timely dispose of foreclosed properties."[103]

On December 21, 1999, Cuomo made headlines by announcing that HUD was seizing control of a program that awards grants to homeless organizations in New York City. Cuomo was outraged that New York City Mayor Rudolph Giuliani refused to deliver HUD money to a homeless advocacy organization that, during a recent audit, was unable to account for $500,000 of a 1997 grant. (Misplacing a half mil, by Clinton administration standards, was about as serious as jay-walking.) Cuomo exploited the situation to try to make Giuliani look heartless. On the same day Cuomo made the decision, his wife, Kerry Kennedy Cuomo, announced at a Manhattan fund-raising event for Senate candidate Hillary Clinton: "Just a few hours ago, my husband pulled up the gauntlet. Next time, Rudy, pick on someone your own size!"[104] The *Wall Street Journal* noted, "Mr. Cuomo is an informal adviser to Mrs. Clinton's Senate campaign. His former HUD regional director for New York, Bill de Blasio, is Mrs. Clinton's campaign chief."[105]

In March 2000, Cuomo announced that HUD was "donating" (as if it was HUD's money in the first place) $200,000 to set up a task force to fight "hate" on the Internet. An alleged former Klansman had created a website that made threats against a Pennsylvania fair housing activist. Cuomo capitalized on the occurrence to proclaim: "Housing discrimination is just as illegal in cyberspace as it is in our cities, our suburbs and our rural areas. The Internet is not sanctuary from the rule of law."[106] It is presumably only a question of time until, thanks to HUD, the Internet is as hate-free as public housing is crime-free.

Cuomo's self-coronation as urban savior has been made more difficult by the continual reports of HUD boondoggles by Inspector General Gaffney. Cuomo responded by seeking to destroy Gaffney (who was appointed by Clinton in 1993). Gaffney in 1998 testified to a Senate committee that she was the victim of "'escalating' attacks on her office by Cuomo and his 'key aides,' including cooked-up charges of racism, insubordination, and malfeasance, and general dirty-dealing."[107] Gaffney testified that Cuomo told her that his top aides saw her as "the embodiment of evil." Cuomo launched an investigation of Gaffney based on charges that she had discriminated against a black official in the IG office. Cuomo then offered to drop the charges if Gaffney would leave HUD. Cuomo's lackeys took the highly unusual step of spending $400,000 to hire an outside lawyer known for taking an extreme position on racial discrimination, rather than relying on HUD lawyers, who could have completed the investigation for $3,000.[108] A GAO investigation found that Cuomo's office violated normal contracting procedures. Senator Fred Thompson (R-Tenn.) denounced Cuomo's aides for having "manipulated the procurement process" in an "extraordinary effort to discredit this longtime public servant."[109]

In 1998, the HUD IG launched in-depth investigations of HUD-related fraud in several major cities. HUD officials blocked the IG's investigations of fraud in New Orleans and San Francisco because they were concerned that targeting cities with black mayors might have been perceived as racist. Senator Phil Gramm, chairman of the Senate Banking, Housing and Urban Affairs Committee, lambasted HUD: "It is an absolute outrage in a democracy when we have an inspector general working with the FBI, and they say taxpayers' money is being stolen, and then a political decision is made to stop that investigation."[110]

CONCLUSION

Secretary Cisneros warned in 1993, "We risk a societal collapse . . . if we tolerate racism and the economic isolation of millions of people."[111] But the surest way to "economically isolate" people is to remove them from the work force and to encourage them to become perpetual dependents on lavish federal handouts. The notion that HUD can give away housing to some people without having any adverse effects on their fellow citizens and neighbors is the ultimate liberal pipedream.

Secretary Cuomo declared in 1998: "Ultimately, the vindication of progressive politics will come only when people believe the government is competent."[112] Alas, progressives are in for a long wait. It is only a matter of time until the next HUD scandal screams across the front pages of the nation's newspapers. The only solution to HUD's problems is to bulldoze the agency itself.

ELEVEN

FREEDOM
TO FARM
WASHINGTON

"I am the only president who knew something about agriculture when I got there [to the White House]."
—Bill Clinton, April 24, 1995, Ames, Iowa[1]

CLINTON'S STATEMENT was a revelation to fans of plantation-owner Washington, vineyard-grower Jefferson, mule-driver Grant, hog-slopper Truman, and peanut-grower Carter. Clinton never had to make a living from raising and selling a harvest. But he played on his stepfather's farm as a boy, and thus became the greatest agricultural expert in the history of the White House.

President Clinton may not have created foolish farm programs but he did fight doggedly to preserve the most absurd subsidies and restrictions on farmers' freedom. Clinton perpetuated a hodgepodge of programs that destabilized markets, increased dependency, and simultaneously encouraged farmers to grow more and paid them to grow less.

Since Clinton took office, federal farm policies have cost taxpayers more than $230 billion.[2] In addition, federal farm policies boosted the cost of food by more than $110 billion since 1993.[3] For the combined cost to taxpayers and consumers of Clinton farm policies since 1993, the federal government could have bought all the farmland in 35 states.[4]

The vast majority of farm products receive no direct federal subsidies. Most of the handouts are confined to fewer than 15 of the 400 farm products produced in America. The only difference between the subsidized and unsubsidized crops is the political pull of those who raise them. For Clinton, the only farmers who mattered were those on the dole.

CLINTON'S FIRST FARM FRAUD

When Clinton took office with a strong majority in both houses of Congress, he had the opportunity to radically reform or terminate failed farm programs. Two days after his first State of the Union address, Clinton went to Hyde Park, New York, the home of Franklin Roosevelt, to brag about his courage in fixing the federal wool program: "There is a program that I think helps a lot of wonderful people, it's a subsidy to sheep growers . . . We had sheep on the farm when I was boy, so I'm more sensitive to this than some are. But when I got to studying this, we started a subsidy to sheep growers in World War I because we needed plenty of wool for uniforms. But the program is still on the books exactly as it was, exactly . . . So I recommended cutting it back. All these things have constituencies, but I can tell you we are going to have to prove that we can cut things."[5]

And what was Clinton's radical wool proposal? To apply the same nonbinding $50,000-a-year handout limitation to each wool grower that already nominally applied to most other farmers. (Wool growers at the time could receive up to $200,000 a year.) The General Accounting Office had repeatedly recommended abolishing the wool program.[6] Lavish wool subsidies encouraged farmers to disdain their customers. American textile mills had long complained that U.S.-produced wool was of lower quality than imported wool. At least one American textile plant refused to buy domestically produced wool because it was so cluttered with briars, hay, twine, and other riffraff. Taxpayers got nothing from the program: the subsidies were a no-strings-attached annual windfall to uncompetitive wool growers. Yet, the best that Clinton offered was to reduce the waste by $12 million in 1994, from $191 million to $179 million. (Congress upped the ante and stunned the Clinton administration by voting to abolish the wool program over the subsequent three years.)

Clinton's wool fix was part of his sweeping agenda to reduce the federal deficit. On February 17, 1993, Clinton proposed ending direct farm subsidies for individuals who earn more than $100,000 per year *off the farm*. OMB Chief Leon Panetta exclaimed to the House Budget Committee: "Let me tell you, those agriculture recommendations are tough with regards to targeting subsidies."[7] Treasury Secretary Lloyd Bentsen explained to the House Budget Committee: "It's only fair that subsidies end for those who do not need them."[8] But no amount of farm income could ever make a farmer non-needy, as far as Clinton was concerned. The largest 17,000 farms had an average net income of over $1 million in 1993, yet Clinton's proposal deigned this group sufficiently needy to continue receiving hefty annual welfare checks (an average of $50,728 per farm in 1993).[9] Clinton's proposed change would have saved taxpayers at most $75 million in 1994—less than one-half of 1 percent of federal farm subsidies. Besides, payment limitations were a charade: gaping loopholes existed so that wives, children, and others each collect the maximum subsidy from the same farm.

Clinton went on national television on February 15, 1993, to assert that he had worked harder than he ever had before to (unsuccessfully) avoid raising taxes on the middle class.[10] His agriculture secretary, Mike "Free Tickets" Espy, bragged two days later that "the overwhelming majority [of farm programs] have been continued without being harmed the least little bit."[11] Espy also asserted "the farm programs have been cut and cut and cut, with corresponding impact on farm income, which, of course, has also been reduced." In reality, 1993 was among the highest years in history for federal farm spending. Spending on the main farm subsidy programs almost doubled in Clinton's first year in office: from $9 to $17 billion. Other farm programs bled taxpayers for another $10-15 billion.

HELL ON ALLIGATORS

The Clinton administration botched a golden opportunity to rescue both alligators and consumers.

Sugar producers have had a starring role in the poisoning of the Everglades. Because the U.S. mainland does not have a natural climate for sugar production, farmers compensate by dousing the land with chemicals to artificially stimulate production. More than 500,000 acres of the Everglades has been converted from swampland to sugar fields. Over the years, phosphorous from the fertilizer used by sugar growers leached into the water of the Everglades and helped destroy the ecosystem of the entire region.[12]

The federal government had sought since 1988 to force sugar growers to cover part of the costs of repairing the fragile south Florida environment. The Clinton administration and Florida sugar growers reached a tentative agreement to finance part of an Everglades cleanup in July 1993. Interior Secretary Bruce Babbitt hailed the agreement as opening the way to "the largest, most ambitious ecosystem restoration ever undertaken."[13]

Under the agreement, Florida sugar growers would pay between $232 million and $322 million in cleanup costs over 20 years—between $11.6 million and $16.1 million per year. This was chicken feed compared to the subsidies they received from import quotas and price supports. In 1993, the world sugar price was 11 cents per pound; the U.S. price was 22 cents per pound. Thus, Florida growers received a government benefit of 11 cents for each of the estimated 3.5 billion pounds of sugar they harvested in 1993—roughly $380 million a year. Under the Clinton administration agreement, the federal sugar program continued providing Florida sugar farmers between $24 and $33 dollars in benefits for each $1 farmers paid to reduce the environmental damage from their farming practices. (The Commerce Department estimated that the sugar program costs American consumers $3 billion a year in higher prices.)[14]

Many environmentalists felt double-crossed by the Clinton administration. As Paul Roberts reported in *Harper's* in November 1999,

> In March 1993, Alfy Fanjul [the largest, wealthiest sugar producer in Florida] met privately with Bruce Babbitt, presenting him with an Everglades restoration plan drawn up by [sugar company] scientists. And lo! When Babbitt unveiled the administration's restoration plan at a July [1993] ceremony, it bore an uncanny resemblance to Fanjul's plan—stipulating, among other things, that state taxpayers would pick up more than half the estimated $700 million for the filtration marshes. Babbitt denied any link between Fanjul campaign dollars and the administration's plan, but Alfy Fanjul himself made no such protestations. Speaking directly after Babbitt at the ceremony, Fanjul held up the new plan as proof that "the Clinton Administration delivers."[15]

The tentative agreement broke down in December 1993.[16] The *St. Petersburg Times* editorialized on December 21, 1993, that Babbitt "has been humiliated by the sugar industry and has thrown away another six months in the fight to save the Florida Everglades."[17] Sugar growers then succeeded in getting the Clinton administration to shift the dispute from federal court to state courts, where they had far more clout.

Sugar growers continued reaping government benefits. Sen. Richard Lugar (R-Ind.), a Republican presidential candidate, championed a plan that would have imposed far more of the cost of the cleanup on sugar growers. The House of Representatives came very close to abolishing the sugar program in early 1996.

But the Clinton administration held the line for perpetuating the existing import quotas and price supports.

In February 1996, Al Gore prepared to roll out a plan for a new clean-up tax on sugar growers. Fanjul called and harangued Clinton for 22 minutes on February 19, 1996—interrupting a two-hour mentoring session Clinton was having with Monica Lewinsky.[18]

When Clinton signed a multi-year farm bill on April 4, 1996, he declared that "the bill would provide $200 million, with the possibility of an additional $150 million, for restoration of the Everglades. This project is one of the Administration's top environmental priorities, and the funds in this bill are a good down payment toward our goal. Moreover, I call on the Congress to enact the Administration's comprehensive Everglades restoration plan, including the one-cent-per-pound marketing assessment on Florida sugar. This assessment would ensure that the benefiting industry pays its fair share."[19] "Fair share" apparently means a dime kickback on a dollar of benefits.

Sugar lobbyists turned up the heat and Clinton changed his tune. In an April 29, 1996, speech in Florida, he declared, "The question is, who is going to pay what in order to save the Everglades? I believe that we can find a way to sustain the economy of Florida in the short run while we move to preserve it in the long run and while we preserve one of the globe's most precious natural resources. We have to save the Everglades. That's what I believe, and I think the National Government has a responsibility to do that."[20] Clinton's proclamation of a "national government responsibility" was a sleight of hand to let the sugar industry off the hook. The "polluter pays" principle vanished, never more to be seen in the Everglades during Clinton's reign.

As Paul Roberts noted in *Harper's,* in July 1999, "Gore presented Congress with an $8 billion, twenty-year Everglades restoration plan, which calls for ripping out hundreds of miles of dikes and claims to let the swamp flow free and wild again. What Gore failed to mention, however, is that the plan is crippled because, at the behest of sugar lobbyists, it leaves virtually untouched the cane farms that helped to create the mess in the first place."[21] Gore bragged that his plan was "terrific for business."[22] Shortly after Gore announced his sugar-friendly Everglades pseudo-rescue, Clinton arrived at Alfy Fanjul's home for a $25,000-per-couple Democratic fundraiser.[23]

In 1995, Clinton declared that he was deeply troubled by an "increasing inequality" in economic opportunity between rural and urban America.[24] But this concern apparently did not extend to the effects of his own actions in exacerbating rural inequality. GAO estimated that 17 of the nation's largest sugar cane farmers received over half of all the benefits provided by the sugar cane subsidies.[25] Nationwide, 1 percent of sugar growers captured almost two-thirds of all the program's benefits. Sugar farmers collected a subsidy more than 30 times larger per acre than did wheat farmers.[26] (In early 2000, the U.S. sugar price was four times higher than the world sugar price.)

The federal sugar program is a quixotic war against Mother Nature. Sugar is cheaper in Canada than in the United States primarily because Canada has almost no sugar growers—and thus no trade restrictions or government support programs. If not for federal subsidies, there would be no cane sugar production in the United States. Third World nations have an overwhelming competitive advantage in sugar production due to climate, lower costs of land, and the availability of cheaper labor. The only thing that could make American sugar cane farmers competitive is massive global warming.

WHISKEY, WINE, AND JAPANESE UNDERWEAR

When Clinton assumed the presidency, the most ridiculed farm program was one that gave federal handouts to American companies for foreign advertisements. The Targeted Export Assistance program was launched in 1985. By 1990, the program had so disgraced itself that it was renamed the Market Promotion Program. In 1995, after exposés about the program paying for ads for Japanese underwear manufacturers (as long as they included a U.S. cotton logo),[27] the Market Promotion Program was renamed the Market Access Program (MAP). Many congressional Democrats longed to abolish MAP, but the Clinton administration staunchly defended the program.

A 1999 Department of Agriculture (USDA) press release on the program declared: "Export promotion is a vital tool in USDA's efforts to expand fair and free trade."[28] But the program has nothing to do with either free trade or fair trade, since it is simply government dumping tax dollars into the coffers of favored groups to bankroll foreign ads. There was no requirement that the advertising be targeted to foreign markets that have "unfair" barriers against American exports.

USDA paid for brand-name foreign advertisements for Ralston Purina Puppy Chow, Tombstone Beef Sticks, Weaver Popcorn, and Sokol & Blossen pâté. USDA gave hundreds of thousands of dollars to McDonald's for foreign ads. GAO studies found no evidence that the program actually boosted American food product exports. However, the cash injections made corporations very happy. Between 1994 and 1997, Gallo Wine Co. received almost $5 million to pay for foreign ads. The Clinton administration also delivered bushels of tax dollars to Robert Mandavi Winery, Fetzer Vineyards, and several other wineries.[29] More than $3 million dollars went to boost whiskey exports, with Jim Beam, Seagrams, Hiram Walker, and Heaven Hill Distilleries on the take. While many Americans could not afford premium Samuel Adams beer, the government forced taxpayers to bankroll $25,000 in foreign ads for that brand. After heavy criticism about freebies for multinationals, the Clinton administration announced that it would only pay for brand-name ads for small and minority-owned companies, such as the Great Western Tortilla Co. of Denver.[30] Money for other corporate ads would be laundered through cooperatives or agricultural associations, who received the bulk of the money under the Clinton-reformed program. And the reformed program did not go on the wagon: $3 million of swill was provided in 1999 for the Wine Institute to hype American booze exports.[31]

Some organizations receiving money for foreign advertisements actively impeded American exports. USDA gave $12 million since 1993 to Blue Diamond Growers and Almond Board of California—even though the Almond Board, with power given to it by USDA, prohibited American farmers from exporting tens of millions of pounds of almonds in an OPEC-style effort to drive up world almond prices.[32] The Raisin Administrative Committee harvested $12 million in federal advertising subsidies since 1993, even though, like the Almond Board, it severely restricts how many raisins can be exported.[33] The Chocolate Manufacturers Association received more than $4 million dollars to promote chocolate exports— exports that are thwarted by federal policies driving U.S. sugar prices to double, triple, or higher than world sugar prices. The U.S. Dairy Export Council received $1.4 million in 1999.[34] But federal price supports sabotage dairy exports by driving U.S. dairy prices to double or triple world dairy prices, thus destroying any market rationale for unsubsidized exports. USDA provided enough handouts that dairy exports had their own rationale. The Cotton Council International was the largest 1999 beneficiary of MAP, raking in $8 million. But U.S. cotton exports are stifled by a byzantine cotton subsidy program that rewards farmers for hoarding their crop rather than selling at world prices (plus another big USDA subsidy).[35]

WHO WAS CRAZIER, FREEMEN OR USDA?

For 81 days in 1996, federal agents and a group consisting largely of disgruntled farmers were locked in a standoff outside of Jordan, Montana. While the stranger aspects of the ideology of the self-proclaimed Freemen were widely reported, little attention was paid to the role of the Agriculture Department in paving the way to this confrontation. Regrettably, farm subsidy policies were even loonier than the Freemen.

Ralph Clark, the grade school dropout who was the mastermind of the Freemen, and his partners had received over $650,000 in farm subsidy payments since 1985.[36] In addition, Clark received almost $2 million in federal farm loans. The federal government generously kept sending him annual payments of almost $50,000 to reward him for not growing crops on land he had bought with government loans—long after he effectively defaulted on those loans.

Why did Clark receive so many government loans? Because he was uncreditworthy. According to the Farmers Home Administration (FmHA), this alone made him worthy of a windfall of capital. And, since he kept losing money year after year, that proved that he deserved new loans. Clark symbolized the type of farmer favored by USDA: big—with a 7,000-acre, government-paid spread—and incompetent. Clark was a poster boy for farm aid lobbyists—portrayed sympathetically in *Life* magazine, with Geraldo Rivera on ABC's *20/20,* and elsewhere. But, after Clark became a racist and a raving anti-Semite, his panache with the Willie Nelson crowd suffered.[37]

For many farmers, the road to hell was paved with cheap government credit. FmHA encouraged many struggling farmers to continue farming until they financially destroyed themselves. According to the agency's own records, by far the most frequent cause of bankruptcy among its borrowers is "poor farming practices." GAO estimated that a quarter of FmHA bankruptcies occurred because the farmers received too many subsidized loans.[38] GAO noted: "In some cases, continued FmHA assistance has actually worsened the financial condition of farmers who have entered the program."[39]

In 1994, the Clinton administration forgave $138 million in losses from 74 farm borrowers—almost $2 million per farmer.[40] In many cases, federal officials made scant effort to collect on the loans, or to compel borrowers to surrender other assets to cover the government's financial bloodbath. As of early 1996, 47 percent of farmers with direct FmHA loans were delinquent—a delinquency rate more than ten times higher than that of the average private bank.[41]

Clinton and Congress looked at a rural landscape littered with loan defaults and rushed to provide more subsidized loans. After the Freemen debacle, USDA continued to give scores of millions to farmers who had defaulted on earlier federal loans.[42] But each inefficient farmer that government kept on a tractor land made it more difficult for efficient farmers to earn an honest living in the marketplace.

The 1996 farm bill authorized the Agriculture Department to make over $20 billion in direct and guaranteed loans to farmers in the following six years. Clinton sought even more subsidized farm loans, declaring in July 1997 that "we should expand eligibility for direct and guaranteed loans."[43] In a teleconference with rural radio stations in July 1998, Clinton summarized his ongoing farm aid deliberations with Congress: "And I, finally, asked for a provision that would improve credit ability and modify the one-strike policy for farmers who have had a debt write-down . . ."[44] The "one-strike policy" meant that if a farmer had defaulted on previous federal loans, he was ineligible for future subsidized loans. Characterizing this as "one-strike" makes the policy seem harsh and unfair—as if any farmer should be entitled to several cracks at fizzling away a few hundred grand of other people's money. New loans for "socially disadvantaged" would-be farmers were a high priority for Clinton's USDA. Unfortunately, there is nothing that a person learns from being socially disadvantaged that qualifies him or her to efficiently grow wheat.

USDA almost doubled the amount of subsidized farm loans and loan guarantees it doled out between 1998 and 1999, reaching almost $4 billion.[45] Congress authorized USDA to make almost $6 billion in subsidized loans and loan guarantees to farmers in fiscal year 2000—the highest amount of federal ag lending since the mid-1980s.[46] The guaranteed loan limit per uncreditworthy farmer was raised to $700,000. Agriculture Secretary Dan Glickman testified to Congress on September 17, 1999: "Demand for USDA loan assistance continues to increase. More and more farmers are becoming highly leveraged, with limited equity and low incomes . . . They are turning to USDA for help. For these farmers, commercial credit sources are not available . . . Additionally, the recently increased loan limits for FSA guaranteed loan programs is increasing the demand for guaranteed loan funding."[47] By Glickman's logic, the fact that there was a strong demand for free money proved farmers were suffering terribly and deserved more loans.

Clinton's pro-deadbeat farm policy continued a cycle that goes back to the 1930s. Politicians create new programs and then pressure bureaucrats to lend farmers as much money as possible. Then, when loan default levels reach politically embarrassing heights, programs are "reformed," lending criteria are tightened, and politicians summon bureaucrats to Capitol Hill and denounce them for their stupidity. Later, when the agricultural economy goes into another cyclical downswing, lending criteria are "loosened" and politicians again arm-twist bureaucrats to bail out as many potential voters as possible.[48] The federal government wrote off $15 billion in bad farm loans between 1989 and 1996.[49] None of that mattered to Clinton and to congressmen who hungered to expand farm lending in the late 1990s.

But the Clinton administration did learn something from the farm lending debacle. The name of the Farmers Home Administration was changed in 1995 to the Consolidated Farm Service Agency. The Clintonites upheld a hallowed tradition: FmHA's predecessor agency, the Resettlement Agency, generated so much bad press that it was re-christened the FmHA in 1946. After FmHA wore out two generations of auditors, its name was retired to the Agricultural Boondoggle Hall of Fame.

REFORM CHARADE:
THE 1995-96 FARM BILL FIGHT

Federal farm programs were scheduled to expire on September 30, 1995. (Congress historically reauthorized farm programs every four or five years.) In early 1995, Congress began examining the programs and crafting a bill to revise them.

The Clinton administration never formally submitted its own farm legislation. Instead, the administration offered speeches, talking points, and "guidance."[50] Secretary Glickman declared that the new farm bill should "loosen the constraints of current policies."[51] Apparently, it would be safe to loosen the ropes a bit but it would be a bad move to completely untie farmers and let them escape.

Clinton set the tone for his farm policy efforts in April 1995, when, at a farm conference in Ames, Iowa, he announced: "Our first rule should be: do no harm."[52] Clinton pretended to take a Hippocratic oath for farm policymaking— as if existing programs harmed no one. Glickman, in a pamphlet entitled "1995 Farm Bill: Guidance of the Administration," declared: "To better reflect our constituency, our programs, and our reason for being, the first recommendation in our farm bill [guidance] is to change the name of the Department itself to the Department of Food and Agriculture—a department for producers AND consumers."[53] A simple name change would be all that was necessary to make all the harm that farm programs do to consumers disappear—or, at least not count. Yet, a few months earlier, Clinton had imposed a new 123 percent tariff on peanut butter imports to protect domestic peanut growers.[54] (Federal farm policies drive U.S. peanut prices to roughly double world prices and cost consumers more than half a billion dollars a year.)[55] But since there was no political controversy over the new peanut butter tariff, the policy had "no harm."

Clinton justified perpetuating subsidies by claiming that farmers had already been sacrificed on the altar of budget austerity. Clinton told an Iowa audience: "I would remind you that . . . the subsidies programs were cut in '85; they were cut in '90. We had a modest reduction in '93."[56] Secretary Glickman hit the same theme: "The farm bill recommendations maintain a level of investment we believe critical to sustaining our food and fiber system, especially given the dramatic spending reductions agriculture has absorbed over the last decade."[57] Calling farm spending an "investment" was a farce, since federal intervention decimated the efficiency of American agriculture. In reality, farm spending was higher during Clinton's first administration than it had been during most of the previous decades. However, because farm spending hit a brief peak in 1986-87, farm-state congressmen could eternally whine that spending had been "cut." Also, in the perverse world of Washington accounting, farm programs were considered to have been "cut" if the agriculture committees forecast lower future spending—even if spending subsequently rose. Since most farm subsidies are entitlements, the money goes out the door regardless of how much congressional agriculture committees promised the programs would cost.

The Clinton administration sought to treat farmers like children. For instance, the administration proposed a "Farm Income Stabilization Plan . . . to encourage producers to save when revenues are high for years when revenues are low. Producers would deposit a percentage of their eligible gross sales into accounts with limited matching contributions by USDA. Withdrawals would be permitted when current-year gross sales fall below a specific percentage of the previous 5-year average."[58] This proposal exemplified how federal aid morally debilitates a group. Prior to the New Deal, farmers were renowned for having among the highest savings rates of any group. Yet, in the Clinton administration's view, the average landowner had become so shortsighted that he needed both a federal bribe to save and a bureaucrat to supervise his withdrawals from "his" savings account.

The 1995-96 farm bill started out on Capitol Hill as the "Freedom to Farm Act"—degenerated into the "Agricultural Market Transition Act"—and finally slithered into law as the "Federal Agricultural Improvement and Reform Act"— with the ultimate bogus Washington acronym: FAIR. Congress and Clinton concocted a seven-year farm plan; even Stalin didn't pretend to plan the economy more than five years ahead. In negotiations with Congress, the Clinton administration continually fought to give more money to farmers and preserve more power for bureaucrats.

Clinton vetoed the first farm bill Congress passed. Congress added more money to the bill and sent it back to the White House. When Clinton grumpily signed the bill on April 4, 1996, he declared: "I believe the bill fails to provide an adequate safety net for family farmers . . . I am firmly committed to submitting legislation and working with the Congress next year to strengthen the farm safety net."[59]

House Speaker Newt Gingrich hyped the farm bill as a triumph of his Republican Revolution, bragging, "We passed the Freedom to Farm Act, which includes ending the [farm] subsidies after 60 years" of government handouts.[60]

But the bill did no such thing. The *Des Moines Register* reported that according to one influential farm lobbyist, House Agriculture Committee Chairman Pat Roberts "convinced Gingrich that several dozen Republicans from farm districts would be jeopardized in the 1996 elections without a generous farm bill."[61] (Similar arguments led the Reagan administration and the Republican Senate to lard the 1985 farm bill with handouts.[62]) The "Freedom to Farm Act" was one of the clearest examples of the hypocrisy of Gingrich and many other Republican congressmen.

In the 1995-96 farm bill fight, the issue was never: Why should taxpayers surrender any more money to farmers?[63] Instead, the issue became: How much extra money should politicians give farmers to compensate them for the possibility that their subsidies might decrease in the next century? Yet farmers had already received a windfall—not only from previous subsidies, but also from farm programs' boosting farmland values by between 15 and 20 percent, according to the USDA. Government subsidies are capitalized in farmland value: the expectation of continued subsidies becomes a key factor in how much people pay for land with a history of subsidized crop production. As the Environmental Working Group, a Washington research organization, noted in early 1995, "windfall benefits to farmland property owners" were "in the range of $83 billion to $110 billion. Because farmland ownership is highly concentrated—just 124,000 owners hold about half of all farmland . . . each of those land owners has gained an average of $167,726 to $223,634 in wealth through the capitalization of farm program payments into farmland values."[64]

Federal farm spending tends to be inversely related to crop prices: the higher the prices, the lower the spending. Crop prices were at historic highs in 1996, and were expected to remain strong in subsequent years.

The 1996 farm act gave subsidized farmers more than 3 times as much in cash handouts in 1996 and 1997 than they would have received under the previous five-year farm bill. Wheat farmers got 50 times more in subsidies for their 1996 crop than they would have gotten if Congress had merely extended existing farm programs.[65] Congressmen relabeled old-fashioned handouts as "market transition payments"—a nice touch that snookered many journalists. Any decision on ending farm subsidies was delayed until the next century. Farmers got their handouts and congressmen could pretend they had paved over one of Uncle Sam's biggest ratholes.

The windfalls of the 1996 farm act provided scant aid to the type of small family farmer that politicians love to invoke. A 1998 USDA study found that most of the 1996 act's benefits went to landowners—often pension or insurance companies—instead of to the people who actually sowed and reaped. Landowners responded to new subsidies by raising the rent farmers pay. (Roughly half of crop land is rented.) The report concluded that "in most cases . . . the resulting [higher] rents . . . essentially passed on much if not all of the [subsidies] to the landlords."[66] By inflating both rents and farmland values, the act boosted the cost of crop production and undermined American competitiveness in world markets. By driving up farmland values, the act also raised entry barriers for young Americans who wanted to buy their own farm.

While Clinton in his last years in office appeared at several photo opportunities calling for increased "food security" and exhorting more people to sign up for food stamps, his administration showed no compassion for low-income Americans not on the dole. Clinton perpetuated federal dairy policies that, according to USDA, add over $8 billion a year to the cost that Americans pay for a mainstay of healthy diets.[67] As a result of a new milk cartel created by the 1996 farm bill (the "Northeast Dairy Compact"), milk prices jumped another 20 cents a gallon in New England states. The 1996 farm bill called for a study of the byzantine system of milk marketing orders that create extensive trade barriers to milk flows between different areas. The Clinton administration perpetuated the current system with few changes—thus guaranteeing that people in the South could not benefit from Wisconsin and Minnesota's lower dairy costs of production. A 1998 study in the *Journal of Consumer Affairs* concluded that the higher dairy prices that result from restrictive federal policies are the primary reason for widespread calcium deficiencies among Americans.[68] But a few million cases of osteoporosis were a small price to pay to keep campaign donors happy.

ANOTHER CONSERVATION FRAUD

When Clinton signed the 1996 farm bill, he declared, "The bill will enhance contributions to environmental quality and farm income from the Conservation Reserve Program, a program whose importance I have repeatedly stressed."[69] Actually, the program was largely another fraudulent means to funnel money to farmers.

In 1985, seeking a politically palatable way to slosh more money to farmers, Congress created the Conservation Reserve Program (CRP). The CRP paid farmers to idle their farmland for ten years. Politicians claimed the program aimed to protect fragile farmland and prevent erosion. However, the program was always far more concerned with idling farmland (thereby seeking

to drive up crop prices) and paying farmers than with maximizing environmental protection.

The CRP was popular with farmers because USDA often paid double or
triple the prevailing local rental rate to reward farmers for not using their land.
The CRP became an early retirement program for many farmers, allowing them
to shut down their businesses and move to Florida. The CRP hurt aspiring young
farmers in many areas by creating a comparative shortage of farmland for rent.
Most of the land enrolled in the CRP could have been farmed with little or no
environmental harm.[70]

In 1997, the Clinton administration announced that most of the cropland
in the United States was in such bad shape that the government would consider
paying to shut it down. When he unveiled the new CRP, Glickman bragged,
"This is the most profound conservation program in the history of the United
States of America."[71] An irony of the new policy was captured by an Associated
Press story: "Up to 240 million acres, two-thirds of the nation's farmland, will
be eligible for the Conservation Reserve Program under the new rules, which
are intended to target the most environmentally sensitive land."[72] If most of the
cropland in the country was eligible, how much targeting was being done? USDA
did somersaults to find pretexts to allow farmers to go on the CRP dole. If only
one-third of a farm was classified as highly erodible, USDA kindly allowed a
farmer to enroll his entire farm in the program. According to Kendell Keith,
president of the National Grain and Feed Association, USDA "grossly exaggerated" the number of highly erodible acres it enrolled in the CRP.[73] Keith blamed
the idling of wheat acres under the CRP for "the 15 percent decline in U.S.
wheat export market share during the past five years."[74]

CLINTON'S "FARM SAFETY NET" FRAUD

Clinton continually used the big lie technique to defend farm handouts. The
big lie was that farmers as a class would financially perish unless the feds
continued indiscriminately raining handouts onto all subsidized farmers.

From 1995 onwards, Clinton ceaselessly proclaimed his devotion to "strengthening the farm safety net."[75] In a September 15, 1998, speech to the National
Farmers Union, Clinton declared that "we have a farm crisis more extensive than
we've had in decades . . . there is suffering on the farm. There is agony on the farm.
This is a horrible affront to everything we have worked so hard to achieve to lift the
economy for all Americans."[76] A few months before, Clinton had proclaimed that
"from the point of view of the farmers, it's a terrible emergency."[77]

Clinton's farm policy was based on the myth of the deserving needy farmer. In 1998, the bankruptcy rate for farmers was less than .05 percent—less than one farmer in 2000.[78] The bankruptcy rate for all households, by comparison, was 1.3 percent—roughly one in 70.[79] Though the bankruptcy rate for all households was more than 25 times higher than the rate for farmers, Clinton favored forcibly transferring more money from average families to farmers. Nor was the average farm family in rags, struggling to find the next meal. According to USDA, the average full-time farmer in 1999 was almost a millionaire, with a net worth of $905,000.[80] By contrast, over half the households in America have a net worth of less than $71,600, according to the Federal Reserve.[81] The average full-time farmer thus has a net worth over 12 times greater than that of half the families of America. Seventy percent of farm program payments go to farmers with a net worth of more than $1 million, according to University of Maryland agricultural economist Kevin McNew.[82] If the same means tests were applied to farmers that applied to other federal handout recipients, few full-time farmers would have qualified for federal aid.

Clinton talked about struggling family farmers as if he had specific individuals in mind for relief. But farm programs blanket the entire nation with handouts, regardless of need. The 1996 bill specifically authorized farmers to collect up to $230,000 in handouts per farm. Farm aid is distributed not according to farmers' need, but according to farmers' size: To him that hath, shall be given. In 1998, the class of biggest farmers each received over 40 times more in direct federal handouts than did the class of smallest farmers.[83] By handing big farmers $50,000, $100,000, or more each year, the federal government provides a war chest to allow big operators to "cannibalize" little operators, as University of Minnesota professor Phil Raup observed. The 1998 and 1999 bailouts were based almost entirely on the number of subsidized acres that a farmer previously planted—the perfect formula to aid large farmers in buying out small farmers.

Thanks to lavish federal handouts and strong crop prices, farm income hit record levels in 1996 and 1997. In 1998, USDA forecast lower farm income—and Washington panicked.

Beginning in the early summer of 1998, Clinton ratcheted up his demands for new farm handouts. In July 1998, Congress voted for $500 million in "disaster payments" to farmers, and for early payment—just before the November 1998 election—of $5 billion in agricultural handouts originally scheduled to be paid in 1999. In September 1998, House Speaker Newt Gingrich and other Republicans rushed to pass a second farm bailout. The Republicans passed a bill with another $4 billion in farm handouts; Clinton vetoed the bill, demanding that Congress ante up $7 billion for farmers. A bipartisan agreement was reached to fleece taxpayers for $6 billion. The second 1998 farm bailout gave favored farmers a 50 percent bonus on their "market transition payments." Congressmen claimed the boost would compensate farmers for low prices—but there was no reduction of federal handouts in 1996 and 1997 to "compensate" taxpayers and consumers for high prices. Sen. Tom Harkin (D-Iowa) correctly labeled the new handouts as "election year panic payments."[84]

Congressmen justified the "emergency" aid to crop farmers because of low wheat and corn prices. In contrast, dairy prices were at all-time highs. However, Rep. David Obey (D-Wis.) warned fellow congressmen that dairy prices might fall in the future, so a $200 million dairy bailout was railroaded through Congress with no hearings and no examination. The bailout meant $2,000 checks for each of the nation's 100,000 largest dairy producers.

Farmers received over $15 billion in federal handouts in the period just before and after the November 1998 election. Direct subsidies to farmers in 1998 roughly doubled the level of 1995—the year before "Freedom to Farm" was enacted.

Clinton justified perpetuating farm subsidies because of the supposed uniqueness of agriculture. Clinton derided subsidy opponents in 1998 for not understanding "the intersection between global impacts on farm prices, the financing challenges that family farmers . . . face, and what happens to you just by getting up in the morning if it happens to be a bad day."[85] Because some farmers feel woebegone or hung over on Monday mornings, Uncle Sam must perennially throw money at them. When Clinton signed a farm bailout package on October 23, 1998, he declared that he was "pleased about other provisions in the bill that address the long-term need for farmers to get a fair income from the market."[86] But the legislation flooded specific favored farmers with cash that they would not have received from voluntary exchanges with their fellow citizens. Clinton's concept of "fair income" simply meant income provided by politicians.

CLINTON'S FARM LEGACY

Clinton's impact on farm policy was stark in the 1999 stampede to throw money at almost any farmer on any pretext.

Some farmers were having a subpar year in 1999 and, as usual, some parts of the nation suffered from bad weather. Prices for many crops had fallen from 1996-97 heights. Clinton and congressional Democrats demanded another farm relief package. Most Republicans either put up little fight or were happy to jump on the bandwagon. The final bill doubled the so-called market transition payments for all subsidized farmers (Congress assumed that the best way to wean farmers from federal subsidies was to drown them in handouts). This gutted the feeble payment limits in the law. An analysis by the Food and Agriculture Policy Research Institute at the University of Missouri and Iowa State University found that the 1999 bailout would deliver $778,000 in subsidies to a typical 6,000-acre California cotton operation, $632,000 in subsidies to a 3,750-acre Texas rice farm, and $605,000 to a typical 4,000-acre Missouri rice farm.[87] The *Chicago Tribune* reported in late 1999 that "Illinois grain farmers will reap more profits from the $6 billion in federal disaster aid alone than from selling their crops, according to a recent study by the University of Illinois at Urbana-Champaign."[88] One study found that grain producers would collect 40 cents out of every dollar of gross income in 1999 from the federal government.[89]

The act delivered $328 million in special payments to tobacco farmers, who had been emotionally traumatized by the Clinton administration's denunciations of their crop. Tobacco farmers had perennially clamored for high price supports. As a result of high U.S. tobacco prices, export markets were lost and USDA cut the tobacco quota allotments (the precise amount that each farmer was permitted to grow). Tobacco farmers essentially received a reward for their own efforts in making their crop uncompetitive.

A $49 million payout to peanut farmers was justified because of a sharp increase in the cost of production of peanuts.[90] Yet, no one in Washington chose to mention that the single largest item in production costs is the cost of renting or buying a federal quota license to grow peanuts for the U.S. market.[91] The aid package was based solely on the amount of peanuts produced, thus favoring large farmers over small farmers. And the program was structured in a way that much, if not most, of the bailout actually went to the doctors, lawyers, and others who own the peanut quota licenses and rent them to farmers.

When he signed the farm bailout package in October 1999, Clinton declared: "While these additional funds have been absolutely critical, the very fact that we've needed them points out the underlying flaws in the 1996 farm bill."[92] Clinton demanded that Congress appropriate more handouts for farmers: when Congress did so, Clinton cited that as proof that the 1996 farm bill had not given enough money to farmers. According to Clinton's logic, the more handouts Congress gave, the more it proved that farmers need perpetual subsidies.

Since President Clinton took office,

- Taxpayers have been forced to spend over $16 billion for subsidies for wheat farmers.[93]
- Corn farmers have received over $30 billion from the government.
- Cotton farmers have received almost $10 billion from the federal government.
- Rice farmers have received more than $6 billion.
- Sugar farmers have received a de facto subsidy of $20-30 billion in higher prices as a result of import quotas and price supports.
- Dairy farmers have received a de facto subsidy of $40-plus billion in direct handouts, byzantine milk marketing restrictions, and trade barriers.

Taxpayers gained nothing from these subsidies other than the quiet satisfaction of knowing that they helped embellish the USDA's annual estimates of gross farm income.

An early 2000 USDA press release entitled "Glickman Reviews 1999 Accomplishments" bragged that "USDA provided a record $22.7 billion in assistance to America's farmers and ranchers."[94] Thanks to this generosity, net cash farm income in 1999 was the second highest on record.[95]

As the new century began, federal farm policy was an array of programs that, by any reasonable standard, should long since have been judged as crashed and burned. For instance, the cotton program was severely disrupting both domestic and foreign sales. Cotton prices were so distorted by the maze of federal interventions that the Clinton administration felt obliged to revive a special subsidy to persuade domestic textile mills to purchase U.S. cotton. The new program was essentially a very expensive cover-up of the failure of the existing cotton program. The American Textile Manufacturers is one of the most outspoken protectionist lobbies in Washington—but their own members needed a bribe to "buy American." Because there was no political controversy about the payments to U.S. textile mills, the new program was a success. The payments to cotton mills epitomized the total loss of political will to even attempt to make farm programs operate in a way that does not parody the public interest—the ultimate symbol that farm policymakers have given up even trying to get policies right.

Farm policy in the mid-to-late 1990s suffered from Clinton's view of himself as a great reformer. Repeatedly, Clinton would propose meager reductions or petty screw-tightening reforms in the most wasteful programs—and then pretend that his changes had turned programs into paragons of good government. Clinton's love of throwing money at suffering situations played into the hands of farm-state congressmen who cared only about maximizing handouts to their campaign contributors and constituents. As a result, taxpayers will continue to be pillaged to perpetuate dozens of programs that have no right to exist.

DISABILITIES
DEMENTIA

PRESIDENT CLINTON DECLARED ON JULY 26, 1994, "The Americans with Disabilities Act (ADA) is a national monument to freedom. Contained within its broad pillars of independence, inclusion, and empowerment is the core ideal of equality that has defined this country since its beginnings."[1] The ADA exemplified Clinton's concept of freedom: something that results from threats, lawsuits, and federal agents who will, in Attorney General Reno's words, "kick down the doors."[2] Clinton's disability policy sought to allow scores of millions of additional people to label themselves disabled and claim a right to special accommodations. Clintonites sought to create special privileges to employees who proclaimed themselves depressed, to make the ADA more fraud friendly, and to sacrifice public health to protect the sensitivities of people with contagious diseases.

The Americans with Disabilities Act was enacted in 1990 with the support of President George Bush, who, along with Congress, deserves initial blame for unleashing a flood of lawsuits and generating thousands of unnecessary conflicts. However, the Clinton administration made a foolish law much worse. The intentions of the original ADA were laudable—but the mixture of good intentions and political coercion generated tragic-comic results.

The 1990 act defined disability as "(A) a physical or mental impairment that substantially limits one or more of the major life activities of [an] individual; (B) a record of such an impairment; or (C) being regarded as having such an impairment."[3] This definition means everything and nothing. Employers and others must provide "reasonable accommodation" to the disabled, unless providing such accommodation would be an "undue hardship." Regrettably, the EEOC is in charge of defining "reasonable." The U.S. Civil Rights Commission lamented in a 1998 report that "the EEOC had not developed policy documents on some of the most heavily disputed disability issues, such as reasonable accommodation and undue hardship."[4]

The EEOC preferred to let the law remain vague and confusing, thereby maximizing the number of lawsuits and the chilling effect on everyone involved in dealing with the disabled. Federal judge Franklin Waters observed in 1997 that the ADA "has the potential to be the biggest instigator or flashpoint for litigation that we've seen in a long time. Not one out of 10 of the [ADA] cases that are filed involve what we traditionally thought of as . . . handicapped."[5]

EQUAL OPPORTUNITY TO INFECT, CRASH, AND POLLUTE

For the Clinton administration, public safety precautions became potential federal crimes. The 1990 act stated that disabled citizens must be accommodated unless doing so would result in a "direct threat" to other people's health and well-being. But for the EEOC and Clinton's Justice Department, nothing is more threatening than unequal treatment.

In 1999, on the ninth anniversary of the ADA's enactment, Clinton bragged, "Throughout our administration, Vice President Gore and I have endeavored to empower [disabled] individuals with the tools they need to bring their tremendous energy and talent to the American work force."[6]

And how did Clinton's prosecutors achieve this lofty goal? The EEOC sued Bell Helicopter Textron because the company fired an epileptic after he had a seizure while working as a rotary shaper operator.[7] The EEOC sued Harvest Foods of Arkansas after it refused to rehire a former truck driver who suffered from panic attacks.[8] The EEOC sued Amego, Inc., of Massachusetts, after it fired a woman suffering from depression and bulimia after she attempted suicide with prescription medicine. She had been a team leader, in charge of "ordering and administering clients' medication at the employer's day treatment program for autistic and severely behaviorally disordered adolescents and adults."[9] A federal judge and appeals panel both threw the EEOC's case out the door.

As U.S. Civil Rights Commissioner Russell Redenbaugh noted, "In January 1997, the EEOC won a $5.5 million verdict for a former Ryder

Systems truck driver, claiming under the ADA that the company unfairly removed him from his position citing safety concerns after he had suffered an epileptic seizure. The driver was hired by another firm, had a seizure while driving, and crashed into a tree."[10]

The ADA, with its "accommodate almost everything" mandate, threatens nondisabled workers. *Crain's Chicago Business* reported the following case: "A factory crane operator was diagnosed with bipolar personality disorder [also called manic depression]. He took lithium to control it, and had never exhibited any aberrant behavior on the job. Still, co-workers feared that a manic episode would occur while he was operating the crane, resulting in serious injury to others . . . However, in this case, the crane operator was protected by the ADA because of his excellent track record on lithium."[11] But a crane operator who forgets his medicine can do far more damage with a 500-pound wrecking ball than a listless government file clerk with the same condition who goes over the edge and shreds a memo.

The ADA protects people with alcohol and illicit drug problems, as long as they promise they are recovering, or are seeking treatment, or they make some type of plausible excuse for their behavior. Thanks to the ADA, Northwest Airlines rehired an airplane pilot who had been fired after he was caught flying a passenger jet while legally drunk. The fired pilot entered a rehab program, then got his job back after threatening a suit, as author Walter Olson reported.[12]

After the *Exxon Valdez* hit a reef and dumped 11 million gallons of oil along the Alaskan coast in 1989, the Justice Department sued Exxon for allowing a former alcoholic to captain the ship. Exxon adopted a strict policy that banned "all employees who currently have a substance abuse problem and all employees with a history of substance abuse from working in" positions in which "there is a high exposure to catastrophic public, environmental, or employee incidents . . . and there is either no direct supervision or very limited supervision."[13] Roughly 10 percent of Exxon's positions were placed in this category.

EEOC Chairman Gilbert Casellas was outraged and complained that Exxon's policies were "based on irrational fears or stereotypes about individuals with a record of past substance abuse." The EEOC sued, demanding that Exxon do an "individualized assessment" for each allegedly rehabilitated addict seeking a high-risk job. The EEOC contended that "when a policy, like Exxon's, is grounded in safety, the business necessity defense can only be satisfied by establishing that the individuals excluded from the positions pose a direct threat to the health or safety of other individuals in the workplace."[14] The EEOC did not explicitly specify that each former addict or alcoholic should be allowed to crash one oil tanker before being presumed unfit for such tasks. The case percolated through the federal courts throughout the mid to late 1990s and was still being fought in early 2000. Exxon sought expert testimony from two Justice Department lawyers who had prosecuted Exxon for criminal violations related to the *Exxon Valdez* accident. But the Justice Department sought to block their testimony, claiming it would be a violation of the Ethics in Government Act.[15] The Justice Department may have feared that the two witnesses would have revealed how the federal government earlier demanded that Exxon adopt the same type of policies for which it was being sued.

Clinton's Justice Department imposed one extreme version of the ADA after another. Roger Clegg of the Center for Equal Opportunity, observed that, after the Justice Department intervened, "A bar in Illinois agreed to modify its policy of refusing to serve alcohol to customers who appear to be drunk based on the way they walk because a customer with Parkinson's disease had been refused service."[16]

The ADA has had a major effect on policies aimed at preventing the spread of contagious diseases. Because people with contagious diseases are perceived to be disabled, they often fall under the protection of the ADA, and the onus falls on anyone seeking to minimize the spread of the disease. In a December 1, 1993, speech marking World AIDS Day, Attorney General Janet Reno declared, "The administration is determined to open doors of opportunity to people with AIDS . . . [T]he department is prepared to kick down the door with firm, fair enforcement actions. No American, including those with AIDS, should be made to suffer discrimination in the workplace or in the doctor's office."[17] The Justice Department warned that dentists who take extra precautions while treating HIV/AIDS patients would be breaking the law. The Justice Department and the EEOC apparently concluded that it is more important to seek to minimize public prejudice against people with infectious diseases than it is to minimize the spread of the disease itself.

The Supreme Court in 1998 heard the case of a Maine dentist, Randon Bragdon, who was accused of violating the ADA because he refused to fill the cavity of an HIV-positive patient, Sidney Abbott, in his office; instead, he offered to treat her at a hospital. (Hospital facilities provide far better protection against infection than exists in the average dental office.) Abbott sued, claiming that Bragdon had violated her civil rights by not treating her in the same way as any patient without a contagious, fatal disease. The Justice Department, in its brief, insisted that Bragdon had no right to refuse to treat the patient in his office because the risks to him and his staff were not significant enough to override the ADA's imperatives. But the federal Centers for Disease Control reported in 1994 that 37 health care workers had been infected with HIV while treating HIV-positive patients, including 7 suspected occupational transmissions of HIV to dental workers.[18] Bragdon's lawyer noted that filling cavities "entails giving oral injections to nervous patients, working in bloody aerosol mists, and poking with sharp instruments in bloody mouths."[19] One expert testified at the trial that dentists suffer 1.5 accidental needlesticks per 100 injections. The Food and Drug Administration in 1992 ordered blood banks not to accept blood donations from anyone who had been directly exposed to the blood of anyone with HIV in the previous year. As Bragdon's brief asked, "If the blood bank may deem the risk significant, why not the dentist himself?"[20] According to Clinical Research Associates, half the face masks commonly used by dentists fail to block the passage of aerosolized bacteria and seven percent of latex gloves contain pinholes.[21] The American Association of Forensic Dentists warned that the use of latex gloves did not reduce the risk of AIDS transmissions to dental workers to "insignificant levels." Refusing to allow the dentist to take extra precautions when treating an HIV-positive patient also places the dentist's other patients at greater risk.

Abbott won. The Supreme Court effectively ruled that politically correct dentistry was more important than dead dentists. Chief Justice William Rehnquist dissented: "Given the 'severity of the risk' involved here, i.e., near certain death, and the fact that no public health authority had outlined a protocol for eliminating this risk in the context of routine dental treatment, it seems likely that [Bragdon] can establish that it was objectively reasonable for him to conclude that treating respondent in his office posed a 'direct threat' to his safety."[22] President Clinton issued a statement announcing that he was "pleased" with the decision: "I am firmly committed to protecting all Americans, including those living with HIV and AIDS, from discrimination, and ensuring that each of us can benefit from all America has to offer. Today's decision will help in fulfilling that commitment."[23]

While the Clinton administration's policies were driven by concern about prejudice against people with HIV/AIDS, the same policies make it far more difficult to restrict public exposures to medical professionals with hepatitis. While the risk of transmitting HIV/AIDS in a medical setting is relatively very low, the risk of transmitting hepatitis is very high. One UCLA surgeon spread hepatitis to 18 heart patients in the early 1990s; though the hospital knew the surgeon was infected, he was permitted to continue operating (with no warning to his patients). The *New York Times* noted that "the hospital's decision to allow the surgeon to keep on operating even after he was found to be infected . . . is in compliance with Federal guidelines."[24]

THE ADA'S MENTAL DRIFT NET

Cases claiming emotional or psychiatric impairment are now the most common type of ADA lawsuit. People claiming to suffer from depression are the most common "mental disability" complaint. The ADA is degenerating into a federal entitlement program for people who claim to be unhappy—with the bill sent to whoever happens to be paying their salary at the time.

The EEOC issued "Enforcement Guidance" on psychiatric disabilities in 1997. The EEOC declared that "mental impairments restrict major life activities such as learning, thinking, concentrating, interacting with others, caring for oneself, speaking, performing manual tasks, or working."[25] The EEOC noted, "An impairment substantially limits an individual's ability to concentrate if, due to the impairment, s/he is significantly restricted as compared to the average person in the general population. For example, an individual would be substantially limited if s/he was easily and frequently distracted, meaning that his/her attention was frequently drawn to irrelevant sights or sounds or to intrusive thoughts." This is practically a description of daily life for many cubicle dwellers in corporate America. Should every employee who cannot resist occasionally playing games on his computer be considered mentally disabled? Alan Zametkin, a National Institute of Mental Health researcher, observed that, after a 1994 bestseller on attention deficit disorder (ADD), "everybody with a messy desk thinks he has ADD."[26]

The ADA earned the nickname "Attorneys' Dreams Answered" because of all the meritless lawsuits the law generated. But even a ludicrous lawsuit can bleed a business. The National Federation of Independent Business estimated that companies spend an average of $12,000 in legal fees to defend themselves against an ADA suit; the cost can rise to $100,000 if the case goes to a jury.[27] Because the legal costs of defending against suits are relatively high, companies have an incentive to settle bogus suits for a few thousand dollars. Miami lawyer Michael Casey observed that many ADA claims are "a legal form of extortion, and the ADA is all-purpose extortion."[28] The profusion of absurd lawsuits included the following:

- Aryeh Motzkin, a 60-year-old philosophy professor, sued Boston University after he was fired for allegedly sexually assaulting a female professor and for sexually harassing three students. Motzkin denied the charges but admitted that the tranquilizers and antidepressants he was taking "loosened his inhibitions."[29] Motzkin sued BU for violating the ADA, claiming that he is mentally handicapped. The *Boston Globe* reported,

"Once students complained about his behavior, Motzkin alleges, the university was aware of his handicap and had an obligation to help him deal with it."[30] (A federal judge spiked his case.[31])

- A government clerk in Howard County, Maryland, was fired after repeated rude outbursts and loud denunciations of her supervisors. She sued, claiming that the firing violated her civil rights because she was a manic depressive and that the employer was obliged to strip her job of all its inherent stress.[32]

- A Massachusetts truck driver sued under the ADA, demanding that he be permitted to drive special routes to accommodate his fear of crossing bridges. The company claimed that he had been fired after he was caught falsifying federally required travel logs. (A federal appeals court spiked his suit in 1998.)[33]

- A Madison, Wisconsin, telephone operator sued her employer after it refused to provide reasonable accommodation for her narcolepsy. The woman was routinely late for work and sought permission to continue arriving late because of her "disability."[34]

- Even the most virtuous of workers are susceptible to the blues. Two investigators with the Nebraska Equal Opportunity Commission claimed to be disabled by depression.[35] They sued the state of Nebraska and won a jury award of $295,000 to compensate them for the lack of consideration the state government showed to their unhappiness. But, as Steve Grassz of the Nebraska attorney general's office observed, "It's not a reasonable accommodation for the state to pay them for not getting any work done."[36]

The ADA begets boutique disabilities. "Multiple chemical sensitivity" (MCS) is one of the most popular new disabilities. Even though MCS has never been recognized by the feds as a legitimate disability, disability activists in California have blanketed businesses and other organizations with lawsuit threats if they fail to cease and desist their olfactory offenses. The Chemical Injury Litigation Project in northern California put together a blank form for MCS sufferers, enabling them to photocopy and mail out threats to sue every business within a 20-mile radius.[37] The products targeted by this "Notice of Noncompliance" included "maintenance products that contain scent, fragrance, perfume, active chlorine, phenol compounds, and/or terpenes such as pinene or that emit any other toxic VOCs or sensitizers into the air," as well as products commonly used for "Floors/Windows/Counters/Tables/Restrooms." Among the allegedly illegal practices targeted are "air fresheners [that] contain fragrances and/or odor-masking compounds."[38] Perhaps MCS activists will launch a national campaign to sue any gas station whose restroom does not smell like an open sewer.

Lucky Stores, a California-based grocery chain, got burned in federal court because of its treatment of a supermarket manager, Richard Holihan, who generated scores of complaints for shoving, screaming at, and threatening his subordinates, as well as for throwing items off grocery shelves and ordering his underlings to pick them up.[39] A company official asked Holihan if he was having any "problems" that the company could help with. Holihan denied having problems, but the complaints from other employees continued. A company vice president met with Holihan and suggested he seek counseling. Lucky Stores provided him nine months paid leave, during which he "got a license and started selling real estate. He opened a sign business. He worked, he said, about 80 hours a week on these two ventures."[40] The company wanted Holihan to come back to work at that time, but he refused. A year later, Holihan contacted them and said he wanted his old job back, but the company had no openings for managers. He sued, claiming that because the company had recommended counseling, it perceived him as disabled. Federal judges agreed and Lucky Stores paid Holihan an undisclosed sum to settle the case. One analysis of the case noted, "Lucky Stores . . . was found guilty of handling employee problems such as Holihan's in exactly the way that the Equal Employment Opportunity Commission wants them handled. In doing so, however, the company also appeared to 'regard' Holihan as disabled."[41]

The ADA has been a boon to lawyers in more ways than one. The *Recorder*, a California legal newspaper, noted in 1996: "Attorneys cited for transgressions ranging from neglect of their cases to stealing from clients have asserted that their actions are mitigated by mental impairment or substance abuse, and thus are entitled to leniency under the ADA."[42]

The ADA is routinely invoked as a shield or a bargaining chip by employees who despise their bosses. A 1999 *New York Law Journal* piece noted,

Mental disability claims are rife with allegations that the employee was unable to get along with a particular person at work, often the boss. The employee may even claim that her supervisor is the cause of a stress-related impairment . . . In some cases, the inability to get along with a supervisor or co-worker results in threats, or even acts of aggression or violence. When a mentally disabled employee is terminated or disciplined for such conduct, he or she is likely to challenge the termination on the ground that the "disability made me do it," or allege that the employer should have accommodated the condition.[43]

Claims of learning disabilities are booming, thanks to the ADA. According to the National Center for Learning Disabilities, "15-20 percent of the U.S. population has some sort of learning disability."[44] Kevin McGuinness flunked out of the University of New Mexico medical school and then sued the school for failing to accommodate his physics and chemistry "test-taking anxiety." A federal appeals court rejected his plea, ruling that "Mr. McGuinness must demonstrate that his anxiety impedes his performance in a wide variety of disciplines, not just chemistry and physics."[45]

Boston University was widely respected for accommodating learning disabled students: they received extra time for test taking, exemption from mandatory foreign language courses, and free assistants to take notes for them during lectures. The number of Boston University students requesting disabilities accommodations rose tenfold between 1991 and 1995.[46] When Jon Westling became president of Boston University in 1995, he publicly expressed doubts about the legitimacy of many learning disability claims and announced that students must undergo independent evaluation to confirm their disability. A group of students responded by suing the university for inflicting emotional distress on them, creating a "hostile environment" for the disabled, and discriminating against them. The lawsuit also demanded that "the university grant course substitutions to any student making such a request."[47] A federal judge ruled in 1998 that some of BU's policies violated federal law; six students split a settlement of roughly $30,000.[48] The students' lawyers noted in the *Journal of Learning Disabilities*: "In the view of Disability Rights Advocates, BU invited an unnecessary battle over ideology. They argued for an abstract conception of 'academic freedom.'"[49]

The ADA is increasingly invoked by people taking bar exams. In 1998, a federal appeals court ruled that Marilyn Bartlett, a slow-reading applicant for the New York bar exam, was entitled to "reasonable accommodations."[50] Bartlett scored in the bottom 4 percent of college students and could read only "slowly, haltingly, and laboriously."[51] Bartlett "had asked for extended time on the bar exam, permission to tape record her essays and the opportunity to circle multiple-choice answers in the test booklet rather than use the computerized answer sheet."[52] On her fifth try, the bar examiners paid for an assistant to read Bartlett the questions out loud in a side room. After Bartlett again flunked, she blamed the assistant for distracting her by munching on snack food.[53] The appeals court ruled that the issue was simply whether Bartlett's "opportunity to take the examination on a level playing field with other applicants" had been violated.[54]

The vast majority of routine lawyering involves paperwork, and the inability to read more than two miles per hour means that either the lawyer is uncompetitive or her clients are shafted. And in such cases, the ADA comes down in favor of shafting the customers. Instead of *caveat emptor* (let the buyer beware) it is *damnet emptor* (let the buyer be damned).[55]

The number of people claiming the right to special accommodations could skyrocket in the coming years. In December 1999, Surgeon General David Satcher issued a report declaring that "22 percent of the population has a diagnosable mental disorder."[56] However, because of expansive new mental illnesses ordained by the American Psychiatric Association, the concept of "diagnosable mental disorder" now means little or nothing. The list now includes "'anti-social personality disorder' ('a pervasive pattern of disregard for . . . the rights of others . . . callous, cynical . . . an inflated and arrogant self appraisal'); 'histrionic personality disorder' ('excessive emotionality and attention-seeking . . . inappropriately sexually provocative or seductive'); 'narcissistic personality disorder' ('grandiosity, need for admiration . . . boastful and pretentious . . . interpersonally exploitative . . . may assume that they do not have to wait in line'); and 'avoidant personality disorder' ('social inhibition, feelings of inadequacy')," as columnist George Will noted.[57]

ACCESS ABSURDITIES

"Access police" are trolling for ADA violators across the land:

- The city of Bellevue, Washington, threatened to levy a $4,500 fine on Papagayo's, a strip club, because it did not have a wheelchair lift attached to the stage for performers. An exasperated representative of the company that hires the strippers said of the government policy: "It's just asinine. If you can't dance, why should you even be on stage?"[58]
- A deaf woman in Santa Monica, California, sued Burger King, claiming that its drive-through windows illegally discriminated against deaf people. Burger King settled the lawsuit by agreeing to install visual electronic ordering devices at 10 restaurants.[59]
- A group of deaf people in Cleveland sued the National Football League, claiming that the "blackout rule," which prohibits television broadcast of home football games that have not been sold out at least 72 hours before the game, violates the rights of the hearing impaired. (The games can be broadcast on radio, but that does not do deaf people a lot of good.) A federal judge ruled that the blackout policy does not discriminate, since it aggravates both deaf and nondeaf people.[60]

- Robert Johnson was terminated from a position as a telemarketer because of his alleged excessive mumbling on the phone during a training course. Johnson denied that he mumbled and sued his employer, claiming that the company was biased against him because he was missing 18 teeth. A federal appeals court upheld his suit, noting that "[U]nlike Johnson, the Americans with Disabilities Act has teeth."[61]

- A group of older female Delta Airlines flight attendants sued the airline, claiming that the company's weight restrictions illegally discriminated against them. The Equal Employment Opportunity Commission ruled that the airline's policy was biased against female flight attendants.[62] The EEOC did not explain how women "of a certain size" could slide around a drinks cart in scandalously narrow airplane aisles.

The federal Department of Transportation in 1998 proposed "peanut-free zones" on airplanes to protect those who might have allergies to peanuts.[63] Some schools have banned peanut butter from their cafeterias because of fear that "peanut allergies might qualify as a disability that must be accommodated" under the ADA. Other school systems have responded to the threat of disability suits by banning all children from bringing peanut butter sandwiches or other peanut products to school.[64] Since there are people with allergies to almost all the most common foods, why not simply ban eating? Or would fear of looking anorexic also qualify as a disability, thus trumping the eating ban?

The Justice Department brought Wendy's fast-food restaurants to their knees in 1998 because their "serpentine" queue lines were not wide enough for a wheelchair to pass through or turn in. Such lines provide faster, more equitable service, and also allow customers to focus on the menu rather than on studying which cashier is least incompetent. Even though wheelchair customers were usually called to the front of the line as soon as they entered the store, the Justice Department claimed that the existence of the serpentine queues abused the disabled. Steven Grover, vice president of technical services for the National Restaurant Association, said: "Is it necessary for the Justice Department to go around with a micrometer and measure everything, or should we be happy that we have good access [for wheelchairs] to restaurants?"[65] Attorney General Janet Reno hailed the eventual settlement: "Integrating people with disabilities into society, even into a fast-food line, is what the ADA is all about. People with disabilities do not want special treatment—they just want to be treated like everyone else."[66] But, thanks to the Justice Department's threats and the settlement, service for many, if not most customers will be slower.

In November 1999, the Occupational Safety and Health Administration (OSHA) proposed new rules to protect workers from repetitive-stress injuries such as carpal tunnel syndrome. The *New York Times* noted that "the rules would require employers to adopt full-scale ergonomics programs to minimize hazards if even a few employees had suffered such injuries."[67] The Small Business Administration estimated that compliance with the new rules would cost $18 billion a year; the regs evoked an outcry from business groups.[68] However, the EEOC did its best to protect the jobs of orthopedic surgeons. The EEOC sued Helcris, Inc., of Indiana in 1997 after the company withdrew an offer of a cashier's job to someone suffering from carpal tunnel syndrome.[69] The EEOC began battling Rockwell Corporation in 1995 over nerve conduction tests it administered to potential assembly line workers at a Centralia, Illinois, auto plant to determine the likelihood of their getting carpal tunnel syndrome.[70] Rockwell argued in court that hiring people who showed a high likelihood of developing carpal tunnel syndrome would pose "a direct threat to their own health and safety."[71] But the EEOC was not fooled.

OTHER EEOC TRIPWIRES

The EEOC outlaws informed consent in dealings with the handicapped. The EEOC bans employers from asking almost any questions during job interviews that "are likely to elicit information about a disability." If an employer asks too directly about a disability during a job interview, the employer is presumed to be discriminating against the handicapped person and can be forced to pay large settlements to avoid a lawsuit. In New Mexico, a Wal-Mart store was sued by the EEOC after a job applicant with an amputated arm was asked during an interview: "What current or past medical problems might limit your ability to do a job?" The rejected applicant got $157,500 in "damages" for what, before the ADA, would have been considered a reasonable, if rude, question.[72] As Civil Rights Commissioner Russell Redenbaugh noted in 1998, "An employer may not ask, at the pre-offer stage, how many days an applicant was sick or on sick leave in his or her former position, because this question relates directly to the severity of an individual's impairment, and severity is a criterion for determining whether an impairment is 'substantially limiting' to a 'major life activity' and thus a disability under the ADA . . . Potential employers may not ask applicants questions about their workers' compensation history because, again, such questions are likely to elicit information about a disability."[73] This can turn job interviews into games of "gotcha!" The applicant has an incentive to withhold as much information as possible from—if not to actively mislead—a potential employer about his ability to do the job without massive and costly assistance. The EEOC assumes that the only way that disabled job applicants can receive fair treatment is to blindfold employers and turn them into sacrificial animals. Once a job offer has been made, the employer faces potentially unlimited additional demands.

On March 1, 1999, the EEOC finally revealed what it considered to be "reasonable accommodation" of the disabled. The EEOC proclaimed that "a reasonable accommodation will be effective if it allows an employee with a disability an equal opportunity to enjoy the benefits and privileges of employment that employees without disabilities enjoy."[74] But this is "equal opportunity" that requires perennially treating people unequally. The EEOC has stated in the past that hiring a job coach or a page turner for a disabled employee is a reasonable accommodation, regardless of how much it costs the employer. The EEOC stressed in 1999 that there is no point at which a disabled employee must cease asking for additional special treatment.[75]

The EEOC surprised many corporations by announcing, in its March 1, 1999, proclamation that companies must allow disabled employees "to work at home as a reasonable accommodation."[76] As *Human Resources* magazine noted, "EEOC guidelines and recent court decisions will force employers to justify their attendance requirements in ADA cases and reconsider attendance rules."[77]

Some EEOC policies risk inducing temporary insanity among corporate personnel officials. The Equal Employment Advisory Council, a consortium of large businesses, observed: "According to the agency's guidance on Workers Compensation and the ADA, an employer is expected to hold a position open for an employee who cannot work due to a disability, unless doing so would impose an undue hardship. If the employer cannot hold the position open without undue hardship, the agency expects the employer to reassign the employee to another position from which to be absent." This consortium complained that such rules "defy common sense."[78] Labor lawyer Jacqueline Rolfs observed, "Although many courts have held that an indefinite leave of absence is unreasonable, the EEOC disagrees. By forcing employers to hold positions open virtually without limit—and by requiring reassignments to vacant positions on an almost automatic basis—the EEOC essentially is creating a right of lifetime employment at a specific company for disabled workers."[79]

The EEOC has consistently contorted the ADA to claim that it covers far more people than even Congress intended. In 1999, the EEOC and the Justice Department argued before the Supreme Court that anyone who has mitigated a physical problem could still be classified as disabled. This meant that anyone who wore glasses, for instance, could be considered disabled because their uncorrected vision was not 20/20. The EEOC effectively sought veto power over the work situations and contracts of more than 100 million Americans. The Supreme Court torpedoed their imperialist gambit, ruling that such an expansive interpretation of the law was unjustified.[80]

Federal judge Samuel Kent denounced an ADA suit in 1995 as "a blatant attempt to extort money." The plaintiff previously had been awarded permanent disability benefits from the Santa Fe Railroad; eight days after he received disability status, he sued the railroad for refusing to rehire him because of his disability. The judge condemned the suit as "either blatantly fraudulent or utterly ridiculous."[81] *Federal EEOC Adviser* magazine noted: "Once you've applied for benefits, however, you're saying, 'I can't work anymore, because I'm disabled.' The courts are generally saying you can either have one or the other. When you try to have both, it's fraud."[82]

But not according to the EEOC—which ruled in 1997 that applying for disability benefits cannot bar employees from also suing their employer for alleged bias against the disabled.[83] The EEOC joined several lawsuits against companies that would not hire applicants who, in lawsuits against their previous employers, claimed to be disabled.[84]

FALSE DELIVERANCE

President Clinton declared on July 26, 1995: "The ADA has meant more opportunity for 49 million Americans with disabilities to do their part to make us a stronger and better country. It has meant that more people can go to work."[85] But a 1998 study by Massachusetts Institute of Technology economists concluded: "The ADA had a negative effect on the employment of disabled men of all working ages and all disabled women under age 40."[86] A 1998 survey for the National Organization on Disability "found that 29 percent of disabled persons are employed full or part time . . . In 1986, 33 percent of the disabled were employed."[87] Whatever pro-employment effect the ADA might have has been swamped by the disincentive effects of federal aid programs. The General Accounting Office concluded in 1996 that Social Security Disability Insurance (SSDI) and Supplemental Security Income (SSI) for the disabled "encourage dependency on benefits, rather than fostering a sense of independence," as the *National Journal* summarized."[88]

Civil Rights Commissioner Russell Redenbaugh, who is blind, warned in 1998 that the EEOC's ADA regulations "may actually encourage discrimination, insofar as they tend to reduce the thousand-fold considerations of hiring down to one: membership in a protected class . . . An overexpansive application of ADA may create the impression that members of the class it protects essentially become . . . 'fire-proof.'"[89] Redenbaugh observed that "the fear of a litigious, activist EEOC may discourage hiring of the very disabled persons the law was meant to help. An employer faced with the prospect of hiring a disabled but nonetheless qualified applicant or hiring a less-qualified but non-disabled applicant must take into consideration this potentially ruinous EEOC 'tax.'"[90]

CONCLUSION

American attitudes toward the handicapped have become far more humane and rational in recent decades. However, the ADA, by maximizing legal conflicts, undermines citizens' incentives to voluntarily accommodate one another. The Civil Rights Commission in 1998 complained that inaccurate news media coverage of the ADA was resulting in "increased hostility to individuals with disabilities."[91] But the hostility is not the result of the news coverage but of a completely inept law and vigilante federal agencies.

The ADA is essentially a federal command for people to treat certain other people "nice"—with harsh penalties for any behavior considered not nice—and with niceness to be defined on a case-by-case basis through endless court cases and complaint settlements. The disabled-rights provisions in the ADA are a stark example of Congress dictating a hierarchy among the citizenry—dictating that some citizen's needs are superior to others and that those others should be forced to pay any price or suffer any burden to serve the group with superior rights. The greater the physical or mental inequalities between people, the more coercion will be necessary to create the illusion of equality of opportunity between disabled and normal workers.

The ADA illustrates how the moral ideals and goodwill of the American people toward a group that most people want to help are exploited by politicians and government bureaucrats. Once that good will supposedly gets canonized in the law, the sky is the limit to how much power government can extort. The more benefits the government mandates, the more incentive people have to declare themselves disabled. A policy designed to help the disabled instead mushrooms the number of people claiming to need help.

The ADA is a case of the absurd pursuit of perfect fairness based on the notion that everyone is entitled to "reasonable accommodation" from everyone else in everything that they do. The more accommodations the EEOC announces as "reasonable," the more power EEOC bureaucrats capture, and the further they will be able to inflict their agenda on everyone else.

THE
GREEN IRON FIST

THE COMMON THREAD OF CLINTON-GORE ENVIRONMENTAL POLICY was command-and-control: a presumption that government knows best and that the surest way to a cleaner, safer environment was to multiply the pretexts under which government agents could punish private citizens. If environmental problems still occurred it simply proved that not enough victims had been flayed—or that the flayings must be better publicized. Clinton's environmental policy was based on faith in sheer power—power that did not have to answer to anyone, not to federal judges, not to Congress, and not to any American citizen unlucky enough to fall under federal thumbs. There was no environmental problem that could not be solved by seizing more land, criminalizing more behavior, and turning more peaceful citizens into felons.

Since Clinton took office, federal environmental policies have cost Americans more than $1.2 trillion dollars.[1] This exceeds the total value of all the investments in the United States in new factories to produce high tech equipment—from semiconductors, to computers, to cell phones—since 1993.[2] The vast majority of these costs were shouldered by the private sector. Unfortunately, much, if not most, of these compliance costs were wasted—as far as making America a safer place for citizens. Political priorities mandated bottomless-pit spending in the name of environmental safety: protecting the environment by compelling people to burn money on the green altar of the month.

Some of the worst excesses in environmental enforcement developed during the Bush administration, but the Clinton administration fought both to perpetuate abuses and to deceive courts and the public about what the government was actually doing. Clinton administration environmental policy was often imbued with a messianic mission to save humanity. This attitude is evident in Vice President Gore's 1992 bestseller, *Earth in the Balance*—"[t]he struggle to save the global environment is in one way much more difficult than the struggle to vanquish Hitler, for this time the war is with ourselves."[3]

SUPERFUND

In a February 11, 1993, speech to business leaders, Clinton declared of the most prominent environmental program: "We all know it doesn't work: the Super- fund has been a disaster. All the money goes to lawyers, and none of the money goes to clean up the problems that it was designed to clean up."[4] Congress enacted Superfund in 1980 to deal with the problem of abandoned hazardous waste sites. But the program mushroomed after the melodramatics of hazardous waste proved politically irresistible. Superfund has already cost the private sector and government scores of billions of dollars. Clinton rightfully portrayed Superfund as the poster boy for failed environmental policy—a program in which the government dutifully repeated the same mistakes year after year, with zero learning curve. But he exaggerated slightly. Every now and then, a cleanup dollar did evade a lawyer's grasp and pay to move dirt—and helped the program win laurels for "moving a dump a day." A GAO study found that only 44 percent of federal spending for Superfund went for cleanups—the rest was fizzled away on administrative overhead and legal fees.[5]

And what did Clinton do? More of the same, spiced with occasional accusations that Republicans favored poisoning America.

Superfund is so wasteful, in large part, because it is so unjust. EPA relies on "joint and several liability": anyone who sent anything to a dump that later became a Superfund site can be held personally liable for the *entire* cleanup cost of that dump. EPA is not required to prove that a company sent waste to a Superfund site; instead, the company must prove itself innocent. Political Economy Research Center economist Richard Stroup noted, "There is no impartial review of EPA decisions. The law exempted the EPA from judicial oversight except at a few points in the Superfund process . . . Accused parties can do little to challenge the EPA's decisions, except at the very end of the remediation process (typically expected to be 12 years)."[6]

Superfund made cleaning up abandoned waste sites far more hazardous than it otherwise would have been. Any company that came in to clean up a site could be held liable for the entire cleanup cost, even if it had had nothing to do with the original contamination. This is like holding a Boy Scout liable for all the future medical expenses of any old lady he helped cross the street.

Superfund strangled cities. Rep. Michael Oxley (R-Ohio) denounced the EPA for creating a "brownfields Berlin Wall" and complained that Superfund and its implementation of regulations "have driven jobs away, discouraged new investment, and exposed residents to contamination for a longer period of time."[7] Lawyer James Thunder noted in 1998, "Superfund's liability scheme caused developers to shun city 'brownfields' in favor of developing non-urban 'greenfields' . . . The Superfund law, and EPA's administration of it, virtually suspended all cleanup of property unless EPA was in charge, delaying cleanup interminably. This placed the health of urban residents at risk."[8] A U.S. Conference of Mayors inventory of brownfields sites found "180 cities reporting 19,000 sites representing more than 178,000 acres . . . a land area larger than the cities of Atlanta, Seattle and San Francisco combined."[9]

Superfund has also been a fiasco because of absurd cleanup standards. EPA presumes that children will visit former Superfund sites on a near-daily basis and eat the dirt.[10] EPA christened the Idaho Pole Company in Bozeman, Montana, a Superfund site; PCPs had leaked onto the ground during the treatment of telephone poles. EPA justified the Superfund designation based on the bizarre assumptions that the local government would authorize using the former industrial site for a mobile-home park; that the new mobile-home residents would insist on drilling private wells directly below them to tap and drink only the most polluted water they could find; and that the new residents would insist on growing their own food in back of their trailers, thus scarfing down a few more carcinogens.[11] Duke professor Kip Viscusi noted, "This hypothetical enthusiasm for living on Superfund sites is implausible in light of the fact that hazardous waste sites rank number one on the public's list of environmental fears."[12] Viscusi analyzed spending for Superfund cleanups and concluded: "The first 5 percent of expenditures eliminates 99.46 percent of the total expected cases of cancer averted by hazardous waste cleanup efforts. The remaining 95 percent of all cleanup costs achieves virtually nothing in terms of health risk reduction."[13] Even more surprising, Viscusi found that "55 percent of the expenditures are made to eliminate under 0.1 percent of the risk."[14] Viscusi concluded that the risk threshold that EPA used to launch Superfund sites was "quite comparable to many of the risks that we encounter in our daily lives, e.g., eating 40 tablespoons of peanut butter or traveling 10 miles by bicycle."[15]

William Cooper, an ecologist at Michigan State University, conceded that "if you had to do it [Superfund cleanups] on risk alone, you wouldn't spend any money on these things."[16] A GAO report found that one-fifth of the Superfund cleanups it examined were not necessary to protect public health.[17] Superfund also suffered from a fixation on doing something—anything. A 1991 National Research Council study concluded: "In some cases, unnecessary or inappropriate remediation might create more of a hazard than would be caused by leaving such materials undisturbed."[18]

The Clinton administration put forward a feeble bill in 1994 to purportedly address Superfund's worst problems. As an *Arizona Republic* editorial noted, "Instead of real reform, the proposed rewrite set up an entirely new bureaucracy to administer a new tax on commercial insurance policies and did not address the two major problems of the old law—protracted liability disputes and inflexible cleanup standards. Moreover, amendments added by congressional Democrats to require union wages on cleanup projects and to establish a trust fund to underwrite toxic-site 'investigations' by environmental activists only ensured that Superfund would become even more superexpensive."[19]

Republican senators balked: since even the president had labeled the program a "disaster," there was little point in perpetuating its worst elements. Clinton exploited the disagreement to prove to voters that the Republican Party wanted to poison America. At a November 1, 1994, campaign rally in Cleveland, Clinton declared that the Republicans who opposed his Superfund bill wanted to "leave the poison in the ground and try to put some poison in the political atmosphere. I say it's time to take the poison out of the ground and out of the political atmosphere and start building this country again and doing what's right for the people of America for a change."[20] This was not an overheated slip of the tongue; the previous day, at a rally in Pittsburgh, Clinton denounced Republicans because "they preferred to leave the poison in the ground so they would have a political issue."[21]

Once the congressional election was over, it was again safe for Clinton to denounce Superfund. In an April 6, 1995, environmental message to Congress, Clinton declared, "For far too long, far too many Superfund dollars have been spent on lawyers and not nearly enough have been spent on clean-up. I've directed my Administration to reform this program by cutting legal costs, increasing community involvement, and cleaning up toxic dumps more quickly. The reformed Superfund program will be faster, fairer, and more efficient—and it will put more land back into productive community use."[22] EPA did little or nothing to fulfill Clinton's promises.

Later that year, Superfund again became a valuable hobgoblin. In a December 18, 1995, veto message of a congressional appropriations bill, Clinton whined: "Particularly objectionable is the bill's 25 percent cut in Superfund, which would continue to expose hundreds of thousands of citizens to dangerous chemicals."[23] In reality, it was the law and the cleanup mechanism defended by Clinton that perpetually delayed most cleanups in urban America.

In his 1996 reelection campaign, an unreformed Superfund again became a success. On August 28, 1996, Clinton bragged to a Kalamazoo, Michigan, audience: "When I came into office, I vowed to strengthen and improve the Superfund's cleanups. In the last 3 years . . . we have cleaned up 197 toxic waste sites, more than in the previous 12 years. We're doing 3 times more a year than were done before."[24] The vast majority of cleanups finished in those years were actually started during the Reagan and Bush administrations. GAO found that Superfund cleanups slowed down during the Clinton administration. GAO reported in 1997 that "the time taken to select remedies has increased greatly over the years."[25]

Clinton repeatedly thwarted efforts by congressional Republicans to reform Superfund's liability mess. EPA Administrator Carole Browner gushed in a 1997 congressional hearing that "we want to protect the 'little guys,' the small businesses, the Mom-and-Pop operations, that we all agree have become unfairly entangled in Superfund litigation."[26] But the Superfund juggernaut kept dragging more and more innocent victims under its treads. In early 1999, EPA sent letters to 165 small businesses, schools, individuals, and churches in Quincy, Illinois, threatening to sue them unless they paid more than $3 million to pay for the cleanup of a city dump that had been closed 15 years before. None of the businesses were accused of violating environmental law at the time they sent their garbage to the dump. But, because the dump was later designated a Superfund site, EPA had a turkey shoot.

Mike Nobis, the general manager of Creative Printers of Quincy, Illinois, testified to Congress in September 1999 about the impact of the EPA's action: "The document [the EPA sent him] made it sound as though we were major hazardous waste dumpers. Yet, nowhere in the document did it list what waste we were accused of dumping. It only said that our trash was hauled to the landfill during the time in question and we now have to help pay for the cleanup, regardless of the fact that there was no other place to dump our trash . . . They knew many of us didn't send hazardous waste and they knew we couldn't afford to fight them. The attorney for the EPA admitted that it would cost us more to fight them in court to prove we didn't haul hazardous waste to the landfill than to just go ahead and settle. It all came down to money . . . and they had more than we did."[27] Nobis lamented, "We have some men in their late 70's and early 80's that could lose their life's savings when they should be enjoying their retirement years. They are spending their time and money paying the EPA for something they did 25 years ago that was legal."[28]

When congressmen pressured EPA to fix the Superfund liability maze, EPA insisted that they had already made sufficient adjustments to the system. Yet EPA refused to disclose precisely what standards the agency was then using to hold small businesses liable.[29]

But EPA did come up with a brilliant solution to part of the liability problem. In 1997, the EPA proposed to exempt state and local governments from most of the liability for sites they were involved with—even sites that they owned and operated. As the *Washington Post* noted, "The EPA and the Justice Department felt towns and cities were getting trashed in Superfund cleanups, so they have stepped in to help."[30] The Clinton administration's compassion on this issue appeared to be limited to fellow government employees.[31]

DICTATORSHIP OUT OF THIN AIR

On July 12, 1999, the Justice Department announced that it was suing Toyota for $58 billion because of alleged violations in the emission control system installed in late-model autos.[32] This was the largest penalty ever sought in a federal regulatory proceeding, and would have been the equivalent of confiscating all of the Toyota factories in the world. The feds sought a penalty of $27,500 for hypothetical violations on each of more than 2 million cars. EPA Chief Browner harrumphed: "Today's action shows this Administration's commitment to insure that companies will not profit from polluting and that the public health will be protected."[33]

What was Toyota's crime? The "check engine" light on the dashboards of late-model Lexuses and Toyotas did not illuminate often enough. Toyota had the highest rated in-use emission control systems of any major auto maker. EPA had no evidence that fuel vapors were actually leaking. Instead, EPA wanted Toyota to do a massive recall of millions of vehicles to modify an emissions control system that the feds had formally approved a few years earlier.

Under the 1990 amendments to the Clean Air Act, auto makers were required to get EPA approval for their catalytic converters and emission control maintenance systems. All major manufacturers complied. But, beginning in 1997, EPA began going back and demanding that auto makers pay fines for violations of rules that did not exist until the EPA made them up a few weeks before issuing its demands. Honda and Ford rolled over in 1998, paying multimillion-dollar fines and agreeing to recalls.

The issue in the Toyota case was more heresy than public health—the heresy that Toyota refused to kowtow to EPA demands. Toyota estimated that, in a worst-case scenario, the total amount of hydrocarbon evaporation from all its cars would not exceed the amount of hydrocarbons that are emitted from painting the exterior of a dozen houses.[34] The Justice Department threatened to destroy one of the world's largest car makers because of an arcane retroactive dispute over hypothetical trace amounts of possible pollutants. In the week before filing the lawsuit, the Justice Department offered to settle the charges against Toyota if the company would agree to pay a roughly $100 million fine and recall the vehicles to modify their emission control systems.[35] The difference between the $100 million settlement offer and the $58 billion penalty sought was the precise measure of federal browbeating and regulatory extortion.

The EPA had approved Toyota's emission diagnostics system in 1995. Holman Jenkins noted in the *Wall Street Journal:* "Toyota's crime, based on [1997] tests of fewer than a dozen rental cars and cars owned by employees of the California Air Resources Board, was to have a system that did not shriek alarm at every loose gas cap or other momentary escape of fuel vapors."[36] The EPA piled on to demand that Toyota recall more than two million cars sold in other states.

The changes that EPA demanded would have greatly increased the number of false positive alerts in the engine maintenance light, needlessly hassling hundreds of thousands of irate consumers who returned with their car to the dealer. On the bright side, the change would allow bureaucrats to pretend that they deserved an "outstanding" rating in their next semiannual performance evaluation.

The charges by the California Air Resources Board were heard by administrative law Judge Jaime Roman who concluded in a February 25, 2000, ruling that "there are no incremental or excess emissions from the Toyota recall class vehicles."[37] The judge found that the "overdesign" of the emissions control systems actually meant that Toyotas and Lexuses performed better than California law required. The acquittal in a California court had no influence on the Justice Department's pursuit of Toyota, even though the factual basis for the federal suit collapsed.

The torpedo fired at Toyota exemplified federal absolutism in enforcing the Clean Air Act. Shortly after the 1996 presidential election, EPA announced plans to impose entirely new standards for ozone and fine particulate emissions. Any state or county with air not as pure as the new standards demanded could lose its federal highway funds, be required to radically curtail factory operations and criminalize backyard barbecues. Browner promised that the new rules would cost less than $10 billion a year. But Clinton's Council of Economic Advisers estimated that the rules could cost $60 billion a year,[38] and economists at George Mason University's Center for the Study of Public Choice estimated that compliance with the new regs could cost $380 billion per year.[39]

Surprisingly, the new regs were expected—even by EPA's own Clean Air Science Advisory Committee—to have little or no health benefit.[40] The new regs were based largely on research done for EPA by Harvard professors. However, the EPA refused to make public the information on which it based the new standards for human exposure.[41]

EPA's actions were so extreme that even federal judges sat up and took notice. In May 1999, a federal appeals court struck down EPA's new regulations as "an unconstitutional delegation of legislative power . . . What EPA lacks is any determinate criterion for drawing lines." The court noted that EPA was "free to pick any [pollution standard] between zero and a hair below the concentrations yielding London's Killer Fog of 1952."[42] EPA Chief Browner denounced the appeals court decision as "one of the most bizarre and extreme decisions in the annals of environmental jurisprudence."[43]

In the debate over the new Clean Air regs, Clinton pushed the hottest button available. In a May 1, 1999, radio address, he declared: "We've set the toughest standards in decades for smog and soot, which will prevent millions of cases of childhood asthma."[44] Clinton's claim was ludicrous: even EPA's own experts believed that the new standards would do little to reduce the number of asthma cases.[45] Hitting a similar theme, EPA's Browner, shortly after she announced the new Clean Air Act standards, told a children's health conference: "When it comes to protecting our kids, I will not be swayed."[46]

But EPA's affection for children was like a struggling asthmatic's breathing—sporadic. On March 6, 1997, the Food and Drug Administration (FDA) announced that—in collaboration with the EPA—it planned to ban the inhalers that 30 million Americans rely on to protect their daily breath. The EPA was concerned that, because the inhalers contained trace amounts of chlorofluorocarbons (CFCs), they contributed to greenhouse gas emissions. As soon as a single non-CFC inhaler got FDA approval, the Clinton administration started the process to outlaw the 42 types of inhalers widely used in this country. (Many different inhalers are used because different people and different illnesses require different methods of treatment.) The FDA-EPA proposal generated nearly 10,000 negative responses from medical professionals and others. Health and Human Services Secretary Donna

Shalala declared that the proposal "would be more than dangerous."[47] Former Surgeon General C. Everett Koop wrote that there is "no comparison between the infinitesimal improvement in ozone depletion [that would result from the FDA's ban] and the direct impact of forced elimination of medications on 14 million American asthmatics."[48] Ben Lieberman of the Competitive Enterprise Institute noted, "Numerous medical societies raised concerns that the wide variety of CFC inhalers currently in use will be replaced with a handful of unproven substitutes that may be inadequate for some patients." But banning CFC inhalers would have given Clinton administration officials new bragging rights at international environmental conclaves. (The Clinton administration downshifted on this initiative after the backlash.)

The only thing that Clinton seemed to care about more than clean air was campaign contributions and political posturing. Clinton's ethanol policy knowingly sacrificed air quality so that he could continue the masquerade that ethanol is the agricultural equivalent of holy water.

Stumping for Iowa candidates on the eve of the 1994 congressional election, Clinton reminded farmers that he told them in 1992: "Well, if you'll vote for me, I won't just talk about ethanol. I'll go to Washington and try to do something about it."[49]

Ethanol is first and foremost a farm welfare program. A 1986 USDA study concluded that increased production of ethanol costs consumers and taxpayers roughly $4 for each $1 of extra farm income. The report stated: "Increases in consumer food expenditures caused by additional ethanol production *far exceed* the increases in farm income. Consumers would be *much better* off if they burned straight gasoline in their automobiles and paid a direct cash subsidy to farmers in the amount that net farm income would be increased by ethanol production."[50] But, because ethanol is a religious issue in farm-belt states, politicians have been willing to force other Americans to pay any price to launder money to farmers via gas tanks.

While Clinton perennially stressed ethanol's environmental benefits, the Clean Air Act of 1977 actually banned products such as ethanol. EPA announced in 1978 that "recent EPA and Department of Energy tests . . . show slight increases in nitrogen oxide emissions and substantial increases in evaporate hydrocarbon emissions" in cars using gasohol (a combination of gasoline and ethanol).[51] A 1986 USDA report noted, "Alcohol blends are significantly more volatile than alcohol-free gasolines. Evaporative emissions reported for ethanol blends are 5 percent to 220 percent above emissions for straight gasoline."[52] Ethanol in gasoline significantly increases summertime smog, especially in heavily populated areas.

But the farm lobby and Archer Daniels Midland (ADM) railroaded through a provision to the Clean Air Act amendments of 1990 that requires gasoline sold in most major metropolitan areas to contain 2 percent oxygenates. ADM is renowned for buying politicians of both parties. (ADM's initials were sometimes thought to stand for Always Delivering Money.)[53] ADM produced over half of all the ethanol used in the United States in the early to mid 1990s.

When EPA proposed its initial implementing regulations for the Clean Air Act in March 1992, the new standard for gasoline volatility would have blocked the use of ethanol during the summer in the nation's most polluted cities.[54] Bush promised to gain an exemption for ethanol but was whisked out of office by voters before he could lock in the new policy.

On June 30, 1994, Clinton announced that gasoline companies would henceforth be required to use ethanol in at least 30 percent of the reformulated gasoline (RFG) sold in polluted urban areas. Clinton justified the ethanol mandate by declaring that it would provide "thousands of new jobs for the future . . . this policy is good for our environment, our public health, and our nation's farmers—and that's good for America."[55] EPA Administrator Carol Browner claimed that "it is important to our efforts to diversify energy resources and promote energy independence."[56] Assistant Secretary of Energy Sue Tierney told a congressional panel a few days before the decision was announced that "the primary beneficiary will be ADM, since their ethanol profits would increase."[57] Assistant EPA administrator Mary Nichols conceded at the time that, as the *Washington Post* reported, "ethanol use probably will not reduce greenhouse gas emissions in the short term because the production of corn requires substantial amounts of energy, some of which results in greenhouse gas emissions."[58]

The EPA waiver for ethanol's use in gasoline was the equivalent of allowing city trash trucks to drop as much trash on the streets as they pick up from the curbsides—and to double bill their customers at the same time. Environmentalists were outraged. As *National Journal* noted, "Environmental activists cite a recent Energy Department study suggesting that the EPA rule could lead to a slight increase in pollution because of ethanol's volatility. And some state environmental officials testified at congressional hearings last spring that the mandate could worsen air quality and contribute to an increase in greenhouse gas emissions."[59] The *New York Times* editorialized: "Ethanol will not clean the air beyond what the 1990 Clean Air Act would already require . . . What the EPA's rule will do is take money from consumers and taxpayers and hand it over to Archer Daniels Midland."[60] Forty-eight U.S. senators sent a letter complaining to EPA Administrator Carol Browner stating: "This rule will create chaos in the marketplace, cause serious RFG [reformulated gasoline] deliverability problems, and unnecessarily increase the cost of RFG to consumers. Lastly, and most importantly, the rule will result in no clear environmental benefits . . . The ethanol industry is already one of the most subsidized industries in the world."[61]

Clinton ignored the criticism. However, on April 28, 1995, a federal appeals court zapped the mandate, ruling: "The sole purpose of the RFG program is to reduce air pollution, which it does through specific performance standards for reducing . . . toxics emissions. EPA admits that the [ethanol rule] will not give additional emission reductions for VOCs or toxics . . . and has even conceded that the use of ethanol might possibly make air quality worse."[62]

The court defeat did not dint Clinton's ethanol evangelicalism. Clinton declared in July 1997: "By now, all Americans should be aware of the important role ethanol plays in cleaning our air and in providing economic development for rural America."[63]

Despite such eloquent rhetoric, further evidence piled up of ethanol as an environmental bust. A National Academy of Sciences study concluded in 1999 that "it is not possible to attribute a significant portion of past reductions in smog to the use of these gasoline additives [ethanol and methyl tertiary butyl ether, commonly known as MTBE]."[64] The report also concluded that "reformulated gasoline made with ethanol is less effective [than that made with MTBE in reducing smog] . . . the overall impact of either oxygen additive in reducing ozone—a major component of smog—is very small."[65]

Most gasoline producers relied on MTBE to meet the oxygenate requirement—in part because it was much more efficient, boosted octane, and was cheaper to produce than ethanol. EPA championed both ethanol and MTBE, and continually downplayed any of the additives' adverse side effects.

Yet, from 1994 onwards, from Wisconsin to Maine, complaints arose about the adverse health effects of MTBE. In 1998, California scientists reported that MTBE had leaked into the water supply and contaminated more than 10,000 wells and two large lakes. In March 1999, California governor Gray Davis ordered that all MTBE be removed from California fuel by the year 2002. An EPA advisory panel reported in July 1999 that MTBE is a "risk to our environment and public health."[66] The panel concluded that the carcinogenic substance had contaminated between 5 and 10 percent of the drinking water supplies where MTBE was used.[67] Sen. Barbara Boxer (D-Cal.) called for a nationwide ban on the use of MTBE. Gasoline companies argued that neither ethanol nor MTBE were still necessary since new processes for reformulating gasoline greatly reduced the environmental damage from gas.

On March 20, 2000, EPA's Browner called a press conference and announced: "Americans deserve both clean air and clean water, and never one at the expense of the other."[68] Browner announced that the Clinton administration now favored ending the use of MTBE—more than five years after reports initially surfaced of MTBE's adverse health effects. But, rather than recognizing the futility of Washington dictating gasoline standards for all parts of the country, Browner announced instead that the administration would seek to persuade Congress to impose a mandate to force much greater use of ethanol. Experts estimated that such a mandate would add a billion dollars a year to the price of gasoline in California alone.[69]

SWAMP JUSTICE

In 1972, Congress passed the Clean Water Act to, among other things, reduce the pollution of navigable waters. The Army Corps of Engineers received the power to approve or deny permits to discharge dredged or fill materials into navigable waters, and Congress gave the EPA the power to veto Army Corps' permits. In 1975, a federal judge decided that this provision also applied to wetlands that were adjacent to navigable waters. Subsequent regulatory and court decisions further expanded federal power. Roughly 100 million acres of land—most of it privately owned—thereby fell under federal jurisdiction.[70] To claim that wetlands were navigable waters made little or no sense: but few judges were willing to stand in front of the regulatory juggernaut.

In August 1993, the Clinton administration announced a new policy that tightened the federal noose over private lands. The White House Office on Environmental Policy (echoing a 1988 George Bush campaign promise) proclaimed a national goal of no net loss of wetlands, creating a presumption that any citizen whose land was labeled "wet" by a federal bureaucrat lost his right to use his land. Previous wetlands definitions specifically prohibited only activities such as dumping dirt or otherwise building on so-called wetlands. But the Clinton administration announced that it was banning any activities on so-called wetlands that "have environmental effects of concern."[71] A federal attorney told an appeals court that, under the new policy, the Army Corps "could require a permit to ride a bicycle across a wetland"—though the Corps was careful not to outrage the cycling lobby.[72] A White House press release suggested that "Congress should amend the Clean Water Act to make it consistent with the agencies' rulemaking."[73] It was unusual for federal officials to declare openly that Congress should be a rubber stamp; usually, agencies expand their own power and assume that no one in Congress will notice or have the gumption to stop them.

Federal agencies prosecuted private citizens based on laws that had never been written, on memos that had never been made public, and on assumptions that could not stand the light of day. Nancy Cline, a mother of five young children, testified to Congress in 1995 about how federal bureaucrats had hounded her and her husband for years. Her husband bought 350 acres of farmland in Sonoma County, California, to establish a winery. The fact that the land had been farmed for more than half a century did not stop an official from the Army Corps from ordering the Clines to cease farming because the land had been reclassified as a wetland. The Clines were threatened with fines of $25,000 per day and imprisonment of up to one year if they continued farming. The Clines repeatedly requested meetings with Army Corps officials but were denied a chance to resolve the issue.

When the Clines refused to bow to the Army Corps' demands, the feds upped the ante and launched a criminal investigation. As Ms. Cline told the House Judiciary Committee,

> In January 1994, the FBI showed up. Obviously the Corps had no desire to discuss or resolve this issue. We were told to hire a criminal attorney . . . Their issue was power and control. Their issue was an edict from the U.S. Attorney General demanding more criminal environmental convictions in the Ninth Circuit apparently short of the prescribed quotas.
>
> The FBI and EPA interrogated neighbors, acquaintances and strangers. They asked about our religion, whether we were intelligent, did we have tempers. They asked how we treat our children.
>
> Our property was surveyed by military Blackhawk helicopters. Their cars monitored our home and our children's school. They accused Fred of paying neighbors to lie. The FBI actually told one terrified neighbor that this investigation was top secret, with national security implications. The community reeled, as did we.
>
> Our personal papers were subpoenaed. The grand jury was convened.
>
> We spent thousands of additional dollars to hire more attorneys. The Justice Department told our attorneys that—unless we would plead guilty and surrender our land they would seek a criminal indictment of both Fred and me. According to one government attorney, I was to be included because I had written a letter to the editor of a local paper in their opinion, "publicly undermining the authority of the Army Corps."[74]

In December 1994, shortly after Republicans had recaptured Congress based in part on a "Contract with America" that called for greater respect for private property rights, a Justice Department attorney informed the Clines' attorney that the government had chosen not to proceed on criminal charges.

The Army Corps has long claimed jurisdiction even over isolated wetlands that have no impact on the nation's waterways. It has justified this, in part, by the "glancing geese" test: if a migrating bird glances a wet spot below, then that spot is automatically part of interstate commerce—because a hunter in some other state might subsequently shoot the bird.[75]

In 1995, the Justice Department sued James Wilson and his development company for disturbing four little wetlands in a housing project he built in Charles County, Maryland. The Army Corps had initially approved Wilson's development plans in 1989; federal regulators subsequently changed the definition of wetlands and ordered him to cease and desist in 1990. Wilson responded by suing the federal government for violating his property rights. The feds were outraged that Wilson had some loads of dirt deposited on the land to stabilize the area where houses were to be built. At a federal trial, the feds conceded that Wilson's development was in an area that was far from pristine, and that Wilson's action caused no evident environmental damage. As a court decision noted, the land in question was "more than ten miles from the Chesapeake Bay, more than six miles from the Potomac River, and hundreds of yards from the nearest creeks."[76] The main evidence the feds offered that the land was involved in interstate commerce came from a fur trapper who testified at trial that beavers and muskrats had been hunted someplace in the county in which Wilson built: no evidence linked Wilson's site to trapping.[77] Wilson was convicted of violating the Clean Water Act and sentenced to 21 months in prison and fined $1 million; the judge imposed another $3 million fine on Wilson's company.[78]

In December 1997, a federal appeals court overturned the conviction, ruling that "the Corps' regulation of such wetlands is based solely on its definition of wetlands as 'waters of the United States'"—for which the court found no basis in the Clean Water Act.[79] On May 29, 1998, the EPA and Army Corps issued a guidance memo detailing their plans to evade the court decision. The EPA and Army Corps informed agency personnel that the decision would be completely disregarded in any area outside of the fourth circuit court of appeals (Virginia, West Virginia, Maryland, North Carolina, and South Carolina). And, even within those states, the EPA and Army Corps planned to continue prohibiting owners from using their land when the feds could argue that the land would be used "by migratory waterfowl, other game birds, or other migratory birds that are sought by hunters, bird watchers, or photographers, or are protected by international treaty, and thereby affect interstate commerce."[80] According to the Clinton administration, it still takes only a few clicks of a camera to nullify property rights.

ENDANGERED SPECIES

In 1996, Clinton praised one environmental activist: "As a direct result of her efforts to make the Endangered Species Act work better, Americans everywhere have voluntarily joined in conserving and restoring the landscapes and open spaces that surround them."[81] To preserve the law's image as one big feel-good experience, it was necessary to deny that the Endangered Species Act (ESA)— as administered by the Clinton administration—had scores of thousands of innocent human victims.

At the time ESA was enacted in 1973, most congressmen and most Americans believed that the act would apply only to high-profile cases such as bald eagles. But, while Clinton sought to invoke that image whenever possible, the ESA was a parody of its public image. Of the 938 species that have been classified as endangered, there are as many clams on the list as there are mammals (61). There are 18 types of snails, 28 types of insects, and 550 types of plants.[82] The Clinton administration perennially used the most cuddly animals to symbolize the law, even though mammals made up less than 10 percent of the officially endangered species.

The ESA can be profoundly disruptive.[83] After the Delhi Sands fly was officially listed as endangered, the Interior Department forced San Bernardino County, California, to spend more than $10 million to shift the site of a new hospital and to create a special ten-acre preserve for the flies.[84] Columnist Paul Craig Roberts noted in late 1999 that the fly has thus far "stopped the construction of a hospital, a school, a golf course, single-family housing developments, sewer and flood-control projects, an electrical substation, industrial projects, shopping centers, roads and intersections, and warehouses."[85] The *Riverside (California) Press-Enterprise* reported, "Developers can't proceed until they give up part of their land for habitat or complete two-year studies showing that the fly does not inhabit their property."[86] In August 1999, the Interior Department shocked local officials by calling for 2,200 additional acres to be designated as fly habitat. The land the feds targeted was worth more than $200 million; if it becomes fly habitat, its value will fall to a tiny fraction of that value.[87]

Federal officials administering the ESA appeared at times prejudiced against human beings. The FWS designated 77,000 acres in Riverside County, California as a "rat preserve" to protect habitat for the kangaroo rat. This southern California area was at high risk for fires—but the FWS warned homeowners that they could be sent to prison or fined $100,000 if they cleared brush from around their houses in order to reduce the danger of fires. On October 26, 1993, dozens of homes and tens of thousands of acres in Riverside County went up in flames thanks to the FWS policies. Ike Sugg of the Competitive Enterprise Institute, the most diligent and effective critic of the ESA, observed, "The designation of brush as protected habitat—and restrictions on controlled burns and other methods to keep brush down—fueled the destructiveness of the fires . . . To protect the kangaroo rat from people, the Fish and Wildlife Service prevented people from protecting themselves and their property from fire."[88] One home-owner saved his home by disobeying the FWS threats and using a tractor to create firebreaks on his land shortly after the fire broke out.

The Clinton administration used the ESA as a battering ram against private property. The National Biological Survey was launched in 1993, on the order of Interior Secretary Bruce Babbitt—after Congress refused to approve or finance the operation. The original proposal sought to give government agents unlimited power to trespass on private land to research whatever animal, plant, or bug species they might find. The proposal specifically declared that no property owner would have the right to see any biological data government agents found—or claimed to find—on his land. Instead, government would use its secret findings to invoke the Endangered Species Act and thus prohibit the owner from making any use of his land.[89]

The essence of the Endangered Species Act is that every type of threatened insect and animal must have absolute superior rights over human beings. As a Wall Street Journal editorial noted, "Enforcement of the act is being effectively steered by the BANANA: Build Absolutely Nothing Anywhere Near Any-thing."[90] Each endangered species that the government adds to its list increases the arbitrary power of Fish and Wildlife Service (FWS) agents to confiscate and control other Americans' property.

In 1995, the Supreme Court heard a case that went to the heart of the ESA's coerciveness. A Clinton administration brief in the 1995 case of Babbitt v. Sweet Home declared that "the carefully tailored 'harm' regulation . . . is limited to such actions that actually kill or injure" endangered species.[91] Actually, the Interior Department defined "harm" in a way that empowered the agency to ban almost any use of any private property within miles of where endangered species had allegedly been sighted—or might choose to reside in the future. For instance, in December 1993, the federal government banned a logging company from harvesting timber on a 73-acre private plot in Washington state because a couple of spotted owls were nesting 1.6 miles away.[92] Interior Secretary Babbitt declared in 1994: "When a species is listed, there is a freeze across all of its habitat for two to three years while we construct a habitat conservation plan which will later free up the land."[93] As the brief for the Competitive Enterprise Institute in Babbitt v. Sweet Home noted, "For purposes of this case, whether the Secretary really ever 'will later free up the land' is immaterial. The real issue is whether he has the authority to 'freeze' it in the first place."[94] Law professor Richard Epstein noted, "Under the challenged definition, any human act of productive labor can be regarded as causing harm because any such action could modify some habitat of some endangered species."[95]

The FWS can impose a fine of up to $200,000 and imprisonment for up to one year for each "take" of an endangered species—and the number of "takes" is limited solely by bureaucrats' imagination. As CEI noted in their brief, "The FWS equates 'taking' habitat with 'taking' wildlife . . . the FWS routinely uses the number of acres rather than the number of animals to determine 'take.'"[96] After the golden-cheeked warbler was labeled endangered, the ESA prohibited owners of hundreds of thousands of acres in Texas from developing their land. The ban devastated Margaret Rector, a 75-year-old retiree; the 15 acres of prime real estate she bought in 1973 as a retirement nest egg fell 95 percent in value. The FWS warned Rector in 1993: "We believe this property would be suitable habitat for the federally listed endangered golden-cheeked warbler."[97] FWS officials had not spotted any of the birds on Rector's land but because the species might perchance enjoy her land, she was banned from building on it.

The Fish and Wildlife Service announced in 1997 that it expected to soon have 18 million acres of private and state government land locked up under so-called habitat conservation plans restricting owners' use.[98] In addition, over 10 million other acres of private and public land have come under either temporary or quasi-permanent control of federal environmental dictates as a result of the Endangered Species Act. The total amount of land impacted by the ESA is equivalent to cordoning off the entire states of Massachusetts, Vermont, New Hampshire, and Connecticut. And the owners have not received a cent of compensation from the government for the nullification of their property rights. This is just fine with Secretary Bruce Babbitt, who has called for "discarding the concept of property and trying to find a different understanding of natural landscape."[99]

The federal government was empowered by the ESA to spend tax dollars to purchase key habitats to protect endangered species. However, in the first 22 years after the ESA's enactment, the feds spent barely $250 million on purchasing habitats for endangered species. The costs that the feds have imposed on private landowners are likely to be at least a hundred times larger. The recovery plan for the Spotted Owl (largely a Bush administration fiasco) was estimated to cost between $21 and $46 billion.[100]

The ESA was widely criticized for heavily burdening landowners while doing little or nothing to help targeted species. On May 6, 1998, Interior Secretary

Babbitt held a press conference beneath a bald eagle nest in Massachusetts and proclaimed: "'We can now finally prove one thing conclusively: The Endangered Species Act works. Period."[101] Babbitt announced a list of 34 endangered species that the Interior Department was planning to soon "de-list"—that is, certify as no longer endangered.[102] The Interior Department press release noted, "Critics of the act often claim that once a species is placed on the list, it stays there forever, citing that as evidence that the act is ineffective and should be weakened or even repealed. With future delistings, their argument becomes moot."[103]

But there was a glitch. The heavily covered media event was based solely on a memo that someone in the Interior Department's press office completely misunderstood.[104] Of the 34 species that Babbitt touted as success stories, 5 were already extinct. Twelve of the species should never have been listed as endangered, according to the Interior Department's own standards; their listing was attributed later to "data entry" errors. Sixteen of the species had shown improvement, but not due to anything that the Interior Department or the Endangered Species Act had done.[105] Fish and Wildlife Service director Jamie Rappaport Clark sent a letter to Congress apologizing for the error, stating that she was "personally embarrassed by [an] unfortunate error" and conceding that a number of species were being considered for delisting because of "new scientific information concerning their taxonomy or abundance."[106] Though it confessed the error to Congress, the Fish and Wildlife Service made no effort to correct the false impression its media event made on the public.

The Clinton administration approach to the Endangered Species Act presumed that landowners are implacable enemies of Mother Nature. Sam Hamilton, former U.S. Fish and Wildlife Service administrator for Texas, observed: "The incentives are wrong here. If a rare metal is on my property the value of my land goes up. But if a rare bird is on my property the value of my property goes down."[107] Dr. Larry McKinney, director of resource protection for the Texas Parks and Wildlife Department, declared: "I am convinced that more habitat for the black-capped vireo, and especially the golden-cheeked warbler, has been lost in those areas of Texas since the listing of these birds than would have been lost without the ESA at all."[108] A 1996 Environmental Defense Fund report concluded that, because of the ESA's penalties, landowners "are afraid that if they take actions that attract new endangered species to their land or increase the populations of endangered species that are already there, their 'reward' for doing so will be more regulatory restrictions on the use of their property."[109]

The issue was not whether the government should make any effort to protect endangered species—but whether merely invoking the name of an allegedly endangered fly, rat, or clam automatically conferred absolute power on federal agents. A law enacted to prevent people from killing endangered species became a license for federal agents to prevent people from living their own lives.

MISCELLANEOUS ABUSES

As environmental laws and regulations have proliferated, reporting require-ments have skyrocketed—and prosecutors sometimes seek to destroy compa-nies for the most piddling of alleged violations. Ben Lacy, the 74-year-old owner of an apple-cider-making operation in Linden, Virginia, was prosecuted by the feds for eight errors in the thousands of lines of reports he submitted between 1991 and 1993 for waste water from his cider operation and the treated sewage from the restrooms at his gift shop, which was piped into a nearby stream. At federal trial, prosecutors blocked a local environmental group from testifying that Lacy's actions did no harm to the stream. After Lacy was convicted of violating the Clean Water Act in his first trial and faced a sentence of up to 24 years and $2 million in fines, Assistant U.S. Attorney Nancy Spodick told reporters: "A lot of small companies are under the perception that the government shouldn't regulate them because they are small. I hope this serves to be a deterrent to companies big and small."[110] Federal judge Sam Wilson outraged the Justice Department by refusing to send the elderly Marine Corps veteran and highly respected pillar of the local community to prison. The *Richmond Times-Dispatch* editorialized: "The federal government clearly wanted to use the Lacy case to intimidate other small businessmen and silence criticism of federal regulation."[111] The key witness in the case was Jeff Morris, a former Lacy employee who turned state's evidence and testified that Lacy ordered employees to falsify records. After the trial, Morris admitted to a private investigator hired by Lacy's lawyers that he had lied on the stand—and said that he had been encouraged to do so by federal prosecutors. Morris stated, "It is very hard, and this was the federal government that was telling me this, it is very hard to convict someone of perjury. It is."[112] (Naturally, the prosecutors themselves faced no penalties from the Justice Department for possibly encouraging perjured testimony.) After a federal judge dismissed the original conviction and ordered a new trial, Lacy pled guilty to one misdemeanor and agreed to pay a $2,500 fine.[113] Lacy continued to insist that he was innocent but after suffering $250,000 in legal expenses to prevent the feds from destroying him, he could no longer afford to continue fighting "the biggest law firm in the world"—the U.S. Justice Department.

By contrast, in late 1997, after the U.S. Park Police effectively dumped 50 cases of confiscated beer into a tributary of the Potomac River, no charges were filed over what was a blatant violation of the Clean Water Act. A Park Police spokesman explained: "We didn't know. We were ignorant of it."[114] The beer binge was a minor violation by National Park Service standards. In the summers of 1998 and 1999, "tens of thousands of gallons of raw sewage . . . flowed untreated into the lakes and streams of Yellowstone National Park, in clear violation of the federal Clean Water Act" because of the park's outdated, unreliable sewage treatment system.[115]

Clinton's environmental policy presumed that, because the federal government is morally superior to the private sector, federal agents need unlimited power to protect and punish. However, as a November 1999 *Boston Globe* series noted, "The United States government, which acts as steward and protector of the nation's environment, is itself the worst polluter in the land. Federal agencies have contaminated more than 60,000 sites across the country and the cost of cleaning up the worst sites is officially expected to approach $300 billion, nearly five times the price of similar destruction caused by private companies."[116] Jonathan Turley, a lawyer who directs George Washington University's Environmental Crimes Project, declared that "the government remains the nation's premiere environmental felon."[117] The *Boston Globe* noted, "Federal facilities are more likely to violate water standards than private companies, EPA records show . . . Federal agencies are increasingly violating the law, with 27 percent of all government facilities out of compliance in 1996, the latest year figures were available, compared to 10 percent in 1992."[118] One EPA official told the *Boston Globe:* "The fact is the federal government is getting away with murder and the EPA is not legally or politically powerful enough to turn the tide."[119]

TWO CENTS ON GLOBAL WARMING

No survey of the environmental achievements of the Clinton administration would be complete without a few words on global warming. In his 1992 bestseller, Vice President Gore called for much higher energy prices—and for the ban of the internal combustion engine. Gore railed against automobiles: "Their cumulative impact on the global environment is posing a mortal threat to the security of every nation that is more deadly than that of any military enemy we are ever again likely to confront."[120] The Kyoto Treaty on Global Warming that the administration negotiated would require the United States to cut its annual energy consumption to 40 percent below the 1990 level. A study by

Wharton Econometric Forecasting Associates estimated that this would destroy 2.4 million jobs and cost the average American household $2,700 a year.[121]

While average temperatures may have increased slightly in the last two decades, there is no clear causal link between modern civilization and global warming. Temperatures have shifted broadly over the centuries. The United Nations Intergovernmental Panel on Climate Change concluded: "Overall, there is no evidence that extreme weather events, or climate variability, has increased, in a global sense, through the 20th century."[122] It is difficult to have confidence in long-range weather forecasts when the most sophisticated computer analyses sometimes fail to predict next-day snow storms. Manhattan Institute author Peter Huber observed, "Gore's notion of 'green' environmental values doesn't center on wilderness and wildlife in America today. It centers on computer models, the pursuit of the invisible, and the long, long term."[123] It would be folly to vest politicians with sweeping veto power over everyday life on the mere possibility that this power might generate environmental benefits in the distant future—especially considering politicians' batting record of achieving environmental triumphs in current lifetimes.

CONCLUSION

The issue is not whether businesses and others should be held liable for the injuries they inflict on other Americans or whether people should be free to poison their neighbors. Even under common law dating back centuries, people were held liable for the damage they did to others' property and health. Instead, the issue is whether the existence of environmental problems automatically nullifies all limits on government power, whether the discovery of an old junkyard is the equivalent of a national emergency that necessitates vesting absolute power in the hands of federal agents.

The environmental policies of the Clinton administration were far more effective at demonizing enemies than in protecting citizens. Clinton administration environmental policy was permeated by a disdain for evidence that the laws were failing to protect the environment and public health and were wasting vast sums of money. Instead, Clintonites were fixated on political appearances, on using law after law to grandstand, and on frightening people into running to the government for shelter.

FOURTEEN

CLINTON'S WAR ON THE SECOND AMENDMENT

"A crucial part of our job here in Washington is to help arm the American people, through our police officers, to fight crime and violence. The Brady law, in that sense, is one of the things that I'm proudest of."

—Bill Clinton, February 28, 1995[1]

BILL CLINTON HAS BEEN BY FAR THE MOST ANTI-GUN PRESIDENT in American history. In each year of his presidency, Clinton proposed or endorsed sweeping new restrictions on firearms and firearms ownership:

- In 1993, 1994, and 1999, Clinton signaled his desire to ban ownership of up to 35 million guns.
- In 1996, he championed legislation that led to the creation of 100,000 gun-ban zones around the country.
- Also in 1996, he helped enact a law that retroactively turned more than a million gun owners into felons.
- In 1997, 1998, and 1999, Clinton sought to compel tens of millions of gun owners to store their weapons in a manner that made them practically useless for self-defense against burglars.

- Clinton's FBI created an illegal national registry of all people who bought firearms after November 1998.

The Clinton administration explicitly argued before the Supreme Court that every gun owner must be presumed guilty, the same as drug dealers—simply because he should have known that guns are dangerous items subject to regulation.[2]

Each time a high-profile shooting occurred, Clinton seized the opportunity to demand new federal gun legislation—even if his proposed law would not have prevented the shooting. Clinton did everything he could to maximize people's fears about the private ownership of guns by their neighbors, young people, rural residents, et cetera. In eight years of comments about guns and firearm policy, Clinton never mentioned or conceded any case of any private citizen using a gun for self-defense.

BRADY ACT BLARNEY

When the Senate passed the Brady Handgun Violence Prevention Act in November 1993, Clinton commented that "we believe very passionately in the Brady bill, . . . I spoke about it at every campaign stop and every country crossroads in this country."[3]

The Brady Act required a five-day waiting period and a background check by the local chief law enforcement officer before a person was permitted to buy a handgun. States that already had more restrictive gun purchase legislation or instant check systems for gun buyers were exempted from the Brady Act's requirements. The law was limited to handguns because the vast majority of violent criminals used handguns, not rifles.

Clinton mentioned the Brady Act over 300 times in speeches and interviews in his first term and made the act a centerpiece of his reelection campaign. In his August 29, 1996, acceptance speech at the Democratic National Convention, Clinton proclaimed that "we stopped 60,000 felons, fugitives and stalkers from getting handguns under the Brady Bill."[4] Seven days later, speaking to supporters in Michigan City, Indiana, Clinton upped the ante, proclaiming, "We did pass the Brady Bill and 100,000 felons, fugitives and stalkers lost their handguns."[5] Why the miraculous jump in the enforcement numbers in only a week? White House Deputy Press Secretary Mary Ellen Glynn explained, in response to my inquiry, that the President "misspoke" as "he was reaching the end of a train trip."[6]

Actually, both the 60,000 and 100,000 figures were hoaxes. The Brady Act may have resulted in denying 60,000 people permission to buy a handgun at a specific store. But to claim that those people were thereby prevented from getting a gun makes as much sense as deducing the number of homeless by counting how many people have ever been turned down for a mortgage loan—regardless of whether they subsequently got a loan or found other lodging.

Few criminals bother filling out federal firearms purchase forms when they acquire weapons. A national survey of police chiefs found that 85 percent believed that the Brady Act has not prevented any criminal from obtaining a handgun from illegal sources in their jurisdictions.[7] According to a 1991 Justice Department survey of convicts, the vast majority of guns used to commit crimes are acquired illegally or on the black market.[8]

The only way that Clinton could confidently assert that 60,000 or 100,000 "felons, fugitives and stalkers" didn't get guns is if his administration had prosecuted and locked them all away. (It is a federal crime, carrying a prison sentence of ten years, for a convicted felon to attempt to purchase a handgun.) However, federal prosecutors in the first 15 months of the new law locked away only three people. A January 1996 GAO report noted, "None of the prosecutions involved prospective gun purchasers with previous convictions for violent offenses."[9]

The lack of prosecutions was especially surprising since would-be handgun buyers must supply their address in filling out the purchase application. Federal agents needed merely to drive to the person's residence and slap on the handcuffs. The Justice Department, responding to GAO criticism about the lack of prosecutions, noted that "prosecutions for false statements on handgun purchase applications are inefficient and ineffective."[10] A high-ranking Justice Department official also justified non-prosecutions because "no new resources were provided to U.S. Attorney Offices, which already must make resource allocation decisions to address competing demands."[11]

Clinton and Congress cavalierly dumped a huge administrative headache on local law enforcement when the Brady Act was passed. Dennis Martin, president of the National Association of Chiefs of Police, estimated in late 1993 that enforcement would require at least 10 million hours a year of police and law enforcement employees' time. Martin noted, "Ironically, we may expect an increase in crime as understaffed, overworked law enforcement agencies throughout the nation spend millions of hours away from patrols and crime-solving to engage in background checks not funded by the Brady bill."[12]

Nor was there any credibility to Clinton's claim that all the 60,000 or 100,000 blocked purchasers were "felons, fugitives and stalkers." GAO found that, in the first 15 months of the law's enforcement, 38 percent of would-be gun buyers had their applications rejected because of administrative reasons (primarily paperwork snafus), 7.6 percent were rejected because of traffic violations, 2 percent were rejected because of minor drug violations, and 0.8 percent were denied because they were illegal aliens.[13] Only 48.7 percent were denied as a result of felony convictions, arrests, warrants, or indictments. (Another 1 percent were denied because they were classified as "fugitives from justice;" the remainder of the denials were for reasons such as individuals adjudicated mentally defective, persons dishonorably discharged from the armed services, and individuals who have renounced their U.S. citizenship.) GAO found that the vast majority of felons denied handguns had no history of violence. In Fort Worth, Texas, only 2.3 percent of those denied handgun purchases were violent felons; nationwide, only 7 percent of the denied applicants had violent felonies on their records.[14]

Law enforcement officials in some of the jurisdictions GAO surveyed (such as Arkansas and Nevada) routinely denied handgun purchase applications based on records showing a felony arrest, even when no evidence was found of a conviction. Some jurisdictions also denied the right to buy a handgun to anyone who had ever been arrested for "minor drug offenses," regardless of whether the person was convicted.[15] Because someone was accused of possessing a joint decades ago, police could prohibit that person from ever owning a handgun for his family's self-defense.

Clinton's proudest anti-gun achievement was administered largely to gin up statistics for applause lines for his speeches. When the constitutionality of the act was challenged in 1994, the Clinton administration responded in a court brief that a local sheriff need only make a "reasonable" effort to conduct a background check; if the sheriff's department was too busy at that time, "a 'reasonable' effort may be no effort at all."[16] (The Supreme Court struck down the Brady Act as an unconstitutional violation of the Tenth Amendment in 1997, but the court's decision had no impact on the Clinton administration's Brady Act policies and pronouncements.)

As time passed, Clinton's comments on the Brady Act became increasingly visionary. The Justice Department announced on June 21, 1998, that presale handgun background checks mandated by the Brady law and by state laws resulted in 69,000 people being denied permission to purchase guns in 1997.[17] The White House issued a statement the same day in which President Clinton proclaimed that, thanks to the Brady law, "law enforcement officials have stopped hundreds of thousands of felons, fugitives and stalkers from buying handguns every year."[18] White House spokeswoman Nanda Chitre, in response to my inquiry, attributed the gaping discrepancy between the Justice Department number and the Clinton number to an "editing mistake."[19]

Yet, as in 1996, the Justice Department and Clinton should have known that their data was as flawed as an Arkansas land deal. The *Indianapolis Star* reported three days later that the Justice report overstated by more than 1,300 percent the number of handgun purchases that were blocked in Indiana in 1997.[20] Other states also signaled that federal data exaggerated the number of denials in their domain.

In an April 29, 1999, interview, Clinton declared: "Just the Brady bill alone has kept a quarter of a million people from getting guns who had questionable backgrounds."[21] Unfortunately, "questionable" often meant merely that some government employee had a question.

On July 24, 1999, Clinton told a Democratic National Committee luncheon in Aspen that "400,000 people with criminal backgrounds have not gotten a handgun because of the Brady bill."[22]

In his final State of the Union address on January 27, 2000, Clinton proclaimed that "the Brady law stopped half a million criminals from getting guns."[23]

But Clinton's claims about the number of people the Brady Act has stopped from getting guns were still a farce. In the first nine months of 1999, during which FBI computers tagged more than 23,000 potential felony cases of prohibited individuals seeking to buy guns, the Bureau of Alcohol, Tobacco and Firearms (ATF) bothered to arrest only 65 violators.[24] Only 29 people were convicted in 1999 as a result of lies about their criminal records on gun purchase applications.[25] Susan Long, co-director of the Transactional Records Access Clearinghouse at Syracuse University, testified to Congress in late 1999 that the number of cases that ATF agents "sent to federal prosecutors declined by 44 percent" between 1992 and 1998.[26] Long noted "an overall decline in the magnitude of ATF enforcement activity at all levels."

When federal officials were asked about the shortage of smoking-gun Brady success stories, their true intentions came out. According to Justice Department spokesman Gregory King, the law's objective was "to keep people from getting guns—not to increase federal prosecutions."[27] Neither the Justice Department nor the White House showed any interest in determining the number or investigating the cases of citizens who had wrongly been denied the right to purchase a handgun because of the Brady Act. For gun control advocates, this is the ultimate "harmless error." Sen. Orrin Hatch (R-Utah) observed, "Law-abiding citizens are often incorrectly denied as 'criminals' because their names or other identifying information are similar to those of criminals, triggering 'false hits' during records checks."[28] Paul Blackman of the National Rifle Association noted, "No one has a clue how many false positives are in the system. My guess would be that it would be somewhere in the neighborhood of four-fifths" of denials, based on the experience of state systems.[29]

The Clinton administration, in a deal with Congress, agreed in 1993 that the waiting requirement for handgun purchases would end after five years, after computer systems allowing for nationwide instant background checks were in place. But Clinton reneged. As the five-year period neared its end, White House aides hyped the waiting periods as the only thing standing between America and mass carnage. Clinton adviser Rahm Emanuel announced on NBC's *Meet the Press* on June 14, 1998, that "20 percent of the guns . . . used in murder are purchased within the week of the murder."[30] There was no evidence for Emanuel's assertion. White House spokeswoman Chitre later explained that Emanuel "misspoke on that one."[31]

The Brady Act prohibited law enforcement agencies from using background check information to compile registration lists of gun owners. The FBI, which runs the National Instant Check System (NICS), announced in 1998 that it intended to retain records of approved gun buyers for 18 months. (Gun owners feared that the registration list would pave the way for eventual gun confiscation, as has happened in many foreign countries.) When the NRA sued to compel the FBI to follow federal law, Clinton became indignant. In a December 5, 1998, radio address, the president denounced the NRA: "They'll stop at nothing to gut the Brady law and undermine our efforts to keep more guns from falling into the wrong hands, even though we now have five years of evidence that it works."[32] Clinton warned: "We can't go back to the days when dangerous criminals walked away from stores with new guns, no questions asked."[33] This totally misrepresented federal law prior to the enactment of the Brady Act; the Gun Control Act of 1968 required all persons who purchased a firearm from a federally licensed firearm dealer to fill out a form attesting that they had no felony convictions.

The Brady Act failed to reduce violent crime. Former Clinton administration Deputy Attorney General Philip Heymann wrote in 1997 that "none" of the decline in murder rates in the 1990s was the result of the Brady Act.[34] GAO concluded that the "Brady [Act] may not directly result in measurable reductions of gun-related crimes." Total violent crime and firearm-related violent crime have declined nationwide during the 1990s, but since 1993 crime rates have declined less in states upon which the five-day waiting period has been imposed.[35] University of Chicago professor John Lott, author of *More Guns, Less Crime,* concluded that the Brady Act is actually responsible for "significant increase in rapes and aggravated assaults" by creating impediments to victims acquiring the means to defend themselves.[36]

ASSAULTING 30 MILLION GUNS

In 1993, Clinton proposed the "Public Safety and Recreational Firearms Use Protection Act." Clinton sought to protect recreational firearms by preventing people from buying many types of guns. This was later rolled into a swollen congressional crime bill and became known as the "assault weapons ban." Clinton's campaigning for the ban quickly took on evangelical dimensions.

"Assault weapons" is a term that has little or no coherent meaning—at least as used by politicians. According to the Defense Department, an assault weapon is a rifle that is capable of both automatic (machine gun) fire and semiautomatic (one shot per trigger pull) fire. But most of the media implicitly define "assault weapon" as any politically incorrect rifle. The proposed federal ban dealt with semiautomatic rifles and pistols. Clinton sought to make so-called assault weapons appear vastly more destructive than they actually were by claiming his ban aimed at machine guns. Clinton declared on October 21, 1993, that "I so desperately want to do something to reduce the number of automatic weapons that are in the hands of teenagers on the streets of the city, assault weapons."[37] Clinton declared at a Beverly Hills reception on December 4, 1993, that "no society can go on . . . allowing huge sections of cities to be no man's lands, where the law of the automatic assault weapon controls."[38]

Ownership of machine guns has been severely restricted by the federal government since 1934, and the violent crime rate of properly registered machine gun owners is among the lowest of any group. Clinton's proposed assault weapons ban did nothing to regulate machine guns that the federal government was not already doing.

Clinton portrayed assault weapons as the preferred guns of the most demented criminals. On May 2, 1994, Clinton declared, "Five years ago, a gunman using an AK-47 killed five elementary school kids. This happens every day."[39] (No one in the subsequent five years used an AK-47 in a school killing.) On May 5, 1994, on the afternoon of the House vote on assault weapons, Clinton declared, "Members are having to choose . . . between supporting the local police in their efforts to disarm criminals who can use these weapons to kill lots of people and those who are spreading fears about the reach of this law."[40] Actually, so-called assault weapons had rarely been involved in crimes. Lieutenant Dennis Gibson of the San Diego police department estimated in 1991 that "of 3,000 firearms seized in the three-year period 1989 to 1991, only nine could be labeled assault weapons."[41] A 1993 report by the Connecticut State Police found that fewer than 2 percent of the 11,700 guns seized in the state were assault weapons.[42] Torrey Johnson of the California Bureau of Forensic Services concluded in a confidential 1993 report, "It is obvious to those of us in the state crime lab system that the presumption that [assault weapons] constitute a major threat in California is absolutely wrong."[43]

The actual details of the proposed ban made it clear that cosmetics, not public safety, was the real target. The bill banned semiautomatic guns that had grenade launchers and bayonet-mount attachments. But neither the Justice Department nor the ATF could provide a single example of either grenade launchers or bayonets attached to assault weapons being used in any violent crime in the United States. Clinton had no reason to presume that bayonet lugs induced temporary insanity among gun owners.

Clinton persuaded his Democratic colleagues that banning assault weapons would be good for them. Speaking a few days before the House vote on assault weapons, Clinton declared, "No good Member of the House or Senate, no Republican or Democrat, no rural legislator should ever fear losing their seat for voting for this bill."[44] After the assault weapons ban had been enacted and after the Democratic Party lost its controlling majority in the House of Representatives for the first time since 1954, Clinton blamed the gun lobby for the loss. Clinton complained in 1999 that "in 1994 the NRA beat somewhere between 12 and 20 of our Members . . . by scaring legitimate gun owners into thinking the Brady bill and the assault weapons ban were going to do terrible things to them."[45]

The goal of the assault weapons ban was to compel gun manufacturers to cease producing specific firearms. In that sense, the law was a stunning success: the number of bayonet lugs and grenade launchers on rifles made and sold after 1994 fell by 100 percent. Once gun manufacturers complied with the law and changed their weapon designs, Clinton pretended that Congress had passed a completely different law than it actually enacted. Clinton denounced gun makers for acting in bad faith for not ceasing production of entire lines of weapons that fully complied with the 1994 law. Beginning in 1997, he played the victim, talking as if the gun manufacturers had deceived him, betrayed the country, and, regrettably, far more sweeping prohibitions would be necessary.

In late 1997, 31 senators sent a letter to Clinton asking him to restrict the import of weapons that, though they complied with the 1994 law, served no "sporting purpose."[46] Arms importers responded by sharply increasing the number of permits for imports, fearing that the borders might soon be closed. Clinton then seized upon the large number of permit requests to justify new anti-import policies. In a November 15, 1997, radio broadcast, Clinton declared: "We know that some foreign gun manufacturers are getting around the ban by making minor modifications to their weapons that amount to nothing more than cosmetic surgery. We didn't fight as hard as we have—to pass the assault-weapons ban in the first place— only to let a few gun manufacturers sidestep our laws and undermine our progress."[47] Jose Cerda, a White House official who specialized in gun control, bragged to the *Los Angeles Times:* "We are taking the law and bending it as far as we can to capture a whole new class of guns."[48]

For Clinton, the phrase "assault weapons ban" was the most important part of the law. Clinton asserted, at a May 14, 1999, Democratic National Committee dinner, that "we abolished assault weapons" with the 1994 legislation.[49] In reality, all the existing "assault weapons" were grandfathered under the new law. Clinton's comment implied that any private ownership of assault weapons showed bad faith or was some type of loophole that must be closed. Clinton fanned confusion over the law and then exploited that confusion to delegitimize and stigmatize a large class of peaceful gun owners.

In an April 29, 1999, interview on NBC, Clinton complained, "The assault weapons ban is a good thing, but there are too many loopholes in it, and we want to close them."[50] Yet, during the original 1994 battle over the bill, Clinton denounced the "so-called camel's-nose-inside-the-tent theory. A lot of our Members are being told by folks back home that . . . today it's these assault weapons, which they don't own, and tomorrow it'll be some legitimate hunting weapon, which they do own."[51]

Was Clinton acting in good faith when he said he wanted to ban only specific military-style "assault" weapons? A few weeks after taking office in 1993, Clinton declared that "I don't believe that everyone in America needs to be able to buy a semiautomatic or an automatic weapon . . . in order to protect the rights of Americans to hunt and to practice marksmanship."[52] Since no American could legally buy an automatic weapon without a federal license and approval, his comment had meaning only regarding his desire to restrict semiautomatics. In January 1994, the Clinton administration's official federal budget presentation for fiscal year 1995 announced, "The administration also supports a ban on semiautomatic firearms."[53] If all semiautomatic guns were banned, the federal government would confiscate more than 35 million weapons. (Clinton administration officials later disavowed the statement, claiming that they didn't know how that sentence managed to get into the official budget plans of the president—as if the sentence was a typo caused by a malfunctioning spellcheck program. More likely, the statement was a trial balloon to test public reaction.)

In a June 1999, television interview exchange with a high school student, Clinton was asked: "Mr. President, I was just wondering why semiautomatic guns . . . and stuff that are obviously not used for hunting purposes are sold in stores. What purpose do they serve?"

Clinton replied: "I tried to ban them all in 1994, and we were able to ban 19 kinds of assault weapons . . . So I spent the last five years trying to get rid of all them. I think they should all be rendered illegal. They also grandfathered in those that were in existence before '94, but I think all of them ought to be taken off the markets. That's what I think. And I'm going to try to keep making progress with Congress to do that."[54] If the Democratic Party had not lost both houses of Congress in the 1994 election, Clinton likely would have pushed far more prohibitive gun legislation in the subsequent years. As it was, he bided his time, waiting for opportunities to inflame public opinion and proscribe more guns.

BANNING BULLETS

Clinton continually sought to redefine gun issues to frighten the average non-gun-owning American. Few issues showcased Clinton's demagogic talents better than "cop-killer bullets." Congress banned specific types of handgun bullets (such as those with depleted uranium) that could penetrate police armored vests in 1986; that legislation enjoyed broad support from both police organizations and the National Rifle Association. Standard police body armor is designed to stop handgun rounds—the type of bullet that police are most often exposed to. Special, much heavier body armor can also stop most rifle rounds, but the weight of such armor makes it impractical for police to wear on a daily basis.

On June 30, 1995, Clinton proposed legislation to severely restrict the types of ammunition Americans could buy. Clinton made a speech in Chicago that day and invoked the memory of a Chicago policeman, Daniel Doffyn, who had recently died of gunshot wounds. Clinton declared, "[A]s we remember Officer Doffyn, I say there is at least one more thing we must do . . . If a bullet can rip through a bulletproof vest like a knife through hot butter, then it ought to be history. We should ban it."[55] But Doffyn died after being shot in the head, as well as being shot in the chest by a bullet that passed through an opening in his vest: no bullet penetrated his body armor.[56] A month later, Clinton appealed to a group of teachers to help him "oppose [the gun lobby's] efforts to keep us from getting all these horrible police-killing bullets out of our lives."[57]

Clinton implied that the ban would affect only a tiny percentage of the ammunition sold in the United States. However, the standard he repeatedly invoked would have banned almost all rifle ammunition (except for .22 and similar rifles) and most handgun ammunition (except for small-caliber pistols).

Cop-killer bullets had a starring role in Clinton's reelection campaign. On October 24, 1996, during a campaign stop in Marrero, Louisiana, Clinton invoked the death of policeman Jerome Harrison Seaberry to boost his bullet ban. Clinton declared, "I still think we ought to ban those bullets that are built only for one purpose, to pierce the bullet-proof vests that our police officers wear." Clinton then solemnly told the crowd: "In Lake Charles, I met with that officer's widow and two beautiful, beautiful young sons. And I thought to myself, 'You know, if people like these folks here are going to put their lives on the line for us, the least we can do is tell them if they put on a bulletproof vest, it will protect them from being killed.' That's the least we can do for them."[58] But, as the *Washington Post* later reported, Seaberry died when he "was responding to a radio call for backup on Christmas night last year when 'he lost control of his vehicle, going too fast . . . hit a tree head-on and the vehicle burst into flames,' said Lake Charles Police Chief Sam Ivey."[59]

On March 5, 1997, Clinton repeated his demand to Congress: "We don't need to study this issue any more to determine what specific materials can be used to make armor-piercing bullets. We need a simple test and a straightforward ban."[60]

And then complications developed. An ATF panel, convened in response to a 1996 law and consisting of the nation's top experts, finished a draft of their study on the role of cop-killer bullets in the deaths of law enforcement officers. Their report found that no U.S. law enforcement officer "who was wearing a bullet-resistant vest died as a result of any round or ammunition having been fired from a handgun penetrating that officer's armor."[61] The study concluded that "existing laws [narrowly limiting ammunition availability] are working, and no additional legislation regarding such laws is necessary." The report observed, "To prohibit any . . . commonly used [handgun] cartridges because they might defeat a Level I bullet-resistant vest would create an unreasonable burden on the legitimate consumers of such cartridges."[62]

After the draft version of the ATF study leaked out, the Treasury Department (which oversees ATF) issued a press release denouncing the study. Treasury Department Undersecretary Raymond Kelly announced that the ATF study "is wrong and does not reflect the Treasury Department's position on cop-killer bullets."[63] The Clinton administration refused to release the study to the public. However, Clinton avoided mentioning cop-killer bullets in his speeches.

Clinton's whining about ineffective bulletproof vests may well have encouraged some police officers not to wear the vests—and thus put them in greater danger. The ATF study concluded that officers who are shot in an armed confrontation are 13.5 times more likely to be killed if they do not wear protective armor.[64] Police officer Bruce Blum complained in the *Washington Post* in 1995 (shortly before Clinton turbo-charged the issue) that the political grandstanding over so-called cop-killing bullets had made people more aware that police wear body armor. Blum blamed the controversy for the fact that, according to the FBI's Uniform Crime Reports, "the incidence of police officers being shot in the head has increased dramatically."[65]

CLINTON'S ALAMO FOR GUN CONTROL

On April 20, 1999, students Eric Harris and Dylan Klebold went on a shooting spree in Columbine High School in Littleton, Colorado. By the time they ended their 46-minute rampage by committing suicide, 12 students and 1 teacher were dead or mortally wounded.

Clinton formally proposed new gun control legislation a week after the shooting, announcing, "We have to redefine the national community so that we have a shared obligation to save children's lives."[66] First Lady Hillary Clinton proclaimed at a Rose Garden event on June 1: "As a nation, we've reacted to the shootings at Columbine High School like almost no other event . . . in recent memory. It has literally pierced the heart of America."[67] On June 9, Clinton denounced the House of Representatives for not enacting gun control legislation and demanded that "if we can still remember Littleton—it hasn't even been two months—then we ought to speak up and be heard." He labeled the House's failure to kowtow as "a classic, horrible example of how Washington is out of touch with the rest of America."[68] Clinton's 1999 gun control proposals effectively banned gun shows, prohibited people under the age of 21 from purchasing handguns, and imposed numerous other new restrictions. Clinton's proposal, by making it more difficult for people to buy firearms, would leave them more dependent on police for their own personal safety.[69] But Clinton's panacea completely ignored the gross failure of law enforcement at the scene of the crime.

Federal and Colorado officials sought to transform the Littleton disaster into a law enforcement triumph. Attorney General Janet Reno praised the local police response as "extraordinary," "a textbook" example of "how to do it the right way."[70] President Clinton declared that "we look with admiration at the . . . the police officers who rushed to the scene to save lives."[71]

Considering the prominent place that the Columbine High School shootings took in Clinton's Gun Demonology Hall of Fame, it is worth considering what actually happened that day. The excruciatingly slow response by SWAT teams and other lawmen to the killings in progress turned a multiple homicide into a historic massacre. The excuses offered by police vivified how law enforcement has no legal liability to the people they fail to protect. And federal aid to local law enforcement, by spawning the proliferation of heavily armed but often flat-footed SWAT teams, may actually have undermined public safety.

For the first four days after the shooting, the Jefferson County Sheriff's Department claimed that, as the *Denver Rocky Mountain News* reported, once the boys' attack began, Deputy Neil Gardner "ran into a [school] hallway and faced off with one of the two gun-toting teenagers. Gardner and the gunman shot it out before the Jefferson County deputy retreated to call for help."[72] Law enforcement was criticized by Denver radio hosts and others for the failure of the deputy to stand his ground. Five days after the shooting stopped, Gardner went on *Dateline NBC* and revealed that he had been outside in his patrol car, that he had driven up when he heard shooting, and that he stopped 50 yards away and fired several shots at Harris, but missed.[73] A *Time* magazine analysis published eight months after the shooting noted that Gardner "was terrified of shooting someone else by accident—and his training instructions directed that he concentrate on guarding the perimeter, so no one could escape."[74] Keeping the perpetrators confined inside the school made it unlikely that they would kill more than 2,000 people.

SWAT team members did not reach the room in Columbine High School where the killers lay until at least three hours after the shooting stopped. A badly wounded school teacher, Dave Sanders, bled to death because the SWAT team took four hours to reach the room he was in—even though students placed a large sign announcing "1 Bleeding to Death" in the window.

Jefferson County Sheriff John Stone later explained: "We had initial people there right away, but we couldn't get in. We were way outgunned."[75] Jefferson County SWAT team Commander Terry Manwaring, whose team entered the school but proceeded at a glacier-like pace, explained: "I just knew [the killers] were armed and were better equipped than we were."[76] However, the SWAT team members had flak jackets and submachine guns—far better protection and weaponry than the black trench coats, the unreliable TEC-9 handgun (which Clinton ludicrously described as an "assault pistol"), the single semiautomatic rifle, and the shotguns that Klebold and Harris had.

SWAT teams made no effort to confront the killers in action; instead, they devoted their efforts to repeatedly frisking students and marching them out of the building with their hands on their heads. Jefferson County Undersheriff John Dunaway bragged to the *Denver Post* that the evacuation of students "was about as close to perfect under the circumstances as it could be." Even though none of the SWAT teams came under hostile fire, Denver SWAT officer Jamie Smith whined: "I don't know how you could have thrown in another factor that would have made things more difficult for us."[77]

Many local SWAT teams descended on the high school parking lot and vicinity after the shooting started. Police spokesmen said most of the SWAT teams were not sent in "for fear that they might set off a new gunfight," as the *New York Times* reported.[78] Sheriff Stone justified the non-response: "We didn't want to have one SWAT team shooting another SWAT team."[79]

The police response was paralyzed by concerns for "officer safety." Steve Davis, spokesman for the Jefferson County Sheriff's Department, said, "We had no idea who was a victim and who was a suspect. And a dead police officer would not be able to help anyone."[80] Donn Kraemer of the Lakewood SWAT team explained: "If we went in and tried to take them and got shot, we would be part of the problem. We're supposed to bring order to chaos, not add to the chaos."[81] A former law enforcement officer who now helps train Colorado police observed: "Everything the SWAT teams did that day was geared around fear. A great flaw in the training for SWAT teams is that they're so worried about officer safety that they've lost their ability to fight."[82] Evan Todd, a Columbine student who was wounded in the initial attack, escaped outside and then explained to a dozen policemen exactly what was happening inside: "I described it all to them—the guns they were using, the ammo. I told them they could save lives [of the wounded still in the library if they moved in right away]. They told me to calm down and take my frustrations elsewhere."[83]

At 12:20 P.M. on the day of the shooting, police on the scene radioed that they needed to be resupplied with ammunition. SWAT teams laid down "cover fire" as they advanced toward the building. Spokesman Davis could not estimate how many shots were fired by the SWAT teams.[84] Denver attorney Jack Beam stated that the sheriff's department may be a target of lawsuits because of possible "friendly fire" casualties.[85] (Jefferson County Coroner Nancy Bodelson persuaded a Colorado judge to seal the autopsy reports on the victims—thus making it much more difficult to determine who shot whom.[86])

Clinton doggedly sought to turn the high school shooting into the Alamo for gun control. Clinton invoked the shooting almost every day from April 20 through mid-June, when the House narrowly defeated Clinton-championed gun control legislation.

Typically, Clinton sought to characterize the issue in a televised meeting with children in the White House in early June as "a special problem—problems of violence against children by guns." Clinton proudly told the children that "since I've been President, we instituted a zero tolerance for guns in schools." Harris and Klebold violated at least 17 state or federal firearms laws.[87] Yet, another law—or two—or three—would supposedly solve the problem.

While Clinton talked as if school homicides were at an epidemic level, less than one percent of youth firearm homicides occur in schools, and the number of shootings in schools had decreased in the preceding decade, according to the federal Centers for Disease Control.[88]

Clinton's reaction to Columbine fit into his continual efforts to portray police as among the most abused groups in American society. Police safety was one of Clinton's favorite pretexts for new gun restrictions. However, in a landmark study in *Applied Economics* in May 1998, economist Lawrence Southwick analyzed murder rates for police in the United States and found that a police officer's "risk of being murdered is actually less than for other people of the same age and sex."[89] In 1993, 70 police officers were killed by felons nationwide. The risk of police being killed by felons was roughly 40 percent lower than that of the comparable private population. Southwick also found that the surge in weapon sales in recent decades has actually made police safer than they otherwise would be: "In every measure used, the [increase in the total private] gun stock was significantly negatively associated with the relative risk for police . . . Apparently, more guns in civilian hands makes police relatively safer."[90] Southwick concluded that the 47 percent increase in real wages police received in recent decades made them more risk averse.

JIGGERING CONVICTIONS

The Clinton administration, in administrative and court actions, consistently acted as if gun owners had no right to a scintilla of due process.

Harold Staples of Jenks, Oklahoma, owned an AR-15, a semiautomatic rifle. The ATF raided his home, confiscated his gun, and charged him with owning an unlicensed automatic weapon, a crime that carried a prison sentence of ten years. Staples swore that, when he operated the gun, it fired only one shot per trigger pull, and functioned poorly at that. Staples was convicted; an appeals court overturned the decision. The Clinton administration appealed and, in 1994, the Supreme Court heard the case. As the brief for Staples pointed out, "Upon seizure, the AR-15 at issue was inoperable, absent critical parts and in a state of disrepair."[91] The gun was disassembled and rebuilt by federal agents with "different parts, cleaned and oiled thoroughly and fired with soft primer ammunition. The weapon was reassembled by the government with a bolt carrier which was not the bolt that originally fit this AR-15."[92] One of Staples's lawyers, Stephen Halbrook, noted that the ATF, after it confiscates a person's guns, routinely tampers with them to make them shoot automatically, and then drags the person into court on trumped-up charges.[93]

The brief for the Clinton administration asserted: "A defendant may be convicted of such offenses so long as the government proves that he knew the item at issue was highly dangerous and of a type likely to be subject to regulation."[94] To justify their claim that gun owners must be presumed guilty, the Justice Department cited cases involving the presumption of guilt under the federal Narcotics Act of 1914. Federal prosecutors argued that "one would hardly be surprised to learn that owning a gun is not an innocent act."

The Supreme Court, by a 7-2 margin, disagreed. Justice Clarence Thomas, writing for the majority, declared, "The government's position, is precisely that 'guns in general' are dangerous items. [For] the Government . . . the proposition that a defendant's knowledge that the item he possessed 'was a gun' is sufficient for a conviction."[95] Justice Thomas pilloried the Clinton administration's position: "In the Government's view, any person . . . who simply has inherited a gun from a relative and left it untouched in an attic or basement, can be subject to imprisonment, despite absolute ignorance of the gun's firing capabilities, if the gun turns out to be an automatic."

The ATF engaged in institutionalized perjury to boost its conviction rate of gun owners. The ATF's National Firearms Branch keeps the National Firearms Registration and Transfer Records—the records of all the owners of machine guns, short-barreled rifles and shotguns, and other destructive devices. Anyone found in possession of a machine gun or other prohibited device who is not listed as the owner in the official records faces ten years in prison. ATF officials testify in up to a thousand federal prosecutions a year of violators of the National Firearms Act. On October 18, 1995, Thomas Busey, chief of the ATF's National Firearms Act Branch, in a videotaped presentation at ATF headquarters, declared that "when we testify in court, we testify that the database is 100 percent accurate. That's what we testify to, and we will always testify to that. As you probably well know, that may not be 100 percent true . . . When I first came in a year ago, our error rate was between 49 and 50 percent, so you can imagine what the accuracy of the NFRTR could be, if your error rate's 49 to 50 percent."[96] By claiming that the records were 100 percent accurate, the ATF generated an illegal basis for confiscating firearms that actually were legally owned by collectors of "curios and relics"—guns more than 50 years old.[97]

The Treasury Department Inspector General investigated ATF's record system and concluded that ATF employees had intentionally destroyed records of machine gun and other registrations. Eric Larson, who testified to Congress on behalf of the Collectors Arms Dealers Association, noted, "The IG also found that ATF improperly registered NFA firearms, and that more than 100,000 NFA firearms are registered to people who are dead."[98] The ATF admitted in correspondence to Larson that the NFRTR database in 1998 "as a whole does not reflect reliable data."[99] Yet, ATF officials continue to testify in court that the database is accurate and reliable—and thus that any citizen whose firearm registration cannot be found because ATF destroyed it should be sent up the river.

OTHER ANTI-GUN GAMBITS

At Clinton's behest, Congress in September 1996 passed the Lautenberg Domestic Violence Prevention Act. Any person with a domestic violence misdemeanor on his record who was found in possession of a gun—or even a single bullet—can face a $250,000 fine and ten years in prison.[100] Experts estimated that overnight the law created one million new felons, since few people were aware of the act's requirement for people with such misdemeanors to surrender their firearms.[101] The proponents of the law talked as if it was carefully targeted against the lowest class of wife beaters. (Such violent sociopaths should have already been barred from owning firearms after collecting a felony assault conviction.) But state laws are both expansive and inconsistent in their definition of assault. In some states, a husband who mimicked Jackie Gleason and shook his fist in the air toward his wife shouting, "One of these days, Alice!" could be permanently stripped of his right to own firearms.

Dr. Peter Proctor, a forensic expert in Houston, observed: "Many domestic violence charges are false—perhaps as many as one-third where child custody or divorce issues are involved."[102] Many people who plea bargained 20 years ago on such a charge and paid a small court fine (instead of spending $5,000 in legal fees to defend themselves) could be surprised to discover that they have lost one of their constitutional rights.

Many localities now require police to make arrests when answering domestic violence calls, and some Virginia counties have seen a tripling of domestic abuse charges against women in recent years. Jeanne MacLeod, director of the Maryland Network Against Domestic Violence, stated: "I think there are many cases when women are being victimized by the mandatory arrest policies. You tell the police they have to arrest someone, and sometimes they can't tell who did what to whom, and they'll arrest both people to safeguard themselves."[103] Firearms often provide the best chance for women to defend themselves against stronger men. Sarah Thompson, a Utah doctor and gun rights activist, observed, "Since both partners are often charged in domestic violence disputes, it effectively prevents battered women from obtaining the safest and most reliable form of self defense, a gun."[104]

The Gun-Free Schools Act of 1996, also passed at Clinton's behest, created 100,000-plus federal gun-ban zones across the country. All land within a thousand feet of any school was declared a gun-ban zone—a total acreage equivalent to the entire state of Florida. Since an estimated five million Americans routinely carry guns with them in their cars or on hunting trips, the potential for arrests and convictions from roadblock dragnet searches is potentially endless. (Congress enacted this law even though the Supreme Court had struck down an almost identical law in 1995 as unconstitutional.)[105]

Clinton bragged on September 11, 1999: "We enacted a national zero tolerance policy for guns in schools, helping to expel 4,000 students for carrying guns to school."[106] But some of the expulsions were less than public safety triumphs. Tawana Dawson, a 15-year-old sophomore at Pensacola High School in Florida, was expelled in 1999 after she was detected lending a weapon to a classmate. Dawson confessed to bringing the weapon to school. The weapon was a pair of toenail clippers with a two-inch filing blade.[107] "Students have been expelled for Halloween costumes that included paper swords and fake spiked knuckles, as well as for possessing rubber bands, slingshots and toy guns—all violations of anti-weapons policies," *USA Today* reported.[108]

DISABLING GUNS
AND MAKING CRACK HOUSES SAFE

A senior White House official told the *Washington Post* in December 1999 that the Clinton administration will "prepare an all-out offensive on guns in the coming year."[109] Guns became the number one enemy for Clinton & Co. in the following months. At a March 15, 2000 anti-gun rally, Clinton declared: "Once again, we battle not just for the safety of our families, but for the soundness of our democracy."[110]

Clinton bravely took the lead in calling for mandatory trigger locks for guns in crack houses. On February 29, 2000, a six-year-old boy took a pistol from the suspected crack house where he lived with his uncle and killed a six-year-old girl at a school in Mt. Morris Township, Michigan. Clinton pounced on the shooting to demand mandatory trigger locks for all guns. In one television interview, Clinton declared: "I'm not at all sure that even a callous, irresponsible drug dealer with a 6-year-old in the house wouldn't leave a child trigger lock on a gun."[111] Vice President Gore, campaigning in the weeks before the Super Tuesday primaries, declared in a speech in Buffalo: "If there are shootings in the first grade and still [Republicans] are not willing to support child trigger locks, what will it take? Shootings in kindergarten? Shootings in nursery school?"[112] Clinton and Gore exploited the tragedy both to stir up antipathy toward all guns—and to foster the delusion that a new federal law would suddenly turn residents of crack houses into model citizens.

One of Clinton's anti-gun allies, Maryland Governor Parris Glendening inadvertently highlighted the danger of gun locks at a March 22, 2000 press conference. With the television cameras rolling, Glendening fumbled for two minutes trying to get a lock off of a gun used by the U.S. Park Police. Glendening shared a laugh with Maryland Lt. Gov. Kathleen Kennedy Townsend during his exhibition. After the National Rifle Association made a television ad showing the governor's gaffe, Glendening accused the NRA of making an "outrageous attack" on him.[113]

In December 1999, the White House announced that HUD would be bankrolling lawsuits against gun manufacturers. The culprits for the stratospheric crime rates in public housing projects had finally been discovered: Smith and Wesson, Colt, et al. The Justice Department reportedly advised HUD that there was no legal basis for HUD's involvement in the lawsuits— but to no avail.[114]

On March 17, 2000, Clinton announced that Smith and Wesson, the nation's largest gun manufacturer, had agreed to sweeping new controls over its gun designs, marketing, and new restrictions on gun buyers. Treasury Secretary Lawrence Summers hailed the settlement: "Because of the agreement reached today, fewer parents will have to bury their children."[115] HUD Secretary Cuomo, the prime architect of the deal, declared of the new specifications for firearms: "This is a product that did not exist last week . . . This will do to the [gun] industry what FedEx did to the [delivery] industry. This is a better mousetrap."[116]

For the Clinton administration, the more difficult a gun is to fire, the safer it is. This is the Rosetta Stone that is necessary to understand Clintonite claims that the "agreement" improves gun safety.

- According to a HUD press release, "Within 12 months, handguns will be designed so they cannot be readily operated by a child under 6."[117] The feds thus apply the "childproof cap" panacea to guns. However, according to a study by Duke University economist Kip Viscusi, the federal mandate for childproof caps on drug prescriptions actually resulted in an increase in fatalities since parents were lulled into a false sense of security and were more likely to fail to keep drugs securely stored away from children. Besides, while people with a headache usually have some margin of time to struggle with the top of an aspirin bottle, people confronting a burglar cannot request a time-out.

- The agreement obliges gun stores to see that "guns and bullets must be kept locked and separated."[118] There have been no reports of shootings in gun stores from customers combining guns and bullets in recent years. Perhaps HUD's negotiators have watched the Arnold Schwarzenegger movie *The Terminator* one too many times.
- The agreement requires Smith and Wesson to "not market guns in any manner designed to appeal to juveniles or criminals."[119] HUD had no evidence that Smith and Wesson had been running advertisements in prison magazines—but the provision aided the Clinton administration's efforts to cast an aura of illegitimacy around firearms.
- The agreement requires "persons under 18 to be accompanied by adults in gun stores or gun sections of stores."[120] This is an effort to classify guns as pornography—something that is so obscene that no child can be exposed to it. The Clinton administration apparently believes that a 17-year-old deer hunter cannot even be trusted with looking at a rifle in a locked case without going beserk.
- Smith and Wesson is required to "refrain from selling any modified/sporterized semi-automatic pistol of type that cannot be imported into U.S."[121] This illustrates how the Clinton administration uses each new restriction to leap-frog toward broader firearms bans. When Clinton banned imports of certain semiautomatics in 1997, he justified it because the guns violated the "spirit" of the 1994 assault weapons ban (even though such guns could be legally sold under existing federal law).
- The settlement created an "Oversight Commission . . . empowered to oversee implementation of the Agreement. The Commission will have five members selected as follows: one by manufacturers; two by city and county parties; one by state parties; one by ATF."[122] Four government officials and one private representative is the Clinton administration's idea of fairness.
- Most importantly, there is an exemption for the new design specifications for purchases by law enforcement agencies. Thus, Smith and Wesson can continue to manufacture certain types of firearms that would be otherwise banned—but only for government employees.

Thanks to the threat of a lawsuit from HUD and from local governments, Smith and Wesson will impose draconian new restrictions on retailers selling its guns and a de facto ban on its guns from being sold at most gun shows. In an op-ed published two days after the agreement was announced, Cuomo declared: "This agreement sends a historic, yet simple, message. We can accomplish so much more through cooperation and negotiation than we can through confrontation and denigration." Yet the entire basis of the agreement was HUD's extortionate threat to bleed gun companies through endless bogus lawsuits. (Several such lawsuits by city governments had already been thrown out of court on summary judgment because of their complete lack of merit.) It is bizarre that Cuomo became the Clinton administration's point man in the attack on "gun violence"—since, in many big cities, HUD-financed public housing projects are both the center of the drug trade and the areas with the highest murder rates.

SELF-DEFENSE:
THE USE THAT CLINTON FORGOT

In his years in office, Clinton never made a single public remark recognizing that any citizen has ever legitimately used a firearm for self-defense.

Clinton declared in 1995: "A crucial part of our job here in Washington is to help arm the American people, through our police officers, to fight crime and violence. The Brady law, in that sense, is one of the things that I'm proudest of."[123] The surest way to "help arm the American people" is to block citizens' access to guns while deluging police departments with federal grants so that they can upgrade their armaments. Yet, armed citizens, acting in self-defense, kill three times as many criminals each year as do police officers.[124]

In his December 5, 1998, radio address calling for a reimposition of a waiting period for handgun purchases, Clinton declared: "We must do even more to support the people [the police] and the laws that protect our children and families."[125] Clinton implied that delaying or denying people's access to firearms was harmless since no citizen ever defended his own family with a firearm.

During a June 4, 1999, television interview with schoolchildren, Clinton agreed with a young girl's suggestion that "it was important to raise the price of weapons as high as possible."[126] Clinton desired to price self-defense out of the reach of as many Americans as possible.

Clinton's disdain for firearms was made stark in a national gun buying crusade that HUD launched in late 1999. "Every gun turned in through a buy-back program means potentially one less tragedy," Clinton declared at a

September 9, 1999, White House photo op with mayors and police chiefs.[127] Clinton announced that HUD would be allocating a $15 million slush fund to buy up to 300,000 guns from private citizens. The program presumed that every gun removed from private ownership made America a safer place.

But, as Prof. Gary Kleck, a criminologist at Florida State University, observed, "Support for turn-in programs among government officials yields real political benefits, in the form of favorable press coverage and positive feedback from gun control supporters. . . . Nevertheless, these programs have no demonstrable impact on crime."[128] "Pretty much, globally, across the board, all of the research shows they're ineffective. You may have a 60-year-old man who's had a gun sitting in the back of his closet for the last 40 years. It either doesn't work or it's old," said Tonya Aultman-Bettridge of the University of Colorado's Center for the Study and Prevention of Violence.[129] Also, Clinton's gun buyback initiative was undercut by police departments dumping tens of thousands of used revolvers onto the private market after they used federal funds and other money to buy fancy new semiautomatics.[130]

According to several national studies, guns are used by private citizens to prevent crimes roughly two million times per year.[131] Economist John Lott concluded that "of all the methods studied so far by economists, the carrying of concealed handguns appears to be the most cost-effective method for reducing crime."[132]

SPORTING WITH FREEDOM

Throughout his presidency, Clinton snubbed the higher political purpose behind the Second Amendment.

On May 5, 1994, after the House of Representatives voted to ban assault weapons, Clinton declared, "Most importantly, that is what the American people want, the right to be safe and secure without having their freedoms taken away by criminals or by an unresponsive or unreasoning National Government."[133] For Clinton, the only threat that government poses to freedom is being insufficiently restrictive.

Clinton's view of the Second Amendment received an ice-water dousing from a March 30, 1999, decision by federal judge Sam Cummings. Judge Cummings struck down as unconstitutional a provision in a 1994 law that routinely turned husbands and others targeted by domestic restraining orders into felons.[134]

In many states, domestic restraining orders are issued almost automatically as part of divorce proceedings. As Judge Cummings noted, thanks to the 1994 federal law, "a person can lose his Second Amendment rights not because he has committed some wrong in the past, or because a judge finds he may commit some crime in the future, but merely because he is in a divorce proceeding."[135] And because millions of Americans get divorced each year, this creates the opportunity for the Justice Department to wrongfully prosecute many peaceful gun owners.

Cummings explained the historical origins of the Second Amendment: "The individual right to bear arms, a right recognized in both England and the Colonies, was a crucial factor in the Colonists' victory over the British Army in the Revolutionary War . . . A foundation of American political thought during the Revolutionary period was the well-justified concern about political corruption and governmental tyranny."[136] Cummings quoted James Madison, who, writing in *Federalist*, Number 46, derided European despotisms "afraid to trust the people with arms." Cummings also quoted Patrick Henry's classic declaration: "The great object is that every man be armed . . . everyone who is able may have a gun."

The Clinton administration, outraged at Judge Cummings' decision, took the case to the Fifth Circuit Court of Appeals. The Justice Department brief asserted: "Of course . . . there should be no doubt that the Second Amendment does not grant a right to bear arms apart from militia service . . . The Amendment was enacted specifically to benefit the states, by ensuring that the federal government would not thwart their ability to organize and regulate local militia. Rather, an individual has the right to bear arms only insofar as the right advances the state's interest in a 'well-regulated Militia.'"[137] The position of the Clinton administration flew in the face of the consensus of most law journal articles in recent decades on this subject; even Harvard law professor Lawrence Tribe recently conceded that the Second Amendment recognizes the right of individuals to own firearms.[138] The ten amendments of the Bill of Rights recognize the rights of individuals; the Clinton administration did not even attempt to explain why the Second Amendment alone was a charter of right only for governments.

CONCLUSION

Clinton showed the classic mindset of a gun controller: obsessively focusing on the next step of control rather than on the dismal failure of all the previous legislation on the books. The solution was always another law, not a re-thinking of the attempt to achieve perfect safety through creeping prohibition. The problem was always the behavior that the government could not yet punish, not all the failures of previous edicts.

Underlying almost everything Clinton did on guns was the belief that no citizen should be allowed to own the means to resist government power. According to Clinton, the only good guns are those in the hands of government agents. Clinton's policies aimed to leave private citizens in servile dependency on government employees for the preservation of their own lives.

For Clinton, every dispute over gun control was a simple question of good versus evil. Clinton was not against guns per se; he proudly claimed that his administration bankrolled 100,000 new police officers. For Clinton, the question of whether a gun is good or evil depends simply on whether a government employee's finger is on the trigger.

Gun control laws ultimately rest on the trustworthiness of the political ruling class. Every lie or deception that government officials use regarding firearms undermines the legitimacy of restrictions on peaceful citizens' right to own the means of self-defense.

Clinton perennially denounced the "loopholes" in federal gun laws. But the ultimate loophole is freedom: the principle that citizens should not be forced to be dependent on often lackadaisical government employees for their own safety and survival. Every restriction on citizens' rights to acquire and carry firearms means increasing citizens' subordination to government employees who are authorized to carry such weapons.

FIFTEEN

WACO

*"I do not think the United States government is responsible for
the fact that a bunch of fanatics decided to kill themselves."*
—President Bill Clinton, April 23, 1993[1]

WACO IS THE PREEMINENT SYMBOL of government out of control, of law
enforcement turning into a marauding army, and of federal agencies acting as if
they are responsible to no one. Waco is also a classic example of the Clinton
administration continually spinning its way out of a catastrophe, showing how
any problem can be "solved" if the truth is sufficiently delayed and rationed.

SHOWTIME FOR THE ATF

The investigation of David Koresh by the Bureau of Alcohol, Tobacco and
Firearms (ATF) began in the final year of the Bush administration. ATF agent
Davy Aguilera visited Koresh's gun dealer, Henry McMahon, in July 1992 and
raised questions about whether Koresh and his Branch Davidian followers were
violating the National Firearms Act by illegally converting semiautomatic
firearms to fully automatic weapons. The dealer sought to resolve the problem
by picking up the phone and dialing Koresh. When Koresh heard the agent's
concerns, he invited the agent to visit the Davidians' residence and carry out an
inspection on the spot. Aguilera refused the invitation.[2]

Seven months later, agent Aguilera submitted an affidavit to a federal magistrate alleging that the Davidians were violating federal firearms laws. The affidavit dealt at length with the Davidians' unusual religious practices and polygamy, as well as their hostility to the federal government. Aguilera mentioned reports that "clandestine" publications such as *Shotgun News* (a widely read gun publication) and a Gun Owners of America video criticizing the ATF had been spotted inside the Davidians' residence. (A subsequent congressional investigation concluded that that "the affidavit . . . contained an incredible number of false statements.")[3]

In early January 1993, the ATF rented a house near the Davidians' sprawling, ramshackle, wooden home to use as an undercover surveillance post. Eight ATF agents were stationed in the building. The Davidians immediately became suspicious when their new neighbors—who were in their 30s, carried briefcases, and drove late-model cars—claimed to be college students.

The ATF could easily have arrested Koresh and, after he was in custody, carried out a peaceful search of the Davidians' home. Koresh routinely went into nearby Waco on shopping trips and regularly jogged outside of the building. On February 19, nine days before the eventual raid, two undercover ATF agents (recognized as such by Koresh and other Davidians) knocked on the door of the Davidian residence and invited Koresh to go shooting. Koresh, two other Davidians, and the two agents proceeded to have a pleasant time shooting with two AR-15s (so-called assault rifles), an ATF agent's .38 Super pistol, and two Sig-Sauer semiautomatic pistols. Koresh provided much of the ammo for the plinking. The undercover agents' official report noted: "Mr. Koresh stated that he believed that every person had the right to own firearms and protect their homes."[4]

Yet, the ATF still insisted that Koresh could not be arrested without a small army—and lots of accompanying television cameras. A congressional investigation subsequently concluded: "The ATF deliberately chose not to arrest Koresh outside the Davidian residence and instead determined to use a dynamic entry approach. The bias toward the use of force may in large part be explained by a culture within ATF . . . Management initiatives, promotional criteria, training, and a broad range of other cultural factors point to ATF's propensity to engage in aggressive law enforcement."[5] The more force the ATF used in attacking the Davidians, the easier it would be to subsequently vilify them in the national press and in federal court.

The ATF received extensive aid and training from the U.S. military before launching its raid. The Posse Comitatus Act of 1878 prohibits any involvement of the U.S. military with domestic law enforcement. In 1981, Congress created an exception to this ban for cases involving narcotics. ATF officials were told the U.S. military could not aid them unless there was a "drug nexus." A few days later, the ATF informed U.S. military officials that they suspected that the Davidians had a methamphetamine lab in their basement.[6] ATF agents were then trained in close-quarters combat. The ATF also called in military helicopters from the Texas National Guard to assist in their assault. The ATF requested that the military supply it with "100 gas masks, 500 sandbags, 90 sleeping bags, 15 night-vision goggles, a water tank truck, ten tents (including one for 'VIP sleeping'), along with electric generators and smoke generators 'to cover two square kilometers with concealment smoke.'"[7] The drug charge vanished immediately after the raid; federal prosecutors never raised the issue at the Davidians' 1994 trial. A subsequent congressional investigation noted, "The only consistent mention of any drug activity by Branch Davidians in any of the ATF Waco documents is in requests for military assistance which required drug activity to justify military intervention and assistance."[8]

The ATF faced congressional appropriations hearings shortly after the planned raid. The agency had been badly embarrassed by a television news magazine episode in January 1993 detailing sexual harassment by agency supervisors.[9] The ATF, which alerted several television stations to provide coverage of its triumphant raid, sought to grab a big cache of weapons to impress Congress. CBS's *60 Minutes* later reported: "Almost all the agents we talked to said they believe the initial attack on that cult in Waco was a publicity stunt—the main goal of which was to improve ATF's tarnished image."[10]

The ATF raid required the element of surprise to succeed. ATF undercover agent Robert Rodriguez was inside the Davidian building, attending a Bible study class with Koresh, on the morning of February 28, 1993, when Koresh received warning of the imminent raid from a Davidian who had stopped to help a lost television cameraman. Koresh, obviously agitated, declared to Rodriguez: "Robert, neither the ATF or the National Guard will ever get me." Koresh had long suspected that Rodriguez was an undercover agent but allowed him to leave the building prior to the raid. Rodriguez raced to the undercover house and phoned raid commander Chuck Sarabyn: "Chuck, they know. They know we're coming."[11]

Forty-five minutes later, 76 ATF agents roared up to the front of the Branch Davidians' residence in two large cattle trailers, and then shouted "ShowTime!" as they raced out for the attack. The ATF planned for one group of agents to storm the front door while a second group carried ladders and smashed in through second-story windows. A subsequent congressional investigation noted, "There was little else to the plan and, importantly, little or no discussion of what might go wrong."[12]

When Koresh saw the cattle trailers pull up and ATF agents dressed in military-style uniforms race out, he opened the front door and asked, "Can't we talk about this? There's women and children in here."[13] The ATF answered with a hail of bullets. Koresh was hit in two places, and his father-in-law, standing behind him, was mortally wounded.

While ATF agents assaulted the front of the building, other ATF agents in Texas National Guard helicopters opened fire from above. One elderly Branch Davidian died when he was shot while lying in his bed on the upstairs floor; bullet holes in the ceiling of his room indicated that the shots entered from above. Wayne Martin, Koresh's top aide, called 911 and frantically complained "Another chopper with more people and more guns going off. Here they come!"[14]

The raid went awry; after the shooting stopped, 4 ATF agents were dead, 16 were wounded, and six Davidians were dead. After a bitter gun battle, the Davidians agreed to a cease-fire and permitted the ATF agents to retreat out of the area. Many ATF agents had run out of ammunition, in part because of their wild firing. The Davidians allowed the ATF agents to gather their dead and wounded and withdraw from the scene. The fact that the Davidians limited the carnage they inflicted was quickly swept aside in the coming weeks because it did not fit the feds' attempt to demonize the Davidians.

ATF agent Roland Ballesteros, one of the first agents out of the cattle trailer, later told the Texas Rangers that he believed federal agents fired the first shots—perhaps to kill five dogs out front to make sure that none of the agents got their tails bitten.[15]

ATF Director Steven Higgins claimed in the subsequent days that ATF agents had been "ambushed."[16] However, as the siege of the surviving Davidians dragged on, bitter ATF agents confided to reporters that raid commanders announced, "They know we are coming! Hurry up!" before the agents left their staging area. The ATF raid co-commander, Phil Chojnacki, later claimed that when ATF agent Rodriguez phoned in his warning—"They know we're coming!"—he thought that Koresh believed they were coming in a "metaphysical sense," not in an actual raid.[17]

ATF officials later claimed that no one crafted a formal, written raid plan prior to launching the largest military-style attack in the agency's history. As early as 36 hours after the initial raid, the government abandoned routine law enforcement procedure to avoid gathering potentially embarrassing evidence. According to a confidential September 17, 1993, Treasury Department memo, the ATF had initiated a shooting review on March 1 and "immediately determined that these stories [of agents involved] did not add up."[18] Justice Department attorney Bill Johnston "at this point advised [ATF supervisor Dan] Hartnett to stop the ATF shooting review because ATF was creating" exculpatory material that might undermine the government's prosecution of the Davidians. No ATF agents made written statements after a raid in which four ATF agents died.

On April 14, 1993, Treasury Department Assistant General Counsel Robert McNamara sent a memo to several top-ranking Treasury officials stating that the Justice Department "does not want Treasury to conduct any interviews or have discussions with any of the participants who may be potential witnesses" because "anything negative, even preliminary, could be grist for the defense mill."[19] The memo noted, "While we may be able to wait for some of [the witnesses] to have testified in the criminal trial, the passage of time will dim memories." The Justice Department also warned the Treasury Department not to contact outside experts to analyze the original raid: "DOJ does not want us to generate gratuitous 'expert witness' materials; the prosecutors are concerned that these people won't have all the facts upon which to base a thoughtful opinion and could play into defense hands."[20]

THE FBI TO THE RESCUE

After the ATF botched the initial assault, the FBI's Hostage Rescue Team was called in to take charge and begin surrender negotiations. When a group of Davidians came out in the first days of the siege, all of the adults were quickly arrested, slapped into handcuffs and leg irons, and paraded in front of the television cameras in bright orange prisoner suits. Dick DeGuerin, David Koresh's attorney, complained, "The first two ladies that came out, one of them was 77 years old and practically blind. She was charged with a false affidavit, with having participated in the shooting that occurred on February 28. An agent actually testified that she held a gun and pointed it. She . . . just couldn't have done it."[21] Davidians still inside were also agitated by the fact that the authorities had taken away the personal Bibles from those who exited.[22]

After the first weeks of the siege, FBI spokesmen bitterly complained that none of the Branch Davidians would come out and surrender. However, in at least seven instances, FBI agents threw flash-bang hand grenades—which emit a deafening explosion and blinding flash—at people who had left the residence, effectively driving them back into the building. FBI agents at Waco sought permission from headquarters to shoot Branch Davidians who were leaving the building—regardless of whether they posed a direct threat to federal agents.[23]

The FBI placed a stranglehold on communications with the Davidians. Many Davidians' families on the outside sought to contact their relatives, hoping to be able to talk them into coming out peacefully. The FBI prohibited all such calls. McLennan County Sheriff Jack Harwell had dealt with Koresh amicably numerous times in the past and was trusted by the Davidians. Despite Harwell's long record of winning the confidence of Koresh and the Davidians, he did not play a significant role in resolving the stalemate. The Davidians had far more respect for the Texas Rangers than they had for federal law enforcement. But the FBI barred the Rangers from any constructive role in resolving the confrontation. Both the ATF and the FBI were intent on portraying Davidians as a group that murdered federal agents because they hated all law enforcement. If the local sheriff or the Texas Rangers had negotiated a peaceful settlement, the ATF's violent raid would have looked even more unprovoked in a federal courtroom.

On the day after the final assault on the Davidians' home, President Clinton declared: "Given [Koresh's] inclination toward violence and in an effort to protect his young hostages, no provocative actions were taken for more than seven weeks by federal agents against the compound."[24] Actually, the FBI was split between its negotiators and its tactical side during the 51-day siege. While the negotiators sought to win Koresh's trust and make him confident that he could gain a fair trial if he surrendered, other FBI agents used tanks to crush the Davidians' cars in front of the building, to crush the children's bicycles and race carts, and to flatten the Davidians' cemetery. The tanks were used aggressively during the siege in violation of the direct orders of FBI Chief William Sessions.[25] The tactical team set up massive amplifiers and blasted the Davidians with around-the-clock recordings of sound tapes of rabbits being slaughtered and Nancy Sinatra singing. The FBI also targeted the premises with flood lights and cut off its power and water. (Attorney General Janet Reno later justified her final assault because she had been told that "conditions were deteriorating" on the inside—just as the FBI intended.)[26] Lawyer DeGuerin later noted: "Increasing the pressure on Koresh had the effect of bonding [the Davidians] closer together. It played right into the apocalyptic vision they had."[27]

On April 17, 1993, an FBI consultant sent a memo to high-ranking FBI officials warning that the agency's image would suffer if the siege continued: "The authority of the FBI in all its operations will continue to weaken, and the press will focus increasingly on whether the situation might have called for a more courageous approach."[28]

At 5:56 A.M., April 19, 1993, FBI chief negotiator Byron Sage phoned into the Davidian's residence and announced: "We are in the process of putting tear gas into the building. This is not an assault. We will not enter the building."[29] Two tanks drove up to the side of the Davidian's residence, smashed boom-like arms through its walls, and began pumping the residence full of a combination of CS gas and methyl chloride. At the same time, other tanks and Bradley Fighting Vehicles maneuvered around the Davidians' home; grenade launchers on those vehicles fired almost 400 ferret rounds of CS through the thin wooden walls and the windows of the building. Throughout the morning, FBI loud-speakers blared: "This is not an assault."

The FBI originally planned to gas the building incrementally over a 48-hour period. A few minutes after the FBI gas attack began, the Davidians allegedly fired upon the tanks injecting the gas into their home. (The Pentagon subsequently refused to provide any damage reports for the tanks it provided the FBI.) The FBI then greatly accelerated its gassing—injecting all the gas it planned to use over two days in a six-hour period. FBI Commander Jeffrey Jamar later stated that he believed before the final assault that the chances of the Davidians' firing on the tanks was 99 percent, so the speedup of the gassing of the Davidians' home was a virtual certainty.[30]

FBI Director Sessions told a congressional committee shortly after the assault: "CS is non-lethal, and studies have shown that it is not harmful to adults or children."[31] However, in a meeting shortly before she approved the raid, Attorney General Reno was warned that CS gas could cause "some people to panic. Mothers may run off and leave infants."[32]

CS gas can kill. United Nations officials estimated that the use of CS gas resulted in 44 fatalities in the Gaza Strip in 1988, as well as over 1,200 injuries and numerous miscarriages.[33] Benjamin Garrett, executive director the Chemical and Biological Arms Control Institute in Alexandria, Virginia, observed that the CS gas "would have panicked the children. Their eyes would have involuntarily shut. Their skin would have been burning. They would have been gasping for air and coughing wildly. Eventually, they would have been overcome with vomiting in a final hell."[34] A subsequent analysis concluded that many areas of the Davidians' residence were saturated with doses of CS and methyl chloride that were nearly double the levels considered "an immediate risk to life and health."[35] Chemistry professor George Uhlig later testified that the gassing may have turned the poorly ventilated area where many of the children's bodies were found "into an area similar to one of the gas chambers used by the Nazis at Auschwitz."[36] Uhlig estimated that "there was a 60 to 70 percent chance that the gases used to propel the poison powder 'suffocated the children early on' in the FBI assault."[37] A few months earlier, U.S. government officials signed an international Chemical Weapons Convention treaty pledging never to use CS gas against enemy soldiers. But the treaty contained an exemption that entitled governments to use CS on their own subjects.[38]

FBI Deputy Director Floyd Clarke told Congress nine days after the assault that the FBI's plan was to "immediately and totally immerse the place in gas, and throw in flash-bangs which would disorient them . . . and cause people to . . . think, if not rationally, at least instinctively, and perhaps give them a way to come out."[39] The FBI assumed that maximizing terror inside the building would make people come out and surrender to the government.

After four and a half hours of gassing, there were no signs that the Davidians would be coming out. The FBI was running low on CS grenades and had put out an emergency request to Houston for resupply. The FBI knew that nearly a hundred people were still inside the building. And, after hours of exposure to CS, many of these people would likely have been semiparalyzed. A 1975 U.S. Army publication on the effects of CS gas noted, "Generally, persons reacting to CS are incapable of executing organized and concerted actions, and excessive exposure to CS may make them incapable of vacating the area."[40]

At this point, the FBI tank drivers received the order to demolish the building. In the next hour, the tanks smashed into the residence eight times and collapsed at least 25 percent of the Davidians' home.[41] The FBI's Clarke later admitted that "the destruction of the building was part of the ultimate plan" for bringing the siege to an end.[42] FBI commanders, in a post-action report, recommended that the two agents in the tank that did the most to destroy the building receive special medals; the official report stated, "At mid-morning . . . [the two agents] were given the mission of slowly and methodically beginning dismantling . . . the gymnasium."[43] The *Dallas Morning News* summarized government documents on the tank assault: "Just before noon, [FBI on-scene commander Dick] Rogers ordered tanks in front to drive deep [into the building] toward the compound tower. At its base was a concrete room where officials believed the 'hostiles' were hiding, records show."[44] Harvard University professor of law and psychiatry Alan Stone, one of the experts brought in by the Justice Department in 1993 to evaluate the agency's action at Waco, noted, "Some of the government's actions may have killed people before the fire started. I cannot tell whether the tanks knocked down places where people were already. I don't know if there were people in there crushed by the collapsing building as a result of FBI tanks plowing into the structure before the fire started."[45]

Around noon, fires broke out. Within a few minutes, the building was a raging inferno.

The FBI knew that the Davidians were lighting and heating their residence with candles and kerosene lamps and had bales of hay around the windows; also, the wooden building was as dry as tinder.[46] The FBI realized from the first that their operation posed a significant risk of fire. As former federal lawyer David

Hardy concluded from examining confidential FBI documents provided in response to his Freedom of Information Act (FOIA) requests, "There is some evidence suggesting that ending the siege by starting a fire was being considered. FBI had ended an earlier siege by firing illuminating [pyrotechnic] rounds into the building. An Army memo obtained under FOIA shows that FBI requested training for their 40mm grenade launchers. Two types of ammunition were to be used; the usual target/practice rounds . . . and illuminating rounds. It's hard to see much use for illuminating when a building is surrounded by floodlights."[47]

A few minutes after the fire started, a nearby resident called 911 and a local volunteer fire department promptly dispatched trucks to the scene. The FBI stopped the trucks far from the burning building, claiming that it was not safe to allow them to get any closer because the Davidians might shoot people dousing the fire that was killing them. The FBI's "fire plan" consisted of preventing fire trucks from coming close to the Davidians' home until all fires were out.[48] The official plan for the FBI's assault that day included a list of nearby hospitals with burn units.[49] The FBI was aware of the possibility of a fire during the final assault; however, notes from a phone call from FBI officials in Waco to FBI headquarters on April 9 specified that "there would be no plan to fight a fire should one develop in the Davidian compound."[50]

Eighty bodies were discovered in the rubble.

Federal officials quickly disavowed any responsibility for the fire. But a U.S. Army field manual warned: "When using the dry agent CS1, do not discharge indoors. Accumulating dust may explode when exposed to spark or open flame." The flash-bang grenades the FBI used were another possible incendiary. A Fitchburg, Massachusetts, SWAT team raided an apartment building in 1996 and used flash-bang grenades to terrify and disorient people inside; one flash-bang set fire to a couch, the building burned down, and 24 people were left homeless.[51] The FBI's Larry Potts, who supervised the standoff from the FBI's Washington headquarters, later testified: "The autopsies revealed that no one was harmed by the tear gas or had toxic levels of any component of tear gas in their systems."[52] Actually, the autopsies showed no such thing, since there was too little left of most of the corpses to determine the cause of death.

Even before the fires were out, federal spokesmen raced to portray the Davidians' deaths as a mass suicide. However, the government may have provided more assistance to the Grim Reaper than the FBI would like to admit. New infrared footage from an FBI plane (shown in a 1999 film *Waco: A New Revelation*), circling 9,000 feet above the Davidians' home on the final day, indicates that federal agents unleashed automatic weapons fire at or into the back of the Branch Davidians' home, both shortly before and just after the fire broke out. The FBI may have attempted to keep the Davidians inside while its tanks crushed in the walls and collapsed the roofs—long after the air inside was nearly unbreathable because of the six-hour gas attack.

According to former CIA Officer Gene Cullen, members of the U.S. military's Delta Force commando unit were "present, up front and close" in the tanks during the final day's action at Waco.[53] Cullen said that Delta Force members bragged to him of their role when he subsequently served with them in Europe. James Francis Jr., chairman of the Texas Department of Public Safety, confirmed in 1999 that there was evidence that the Delta Force participated in the final assault against the Davidians.[54]

Congressional investigators in 1999 were stunned when, in response to their inquiries into the final day at Waco, federal agencies invoked "national security." The *Dallas Morning News* reported in September 1999: "The military has estimated that at least 6,000 pages of its documents are classified, and CIA, FBI, Treasury, ATF and Justice Department officials have indicated that their agencies have a number of secret documents relating to the standoff."[55] The Texas Department of Public Safety in September 1999 blocked the release of a report listing all the evidence they collected after the fire because the information contained military secrets.[56] The military may have been testing new weapons on American citizens during the standoff.

While the fire still burned, FBI tanks, using bulldozer plows, pushed doors, remaining walls, and other items in the vicinity into the raging fire. A few weeks later, the FBI razed the crime scene.[57] A former arson investigator for the ATF, whose wife was still on the ATF payroll and whose business cards included the ATF insignia, came in and did an "independent investigation" that supposedly proved the Davidians started the fire; however, this investigation was later widely criticized as a slapdash job with a preordained conclusion (which the investigator denied).[58] Lawyers for surviving Davidians complained that the destruction of the crime scene "prevented examination of the blast hole in the ceiling, the scraping and removal of the remains of the building including concrete foundation slabs and dirt which contained thousands of expended bullet slugs from government firearms, evidence of lethal chemicals, accelerants and other dangerous elements used in the assault and other evidence."[59]

On the day after the Waco fire, the FBI's Larry Potts explained the rationale for the final onslaught: "Those people thumbed their nose at law enforcement."[60] After the fire burned itself out, FBI supervisors proposed giving "substantial cash incentive awards" and medals to all the Hostage Rescue Team agents for their "brave and selfless actions." FBI headquarters spiked the idea.[61]

Attorney General Janet Reno went on *Nightline* the evening of the Waco fire and announced: "I made the decision. I'm accountable. The buck stops with me."[62] Reno then asserted that the fiery end was all somebody else's fault: "I don't think anybody has ever dealt with a David Koresh, who would purposely set people afire in that number." *Nightline* host Ted Koppel asked Reno why the feds used "tanks to ram the compound down." Reno replied, "I think that what we were trying to do was to give everybody an opportunity to come out in the *most unobtrusive way* possible, not with a frontal assault."[63]

At a press conference the day after the fire, Clinton attacked Koresh: "The bureau's efforts were ultimately unavailing because the individual with whom they were dealing, David Koresh, was dangerous, irrational, and probably insane. Mr. Koresh's response to the demands of his surrender by Federal agents was to destroy himself and murder the children who were his captives as well as all the other people there who did not survive."[64]

Clinton also declared, "I was frankly—surprised would be a mild word—to say that anyone that would suggest that the Attorney General should resign because some religious fanatics murdered themselves."[65] According to a Federal News Service transcript, the White House press corps applauded Clinton's comment on Reno.[66] (It is rare for journalists to applaud at a press conference.) Eighty-nine percent of the Washington press corps had voted for Clinton in the presidential election the preceding fall.[67] (The pro-government slant of the press corps was captured by the subtitle of a 1996 book by two *Washington Post* reporters: *Main Justice: The Men and Women Who Enforce the Nation's Criminal Laws and Guard Its Liberties*.[68] The possibility that Justice Department employees could threaten people's liberties was inconceivable to much of the establishment media—regardless of how many tanks the FBI sent in.)

Snap polls just after the Waco fire showed that the American people overwhelmingly supported the FBI action. A few days later, the opening of a Senate Appropriations Committee hearing had to be delayed so senators could have their pictures taken with Attorney General Janet Reno, who had become a national hero for her "the buck stops with me" post-Waco statement.

Reno received a different reception from Rep. John Conyers (D-Mich.) when she testified at a House hearing. Reno cried when Conyers berated her for authorizing the final assault. Reno pretended to stand on principle, asserting: "Most of all, congressman, I will not engage in recrimination."[69] As the *New Republic*'s Mickey Kaus noted, Reno "was shielding her agency from criticism for its role. It was this refusal to criticize the FBI, not Reno's willingness to accept criticism herself, that led some FBI agents to call her a 'stand-up guy.' Reno did call for a post-Waco 'examination,' but only one that would 'focus on the future'—analyzing the need for more 'training' and 'staffing' rather than fixing blame. Here is a virtue Washingtonians can appreciate."[70]

COVER-UP CAPERS

At his press conference on the day after the fire, Clinton declared: "There is nothing to hide here. This was probably the most well-covered operation of its kind in the history of the country."[71] As he spoke, Reno raced to put the fix in on the Justice Department's Waco investigation. Reno chose Edward Dennis, a former assistant attorney general in the Bush administration, to head the investigation. Dennis was a fishy choice to evaluate the Justice Department's behavior since his law firm had many clients with cases currently before the Department.[72] The *New York Times* reported on May 16, 1993, that acting Deputy Attorney General Philip Heymann said "that investigators would not look at the decision to batter the compound with tanks and spray tear gas."[73] The *Times* noted: "Officials said that since Ms. Reno has been widely supported in Congress, and since polls show that the majority of Americans supported her decision to use tear gas and blame the cult members themselves for the final deadly fire, department officials concluded that nothing could be gained by looking more closely at her order to carry out the assault."

The Justice Department's final report was widely derided as a whitewash.[74] Edward Dennis announced at a Washington press conference that he found "no fault in the performance of law enforcement during the standoff and the tear gas assault."[75] Reno initially justified the final assault because of ongoing child abuse; the report found no evidence to support that charge. Reno announced, "I now understand that nobody in the [FBI] told me that it was ongoing. We were briefed, and I misunderstood."[76] Reno refused to answer any questions about the contradictions between the report and her initial comments on the final assault because she claimed it might undercut the prosecution of surviving Davidians in federal court. (The Treasury Department wrote a separate report, which concluded that several ATF officials had lied and the agency had committed blunders; the report avoided or swept under the rug the most serious allegations of ATF wrongdoing.)[77]

Eleven surviving Branch Davidians were tried for murder and various other charges in early 1994. A grand jury indictment accused them of conspiring "with malice aforethought" to kill ATF agents "on account of the performance of their duties."[78] According to the charges, this conspiracy was led by Koresh, who "would and did advocate and encourage an armed confrontation" with the ATF.[79] The Davidians were living peacefully off to themselves; but because the ATF decided to launch a frontal military-style attack on their home—that proved that they lusted for an "armed confrontation." (No ATF officials have ever been charged with "advocating an armed confrontation" with American citizens.)

The trial was presided over by federal judge Walter Smith, a former personal injury lawyer and chairman of the McLennan County Republican Party.[80] A 1994 *Washington Times* profile noted that Smith "is known as a jurist who will bend over backward to give the government the benefit of the doubt in most criminal cases."[81] Smith had no qualms about the government killing nonviolent offenders; in a 1989 speech at a local church, Smith advocated the death penalty for all drug offenses.[82] Smith had played a key role in maintaining the credibility of the ATF's first clash with the Davidians by keeping the original search and arrest warrants for Koresh sealed until the day after the fatal fire.[83] This helped postpone serious questioning of the basis for the ATF's assault until after most Davidians were dead.

Judge Smith proclaimed that "the government is not on trial."[84] He announced at the end of jury selection: "I've said the last thing I'm going to say to them about self-defense. I think it's a very iffy thing at best. I don't want to waste time putting it in [jurors] minds."[85] Smith limited defense attorneys in offering evidence that the Davidians acted in self-defense when the ATF attacked their home. Smith even prohibited the attorneys from introducing into evidence the official Treasury Department report on ATF actions at Waco. Since the credibility of ATF witnesses was crucial to the government's case, the Treasury Department's findings of false statements and incompetence by ATF officials could have been decisive. Smith also denied requests by defense attorneys to compel testimony from ATF Chief Stephen Higgins and from Janet Reno. As David Kopel and Paul Blackman noted in their excellent 1997 book, *No More Wacos*, "The judge refused to allow defense attorneys to call ATF agents who had been in the Blackhawk helicopters to determine whether shots had been fired from the helicopters . . . At the trial, pictures of the four dead ATF agents were displayed for long periods of time, but the judge refused to let jurors see pictures of the dead children."[86]

It is still unclear whether the Davidians actually had any illegal machine guns. During the trial, as Kopel and Blackmun noted, "The defense's gun expert was not allowed to examine the guns. Instead he was only permitted to view the guns through a plastic covering, supposedly because the guns still had such a heavy stench. Changing a semiautomatic to full automatic involves complex modifications of small internal components; depriving the defense expert of an opportunity to examine the guns in detail and to disassemble them made it impossible to verify if the guns had been converted at all."[87] FBI expert witness James Cadigan testified that "he had actually tested only one AR-15 which had been converted to full auto. And that one was 'damaged beyond repair,' so he supplied his own upper receiver and barrel and then test fired it. The rest he simply looked at, using a magnifying glass, perhaps, but no x-ray equipment and no test-firing," as Kopel and Blackman noted.[88] (As noted in chapter 14, federal judges have derided federal agents for manipulating legal guns to cause them to fire two shots per trigger pull—thus making their ownership a felony.) The FBI laboratory where Cadigan worked was plunged into controversy shortly after the trial when revelations concerning shoddy work, tampering with evidence, and misleading testimony by FBI experts surfaced.[89]

Prosecutors compared Koresh to Hitler and Stalin and declared that the 11 defendants were "as much religious terrorists as the people who blew up the barracks in Lebanon, the people who blew up the World Trade Center in New York and Pan Am 103."[90]

The jury on February 28, 1994, found all the Davidian defendants not guilty of murder, though seven were convicted of manslaughter, a charge which was expected to carry a prison sentence of roughly five years. Judge Smith "appeared visibly upset when the jury acquitted" the Davidian defendants.[91] Bill Johnston, the lead federal attorney at Waco, burst into tears in bitter disappointment at the verdict.[92] The *New York Times* characterized the verdict as a "stunning defeat" for the federal government;[93] a *Los Angeles Times* headline declared, "Outcome Indicates Jurors Placed Most Blame on the Government."[94]

Though the jurors found the Branch Davidians not guilty of murder, they found seven guilty of carrying a weapon during commission of a murder. Obviously, this was inconsistent with the murder verdict, and Smith dismissed that finding. (The judge had given the jury 67 pages of convoluted instructions.) If the judge had any doubt about the jury's intent, he could have easily polled the individual jurors or sent the jury back to reconcile the verdict. Instead, he dismissed them.

Once the jurors were safely away from the scene, Smith chose to revive the dismissed charge. Though federal prosecutors had not charged any of the defendants with firing machine guns at federal agents, the judge decreed that all of those convicted of manslaughter were also guilty of using a machine gun. They were pronounced guilty of "constructive possession" of machine guns, simply because the government alleged that machine guns were in the Davidians' home.[95] Under federal criminal procedures, judges have wide leeway to sentence people for behavior that they were not convicted of but that judges believe they are guilty of. Smith's decision meant an additional 30 years each for five Davidians.

When Reno traveled to Oklahoma City to hype Clinton's crime bill in April 1994, FBI agent Bob Ricks—who had been the agency's daily spokesman during the 51-day siege—told Reno that many people were still agitated by Waco. Ricks asked that the gag order be lifted on himself and other officials. Reno replied, "I don't think the American people care about Waco anymore."[96]

Phil Chojnacki, one of the two Waco ATF raid commanders, was fired in 1994 after his Treasury Department bosses concluded he lied about knowing that the "element of surprise" had been lost in the initial assault that resulted in the deaths of four ATF agents. But Chojnacki was rehired two months later (after he formally protested his firing); his new job description included serving "as an expert witness to present evidence and facts in civil or criminal trial hearings." Rep. John Mica (R-Fla.) demanded to know, "Does it make sense to you to put someone you just fired for lying into a job where one of the major duties is testifying for the government in court?"[97] (Republicans suspected that Chojnacki was rehired in return for keeping silent about Waco details that would embarrass high-ranking Clinton administration officials.)

On April 19, 1995, the second anniversary of the FBI's final assault at Waco, an explosion at a federal office building in Oklahoma City killed 167 people. A state trooper arrested Timothy McVeigh, an Army veteran who was deeply agitated by the FBI's final assault at Waco. The Oklahoma City bombing once again returned Waco to the front burner. (McVeigh was convicted for the bombing and received a death sentence in 1997.)

On a live episode of *60 Minutes,* a few days after the bombing, Clinton was asked if he had "any second thoughts" about the raid at Waco. Clinton exploded: "Before that raid was carried out, those people murdered a bunch of innocent law enforcement officials . . . and when that raid occurred it was the people who ran that cult compound who murdered their own children, not the federal officials. They made the decision to destroy all the children that were there."[98]

Attorney General Janet Reno declared in a May 5, 1995, speech to federal law enforcement agents: "There is much to be angry about when we talk about Waco—and the government's conduct is not the reason. David Koresh is the reason."[99] Reno also revealed that the "first and foremost" reason for the tank-and-gas assault was that "law enforcement agents on the ground concluded that the perimeter had become unstable and posed a risk both to them and to the surrounding homes and farms. Individuals sympathetic to Koresh were threatening to take matters into their own hands to end the stalemate and were at various times reportedly on the way."[100] This new "first and foremost" reason was a convenient ex post facto rationale after the Oklahoma City bombing. There was no evidence that FBI agents faced any real threats from an uprising during the Waco siege.

CONGRESS CURTSIES TO WACO

In November 1994, Republicans captured control of Congress and, in the summer of 1995, held the first substantive hearings on Waco—much to the dismay of the White House and congressional Democrats. Rep. Charles Schumer (D-N.Y.)

sneered: "We know what that was all about. That was an attack on the ATF. This planned hearing was simply some red meat to some of those extreme right forces."[101] White House Chief of Staff Leon Panetta denounced proposals for new hearings as "despicable."[102] Treasury Undersecretary Ron Noble warned that extremists might view the hearings "and decide to blow up some other building."[103] After the main hearings began, President Clinton, in a speech to directors of federal law enforcement agencies, denounced Republicans: "It is irresponsible for people in elected positions to suggest that the police are some sort of armed bureaucracy acting on private grudges and hidden agendas. That is wrong, it's inaccurate, and people who suggest that ought to be ashamed of themselves."[104] The president condemned the hearings as part of a Republican "war on police," and declared that "there is no moral equivalence between the disgusting acts which took place inside that compound in Waco and the efforts law enforcement officers made to protect the lives of innocent people." The Treasury Department press office mass-faxed a July 6, 1995, letter from Secretary Robert Rubin warning journalists that federal action at Waco "cannot be understood properly outside the context of Oklahoma City."[105] Thus, a truck bomber invoking Waco in 1995 somehow vindicated a federal assault against American citizens in 1993.

The FBI's Larry Potts presented the FBI's official statement on Waco: "It is always the goal of the FBI, as it was in Waco, to ensure that law and order prevail over the criminal elements which threaten our civilization on a daily basis . . . the FBI personnel acted with incredible professionalism, skill and restraint. I am immensely proud of all the FBI personnel who worked so conscientiously for so long to bring peace and justice to Waco."[106]

When Janet Reno appeared before the committee on August 1, she was far more enthusiastic about talking about her feelings than about explaining her decisions:

- "This was the hardest decision I've ever had to make. It will live with me for the rest of my life."
- "I don't think you comprehend—if you talk to me about children—the fact that this instance will be etched on my mind for the rest of my life."
- "I stayed awake at night, wondering what was the right thing to do."[107]

For Reno, her professions of remorse were far more important than the children she ordered gassed. The tone of her responses also made clear that she felt morally superior to the Republican congressmen questioning her.

In response to a specific question about why the FBI tanks began destroying the building before the fire, Reno responded: "I share your frustration when you have such a tragedy as this, and you try to figure out what to do in the future to avoid the recurrence of it, not in an experiment, but in a thoughtful way."[108]

The confidential FBI report that Reno received before approving the attack stated that the impact of the CS gas on "infants and children cannot be ignored because gas masks are not available for infants and younger children."[109] When Rep. John Mica (R-Fla.) presented Reno with a gas mask to illustrate the point that it could not have fit children, Reno casually tossed the gas mask on the floor and announced that "it's not very helpful, in terms of trying to understand what happened there, to just show gas masks. We've got to show the people what went into the process."[110]

The highlight of Reno's testimony was her revelation that the 54-ton tanks that smashed through the Davidians' ramshackle home should not be considered military vehicles—instead, they were "like a good rent-a-car."[111] Reno explained that it would be wrong to focus on the "menacing quality" of the tanks since "those tanks had been around. People [inside] knew about the tanks. I think they were very accustomed to the tanks, at that point." But the Davidians were not accustomed to the tanks flattening their home. Earlier in the hearings, Rep. Bill Zeliff (R-N.H.) complained that the Clinton administration sent more than a dozen tanks and Bradley fighting vehicles to Waco—yet refused to send similar vehicles to Somalia, where 18 U.S. soldiers died in a Somali ambush largely due to a lack of armor to protect them.[112]

When the House hearings on Waco ended in August 1995, many Americans believed that the Justice Department, the FBI, and the Clinton administration had been caught repeatedly lying about what happened at Waco. However, Republicans allowed the story to return to hibernation. Respectable opinion—at least in Washington—resumed pretending that the Waco debacle never occurred. The Women's Bar Association of the District of Columbia created a special award to honor the nation's first female attorney general: the Janet Reno Torchbearer Award. The first recipient, in 1997, was Supreme Court justice Sandra Day O'Connor; the award was presented by Justice Ruth Bader Ginsburg.[113]

In July 1999, federal judge Walter Smith shocked the Clinton administration by allowing wrongful-death lawsuits against the federal government by Davidian survivors and relatives to proceed.[114] Private investigations, an academy-award-nominated documentary (*Waco: Rules of Engagement,* by the team of Dan Gifford, Mike McNulty, and William Gazecki), and damning responses from Freedom of Information Act requests resulted in a growing surge of new information, which eventually broke the dam of media apathy in August 1999.

News leaked out that the feds had knowingly suppressed information about the FBI using pyrotechnic CS-gas rounds, which might have started the fires on

April 19, 1993. Reno was shaken to her core by the revelations; she announced to the media on August 27, 1999: "I am very, very upset. I don't think it's very good for my credibility."[115] White House press spokesman Joe Lockhart chimed in from Martha's Vineyard (where Clinton was vacationing) that Clinton "stands with the attorney general in her determination to get all the facts in this case and to make them available, to Congress and the public, as soon as possible."[116] After further evidence revealed that Reno had grossly misled Congress and the American people, she redeemed herself by invoking the word "truth"—that is, promising to find that damn thing—25 times at a September 3, 1999, press briefing.[117] This was a new record for her. Reno also played the victim, lashing out at the FBI for supposedly withholding key information from her. But Reno bore responsibility for whatever she did not find out, since she had orchestrated the initial Justice Department investigation to whitewash both herself and the FBI.

Other evidence surfaced throughout late 1999 that further undermined federal credibility:

- The FBI deceived Congress and a federal judge by withholding information that it had six closed-circuit television cameras monitoring the Davidians' home throughout the siege. The resulting films could have key information that could resolve the major issues of Waco. The FBI claimed that none of the cameras contained tape.[118]
- Lawyers for surviving Branch Davidians were given a massively doctored infrared FBI tape of the final day's assault. The tape has large gaps—including a suspicious gap just before the fire started and numerous splices—bringing back memories of Nixon secretary Rosemary Woods.

It became clear that a massive cover-up had occurred. *Newsweek* reported that, according to a senior FBI official, "as many as 100 FBI agents and officials may have known about" the military-style explosive devices used by the FBI at Waco, despite Reno's and the FBI's repeated denials that such devices were used.[119]

At the same time that Reno said she wanted to get to the truth, the Justice Department fought federal judge Walter Smith's orders to take control of the evidence from the crime scene. (Smith was presiding over the civil wrongful-death suits.) Smith was very concerned that evidence would be destroyed or "lost" until after the civil trials finished.

Reno could have recused herself from any role in choosing a new person to reinvestigate Waco. Instead, she personally chose John Danforth, a former senator and a golfing buddy of Clinton's, to be in charge of the reinvestigation. (Danforth may have won the attorney general's affection when he was one of the few Republican senators to support the assault weapons ban; Danforth declared in 1993 that "it is time to add my voice to the growing call to stop our country's obsession with guns."[120]) It was peculiar to allow someone implicated in six years of falsehoods to choose the person to investigate her and her agency. Danforth reported to Eric Holder, Reno's top assistant at the Justice Department.

Danforth promptly decimated his credibility by choosing federal attorney Edward Dowd as his chief investigator. Dowd used federal funds in 1999 to campaign against a Missouri state referendum on citizens' right to carry concealed firearms. As Yale Law School's John Lott, who actively supported the referendum, recalled, "Dowd used taxpayer money to set up a 1-800 line to answer people's questions about the initiative. He used federal money to send out a letter to state law enforcement to try to get them to oppose the initiative."[121] Dowd was under investigation for violating federal law by the Justice Department Inspector General when Danforth picked him. The *Washington Times* ran a front-page story about the investigation and voila!—the Justice Department announced the same day that Dowd had been cleared of all charges.[122] When Sen. Kit Bond (R-Mo.) asked to see the official report, the Justice Department refused to provide him any information, claiming that it was protected by the Privacy Act.[123]

Danforth asked federal judge Walter Smith to temporarily bar private lawyers in the wrongful-death suit from interviewing key witnesses. The judge granted a 30-day freeze. Danforth's actions, along with Clinton administration requests for more time to produce documents, resulted in a six-month delay of the trial.

The delay was a godsend for the Clinton administration. Clinton appointees excel at "telling the truth slowly," in the words of former White House Press Secretary Mike McCurry—at rationing out the truth in small enough dribbles to blunt its impact.[124] The Justice Department may try to run the clock out on both the Clinton administration's tenure and on the attention span of the American public.

The wrongful death lawsuits could yet be derailed by Judge Smith, who proclaimed in a September 1999 letter to Danforth his "fervent hope" that his investigation and the civil trial will "help restore the public's confidence in the government."[125] The lead federal attorney on the case, Marie Hagen, urged the judge to postpone the trial until 2001: the judge refused.[126]

Congress, as usual, seemed spooked by Waco. Rep. Mark Souder (R-Ind.) declared that Republicans were suffering from "Waco fatigue... There's a feeling that the political risk may be higher than the political gain of pursuing this subject at this time."[127] However, any fatigue on Capitol Hill was most likely the result of strenuous dodging of the issue.

In January 2000, federal agents finally made sworn statements in court denying any shooting on the final day at Waco. But the Defense Department's denial did not inspire confidence. As the *Dallas Morning News* noted, "A separate Department of Defense statement said that no one from the military or under its control fired that day 'based on currently available information.'"[128] Almost seven years after the April 19, 1993, finale, Pentagon officials were still hedging their bets.

In March 2000, a re-enactment of the final day's assault was carried out by U.S. army units in order to help determine whether the FLIR videotapes from the original assault actually showed automatic weapons fire from government positions. Special counsel Danforth recommended that Vector Data Systems be chosen to record and analyze the test results, and Judge Smith obliged Danforth; the Justice Department paid the bill. The Justice Department continually identified Vector Data Systems as an independent British company; however, Vector was actually owned by Anteon, a large American corporation that had extensive contracts with the Justice Department, the CIA, and the Pentagon. (Vector also had an office in the Washington suburbs.) At Danforth's request, the public and the news media were banned from the re-enactment. A month after the re-enactment, Vector reported that the tapes of the action and its analysis of the tapes from April 19, 1993 showed zero gunfire. This was peculiar—since the FBI had claimed that the Branch Davidians had been firing at the tanks throughout the morning of the final assault. Jim Brannon, a lawyer for Branch Davidian survivors, complained: "Vector was either incompetent or they willfully sabotaged the test."[129] Judge Smith ruled that the Vector report was not "conclusive evidence" and added that lawyers had a right to controvert the report's findings.

On April 24, 2000, the Supreme Court heard oral arguments over the 30-year sentences that Judge Smith slapped onto five Waco defendants in 1993. Clinton Assistant Attorney General James Robinson implored the Justices to recognize that automatic weapons are so heinous that there is no need to have a jury verdict on whether defendants actually used them; instead, a judge should have authority to cast people in prison for most of the remainder of their lives based simply on an allegation that such weapons were in the same building with the defendants. The rigorous questioning that Robinson endured led some observers to conclude that the Supreme Court would overturn the sentences.

On April 28, police discovered the dead body of Carlos Ghigliotti at the offices of his company, Infrared Technologies Corp. in Laurel, Maryland.[130] Ghigliotti, a former FBI consultant and a widely respected thermal imaging expert, had been working for the House Government Reform Committee, analyzing the evidence of gunfire during the final assault at Waco. According to

Ghigliotti's friend, David Hardy, Ghigliotti's analysis—based in part on material available only to the congressional committee—showed far stronger evidence of gunfire than did any previously publicly available material.[131] Police initially investigated the death as a homicide. An autopsy on the badly decomposed body concluded that the 42-year-old Ghigliotti had died from a heart attack caused by arteriosclerosis. Plaintiff lawyer Mike Caddell, who had listed Ghigliotti as an expert witness for the coming trial, observed, "The death of Carlos is a tremendous loss for our cause. There's no one who had done as much work of the same quality in this area as Carlos."[132]

Attorneys for the plaintiffs were given permission by Judge Smith to take a deposition from Attorney General Reno. Justice Department attorneys raced to minimize the questioning, stating in a brief that "there is good cause for limiting the attorney general's deposition to two hours because the national interest requires that she be protected from any undue burden on her ability to perform her governmental duties."[133] Despite Reno's protestations that she wanted the truth to out, she could afford less time for the deposition than she spent preparing and presenting her reading of "Voyage to the Bunny Planet" at the annual White House Easter egg roll a few weeks later. Given Reno's experience with filibustering during congressional testimony (to run out the time allotted to congressmen who were questioning her), a two-hour limit to question her was the equivalent of a ten-minute limit for a non-politician. During the deposition, plaintiff attorneys pressed Reno about the FBI's destruction of the Davidians' home; Reno replied, "Any time you effect an arrest . . . and try to ensure the safety of everyone, there are going to be variables, and the on-scene commanders would be responsible for dealing with those variables as they developed."[134] Former FBI Director William Sessions had stated in a deposition that demolishing the building was clearly not authorized by the action plan FBI headquarters approved. But Reno clung to the charade that it was all an accident: "Based on what I know to date, this was not an effort to tear down the building. If it had been, there may have been situations at the scene that suggested that it should be done and it could be done consistent with the plan."[135] A Justice Department brief filed in federal court in April insisted that federal officials could not be held liable for their actions at Waco even if their "discretion has been abused" and even if "wrongful acts" had been committed.[136] The Justice Department is adamant that no federal agent or official deserves even a judicial wrist slap—not even the equivalent of a ticket for jay walking—for carrying out a military-style assault on Americans civilians that ended with 80 dead.

THE
RUBY RIDGE
COVER-UP

"The real measure of our progress is whether responsibility and respect for the law are on the rise."
—President Bill Clinton, April 6, 1998[1]

NOTHING ELUCIDATES THE CLINTON ADMINISTRATION philosophy of civil rights better than the investigations and lawsuits involving Ruby Ridge. The shootings at Ruby Ridge, Idaho, occurred during the waning days of the Bush administration. But most of the cover-up and almost all of the whitewashing occurred on Clinton's watch. Ruby Ridge became a symbol of federal agents above the law and spurred millions of Americans to distrust Washington.

The Ruby Ridge case involved the entrapment of Randy Weaver on firearms charges by an informant for the Bureau of Alcohol, Tobacco and Firearms (ATF), false ATF reports to federal prosecutors, and dozens of intrusions by U.S. marshals on Weaver's land. On August 21, 1992, three U.S. marshals dressed in ninja outfits with face masks ambushed Weaver's 14-year-old son Sammy and 25-year-old family friend Kevin Harris, firing submachines guns at them as they came down a road in the woods. Marshal Arthur Roderick started the clash by shooting the boy's dog. A firefight ensued in which Marshal William Degan was killed. As Sammy Weaver was leaving the scene and running back toward the family's shack, Marshal Larry Cooper shot him in the back and killed him.[2]

The next day, FBI snipers arrived on the scene and received "rules of engagement," which declared that "any armed male adult observed in the vicinity of the Weaver cabin could and should be killed."[3] Within an hour of the snipers taking position, every adult in the cabin was either dead or severely wounded—even though they had not fired a shot at the FBI, and even though the FBI never called out for them to surrender. FBI sniper Lon Horiuchi shot Randy Weaver in the back as he stood outside his shack, and then fired a shot that killed Vicki Weaver as she stood in the cabin doorway holding their 10-month-old baby. (The second shot passed through Vicki Weaver and struck Kevin Harris.) The FBI initially proclaimed Ruby Ridge a great success.[4]

Weaver and Harris went on trial in April 1993 for the killing of Marshal Degan and on other charges. Federal prosecutors sought to prove that Weaver had conspired for nine years to have an armed confrontation with the government. Among the evidence the government offered to prove conspiracy: the Weaver family moved from Iowa to Idaho in 1985 and then bought a plot of land in an isolated area.[5] This argument collapsed after it became obvious that Weaver's confrontation with the government began only after being entrapped by an undercover federal agent; the subsequent conflict was initiated by heavily armed federal agents who trespassed on his land and opened fire. The government tried to prove that Harris had fired first in the initial confrontation, but this claim was contradicted by other government witnesses. The feds claimed that Marshal Degan had never fired a shot before he was hit; however, ballistics evidence showed that he had pumped out seven rounds.[6]

Weaver's lawyer, Gerry Spence, did not call a single witness for Weaver's defense, relying instead on all the contradictions provided by the government's witnesses. A jury found Weaver and Harris not guilty on almost all charges, effectively deciding that the shooting of the marshal was an act of self-defense. (Weaver was found guilty for not showing up for his original court hearing—even though prosecutors admitted during the trial that he was sent the wrong date for the appearance.) Federal judge Edward Lodge condemned the FBI: "The actions of the government, acting through the FBI, evidence a callous disregard for the rights of the defendants and the interests of justice and demonstrate a complete lack of respect for the order and directions of this court."[7] Judge Lodge issued a lengthy list detailing the Justice Department's misconduct, fabrication of evidence, and refusals to obey court orders.

After the trial verdict debacle, the FBI and Justice Department launched separate investigations. A 1994 Justice Department report concluded that numerous federal officials may have obstructed justice, perjured themselves, or otherwise broken the law. A task force of 24 Justice Department and FBI officials recommended that sniper Horiuchi face federal charges for the killing of Vicki Weaver.[8] After that report was completed, the Justice Department's Office of Professional Responsibility (OPR) came in, added their own spin, and urged that neither Horiuchi nor any other fed face charges.[9] (OPR is renowned for discovering reasons not to prosecute suspected government wrongdoers.[10]) Assistant Attorney General for Civil Rights Deval Patrick, in an October 15, 1994, memo, disregarded the initial task force and ruled that the federal agents had not used excessive force in the killings of Sammy and Vicki Weaver. The Justice Department refused to release Patrick's memo. However, a *New York Times* article noted that Patrick "said that when the sharpshooter fired the fatal shot, the agents had a reasonable belief that their lives were in danger. Agents had not intentionally used excessive force, the memorandum said."[11] The Justice Department refused to release any of the reports.

A few weeks later, on January 6, 1995, FBI Director Louis Freeh announced the results of the FBI's internal investigation. Freeh declared that the Randy Weaver "crisis was one of the most dangerous and potentially violent situations to which FBI agents have ever been assigned."[12] This was peculiar, considering that camouflaged FBI snipers had been hiding in the woods 200 yards away when the Weavers were gunned down.

Freeh found 12 FBI officials guilty of "inadequate performance, improper judgment, neglect of duty and failure to exert proper managerial oversight."[13] However, the heaviest penalty that Freeh imposed was 15 days unpaid leave, and that on only four agents. Freeh had imposed heavier penalties on FBI agents who used their official cars to drive their children to school.[14] Freeh gave especially lenient treatment to Larry Potts, an old friend and Freeh's pick as acting deputy FBI director. Potts was the senior FBI headquarters official in charge of the Idaho operation. Despite the finding of a Justice Department confidential report that the rules of engagement had violated the Constitution, Freeh recommended that Potts face only the penalty of a letter of censure—the same penalty that Freeh had imposed on himself when he lost an FBI cellular telephone.[15] (In Senate testimony a month later, Freeh declared that "no misconduct" by FBI officials had occurred in the handling of the Weaver case.[16])

The FBI falsely claimed in a press release issued the same day as Freeh's announcement that Weaver had been convicted of the original weapons violations charge.[17] The FBI claimed to have been studying the Weaver case for more than two years—but did not even get the basic facts straight. (A few months later, the *Washington Post* published an op-ed piece by FBI Spokesman Frank Scafidi who falsely asserted that the bullet that killed Vicki Weaver first hit and passed through Kevin Harris—perhaps part of the FBI's concerted effort to derail criticism.)[18]

Freeh justified the FBI shooting of Randy Weaver by saying that sniper Lon Horiuchi "observed one of the suspects raise a weapon in the direction of a helicopter carrying other FBI personnel."[19] But other federal officials testified at the trial that no helicopters were flying in the vicinity of the Weavers' cabin when Horiuchi opened fire. Chuck Peterson, an Idaho lawyer who was part of Weaver's defense team, observed, "The federal judge threw out the [charge that Weaver aimed at] the helicopter because it was so incredibly weak—it was not supported by anything."[20] Dean Miller, a reporter for the *Spokane Spokesman-Review*, who had covered the original siege and subsequent federal trial, called Freeh's assertion the "Horiuchi fig leaf"—a desperate effort to give respectability and legality to the shooting.[21]

Freeh was also satisfied that Horiuchi's second shot was justified and that the killing of Vicki Weaver was an accident.[22] (An internal FBI report completed shortly after the confrontation justified the killing of Mrs. Weaver by asserting that she had put herself in harm's way. A Senate report later noted that the FBI "assault plan . . . was based on the premise that Vicki Weaver would kill her children."[23]) Freeh declared, "The question is whether someone running into a fortified position who is going to shoot at you is as much a threat to you as somebody turning in an open space and pointing a gun at you. I don't distinguish between those."[24]

But Weaver had never fired upon the FBI agents—he was merely a wounded man trying to struggle into his home and the arms of his family. According to Freeh, if a government agent shoots and wounds a private citizen, the agent acquires an unlimited right to kill the target—because otherwise the citizen might shoot back at the government agent.

Besides, Freeh's allegation that Weaver was "running into a fortified position" was an absurdity. As Gerry Spence, Weaver's lawyer, observed, "The cabin was built with sticks and plywood so fragile a wolf could have blown it down."[25]

The establishment press rallied around the Clinton administration. The *Washington Post*, in a January 9, 1995, editorial titled "Ruby Ridge and Waco," declared: "No criminal charges against law enforcement agents are contemplated, and none would be justified."[26] The *Post* rushed to judgment despite the Justice Department's refusal to make public its 500-plus page report of its internal investigation. A July 14, 1995, *New York Times* editorial described Randy Weaver, his wife, their 10-month-old baby, 13-year-old son, 16-year-old daughter, and family friend Kevin Harris as "an armed separatist brigade."[27] The *Post* and *Times* editorials were, on occasion, as vacuously pro-government as many Southern newspapers had been in the late 1950s and early 1960s regarding vicious police attacks on civil rights protesters.

Deputy Attorney General Jamie Gorelick strongly opposed the proposed promotion of Potts to deputy FBI director, and instead recommended a 30-day suspension for Potts. Freeh protested bitterly in a March 7, 1995, memo to Gorelick: "For you to increase the proposed discipline inevitably sends a wrong message to both the public and the employees of the FBI. First, there is an oft-repeated misconception in the public press that FBI employees must be disciplined for the shooting death of Vicki Weaver . . . To now increase the discipline proposed for Mr. Potts to a thirty-day suspension will signal, wrongly or not, that there is culpability among FBI employees for the shooting death of Mrs. Weaver . . . This will undoubtedly and unjustifiably harm Mr. Potts, the FBI and the Department . . . I am also concerned about the impact this decision would have on my credibility as Director . . . The potential for damage to my personal credibility is apparent and is not warranted."[28] Gorelick acceded to Freeh's demand.

Janet Reno approved Potts's promotion in May 1995. The Potts promotion set off a political firestorm. Eugene Glenn, the on-site FBI commander at Ruby Ridge, formally protested that the FBI's review of the Ruby Ridge case was incomplete and compromised by flaws that "reveal a purpose to create scapegoats and false impressions."

In June 1995, the confidential 542-page Justice Department report on Ruby Ridge leaked out and was placed on the Internet by *Legal Times*. The revelations in the report made a mockery of Deval Patrick and Louis Freeh's earlier statements. The task force was especially appalled that the adults were gunned down before receiving any warning or demand to surrender: "There was no attempt by the FBI to give notice to the individuals in the cabin prior to the shots taken by Horiuchi . . . While the operational plan included a provision for a surrender demand, that demand was not made until after the shootings . . . The absence of such a [surrender demand] subjected the Government to charges that it was setting Weaver up for attack."[29]

The report concluded that the FBI's rules of engagement at Ruby Ridge flagrantly violated the U.S. Constitution: "The Constitution allows no person to become 'fair game' for deadly force without law enforcement evaluating the threat that person poses, even when, as occurred here, the evaluation must be made in a split second." The report portrayed the rules of engagement as a license to kill: "The Constitution places the decision on whether to use deadly force on the individual agent; the Rules attempted to usurp this responsibility."[30] The report concluded that the rules were a decisive factor in the wrongful killing of Vicki Weaver.

On July 12, 1995, Michael Kahoe, the director of the FBI's Violent Crimes and Major Offenders Section, was suspended because he was suspected of shredding the FBI after-action report on Ruby Ridge.[31] A month later, Deputy Director Larry Potts and four other high-ranking officials were suspended from their positions (with full pay) because they were suspected of having destroyed evidence, or for their role in issuing illegal rules of engagement. A new investigation was launched. The *Los Angeles Times* noted, "The revelations of suspected wrongdoing inside the nation's premier law enforcement agency are more sweeping than the ethics violations that led to President Clinton's firing of former FBI director Bill Sessions and the burning of Watergate-related evidence in his fireplace that led to the 1973 resignation of acting FBI director Patrick Gray."[32]

On August 15, 1995, the U.S. government paid the Weaver family $3.1 million to settle their civil suit against the United States for the deaths of Sammy and Vicki Weaver. One Justice Department official told the *Washington Post* that, if the suit had gone to trial in Idaho, the Weavers probably would have collected $200 million from the feds.[33] The official Justice Department press release noted, "By entering into a settlement, the U.S. hopes to take a substantial step toward healing the wounds the incident inflicted . . . The U.S. does not admit wrongdoing or liability to the plaintiffs."[34] If the Justice Department was serious about denying wrongdoing, the officials who approved the payoff should have been indicted for squandering taxpayers' money.

Thanks to the doggedness of Sen. Arlen Specter (R.-Pa.), the Senate Subcommittee on Terrorism, Technology and Government Information held hearings on Ruby Ridge in September and October 1995. Shortly after Specter proposed hearings, the Justice Department announced plans to investigate FBI perjury regarding Ruby Ridge. Deputy Attorney General Jamie Gorelick then complained in mid-August that the Senate investigation might "undermine the integrity and confidentiality of [the Justice Department] investigation."[35]

Throughout the hearings, senators struggled to understand why the federal government had invested so much effort in going after Weaver, who was, at worst, an outspoken, penny-ante firearms law violator. U.S. marshal Dave Hunt stressed again and again in his testimony that Weaver had criticized the federal government as a "lawless government." Weaver's political and racist beliefs clearly resulted in the feds making a far higher priority of his apprehension and subjugation. One almost got the impression that federal agents felt compelled to silence any citizen who publicly proclaimed that the government was lawless.

It emerged during the hearings that ATF agent Herb Byerly, the person who set up Weaver to violate firearms law, had lied about Weaver, telling the U.S. attorney that Weaver had previous convictions. Weaver had never been convicted of anything in his life. Asked about these slanders during his testimony, Byerly insisted they had been merely "typographical errors"— eliciting peals of laughter from the hearing room.[36]

ATF Chief John Magaw, in his appearance before Sen. Specter's Ruby Ridge committee, repeatedly maintained that his agents' "conduct was lawful and proper in every respect."[37] When pressed by Specter as to why he kept ignoring the court verdict and saying that Weaver had not been entrapped, Magaw responded: "Do you believe Randy Weaver—or do you believe the federal agents who have sworn to tell the truth and are carrying out a career in this government?" Regardless of how many lies federal agents had been caught telling, Magaw believed that every federal agent was still entitled to absolute credibility.

On October 19, Louis Freeh formally presented the FBI's case to the Senate and the American people. Freeh repeatedly sought to vindicate the FBI's action by referring to the "murder" of Marshal Degan. Sen. Charles Grassley challenged him on that point: "The jury acquitted Mr. Harris of murder. If you've learned anything from the mistakes of government hyperbole and you respect our jury system, then why are you still calling it murder and what kind of signal does that send when you do call it murder?" Freeh responded, "Senator, there's no one who has more respect for the jury system in determination as I do. On the facts, however . . . I view that unfortunate killing as a murder and that's how I've described it."[38]

Freeh proffered his ritual denunciations of perjurious FBI agents, and then proceeded to grossly misstate the facts of Ruby Ridge. Seeking to justify an FBI sniper opening fire without warning on two men who were merely standing outside the cabin, Freeh claimed, "Special Agent Horiuchi testified that he took the first shot when he observed a man later determined to be Randy Weaver . . . raise his rifle. At that time, Special Agent Horiuchi perceived that Weaver 'was trying to get a shot off' at a law enforcement helicopter that was flying overhead. Special Agent Horiuchi said he took the first shot for only one reason: he believed he was protecting fellow law enforcement officers who were in the helicopter."[39] However, at the federal trial in 1993, Horiuchi testified that he never saw Weaver holding a gun before he tried to kill him. Horiuchi explained the plan of the FBI snipers at Weaver's trial: "We were planning to shoot the adult males."[40]

Horiuchi also explained that he did not open fire until both adult males were out of the cabin because he hoped to be able to shoot both of them at the same time. FBI sniper Peter King told the Senate committee that the shoot-to-kill rules of engagement were "crazy."[41]

Louis Freeh was the director who brought the Fifth Amendment to FBI agents. Five FBI agents took the Fifth Amendment rather than tell the incriminating truth about their activities on the Ruby Ridge case.[42] (The Justice Department had long argued that any citizen who invoked the Fifth Amendment in asset forfeiture cases must be presumed guilty and automatically forfeit his property.) And, to help the G-men avoid telling the truth about their conduct, each one was entitled to a free attorney, courtesy of the U.S. taxpayers. Sen. Herbert Kohl complained, "I would be asked by the FBI to believe [Ruby Ridge] was almost a model of [good] conduct. The conclusion, is drawn, from . . . all the people we've heard, that no one did anything wrong of significance or consequence."[43]

The FBI's attitude toward the American people was best captured by a single image from the Senate hearings: an FBI robot outside the cabin holding a 12-gauge shotgun in one arm and a phone in the other. FBI siege negotiators continually demanded that Weaver come out of his cabin, pick up the phone, and talk to FBI agents at the other end of the line. But the robot's shotgun was pointing right at the door. FBI press spokesmen repeatedly complained to the news media during the 11-day siege that Weaver refused to negotiate—but never mentioned the shotgun.

The Senate subcommittee, in a subsequent report, concluded that the five successive FBI reports of internal investigations of the episode "are variously contradictory, inaccurate, and biased. They demonstrate a reluctance on the part of the FBI initially to take the incidents at Ruby Ridge seriously . . . Rather than attempting to uncover and resolve any discrepancies, FBI agents avoided uncomfortable facts and coddled their own people."[44] The FBI did not even attempt to make its investigations appear untainted. The Senate report noted, "The various Ruby Ridge reports reveal several instances of friends reviewing friends' conduct and the subjects of the reviews later sitting on the promotion boards of the very agents who reviewed their conduct."[45]

Shortly after the hearings ended, the Justice Department sent a team of investigators back to Ruby Ridge to reconstruct Horiuchi's angle of vision for the shootings. Idaho Defense Attorney David Nevin, who played a key role in the 1993 federal trial of Weaver and Kevin Harris, later observed: "When you look through the scope [of Horiuchi's rifle] at the door, you can see a wedding ring on the hand of someone standing behind the window of the door. You can see someone standing back there with great resolution and great visibility."[46]

"BETTER LATE THAN NEVER" HEROES

On March 1, 1996, the U.S. Marshals Service gave its highest award for valor to the five surviving U.S. marshals involved at Ruby Ridge, including the marshal who shot 14-year-old Sammy in the back and killed him and the marshal who started a firefight by shooting the boy's dog without provocation. (The awards were approved by Attorney General Janet Reno; the Marshals Service is part of the Justice Department.) The marshals received the awards, according to U.S. Marshals Service Director Eduardo Gonzalez, for "their exceptional courage, their sound judgment in the face of attack, and their high degree of professional competence during this incident."[47]

Gonzalez declared: "When gunfire broke out on Ruby Ridge on that summer day, every member of the team came under fire at some point." Gonzalez labeled the men "heroes." However, the federal government never presented any evidence at trial to show that three of the men (part of a separate team far away from the firefight) were ever shot at, and grave doubts remained over the actions of the other two marshals. Asked by a reporter why the Marshals Service waited three and a half years to make the awards, Gonzalez replied: "It was the first opportunity we had after we had the formal hearings on Ruby Ridge. I didn't think it was appropriate while the hearings were going on."[48] (The senators who were stunned and mystified by the marshals' testimony would not have been amused.)

Rather than valor awards, some marshals may have deserved perjury indictments. Several places in the confidential Justice Department report dealt with the possibility of a cover-up. After the firefight between the U.S. marshals and the Weavers and Kevin Harris, the surviving marshals were taken to a condominium to rest and recuperate. The report observed: "We note that the marshals were kept together for several hours before giving their statements. We question the wisdom of keeping the marshals together at the condominium for several hours, while awaiting interviews with the FBI. Isolating them in that manner created the appearance and generated allegations that they were fabricating stories and colluding to cover-up the true circumstances of the shootings."[49] The Senate report also noted: "FBI agents who were briefed in Washington and in Idaho during the early stages of the crisis at Ruby Ridge received a great deal of inaccurate or exaggerated information concerning . . .

the firefight."[50] The Marshals Service denied FBI requests to interview the marshals until 2 P.M. on the following day—long after the Hostage Rescue Team was set in motion on its fatal mission—because the Marshals Service insisted on giving "the Deputies time to compose themselves after their ordeal."[51] The marshals' gross mischaracterization of the clash on August 21 paved the way to the FBI's shoot-to-kill orders.

When Marshals Roderick and Cooper testified at the 1995 hearings, they stunned the senators by announcing that Randy Weaver had accidentally shot his own son. Though Sammy Weaver was shot as he was running in the direction of his father, and though Randy Weaver was far away from the scene of his son's death and was located in front of him and at a higher elevation, and though his son was shot in the back by a bullet with an upward trajectory, Cooper insisted the father shot the son. The only plausible theory to support this claim was if Randy Weaver had been using "Roger Rabbit" cartoon bullets—bullets that could twist around trees, take U-turns, and defy all the laws of physics. The Senate report concluded: "The Subcommittee . . . has seen no evidence which would support the Marshals' claim." The Senate report noted: "We were disappointed to learn that, based on his desire to avoid creating discoverable documents that might be used by the defense in the Weaver/Harris trial . . . former [Marshals Service] Director Henry Hudson decided to conduct no formal internal review of USMS activities connected with the Weaver case and the Ruby Ridge incident."[52] When the marshals were named as defendants in the civil damage lawsuit filed by Kevin Harris, a 1997 federal appeals court decision noted that Marshals "Cooper and Roderick contend that they have absolute immunity from claims that they gave false testimony: (a) in official reports; (b) before the grand jury that indicted Mr. Harris on the federal charges; and (c) at his trial on those charges."[53] The court derided the marshals' "specious reasoning": "The argument here is, in essence, that if a conspiracy to lie is so successful that on the basis of the lies a grand jury finds probable cause, the conspirators become immunized for the constitutional injury they have caused. We disagree."[54]

A PLEA FOR A PENSION

The FBI's Michael Kahoe copped a plea bargain in October 1996 and was sentenced to serve 18 months in prison and pay a $4,000 fine. Kahoe could have received up to 10 years in prison and a $250,000 fine. Luckily for Kahoe, confessing to obstruction of justice did not disqualify him from continuing to receive a paycheck from the Justice Department. The real lesson of the Kahoe sentence was: Cover Up a Killing, Get a Pension. Kahoe was permitted to stay on the FBI payroll (at $112,000 a year) for several months after he pled guilty—until he turned 50—so that he could qualify for a pension of $67,000 per year.[55] If he had been fired at the time he pled guilty to obstruction of justice, his pension would have been much less. (Kahoe also collected 15 months of paychecks from the FBI after he was suspended.)

ONCE AGAIN, NOBODY DID NOTHING

The re-reinvestigation that began in 1995 dragged into the summer of 1997. On August 15—on a Friday afternoon, when most news reporters were off duty—the Justice Department announced that it would file no criminal charges against high-ranking FBI agents in the Ruby Ridge case. After bragging about the number of pages examined, computer disks checked, and people interviewed, the official press release declared that there was nothing prosecutable that had not already been known at the beginning of the process and that "the little circumstantial evidence from which it could be argued that there may have been an intent [by FBI snipers] to use more force than was necessary was far outweighed by a significant amount of evidence that law enforcement had no such intention here. Instead, there was substantial evidence that FBI law enforcement efforts were undertaken by on-site supervisors with the actual, although not completely accurate, belief that Randall Weaver and Kevin Harris posed a severe threat to law enforcement officers requiring the use of deadly force."[56]

To call it "not completely accurate" that Weaver and Harris "posed a severe threat to law enforcement officers" fails the laugh test. A 1997 federal appeals court decision noted: "Horiuchi and his fellow officers were safely ensconced on the hill overlooking the Weaver cabin. No threatening movement was made by Harris with respect to Horiuchi or anyone else, even after Horiuchi shot Randy Weaver."[57] The appeals court called the rules of engagement "a gross deviation from constitutional principles and a wholly unwarranted return to a lawless and arbitrary wild-west school of law enforcement."

No one in the FBI was held responsible by the Justice Department for the "go kill them on the mountain" orders. The only official who received any legal penalty—Kahoe—admitted destroying evidence. To Justice Department investigators, shredding paper was apparently a worse offense than killing innocent civilians.

Newsweek reported that the Justice Department chose not to prosecute Potts and his deputy Danny Coulson, the two supervisors of the Ruby Ridge operation, "even though investigators turned up deeply troubling evidence that the two may have lied about approving the illegal shoot-to-kill orders . . . During the investigation, Potts belatedly produced an undated memo that he offered as proof that he never signed off on the orders. In the document, which he claims he dictated to an FBI secretary, he lays out a far more restrictive deadly-force policy. But [forensic testing] . . . strongly suggests to investigators that the note was fabricated after the fact . . . Both [Potts and Coulson] can retire with full pensions—and they plan to do so before Reno can discipline them."[58]

Potts' exit provided one more example of how FBI bigwigs put themselves above the law. After Potts announced his intention to retire, several high-ranking FBI officials "flew into Washington from around the country for a farewell dinner. They billed the government, claiming official business—a nonexistent ethics seminar at the FBI training academy . . . Instead of being accused of fraud, the charge [against the lying FBI officials] was softened to inattention to detail," as *Newsweek* reported in 1999.[59]

On August 21, 1997, a week after the Justice Department whitewashed the FBI defendants, Boundary County, Idaho, Prosecutor Denise Woodbury announced the indictment of FBI sniper Lon Horiuchi for involuntary manslaughter in the killing of Vicki Weaver. FBI Director Freeh was outraged that a local court would seek to hold an FBI agent legally responsible for the killing, declaring that Horiuchi had an "exemplary record" and is "an outstanding agent and continues to have my total support and confidence." Freeh declared: "The FBI is doing everything within its power to ensure [Horiuchi] is defended to the full extent and that his rights as a federal law enforcement officer are fully protected."[60] Justice Department lawyers persuaded a judge to move Horiuchi's case from a state court to a federal court, where federal agencies have far more procedural advantages. Although a confidential Justice Department report concluded that Horiuchi acted unconstitutionally, Justice Department lawyers argued vigorously that Horiuchi was exempt from any state or local prosecution because he was carrying out federal orders at the time he gunned Vicki Weaver down. The Justice Department and the FBI warned in March 1998 that permitting Horiuchi to be prosecuted would have "an enormously chilling effect on federal operations, especially law enforcement."[61]

On May 14, 1998, federal judge Edward Lodge ruled that Horiuchi could not be tried for killing Vicki Weaver because he was a federal agent on duty, and thus effectively exempt from any jurisdiction of state courts. Lodge focused on Horiuchi's "subjective beliefs": as long as Horiuchi supposedly did not believe he was violating anyone's rights or acting wrongfully, then he could not be guilty. The judge blamed Vicki Weaver for her own death. Lodge decreed that "it would be objectively reasonable for Mr. Horiuchi to believe that one would not expect a mother to place herself and her baby behind an open door outside the cabin after a shot had been fired and her husband had called out that he had been hit."[62] Thus, if an FBI agent wrongfully shoots one family member, the government automatically receives a presumptive right to slay the rest of the family unless they run and hide.

SEVENTEEN

THE RENO-FREEH WHITEWASH TEAM

THE PRESTIGE OF FEDERAL LAW ENFORCEMENT suffered a meltdown during the Clinton administration. Whether it was the Justice Department obstructing justice, or the FBI tyrannizing innocent citizens, or both the Justice Department and the FBI competing for the best imitation of the Keystone Kops, citizens' trust in lawmen plummeted. A few highlights from the Clinton law enforcement record will be examined in this chapter.

WHITEWASH QUEEN

Washingtonian reported in August 1999 that Janet Reno "has much of the [Justice] department working on what she calls her 'legacy' document. It is to comprise 16 chapters that will summarize her accomplishments and spell out the challenges to her successor. Attorneys working on the 'legacy' project say that she has urged them to 'speed it up.'"[1]

Alas, before Reno could retire with one last fawning frenzy by the Washington press corps, the fires of Waco re-ignited. News leaked out that the feds knowingly suppressed information about using pyrotechnics that might have started the fires that killed scores of women and children. Reno stayed on, waiting for a more opportune time to exit.

In reality, Reno's main legacy may be to remind people of H. L. Mencken's quip that the name "Justice Department" is an oxymoron.

Reno saw government as the fount of all good—and government employees as a Brahmin class. Reno informed a group of federal law enforcement officers in 1995: "You are part of a government that has given its people more freedom . . . than any other government in the history of the world."[2] In a 1996 speech to government prosecutors, Reno declared: "All of you public lawyers are but little lower than the angels, and I salute you."[3] Reno showed her belief in angels in 1994 when she decreed that federal prosecutors would no longer be bound by the ethics guidelines of state bar associations.[4] Reno's power grab for federal prosecutors was unanimously condemned by the Conference of Chief Justices, representing all the state supreme courts.

Reno was initially hailed by liberals as their Great White Hope, in part because she had publicly criticized federal drug laws that consign people to prison for nonviolent offenses. Reno declared in 1993: "We've put often vast amounts of dollars into prisons, which are negative monuments against the landscape. Prisons are not an investment in our future."[5] During Reno's jurisdiction, the population of federal prisons rose by more than 50 percent—and the surge was largely the result of new drug offenders being locked away.[6] Reno was initially deeply offended that federal mandatory minimum penalties for crack possession were a hundred times harsher than for powder cocaine. After the White House yanked her chain, she came out in favor of continuing the large disparity, despite its harsh, disproportionate effect on young blacks.[7]

SOCIAL WORKER WITH AN IRON FIST

Reno was the perfect attorney general for an administration that invoked "the children" to stretch its power in almost every direction.

Upholding a venerable tradition of attorney generals in the forefront of sabotaging the Constitution, Reno called for government censorship of television violence. In 1993 Senate testimony, Reno warned: "If immediate voluntary steps are not taken [by television producers] and deadlines established, government should respond and respond immediately. We must move forward to set a schedule for compliance with proper standards, or government should set those standards."[8] Reno demanded that television should also offer shows with plots that repudiate violence and guns[9] (except for violence by government against citizens). Reno did not say when she would be sending in the SWAT teams to take down Beavis and Butthead.

Her intimidation tactics ensured her a tidal wave of positive press as a person who truly cared about children.

In 1996 Congress passed and Clinton signed the Communications Decency Act. The measure would have effectively curtailed all sexual expression on the Internet, imposing a two-year prison sentence and a $250,000 fine on anyone who engaged in speech on the Internet that might be viewed by children and was "indecent" or "patently offensive." A three-judge panel found the law "profoundly repugnant" to the First Amendment.[10] Despite the setback, Reno defended the law. Reno declared in early 1997: "One of the points we have to remember is, if you have an absolutely incredible technology that . . . provides new and incredible opportunities for learning, for communication, and for understanding, it also has incredible opportunities to put stuff on there that can be damaging, harmful, and hurtful, particularly to children. We have seen the problem that exists in this country of children who are unsupervised for many hours of the day . . . We have got to design a system that can ensure the availability of this marvelous tool without damaging the children that will have access. And I think that there are ways and effective means, and I think that this will be the basis of the argument" that Justice Department lawyers made before the Supreme Court to defend the law's draconian penalties.[11] Newsbytes summarized the Clinton administration's argument before the Supreme Court: "The government asserts that a fear of encountering 'indecency' online could deter potential users from exercising their First Amendment interest in accessing the new medium."[12] An ACLU lawyer commented: "It is supremely ironic that the government now says it is protecting the 1st Amendment rights of Americans by threatening people with jail for engaging in constitutionally protected speech."[13] (The Supreme Court trounced the Justice Department, ruling the law unconstitutional.)

POACHING THE FORTUNE 500

Reno's Justice Department seemed at times to bear a little hostility toward some of America's most productive corporations. Nothing better illustrated this than the four years the Justice Department spent hounding Microsoft for antitrust violations. Reno proclaimed: "Forcing PC manufacturers to take a Microsoft product as a condition of buying a monopoly product like Windows is plain wrong."[14] By this standard, the feds could prosecute almost any corporation that bundled together more than one service or product. The Justice Department claimed in court that Microsoft had effectively crippled competition for Internet browsers, thereby devastating Netscape. Annoyingly,

America Online announced a deal to buy Netscape for $4 billion shortly after Justice lawyers held a wake for Netscape. After the Justice Department won a preliminary victory on November 5, 1999, when a federal judge announced preliminary findings of facts favorable to the department's position, Reno appeared at a press conference and announced: "This is a great day for American consumers. We're so pleased with the court's findings, for they fully support the department's view that this case is about the protection of innovation, competition and the consumer's right to choose the products they want."[15] But the case was not about the consumer's right to choose: anyone who wanted Netscape could easily download a free copy from Netscape's website. Instead, the case was about Justice Department lawyers' right to micro-manage how corporations behave.[16] It was ironic to hail a court decision against Microsoft as a victory for "innovation," since Microsoft had done more to bring the world into the computer age than any other single corporation in the preceding 15 years.

On September 22, 1999, Reno invoked one of the most abusive federal laws—the Racketeer Influenced and Corrupt Organizations Act (RICO)—to torpedo the tobacco industry. Reno charged the industry with racketeering based on offenses such as mimicking Al Gore in claiming that air pollution causes respiratory problems. (Reno was outraged that an industry study noted that some problems blamed on cigarettes may actually be due to urban smog.)[17] Reno justified the suit as a way to force tobacco companies to "pay their fair share" of the Medicare and other federal costs for millions of ill smokers. Yet, studies by the Congressional Research Service and the Rand Corporation concluded that smokers, by dying early, actually reduce government health care outlays.[18] Smokers on average actually significantly *over*estimate their chances of dying from coffin nails, according to a study by Duke professor Kip Viscusi.[19] The feds whined that cigarette makers downplayed the risks of smoking—yet every pack sold since the 1960s contained a federally mandated warning that smoking can kill you. Did Reno want a siren attached to every cigarette? Reno filed the civil suit after a five-year federal criminal investigation found insufficient grounds to charge the industry, and after she had informed Congress in 1997 that there were insufficient grounds for a civil suit. But Clinton, in his 1999 State of the Union address, promised a big lawsuit against tobacco, so Janet Reno ginned up a case to satisfy the boss. If Reno's effort to target an entire industry for racketeering is successful, it is only a question of time until prosecutors use the same club to go after firearms makers, fast-food restaurants, and other politically incorrect industries.

SELECTIVE JUSTICE

The Clinton administration railroaded legislation through Congress to crack down on domestic terrorism—a threat that was frequently invoked after the Oklahoma City bombing. But some terrorists were more corrigible than others. On August 11, 1999, Clinton announced he was offering a pardon to 16 members of the FALN—(the Spanish acronym for Armed Forces of National Liberation)—a Puerto Rican terrrorist group that had carried over a hundred bombings, killing six people and wounding 130, in their pursuit of independence for Puerto Rico. Twelve of the 16 had been apprehended with machine guns or sawed-off shotguns[20]—the type of crime that justified a federal search-and-destroy response at both Ruby Ridge and Waco. In previous cases, the person seeking a pardon was required to formally show remorse and, at the least, promise not to engage in violence in the future. However, there was no such obligation for the Puerto Rican terrorists. Justice Department lawyers coached the convicts on how to write their appeal for a pardon. The *New York Times* noted that "the Puerto Rican nationalists did not apply for clemency personally, as is usually required, but department officials processed an application anyway. Under department regulations, a personal application is usually required to start the process, because such a move is taken as a sign of remorse for the criminal acts."[21] Several Justice Department officials urged that a pardon not be granted; the FBI warned that the president's action would return "hardened terrorists to the clandestine movement."[22] One of the terrorists said, during a tape-recorded call from federal prison a few months before Clinton pardoned him, "I don't have to ask for forgiveness from anybody. I have nothing to be ashamed of, or feel that I have to ask for forgiveness. My desire has gotten stronger, to the point where I want to continue. Continue to fight and get involved with my people."[23] A Justice Department report on its "Counterterrorism and Technology Crime Plan" concluded that Clinton's pardon significantly increased the danger of future FALN terrorist attacks.[24] But the pardon was for a worthy cause: helping Hillary Clinton win Puerto Rican votes in pursuit of a U.S. Senate seat.

Justice Department lawyers had to use extra elbow grease to try to exonerate fellow attorneys at the Interior Department and Treasury Department. An outside audit found that the Interior Department was unable to account for more than $2 billion in funds supposedly deposited in Indian Trust Fund Accounts.[25] Attorneys representing the hundreds of thousands of Indians who lost money as a result filed suit. Treasury Department officials responded by shredding 162 boxes of documents that could have explained how the funds vanished.[26] Federal judge Royce Lamberth declared: "Rather than coming forward at that time and making the necessary admissions, the Treasury officials deliberately decided not to tell Justice Department officials about the destruction, arrogating totally to themselves the decision that the documents were not related to this litigation, a decision that everyone involved now admits was wrong."[27] Justice Department lawyers pleaded with Lamberth not to release a critical report because of the danger of "severe and unfair damage" to the reputations of the Treasury shredders, as well as the risk of "eroding confidence" in the Interior Department.[28] The judge in 1999 fined the Treasury and Interior departments $625,000 for disobeying court orders in the case.

THE BEST OF INTENTIONS

Reno's belief that government lawyers, if not all federal officials, are "little lower than the angels" repeatedly influenced her decisions not to prosecute federal officials who clearly violated federal law because they purportedly had no "intent" to violate the law:

- Reno refused to appoint an independent counsel to investigate the tidal wave of illegal foreign money that hit the 1996 Clinton reelection campaign, the use of White House bedrooms and coffee tables to shake down donors, etc. The Justice Department lawyer that Reno hand-picked to investigate the charges, Charles LaBella, concluded that the evidence pointed to "a level of knowledge within the White House—including the president's and first lady's offices—concerning the injection of foreign funds into the re-election effort."[29] Reno brushed off LaBella's recommendation and tried to bury his report. (This may have been the quid pro quo Reno cut to keep her job for Clinton's second term, after it became obvious in early 1997 that the White House wanted her gone.) By confining all the campaign investigations to her own Public Integrity Section, she minimized the danger of integrity breaking out. The *New York Times,* commenting on one of the contortions Reno went through to avoid appointing a special counsel to investigate Clinton, editorialized: "The mystery is why any Attorney General would want his or her chief legacy to be the preservation of a cover-up."[30]
- Reno refused to appoint an independent counsel to investigate Vice President Gore for numerous stark violations of campaign finance law— such as shaking down Buddhist monks and using his White House office to raise hard cash for the Clinton-Gore reelection campaign—because

Reno claimed that Gore had no intent to violate the law. A long-term Gore fund-raiser, Maria Hsia, was convicted in early 2000 for her role in the Buddhist Temple shakedown. On the three occasions when FBI agents interviewed Gore about his fund-raising activities, they politely never asked any questions about the Buddhist Temple.[31] While the Justice Department investigation lagged, many key suspects fled to Asia and other foreign shores. When Gore was questioned by reporters in March 2000 about the conviction of Hsia, he declared: "I made a mistake going to that Buddhist temple. I made a mistake in making telephone calls from my office." Gore then deftly put the entire matter behind him: "I have a passion for campaign finance reform that is fueled in part because of the pain of those mistakes."[32]

The longer Reno clung to office, the more convinced she became that she personified justice. Consider her flip-flop on the independent counsel law. Reno urged Congress in 1993 to renew the independent counsel law because "there is an inherent conflict whenever senior executive branch officials are to be investigated by the department and its appointed head, the attorney general. The attorney general serves at the pleasure of the president . . . It is absolutely essential for the public and process of the criminal justice system to have confidence in the system, and you cannot do that when there is conflict, or an appearance of conflict in the person who is, in effect, the chief prosecutor."[33] But the longer she served as attorney general, the more contemptuous she became of public confidence in the justice system. She reversed her position and announced in June 1999: "Basically, I think the attorney general gets held responsible for it one way or the other, and so the responsibility should lie with the attorney general."[34] Reno suggested to Congress that the existing law be replaced with a system that gave any attorney general unfettered authority to veto any indictments and to fire any special counsel at any time on any pretext, thereby completely and perpetually politicizing the process of investigating wrongdoing by high-ranking government officials. Apparently, the best response to crimes of government officials is to get a bigger broom to sweep them under the rug.

Reno was consistently judged by the media simply on whether she "held her ground" under Republican questioning in congressional hearings. This standard was *de rigueur* in part because many journalists did not want to bother understanding the underlying issues: it was much easier to cast everything simply as a horse race—or, in this case, a mule tug. Reno's modus operandi for her Capitol Hill testimony was to appear holier than thou; regardless of the specific abuses by DOJ employees or herself she might be questioned about, she could pretend that she inhabited some lofty plateau far above the grubby politicians who were doubting her integrity.

HATE CRIME HYSTERIA

While Reno persistently found the motives of government employees above reproach (or at least not prosecutable), she and President Clinton avidly pursued legislation to give the federal government far more prerogative to punish private motives and intentions.

In April 1999, Clinton, "hoping to ride the momentum of headlines from Kosovo," as the Associated Press reported, proposed expanding federal hate crime laws to cover offenses allegedly based on sexual orientation, gender, or disability. Clinton announced that the United States was as vulnerable as Kosovo to "old, even primitive hatreds . . . It's very humbling. We should remember that each of us almost wakes up every day with the scales of light and darkness in our own hearts, and we've got to keep them in proper balance. And we have to be, in the United States, absolutely resolute about this."[35] (Naturally, Clinton's standing order at that time for American planes to bomb cities full of Serb civilians was irrelevant to the "scales of light and darkness" in his own heart.)

Federal hate crime legislation bases the harshness of punishment on the group identity of victims, rather than on the actions of individual offenders. Crimes based on racial or ethnic prejudice could already be pulled under federal jurisdiction under a hate crime law passed in 1990. Anyone convicted of a hate crime—selecting a victim based on the specified criteria—became eligible for far more years up the river than politically correct felons.

Clinton frequently evoked the issue of hate crimes in fund-raising speeches before gay rights and other groups. In a Beverly Hills speech on October 2, 1999, Clinton announced that hate is "America's largest problem . . . We cannot be under the illusion that either material prosperity or technological breakthroughs alone can purge the darkness in our hearts."[36] On October 19, 1999, Clinton announced that hate crimes were "the biggest challenge facing" the nation and the world.[37] By raising hate crimes to the top of the national problem list, all political and governmental abuses were put in the shadows.

Attorney General Reno relied on bait-and-switch tactics to advance the cause. On the "Kids Page" of the Justice Department website, visitors found a big grinning picture of Reno and a banner proclaiming "HATEFUL ACTS HURT KIDS!" The text below declared: "It hurts kids to be treated unfairly because of their race, color, religion, culture, disability, or gender. Have your feelings ever been hurt by someone's words or acts? . . . Did they make fun of your name . . . or how you dressed or talked?" Thus, snideness about someone's shirt becomes the moral equivalent of burning a cross on a black family's yard. As an example of hateful conduct, the website offered the case of a young girl who said that other people did not want to sit with her at the school cafeteria.[38] Under this standard, almost any private restaurant could be considered an incubator of hate, since people usually prefer not to share tables with strangers. Reno also asserted: "When someone makes jokes about people, or labels people because of where they come from, the color of their skin, their religion or gender, it's both a hurtful act and a hateful act."[39] Some ethnic/gender/national-origin humor is tinged with hatred; but it is absurd to assume that every guy who tells a dumb blonde joke hates women, or that every female who tells a dumb jock joke hates men. Reno also encouraged kids to turn informant on anyone who made off-color ethnic remarks in their own homes, suggesting "you might try talking to your parents, teacher, religious leader, counselor or some other adult with whom you feel comfortable." But, as columnist Nat Hentoff noted, this encouraged kids to turn their parents in to government employees, since most school teachers and counselors work for the state.[40]

Reno blurred the distinction between hatred and merely hurtful acts, implying that simply not liking someone was akin to a hate crime. Reno's peculiar examples of hate crimes are typical of how expanding federal power becomes consecrated. First the term "hate crime" is held up for all decent people to applaud and support. Then the definition of the crime is continually expanded. Next, feds finance activist groups (such as those bankrolled by AmeriCorps) to set up reporting systems practically designed to greatly exaggerate the scope of the problem. Then after enough bogus statistics are aggregated, Clinton announces there is a national crisis and the feds need far more power to prevent moral genocide.

Clinton and Reno continually spoke as if the nation was suffering from an epidemic of hate crimes. But FBI data on hate crimes "are all but useless for discerning trends, because of the variation in the number of states and police departments reporting," wrote law professors James Jacobs and Kimberly Potter in their 1998 book, *Hate Crimes: Criminal Law and Identity Politics*.[41] Jacobs and Potter conclude that "conspicuously absent are the data to support the claim that hate crime is increasing."[42]

Existing hate crime laws already encourage federal agents to stampede after publicity. As lawyer Richard Dooling noted in the *Wall Street Journal,*

> One of the witnesses testifying in the Senate [hate crimes hearings] against the
> bill, Kern County, Calif., District Attorney Ed Jagels told the committee that

he had received a memo awhile back from the U.S. attorney's office in California, advising him that federal authorities would no longer investigate or prosecute certain kinds of bank robberies and embezzlement from federally chartered institutions . . . After being told that the feds in his district lacked the resources to handle certain bank robberies, Mr. Jagels was surprised when a small army of federal agents and U.S. attorneys arrived to investigate an altercation involving racial epithets and watermelons, which occurred in the county seat of Bakersfield—a case Mr. Jagels's office could easily have handled alone. Does the federal government take symbolic watermelons more seriously than bank robberies?[43]

Hate crime laws allow prosecutors and politicians to play God, pretending they can determine which perpetrators are truly evil and which are merely greedy robbers, horny rapists, or abused-children-turned-mass murderers. Prosecuting hate crimes takes government out of the mundane and makes it seem to be an avenging angel. Government rises from merely trying to punish and thus prevent violence to being a judge of souls.

LAPTOPS=COPS MIRACLE

Reno's Justice Department masterminded President Clinton's promise to spend federal tax dollars to multiply local police. Clinton promised that his proposal to put 100,000 cops on the streets would make Americans "freer from fear."[44] After Congress enacted the program as part of the 1994 crime bill, Clinton declared that he had promised "to put 100,000 more police on our streets because there is simply no better crime-fighting tool to be found."[45] Vice President Al Gore made this a key boast in his 2000 presidential campaign, declaring on the night of his Super Tuesday primary victories: "We're putting 100,000 new police on our streets! More Americans are safer!"[46]

But, despite $9 billion in federal spending, the Community Oriented Policing Services's 100,000 new cops claim is "voodoo math," as one Florida police chief characterized the Clinton administration's success claims.[47]

Clinton's new cops are often nothing more than federally paid purchases of laptop computers. In Little Rock, Arkansas, 40 of the 82 "new" cops were actually "equivalent in technology"—new cops created by claiming labor savings as a result of purchases of laptop computers and other equipment.[48] The Omaha, Nebraska Police Department was credited with hiring 72.8 new police officers after it received $2.8 million in federal grants to purchase laptop computers—

even though the laptop computers were not purchased.[49] The Justice Department claims that COPS grants to the Washington, D.C. police department (which ranks number one in the nation in donut consumption) allowed for the equivalent of 781 additional police; however, only a few dozen new cops actually hit the streets.[50]

A 1999 DOJ Inspector General report concluded that more than 40,000 of the 100,000 "new cops" were actually "equivalents" concocted as a result of assertions of time savings from new technology or from hiring civilians to supposedly do police paperwork or administrative duties.[51] Such grants have their own acronym: MORE, for Making Officer Redeployment Effective. As usual, the acronym has no relation to how the program actually operates.

Seventy-eight percent of police departments that receive MORE grants cannot show that federal aid actually led to more cops on the street. Almost half of police departments simply substituted federal funds for local spending.[52] Most police departments have no plans to retain the new cops after the federal spigot runs dry. The Justice Department has little idea how the program is actually operating because 94 percent of police departments don't bother submitting mandatory financial status reports (or submit the reports late).

When DOJ Inspector General Michael Bromwich launched an investigation to see how many new cops had been hired, COPS bureaucrats insisted that their goal was merely to have approved grant applications for 100,000 new police by the end of fiscal year 2000. However, Clinton administration officials and COPS documents clearly stated that the goal was to have the 100,000 cops on the street by that time.[53] The IG report noted, "COPS counts an officer as funded when it approves the grantees' application for award of the grant, instead of when the grantee actually accepts the grant."[54] Almost 500 police departments have failed to accept grants because of the requirement that the local government provide 25 percent of the new cop's salary. The feds make no effort to verify claims of new hires. Nassau County, New York received $26 million and was credited with hiring 327 new cops; an IG audit found that the county actually reduced his cop force by 218 officers, in spite of the grant.[55]

Clinton perennially invokes his 100,000 new cops as a way to make average Americans feel that their federal government cares about them. But Kristen Mahoney, who worked in the federal program during its launch stage, observed: "The COPS office started off on a wing and a prayer. They threw us into it and said that . . . we need to spend a billion dollars by the end of the year."[56] The *Chicago Tribune* examined grants to the nation's 50 largest police departments and found "no correlation between the growth in number of officers and crime rates since 1993."[57] The *Tribune* noted: "The COPS program has earmarked $240 million for studies, training and conferences, which Justice Department officials said is critical for spreading the word about community policing and improving local programs. But not a dime has been spent on quantifying what has become the program's main selling point—that more cops mean less crime."[58]

While Clinton claimed that local grant recipients would implement community policing methods, there is no such requirement in the grant application (which is often a mere one page). Federal money is helping turn some police departments into public nuisances. The *Chicago Tribune* noted: "In Johnstown, Ohio, hundreds of residents are threatening to abolish the Police Department because, they say, the addition of COPS officers led not to cooperation with the police, but harassment of average citizens. Residents say that officers stop motorists on any pretext, including having too much snow or rust on a license plate."[59]

FBI ETHICAL TRIUMPHS

In a 1995 commencement address at Catholic University, FBI Director Louis Freeh, speaking of the mission of law enforcement agents, compared himself to the prophet Isaiah and quoted the Old Testament: "Then I heard the voice of the Lord saying, 'Whom Shall I Send? Who Will go for us? Here I am, I said; Send me.'"[60] It was not surprising that Freeh would characterize himself in biblical terms, since he had already been deified by the Washington press corps, members of Congress, and the Clinton administration.

Freeh's biblical invocation at Catholic University was not an aberration. The FBI issued a report in 1998 by Freeh in which he hyped his achievements in his first five years as FBI director. The report began by quoting Psalm 101: "He who walks in the way of integrity shall be in my service. No one who practices deceit can hold a post in my court. No one who speaks falsely can be among my advisors."[61] Freeh bragged: "In the past five years, I have established core values for all FBI employees: obedience to the Constitution, respect for the dignity of all protected by the FBI, compassion, fairness, and total integrity. At the same time, I have developed 'Bright Line' policies to which all FBI employees must adhere. Certain conduct will not be tolerated, including lying, cheating, stealing, sexual harassment, and alcohol and drug abuse."[62] Freeh declared: "One of the major training breakthroughs that has been achieved at the FBI is the addition of ethics and integrity training for the new Special Agent curriculum and management training at the FBI Academy at Quantico. Ethics is the golden thread which runs throughout our training. It often is the difference between correctly applying the awesome power of law enforcement and conduct that undermines the rule of law."

Freeh was selected for FBI director after Clinton fired then-director William Sessions over alleged ethical abuses.[63] (Some critics believed that Sessions was fired largely because Clinton wanted his "own man" at the head of the FBI.) The Clinton spin machine set Freeh up as a savior and a "law enforcement legend," in Clinton's words,[64] when he took the job in August 1993. Freeh had the right attitude for the Clinton administration: he was enamored of government. In a 1994 interview, Freeh recalled that he did not protest the Vietnam War while at college in the 1960s: "For me, it would have been extremely difficult to break the law or protest against the government because I had this sense that the government was always right."[65] But someone who believes government is always right easily assumes that a citizen with a conflict with a government agent is always wrong.

Freeh succeeded in persuading Congress to double the FBI's annual budget (from $1.5 billion to more than $3 billion) and to authorize the hiring of an additional thousand special agents.[66] In November 1994, he issued a special report to FBI employees—naturally, also provided to major media— that claimed that cuts in the FBI budget were gravely endangering FBI agents because the agency could no longer provide agents with sufficient ammunition for target practice. Freeh declaimed, "Every citizen—to say nothing of public officials—should try to imagine the dangers, the sheer lunacy, of FBI agents not even having enough bullets. That is intolerable and will not be allowed to recur."[67] Freeh ignored the Clinton administration's FBI budget request, instead lobbying successfully on Capitol Hill for a higher appropriation. Yet, while Freeh claimed that the FBI did not have enough money to pay for target practice, he had no difficulty finding tax dollars to finance his own pet projects, such as a new FBI international academy in Budapest, 20 new overseas postings for FBI agents, and a massive expansion into counter-intelligence efforts. The *Washington Post* labeled Freeh the "Genghis Khan of turf grabbers" for his efforts to expand the FBI.[68]

We will examine a few FBI ethical triumphs below.

PIPE-BOMB BUST

Thanks to Freeh's reforms, FBI agents receive special training to give them a "deeper intellectual understanding of human rights," as the *Washington Post* reported. But there are one or two loopholes. The official course material used in FBI ethics classes declares: "The harmful effects [of deception] may be counterbalanced by beneficial consequences." The *Post* noted, "Subjects of FBI investigations, according to the academy's study guide, 'have forfeited their right to the truth,' and as a result, agents are justified in the use of decoys, sting operations and other forms of deception when they are investigating a case."[69]

On July 27, 1996, a pipe bomb went off at Centennial Olympic Park in Atlanta, where the world's athletes and media were gathered for the Olympic games. The FBI decided that 33-year-old security guard Richard Jewell, who had found the bomb and helped clear the area and minimize fatalities, had also planted the bomb. FBI agents lured Jewell over to their Atlanta office and asked him to help them make a training film about detecting bombs. The ruse allowed the agents to question Jewell extensively without reading him a Miranda warning—without alerting him that anything he said could be used against him. As *Investor's Business Daily* noted, "Jewell was the bureau's top suspect, a fact that was leaked to the press in time for cameras to catch agents poring over Jewell's home."[70] FBI leaks led to 88 days of hell for Jewell, who saw his life and reputation dragged in the gutter day after day. The FBI did nothing to curb the media harassment of Jewell long after it had recognized that he was innocent. A Justice Department investigation concluded that the training-film scam violated Jewell's constitutional rights. But, in 1997 Senate testimony, Freeh asserted that Jewell's rights were not violated because Jewell did not say anything to incriminate himself.[71] Apparently, only guilty citizens have constitutional rights. Two FBI agents were censured and one was suspended for five days without pay. But, as the *Washington Times* noted, "No similar disciplinary action was recommended against senior FBI officials in Washington who oversaw the probe and were actively involved in the interrogation, including Mr. Freeh, who took part in the hour-long interview, even suggesting a question."[72]

Jewell became a hero-martyr to some Americans. President Clinton identified with Jewell because Clinton felt that he, too, was so often falsely accused by the media. Clinton was asked at a November 1996 press conference whether he thought John Huang should "come forward and answer these questions [about alleged illegal fund-raising]." Clinton responded: "One of the things I would urge you to do, remembering what happened to Mr. Jewell in Atlanta, remembering what has happened to so many of the accusations over the last four years made against me that turned out to be totally baseless, I just think that we ought to make sure we've got— we ought to just get the facts out, and they should be reported."[73] (Huang pleaded guilty to federal election law violations in 1999.[74])Clinton "kept in the file newspaper articles about what he regarded as unfair attacks on [Jewell]," the *New Yorker* reported in late 1999.[75]

FILEGATE

In 1996, news broke that the FBI had illegally delivered to the White House more than 900 confidential background-check files the FBI had compiled on Bush and Reagan administration nominees. Freeh immediately issued a press release announcing: "I and the FBI have been victimized by the White House."[76]

The White House roundup of files was the project of White House personnel security chief and former bar bouncer Craig Livingstone. Disclosing the information in the FBI files—which contain detailed hearsay, innuendo, and rumors about subjects' sexual, financial, social, and other activities—is a federal crime carrying a penalty of a year in prison for each violation. Clinton quickly asserted that the file transfer was simply a "completely honest bureaucratic snafu."[77] (CNN reporter Jill Dougherty, in a segment on the controversy, noted, "The president said he supported the apology his chief of staff offered earlier in the day on Mr. Clinton's behalf."[78])

Freeh responded to the snowballing scandal by appointing FBI General Counsel Howard Shapiro to investigate. Shapiro promptly reported that no one at the FBI or the White House had violated federal law. Shapiro's investigation was discredited after congressional probers discovered that he had not even bothered to talk to any White House officials about what was done with the illegally acquired files.[79]

The question quickly arose as to who had hired Livingstone, and no one at the White House would take credit for his selection. FBI agent Dennis Sculimbrene submitted notes to a congressional committee that he had made of a 1993 interview in which he was told by White House counsel Bernard Nussbaum that Hillary Clinton had insisted on Livingstone's hiring—despite Livingstone's scant professional background. When FBI General Counsel Shapiro learned of Sculimbrene's notes, he dispatched two FBI agents to pay a surprise visit to Sculimbrene at home. Republican congressmen charged that the purpose of the visit was to intimidate Sculimbrene. Shapiro also alerted the White House the day before the FBI provided incriminating information demanded by congressional investigators. This kindly gesture caused an explosion on Capitol Hill. Shapiro quickly publicly admitted that he had made a "horrific blunder," and Freeh issued a press release proclaiming his "full confidence" in Shapiro and declaring that "none of Howard's actions were done in bad faith or for partisan purposes."[80]

The White House sought to blame the scandal on the Secret Service for providing an outdated list of names of political appointees for background checks. However, two Secret Service agents testified in congressional hearings that the White House spin was false.[81] The Treasury Department responded by launching a criminal investigation of the agents. (The investigation turned up nothing and was widely denounced as an attempt to punish the two men.)[82] A House report observed, "It is unconscionable that the White House shifted the blame from its own incompetent appointees to those of the U.S. Secret Service. The White House mounted a stealth campaign consisting mainly of background statements attributed to unidentified sources to blame the Secret Service."[83]

When asked in 1998 what happened to the confidential files before they were sent back to the FBI, Livingstone replied: "I can see a secretary or some poor intern being relegated to typing up somebody's information on the computer so that the president could read it or the chief of staff could read it."[84] Rep. Bill Clinger, who chaired the House investigation, reported that "at least one individual, Anthony Marceca, reviewed every file . . . looking for 'derogatory' information. He even took information home with him and kept it for years after leaving the White House."[85] Marceca and several other White House aides took the Fifth Amendment when forced to testify before Clinger's committee under oath. A House committee recommended two months later that Shapiro be fired because he had a "far too cozy relationship" with the Clinton White House. The report also accused Shapiro of "inexplicable and inexcusable" interference with the congressional FBI files investigation.[86] The Justice Department's Office of Professional Responsibility (headed by a man whom Freeh hailed as a "good friend") investigated and concluded that "Shapiro's actions were not motivated by any alleged personal or political ambitions."[87] When Shapiro left office in 1997 to take a high-paying job with a Washington law firm, Janet Reno declared: "He made a major contribution to the FBI and the Department of Justice, and I'm going to miss him."[88]

LAB FRAME-UPS

In 1991, Frederic Whitehurst, a Ph.D. chemist and the FBI's top bomb-residue expert, formally complained that the revered FBI crime laboratory was engaged in shoddy practices and fabricating evidence. The FBI did an internal investigation that quickly brushed his charges under the table.

In 1995, Department of Justice Inspector General Michael Bromwich launched a new investigation into Whitehurst's charges and issued a 517-page report in April 1997 that left the FBI lab's reputation in tatters. The IG report found that lab experts provided court testimony "that appeared tailored to the most incriminating result" and often involved "speculation beyond [their] scientific expertise."[89] The IG noted that, in the Oklahoma City bombing trial, one FBI lab expert's witness opinion was "misleading and presents the case in a way most incriminating to the defendants . . . In other respects as well, his work was flawed and lacked a scientific foundation. The errors he made were all tilted in such a way as to incriminate the defendants."[90] Other testimony offered by FBI lab experts "repeatedly reached conclusions that incriminated the defendants without a scientific basis." In the New York World Trade Center bombing case, "Williams [an examiner in the Explosives Unit] gave inaccurate and incomplete testimony and testified to invalid opinions that appeared tailored to the most incriminating result." The report stated that the IG was "deeply troubled that his [the agent's] testimony on direct examination may have misled the court."[91] Though the report noted at least one case in which an FBI lab employee "testified falsely," it insisted that no FBI agent was guilty of perjury—as usual, because there was no intent to break the law. Kim Weissman, publisher of *Congress Action,* noted, "That the IG never found a single instance of evidence slanted to favor a defendant, and that all the flaws resulted in evidence and testimony slanted to favor the prosecution, was irrelevant to Bromwich."[92] The IG report found ample damning evidence, yet judiciously concluded that no actual damnation existed. John Kelly and Philip Wearne, in their 1998 book, *Tainting Evidence,* noted that the FBI lab scandal "has affected hundreds, maybe thousands of lives . . . A scandal that demonstrated that . . . the FBI was unaccountable even to the FBI, let alone Congress, the scientific community, or the general public."[93]

Freeh received a draft of the IG report in early March 1997 and testified to a congressional committee a few days later that Whitehurst had been suspended "solely and directly on the basis of the recommendation by the inspector general and their findings." Bromwich was outraged: Freeh almost certainly knew that Bromwich had strenuously opposed FBI efforts to suspend the scientist. As Stuart Taylor noted in the *American Lawyer,* "Bromwich was deeply disturbed by what he saw as an effort by the FBI to put a self-serving slant on the situation, deflecting the blame for what many in Congress saw as a retaliation against the whistle-blower."[94] After a memo Bromwich wrote to Freeh contradicting his testimony became public, the FBI issued a statement declaring that Freeh "totally rejects" any inference that he had lied; the press release also stated that Freeh "regrets his inadvertent omission" in congressional testimony.[95] Sen. Charles Grassley (R-Iowa) responded by denouncing the FBI: "At the heart of its damage-control operation is an effort to mislead. And that effort comes right from the top of the FBI, right from the director himself, Louis Freeh."[96]

In February 1998, the FBI paid Whitehurst more than a million dollars to settle his lawsuit that charged that the agency retaliated against him for blowing the whistle on the lab's problems.[97]

Fifteen months after the IG's report hit the streets, the Justice Department finally took action against the wrongdoers identified in the report. Two FBI employees were given letters of censure. Assistant Attorney General for Administration Stephen Colgate wrote in a memo that "minimal" sanctions were being imposed in part because of the "staleness" of the abuses the IG discovered and because of the "consistent and often spirited opposition" of FBI leadership to harsher penalties.[98] Sen. Grassley declared: "FBI management has succeeded in protecting its rogues in the lab scandal. They lobbied fiercely to protect the wrongdoers from punishment. The bureau pressured the Justice Department and the department rolled over."[99]

Freeh successfully fought off every attempt to allow the Justice Department Inspector General to have full power to investigate FBI abuses. Sen. Grassley told Freeh at a June 1997 hearing: "Beyond the [FBI's] veneer is an ugly culture of arrogance that uses disinformation, intimidation, empire building to get what it wants . . . It resists oversight by an independent body."[100] Christopher Kerr, a 23-year FBI agent and a board member of the FBI Agents Association, observed in late 1995: "Few in the FBI ranks were surprised to learn that the recent Ruby Ridge inquiry was 'fixed' . . . It is a system interwoven with conflicts of interest and an almost total lack of what passes for due process anywhere else in government."[101]

According to David Burnham, a highly respected former *New York Times* police reporter, "The F.B.I. today is a sloppy, unresponsive, badly managed, uncooperative and out-of-touch agency that is aggressively trying to expand its control over the American people."[102] Burnham, using computer and court records, did a pioneering analysis debunking the FBI's mystique. He concluded: "For many years Justice Department prosecutors all over the country have found much of the bureau's investigative work inadequate."[103] Only 26 percent of FBI investigations forwarded to federal prosecutors result in court convictions, a much lower average than those of the DEA or ATF.[104]

On the plus side, the FBI did an admirable job of handling the standoff with the so-called Montana Freemen in 1996. The agency's Hostage Rescue Team was sent to the scene, but FBI headquarters kept them on a leash short enough for a peaceful surrender to be worked out with the malcontents inside a ranch house. The strategy paid off, both in good publicity and in the ultimate results: court convictions of several of the Freemen.

CONCLUSION

At press time, both Reno and Freeh were expected to exit before the end of the Clinton administration. Reno was increasingly debilitated by Parkinson's Disease and was expected to resign before the November election. Freeh was suffering from what French physician Rabelais diagnosed long ago as "a shortage of money." A front-page April 4, 2000 *Washington Post* puff piece on the FBI director revealed that he was being tortured by trying to maintain his family on his $141,000 annual salary.[105] (Freeh was afflicted with a $400,000 mortgage—an act of God that would bring many Americans to their knees.) The *Post* reported that Freeh was shopping around for a private sector job, one that hopefully paid at least $1 million a year. His ten-year term as FBI director would end in 2003—but apparently Freeh could no longer in good conscience subject his family to the deprivations they were enduring on his government salary.

KOSOVO: MORALIZING WITH CLUSTER BOMBS

"Promising too much can be as cruel as caring too little."
—President Bill Clinton, September 21, 1999[1]

TERRORIST ETHNIC CLEANSING was rampant in Kosovo. The *New York Times* reported, "Ethnic Albanians in the Government have manipulated public funds and regulations to take over land belonging to Serbs . . . Slavic Orthodox churches have been attacked, and flags have been torn down. Wells have been poisoned and crops burned. Slavic boys have been knifed."[2] The top ethnic Albanian politician "joked at an official dinner in Prizren last year that Serbian women should be used to satisfy potential ethnic Albanian rapists." The *Times* noted, "A young Army conscript of ethnic Albanian origin shot up his barracks, killing four sleeping Slavic bunkmates and wounding six others."[3] The attack sparked widespread fear because thousands of ethnic Albanians in the army were being incited to slaughter Serbian soldiers. Tens of thousands of Serbs had fled Kosovo in the preceding years as a result of the rising ethnic violence, often abandoning their farms and homes in the process. Ethnic Albanians demanded an "ethnically pure" region and called for the expulsion of all Serbs.

The November 1, 1987, *Times* story was long forgotten by early 1999. The history of Kosovo had been rewritten by the Clinton administration as it began saturation bombing of Serbia in order to create a multiethnic paradise in Kosovo. Clinton declared in June 1999 that "the violence we responded to in Kosovo was the culmination of a 10-year campaign by Slobodan Milosevic, the leader of Serbia, to exploit ethnic and religious differences."[4] Because Clinton chose to start the clock at a time when Serbs responded to persecution, the administration could pretend that they were dealing with a simple case of good versus evil— rather than a situation tangled by centuries of reprisals.

Clinton's war against Serbia epitomized his moralism, his arrogance, his refusal to respect law, and his fixation on proving his virtue via deadly force, regardless of how many innocent people died in the process.

GINNING UP A PRETEXT TO BOMB

Ethnic conflicts exploded throughout the former Yugoslavia in the early 1990s. The casualty toll was highest in Bosnia. In 1995, the Clinton administration backed a sweep by the U.S.-trained Croatian army to recapture Serb-held territory in Croatia. Over a quarter-million Serb civilians were turned into refugees by this attack; much of Croatia was ethnically cleansed in the process.[5] The U.S. government made no protest and refused to recognize the plight of Serb refugees.

By 1998, full-scale civil war was raging in Kosovo, a province of Serbia the size of Connecticut. The Kosovo Liberation Army (KLA) controlled about 40 percent of the territory of the province. Both sides used brutal tactics. For instance, at the State Department daily press briefing of March 4, 1998, department spokesman James Rubin announced that the U.S. government "called on the leaders of the Kosovar-Albanians to condemn terrorist action by the so-called Kosovo Liberation Army." The KLA was known to be heavily involved in drug trafficking and had close ties to Osama bin Laden, allegedly the worst terrorist mastermind in the world. A cease-fire was negotiated between the Serbian government and the KLA in late 1998, but did not stop the fighting. According to former Secretary of State Henry Kissinger, 80 percent of the cease-fire violations in the months before the NATO bombing campaign began were committed by the KLA.[6] The BBC later published confidential minutes of a meeting of the North Atlantic Council, NATO's policymaking body, from shortly before the conflict, which stated that the KLA had "launched what appears to be a deliberate campaign of provocation." The Council concluded that the KLA was "the main initiator of violence."[7]

The United States and its NATO partners pressured the Serbian government to agree to a set of demands purportedly to end the ethnic violence in Kosovo. When Serbian President Slobodan Milosevic refused, NATO bombed. In a speech on March 24, 1999, the day the bombing began, Clinton denounced Milosevic for rejecting "the balanced and fair peace accords that our allies and partners, including Russia, proposed last month, a peace agreement that Kosovo's ethnic Albanians courageously accepted."[8] However, at negotiations in Rambouillet, France, NATO effectively demanded the equivalent of unconditional surrender from the Yugoslavian government. As John Pilger reported in the British *New Statesman,* "Anyone scrutinizing the Rambouillet document is left in little doubt that the excuses given for the subsequent bombing were fabricated. The peace negotiations were stage-managed, and the Serbs were told: surrender and be occupied, or don't surrender and be destroyed. The impossible terms, published in full in *Le Monde Diplomatique,* but not in Britain, show that NATO's aim was the occupation not only of Kosovo, but effectively all of Yugoslavia."[9] The secret agreement specified that NATO forces would have been "immune from all legal process, whether civil, administrative or criminal, [and] under all circumstances and at all times, immune from [all laws] governing any criminal or disciplinary offences which may be committed by NATO personnel in the Federal Republic of Yugoslavia . . . NATO personnel shall enjoy . . . with their vehicles, vessels, aircraft and equipment, free and unrestricted passage and unimpeded access throughout the Federal Republic of Yugoslavia, including associated airspace and territorial waters." The Yugoslavian government would also have been obligated, "upon simple request, [to] grant all telecommunications services, including broadcast services, needed for [the occupation], as determined by NATO. This shall be free of cost." NATO also demanded that the Yugoslavian "economy shall function in accordance with free market principles." (Such principles were only for export; Clinton adamantly opposed free market principles for the U.S. health care sector.)

Former Secretary of State Henry Kissinger characterized the Rambouillet text as "a provocation, an excuse to start bombing" and concluded: "Rambouillet . . . was a terrible diplomatic document that should never have been presented in that form."[10] Former State Department Yugoslavian desk officer George Kenney reported in May 1999: "An unimpeachable press source who regularly travels with Secretary of State Madeleine Albright told this reviewer that, swearing reporters to deep-background confidentiality at the Rambouillet talks, a senior State Department official had bragged that the United States 'deliberately set the bar higher than the Serbs could accept.' The Serbs needed, according to the official, a little bombing to see reason."[11]

A MORAL IMPERATIVE TO KILL

Launching the bombing of Serbia was a family affair in the Clinton White House. Hillary Clinton revealed to an interviewer in the summer of 1999: "I urged him to bomb. You cannot let this go on at the end of a century that has seen the major holocaust of our time. What do we have NATO for if not to defend our way of life?"[12] A biography of Hillary Clinton, written by Gail Sheehy and published in late 1999, stated that Hillary had refused to talk to the president for eight months after the Monica Lewinsky scandal broke. Hillary only resumed talking to her husband when she phoned him and urged him in the strongest terms to begin bombing Serbia; the next day, Clinton announced that the United States had a "moral imperative" to stop Milosevic and the bombing began.[13] Alexander Cockburn observed in the *Los Angeles Times:* "It's scarcely surprising that Hillary would have urged President Clinton to drop cluster bombs on the Serbs to defend 'our way of life.' The first lady is a social engineer. She believes in therapeutic policing and the duty of the state to impose such policing. War is more social engineering, 'fixitry' via high explosive, social therapy via cruise missile . . . As a tough therapeutic cop, she does not shy away from the most abrupt expression of the therapy: the death penalty."[14]

There was no fact that could not be brushed aside or twisted to sanctify the bombing. In a March 27, 1999, radio address, Clinton announced, "Through two World Wars and a long cold war we saw that it was a short step from a small brush fire to an inferno, especially in the tinderbox of the Balkans. The time to put out a fire is before it spreads and burns down the neighborhood."[15] The inference that World War II started in the Balkans would surprise Poles who recalled the Nazi invasion of September 1, 1939.

Clinton went to war against Serbia in part to prove how opposed he was to the Holocaust. Comparisons between Serbia and Nazi Germany popped up again and again in Clinton's speeches. In a 1999 Memorial Day speech at Arlington National Cemetery, Clinton declared, "In Kosovo we see some parallels to World War II, for the government of Serbia, like that of Nazi Germany, rose to power in part by getting people to look down on people of a given race and ethnicity, and to believe they had no place in their country, and even no right to live."[16] In a speech at the National Defense University on May 13, Clinton said that Serbia, like Nazi Germany, had engaged in a "vicious, premeditated, systematic oppression fueled by religious and ethnic hatred."[17] Clinton used the word "Holocaust" as the ultimate trump card, a term to undermine resistance to the use of deadly force by the government—practically the mirror image of the lesson that should have been learned from the original Holocaust. Ironically, many Israelis were very ambivalent about the NATO war, in part because the Serbs had fought valiantly against the Nazis in the 1940s and had historically shown little anti-Semitism; the Kosovar Albanians, by contrast, had flocked to join an SS division during World War II.[18] Israelis were also concerned that an independent Kosovo could become a base for Islamic terrorists.[19]

Clinton claimed on March 24 that one purpose of the bombing was "to deter an even bloodier offensive against innocent civilians in Kosovo and, if necessary, to seriously damage the Serbian military's capacity to harm the people of Kosovo."[20] The CIA warned the Clinton administration that, if bombing was initiated, the Serbian army would greatly accelerate its efforts to expel ethnic Albanians. The White House disregarded this warning and feigned surprise when mass expulsions began. Yet, NATO supreme commander, General Wesley Clark, said on March 26 that the upsurge in crackdowns on ethnic Albanians was "entirely predictable."[21] Since NATO had no ground forces in the area ready to intervene and since NATO planes stayed three miles above the ground to minimize pilot casualties, NATO could do nothing to stop the surge in ethnic cleansing. Violence spurred by the bombing was quickly invoked as the ultimate justification for the bombing.

In a special videotape address to the Serbian people on March 25, Clinton declared that the Serbian attack "was not simply a war against armed Kosovar forces but also a campaign of violence in which tanks and artillery were unleashed against unarmed civilians."[22] But a campaign against unarmed civilians from planes far overhead was different because NATO had a "moral imperative."

The longer the bombing went on, the more brazenly NATO ignored the limits it had initially imposed on its targets. In the final weeks of the 78-day war, all that mattered was finding new targets so that NATO spokesmen could continue their daily bragging about a "record number of sorties flown" and "record number of bombs dropped."

The *Los Angeles Times* detailed many of the "mistakes" made by U.S. and British war planes:

April 5	An attack on a residential area in the mining town of Aleksinac kills 17 people.
April 12	NATO missiles striking a railroad bridge near the Serbian town of Grdelica hit a passenger train, killing 17.
April 14	75 ethnic Albanian refugees die in an attack on a convoy near Djakovica.
April 27	A missile strike in the Serbian town of Surdulica kills at least 20 civilians.

May 1   A missile hits a bus crossing a bridge north of Pristina, killing 47.

May 7   A cluster bomb attack damages a marketplace and the grounds of
           a hospital in Nis, killing at least 15.

May 8   Fighter pilots using outdated maps attack the Chinese Embassy
           in Belgrade, killing 3 journalists and injuring 20 other people.

May 13   87 ethnic Albanian refugees are killed and more than 100 injured
           in a late-night NATO bombing of a Kosovo village, Korisa.

May 20   At least three people are killed when NATO missiles hit a hospital
           in Belgrade.

May 21   NATO bombs a Kosovo jail, killing at least 19 people and injuring
           scores.

May 31   NATO missiles slam into a bridge crowded with market-goers and
           cars in central Serbia, killing at least nine people and wounding 28.[23]

NATO spokesmen responded to each new fiasco by bragging even louder about how smart the bombs were that they were dropping—like defending some mass murderer by talking about his high SAT scores. If Serbian terrorists had blown up hospitals, bridges, neighborhoods and old folks' homes in the United States at the same rate that NATO hit the same targets in Serbia, Americans would have viewed the war differently. According to Human Rights Watch, at least 500 civilians were killed by NATO bombing;[24] the Yugoslavian government claimed that 2,000 civilians were killed.

NATO repeatedly dropped cluster bombs into marketplaces, hospitals, and other civilian areas.[25] Cluster bombs are anti-personnel devices designed to be scattered across enemy troop formations. NATO dropped more than 1,300 cluster bombs on Serbia and Kosovo and each bomb contained 208 separate bomblets that floated to earth by parachute. Bomb experts estimated that more than 10,000 unexploded bomblets were scattered around the landscape when the bombing ended.[26]

The more Serb civilians NATO killed, the more exalted the war aims became. Secretary of Defense William Cohen on April 7 characterized the bombing of Serbia: "This is a fight for justice over genocide, for humanity over inhumanity, for democracy over despotism."[27] British Prime Minister Tony Blair described the fight between NATO and the Serbs as "the battle between good and evil, between civilization and barbarity."[28]

And, as Serb civilian casualties rose, purported Serb atrocities mushroomed. One NATO official later told the *Wall Street Journal* that "as the war dragged on, NATO saw a fatigued press corps drifting toward the contrarian story: civilians killed by NATO's bombs. NATO stepped up its claims about Serb 'killing fields.'"[29] Clinton on May 13 declaimed that "there are 100,000 people [in Kosovo] who are still missing"—clearly implying that they might have been slaughtered.[30] Clinton also claimed that 600,000 ethnic Albanians could be "trapped within Kosovo itself lacking shelter, short of food, afraid to go home or buried in mass graves dug by their executioners."[31] Secretary William Cohen announced on May 26 during a commencement address at the U.S. Naval Academy: "This is no ordinary conflict . . . What is convulsing the United States and our NATO allies is the face of evil, an ethnic and religious nationalism that has at its core a hatred of everything our great democracies treasure."[32] On May 16, Cohen declared that he had seen reports of 4,600 Albanians killed, but he added, "I suspect it's far higher than that . . . We've now seen about 100,000 military-aged men missing. They may have been murdered."[33] By June 1, 225,000 men were missing and 6,000 had been killed "in summary executions," according to NATO spokesman Jamie Shea.[34]

Before the bombing campaign, NATO leaders denounced Milosevic as a ruthless dictator. Once the bombing started, Clinton, Blair, and other NATO leaders decided that every Yugoslavian citizen somehow became personally responsible for all of Milosevic's crimes. Seeking to maximize the misery of the Serbian people became one of the highest priorities of the NATO bombing. Barbara Ehrenreich, author of *Blood Rites: Origins and History of the Passions of War*, observed: "The NATO assault has been conducted as though we're attacking just one individual, not an entire population. It's the one-man theory of the nation-state. And its effect is to eliminate both the psychological impact of nationalism and the guilt produced by civilian causalities since civilians don't fully exist under this theory."[35]

President Clinton opened an April 15 speech to newspaper editors by proclaiming the "stark contrast between a free society with a free press and a closed society where the press is used to manipulate people by suppressing or distorting the truth."[36] However, NATO consistently misrepresented its own actions. The *Washington Post*'s Bradley Graham noted on May 24, 1999, that Pentagon and NATO "briefings about the air operation have . . . acquired a propaganda element aimed at demonizing Milosevic and his Belgrade government and imparting a moral imperative to the conflict. U.S. and NATO spokesmen, in scripts closely coordinated with the help of several public affairs specialists loaned by Washington to Brussels, routinely mix reports on allied strikes with fresh accusations of atrocities by Yugoslav forces."[37] Graham noted that the spokesmen routinely sought to delay admitting NATO responsibility for bombing civilians for "at least one news cycle or two before owning up to attacks gone awry."[38] Since most Americans were getting most of their news from television, the delay usually meant minimal blame on the home front. NATO spokesman Jamie Shea, in a London speech shortly after the war ended, bragged: "One thing we did well during the Kosovo crisis was to occupy the media space. We created a situation in which nobody in the world who was a regular TV watcher could escape the NATO message. It was essential to keep the media permanently occupied and supplied with fresh information to report on. That way, they are less inclined to go in search of critical stories."[39] Shea said that the guiding principle was, "Concern yourself principally with TV and radio . . . TV is the medium of wars . . . and one advantage of TV over newspapers is that we write the script."[40] A study released by the Center for Media and Public Affairs, a nonpartisan research organization, analyzed television coverage and concluded that "the Kosovo crisis was in a sense ideal for Clinton," who "came off more as a pure humanitarian" than did Bush during the war against Iraq.[41]

NATO worked overtime to explain away its "mistakes." On April 12, a NATO pilot sent a missile into a passenger train on a railway bridge, killing 14 people. General Clark took to the press podium to show the video from the nose of the missile, stressing that the pilot was focused on the bridge "when all of a sudden, at the very last instant, with less than a second to go, he caught a flash of movement that came into a screen and it was the train coming in. Unfortunately, he couldn't dump the bomb at that point. It was locked, it was going into the target and it was an unfortunate incident which he and the crew and all of us very much regret."[42] The video was endlessly repeated on Western television stations, driving home the point that, with the speed of modern missiles, there was sometimes nothing pilots could do to avoid catastrophe. However, in January 2000, the *Frankfurter Rundschau* revealed that the video was shown at the NATO press conference at triple the actual speed, thus making the attack on civilians look far more inevitable than it actually was. NATO officials had become aware of the deceptive nature of the video several months earlier but saw "no reason" to publicly admit the error, according to a U.S. Air Force spokesman.[43]

On April 14, NATO bombs repeatedly hit a column of ethnic Albanian refugees a few miles from the Albanian border, killing 75 people. NATO spokesmen initially claimed that Serb planes carried out the attack and used the incident to further inflame anti-Serbian opinion. Five days later, NATO spokesmen admitted that the killings had been done by NATO forces. NATO then released the audio tape from the debriefing of a pilot identified as involved in the attack. As *Newsday* reported, "According to officials, the American pilot was selected because he gave a graphic account of Milosevic's forces torching a series of ethnic Albanian villages near the Kosovo town of Dakojvica Wednesday.

The pilot told how he selected a three-truck military convoy for a laser-guided bomb strike when he saw it pulling away from a village where fires were just starting."[44] However, this gambit backfired when high-ranking military officers protested that NATO, at General Clark's urging, had released the tape of a pilot who had nothing to do with bombing the refugee column. The pilot's words were a red herring to distract attention from the carnage inflicted on the refugees.

On April 8, British Air Commodore David Wilby, the chief spokesman for General Clark, read an official statement threatening to bomb Serb television facilities: "Serb radio and TV is an instrument of propaganda and repression. It has filled the airwaves with hate and with lies over the years. It is therefore a legitimate target in this campaign. If President Milosevic would provide equal time for Western news broadcasts without censorship . . . then his television could become an acceptable instrument of public information."[45] NATO felt entitled to control not only the roads and airports, but also the minds of the Serbian people. The White House was embarrassed by the open threat and ordered Wilby cashiered as spokesman.[46]

Two weeks later, NATO bombed Serb television production facilities in downtown Belgrade, killing 16 people, including several janitors, a make-up woman, and other people on the site late at night.[47] Clinton justified the hit: "Serb television is an essential instrument of Mr. Milosevic's command and control. He uses it to spew hatred and to basically spread disinformation."[48] The *Washington Post* noted: "Clinton portrayed himself as passively accepting the recommendations of NATO military commanders—'That was a decision they made, and I did not reverse it'—but administration sources said he actively lobbied other foreign leaders to build political support for hitting" the television station and other civilian targets.[49] The *Irish Times* noted that "many Serbs believe the destruction of RTS [Radio-Television Serbia] and further bombardments of television transmitters is a personal vendetta by President Bill Clinton and other western leaders who have been mocked by Serb television. The night before it was destroyed, Kosava Television . . . broadcast a pornographic film with Clinton and Monica Lewinsky lookalikes engaging in oral sex and smoking a cigar."[50]

According to the U.S. Constitution, the U.S. government cannot go to war unless Congress passes a declaration of war. Clinton administration officials dodged this requirement by asserting that the Kosovo action was not a "war." Apparently, a war only occurs when a foreign nation attacks the United States not when the United States attacks a foreign nation. In 1973, Congress enacted the War Powers Act, which required the president to get authorization from Congress before committing U.S. troops to any combat situation that lasted more than 60 days. Clinton made it clear that he felt no obligation to consult Congress before unleashing American bombs on a foreign nation. The House of Representatives voted on April 28 and failed to support Clinton's war effort. Thirty-one congressmen sued Clinton for violating the War Powers Act. A federal judge dismissed the lawsuit after deciding that the congressmen did not have legal standing to sue.[51] Clinton's success in waging an illegal war further lifted the presidency above all law and beyond all restraint.

The NATO attack on Serbia could have sparked a far wider war. General Clark favored imposing a military blockade on any ships seeking to enter a port in Montenegro, part of Yugoslavia. Clark told congressmen in background briefings that "if the Russians are going to sail warships into the combat zone, we should bomb them."[52] French President Jacques Chirac warned that stopping and forcibly searching ships on the seas would be an act of war. Russia's Balkans envoy, Viktor Chernomyrdin, warned that NATO's action could ignite World War III.

For Clinton, bombing Serbia was a triumph of idealism. The *Washington Post* reported that, on the day after NATO planes bombed the Chinese embassy, "Clinton complained to British Prime Minister Tony Blair that news coverage was not fully presenting the moral dimensions of the war."[53] In the final days of the bombing, the *Washington Post* reported that "some presidential aides and friends are describing Kosovo in Churchillian tones, as Clinton's 'finest hour.'"[54] The *Post* also reported that one Clinton friend reported that "what Clinton believes were the unambiguously moral motives for NATO's intervention represented a chance to soothe regrets harbored in Clinton's own conscience . . . The friend said Clinton has at times lamented that the generation before him was able to serve in a war with a plainly noble purpose, and he feels 'almost cheated' that 'when it was his turn he didn't have the chance to be part of a moral cause.'"[55]

NATO BRINGS PEACE TO KOSOVO

On June 10, NATO and the government of Yugoslavia reached an agreement to end the bombing. In his June 10 victory speech, Clinton proclaimed: "The demands of an outraged and united international community have been met. I can report to the American people that we have achieved a victory for a safer world, for our democratic values, and for a stronger America . . . We have sent a message of determination and hope to all the world . . . Because of our resolve, the 20th century is ending not with helpless indignation but with a hopeful affirmation of human dignity and human rights for the 21st century."[56]

However, experts who compared the final surrender agreement with the Rambouillet text were surprised to see that NATO dropped many of its most onerous demands from three months earlier. As Brookings Institution fellow Alan Kuperman noted, "Under the new terms, Kosovo will remain part of Serbia and not be permitted to declare independence in three years. NATO troops will be constrained to Kosovo only, not given free rein throughout Serbia. NATO's mission is subject to authorization by the U.N. Security Council, where Yugoslavia's sympathizers, Russia and China, have vetoes."[57] Kuperman noted that the final deal was far more favorable to Milosevic than was the Rambouillet ultimatum and that "Milosevic accepted this deal the first time it was offered to him." As the British *Independent* noted, "On March 23, the day before the bombing began, the elected parliament in Belgrade called for an 'international presence in Kosovo immediately after the signing of an accord for self-administration in Kosovo . . . to be decided by the [UN] Security Council.'"[58] This was a key provision in the June peace settlement— and the Yugoslavians had already accepted it before the bombing began. The final deal was hardly unconditional surrender: NATO acquiesced to Serb demands that Russian soldiers be included as part of any "peace-keeping" force sent to Kosovo.

In a June 11 speech at an Air Force base, Clinton bragged: "Day after day, with remarkable precision, our forces pounded every element of Mr. Milosevic's military machine, from tanks to fuel supply, to anti-aircraft weapons, to the military and political support."[59] Throughout the bombing campaign, NATO and Pentagon spokesmen gushed about the slaughter NATO was inflicting on the Serbian military. However, once the bombing stopped, the Clinton admin-istration was stunned to see the Serbian army withdraw in fine order with polished buttons and good morale. Shortly after the bombs stopped falling, Defense Secretary William Cohen declared, "We severely crippled the [Serb] military forces in Kosovo by destroying more than 50 percent of the artillery and one third of the armored vehicles." Chairman of the Joint Chiefs of Staff Gen. Henry Shelton bragged that NATO had destroyed "around 120 tanks . . . about 220 armored personnel carriers . . . and up to 450 artillery and mortar pieces."[60] However, a confidential post-war U.S. military investigation concluded that the damage claims had been exaggerated nearly ten-fold. In reality, only 14 tanks, 18 armored personnel carriers, and 20 artillery pieces were taken out—despite the claimed dropping of more than 20,000 bombs on the Serbian military.[61] On the other hand, NATO did have a very high "kill-rate" for the cardboard decoy tanks that the Serbs erected all over Kosovo. At the end of the war, the Serbian military largely was unscathed—but the country's civilian infrastructure was in ruins. NATO bombs were far more effective against women, children, hospitals, and retirement homes than against soldiers.

After the peace agreement, NATO was plagued by a surplus of dead Serb civilians and a severe shortage of dead ethnic Albanians. In late October, pathologist Emilio Perez Pujol, who headed a team of Spanish investigators in Kosovo, told *The Times* of London, "I calculate that the final figure of dead in Kosovo will be 2,500 at the most. This includes lots of strange deaths that can't be blamed on anyone in particular."[62] NATO officials had declaimed that the Serbs had dumped a thousand bodies of slaughtered ethnic Albanians into the Trepca mines; however, postwar investigators found no bodies.

In a special videotape address to the Serbian people, Clinton declared, "I want you to understand that NATO only agreed to be peacekeepers on the understanding that its troops would ensure that both sides kept their commitments and that terrorism on both sides would be brought to an end. They only agreed to serve with the understanding that they would protect Serbs as well as ethnic Albanians and that they would leave when peace took hold."[63] In a Thanksgiving 1999 speech to American troops in Kosovo, Clinton proclaimed: "Thanks to you we have reversed ethnic cleansing."[64] Clinton noted that there had been "almost 1 million refugees," but "because we acted quicker [than in Bosnia], they all came home."[65]

Clinton ignored the ongoing massive exodus of Serbs racing north for their lives. Jiri Dienstbier, the UN representative on human rights, declared in late 1999: "The spring ethnic cleansing of ethnic Albanians, accompanied by murders, torture, looting, and burning of houses, has been replaced by the autumn ethnic cleansing of Serbs, Romas [gypsies], Bosniaks, and other non-Albanians accompanied by the same atrocities."[66] One U.S. government official told the *Washington Post* in August 1999: "It looks like it's over for the Serbs. We can talk about peace, love and democracy, but I don't think anyone really knows how to stop this."[67] A November 1999 report by the International Crisis Group concluded that "there are as many killings right now in Kosovo as there were before NATO intervened." The British *Independent* reported: "Of Pristina's 40,000 Serb population, only 400 are left . . . The 300-strong Croat community at Lecnice were preparing to celebrate their 700th anniversary in the province but left en masse last month for Dubrovnik . . . The president of the tiny Jewish community in Pristina, Cedra Prlincevic, left for Belgrade after denouncing 'a pogrom against the non-Albanian population'. He had left Kosovo, he said, 'with only the Talmud'."[68] A December 1999 report by the Organization for Security and Cooperation in Europe noted, "The human rights violations . . . for the period June-October 1999 include executions, abductions, torture, cruel, inhuman and degrading treatment, arbitrary arrests and attempts to restrict freedom of expression. House burnings, blockades restricting freedom of movement, discriminatory treatment in schools, hospitals, humanitarian aid distribution and other public services based on ethnic background, and forced evictions from housing recall some of the worst practices of Kosovo's recent past."[69] Amnesty International reported on December 23, 1999: "Violence against Serbs, Roma, Muslim Slavs and moderate Albanians in Kosovo has increased dramatically over the past month, pointing to a failure by the United Nations mission to protect human rights. Murder, abductions, violent attacks, intimidation, and house-burning are being perpetrated on a daily basis."[70]

The cease-fire agreement specified that "an agreed number of Serb personnel will be allowed to return to Kosovo" for tasks such as "maintaining a presence at sites of Serb heritage" such as Serbian Orthodox religious shrines and churches.[71] However, NATO reneged on that deal. By late September 1999, more than 60 churches and other religious sites had been blown up, burnt, ransacked, or otherwise ruined. Many of the detonations of the churches were very skilled, with massive amounts of explosives—clearly the work of the KLA, which NATO claimed had disbanded months earlier.[72]

The main achievement of the war was that instead of Serbs terrorizing ethnic Albanians, ethnic Albanians terrorized Serbs; instead of refugees fleeing south and west, refugees headed north. This result may not have been entirely unwelcome to NATO. British Defense Minister George Robertson declared in March 1999 that the goal of the operation was "Serbs out, NATO in, refugees back."[73]

Clinton also declared that the Kosovar children "love the United States . . . because we gave them their freedom back."[74] Perhaps Clinton saw freedom as nothing more than being tyrannized by people of the same ethnicity. Once the bombing started, NATO transformed former terrorists into "freedom fighters"—a term explicitly used in the June 1999 agreement between the NATO and the KLA. As the Serbs were driven out of Kosovo, Kosovar Albanians became increasingly oppressed by the KLA, which ignored its commitment to disarm. The *Los Angeles Times* reported on November 20, 1999: "As a postwar power struggle heats up in Kosovo Albanian politics, extremists are trying to silence moderate leaders with a terror campaign of kidnappings, beatings, bombings and at least one killing. The intensified attacks against members of the moderate Democratic League of Kosovo, or LDK, have raised concerns that radical ethnic Albanians are turning against their own out of fear of losing power in a democratic Kosovo."[75]

Before the war, NATO had imposed a trade boycott against Serbia. Many Europeans assumed that the boycott would end once a Kosovo peace agreement was signed. But the Clinton administration refused to lift any sanctions after the war ended—even to permit Europeans to provide heating oil to Serbian cities controlled by politicians opposed to Milosevic. The *New York Times* noted, "American officials have said they fear that the assistance could shore up Mr. Milosevic by alleviating public discontent, which they hope could lead to protests in Yugoslavia, early elections, or even Mr. Milosevic's ouster or resignation."[76] State Department chief spokesman James Rubin said, "We're concerned about proposals that may have appropriate humanitarian goals but may lead to developments that directly or indirectly support the regime."[77] Thanks to the NATO destruction of oil refineries and other energy infrastructure, the Serbs faced dire hardships in the coming winter. A September 20, 1999, report by the UN Office for the Coordination of Humanitarian Affairs warned, "The overall impact of such shortages is expected to be increased morbidity and mortality, particularly in urban areas. The most vulnerable will be the elderly, the very young, the sick and the urban poor."[78]

In November 1999, the United States offered to lift the economic sanctions imposed on Serbia if the Serbs would agree to have an early election. But there was a caveat: if Milosevic's party won, the United States would not consider the elections bona fide and would refuse to lift the sanctions. Secretary Albright observed: "I find it really, really, really hard to believe that Milosevic might win a free and fair election."[79] Serbian Deputy Prime Minister Vojislav Seselj retorted: "For Americans, the only free and fair elections are those won by their lackeys."

In a 1999 talk to troops in Kosovo, Clinton bragged: "You just look around this room today. We just celebrated Thanksgiving, with, I bet you, conservatively, 25 different ethnic groups represented among the American military forces here in this room—maybe 50, maybe it's more."[80] Clinton's standard of virtue seemed to consist of little more than ethnic bean counting: the greater the number of ethnic groups, the greater the virtue. Clinton talked as if every bomb dropped was a triumph for multiculturalism and diversity. Clinton was far more concerned with counting the number of ethnic groups at dinner than in noticing the ongoing purge of the Serbs.

Kosovo became a de facto NATO protectorate—and the United States was far and away the main force behind NATO. Prior to the NATO bombing, American citizens had no responsibility for atrocities committed by either Serbs or ethnic Albanians. However, after American planes bombed much of Serbia into rubble to drive the Serb military out of Kosovo, Clinton effectively made the United States responsible for the safety of the remaining Serbs in Kosovo. This was equivalent to forcibly disarming a group of people, and then standing by, whistling and looking at the ground, while they are slaughtered. Since the United States promised to bring peace to Kosovo, Clinton bears some responsibility for every burnt church, every murdered Serb grandmother, every new refugee column streaming north out of Kosovo. Despite these problems, Clinton bragged at a December 8, 1999, press conference that he was "very, very proud" of what the United States had done in Kosovo.[81]

THE LEGACY OF THE SERBIAN WAR

Clinton's experience in Kosovo gave him great empathy for Boris Yeltsin when Yeltsin sent in the Russian military to obliterate Chechnya. At a summit of Western leaders in Istanbul in November 1999, Clinton declared that "we want Russia to overcome the scourge of terrorism and lawlessness. We believe Russia has not only the right, but also the obligation to defend its territorial integrity . . . Russia has faced rebellion within, and related violence beyond, the borders of Chechnya. It has responded with a military strategy designed to break the resistance and end the terror."[82] At the time Clinton endorsed Yeltsin's policy, the Russian military was flattening Grozny with long-distance rockets and pounding the entire province with its bombers, making little or no effort to limit civilian casualties. A few weeks after Clinton endorsed Yeltsin's policy, the Russian military announced that they would kill any person still residing in Grozny at the end of a 72-hour warning period. (At that time, an estimated 40,000 civilians, largely elderly, were still in the city.) This brutal ultimatum did not stop Clinton from later characterizing the Russian military assault as an effort to "liberate Grozny."[83]

In the same way that Clinton acted domestically as though he were above the Constitution and federal law, his deployment of the U.S. military against the Serbs was in clear violation of international law. As Cornell law professor Jeremy Rabkin observed, "The non-aggression provisions of the U.N. Charter were duly ratified by two-thirds of the Senate and not superseded by the defense provisions of the NATO treaty."[84] The more morally superior Clinton perceived himself, the less bound U.S. policy was by international law.

The bombing of Serbia persuaded many people around the world that NATO had changed from a defensive alliance to an arrogant combination ready to impose Western values with its bombs. Henry Kissinger observed: "In Russia, an outraged sense of humiliation over NATO's actions has spread from the elites to the population at large and threatens to blight U.S.-Russian relations for years to come."[85]

CONCLUSION

In a CNN interview shortly after the peace agreement was announced, the president enunciated what his aides labeled the "Clinton doctrine:" "There's an important principle here . . . While there may well be a great deal of ethnic and religious conflict in the world . . . whether within or beyond the borders of a country, if the world community has the power to stop it, we ought to stop genocide and ethnic cleansing."[86]

The "Clinton doctrine," if strictly followed, would mire the United States in scores of conflicts around the world. But, though there is little danger that Clinton would actually risk following his own doctrine, his all-caring rhetoric generated positive press.

Kosovo was apparently not one of the places that Clinton subsequently favored enforcing this doctrine. The UN High Commissioner for Refugees estimated in early 2000 that roughly a quarter million Serbs, Roma, and others had fled Kosovo since the June "peace agreement."[87] In March 2000 renewed fighting broke out when the KLA launched attacks into Serbia, trying to seize territory that it claimed historically belonged to ethnic Albanians.[88] UN Human Rights Envoy Jiri Dienstbier reported in March 2000 that "the [NATO] bombing hasn't solved any problems. It only multiplied the existing problems and created new ones. The Yugoslav economy was destroyed. Kosovo is destroyed. There are hundreds of thousands of people unemployed now."[89] Dienstbier warned that NATO must send in ground troops to stop the attacks by ethnic Albanians.

As violence proliferated, the Clinton administration concentrated on a single lofty goal. The *New York Times* reported on March 12 that "administration officials acknowledge that an overriding priority is to avoid American casualties and keep Kosovo out of the news during an election year. One administration official, who served in Bosnia, said that the driving force behind the policy now is to keep it 'off the front page.'"[90]

NINETEEN

CONCLUSION: CLINTON'S LEGACY VERSUS AMERICAN LIBERTY

THE BETTER THAT PEOPLE UNDERSTAND what Clinton did in office, the greater the nation's chances for political recovery.

It would be a fatal mistake to assume that, since Clinton's reign will soon end, Americans no longer need to be concerned with his actions in office. The vast majority of Clinton-era misgovernment will survive the end of his administration. Even if Republicans capture the White House, there is little reason at this time to expect that they will have the resolve to shut down HUD, slash the IRS's powers, severely curb the FBI, cease dictating racial hiring quotas, end the war on drug users, plow under farm subsidies, dismantle trade barriers, and respect the Bill of Rights. And, if Vice President Gore is elected president, he can be expected to stretch federal power further in dozens of directions.

The principle of government supremacy is Clinton's clearest legacy. Clinton did more than any recent president to place the federal government above all laws—above the Constitution—and beyond any effective restraint. Clinton ignored federal and Supreme Court decisions limiting his power and Congress rarely had the gumption to check his abuses. Clinton exploited and expanded the dictatorial potential of the U.S. presidency.

Clinton was the Nanny State champion incarnate—the person who taught tens of millions of Americans to look to government for relief from every irritation of daily life—from child safety car seats to unpasteurized cider to leaky basements. Clinton's perennial message was that people should trust political action far more than the voluntary efforts of individuals to improve their own lives. Clinton sought to continually remind people of the greatness of the State and the helplessness of the citizen.

"WRITE A MEMO, SAVE THE WORLD"

The *Los Angeles Times* noted on July 4, 1998: "Fresh from what aides view as a triumphant trip to China, Clinton is reportedly eager to exercise his executive powers to the hilt." Senior White House Counselor Paul Begala declared: "He always comes back from these trips with a big head of steam, and this trip has been especially remarkable. This president has a very strong sense of the powers of the presidency, and is willing to use all of them."[1] Begala summed up the administration's attitude: "Stroke of the pen. Law of the land. Kind of cool."[2]

Clinton used the inspiration from his visit with Chinese communists to issue a fresh volley of executive orders on issues ranging from Medicare to teenage smoking to food safety. Clinton also used executive orders to implement portions of the Kyoto Treaty on global warming—a treaty that he would not submit to the U.S. Senate because he knew the Senate would not ratify it.

Clinton signed his most controversial executive order during a May 1998 visit to England. Clinton's order established expansive principles to justify federal intrusion in state and local affairs, asserting, "Preserving supremacy of federal law provides an essential balance to the power of the states."[3] Clinton's executive order essentially sought to nullify the Tenth Amendment of the Constitution, which states, "The powers not delegated to the United States by the Constitution, nor prohibited by it to the states, are reserved to the states respectively, or to the people." Rep. David McIntosh (D-Ind.) warned that "the new order would wreak havoc on the balance of power envisioned by the Constitution between the States and the federal government."[4] On August 6, 1998, the House of Representatives voted 417-2 to block any funds for the order's enforcement and Clinton suspended the order.[5]

The same devotion to decrees permeated federal agencies under Clinton. For instance, on January 4, 2000, the *Washington Post* gave a front-page splash to an Occupational Safety and Health Administration (OSHA) "guidance document" that announced that OSHA had the right to dictate standards for people who work at home. Because a 1971 law gave OSHA jurisdiction over most work places, and because more employees were telecommuting or finishing memos at home, OSHA claimed jurisdiction over more than ten million homes.[6] The *Washington Post* noted that the new policy "means that employers are responsible for making sure an employee has ergonomically correct furniture, such as chairs and computer tables, as well as proper lighting, heating, cooling and ventilation systems in the home office. The employer must also provide any needed training to comply with OSHA standards, including making sure the home work space has emergency medical plans and a first-aid kit." OSHA warned, "If work is performed in the basement space of a residence and the stairs leading to the space are unsafe, the employer could be liable if the employer knows or reasonably should have known of the dangerous condition."[7]

Congress was not amused. The OSHA guidance letter was withdrawn after fierce protests from Capitol Hill and elsewhere. However, a congressional hearing a month later revealed that OSHA had issued nearly 40,000 pages of "guidance" to employers in recent years, creating widespread legal uncertainty and maximizing pretexts to punish.[8]

Other federal agencies creatively used their power. Commissioner Harold Furchgott-Roth of the Federal Communications Commission (FCC) observed in September 1999 that the majority of FCC commissioners "are engaged in shakedowns, extortions, and things that fall outside the formal regulatory process."[9] Furchgott-Roth observed, "The commission has been very effective in shaking down companies [and deciding] which communities get served first, which communities get served last, [and] who the assets get spun off to." Furchgott-Roth denounced as an "incredible fraud" the tax the FCC illegally imposed on telephone users to bankroll Clinton's promise to subsidize Internet access to schools.[10]

THE MIRAGE OF GOVERNMENT FORCE

Few events better symbolized both the nature and the effect of Clinton's rule than the raid by 130 federal agents in Miami's Little Havana on April 22, 2000. The controversy over the raid also goes to the heart of Clinton's efforts to neuter Americans' concept of government.

The raid went pretty much as planned—the agents got six-year-old Elian Gonzalez and left shattered doors, a broken bed, roughed-up Cuban-Americans and two NBC cameramen on the ground, writhing in pain from stomach-kicks or rifle-butts to the head. The only problem: Associated Press stringer Alan Diaz snapped a photo of a Border Patrol agent pointing his submachine gun towards the terrified boy who was being held by the fisherman who had rescued him six months earlier from the Atlantic Ocean.

Administration officials scrambled to help Americans see beyond the surface of the photo. A few hours after the raid, Deputy Attorney General Eric Holder asserted that the boy "was not taken at the point of a gun." When challenged about the photograph showing the machine gun, Holder explained: "They were armed agents who went in there who acted very sensitively."[11] Holder denied that the agents had raided the house at night—because it was 5:15 A.M., more than an hour before sunrise.

Television footage of an Immigration and Naturalization Service agent absconding out of the house with Elian showed a look of horror on the boy's face. However, INS chief Doris Meissner quieted concerns about the boy's well-being when she announced that Elian was given Play-Doh after he was deposited on a government plane to take him to Washington. Meissner declared, "The squeezing of Play-Doh is the best thing that you can do for a child who might be experiencing stress."[12]

Attorney General Janet Reno called a press conference a few hours after the raid and, when asked about the photo, stressed that the agent's "finger was not on the trigger."[13] The Hechler and Koch MP-5 submachine gun sprays 800 rounds a minute—and a finger a half inch away from the trigger means nothing. Two days later, Reno declared, "One of the things that is so very important is that the force was not used. It was a show of force that prevented people from getting hurt." By Reno's standard, any bank robbery in which no one gets shot is merely a nonviolent exchange of bags of money.

White House spokesman Joe Lockhart, responding to a question about the use of excessive force, stressed that the agents "drove up [to the Gonzalez house] in white mini-vans"—as if the color of the vehicles proved they were on a mission of mercy.[14] President Clinton stepped up to a microphone in the White House Rose Garden that morning and announced that "there was no alternative but to enforce the decision of the INS and the federal court . . . The most important thing was to treat this in a lawful manner, according to the established process."[15]

However, Harvard law school constitutional scholar Lawrence Tribe concluded that "no judge or neutral magistrate had issued the type of warrant or other authority needed for the executive branch to break into the home to seize the child . . . Ms. Reno's decision to take the law as well as the child into her own hands . . . strikes at the heart of constitutional government and shakes the safeguards of liberty."[16]

The news media rushed to help Americans see the "big picture." Less than three hours after the raid, CBS news anchor Dan Rather interrupted the televising of Reno's press conference to assert: "Even if the photographer was in the house legally . . . there is the question of the privacy, beginning with the privacy of the child."[17] Rather was more concerned about photographing the boy's terror than about the terrorizing itself. James Warren, Washington bureau chief of the *Chicago Tribune,* fretted that the picture "will ignite all the crazies."[18] The *Washington Post* ran a laudatory article on how Reno had supposedly personally insured that not all journalists would be knocked out of action during the raid—as if the attorney general had personal authority to choose when the government stooped to respect the First Amendment.[19]Much of the news media—including *Time* magazine and the *New York Times*—gave far greater visibility to the Christmas-card type photo of a father-son reunion snapped by $800-an-hour lawyer Greg Craig (and distributed by Justice Department officials) than to the AP action photo.[20]

New *York Times* columnist Thomas Friedman, in a non-sarcastic article headlined, "Reno for President," declared that the machine gun photo "warmed my heart" and that it symbolized that "America is a country where the rule of law rules. This picture illustrates what happens to those who defy the rule of law and how far our government and people will go to preserve it."[21] Garry Wills, author of *A Necessary Evil: A History of American Distrust of Government,* wrote on the *New York Times* op-ed page: "The familiar picture of the menacing INS agent flourishing a machine gun shows us an officer trying to avoid violence, not one inviting it . . . The readiness of people to deplore 'jack-booted' tactics reveals the intransigence that made the rescue necessary."[22] Thus, the fact that people talk about "jack-booted" federal agents proves that G-men need machine guns when they crash into people's homes. Like a variation of old-time Soviet psychiatry, fear of government agents with machine guns is now a symptom of mental illness.

Clinton had a hang-dog look on his face during his press statement on the morning of the raid because he realized that the soon-to-be-famous photo would undercut his attempt to delegitimize fear of government. However, much of the establishment media did all they could to keep the public pacified. Republicans initially proclaimed their outrage and promised to expose the shenanigans behind the raid; however, after polls showed scant support for congressional hearings, Republicans decided that the truth would be too expensive to find.

REVENUE ÜBER ALLIES

Federal policies in the 1990s were driven by the continual revenue increases that resulted from payroll tax withholding and an expanding economy.

Because federal revenues jumped sharply every year of the Clinton administration, politicians of both parties harvested vast amounts of play money
to spend as they chose. The few budget cuts that occurred were quickly
dwarfed by surges in new spending. The rise in revenue led to an increase
in the size of government that, if the past is any guide, will be very difficult
to roll back.

Federal tax law guaranteed that the government would reap greater profits
from citizens' labor than would citizens themselves. Though the federal government forecast a multi-trillion dollar budget surplus in the decade from 2000 to
2010, Clinton proposed $78 in new federal spending for each net dollar of tax
cuts.[23] Clinton recognized that the more government planned to spend, the more
illegitimate tax cuts would be perceived.

Clinton's tax policy exemplified his "feeling your pain" public policy: the
only pains that don't count are those inflicted by the government. Clinton's
comments on taxation vivified his view that it is never a question of the burden
that government imposes on people, but of the good things government can do
with the money it forcibly seizes from people under its power.

THE NEW TWO-CLASS SYSTEM

Another Clinton legacy is a two-class system in America: those whom the law
fails to restrain, and those whom it fails to protect; those above the law, and
those below it; those for whom there is "no controlling legal authority," in Vice
President Gore's famous words,[24] and those for whom there are few, if any,
constitutional protections.

The notion that "the king can do no wrong" permeated the Clinton
administration's legal and public relations defense strategies. The Clinton
administration perennially invoked sovereign immunity to protect wrongdoing feds—from the FBI sniper who killed Vicki Weaver in the doorway of
her Idaho cabin; to IRS agents who wantonly seized people's property and
disrupted their lives; to Treasury Department employees who shredded 162
cartons of documents detailing how the government robbed hundreds of
thousands of Indians who relied on Bureau of Indian Affairs trust fund
accounts; and to the FBI agents involved in the final attack at Waco. Clinton
sought to raise the reputation of government to lofty new heights—at the
same time that Justice Department lawyers argued that individual federal
agents are exempt from liability for wronging other Americans.

GOVERNING BY LYING

Clinton was a master of the big lie. In a February 4, 2000, speech at a Washington prayer breakfast, Clinton called for reconciliation among all groups clashing around the world, from Northern Ireland to the Middle East to Kosovo. Clinton then revealed, "And here in Washington we are not blameless . . . For we often, too, forget in the heat of political battle our common humanity. We slip from honest difference which is healthy into dishonest demonization."[25]

This from a politician who had proclaimed that Republicans who opposed his Superfund legislation wanted to poison America; who ignored a jury verdict and declaimed that Texas residents were murderers because they resisted federal agents attacking their home; who, in his 1996 reelection campaign ads, accused Republicans of favoring killing older Americans because of their position on Medicare;[26] whose wife went on national television after the Monica Lewinsky story broke and said it was just another concoction of a "vast right-wing conspiracy;" whose vice president compared opponents of affirmative action to people who sought to murder blacks; who scapegoated the Japanese as the ultimate unfair traders because they would not provide affirmative action guarantees to favored American corporations; and who perennially portrayed advocates of tax cuts as favoring throwing old people out on the street via the destruction of Social Security.

And what of Clinton's constant false statements about federal policy? Of his continual proclamations of the need for a better "farm safety net," while his administration forgave million-dollar loans given to uncreditworthy farmers, and while he signed bailout legislation to give up to $430,000 a year to each farmer on the dole? Of his fictitious claim of a record settlement for fair housing violations? Of his characterization of textile import quota agreements as victories for free trade? Of his efforts to demonize any criticism of federal law enforcement? Of his promise to "mend" affirmative action at the same time that federal lawyers continued squeezing employers to use racial hiring quotas? Of his perennial hokum that the Brady Handgun Violence Prevention Act prevented hundreds of thousands of criminals from getting guns?

Clinton repeatedly claimed that, thanks to his reforms, "we now have the smallest Government we've had since 1963."[27] Surprisingly, much of the media and public swallowed this charade. Brookings Institution fellow Paul Light derided Clinton for counting only federal civil servants in this measure; Light observed that, after including the number of government contractors and employees hired to carry out federal mandates, "the true size of [the federal] government in 1996 expands to nearly 17 million, or more than eight times larger than the standard headcount of 1.9 million used by Congress and the President to declare the era of big government over."[28] The number of people in federal prisons has increased more than 500 percent since 1963; more than 700 new crimes have been added to the federal statute book; the length of the Code of Federal Regulations has quintupled; and the number of federal regulators has increased eightfold. The number of levers and thumbscrews available to federal agents pursuing private citizens is far greater now than it was then. As columnist Robert Samuelson observed, "The illusion of small government made government bigger."[29]

The lies that Clinton got away with were far more important than the ones on which he was caught. The discovery of a stained blue dress obliterated Clinton's defense in the Lewinsky scandal. But for most lies, there was nothing as concrete and indisputable that the public and the media were forced to recognize and accept. The vast majority of Clinton's lies and misrepresentations succeeded in sanctifying the expansion of federal power.

ATTENTION DEFICIT DEMOCRACY

For scores of millions of Americans, Clinton's "caring" was more important than his lying. Clinton's "government by verbal fraud" succeeded because most of the citizenry and most of the media paid little attention to what the federal government actually did. Government became much larger, more complex, and more interventionist—and the average citizen did nothing to comparatively increase his oversight of his rulers.

As Clinton's reign ends, representative government is increasingly a parody of the intentions of America's Founding Fathers. America is becoming a nation with more and more subjects and fewer and fewer citizens. More people are willingly becoming wards of the State, either depending on it for their next meal or surrendering their judgment. Rather than a government by the people, America is becoming an Attention Deficit Democracy.[30]

Polls showed that, especially in his second term, most Americans personally distrusted Clinton yet supported some of his proposals for new federal programs. Many Americans concluded that untrustworthy individuals can be trusted with greater power—as long as they promise to do good. A promise to feel people's pain apparently transcends all other legal and constitutional obligations. But the beneficence of government cannot miraculously transcend the venality of politicians.

In 1992, Clinton offered up himself and Al Gore as a better class of ruler to fix the problems of Big Government. The new saviors were oversold. It is time to cease hoping and waiting for rulers who will resolve the myriad contradictions among federal programs and policies and—more importantly—end the damage from the perverse incentives government offers for people to scorn self-reliance. No one is going to ride in on a white horse and wave a magic wand over our political system.

For much of the twentieth century, social reformers insisted that the character of criminals could be redeemed while they were in prison, if only the right environment and encouragement were provided. Few people still swallow this nostrum.

Similarly, some Americans continue to hope that, regardless of how many lies politicians tell on the campaign trail, being elected to office will somehow elevate their character. It is time to recognize that holding elective office is no more likely to uplift the character than is serving time in the pen.

The issue is not how much a politician cares but how much power he seeks. The power a politician acquires for government will survive long after his photo opportunities have been forgotten. People must realize that the government in recent years has become far more of an enemy to their rights and liberty. People must recognize that government is now the most dangerous predator.

The vast majority of government agencies can neither be reinvented nor reformed. If Americans want good government, hundreds of failed government programs must be abolished and legions of laws that turn government into a public nuisance must be repealed. All other "reforms" will merely prolong the abuse of the American people.

The good citizen must recognize and remember the failures of the government that reigns over him. Those who forget past boondoggles shall be perpetually taxed for new boondoggles. Those who ignore past violations of their rights invite new injustices. And those who pretend the system will automatically cure itself open the floodgates to new political pestilences.

ACKNOWLEDGMENTS

I would like to extend a special thanks to Wladyslaw Pleszczynski of the *American Spectator,* James Petersen of *Playboy,* and Jacob Hornberger of *Freedom Daily,* three fine editors I have worked with since 1994 on many of the issues included in this book. I would like to thank the staff of the Competitive Enterprise Institute for their invaluable help on environmental and other regulatory issues. My friend Greg Rushford, publisher of the *Rushford Report,* provided insights into trade policy that severely tested my youthful idealism about government and the political process.

At St. Martin's Press, editor Michael Flamini suggested the title of the book; I greatly appreciated his enthusiasm for the project and his expert judgment. St. Martin's Press Vice President Garrett Kiely suggested a subtitle that perfectly captured the book's gist. (I also want to heartily thank everyone else who sent me email messages suggesting other titles.) Bill Berry did an excellent job of copyediting the book; I especially appreciated his public affairs expertise. Meg Weaver did an excellent job of batting cleanup, bringing patience and exactness to the final polishing of the manuscript. I also want to thank production editor Alan Bradshaw for his fine work in shepherding the manuscript into book form and for expediting the project into print.

Finally, I would like to thank my father for his encouragement and enthusiasm for my work over the last couple of decades. His feedback has meant a great deal to me. And I even appreciate when, after all these years, he still occasionally catches my grammar errors.

NOTES

CHAPTER ONE

1. Quoted in Mary McGrory, "Why Zoe Got Zapped," *Washington Post,* January 24, 1993.
2. "Trends in Federal Revenue Collection," Tax Foundation, February 2000.
3. "Rising Tax Burden on Average Families," Tax Foundation, March 2000.
4. U.S. General Accounting Office, "Tax Administration: Extent and Causes of Erroneous Levies," December 21, 1990. GAO concluded that the IRS conducted 50,000 wrongful levies a year. The number of levies increased sharply in subsequent years and there was no evidence that the accuracy of the levies improved, at least through 1998.
5. "Address Before a Joint Session of the Congress on the State of the Union," *Public Papers of the Presidents,* January 24, 1995, p. 96.
6. "Address Before a Joint Session of the Congress on the State of the Union," *Public Papers of the Presidents,* January 27, 1998, p. 129.
7. "Address Before a Joint Session of the Congress on the State of the Union," *Public Papers of the Presidents,* January 19, 1999, p. 78.
8. "Address Before a Joint Session of the Congress on the State of the Union," *Public Papers of the Presidents,* January 27, 1998, p. 129.
9. "Address Before a Joint Session of the Congress on the State of the Union," *Public Papers of the Presidents,* January 23, 1996, p. 90.
10. Maureen Dowd, "Sadistic Yellow Vitriol," *New York Times,* September 1, 1996.
11. Sandy Grady, "Clinton's State of Al Gore," *Denver Post,* January 29, 2000.

CHAPTER TWO

1. "Remarks at the AmeriCorps National Civilian Community Corps Graduation Ceremony," *Public Papers of the Presidents,* August 9, 1999, P. 1597.
2. Mary Pasciak, "Toy Gun Buyback Sends Disarming Message to Young," *Buffalo News,* January 31, 1999.
3. "Lessons Learned," *Inyo Register* (Bishop, Cal.), December 17, 1998.
4. Congressional Record, May 16, 1997, p. H2863.
5. "Underwear Collection Fills Important Need for Women at Shelter," *San Diego Union-Tribune,* September 20, 1998.
6. Jeff Kass, "AmeriCorps Off to Slow Start," *Los Angeles Times,* July 17, 1995.
7. "Remarks to Summer of Safety Program Participants in Saint Louis," *Public Papers of the Presidents,* June 24, 1994, p. 1134.
8. "Remarks in a Swearing-In Ceremony for AmeriCorps Volunteers," *Public Papers of the Presidents,* September 12, 1994, p. 1754.
9. "Address Before a Joint Session of the Congress on the State of the Union," *Public Papers of the Presidents,* January 24, 1995, p. 96.

10. "Remarks at the 'AmeriCorps Call to Service' in College Park, Maryland," *Public Papers of the Presidents,* February 10, 1999, p. 220.
11. Author interview with Anne Bushman, July 2, 1999.
12. U.S. General Accounting Office, "National Service Programs: Two AmeriCorps Programs Funding and Benefits," February 2000, p. 5.
13. Ibid.
14. Hearing, Departments of Veterans Affairs, and Housing and Urban Development and Independent Agencies, Appropriations, Fiscal year 1998, HR 2158/S 1034, Senate Appropriations Committee, March 4, 1997 (Washington: Government Printing Office, 1997), p. 91.
15. Ron Menchaca, "City Can Help in Relocation," *Charleston Post and Courier,* May 27, 1999.
16. Women in Community Service, Vista, Chicago, IL. Information from http://www.nationalservice.org/stateprofiles/index.html.
17. "Remarks at the AmeriCorps National Civilian Community Corps Graduation Ceremony," *Public Papers of the Presidents,* August 9, 1999, p. 1597.
18. Bruce Ramsey, "Ending Poverty Summons A Variety of Creative Solutions," *Seattle Post-Intelligencer,* February 18, 1998.
19. Grant application to AmeriCorps from Congressional Hunger Center (the parent organization for four anti-hunger AmeriCorps projects), Washington, D.C., March 11, 1999. (There was a separate section in the application for each of the four different projects).
20. Parke Wilde, Paul McNamara, and Christine Ranney, "The Effect of Income and Food Programs on Dietary Quality," *American Journal of Agricultural Economics,* November 1999, p. 959.
21. Author interview with Fanny Woods, August 4, 1999.
22. Grant application to AmeriCorps from Congressional Hunger Center (the parent organization for four anti-hunger AmeriCorps projects), Washington, D.C., March 11, 1999.
23. See http://www.ghn.org/chc/.
24. See http//www.hungercenter.org/beyond_food/mississippi/mace.html.
25. Author interview with Harris Wofford, September 15, 1999.
26. "Remarks at the Presidential Scholars Awards Presentation Ceremony," *Public Papers of the Presidents,* July 1, 1994, p. 1397.
27. Author interview with Nidia Salamanca, July 23, 1999.
28. Memorandum of Agreement between the Opportunity Council, Bellingham, Wash., and Corporation for National and Community Service, May 13, 1999. Included in the agreement was the AmeriCorps application for the Whatcom Human Rights Task Force, dated October 8, 1998.
29. Grant application to AmeriCorps from the National Alliance of HUD Tenants, Boston, Mass., February 17, 1999.
30. Ibid.
31. Grant application to AmeriCorps from Equality Colorado, Denver, Col., April 19, 1999.
32. Ibid.
33. Memo from Deb Jospin to Harris Wofford, July 29, 1997. This memo was in the project file for the LAGLC grant.
34. Memorandum of Agreement between Corporation for National and Community Service and the Los Angeles Gay and Lesbian Center, Project No. CA-31-684-8, July 22, 1999.
35. Project Progress Report, "Safe Haven" Project, L.A. Gay and Lesbian Center, quarter ending March 31, 1999. Received at AmeriCorps headquarters on May 5, 1999.
36. Statement of Irene Gonzales Madrid, attached to Project Progress Report, "Safe Haven" Project, L.A. Gay and Lesbian Center, quarter ending June 30, 1998. Received at AmeriCorps headquarters on August 24, 1998.

37. Author interview with Gwen Baldwin, September 17, 1999.

38. Grant application submitted to AmeriCorps for the Child Victim Rapid Response program, Florida Office of the Attorney General, April 1, 1998.

39. Interview with Cynthia Rodgers, August 13, 1999.

40. "Reno's Dirty Linen; Attorney-General Janet Reno and Child Abuse Cases," *New Statesman and Society,* April 16, 1993.

41. For a survey of some of the worst wrongful child abuse accusation scandals, see Dorothy Rabinowitz, "Only in Massachusetts," *Wall Street Journal,* December 29, 1999.

42. Grant application to AmeriCorps from the Southern California Environmental Resources Management Program, Carson, Cal., April 14, 1999.

43. Ben Lieberman, "Federal Nannies Render Appliances Less Effective," *Las Vegas Review-Journal,* March 20, 1998.

44. "Remarks at the AmeriCorps National Civilian Community Corps Graduation Ceremony," *Public Papers of the Presidents,* August 9, 1999, P. 1597.

45. Author interview with AmeriCorps official who wished to remain anonymous, August 10, 1999.

46. Interview with Robert Sweet, August 10, 1999.

47. Senate Appropriations Committee, Hearing, Departments of Veterans Affairs, and Housing and Urban Development and Independent Agencies Appropriations, Fiscal year 1998, March 4, 1997 (Washington, Government Printing Office, 1997), p. 87.

48. Jill Leovy, "Welfare-to-Work Plan Encounters Some Bumps," *Los Angeles Times,* February 16, 1999.

49. Press Release, "The Myth of the Magical Volunteer Bureaucracy," Office of Rep. Pete Hoekstra, 1996.

50. Interview with Derrick Max, October 3, 1999.

51. Interview with Brian Farar, July 22, 1999.

52. Grant application, "Volunteer Assistant Teachers Train to Become Teachers," Mississippi Department of Education, June 12, 1998.

53. Grant application to AmeriCorps from Rockin' Magicians Sports Assn. Inc., New York, N.Y., April 12, 1999.

54. Hearing, Departments of Veterans Affairs, and Housing and Urban Development and Independent Agencies Appropriations, Fiscal year 1999, HR 4194/S. 2168, Senate Appropriations Committee, March 5, 1998 (Washington: Government Printing Office, 1998), p. 71.

55. The General Accounting Office concluded: "Overall, Title I Programs do not ultimately reduce the effects of poverty on a student's achievement . . . Most title I students failed to exhibit the reading and mathematics skills expected for their respective grade levels." Testimony of Carlotta C. Joyner, Director, Education and Employment Issues General Accounting Office Senate Budget Committee Hearing on Federal Pre-College Education Programs, Federal Document Clearing House Congressional Testimony, November 6, 1997.

56. "Remarks at the AmeriCorps Public Safety Forum in New York City," *Public Papers of the Presidents,* March 10, 1994, p. 419.

57. National and Community Service Trust Act of 1993, Public Law 103-82, September 21, 1993.

58. Information from http://www.nationalservice.org/stateprofiles/index.html.

59. Mary Anne Clancy, "AmeriCorps volunteer writing grants," *Bangor (Maine) Daily News,* September 4, 1998.

60. Central Oregon Intergovernmental Council, Redmond, Oregon. Information from http://www.nationalservice.org/stateprofiles/index.html.

61. YMCA of Snohomish County; Snohomish County Youth Connection Project, Everett, Wash. Information from http://www.nationalservice.org/stateprofiles/index.html.

62. NH Philharmonic Orchestra's AmeriCorps Music Education Program, Manchester, N.H. Information from http://www.americorps.nh.com/programs

63. Youth Garden Project, Moab, Utah. Information from http://www.nationalservice.org/stateprofiles/index.html.

64. City of Pawtucket Partners in Learning/ AmeriCorps, Pawtucket, R.I. Information from http://www.nationalservice.org/stateprofiles/index.html.

65. Grant Application submitted to AmeriCorps by Ohio State University Research Foundation, Ohio Teen B.R.I.D.G.E.S., May 1, 1998.

66. Grant application to AmeriCorps from Congressional Hunger Center (the parent organization for four anti-hunger AmeriCorps projects), Washington, D.C., March 11, 1999. (There was a separate section in the application for each of the four different projects.)

67. Ibid.

68. "AmeriCorps Members Busy Helping with Local Communities," *Indian Valley Record* (Greenville, Cal.), March 17, 1999.

69. Andreas Fuhrmann, "Fun Fest '98 Was Fun for Everyone," *Largo (Florida) Weekly,* August 13, 1998.

70. "EnviroCorps Serves and Educates," *Elkhart (Indiana) Truth,* June 23, 1998.

71. "Remarks by the President to American Society of Newspaper Editors," M2 Presswire, April 19, 1999.

72. Lauren Gelfand, "AmeriCorps Volunteers Greet Clinton," Associated Press, June 3, 1999.

73. "Remarks to the City Year Convention in Cleveland, Ohio," *Public Papers of the Presidents,* June 3, 1998, p. 1027.

74. Letter from Rep. Pete Hoekstra to the White House, June 24, 1998.

75. "Remarks at the AmeriCorps National Civilian Community Corps Graduation Ceremony," *Public Papers of the Presidents,* August 9, 1999, p. 1597.

76. Charles Grassley, "Introduction to the $30,000 'Volunteer'," *Washington Times,* November 1, 1994.

77. Corporation for National and Community Service, Office of the Inspector General, *Report of Investigation of Green Corps,* OIG Report no. 96-026, September 20, 1996.

78. Christopher Lopez, "Cole Leader Apologizes for Blunder," *Denver Post,* July 29, 1995.

79. Author interview with Inspector General Luise Jordan, September 15, 1999.

80. Daniel E. Witte, "Getting a Grip on National Service: Key Organizational Features and Strategic Characteristics of the National Service Corps (AmeriCorps)," *Brigham Young University Law Review,* 1998, p. 772.

81. Corporation for National Service, Office of the Inspector General, *Audit of the Corporation's Procurement and Contracting Processes and Procedures,* Report no. 98-24, August 7, 1998.

82. Corporation for National and Community Service, Office of Inspector General, Semi-Annual Report, September 30, 1998, p. 9.

83. Press Release, "Former Director of AmeriCorps-Funded Program Pleads Guilty," AmeriCorps, Office of Inspector General, January 11, 1999.

84. Sue Loughlin, "State Investigates Missing Records from Programs at Ivy Tech," *Terre Haute Tribune-Star,* June 9, 1999. Also, Sue Loughlin, "Paid Work Can't Get Volunteer Credit," *Terre Haute Tribune Star,* June 10, 1999. Loughlin's reporting broke this story throughout the late spring of 1999.

85. House Committee on Education and the Workforce, Subcommittee on Oversight and Investigations, "Testimony of Brian Sullivan," September 14, 1999.

86. Indiana State Board of Accounts, "Special Report on WinCorps and 21st Century Scholars Program, Ivy Tech State College, Terre Haute, Indiana," July 29, 1999.

87. "Testimony of Luise Jordan," Inspector General, Corporation for National and Community Service, before the Subcommittee on Oversight and Investigations, House Committee on Education and the Workforce, September 14, 1999.

88. Corporation for National Service, Office of the Inspector General, *Assessment of AmeriCorps Service Hour Reporting,* Report no. 98-19, June 19, 1998.

89. Ibid.

90. Ibid.

91. Ibid.

92. Information provided by Washington expert on AmeriCorps who wished to remain anonymous.

93. U.S. General Accounting Office, "National Service Programs: Two AmeriCorps Programs' Funding and Benefits," February 2000. (emphasis added)

94. This was an undated resignation letter provided in response to a Freedom of Information Act request I filed with AmeriCorps. AmeriCorps withheld the name of the member, who was based at an AmeriCorps site in Charleston, South Carolina.

95. "Remarks to the City Year Convention in Cleveland, Ohio," *Public Papers of the Presidents,* June 3, 1998, p. 1027.

96. John Messer, "Disparities Between National Service Outcome Measures and Goals: Core Susquehanna AmeriCorps: A Case Study," Independent Sector 1997 Working Papers, p. 323.

97. Ibid.

98. Interview with Peter Hoekstra, August 12, 1999.

99. Transcript of hearing on Fiscal Year 2000 Appropriations for AmeriCorps, Senate Appropriations Committee, March 11, 1999, p. 32.

100. See http://www.americorpsalums.org.

101. Mary Owen, "AmeriCorps Program has Costly Catch," *Detroit Free Press,* November 10, 1998.

102. John Messer, "Disparities Between National Service Outcome Measures and Goals: Core Susquehanna AmeriCorps: A Case Study," Independent Sector 1997 Working Papers, p. 323.

103. Daniel E. Witte, "Getting a Grip on National Service: Key Organizational Features and Strategic Characteristics of the National Service Corps (AmeriCorps)," *Brigham Young University Law Review,* 1998, p. 772.

104. Author interview with AmeriCorps Press Spokesman Tara Murphy, August 26, 1999.

105. Eugene L. Meyer, "Clinton Attends AmeriCorps Rally," *Washington Post,* February 11, 1999.

106. Interview with Doug Bandow, August 17, 1999. Bandow has published widely on AmeriCorps and is one of the program's most astute critics.

CHAPTER THREE

1. "Remarks on Signing the Second Taxpayer Bill of Rights and an Exchange with Reporters," *Public Papers of the Presidents,* July 30, 1996, p. 1375.

2. Internal Revenue Service, Annual Reports, 1993-99.

3. Various General Accounting Office Reports 1993-1999.

4. Greg Pierce, "IRS Says It's Not Guilty of 'Abuse,'" *Washington Times,* October 28, 1994.

5. "Prepared Statement of Margaret Milner Richardson, Commissioner of Internal Revenue Service, Before the Subcommittee on Oversight, House Committee on Ways and Means," Federal News Service, March 24, 1995.

6. "Testimony of Jennifer Long, Senate Finance, IRS Treatment of Employees and Taxpayers," Federal Document Clearing House, September 24, 1997.

7. Author interview with Carole Ward, April 11, 1998.

8. Author interview with Carole Ward, April 10, 1998.

9. Ibid.

10. "Business Woman Is Awarded $325,000 for IRS's Unauthorized Disclosures. (*Carol Ward v. United States*) (No. 95-WY-810-WD)," *Tax Notes Today,* June 6, 1997.

11. Ibid.

12. Author interview with Denis Mark, April 10, 1998.

13. Author interview with Bob Kammen, October 8, 1997.

14. Author interview with Carole Ward, April 12, 1998.

15. "Prepared Statement of Tom Savage Before the Senate Finance Committee, Subject: Oversight Hearing on the Internal Revenue Service," Federal News Service, September 24, 1997. Also, numerous interviews with Tom Savage and his lawyers, September and October 1997.

16. As Savage related: "The IRS now asserted falsely that TSA and the subcontractor were partners, and that the employees of the subcontractor working on the project were actually employees of this fictitious association between TSA and the subcontractor." "U.S. Senate Committee on Finance, Day 3 of Hearings on Alleged Abuses at the IRS," Federal Document Clearing House, September 25, 1997.

17. "U.S. Senate Committee on Finance, Day 3 of Hearings on Alleged Abuses at the IRS," Federal Document Clearing House, September 25, 1997.

18. Author interview with Tom Savage, October 5, 1997.

19. "Hearing of the Senate Finance Committee; Subject: IRS Oversight," Federal News Service, April 29, 1998.

20. Ibid.

21. "Criminal Tax Defendant May Be Entitled to Recover Attorney's Fees," *Tax Notes Today,* October 14, 1998.

22. Ibid.

23. Ibid.

24. "Hearing of the Senate Finance Committee; Subject: IRS Oversight," Federal News Service, April 29, 1998.

25. David Cay Johnston, "Man Pursued by I.R.S. Wins $75,000 to Pay His Lawyer," *New York Times,* February 9, 1999.

26. David Montgomery, "The Tax Man Cometh," *Washington Post,* April 11, 1999.

27. Ibid.

28. Brett Fromson, "Heavy-Handed IRS Unit Under Scrutiny," *Washington Post,* April 20, 1998.

29. Fax from IRS spokeswoman Susan Stawick, March 10, 2000.

30. Ralph Vartabedian, "IRS 'Rewards-for-Snitches' Program Comes under Fire," *Los Angeles Times,* April 15, 1998.

31. "Full Text: Testimony of Six Current and Former IRS Employees at Finance Hearing on IRS," *Tax Notes Today,* September 26, 1997.

32. "Testimony, William V. Roth, Jr., Chairman, Senate Finance; Subject: IRS Restructuring," Federal Document Clearing House, February 11, 1998.

33. William Roth and William Nixon, *The Power to Destroy* (New York: Atlantic Monthly Press, 1999), p. 32.

34. Ibid., p. 76-77.

35. Ibid., p. 76.

36. "Unofficial Transcript of Finance Hearing on IRS Abuses," *Tax Notes Today,* October 2, 1997.

37. "Enrolled Agents Group's Testimony at Finance Hearing on IRS Treatment of Taxpayers," *Tax Notes Today,* September 24, 1997.

38. "Report on IRS Internal Audit of District's Use if Enforcement Statistics," *Tax Notes Today,* December 24, 1997.

39. "IRS Releases Second Report on Use of Enforcement Stats," *Tax Notes Today,* January 14, 1998.

40. "Prepared Statement of Bruce Strauss before the Senate Finance Committee; Subject: Oversight Hearing on the Internal Revenue Service," Federal News Service, September 24, 1997.

41. Ibid.

42. Roth and Nixon, *The Power to Destroy,* p. 63.

43. "AICPA Says Financial Status Audit Techniques Undermine Taxpayers' Rights," *Tax Notes Today,* April 25, 1996.

44. Treasury Department Inspector General for Tax Administration, "The New Jersey District Needs to Execute Levy Actions Consistent with Sound Tax Administration and Concern for Taxpayer Treatment," September 27, 1999.

45. Fowler Martin, "US IRS To Apologize To 8,500 Mistreated NJ Taxpayers," Dow Jones Newswires, October 29, 1999.

46. Ibid.

47. Ibid.

48. Ibid.

49. General Accounting Office, "Financial Audit Examination of IRS Fiscal Year 1997 Custodial Financial Statements," February 26, 1998.

50. "Bond Warns IRS: Lighten Up on Baseball Fans," Congressional Press Releases, Federal Document Clearinghouse, September 8, 1998.

51. Sheldon Richman, "Of Home Runs and Capricious Tax Men," *Las Vegas Review-Journal,* September 21, 1998.

52. Stephen Barr, "IRS Computer Revamp Faulted by Study Panel," *Washington Post,* August 20, 1993.

53. "Hearing of the Senate Governmental Affairs Committee; Subject: Waste and Abuse at IRS and U.S. Customs Service," Federal News Service, August 4, 1993.

54. Editorial, "Auditing the IRS," *Orange County Register,* August 11, 1993.

55. "Testimony of James F. Hinchman, U.S. General Accounting Office," Federal Document Clearing House, July 19, 1994.

56. Editorial, "Curbing Curiosity," *Cleveland Plain Dealer,* April 14, 1997.

57. Editorial, "IRS: The Problem is Power," *Investor's Business Daily,* April 11, 1997.

58. "IRS' Actions to Implement Public Law 105-35," *Tax Notes Today,* January 27, 1999.

59. Dow Jones Newswire, "Weak IRS Computer Security Is Putting Taxpayer Data at Risk," January 13, 1999.

60. Ibid.

61. "Rubin Asks Roth to Watch Rhetoric on Eve of IRS Abuse Hearings," *Tax Notes Today,* September 23, 1997.

62. "Remarks by Vice President Al Gore, Secretary of the Treasury Robert Rubin, IRS Commissioner Charles Rossotti and IRS Customer Service Task Force Member Marilyn

Smith, Re: Report of the IRS Customer Service Task Force," Federal News Service, March 18, 1998.

63. Jill Young Miller, "Bill Calls on Federal Staffs to Answer the Phones; Senator Aims to Pull Plug on Games and Voice Mail," *Sun-Sentinel* (Florida), July 7, 1997.

64. "Remarks by Vice President Al Gore, Secretary of the Treasury Robert Rubin, IRS Commissioner Charles Rossotti and IRS Customer Service Task Force Member Marilyn Smith, Re: Report of the IRS Customer Service Task Force," Federal News Service, March 18, 1998.

65. "President Clinton's Weekly Radio Address," Federal News Service, May 2, 1998.

66. "Remarks on Signing the Internal Revenue Service Restructuring and Reform Act of 1998," *Public Papers of the Presidents,* July 22, 1998, p. 1453.

67. James Bovard, "The IRS Mess," *American Spectator,* June 1998.

68. "Roth: Outline of IRS Reform Proposal," *Tax Notes Today,* March 27, 1998.

69. Treasury Department Inspector General for Tax Administration, "The Internal Revenue Service Needs to Improve Treatment of Taxpayers During Office Audits," Report no. 093602, April 29, 1999.

70. Treasury Department Inspector General for Tax Administration, "The Internal Revenue Service Has Not Fully Implemented Procedures to Notify Taxpayers Before Taking Their Funds For Payment of Tax," Report no. 199910071, September 29, 1999.

71. Treasury Department Inspector General for Tax Administration, "The Internal Revenue Service Needs to Improve Compliance with Legal and Internal Guidelines When Taking Taxpayers' Property for Unpaid Taxes," Report no. 199910072, September 27, 1999.

72. Treasury Department Inspector General for Tax Administration, "The Internal Revenue Service Should Continue Its Efforts to Achieve Full Compliance with Restrictions on the Use of Enforcement Statistics," Report no. 199910073, September 29, 1999.

73. General Accounting Office, "IRS Employee Evaluations—Opportunities to Better Balance Customer Service and Compliance Objectives," October 14, 1999.

74. John F. Harris and Peter Baker, "White House Memo Asserts a Scandal Theory," *Washington Post,* January 10, 1997.

75. Joseph Farah, "Complicit Criminality in Congress," World Net Daily, November 2, 1999.

76. Joseph Farah, "Fighting Back Against a Political IRS," World Net Daily, May 8, 1998.

77. Editorial, "Abuse and the IRS," *Wall Street Journal,* July 20, 1999.

78. Larry Margasak, "IRS Can't Find Audit Files," Associated Press, November 16, 1999.

79. Ibid.

80. Editorial, "Where's Janet?" *Wall Street Journal,* November 19, 1999.

81. John Solomon and Larry Margasak, "Documents Pinpoint Federal Audits," Associated Press, November 16, 1999.

82. Ibid.

83. "Prepared Testimony of Gregory D. Kutz, Associate Director, Accounting and Financial Management Issues, Accounting and Information Management Division, United States General Accounting Office, Before the House Committee on Government Reform Subcommittee on Government Management, Information and Technology," Federal News Service, February 29, 2000.

84. Ibid.

85. Ibid.

86. Ibid.

87. David Cay Johnston, "I.R.S. Bolstering Efforts to Make Tax Cheats Pay Up," *New York Times,* February 13, 2000.

88. "Testimony of Charles Rossotti, Commissioner, Internal Revenue Service, Senate Governmental Affairs," *Federal Document Clearing House,* October 20, 1999.
89. David Cay Johnston, "I.R.S. Bolstering Efforts to Make Tax Cheats Pay Up," *New York Times,* February 13, 2000.

CHAPTER FOUR

1. "Remarks at the University of California San Diego Commencement Ceremony in La Jolla, California," *Public Papers of the Presidents,* June 14, 1997, p. 876.
2. *Adarand v. Pena,* 515 U.S. 200 (1995).
3. Ibid.
4. Warren Strobel, "Clinton Defends Preferences for Colleges, Hiring," *Washington Times,* June 15, 1997.
5. The report was reprinted in the *Congressional Record,* March 15, 1995, pp. S 3929+.
6. "Remarks of President Bill Clinton Regarding Affirmative Action," *Federal News Service,* July 19, 1995.
7. Ibid.
8. "Remarks by the President on Affirmative Action," White House Office of the Press Secretary, July 19, 1995.
9. Garland Thompson, "Minority Business Summit Weighs Affirmative Action's Survival After Adarand," *US Black Engineer,* October 31, 1995.
10. Dan Felstein, "FTA Letter Puts Metro in Dilemma," *Houston Chronicle,* May 1, 1996.
11. Editorial, "Metro's Dilemma," *Houston Chronicle,* January 25, 1997.
12. Dan Feldstein, "Metro Gets Money despite Lack of Affirmative Action," *Houston Chronicle,* September 27, 1997.
13. David Stout, "Appeals Court Overturns Race-Based School Policy," *New York Times,* March 20, 1996. The lawsuit against the preferences was brought by the Center for Individual Rights, a Washington, D.C., public interest law firm.
14. Linda Chavez, "Clinton Flouts Bias Rulings," *Denver Post,* April 13, 1997.
15. Richard Starr, "Sexual Perversity in Washington: The Brave New World of Norma Cantu," *Weekly Standard,* April 7, 1997.
16. Peter Applebome, "In Shift, U.S. Tells Texas It Can't Ignore Court Ruling Barring Bias in College Admissions," *New York Times,* April 15, 1997.
17. "President Clinton, Remarks to the National Association of Black Journalists," *Federal News Service,* July 18, 1997.
18. Charles Dervarics, "Justice Department Files Proposition 209 Brief," *Black Issues in Higher Education/Ethnic News Watch,* February 20, 1997.
19. Frank J. Murray, "Proposition 209 Faces Administration's Fire," *Washington Times,* January 30, 1997.
20. "Testimony of Michael Carvin, Subcommittee on the Constitution," *Federal Document Clearing House,* May 20, 1997.
21. Frank Murray, "Appeals Court Restores '209' in California; Judge Had Blocked Voter Decision," *Washington Times,* April 9, 1997.
22. Tim Golden, "Federal Appeals Court Upholds California's Ban on Preferences," *New York Times,* April 9, 1997.
23. Michele Collison, "Exam Negotiation; New Law Prevents Reliance on Discriminatory Standardized Tests," *Black Issues in Higher Education,* June 10, 1999.

24. Patrick Healy, "Civil-Rights Office Questions Legality of Colleges' Use of Standardized Tests," *Chronicle of Higher Education,* May 28, 1999.
25. Pete Hoekstra, "Washington's New Guidelines Would Do More Harm to Schools and Minorities," *Insight on the News,* August 30, 1999.
26. John Leo, "The Feds Strike Back," *U.S. News and World Report,* May 31, 1999.
27. Ibid.
28. Roger Clegg and Lenore Ostrowsky, "Test Guidelines Will Coerce Colleges and Cheat Students," *Chronicle of Higher Education,* July 2, 1999.
29. Karen Arenson, "College Board Revises Tests to Improve Chances for Girls," *New York Times,* October 2, 1996.
30. Mark Murray, "Affirmative Action, on the Mend," *National Journal,* February 20, 1999.
31. "Testimony of Roger Clegg, House Judiciary Subcommittee on the Constitution, February 25, 1998," Federal Document Clearing House, February 25, 1998.
32. Linda S. Gottfredson, "Racially Gerrymandered Police Tests," *Wall Street Journal,* October 24, 1996.
33. John Lott, "Does a Helping Hand Put Others At Risk?: Affirmative Action, Police Departments, and Crime," *Economic Inquiry* (published by the Western Economics Association), April 2000.
34. Stuart Taylor, "A Year's Worth of Outrage, Hypocrisy and Pandering," *Legal Times,* January 9, 1995.
35. Pete Du Pont, "Last Gasp for Quotas in a Zero-Sum Game," *Washington Times,* August 1, 1995.
36. Ibid.
37. Ruth Larson, "Forest Service Hit for 'Quota Lunacy'," *Washington Times,* February 6, 1995.
38. U.S. Department of Labor, Office of Public Affairs, San Francisco, Cal., News Release, USDL-3, January 12, 1995.
39. Deborah Billings and Pamela Prah, "Labor Department Expects Data to Show Major Difference from Affirmative Action," *Daily Labor Report,* March 20, 1995.
40. "Policing the Federal Contractors," *Newsday,* April 17, 1994.
41. "Prepared Statement of Shirley J. Wilcher, Senate Labor Committee," Federal News Service, June 15, 1995.
42. "OFCCP Discussion Paper on Affirmative Action Requirements for Construction Contractors Performing Federal and Federally Assisted Work—September 1994," *Daily Labor Report,* October 17, 1994, p. D29.
43. Author interview with Peter Kirsanow, March 28, 1996.
44. Author interview with Mary Jane Sinclair, April 4, 1996.
45. "Prepared Statement by Jennifer Taylor, Supervisor, Employment, City Utilities of Springfield, Before the House Economic and Educational Opportunities Committee," Federal News Service, February 29, 1996.
46. Author interview with Sadie Fox, April 5, 1996.
47. Author interview with Len Wise, April 5, 1996.
48. U.S. Senate, Labor and Human Resources Committee, *Affirmative Action and the Office of Federal Contract Compliance,* June 15, 1995 (Washington: Government Printing Office, 1995), p. 33.
49. Ibid.
50. Equal Employment Advisory Council, "EEAC Files Position Statement with OFCCP on Definition of 'Applicant' and Related Recordkeeping Requirements," no. 95-187, December 15, 1995.

51. Senate Labor and Human Resources Committee, *Affirmative Action and the Office of Federal Contract Compliance*, p. 54.
52. Author interview with James Wesner, March 29, 1996.
53. Author interview with lawyer who wished to remain anonymous, May 17, 1996.
54. Author interview with official who wished to remain anonymous, January 29, 1999.
55. Quoted in Davan Maharaj, "Unequal Pay Is Targeted by Tougher Enforcement," *Los Angeles Times*, January 30, 1999.
56. Equal Employment Advisory Council, "Conducting a Self-Analysis for Potential Discrimination in Compensation," no. 95-44, March 31, 1995, p. 9.
57. Ibid., p. 18.
58. Interview with California attorney who wished to remain anonymous, May 8, 1996.
59. "'OFCCP: Regional Offices Experiencing 'Interesting' Reaction to *Adarand*," *Daily Labor Report*, September 19, 1995, p. D14.
60. Ruth Larson, "New EEOC Chief Inherits Case Crush," *Washington Times*, October 27, 1994.
61. Mike Royko, "U.S. Trying to Pluck a Chicken Company, *Chicago Tribune*, June 17, 1994.
62. Author interview with Mark Kaminsky, March 7, 1995.
63. Mike Royko, "Restaurant Owner Getting a 'Bub' Rap," *Chicago Tribune*, June 3, 1994.
64. Ibid.
65. Joseph Cahill, "Why EEOC Can Spell Trouble," *Crain's Small Business*, June 1995.
66. Ibid.
67. Russell Vernon, "Fighting the Feds," *Wall Street Journal*, March 26, 1997.
68. Ibid.
69. Greg Gattuso, "West Point CEO a 'David' v. Bureaucracy," *Supermarket News*, April 7, 1997.
70. Joseph Cahill, "Why EEOC Can Spell Trouble," *Crain's Small Business*, June 1995.
71. Equal Employment Opportunity Commission, "EEOC Fiscal Year 1999 Accomplishments Report Shows Groundbreaking Progress on All Fronts," Press Release, December 27, 1999.
72. Equal Employment Opportunity Commission, "EEOC Accomplishments Report for Fiscal Year 1999," December 1999.
73. John Beckett, "Freedom of or from Religion?" *Washington Times*, February 15, 1994.
74. Gary Bauer, "Religious Harassment Rules Required," *Washington Times*, May 22, 1994.
75. Thomas Hargrove, "House has Bad News for EEOC," *Washington Times*, June 29, 1994.
76. Press Release, "EEOC Issues Guidance on Remedies for Undocumented Workers under Laws Prohibiting Employment Discrimination," Equal Employment Opportunity Commission, October 26, 1999.
77. Paul Bedard, "White House Fired Chef over Bias Filing," *Washington Times*, September 8, 1997.
78. Paul Bedard, "Judge's Ruling Protects Hillary; Fired-Chef Case Kept Confidential," *Washington Times*, May 7, 1997.
79. Paul Bedard, "White House Fired Chef Over Bias Filing," *Washington Times*, September 8, 1997.
80. Paul Bedard, "Judge's Ruling Protects Hillary; Fired-Chef Case Kept Confidential," *Washington Times*, May 7, 1997.
81. George Benston, "The Community Reinvestment Act: Looking for Discrimination That Isn't There," Cato Institute Policy Analysis, October 6, 1999.
82. "Consultants Cash In," *Boston Globe*, August 15, 1999.
83. Jonathan Macey, "Egalitarianism and Financial Institutions," Competitive Enterprise Institute Conference, Washington, D.C., November 2, 1994.
84. Editorial, "Gramm's Glass-Steagall Beef," *Wall Street Journal*, January 6, 1999.

85. Steve Malanga, "How To Hold Up a Bank," *Crain's New York,* November 1, 1999.
86. Carl Horowitz, "Shaking Down America's Banks," *Investor's Business Daily,* April 3, 1995.
87. Marcy Gordon, "Gramm Focuses on Bank Overhaul Bill," Associated Press, January 13, 1999.
88. William Isaac, "In Reform Bill Talks, Gramm's CRA Stance Merits a Hearing," *American Banker,* September 30, 1999.
89. Senate Banking Committee, "Banks' CRA Agreements To Be Made Public under Senate Version of Financial Services Modernization," Press Release, May 6, 1999.
90. Senate Banking Committee, "Report to the Chairman, Committee on Banking, Housing, and Urban Affairs, United States Senate, on the Involvement of Federal Banking Examiners in Political Activities," September 16, 1999.
91. Stephen Labaton, "White House Used Auditors against a Bill," *New York Times,* September 16, 1999.
92. Ibid.
93. Marcy Gordon, "Financial Overhaul Nears Approval," Associated Press, November 3, 1999.
94. Howard Kurtz, "Gore to Announce Plan to Hike Budget for Civil Rights by 15%," *Washington Post,* January 18, 1999.
95. Ibid.
96. Adam Nagourney, "At N.A.A.C.P. Dinner, Gore Praises Affirmative Action and Declares War on Prejudice," *New York Times,* April 26, 1999. Columnist Jeff Jacoby was the first to point out Gore's subtle influence.
97. Clifford Alexander, "Clinton Lies about Race, Too," *Wall Street Journal,* September 2, 1998.
98. Ibid.
99. "The President's Radio Address," *Public Papers of the Presidents,* June 8, 1996, p. 1015.
100. Remarks on the Church Arson Prevention Act of 1996," *Public Papers of the Presidents,* July 9, 1996, p. 1221.
101. Michael Fumento, "A Church Arson Epidemic? It's Smoke and Mirrors," *Wall Street Journal,* July 8, 1996.
102. "Remarks by the President on Affirmative Action," White House Office of the Press, July 19, 1995.

CHAPTER FIVE

1. "Remarks on the National Performance Review," *Public Papers of the Presidents,* March 27, 1995, p. 481.
2. Author interview with FEMA employee who wished to remain anonymous, June 17, 1996.
3. General Accounting Office, "Disaster Assistance –Information on Declaration for Urban and Rural Areas," September 1995.
4. Carla Rivera, "FEMA Discontinues Unrequested Quake Checks," *Los Angeles Times,* February 4, 1994.
5. Jesse Malkin and Michelle Malkin, "All Abroad the Northridge Gravy Train," *Orange County Register,* February 17, 1994.
6. "Laugh Lines," *Los Angeles Times,* May 9, 1994.
7. Richard Simon and Myron Levin, "Nearly a Year after Quake, U.S. Aid Exceeds $5 Billion," *Los Angeles Times,* January 8, 1995.
8. Paul Sperry, "FEMA," *Investor's Business Daily,* May 19, 1994.
9. Vallee Bunting, "FEMA Responds," *Playboy,* September 1998.
10. General Accounting Office, "Disaster Assistance, Guidance Needed for FEMA's 'Fast Track' Housing Assistance Process," October 1997.

11. FEMA IG, "Options for Reducing Public Assistance Program Costs," Inspection Report I-02-95, July 1995. (emphasis in original)
12. Marc Lacey, "$8 Billion Left in Quake Aid, but Claims Expect That," *Los Angeles Times,* July 19, 1995.
13. FEMA IG, "Options for Reducing Public Assistance Program Costs," Inspection Report I-02-95, July 1995.
14. "Laugh Lines," *Los Angeles Times,* April 6, 1995.
15. Ken Miller, "A Sampling of FEMA's Recreational Relief," Gannett News Service, July 18, 1996.
16. Ibid.
17. Jay Rey, "Officials Seek Aid to Recoup Cost of Clearing January Snow," *Buffalo News,* February 10, 1999.
18. Barbara O'Brien, "Town Gets Reimbursement Check for Snow Removal," *Buffalo News,* May 11, 1999.
19. "Federal Aid Ok'd for Snow Removal," *Buffalo News,* March 18, 1999.
20. Scott Silvestri, "Towns Finding Upside of Blizzard," *Chicago Daily Herald,* April 28, 1999.
21. Jon Hilkevitch, "CTA Left Holding the Bag for Snow Costs; U.S. Pays Only Fraction of $6.3 Million Pricetag," *Chicago Tribune,* June 17, 1999.
22. Jonathan McKernan, "It's Official: County on Disaster List," *Chicago Daily Herald,* January 30, 1999.
23. Stephanie Reitz, "Town Digs into Reserves to Pay for Snow Removal," *Hartford Courant,* June 4, 1996.
24. Vallee Bunting, "FEMA Responds," *Playboy,* December 1998.
25. "President Clinton Declares Major Disaster in Vermont," M2 Presswire, July 28, 1997.
26. Author interview with John McLaughry, September 5, 1997.
27. Anne Wallace Allen, "Flooding Forces Campers to Evacuate, Closes Roads," Associated Press, July 15, 1997.
28. FEMA Inspector General, "Crisis Counseling Expenditures After the Northridge Earthquake," Audit Report H-6-97, March 27, 1997.
29. "Crisis Counselors Extend a Helping Hand," *Disaster Times* (FEMA, North Dakota version), March 1997.
30. *Recovery Times,* (FEMA, Michigan version), March 10, 1997.
31. Alan J. Borsuk, "FEMA Vows Prompt Aid Action," *Milwaukee Journal Sentinel,* July 10, 1997.
32. *Disaster Times,* (FEMA, North Dakota version), March 1997.
33. Tillie Fong, "Many Affected by Flood Eligible for Disaster Aid," *Rocky Mountain News,* August 16, 1997.
34. Jeffrey Savitskie, "Engler Makes Plea for Federal Aid; Storm Costs Likely to Top $76 Million," *Detroit News,* July 10, 1997.
35. Suzette Hackney, "In Metro Detroit—Storm Victims Slow in Filing," *Detroit News,* August 19, 1997.
36. Shawn D. Lewis, "Spirits Lift as Mennonites Repair Storm-Damaged Roofs," *Detroit News,* September 9, 1997.
37. Jonathan Ellis, "On the Road with the Secret Government," *Liberty Magazine,* November 1998.
38. "Telephone Remarks to the National Emergency Management Association Meeting," *Public Papers of the Presidents,* February 26, 1996, p. 380.
39. "Laugh Lines," *Los Angeles Times,* July 10, 1997.
40. John Riley, "Shoreline in Peril: Flood of Claims," *Newsday,* August 18, 1998.
41. Rocky Barker, "The Flood—Next Time," *Idaho Statesman,* March 19, 1997.

42. Ibid.
43. Author interview with Scott Faber, July 8, 1996.
44. John Riley, "Shoreline in Peril: Flood of Claims," *Newsday,* August 18, 1998.
45. "How Often Should Taxpayers Foot Bill for Coastal Rebuilding?" Associated Press, August 30, 1998.
46. Ibid.
47. Greg Jaffe and Motoko Rich, "N.C. Island Attracts Tourists, Hurricanes, Federal Disaster Aid," *Palm Beach Post,* September 6, 1998.
48. George M. Stephens, "Let States Finance Their Own Disasters," *Raleigh News and Observer,* November 24, 1996.
49. "Prepared Statement of the Honorable James L. Witt, Director, Federal Emergency Management Agency, Before the House Committee on Appropriations VA, HUD and Independent Agencies Subcommittee," Federal News Service, April 30, 1996.
50. Author interview with a FEMA employee who wished to remain anonymous, August 1, 1996.
51. James Lee Witt, "Federal Flood Insurance," *Los Angeles Times,* July 2, 1997.
52. "Testimony of James Witt, Director, FEMA, Senate Appropriations," Federal Document Clearing House, April 30, 1996.
53. "Testimony of James L. Witt, Director, Federal Emergency Management Agency, Senate Appropriations, VA, HUD, and Independent Agencies, FY98 VA, HUD Appropriations," Federal Document Clearing House, March 18, 1997.
54. Author interview with Beth Milleman, August 2, 1996.
55. FEMA IG, "Audit of the Enforcement of Flood Insurance Purchase Requirements for Disaster Aid Recipients," Inspection Report, H-14-95, July 1995.
56. James Toedtman, "Curbing Coastal Development: Officials Recommend Revamp of Insurance Policy," *Newsday,* April 11, 1999.
57. Gene Marlowe, "Agency Fed Up with Rebuilding Flood Zones," *Tampa Tribune,* June 15, 1998.
58. "Seeking an End to a Flood Of Claims," National Wildlife Federation, July 1, 1999.
59. Rad Sallee, "Federal Flood Payoffs Crest Here, Study Says," *Houston Chronicle,* July 22, 1998.
60. Bob Schildgen, "Unnatural Disasters: Areas that Suffer Repeat Flooding yet Continue to Rebuild," *Sierra,* May 1999.
61. Mike Clary, "Even Before Landfall, Floyd Drives Unprecedented Flood—of Evacuees," *Los Angeles Times,* September 16, 1999.
62. Dan Lewerenz, "Evacuees Blame Public Officials for Traffic Woes," *Memphis Commercial Appeal,* September 16, 1999.
63. Editorial, "State Must Have Firm Plan to Right Evacuation Wrongs," *Charleston Post and Courier,* September 16, 1999.
64. Bruce Smith, "Mayors Offer Suggestions for Evacuation," Associated Press, September 22, 1999.
65. Mike Clary, "Even Before Landfall, Floyd Drives Unprecedented Flood—of Evacuees," *Los Angeles Times,* September 16, 1999.
66. "Teleconference Remarks with Governors from States Struck by Hurricane Floyd and Remarks to Disaster Relief Workers and an Exchange with Reporters," *Public Papers of the Presidents,* September 16, 1999, p. 1756.
67. "Remarks to the Community in Tarboro, North Carolina," *Public Papers of the Presidents,* September 20, 1999, p. 1776.
68. "White House Fact Sheet on Federal Agency Efforts in Response to Hurricane Floyd," U.S. Newswire, September 20, 1999.

69. "Teleconference Remarks with Governors from States Struck by Hurricane Floyd and Remarks to Disaster Relief Workers and an Exchange With Reporters," *Public Papers of the Presidents,* September 16, 1999, p. 1756.

70. Quoted in James Bovard, "FEMA Money! Come and Get It!" *American Spectator,* September 1996.

71. Jeffrey Tucker, "Life with Morrie," *Free Market,* March 1996.

72. Patrick McGreevy, "FEMA Proposal Could Prove Costly to City," *Los Angeles Times,* July 6, 1999.

73. Ibid.

74. "Testimony James Witt, Director, FEMA, Senate Appropriations Committee," Federal Document Clearinghouse, April 30, 1996.

75. FEMA IG, "Audit of FEMA's Disaster Relief Fund," H-16-95, July 1995, p. 9.

76. Ibid., p. 14

77. Nancy Hill Holtzman, Marc Lacey, and Hugo Martin, "Study of Quake-Recovery Expenses Yields Controversial Results," *Los Angeles Times,* June 7, 1996.

78. "Remarks by Clinton Following His Meeting with the Families of the Victims of TWA Flight 800 of July 17, 1996," Federal News Service, July 25, 1996.

CHAPTER SIX

1. Gary Fields, "Study: Drug Use Up Despite Crackdown," *USA Today,* February 4, 1999.

2. "Remarks on the Zero Tolerance for Drugs in Prison Initiative," *Public Papers of the Presidents,* January 5, 1999, p. 5.

3. Michael Sniffen, "DEA Boss Upset with Murphy Brown," Associated Press, November 5, 1997.

4. Phillip Coffin, "A Duty To Censor: U.N. Officials Want to Crack Down on Drug War," *Reason,* August 1998.

5. Robert Lee Hotz, "Chemicals in Pot Cut Severe Pain, Study Says," *Los Angeles Times,* October 27, 1997.

6. Quoted in Eric Schlosser, "More Reefer Madness," *Atlantic Monthly,* April 1997.

7. "Marijuana Successfully Treats Tourette's Syndrome, Study Shows," NORML Press Release, March 11, 1999.

8. Susan Gilbert, "Health Watch: Marijuana and Strokes," *New York Times,* July 28, 1998.

9. "Cannabis 'Helps MS Sufferers,'" *BBC News Online,* March 2, 2000

10. Quoted in Ellen Beck, "Report: Marijuana May Have Medical Uses," UPI, March 17, 1999.

11. Rick Bayer, "CMA Backs Rescheduling of Marijuana," *DrugSense Weekly,* June 17, 1998.

12. Jacob Sullum, "Polls Apart on Issues," *Washington Times,* September 19, 1999.

13. Sabin Russell, "U.S. Drug Czar Visits Haight, Denounces Medical Use of Pot," *San Francisco Chronicle,* August 16, 1996.

14. "Gen. McCaffrey Defends Federal Law Prohibiting the Medicinal Use of Marijuana," *CNN Today,* Transcript #96123003V13, December 30, 1996.

15. Richard Brookhiser, "Reefer Madness Redefined," *Washington Post,* February 5, 1997.

16. *Dr. Marcus Conant, et al., Plaintiffs, vs. Barry R. McCaffrey,* 1997 U.S. Dist. Lexis 8749, April 30, 1997.

17. "Weekly Media Availability with Attorney General Janet Reno," Federal News Service, October 22, 1998.

18. Joseph Treaster, "Agency Says Marijuana Is Not Proven Medicine," *New York Times,* March 19, 1992.

19. Stephen Chapman, "What's So Bad About Marijuana?" *Chicago Tribune,* May 22, 1997.

20. Rochelle Warrander, "Rochelle Drug-Abuse Groups Hit Back at Claim on Cannabis," *The Daily News* (New Plymouth, New Zealand), July 31, 1998.

21. "Weak Link between Marijuana and Crashes," *Journal of Addiction & Mental Health,* June 1999, p. 6.

22. Joanne Jacobs, "Science Belies the Political Puffing against Marijuana," *Sacramento Bee,* March 24, 1999.

23. David Concar, "Suppressed Study Showed Marijuana Safer than Booze," *Cincinnati Enquirer,* March 8, 1998.

24. Press Release, "NORML Report Highlights Failures of Marijuana Prohibition on NORML 60 Year Anniversary of the Marihuana Tax Act, July 29, 1997.

25. Editorial, "Drug War Bankruptcy," *Orange County Register,* October 25, 1999.

26. George Gedda, "Researchers Look to Fungus as Key To Killing Narcotics Plants," Associated Press, October 23, 1998.

27. Ramsey Campbell, "Lab-Brewed Fungus Could Be Real Horror Show," *Orlando Sentinel,* December 1, 1999.

28. Prepared Testimony of Eric E. Sterling, President, The Criminal Justice Policy Foundation, Before The House Appropriations Committee, Subcommittee on Treasury, Postal Service and General Government," Federal News Service, March 23, 2000.

29. "Address Before a Joint Session of the Congress on the State of the Union," *Public Papers of the Presidents,* January 23, 1996, p. 90.

30. "Remarks by President Clinton to the Community of Monrovia, California," U.S. Newswire, July 23, 1996.

31. "Drug Czar Barry McCaffrey to Keynote National D.A.R.E. Conference; 4,500 Police Attend," Business Wire, July 7, 1999.

32. "Proclamation 7180—National D.A.R.E. Day 1999," *Public Papers of the Presidents,* April 8, 1999, p. 615.

33. Richard Serrano, "Police Board Won't Probe Gates Furor," *Los Angeles Times,* September 19, 1990.

34. Susan Ennett, Nancy Tobler, Christopher Ringwalt, and Robert Flewelling, "How Effective Is Drug Abuse Resistance Education? A Meta-Analysis of Project DARE Outcome Evaluations," *American Journal of Public Health,* September 1994, p. 1394.

35. Bob Banta, "Police Budget: Programs vs. Patrols; Chief Cuts Drug, Crime Prevention Units to Put More Officers on the Streets," *Austin American-Statesman,* August 28, 1996.

36. Quoted in Jennifer Gonnerman, "Truth or D.A.R.E.," *Village Voice,* April 13, 1999.

37. Jeff Gottlieb and Jason Kandel, "Santa Ana Might Just Say No to DARE during School Hours," *Los Angeles Times,* August 12, 1999.

38. Marc Kaufman, "Study Fails to Find Value in DARE Program," *Washington Post,* August 3, 1999.

39. James Bovard, "Turning Kids into Druggies and Informants," *American Spectator,* April 1996.

40. "The President's Radio Address," *Public Papers of the Presidents,* October 26, 1996, p. 2191.

41. "Remarks in Minneapolis, Minnesota," *Public Papers of the Presidents,* October 28, 1996, p. 2211.

42. "The President's Radio Address," *Public Papers of the Presidents,* December 20, 1997, p. 2095.

43. Ralph Frammolino, "Failing Grade for Safe Schools Plan," *Los Angeles Times,* September 6, 1998.

44. Ibid.

45. Ibid.

46. "Message to the Congress Transmitting the Proposed 'Educational Excellence for All Children Act of 1999,'" *Public Papers of the Presidents,* May 21, 1999, p. 964.
47. "Prepared Testimony of Barry R. McCaffrey, Director, Office of National Drug Control Policy, Before the Senate Committee on Health, Education, Labor, and Pensions, Subject—Building a More Effective Safe and Drug-Free Schools and Communities Program," Federal News Service, July 13, 1999.
48. Ralph Frammolino, "Failing Grade for Safe Schools Plan," *Los Angeles Times,* September 6, 1998.
49. Blair Golson, "Drug Czar Aims to Revamp School Aid Program," *Los Angeles Times,* July 13,1999.
50. "The President's Radio Address," *Public Papers of the Presidents,* September 11, 1999, p. 1725.
51. Michelle Malkin, "Ritalins's Problems," *Omaha World-Herald,* November 27, 1999.
52. George F. Will, "Ease Up on the Ritalin and Let Boys Be Boys," *Houston Chronicle,* December 7, 1999.
53. Kathy Koch, "Ritalin: Are We Overdoing It?" *Raleigh News and Observer,* November 7, 1999.
54. Christopher Wren, "Bird Food Is a Casualty of the War on Drugs," *New York Times,* October 3, 1999.
55. Matt Weiser, "U.S. Cracks Down on Hemp-Based Foods," *Arizona Republic,* October 2, 1999.
56. "Cindy Horswell, "Humble Board Upholds Girl's Suspension over Advil," *Houston Chronicle,* November 14, 1996.
57. Dennis Cauchon, "Schools Struggling to Balance 'Zero Tolerance,' Common Sense," *USA Today,* April 13, 1999.
58. Cythnia Hubert, " Drug Sting Tactics Helped 'Poison the Public,' Judge Says," *Sacramento Bee,* April 25, 1998.
59. Josh Meyer, "An Undercover Informant Comes under Suspicion," *Los Angeles Times,* March 5, 2000.
60. David Rovella, "Some Superinformant," *National Law Journal,* November 22, 1999.
61. "Attorney David Chesnoff and DEA Chief of Operations Richard Fiano Talk about the Highest Paid Drug Informant Responsible for Scores of Drug Convictions which Are Now in Question," *ABC World News This Morning,* March 9, 2000.
62. Michael D. Sorkin and Phyllis Brasch Librach, "Drug Agency Suspends Informer Known To Lie in Court," *St. Louis Post-Dispatch,* February 6, 2000.
63. Josh Meyer, "An Undercover Informant Comes under Suspicion," *Los Angeles Times,* March 5, 2000.
64. Nadine Strossen, "Read My Scripts," Intellectualcapital.com, February 24, 2000.
65. Max Frankel, "Plots for Hire," *New York Times,* February 6, 2000.
66. Chris Mitchell, "Salient Facts: Swat Team; Hometown Commandos," *New York Times Magazine,* May 30, 1999.
67. Details of the Garrison case derived from Jeff Jones, "Neighbor Killed by SWAT Team," *Albuquerque Journal,* December 17, 1996; Jeff Jones, "Lawmen Defend Use of SWAT," *Albuquerque Journal,* December 19, 1996; Jeff Jones, "Cops Will Examine 911 Role," *Albuquerque Journal,* December 18, 1996; and Jessie Milligan, "Judge Dismisses Most of Lawsuit in SWAT Death," *Albuquerque Tribune,* March 18, 1999.
68. Nicholas Riccardi, " FBI Probes Man's Killing in Police Raid," *Los Angeles Times,* August 31, 1999.
69. Anne-Marie O'Connor, "Bereft Family Disputes Police Shooting Report," *Los Angeles Times,* August 26, 1999.

70. Richard Espinoza, "Osawatomie Man Was Fatally Shot in Home by Officer," *Kansas City Star,* April 7, 1999.

71. Richard Espinoza, "Drug Raid Shooting Still an Issue in Osawatomie," *Kansas City Star,* July 13, 1999.

72. Kevin Vaughan, "Cop's Allegations Investigated," *Denver Rocky Mountain News,* January 28, 2000.

73. Kevin Flynn and Lou Kilzer, "No-Knocks Net Little Jail Time," *Denver Rocky Mountain News,* March 13, 2000.

74. Jim Dwyer, "Safir Not Sorry for Bad Raids, *New York Daily News,* August 30, 1998.

75. Chris Mitchell, "Salient Facts: SWAT Team: Hometown Commandos," *New York Times Magazine,* May 30, 1999.

76. Edie Gross, "SWAT: 'Be Safe, Be Strong, Be Mean!'" *Palm Beach Post,* June 8, 1997.

77. Thaddeus Herrick, "Marines Misplaced on Border, Study Says," *Houston Chronicle,* September 10, 1998.

78. "Pentagon Has All but Ended Use of Armed Troops on U.S.-Mexico Border," Associated Press, January 29, 1999.

79. Dane Schiller, "Border Shooting Probe Disputed; Inquiry Obstructed, Ranger Says," *New Orleans Times-Picayune,* December 15, 1998.

80. Thaddeus Herrick, "Family To Receive $1.9 Million in Border Shooting," *Houston Chronicle,* August 12, 1998.

81. David Briscoe, "Coast Guard Shooters Disable Boats," Associated Press, September 14, 1999.

82. Ibid.

83. Valerie Alvord, "Customs Burned by Drug Theft," *San Diego Union-Tribune,* December 19, 1998.

84. Marisa Taylor and Ricardo Sandovar, "Border Agent Corruption Said to Be Increasing," *San Antonio Express-News,* March 7, 1999.

85. Rene Sanchez, "LAPD Reeling as Corruption Cases Multiply," *Washington Post,* February 12, 2000.

86. Jane Fritsch, "Squads That Tripped Up Walking the Bad Walk," *New York Times,* March 5, 2000.

87. Anne-Marie O'Connor, "INS Agents Suggested Rampart Deportations," *Los Angeles Times,* March 3, 2000.

88. Adam Cohen, "Gangsta Cops," *Time,* March 6, 2000.

89. "Rampart Set Up Latinos To Be Deported, INS Says," *Los Angeles Times,* February 24, 2000.

90. Jim Newton, Matt Lait, and Scott Glover, "LAPD Condemned by Its Own Inquiry into Rampart Scandal," *Los Angeles Times,* March 1, 2000.

91. Joseph D. McNamara, "When Cops Become Gangsters," *Los Angeles Times,* September 21, 1999.

92. Carlos A. Ball, "Self-Defeating U.S. Polices Are Undermining Latin America's Future," speech at Libertarian Party of Florida Convention, West Palm Beach, October 9, 1999.

93. "Message to the Congress Transmitting the 1999 National Drug Control Strategy," February 8, 1999, *Public Papers of the Presidents,* p. 216.

94. General Accounting Office, "Drug Control: Status of U.S. International Counternarcotics Activities," 1998.

95. Larry Rohter, "U.S. Official Proposes $1 Billion for Colombia Drug War," *New York Times,* July 17, 1999.

96. Robert Novak, "The Colombia Casualty," *New York Post,* August 5, 1999.

97. Karen DeYoung, "U.S. Colonel to Plead Guilty in Colombia Drug Probe," *Washington Post,* April 4, 2000.

98. Tod Robberson, "U.S. Counters Colombia Rebels with Covert Plan," *Dallas Morning News,* August 19, 1998.

99. Tim Johnson, " Colombian Police Challenge CIA's Coca Assessments," *Fort Worth Star-Telegram,* March 26, 1999.

100. Jared Kotler, "New Colombian Environment Minister: Crop Eradication Program a Failure," Associated Press, August 16, 1998.

101. Diana Jean Schemo, "Pushed by U.S., Colombia Plans New Chemical Attack on Coca," *New York Times,* June 20, 1998.

102. Ibid.

103. The cases in this section are drawn from James Bovard, "Politically Connected," *Playboy,* April 1997. The author would like to thank *Playboy* for permission to use this material.

104. Peter Grier and James N. Thurman, "Illegal Drug Use Tapers Off in US, but Supplies Are Plentiful," *Christian Science Monitor,* March 24, 2000.

105. Quoted in Prepared Testimony of Eric E. Sterling, President, The Criminal Justice Policy Foundation, Before the House Appropriations Committee, Subcommittee on Treasury, Postal Service and General Government," Federal News Service, March 23, 2000.

106. Marsha Rosenbaum, "Are We Really Winning the War on Drugs?" *San Francisco Chronicle,* March 24, 2000.

107. Prepared Testimony of Eric E. Sterling, President, The Criminal Justice Policy Foundation, Before the House Appropriations Committee, Subcommittee on Treasury, Postal Service and General Government," Federal News Service, March 23, 2000.

108. Ibid.

109. "Prices Down for Heroin, Cocaine Despite War on Drugs," Associated Press, March 22, 2000.

110. Marsha Rosenbaum, "Are We Really Winning the War on Drugs?" *San Francisco Chronicle,* March 24, 2000.

111. John Donnelly, "Drug Deaths Reach A Peak as Prices Fall," *Boston Globe,* March 22, 2000.

112. "Remarks by Vice President Al Gore at an Anti-Drug Event," Federal News Service, February 8, 1999.

113. Kevin Zeese, "Ending the Drug War Is Popular," *Weekly Standard,* January 3, 2000.

114. Author interview with Julie Stewart, December 18, 1996.

115. James Bovard, "Time Out for Justice: Why Talking about Drugs Is Worse Than Murder," *Playboy,* December 1997.

116. Mathew Brelis, "A Big Time Bust," *Boston Globe,* November 8, 1998.

117. Quoted in Steve Chapman, "In the Drug War, Fantasy Beats Reality," *Chicago Tribune,* July 23, 1998.

118. Kevin Zeese, "General McCaffrey's History of Misinformation," *DrugSense Weekly,* October 15, 1999.

119. Gary Fields, "DEA chief: Drug Fight Lacks Desire," *USA Today,* February 19, 1999.

120. Gary Fields, "Drug Policy Adviser: Time to 'Get Serious'," *USA Today,* March 19, 1999.

CHAPTER SEVEN

1. *Boyd v. U.S.,* 116 U.S. 616 (1886).

2. Jeffrey Standen, "Searching Questions: Is a Purse a House or a Car?" *Legal Times,* June 7, 1999.

3. "Memorandum on Fairness in Law Enforcement," *Public Papers of the Presidents,* June 9, 1999, p. 1067.

4. "Opening Remarks at a Roundtable Discussion on Increasing Trust Between Communities and Law Enforcement," *Public Papers of the Presidents,* June 9, 1999, p. 1065.
5. "Hispanic Business Roundtable: Clinton Lacks the Moral Authority to Lead Fight Against Racial Profiling," *U.S. Newswire,* June 10, 1999.
6. James Merriweather, "Most of Proposal Shelved: Clark Suspicious," *Arkansas Gazette,* October 24, 1989.
7. David Cole, "Pervasive Racial Profiling is Abundantly Evident and a Barrier to Equal Justice," *Insight on the News,* July 19, 1999.
8. Ibid.
9. Jeffrey Goldberg, "The Color of Suspicion," *New York Times Magazine,* June 20, 1999.
10. David Heinzmann, "Customs Agents Get Better Look; Scanner to Cut Strip Searches," *Chicago Tribune,* November 23, 1999.
11. Maishah English, "Congressional Roundup: Customs Agents Profiling Blacks," *Washington Afro-American,* April 23, 1999.
12. General Accounting Office, "U.S. Customs Service: Better Targeting of Airline Passengers for Personal Searches Could Produce Better Results," March 17, 2000.
13. Connie Cass, "Customs Searches Prompt Lawsuits," Associated Press, December 3, 1998.
14. "New Airport Scanners Offer X-Ray Image," *Washington Post,* December 30, 1999.
15. Ismail Turay, "Airport X-Rays Protested As 'X-rated'," *Atlanta Journal and Constitution,* January 17, 2000.
16. Tim Vanderpool, "Locker Searches at the Border," *Christian Science Monitor,* June 7, 1999.
17. Author interview with Layne Lathram, March 3, 2000.
18. Brief for the Solicitor General, *Bond v. U.S.,* no. 98-9349, 1998 U.S. Briefs 9349, January 7, 2000.
19. "The President's Radio Address," *Public Papers of the Presidents,* October 19, 1996, p. 2109.
20. Timothy Lynch, "In Defense of the Exclusionary Rule," Cato Institute Policy Analysis #319, October 1, 1998. Quote is a paraphrase.
21. "Radio Remarks on Drunk Driving," *Public Papers of the Presidents,* September 2, 1999, p. 1682.
22. Jon E. Dougherty, "Checkpoints for Seat Belt Compliance? Federal Government Spends Millions on New Plan," World Net Daily, January 15, 1999.
23. U.S. Department of Transportation, "Stepping up to Buckle Up America—Added Benefits from a High Visibility Enforcement," Press Release, 1999.
24. Matthew L. Wald, "3 Issues Test Resolve Of Federal Regulators," *New York Times,* February 27, 1998.
25. "Holiday Traffic Law Blitz Announced," *Albuquerque Journal,* November 4, 1999.
26. Erik Tryggestad, "'Gray Area' of Seat-Belt Law Debated," *Jacksonville (Florida) Times-Union,* April 3, 1999.
27. Courtland Milloy, "Zero Tolerance's Negative Side," *Washington Post,* March 22, 1998.
28. Ibid.
29. Ricky Young, "Cops Won't Buckle Under on Seat-Belt Stops," *Denver Post,* November 29, 1998.
30. "Police Roll Call Kicks Off the Largest-Ever Nationally Coordinated Effort by Law Enforcement to Buckle Up Children; In All 50 States Officers Mobilize Against the Leading Cause of Death to Children," *PR Newswire,* May 18, 1998.
31. Nadine Strossen, "*Michigan Department of State Police v. Sitz:* A Roadblock to Meaningful Judicial Enforcement of Constitutional Rights," *Hastings Law Journal,* vol. 42, January 1991, p. 287.

32. U.S. Department of Transportation, "Buckle Up America report to Congress," 1998.

33. David Ottaway and Warren Brown, "From Life Saver to Fatal Threat; How the U.S., Automakers And a Safety Device Failed," *Washington Post,* June 1, 1997.

34. Quoted in "Prepared Testimony of Sam Kazman, Competitive Enterprise Institute, Before the House Committee on Commerce, Subject: Reauthorization of the National Highway Traffic Safety Administration," Federal News Service, May 22, 1997.

35. Charles Lave and Patrick Elias, "Resource Allocation in Public Policy: The Effects of the 65-mph Speed Limit," *Economic Inquiry,* July 1997, p. 614.

36. Dean Anason, "Former Fed Governor: Law Meant to Detect Dirty Money Ineffective," *American Banker,* December 8, 1997.

37. Katherine Walsh, "IRS Broadens Definition of Cash in Efforts to Battle Drug Money," *Regulatory Compliance Watch,* June 7, 1991.

38. Memo from Win Swenson, Money Laundering Working Group, to Phillip J. Newton, Staff Director, U.S. Sentencing Commission, October 14, 1992, p. 24.

39. "Brief for the United States," *Waldemar Ratzlaf and Loretta Ratzlaf v. United States,* no. 92-1196, August 20, 1993.

40. *Ratzlaf v. United States,* 510 U.S. 135 (1994).

41. "Clinton to Sign New Law After Easy Passage," *Money Laundering Alert,* August 1994.

42. *Lee v. Bankers Trust Co.,* 166 F. 3d 540 (1999).

43. "Prepared Statement of Gregory T. Nojeim, Legislative Counsel, American Civil Liberties Union, Washington National Office, Before the House Committee on the Judiciary, Commercial and Administrative Law Subcommittee, Subject: Financial Privacy and the Proposed 'Know Your Customer' Regulations," Federal News Service, March 4, 1999.

44. Edmund Sanders, "Reporting Laws Turn Banks into Government Agents," *Los Angeles Times,* December 24, 1999.

45. *Federal Register,* December 7, 1998, pp. 67515-67424.

46. Ibid.

47. Ibid.

48. "KYC Rule Will Give Enforcement Agents New Information Sources," *Money Laundering Alert,* November 1998.

49. Marcy Gordon, "Senate Tells Regulators to Withdraw New Anti-Money Laundering Rules," Associated Press, March 5, 1999.

50. Scott Barancik, "Know Your Customer Is Out; Agencies' Next Step Unclear," *American Banker,* March 23, 1999.

51. Deborah Thoren-Pedenand and John Byrne, "'Know Your Customer' Lives On: Guidelines for Compliance," *ABA Bank Compliance,* September-October 1999.

52. Ibid.

53. "Bank Says New Regulation Could Compromise Sanctity of SARs," *Money Laundering Alert,* February 1999.

54. "SAR Information Could be Falling into Wrong Hands, GAO Says," *Money Laundering Alert,* August 1998.

55. Ibid.

56. Declan McCullagh, "No Deposit, Less Return," *Wired News,* October 27, 1999.

57. Ibid.

58. Ibid.

59. See James Bovard, "'On-Time' Delivery: The Great Mail Fraud," *Wall Street Journal,* January 30, 1991; and James Bovard, "Mail Monopoly Says Happy New Year," *Wall Street Journal,* December 29, 1989.

60. "Testimony on October 19, 1999, of Edward L. Huggins, Director, Cato Institute, House Small Business, Regulatory Reform and Paperwork Reduction, Regulation of Private Mailbox Providers," Federal Document Clearing House, October 22, 1999.

61. Author interview with Juley Fulcher, July 6, 1999.

62. Robin Fields, "New Mailbox Rules May Limit User's Privacy, Convenience," *Los Angeles Times,* April 30, 1999.

63. Author interview with a congressional aide who wished to remain anonymous, July 7, 1999.

64. See U.S. Congress, House Post Office and Civil Service Committee, *Implementation of New First-Class Mail Delivery Standards,* September 27, 1990 (Washington, D.C.: Government Printing Office, 1990).

65. American Civil Liberties Union, "Big Brother in the Wires: Wiretapping in the Digital Age," March 1998.

66. Quoted in Ted Bunker, "Is it 1984? Overview of Clipper Security Chip Controversy," *LAN Magazine,* August 1994.

67. American Civil Liberties Union, "Big Brother in the Wires Wiretapping in the Digital Age," March 1998. (Emphasis added.)

68. Ibid.

69. Steven Levy, "Battle of the Clipper Chip," *New York Times,* June 12, 1994.

70. Elizabeth Corcoran, "U.S. Closes Investigation In Computer Privacy Case; Export of Encryption Program Was at Issue," *Washington Post,* January 12, 1996.

71. "Interview: Phil Zimmermann; Pretty Good Policy," *Network Solutions,* July 1, 1999.

72. "Testimony on April 6, 1995, Louis Freeh, House Judiciary, International Terrorism," Federal Document Clearing House, April 6, 1995. (emphasis added)

73. American Civil Liberties Union, "Big Brother in the Wires: Wiretapping in the Digital Age," March 1998.

74. Federal Register, October 16, 1995, p. 53643.

75. "Big Brother in the Wires Wiretapping in the Digital Age," American Civil Liberties Union, March 1998.

76. John Markoff, "F.B.I. Wants Advanced System to Vastly Increase Wiretapping," *New York Times,* November 2, 1995.

77. Meg McGinity, "FCC Decision To Open Up Access To Law Enforcers Raises Cost Concerns," *tele.com,* September 20, 1999.

78. Sharon LaFraniere, "FBI Asks Wiretap Access to Digital Phone Systems," *Washington Post,* March 7, 1992.

79. Nancy Konish, "Tapping Into Wireless Phone Privacy; Government Activity," *Electronic Design,* December 17, 1999.

80. Stephen Labaton, "U.S. Expands Police Powers to Monitor Cellular Phones," *New York Times,* August 28, 1999,

81. "CTIA, Civil Liberties Groups Join Legal Forces on Calea," *Wireless Today,* December 8, 1999.

82. Ibid.

83. Robert O'Harrow and Liz Leyden, "U.S. Helped Fund Photo Database of Driver IDs," *Washington Post,* February 18, 1999.

84. Robert O'Harrow, "Justice Dept. Pushes for Power to Unlock PC Security Systems," *Washington Post,* August 20, 1999.

85. Declan McCullagh, "Clinton Favors Computer Snooping," *Wired,* January 19, 2000.

86. Ibid.

87. David McGuire, "Barr Slams Electronic 'Trapdoor' Surveillance Plan," Newsbytes, October 25, 1999.

88. John Schwartz, "A Wiretap-Friendly Net?: Group Weighs Aid to Law Enforcement," *Washington Post,* November 10, 1999.

89. Robert MacMillan, "ACLU Asks Internet Task Force To Drop Wiretap Plan," Newsbytes, November 5, 1999.

90. Constant Brand, "Europeans Shocked Over Spy Charge," Associated Press, February 24, 2000.

91. Kathryn Balint, "Spy in the Sky? That Could Be Echelon," *San Diego Union-Tribune,* October 17, 1999.

92. Alice Ann Love, "NSA Defends Eavesdropping Policy," Associated Press, February 27, 2000.

93. Letter from Kenneth Heath, Chief of Staff, Legislative Affairs Office, National Security Agency, to all members of Congress, February 24, 2000.

94. James Woolsey, "Why We Spy on Our Allies," *Wall Street Journal,* March 17, 2000.

CHAPTER EIGHT

1. Author interview with Dotty Slovak of the Justice Department, May 27, 1999.

2. *U.S. v. Twelve Thousand, Three Hundred Ninety Dollars,* 956 F. 2d 801, 808 (1992).

3. David Rosenzweig, "Undercover Informant Got $2 Million for Aiding Drug Probe," *Los Angeles Times,* January 30, 1999.

4. *U.S. vs. $30,060,* 39 F. 3d 1039 (1994).

5. *U.S. v. $277,000 U.S. Currency and One Dodge Ram Charger,* 69 F. 3d 1491 (1995).

6. *Muhammeds v. DEA,* 92 F. 3d 648 (1996)

7. *Muhammeds v. Department of Treasury, Internal Revenue Service, and DEA,* 1998 U.S. District lexis 20830, November 18, 1998.

8. *U.S. v. One Lot of U.S. Currency Totaling $14,665; Manuel J. Espinola, Claimant,* 33 F. Supp 2d 47 (1998).

9. *U.S. vs. Funds in the Amount of $9,800,* 952 F. Supp. 1254 (1996).

10. *U.S. vs. $40,000. U.S. Currency,* Defendant; Carlos Maldonado, claimant, 999 F. Supp. 234 (1998).

11. Steve Stephens, "Metro Column," *Columbus Dispatch,* January 18, 1999.

12. Congressional Record, October 9, 1998, p. 12223.

13. Editorial, "Forfeit: U.S. Attorney Here Overstepped Bounds in Motel Seizure," *Houston Chronicle,* March 12, 1998.

14. Deborah Tedford, "Hotel Owners Agree to Beef Up Security," *Houston Chronicle,* July 10, 1998.

15. Author interview with lawyer Terry Reed, May 25, 1995.

16. Rep. Henry Hyde, "Civil Asset Forfeiture Reform Act of 1993—A Briefing Paper," June 1993, p. 10.

17. "Hearing of the Crime Subcommittee of the House Judiciary Committee, Subject: Criminal Asset Forfeiture," Federal News Service, September 18, 1997.

18. *Congressional Record,* October 9, 1998, p. 12223.

19. Deborah Pines, "Government Returns Forfeited Cash to Refugee," *New York Law Journal,* February 26, 1999.

20. Ibid.

21. *Congressional Record,* June 24, 1999, p. H4857.

22. Author interview with David Smith, August 6, 1999.

23. Oral hearings before the Supreme Court, *U.S. v. Bajakajian,* no. 96-1487, November 4, 1997.

24. Ibid.
25. "Petition for a Write of Certiorari," *U.S. v. Bajakajian,* no. 96-1487, March 18, 1997.
26. *U.S. v. Bajakajian,* 84 F. 3d 334 (1996).
27. "Brief for the United States," *U.S. v. Bajakajian,* no. 96-1487, July 14, 1997.
28. *U.S. v. Bajakajian,* 524 U.S. 321 (1998).
29. "Testimony of Raymond W. Kelly, Customs Service Commissioner, Senate Appropriations," Federal Document Clearing House, April 20, 1999.
30. Customs Service Press Release, "Customs Turns up the Heat on Currency Smugglers," PR Newswire, May 17, 1999.
31. Joel Millman, "'Operation Buckstop' Is Meant to Catch Money Launderers, but Irritates Mexicans," *Wall Street Journal,* December 29, 1999.
32. Ibid.
33. Ibid.
34. "Administration Seeks to Extend 'Long Arm' of U.S. Laundering Law," *Money Laundering Alert,* January, 2000.
35. "Prepared Statement of Mary Lee Warren, Deputy Assistant Attorney General, Criminal Division, Before the House Committee on Banking and Financial Services, Subcommittee on Financial Institutions and Consumer Credit and Subcommittee on General Oversight and Investigations, Subject: Trends in Money Laundering," Federal News Service, April 15, 1999.
36. Lyle Denniston, "Supreme Court Widens Seizures," *Baltimore Sun,* March 5, 1996.
37. "Brief for the United States as Amicus Curiae Supporting Respondent," *Bennis v. Michigan,* September 18, 1995.
38. *Bennis v. Michigan,* 516 U.S. 442 (1996).
39. "Respondents' Brief on the Merits," *City of West Covina, Petitioner v. Lawrence Perkins, et al.,* no. 97-1230, September 11, 1998.
40. Brief for the United States as Amicus Curiae Supporting Petitioner," *City of West Covina, Petitioner v. Lawrence Perkins, et al.,* no. 97-1230, July 18, 1998.
41. *City of West Covina v. Perkins,* 525 U.S. 234 (1999).
42. Ludmilla Lelis, "Will Ruling Put Brakes on Volusia I-95 Squad?" *Orlando Sentinel,* February 27, 1998.
43. Brief for the United States as Amicus Curiae Supporting Petitioner," *Florida v. Tyvessel Tyvorus White,* no. 98-223, January 1999, p. 1.
44. John Dillin, "Reno to Review Controversial Asset-Forfeiture Policies," *Christian Science Monitor,* October 25, 1993.
45. Earle Eldridge, "No Action Expected Soon on Civil Forfeiture Bills," Gannett News Service, August 12, 1994.
46. Author interview with Stefan Cassellas; quoted in James Bovard, "The Dangerous Expansion of Forfeiture Laws," *Wall Street Journal,* December 29, 1997.
47. Author interview with Bob Barr, November 18, 1997.
48. *Congressional Record,* June 24, 1999, p. H4867.
49. Ibid.
50. Ibid., p. H4868.
51. Ibid., p. H4859.
52. Ibid., p. H4873.
53. Congressional Record, June 24, 1999, p. H4873.
54. Cassandra Burrell, "Officials Want New Forfeiture Bill," Associated Press, July 22, 1999.
55. "Testimony of Richard Fiano, Senate Judiciary, Administrative Oversight and the Courts, Asset Forfeiture," Federal Document Clearing House, July 26, 1999.

56. Senate Judiciary Committee, Hearing on Asset Forfeiture, "Testimony of Eric Holder, Deputy Attorney General, U.S. Department of Justice," July 22, 1999.

57. For examples of the wide array of Food and Drug Administration forfeitures, see James Bovard, "Double-Crossing to Safety," *American Spectator,* January 1995.

58. "Testimony of James E. Johnson, Senate Judiciary, Administrative Oversight and the Courts, Asset Forfeiture," Federal Document Clearing House, July 26, 1999.

59. "Prepared Statement of David B. Smith Before the House Judiciary Committee, Subcommittee on Crime, Subject: Hearing on Money Laundering Act of 1999," Federal News Service, February 10, 2000.

60. David Rovella, "Defenders Argue Asset Seizure Bill Is Too Mild, "*National Law Journal,* April 24, 2000.

CHAPTER NINE

1. "State of the Union Address," White House Office of the Press Secretary, January 27, 1998.

2. Clinton's deceptive use of trade agreement numbers was first exposed in "Clinton's Real Record on Trade," *Rushford Report,* July 1996. A later analysis of the vice president's abuse of the numbers was in "At the Races: A Weekly Review of Campaign 2000," *National Journal,* April 8, 2000. I phoned the office of the U.S. Trade Representative several times in early April 2000 but no one there could provide a list of market-opening trade agreements that came within a country mile of Clinton and Gore's claims.

3. Interview with Gary Hufbauer, February 28, 2000. Hufbauer was the key author in the Institute for International Economic's 1994 estimate on the cost of trade barriers. Hufbauer stated that since the large majority of trade barriers analyzed earlier remained in place, the current cost of trade barriers could be estimated by multiplying the current gross domestic product by the GDP at the time of the original estimate. Gary Clyde Hufbauer and Kimberly Ann Elliot, *Measuring the Costs of Protection in the United States* (Washington: Institute for International Economics, 1994), p. 3.

4. Nancy Dunne, "Kantor Supports 'New Trade Rules'," *Financial Times* (London), March 5, 1993.

5. For more information on the origin and successes of U.S. textile protectionism, see James Bovard, *The Fair Trade Fraud* (New York: St. Martin's Press, 1991), pp. 35-64.

6. The White House, *Economic Report of the President* (Washington, D.C.: Government Printing Office, 1989), p. 172.

7. *Federal Register,* June 3, 1993, p. 31509. For further details, James Bovard, "The U.S. War on Macedonia," *Wall Street Journal,* June 9, 1993.

8. *Federal Register,* May 18, 1994, p. 25893. For further details, see James Bovard, "The Latest Salvo in Clinton's Textile Trade War," *Wall Street Journal,* July 5 , 1994.

9. Ibid.

10. James Bovard, "The Latest Salvo in Clinton's Textile Trade War," *Wall Street Journal,* July 5, 1994.

11. "Remarks to Future Leaders of Europe in Brussels," *Public Papers of the President,* January 9, 1994, p. 11.

12. Jane Perlez, "In Ukraine, a Free-Market Lesson Learned Too Well," *New York Times,* January 1, 1995.

13. Elizabeth Edwardsen, "Woolen Mills Battle Ukrainian Imports," Associated Press, July 21, 1994.

14. Jane Perlez, "In Ukraine, a Free-Market Lesson Learned Too Well," *New York Times,* January 1, 1995.
15. Paula Green, "US Fastens Impost Quotes onto Salvadoran Skirts," *Journal of Commerce,* July 15, 1996.
16. *Federal Register,* October 21, 1994, p. 53139.
17. James Bovard, "U.S. Hits Haiti with Double Whammy," *Wall Street Journal,* October 25, 1994.
18. James Bovard, "Trade Quotas Buil New Chinese Wall," *Wall Street Journal,* January 10, 1994.
19. Quoted in James Bovard, "Silken Import Disport," *Washington Times,* March 15, 1994.
20. Paula Green, "U.S. Textile Importers Say that Pact with Cambodia Is Restrictive," *Journal of Commerce,* January 28, 1999.
21. Ibid.
22. "Textile Development Memo," December 3, 1999 (Prepared by Brenda A. Jacobs of the Washington law firm of Powell, Goldstein, Frazer & Murphy).
23. Thomas L. Friedman, "U.S. Pares Imports of China's Fabrics in a Punitive Move," *New York Times,* January 7, 1994.
24. At a press briefing on January 6, a senior Clinton administration official (probably Kantor or one of his top USTR aides) was pressed by a journalist to explain how the $2 billion figure was reached; the official replied, "Look, it's a real difficult thing to do. There's no scientific procedure to it . . . It is merely an estimate. That's all it is." "Background Briefing on the Imposition of Lower 1994 Quotas on Textile Products from the People's Republic of China," Federal News Service, January 6, 1994.
25. Ibid.
26. Patrick Tyler, "Textile Accord with China Averts Trade Clash," *New York Times,* January 18, 1994.
27. James Bovard "Clinton's Fraudulent Trade Policy," *Wall Street Journal,* February 11, 1994.
28. Author interview with USTR official who wished to remain anonymous, January 12, 1994.
29. "When Is a TV Duck Really a Bedspread?," *Rushford Report,* July 1995.
30. The Item Company d/b/a, Blue Ridge Company v. U.S., 98 F.3d 1294, October 11, 1996.
31. Greg Rushford, "Trade Chiefs Suit Themselves," *Wall Street Journal,* October 7, 1998.
32. "Bill Clinton's Hat Trick," *Rushford Report,* March 1995.
33. "Telephone Interview with Michael Paulson of the *Seattle Post-Intelligencer* from San Francisco, California," *Public Papers of the Presidents,* November 30, 1999, p. 2485.
34. "The President's News Conference," *Public Papers of the Presidents,* December 8, 1999, p. 2537.
35. Brink Lindsay, "The U.S. Antidumping Law: Rhetoric versus Reality," Cato Institute, August 16, 1999.
36. James Bovard, "Steel Rulings Dump on America," *Wall Street Journal,* June 23, 1993.
37. Ibid.
38. "The Principles and Future of U.S.-Polish Relations: Vice President Gore, Address Delivered in Warsaw, Poland, April 20, 1993," Department of State Dispatch, U.S. Department of State, May 3, 1993.
39. *Federal Register,* July 9, 1993, p. 37205. (The ruling was published in the *Federal Register* a few weeks after the Commerce Department officially disseminated its findings.)
40. Author interview with David Phelps, January 17, 2000.
41. U.S. Commerce Department, "Agreement Concerning Trade in Certain Steel Products from the Russian Federation," July 12, 1999.

42. U.S. Commerce Department, "Agreement Suspending the Antidumping Investigation on Hot-Rolled Flat-Rolled Carbon-Quality Steel From Brazil," 1999.

43. David E. Sanger, "Clinton Restricts Imports of Brazilian Steel and Australian Lamb," *New York Times,* July 8, 1999.

44. Brink Lindsey, "The U.S. Antidumping Law: Rhetoric versus Reality," Cato Institute, August 16, 1999.

45. Ibid.

46. Congressional Budget Office, "Antidumping Action in the United States and around the World," June 1998.

47. Brink Lindsey, "The U.S. Antidumping Law: Rhetoric versus Reality," Cato Institute, August 16, 1999.

48. Congressional Budget Office, "Antidumping Action in the United States and around the World," June 1998.

49. Brink Lindsey, "Trade Policy in the Dumps," *Regulation,* no. 3, 1998.

50. A 1998 World Bank study found that U.S. exports are now hit by antidumping cases more often than those of any other nation. Brink Lindsey, "Trade Policy in the Dumps," *Regulation,* no. 3, 1998.

51. Kelly McParland, "U.S. Wheat Tariffs Set for July 1," *Financial Post,* April 23, 1994.

52. Noel Uri and Douglas Beach, "The Significance of Quality Differences for the United States and Canada Wheat Trade," *Applied Economics,* August 1996, p. 985.

53. "Hearing of the Senate Finance Committee, Subject: North American Free Trade Agreement," Federal News Service, September 15, 1993.

54. Shawn McCarthy, "Canada's Farmers Set for Wheat War," *Toronto Star,* April 18, 1994.

55. Greg Ip, "Trade Feud Stirs Up U.S. Pasta Industry," *Financial Post* (Toronto), September 9, 1995.

56. Carol Goar, "U.S. Backs Down in Grain Dispute; But Continues to Rattle Scythes Over Our Wheat," *Toronto Star,* September 14, 1995.

57. Philip Brasher, "Administration Officials to Look into Alleged Canadian Wheat Dumping," Associated Press, July 31, 1997.

58. Leslie Helm, "U.S., Japan Face Rough Seas on Trade Imbalance," *Los Angeles Times,* April 19, 1993.

59. James Gerstenzang, Trade Flap Casts Shadow Over Hosokawa's U.S. Visit," *Los Angeles Times,* February 10, 1994.

60. "Remarks and a Question-and-Answer Session at Waseda University in Tokyo," *Public Papers of the Presidents,* July 7, 1993, p. 1274.

61. "Press Conference With U.S. Trade Representative Mickey Kantor," Federal News Service, March 3, 1994.

62. Tony Munroe, "U.S. to Hit Japan with 100% Tariffs," *Washington Times,* May 17, 1995.

63. William Cline, "Car Crash: Clinton Ignores Trade Facts," *Wall Street Journal,* May 15, 1995.

64. "Easy Rider," *Rushford Report,* December 1999.

65. Ibid.

66. James Bovard, "NAFTA's Protectionist Bent," *Wall Street Journal,* July 31, 1992.

67. James Bovard, "Threats, and Pseudo-Threats, to Free Trade," *Wall Street Journal Europe,* September 21, 1994.

68. "Remarks in an On-Line Townhall Meeting," *Public Papers of the Presidents,* November 8, 1999, p. 2293.

69. David Sanger, "After Clinton's Push, Questions about Motive," *New York Times,* December 3, 1999.

70. Celia W. Dugger, "Why India and Others See U.S. as Villain on Trade," *New York Times,* December 17, 1999.

71. "Remarks at a World Trade Organization Luncheon in Seattle," *Public Papers of the Presidents,* December 1, 1999, p. 2494.

72. Bruce Ramsay, "Clinton Sabotaged Any Chances of Success at the WTO Summit," *Seattle Post-Intelligencer,* December 15, 1999.

73. Joseph Kahn and David E. Sanger, "Trade Obstacles Unmoved, Seattle Talks End in Failure," *New York Times,* December 4, 1999.

74. David E. Sanger, " The Shipwreck in Seattle," *New York Times,* December 5, 1999.

75. Jagdish Bhagwati, "The Folly of Fair Trade," *Wall Street Journal,* March 11, 1999.

76. James Bovard, "Bush Protection: The President and Free Trade," *New Republic,* January 20, 1992.

77. Jim Ostroff, "China Quotas Cut Jan. 17 if There Is No New Pact; Kantor Delivers Ultimatum," *Daily News Record,* January 7, 1994.

CHAPTER TEN

1. Stephen Engelberg, "Leader of H.U.D. Assesses It Harshly," *New York Times,* June 23, 1993.

2. Guy Gugliotta, "Redoubled Effort Targets Derelict Public Housing," *Washington Post,* May 31, 1996.

3. David Nyhan, "Restoring a Dilapidated Reputation: Cuomo and HUD," *Boston Globe,* February 7, 1999.

4. Michael Grunwald, "HUD's Cuomo Raises Voice In Anti-Poverty Campaign," *Washington Post,* May 29, 1999.

5. Department of Housing and Urban Development, Office of Inspector General, "Department of Housing and Urban Development's Loss Mitigation Program," Audit Report no. 99-DE-121-0001, September 30, 1999.

6. "Clinton Remarks to AmeriCorps Volunteers, Regency House Residents," U.S. Newswire, January 18, 1999.

7. "Agreement Between Colombia National Mortgage and the Fort Worth Human Relations Commission," January 1999.

8. Ibid.

9. Author interview with Dave Gallitano, January 21, 1999.

10. Ibid.

11. "Agreement Between Colombia National Mortgage and the Fort Worth Human Relations Commission," January 1999.

12. Ibid.

13. Author interview with Dave Gallitano, January 21, 1999.

14. "Clinton Announces $11.5 Million in Grants to Help Groups in 42 Cities Crack Down on Housing Discrimination," U.S. Newswire, November 25, 1998.

15. "Clinton Administration Cracks Down on Housing Discrimination with New Charges, $15 Million in Grants," U.S. Newswire, September 30, 1997.

16. "HUD Secretary Announces Nationwide Audit of Housing Discrimination," U.S. Newswire, November 16, 1998.

17. Author interview with AccuBanc official who wished to remain anonymous, January 25, 1999.

18. Ibid.

19. "Cuomo Announces Record $2.1 Billion Lending Discrimination Settlement, Commemorates Fair Housing Act Anniversary," U.S. Newswire, April 3, 1998.

20. George Anderson, "Housing and the Poor: An Interview with Andrew Cuomo, Secretary of the Dept. of Housing and Urban Development," *America,* May 30, 1998. (emphasis added)

21. "President Clinton and Vice President Al Gore Announce Largest Lending Discrimination Settlement in American History at 1999 Martin Luther King Day Service Project," U.S. Newswire, January 18, 1999.

22. Author interview with Vanessa Ruiz Boling, February 8, 1999.

23. Steve Cocheo, "HUD Renews Fair-Lending Drive with Texas Roundup," *ABA Banking Journal,* May 1998.

24. Jonathan Macey, "Banking by Quota," *Wall Street Journal,* September 7, 1994.

25. Ibid.

26. Paul Craig Roberts, "In the Footsteps of Charles I," *Washington Times,* November 4, 1994.

27. Paul Mondor, "The Quasi-Law of Fair Lending," *Mortgage Banking,* November 1996.

28. For further information on fair housing enforcement, see James Bovard, *Lost Rights: The Destruction of American Liberty* (New York: St. Martin's Press, 1994), pp. 314-316; and James Bovard, *Freedom in Chains: The Rise of the State and the Demise of the Citizen* (St. Martin's Press, 1999), pp. 153-55.

29. "HUD Secretary Announces Nationwide Audit of Housing Discrimination," U.S. Newswire, November 16, 1998.

30. "Federal Jury in Alabama Clears Lowder Companies in Housing Discrimination Suit," PR Newswire, December 17, 1998.

31. Malcomb Daniels, "Verdict Favors Lowder," *Montgomery Advertiser,* December 18, 1998.

32. "Point Papers on the Department of Housing and Urban Development and the Central Alabama Fair Housing Center," Lowder Real Estate Co., Montgomery, Ala., July 7, 1999.

33. Wendy Davis, "Government Loses Race Case After Failing To Prove Bias by Landlord," *New Jersey Law Journal,* January 17, 2000. The Justice Department press office failed to return numerous calls the author made in March 2000 looking for their comments on this fact.

34. HUD, Office of Inspector General, "Internal Audit: Office of Fair Housing and Equal Opportunity," Audit Report no. 98-SF-174-0002, September 15, 1998.

35. Robert Detlefsen, "Thin Red Line," *National Review,* December 21, 1998.

36. "Cuomo, Richmond Fair Housing Group Praise Housing Discrimination Verdict Against Nationwide Insurance," U.S. Newswire, October 27, 1998.

37. Gordon Hickey, "Insurance Firm Plans Home Gift," *Richmond Times-Dispatch,* May 7, 1999.

38. Deborah Lohse, "Huge Judgment Against Nationwide For Alleged Bias Is Thrown Out," *Wall Street Journal,* January 17, 2000.

39. Robert Detlefsen, "HUD's Insurance Obsession," *Journal of Commerce,* February 26, 1999.

40. Chris Barnett, "HUD: Little Insurance Discrimination," *Journal of Commerce,* January 6, 1999.

41. "Cuomo Says HUD Seeking to End Mortgage Lending Discrimination, " U.S. Newswire, August 06, 1998.

42. Peter Kilborn, "Good Times Don't Extend to Minority Homebuyers," *Deseret News* (Salt Lake City), September 16, 1999.

43. Albert R. Karr, "Fed Study Challenges Notion of Bias Against Minorities in Mortgage Lending," *Wall Street Journal,* January 26, 1995.

44. Cindy Loose, "Racial Disparity Found in Credit Rating," *Washington Post,* September 21, 1999.

45. Ibid.
46. Ibid.
47. Editorial, "Fair-Housing Law Carried to Extremes," *Bismarck Tribune,* September 13, 1999.
48. Larry Witham, "HUD Probes Have Yellow Pages Sending Religious Icons Walking," *Washington Times,* February 17, 1994.
49. Pete Hamill, "Diversity Blarney," *Wall Street Journal,* August 12, 1999.
50. Emily Gurnon, "Berkeley Neighbors Win One Over HUD," *San Francisco Examiner,* December 24, 1998.
51. Andrea Hamilton, "HUD Backs Off After Outcry Over Protest Investigations," Associated Press, February 12, 1995.
52. Roberta Achtenberg, "Sometimes on a Tightrope at HUD," *Washington Post,* August 22, 1994.
53. Emily Gurnon, "Judge Castigates HUD in Ruling," *San Francisco Examiner,* December 24, 1998.
54. Editorial, "When Speech Becomes a Crime," *Washington Times,* January 8, 1999.
55. John Machacek, "Cisneros Pushes Fair Housing Plans," Gannett News Service, September 29, 1993.
56. Jane Lehman, "Opening Low-Income Housing Frontiers," *Washington Post,* September 11, 1993.
57. *Federal Register,* December 28, 1999, p. 72722.
58. *Federal Register,* October 1, 1999, pp. 53450+.
59. "Q&A: Housing and Urban Development Secretary Henry Cisneros Discusses Some Solutions to the Country's Many Housing Problems," *Norfolk Virginian-Pilot,* June 19, 1994.
60. Editorial, "A Place in the Suburbs," *Boston Globe,* April 5, 1993.
61. Diana Rojas, "Public Housing Protest Effective: Haledon Receives Only 4 Requests," *The Bergen County (N.J.) Record,* May 24, 1994.
62. Tod Robberson, "Fairfax Officials Fret About Rent Voucher Cluster Along Route 1," *Washington Post,* August 25, 1996.
63. E. Thomas McClanahan, "The Housing Fiasco," *Kansas City Star,* June 1, 1997.
64. "Borough Has Most Section 8 Housing," *Pittsburgh Post-Gazette,* January 6, 1999.
65. U.S. Department of Housing and Urban Development, *Crime in Public Housing: A Review of Major Issues and Selected Crime Reduction Strategies,* vol. 1 (Washington, D.C.: Government Printing Office, 1979), p. i.
66. Andrew Cuomo, "Setting Goals for HUD," *National Mortgage News,* November 2, 1998.
67. "Clinton Statement on Housing Vouchers," U.S. Newswire, December 30, 1999.
68. John F. Harris, "Clinton Will Request Expansion of Rental Subsidies," *Washington Post,* December 29,1999.
69. Marc Lacey, "Clinton Plans New Vouchers for Working-Class Housing," *New York Times,* December 29, 1999.
70. George Archibald, "GOP Calls Cuomo Poor HUD Leader," *Washington Times,* March 31, 2000.
71. "Philadelphia Receives $4.9 Million for Demolition Projects," Associated Press, September 10, 1999.
72. "HUD Is Rolling Out $571 Million for Demolition, Reconstruction," *Engineering News-Record,* September 13, 1999.
73. Leon Tucker, "Less Room for Poor in Hope's Housing; Critics Call Program 'Urban Removal,'" *Nashville Tennessean,* September 21, 1999.
74. Matea Gold, "Reviving Pride in the Projects," *Los Angeles Times,* September 20, 1999.

75. Ibid.
76. Louis Jacobson, "High Hopes," Government Executive, July 1999.
77. Ibid.
78. Daniela Deane, "A New Face for Public Housing," *Washington Post,* May 8, 1999.
79. Ibid.
80. K. L. Billingsley, "Luxury Public Housing Project Blasted as "Monument to Waste," *Washington Times,* August 6, 1994.
81. Michael Cottman, "District Gets $30 Million for Housing: HUD Grant to Finance Mixed-Income Dwellings in Blighted SE Neighborhoods," *Washington Post,* September 11, 1999.
82. Darla Carter, " Innovation May Revive West End: Development Seeks To Mix Poor, Well-Off Residents," *Louisville Courier-Journal,* September 7, 1999.
83. U.S. Department of Housing and Urban Development, Office of Inspector General, "Audit of Housing Authority of the City of Newport," Report no. 99-BO-202-1003, July 1, 1999.
84. Michael C. McDermott, "HUD Grants Town $215,000 To Raze Much of Decrepit Cadman Towers," *Quincy (Mass.) Patriot Ledger,* September 14, 1999.
85. Howard Husock, "Public Housing as a 'Poorhouse,'" *Public Interest,* Fall 1997, p. 73.
86. Tracie Rozhon, "Old Baltimore Row Houses Fall Before Wrecking Ball," *New York Times,* June 13, 1999.
87. Michael Grunwald, "HUD's Cuomo Raises Voice In Anti-Poverty Campaign," *Washington Post,* May 29, 1999.
88. Mark Murray, "Revving up the Minivan Corps," *National Journal,* May 23, 1998.
89. Ibid.
90. "Community Builders," U.S. Department of Housing and Urban Development, Office of Inspector General, 99-FW-177-0002, September 30, 1999.
91. Ibid.
92. William Murphy, " HUD Program Builds Only PR," *Newsday,* October 15, 1999.
93. "Testimony of Michael Beard, District Inspector General for Audit, Southwest District, House Government Reform, Government Management, Information and Technology, Conflicts in HUD's Role," Federal Document Clearing House Congressional Testimony, November 3, 1999.
94. Ibid.
95. Department of Housing and Urban Development, Office of Inspector General, "Community Builders' Role in Multifamily Property Disposition, Multifamily Housing Property Disposition Center, Fort Worth, Texas," Audit Memorandum no. 99-FW-177-0803, September 30, 1999.
96. "Testimony of Michael Beard, District Inspector General for Audit, Southwest District, House Government Reform, Government Management, Information and Technology, Conflicts in HUD's Role," Federal Document Clearing House, November 3, 1999.
97. Department of Housing and Urban Development, Office of Inspector General, "Nationwide Audit, Community Builders," Audit Report no. 99-FW-177-0002, September 30, 1999.
98. David Goldstein, "Bond, Cuomo Take Political Wrangling to Another Level," *Kansas City Star,* September 18, 1999.
99. George Archibald, "Community Builders Are Blamed," *Washington Times,* October 20, 1999.
100. "Prepared Testimony of Susan Gaffney Inspector General, Department of Housing and Urban Development, Before the House Budget Committee," Federal News Service, February 17, 2000.
101. Ibid.
102. Ibid.

103. George Archibald, "GOP Calls Cuomo Poor HUD Leader," *Washington Times,* March 31, 2000.

104. Micah Morrison, "Clinton to New York: Drop Dead," *Wall Street Journal,* February 7, 2000.

105. Ibid.

106. Doug Brown, "HUD Takes Full Aim at Internet Hate," *Interactive Week,* March 16, 2000.

107. Sam Dealey, "Boyz-n-the HUD," *American Spectator,* April 1999.

108. Audrey Hudson, "HUD Flouted Rules in Hiring Outside Probers, GAO says," *Washington Times,* October 15, 1999.

109. Stephen Barr, "HUD Contracts Questioned by Congress," *Washington Post,* October 15, 1999.

110. Press Release, "Gramm Calls for Committee Investigation of HUD's Cancellation of Criminal Audits," Senate Banking, Housing and Urban Affairs Committee, March 23, 1999.

111. J. Linn Allen, "Old Demons Still Blocking Fair Housing," *Chicago Tribune,* November 14, 1993.

112. David Nyhan, "Restoring a Dilapidated Reputation: Cuomo and HUD," *Boston Globe,* February 7, 1999.

CHAPTER ELEVEN

1. From an interview with George Anthan and other Des Moines Register editors and reporters. See George Anthan, "Rural 'Inequality' Cited; Clinton Seeking a Program for the Future," *Des Moines Register,* April 25, 1995.

2. *Agricultural Policies in OECD Countries, Monitoring and Evaluation 1999* (Paris: Organization for Cooperation and Development, 1999), p. 252.

3. Ibid.

4. Information on state farmland values can be found at http://www.ers.usda.gov/epubs/other/usfact/

5. "Remarks on the Economic Plan in Hyde Park, New York," *Public Papers of the Presidents,* February 19, 1993, p. 245.

6. General Accounting Office, *Congressional Decision Needed on Necessity of Federal Wool Program* (1982).

7. "Hearing of the House Budget Committee, Subject: President Clinton's Economic Program," Federal News Service, February 18, 1993.

8. Ibid.

9. Janet Perry and Mitch Morehart, "Characteristics of Commodity Program Recipients," Agriculture Income and Finance, Situation and Outlook Report, December 1994, p. 23; also, USDA, Economic Indicators of the Farm Sector, National Financial Summary, 1993, pp. 70-71.

10. "Address to the Nation on the Economic Program," *Public Papers of the Presidents,* February 15, 1993, p. 207.

11. "Department of Agriculture Briefing on the Clinton Economic Proposal, Briefer: Secretary of Agriculture Mike Espy," Federal News Service, February 17, 1993.

12. Jonathan Tolman, "Federal Agricultural Policy: A Harvest of Environmental Abuse," Competitive Enterprise Institute, August 1995.

13. Rita Beamist, "Cleanup Talks Collapse," Associated Press, December 16, 1993.

14. U.S. Department of Commerce, *United States Sugar Policy—An Analysis* (Washington, D.C.: Government Printing Office, 1988).

15. Paul Roberts, "The Sweet Hereafter," *Harper's,* November 1999.

16. Rita Beamish, "Cleanup Talks Collapse," Associated Press, December 16, 1993.

17. Editorial, "Babbitt vs. Big Sugar," *St. Petersburg Times,* December 21, 1993,

18. Francis Wheen, "More Sweet Talk at the White House," *Guardian* (London), September 16, 1998.

19. "Statement on Signing the Federal Agriculture Improvement and Reform Act of 1996," *Public Papers of the Presidents,* April 4, 1996, p. 614.

20. "Remarks at a Democratic Dinner in Coral Gables, Florida," *Public Papers of the Presidents,* April 29, 1996, p. 758.

21. Paul Roberts, "The Sweet Hereafter," *Harper's,* November 1999.

22. Ibid.

23. Paul Roberts, "The Sweet Hereafter," *Harper's Magazine,* November 1999.

24. George Anthan, "Rural 'Inequality' Cited; Clinton Seeking a Program for the Future," *Des Moines Register,* April 25, 1995.

25. General Accounting Office, *Sugar Program: Impact on Sweetener Users and Producers,* May 24, 1995.

26. This information is from the Coalition for Sugar Reform website at http://www.sugar-reform.org.

27. James Bovard, "Stop Subsidizing Puppy Chow," *Advertising Age,* April 6, 1992.

28. Press Release, "USDA Announces Map Allocations for Fiscal 1999," U.S. Department of Agriculture, Release No. 0265.99, June 25, 1999.

29. Michael Doyle, "Marketing Program Entering Populist Stage," *Fresno Bee,* September 6, 1998

30. Stephen Moore, "Those Dancing Raisins," *Journal of Commerce,* July 20, 1998.

31. U.S. Department of Agriculture, "USDA Announces Map Allocations for Fiscal 1999," Press Release no. 0265.99, June 25, 1999.

32. *Federal Register,* November 2, 1999, p. 59107: "Almonds Grown in California; Salable and Reserve Percentages for the 1999-2000 Crop Year."

33. See *Federal Register,* June 7, 1999, p. 30233: "Raisins Produced From Grapes Grown In California; Final Free and Reserve Percentages for 1998-99 Zante Currant Raisins." As USDA's Agricultural Marketing Service explained in a later *Federal Register* notice, "When volume regulation is in effect, a certain percentage of the crop may be sold by handlers to any market (free tonnage) while the remaining percentage must be held by handlers in a reserve pool (or reserve) for the account of the [Raisin Administrative] Committee. *Federal Register,* December 10, 1999, p. 69204.

34. U.S. Department of Agriculture, "USDA Announces Map Allocations for Fiscal 1999," Press Release no. 0265.99, June 25, 1999.

35. General Accounting Office, "Cotton Program: Costly and Complex Government Program Needs to be Reassessed," June 1995. The flaws in the program were not fixed in the 1996 farm bill.

36. James Brooke, "Freeman Depended on Subsidies," *New York Times,* April 30, 1996.

37. Ibid.

38. General Accounting Office, "Farmers Home Administration: Problems and Issues Facing the Emergency Loan Program," November 1987.

39. General Accounting Office, *Farmers Home Administration: Billions of Dollars in Farm Loans Are at Risk,* April 1992.

40. Office of Sen. Richard Lugar, Press Release, "Lugar Urges Drastic Reform of USDA's Farm Loan Practices," March 21, 1995. Lugar's release was based on GAO analyses.

41. General Accounting Office, "Emergency Disaster Farm Loans: Government's Financial Risk Could be Reduced," March 1996.

42. General Accounting Office, "Farm Service Agency—Information on Farm Loans and Losses," November 27, 1998.

43. "Remarks Following a Meeting on Agricultural Assistance and an Exchange with Reporters," *Public Papers of the Presidents,* July 23, 1998, p. 1458.

44. "Remarks in a Teleconference with Rural Radio Stations on Agricultural Issues and Farming," *Public Papers of the Presidents,* July 23, 1998, p. 1458.

45. U.S. Department of Agriculture, "Glickman Reviews 1999 Accomplishments, Sets Goals for 2000," Press Release no 0008.00, January 10, 2000.

46. *Agricultural Income and Finance, Situation and Outlook,* Economic Research Service, U.S. Department of Agriculture, March 7, 2000.

47. "Dan Glickman, Secretary, Department of Agriculture, House Agriculture, Farm Crisis," Federal Document Clearing House, September 17, 1999.

48. For details on the farm loan bubble and bust in the 1970s and 1980s, see James Bovard, *The Farm Fiasco* (San Francisco: ICS Press, 1989), p. 127-153.

49. General Accounting Office, "Emergency Disaster Farm Loans: Government's Financial Risk Could be Reduced," March 1996.

50. "News Conference with Secretary of Agriculture Dan Glickman to Unveil the Clinton Administration Farm Bill," Federal News Service, May 10, 1995.

51. U.S. Department of Agriculture, "1995 Farm Bill: Guidance of the Administration," May 1995.

52. Todd Purdum, "Clinton Pledges to Defend Farm Subsidies," *New York Times,* April 26, 1995.

53. "1995 Farm Bill: Guidance of the Administration," U.S. Department of Agriculture, May 1995.

54. Greg Rushford and T. R. Goldman, "Lobbying Stakes: Not Just Peanuts," *Legal Times,* April 4, 1994.

55. General Accounting Office, *Peanut Program: Impact on Peanut Producers, Users, and the Government,* June 8, 1995.

56. "Remarks at the Opening Session of the National Rural Conference in Ames, Iowa," *Public Papers of the Presidents,* April 25, 1995, p. 707.

57. Letter to Members of Congress from Secretary of Agriculture Glickman, May 10, 1995.

58. U.S. Department of Agriculture, "1995 Farm Bill: Guidance of the Administration," May 1995.

59. "Statement on Signing the Federal Agriculture Improvement and Reform Act of 1996," *Public Papers of the Presidents,* April 4, 1996, p. 614.

60. Cable News Network, "Late Edition, Text of Gingrich Interview," Transcript no. 770-1, April 21, 1996.

61. George Anthan, Column, *The Des Moines Register,* April 23, 1996.

62. James Bovard, "The '85 Farm Bill Will Hurt Exports," *New York Times,* December 12, 1985.

63. James Bovard, "Kill Farm Subsidies Now," *Washington Post,* October 13, 1995

64. Environmental Working Group, "Analysis of 1995 Farm Bill Options," February 1995.

65. George Anthan, "$ 8.5 Billion Windfall for Farmers Justified?" *Des Moines Register,* January 11, 1998.

66. George Anthan, "Report: Subsidies Going to Landowners," *Des Moines Register,* May 3, 1998.

67. Frederick Nelson, "Measuring Domestic Support for U.S. Agriculture," WTO Briefing Paper, USDA, Economic Research Service, November 1997.

68. Dale Heien and Cathy R. Wessells, "The Nutritional Impact of the Dairy Price Support Program," *Journal of Consumer Affairs,* Winter 1998, p. 201. Cited in Kevin McNew, "Milking the Sacred Cow," Cato Institute Policy Analysis, December 1, 1999.

69. "Statement on Signing the Federal Agriculture Improvement and Reform Act of 1996," *Public Papers of the Presidents,* April 4, 1996, p. 614.

70. For details on the failure of the CRP to target the most erosive land, see J. Wu, M. D. Nellis, M. D. Ransom, K. P. Price, and S. L. Egbert, "Evaluating Soil Properties on CRP Land Using Remote Sensing and GIS in Finney County, Kansas," *Journal of Soil and Water Conservation,* September – October 1997, p. 352; David Dukes, "CRP: A Wake-Up Call for Agriculture," *Journal of Soil and Water Conservation,* March – April 1996, pp. 140-141; and General Accounting Office, "Conservation Reserve Program: Cost-Effectiveness is Uncertain," 1993.

71. Philip Brasher, "USDA Increases Eligibility for Conservation Reserve Program," Associated Press, February 12, 1997.

72. Ibid.

73. "C.R.P., under New Rules, Still Idles Productive Cropland," *Milling and Baking News,* August 5, 1997.

74. "National Grain and Feed Association Statement on the CRP," *Milling and Baking News,* December 30, 1997.

75. "Message to the House of Representatives Returning Without Approval the 'Agriculture, Rural Development, Food and Drug Administration, and Related Agencies Appropriations Act, 1999.'" *Public Papers of the Presidents,* October 7, 1998, p. 2006.

76. "Remarks to the National Farmers Union," *Public Papers of the Presidents,* September 15, 1998, p. 1796.

77. "The President's News Conference," *Public Papers of the Presidents,* June 25, 1999, p. 1189.

78. Fax from Jerome Stam, USDA Economic Research Service farm bankruptcy expert, April 6, 2000.

79. American Bankruptcy Institute statistical table at *http://www.abiworld.org/stats/newstats-front.html*

80. U.S. Department of Agriculture, Economic Research Service, Agricultural Income and Finance, Situation and Outlook Report, February 2000, p. 39.

81. Albert Crenshaw, "Net Worth of U.S. Families Up Sharply," *Washington Post,* January 19, 2000.

82. Julia Malone, "Special Interests Find Free Ride in Farm Emergency," Cox News Service, August 6, 1999.

83. U.S. Department of Agriculture, Economic Research Service, Agricultural Income and Finance, Situation and Outlook Report, December 1999, p. 11.

84. Janelle Carter, "Dems Assail GOP Farm Aid Package," Associated Press, September 18, 1998.

85. George Anthan, "Clinton Supports Added Farm Aid," *Des Moines Register,* June 30, 1999.

86. "Statement on Emergency Assistance to Farmers and Ranchers," *Public Papers of the Presidents,* October 23, 1998, p. 2114.

87. George Anthan, "Subsidies May Bring Big Bucks," *Des Moines Register,* October 24, 1999.

88. Greg Burns, "Big Harvest: Farm Aid," *Chicago Tribune,* November 28, 1999.

89. Ibid.

90. U.S. Department of Agriculture, "USDA Announces Market Assistance Program for 1999: Crop Peanuts," Press Release no. 0498.99, December 20, 1999.

91. James Bovard, "This Program Is Just Plain Nuts!" *Wall Street Journal,* August 30, 1995. See also, General Accounting Office, "Peanut Program—Changes Are Needed to Make the Program Responsive to Market Forces," February 1993.

92. Philip Brasher, "Clinton Critical of 1996 Farm Bill; President Signs Assistance Measure," *Bismarck Tribune,* October 23, 1999.

93. Data on spending for each farm program is taken from the annual Budget Summary published by the Office of Budget and Program Analysis, U.S. Department of Agriculture, 1993-2000.

94. U.S. Department of Agriculture, "Glickman Reviews 1999 Accomplishments, Sets Goals for 2000," January 10, 2000.

95. *Agricultural Income and Finance, Situation and Outlook,* Economic Research Service, U.S. Department of Agriculture, March 7, 2000.

CHAPTER TWELVE

1. "Proclamation 6708—Anniversary of the Americans with Disabilities Act, 1994," *Public Papers of the Presidents,* July 26, 1994, p. 1559

2. "Remarks by Attorney General Janet Reno and FBI Director Louis Freeh," Federal News Service, December 1, 1993.

3. Ibid.

4. "Civil Rights Commission Finds Federal Enforcement of the ADA Falls Short," PR Newswire, October 2, 1998.

5. Mark Johnson, "And Justice for All," *Tampa Tribune,* August 10, 1997.

6. "Statement on the Ninth Anniversary of the Americans with Disabilities Act," *Public Papers of the Presidents,* July 26, 1999, p. 1493.

7. *EEOC v. Bell Helicopter Textron, Inc.,* Civil Action No. 4-98CV-0181Y (N.D. Tex.) (Lawsuit filed February 25, 1998).

8. *EEOC v. Harvest Foods,* Civil Action No. LR-C-95-408 (E.D. Ark.) (Lawsuit filed June 30, 1995).

9. Summary of case from EEOC Docket of Americans with Disabilities Act (ADA) Litigation As of March 31, 1998. Available on the EEOC website (www.eeoc.gov).

10. "Statement of Commissioner Russell G. Redenbaugh," in U.S. Civil Rights Commission, *Helping Employers Comply with the ADA—An Assessment of How the United States Equal Employment Opportunity Commission Is Enforcing Title I of the Americans with Disabilities Act,* 1998, pp. 274+.

11. Joanne Cleaver, "Lenthening Arm of the ADA Law's Broad Scope Covers Not-So-Obvious Conditions," *Crain's Chicago Business,* June 13, 1994

12. Cited in David R. Henderson, "Why You Can't Fire Anybody: The Invisible Foot of Government," *Fortune,* June 23, 1997.

13. Jeffrey A. Van Detta, "'Typhoid Mary' Meets the ADA: A Case Study of the 'Direct Threat' Standard Under the Americans with Disabilities Act," *Harvard Journal of Law & Public Policy,* vol. 22, Summer 1999, p. 849.

14. Ibid.

15. "Former Attorneys May Testify as Experts in Exxon ADA case," *Federal Discovery News,* March 15, 2000.

16. Roger Clegg, "The Costly Compassion of the Americans with Disabilities Act," *Public Interest,* Summer 1999.

17. "Remarks by Attorney General Janet Reno and FBI Director Louis Freeh," Federal News Service, December 1, 1993.

18. Reply Brief for the Petitioner, *Randon Bragdon v. Sidney Abbott, et al.,* no. 97-156, March 5, 1998.

19. Ibid.

20. Ibid.

21. "Maine Dentists Says Patient's Lawyers Cannot Support No Significant Risk' Claim," *AIDS Litigation Reporter*, May 24, 1999. Clinical Research Associates and the Association of Forensic Dentists filed briefs in the re-hearing of one specific aspect of the case by a lower federal court after the Supreme Court had ruled in Abbot's favor.

22. *Bragdon v. Abbott*, 524 U.S. 624 (1998).

23. "Statement on the Supreme Court Decision in *Bragdon v. Abbott*," *Public Papers of the Presidents*, June 26, 1998, p. 1238.

24. Lawrence K. Altman, "Investigating a Medical Maze: Virus Transmission in Surgery," *New York Times*, March 22, 1994.

25. Equal Employment Opportunity Commission, "Enforcement Guidance on the Americans with Disabilities Act and Psychiatric Disabilities," number 915.002, March 25, 1997.

26. Kathy Koch, "Ritalin: Are We Overdoing It?" *Raleigh News and Observer*, November 7, 1999.

27. Meredith May, "U.S. Disability Act Being Redefined to Include Psychological Stress," *Contra Costa Times*, April 5, 1999.

28. Mark Johnson, "And Justice for All," *Tampa Tribune*, August 10, 1997.

29. Lucy Howard and Carla Koehl, "Law: New Defense," *Newsweek*, April 17, 1995.

30. Judy Rakowsky, "BU Fires Accused Professor; Focus of Complaints of Sexual Misconduct," *Boston Globe*, April 4, 1995.

31. Alice Dembner, "Lawsuit by BU Professor Fired for Sex Harassment Is Dismissed," *Boston Globe*, June 12, 1996.

32. Janice Heller, "Separating Use from Abuse," *Legal Times*, April 10, 1995.

33. *Champagne v. Servistar Corp*, 138 F. 3d 7 (1ª. Cir. 1998).

34. "Narcoleptic Woman Sues over Lost Job," *Chicago Tribune*, April 24, 1995.

35. Robyn Tysver, "Disability Law's Future Doubted," *Omaha World-Herald*, August 12, 1999.

36. Stephanie Armour, "Disabilities Act Abused? Law's Use Sparks Debate," *USA Today*, September 25, 1998.

37. Carl Nolte, "Perfume Protest at Fairmont Hotel; Mask-Wearing Demonstrators Say Scents Make Them Sick," *San Francisco Chronicle*, October 25, 1994.

38. James Bovard, "Get a Whiff of This!" *Wall Street Journal*, December 27, 1995.

39. Martin Paskind, "Lucky Stores Was Not So Lucky in This Case," *Albuquerque Journal*, September 9, 1996.

40. Ibid.

41. Ibid.

42. Rob Rossi, "The Law of Unintended Consequences," *Recorder*, October 11, 1996.

43. James A. A. Pabarue and K. Tia Burke, "ADA Meets Workplace Mental Disability," *New York Law Journal*, August 23, 1999.

44. Samuel S. Heywood, "Without Lowering the Bar: Eligibility for Reasonable Accommodations on the Bar Exam for Learning Disabled Individuals under the Americans with Disabilities Act," *Georgia Law Review Association*, vol. 33, Winter 1999, p. 603.

45. Richard Benke, "Test Anxiety No Disability, Court Rules in UNM Case," *Albuquerque Tribune*, December 2, 1998.

46. Sid Wolinsky and Amy Whelan, "Federal Law and the Accommodation of Students with LD: The Lawyers' Look at the BU Decision," *Journal of Learning Disabilities*, July 1, 1999, p. 286.

47. Lawrence Elswit, Erika Geetter, and Judith Goldberg, "Between Passion and Policy: Litigating the Guckenberger Case," *Journal of Learning Disabilities*, July 1999, p. 292.

48. Mark Mueller, "Court Gets Tough in BU Case; Learning-Disabled Student Policy Unlawful," *Boston Herald*, August 16, 1997.

49. Wolinsky and Whelan, "Federal Law and the Accommodation of Students with LD," p. 286.

50. Tamar Lewin, "Court Backs Reading-Disorder Allowances for Bar Exams," *New York Times*, September 16, 1998.

51. Heywood, "Without Lowering the Bar," p. 603.

52. Tamar Lewin, "U.S. Court Upholds Aid for the Disabled on State Bar Exams," *New York Times*, September 16, 1998.

53. John Leo, "Let's Lower the Bar," *U.S. News and World Report*, October 5, 1998.

54. "Bar Exam Applicant to Get Reasonable Accommodations," *National Law Journal*, October 5, 1998.

55. One solution to this problem is to end bar associations' monopoly over who is permitted to hire out as a lawyer. Bar associations have greatly abused this monopoly in the past and there is no reason to extend it into the future. For examples of bar association licensing abuses, see James Bovard, *Lost Rights: The Destruction of American Liberty* (New York: St. Martin's Press, 1994), pp. 88-89. For a good book on the abuses of lawyers, see Nicholas Carroll, *Dancing with Wolves* (Lafayette, Cal.: Royce Baker Publishing, 1992).

56. Robert Pear, "Mental Disorders Common, U.S. Says," *New York Times*, December 13, 1999.

57. George F. Will, "Protection for the Personality-Impaired," *Washington Post*, April 4, 1996.

58. Keith Ervin, "Strip Club Told to Open Stage to Dancers in Wheelchairs," *Seattle Times*, May 12, 1995.

59. *ADA Compliance Guide*, June 1994.

60. Ben Kaufman, "NFL Blackouts Not Discriminatory," *Cincinnati Enquirer*, August 27, 1995.

61. Mark Johnson, "And Justice for All," *Tampa Tribune*, August 10, 1997.

62. "EEOC Says Delta Weight Policy Was Discriminatory," *Aviation Daily*, January 30, 1995.

63. "Airline Snack Foods: The Peanut Potential," *Child Health Alert*, September 1, 1999.

64. Brigid Schulte, "Peanut-Free School Zone," *Washington Post*, September 5, 1999.

65. Amy Zuber, "Wendy's to Make Stores more Accessible to Disabled," *Nation's Restaurant News*, September 21, 1998.

66. Anne Gearan, "Justice Department, Fast-Food Chain Reach Wheelchair Agreement," *Associated Press*, August 28, 1998.

67. Robert Pear, "After Long Delay, U.S. Plans to Issue Ergonomic Rules," *New York Times*, November 22, 1999.

68. Ibid.

69. *EEOC v. Helcris, Inc., d/b/a Vogue Cleaners*, civil action no. 2:97CV29OR/K (N.D. Ind., filed August 15, 1997).

70. Kirstin Downey Grimsley, "Pre-Hiring Medical Screening Put to Test," *Washington Post*, October 27, 1998.

71. "Judge Sets Status Hearing for EEOC Challenge to Pre-Hiring Tests," *Repetitive Stress Injury Litigation Reporter*, July 1999.

72. "Employment Prohibited Pre-employment Inquiry Leads to $157,500 Jury Award," *Disability Compliance Bulletin*, August 27, 1998.

73. "Statement of Commissioner Russell G. Redenbaugh," in U.S. Civil Rights Commission, *Helping Employers Comply with the ADA—An Assessment of How the United States Equal Employment Opportunity Commission Is Enforcing Title I of the Americans with Disabilities Act*, 1998, pp. 274+.

74. The U.S. Equal Employment Opportunity Commission, "Enforcement Guidance: Reasonable Accommodation and Undue Hardship Under the Americans with Disabilities Act," March 1999.

75. Ibid.

76. Ibid.

77. Peter Petesch, "Are the Newest ADA Guidelines 'Reasonable?'" *Human Resources*, June 1, 1999.

78. Comments on the Americans with Disabilities Act submitted by the Equal Employment Advisory Committee to the U.S. Civil Rights Commission, March 2, 1998.

79. Jacqueline Rolfs, "When Is 'Reasonable Accommodation' Unreasonable?" *Minneapolis Star Tribune,* August 8, 1999.

80. *Sutton v. United Air Lines,* no. 97-1943, 1999 U.S. Lexis 4371 (June 22, 1999).

81. *United States Law Week,* May 2, 1995, p. 2671.

82. "Q&A: What Courts and EEOC Say About Mental Disabilities," *Federal EEO Advisor,* February 1998.

83. Equal Employment Opportunity Commission, "New EEOC Policy Guidance Explains that Applications for Disability Benefits Do not Bar Claims Under the ADA," Press Release, February 12, 1997.

84. *Cleveland v. Policy Management Systems Corp.,* 120 F. 3d 51 (1997).

85. "Remarks to the Americans with Disabilities Act Roundtable," *Public Papers of the Presidents,* July 26, 1995, p. 1299.

86. Editorial, "Good Intentions, Bad Results," *Investor's Business Daily,* October 29, 1998.

87. Barbara Vobejda, "Survey Finds No Job Gains for Disabled," *Washington Post,* July 23, 1998.

88. "Federal Disability Programs Criticized by the GAO," *National Journal's Congress Daily,* May 24, 1996.

89. "Statement of Commissioner Russell G. Redenbaugh," in U.S. Civil Rights Commission, *Helping Employers Comply with the ADA—An Assessment of How the United States Equal Employment Opportunity Commission Is Enforcing Title I of the Americans with Disabilities Act,* 1998, pp. 274+.

90. Walter Olson, "Standard Accommodations: The Road to Universal Disability," *Reason,* February 1999.

91. "Civil Rights Commission Finds Federal Enforcement of the ADA Falls Short," *PR Newswire,* October 2, 1998.

CHAPTER THIRTEEN

1. "The Changing Burden of Regulation, Paperwork, and Tax Compliance on Small Business: A Report to Congress," U.S. Small Business Administration, October 1995. (The 1995 report contained estimates of the cost of environmental regulation for each year for the rest of the decade; since there were no major deregulations in environmental policy, the estimates remain credible). Cited in Clyde Wayne Crews, "Ten Thousand Commandments: An Annual Policymaker's Snapshot of the Federal Regulatory State," Competitive Enterprise Institute, March 1, 1999.

2. U.S. Department of Commerce, Bureau of Economic Analysis, unpublished data on investment in SIC-35 and SIC-36.

3. Al Gore, *Earth in the Balance: Ecology and the Human Spirit* (New York: Houghton Mifflin, 1992), p. 275.

4. "Remarks to Business Leaders," *Public Papers of the Presidents,* February 11, 1993, p. 185.I.

5. Joyce Price, "Superfund Spending Questioned by GAO," *Washington Times,* September 22, 1997.

6. Richard Stroup, "Superfund: The Shortcut That Failed," Political Economy Research Center, May 1996.

7. Michael Oxley, "Tear Down the Brownfields Berlin Wall," *Environmental Forum,* May-June 1995.

8. James M. Thunder, "EPA's Missteps on Brownfields: What Lessons Can We Learn?" Legal Backgrounder, Washington Legal Foundation, May 15, 1998.

9. Thomas Cochran and Jack Faris, "Superfund Cleanup Required," *Washington Times,* October 28, 1999.

10. John Shanahan, "How To Rescue Superfund: Bringing Common Sense to the Process," Heritage Foundation Backgrounder no. 1047, July 31, 1995.

11. Richard Stroup, "Superfund: The Shortcut That Failed," Political Economy Research Center, May 1996.

12. Kip Viscusi and James Hamilton, "Cleaning Up Superfund," *Public Interest,* Summer 1996.

13. "The Economy," *Investor's Business Daily,* March 17, 1999.

14. Kip Viscusi and James Hamilton, "Cleaning Up Superfund," *Public Interest,* Summer 1996.

15. Ibid.

16. "Testimony of Jerry Taylor, Director, Natural Resource Studies, CATO Institute, House Transportation, Water Resources and Environment, Superfund Reauthorization," Federal Document Clearing House, June 22, 1995.

17. Quoted in Dana Joel Gattuso, "Superfund Legislation: True Reform or a Hazardous Waste?" Competitive Enterprise Institute, November 3, 1999.

18. Quoted in Dana Joel Gattuso, "Superfund Legislation: True Reform or a Hazardous Waste?" Competitive Enterprise Institute, November 3, 1999.

19. Editorial, "Superfund Cleanup; Congress' Tainted Reform," *Arizona Republic,* October 12, 1994.

20. "Remarks at a Rally for Democratic Candidates in Cleveland, Ohio," *Public Papers of the Presidents,* November 1, 1994, p. 2225.

21. "Remarks at a Rally for Democratic Candidates in Pittsburgh, Pennsylvania," *Public Papers of the Presidents,* October 31, 1994, p. 2207.

22. "Message to the Congress on Environmental Policy," *Public Papers of the Presidents,* April 6, 1995, p. 558.

23. "Message to the House of Representatives Returning Without Approval the Department of Veterans Affairs and Housing and Urban Development, and Independent Agencies Appropriations Act, 1996," *Public Papers of the Presidents,* December 18, 1995, p. 2199.

24. "Remarks in Kalamazoo, Michigan," *Public Papers of the Presidents,* August 28, 1996, p. 1567.

25. U.S. General Accounting Office, "Superfund—Times to Complete the Assessment and Cleanup of Hazardous Waste Sites," May 8, 1997.

26. "Prepared Testimony of Mike Nobis of Creative Printers, Quincy, Illinois, before the House Commerce Committee Subcommittee on Finance and Hazardous Materials, Subject: Municipal Superfund Liability Relief Is Needed," Federal News Service, September 22, 1999.

27. Ibid.

28. Ibid.

29. "House Panel Grills EPA's Fields on Specifics of Liability Relief," *Hazardous Waste News,* September 27, 1999.

30. Cindy Skrzycki, "EPA Moves to Clean Up Liability Issues in Waste Disposal," *Washington Post,* August 22, 1997.

31. David Kopel, "Privileged Polluters: The Case against Exempting Municipalities from Superfund," Competitive Enterprise Institute, March 1998.

32. Warren Brown, "U.S. Accuses Toyota of Clean-Air Violations; Justice, EPA Seek $58.5 Billion Penalty," *Washington Post,* July 13, 1999.

33. Keith Bradsher, "U.S. Lawsuit Faults Toyota on Pollution Warning Lights," *New York Times,* July 13, 1999.

34. Author Interview with Toyota spokeswoman Martha Voss, December 17, 1999. Also, Press Release, "Toyota Remains Firm in Position on Emissions Performance," Toyota U.S.A., July 12, 1999.

35. Michael Sniffen, "U.S. Sues Toyota over Smog Control," Associated Press, July 12, 1999.

36. Holman Jenkins, "Who Controls the Idiot Light?" *Wall Street Journal,* July 21, 1999.

37. Quoted in untitled press release, Toyota USA, Torrance, Cal., February 25, 2000.

38. Editorial, "Clintonites vs. the EPA," *Investor's Business Daily,* March 19, 1997.

39. Eric Peters, "Protecting Us from the EPA," *Investor's Business Daily,* June 9, 1999.

40. Ben Lieberman, "Clean Air Act," Competitive Enterprise Institute Issue Brief, March 1, 1999.

41. James Miller, "Hiding the Truth," *Investor's Business Daily,* August 11, 1999.

42. Robert L. Jackson and James Gerstenzang, "Air Quality Standards Rejected by Appeals Court," *Los Angeles Times,* May 15, 1999.

43. "Justice Says Court 'Erred' in Decision," *Washington Times,* June 29, 1999.

44. "The President's Radio Address," *Public Papers of the Presidents,* May 1, 1999, p. 782.

45. Ben Lieberman, "EPA's Asthma Miasma," Competitive Enterprise Institute, April 2, 1998.

46. Michael Fumento, "EPA's Pollution-Asthma Theory Is Full of Bugs," *Investor's Business Daily,* May 27, 1997.

47. Editorial, "Let 'Em Wheeze," *Investor's Business Daily,* October 24, 1997.

48. Ibid.

49. "Remarks to the Community in Des Moines, Iowa," *Public Papers of the Presidents,* November 3, 1994, p. 2255.

50. U.S. Department of Agriculture, Office of Energy, "Fuel Ethanol and Agriculture: An Economic Assessment," Agricultural Economic Report no. 562, August 1986.

51. Larry Kramer, "EPA Will Allow Continued Sale of Fuel 'Gasohol," *Washington Post,* December 16, 1978.

52. Office of Energy, "Fuel Ethanol and Agriculture: An Economic Assessment," U.S. Department of Agriculture, Agricultural Economic Report No. 562, August 1986.

53. For the sad, sordid details of ADM's influence, see James Bovard, "Archer Daniels Midland: A Case Study in Corporate Welfare," Cato Institute, September 1995.

54. David Greising, "Big Stink on the Farm," *Business Week,* July 20, 1992.

55. Peter Stone, "The Big Harvest," *National Journal,* July 30, 1994, p. 1790.

56. "EPA to Require Cleaner-Burning Gas in Polluted Areas," *New York Times,* July 1, 1994.

57. Gary Lee, "EPA Backs Ethanol for Fuel," *Washington Post,* July 1, 1994.

58. Ibid.

59. Peter Stone, "The Big Harvest," *National Journal,* July 30, 1994, p. 1790.

60. Editorial, "This Clean Air Looks Dirty," *New York Times,* July 18, 1994.

61. Laurie Lande, "Senators Protest Ethanol Mandate," *Oil Daily,* March 4, 1994.

62. Jonathan Adler, "Alternative Fuel Follies with Ethanol Vapors," *Washington Times,* May 3, 1995.

63. Statement on Renewable Fuels Tax Incentives," *Public Papers of the Presidents,* July 31, 1997, p. 1162.

64. George Anthan, "Ethanol Back in the (Political) Limelight," Gannett News Service, December 22, 1999.

65. Rich Hein, "Ethanol Doubts Surface; Reports Haven't Fazed Politicians," *Chicago Sun-Times,* October 13, 1999.

66. Scott Rubush and Amy R. Gershkoff, "One Step Forward, Two Steps Back," *Insight on the News,* August 23, 1999.

67. John Rather, "Contaminant from Gas Is Found in Water," *New York Times,* August 29, 1999.

68. David Stout, "E.P.A. Urges Substitution of an Additive to Gasoline," *New York Times,* March 21, 2000.

69. Paul Rogers, "Clinton's Ethanol Proposal Could Cost Californians $ 1 Billion a Year," *San Jose Mercury News,* March 22, 2000.

70. National Mining Association v. Army Corps of Engineers, 330 U.S. App. D.C. 329; 145 F. 3d 1399 (1998).

71. White House Office on Environmental Policy, "Protecting America's Wetlands: A Fair, Flexible, and Effective Approach," August 24, 1993.

72. *National Mining Association v. Army Corps of Engineers,* 330 U.S. App. D.C. 329; 145 F.3d 1399 (1998).

73. White House Office on Environmental Policy, "Protecting America's Wetlands: A Fair, Flexible, and Effective Approach," August 24, 1993.

74. "Testimony of Nancy Cline, Private Citizen, Sonoma, California, House Judiciary, The Constitution, Regulatory Takings and Property Rights," Federal Document Clearing House Congressional, February 10, 1995.

75. Federal judge Daniel Manion skewered this doctrine in a 1992 decision; unfortunately, an appeals court overturned his ruling. See *Hoffman Homes, Inc., v. Administrator, United States Environmental Protection Agency,* no. 90-3810, United States Court of Appeals for the Seventh Circuit, 1992 U.S. App. LEXIS 7329, April 20, 1992.

76. *U.S. v. Wilson,* 133 F. 3d 251 (1997).

77. Editorial, "A Crime in Search of a Criminal," *Washington Times,* January 13, 1998.

78. Max Boot, "The Wetlands Gestapo," *Wall Street Journal,* March 3, 1997.

79. *U.S. v. Wilson,* 133 F. 3d 251 (1997).

80. Robert Wayland, director, Office of Wetlands, Oceans, and Watersheds, Office of Water, EPA and Charles Hess, chief, Operations, Construction, and Readiness Division, Directorate of Civil Works, Army Corps of Engineers, "Joint Memo/Policy Guidance, Guidance for Corps and EPA Field Offices Regarding Clean Water Act Section 404 Jurisdiction over Isolated Waters in Light of U.S. v. James J. Wilson," May 29, 1998.

81. "Statement on Signing the Mollie Beattie Wilderness Area Act," *Public Papers of the Presidents,* July 29, 1996, p. 1366.

82. "Endangered Species Listings and Recovery Plans as of September 30, 1999," U.S. Fish and Wildlife Service, Department of Interior.

83. Ike Sugg, "Flies Before People," *Wall Street Journal,* February 11, 1997.

84. Lynda Gorov, "Protecting a Fly May Endanger Calif. Towns," *Boston Globe,* September 25, 1999.

85. Paul Craig Roberts, "Giving Development a Bad Name," *Washington Times,* November 7, 1999.

86. Dan Lee, "City Wants Delhi Fly Taken Off U.S. List," *Riverside (California) Press-Enterprise,* October 5, 1999.

87. Ibid.

88. Ike Sugg, "California Fires—Losing Houses, Saving Rats," *Wall Street Journal,* November 10, 1993.

89. Ike Sugg, "Babbitt's Ecobabble," *National Review,* September 20, 1993.

90. Editorial, "The Emotional Species Act," *Wall Street Journal,* November 2, 1993.

91. Quoted in Brief of the Competitive Enterprise Institute (Sam Kazman and Ike Sugg), *Bruce Babbitt v. Sweet Home Chapter of Communities for a Great Oregon,* March 24, 1995.

92. Ibid.

93. Ibid.

94. Ibid.

95. "Brief of the Institute for Justice" (Richard Epstein), *Bruce Babbitt v. Sweet Home Chapter of Communities for a Great Oregon,* No. 94-859, March 24, 1995.

96. "Brief of the Competitive Enterprise Institute" (Sam Kazman and Ike Sugg), *Bruce Babbitt v. Sweet Home Chapter of Communities for a Great Oregon,* March 24, 1995.

97. Ibid.

98. "List of Protected Habitats," Associated Press, May 4, 1997.

99. Quoted in "Babbitt: *Rolling Stone* Asks 'Is He Tough Enough?'" Greenwire, June 24, 1993.

100. "Brief of the Competitive Enterprise Institute" (by Sam Kazman and Ike Sugg), *Bruce Babbitt v. Sweet Home Chapter of Communities for a Great Oregon,* March 24, 1995.

101. "Babbitt Announces New Policy, Plans to 'Delist' Endangered Species," Press Release, Department of the Interior, U.S. Newswire, May 6, 1998.

102. Joby Warrick, "Babbitt Sets Plan to Pare Endangered Species List; Protected Status Aided Recoveries," *Washington Post,* May 6, 1998.

103. "Babbitt Announces New Policy, Plans to 'Delist' Endangered Species," Press Release, Department of the Interior, U.S. Newswire, May 6, 1998.

104. Editorial, "A Correction Please, Secretary Babbitt," *Investor's Business Daily,* July 16, 1998.

105. Ike Sugg, "Saving Species or Saving Face?" *Wall Street Journal,* June 30, 1998.

106. Steve Davies, "The Fish and Wildlife Service Has Apologized for an Announcement," *Inside Energy/with Federal Lands,* September 7, 1998.

107. Alexander Annett, "Reforming the Endangered Species Act to Protect Species and Property Rights," Heritage Foundation Backgrounder no. 1234, November 13, 1998.

108. Ike Sugg, "Saving Species or Saving Face?" *Wall Street Journal,* June 30, 1998.

109. Quoted in Ike Sugg, "The Ark That Wouldn't Float," Competitive Enterprise Institute, March 1, 1997.

110. Wes Allison, "Bitter Fruit for Cider Maker," *Richmond-Times Dispatch,* April 8, 1996.

111. Editorial, "A Man's Word," *Richmond Times-Dispatch,* July 14, 1996.

112. Ibid.

113. Editorial, "Bully for Them," *Richmond Times-Dispatch,* March 22, 1998.

114. Linda Wheeler, "Beer Flowed on Wrong Side of the Law," *Washington Post,* November 20, 1997.

115. David Armstrong, "Environmental Injustice; Government as Polluter," *Boston Globe,* November 14, 1999.

116. Ibid.

117. Ibid.

118. Ibid.

119. Ibid.

120. Quoted in Kenneth Smith, "Friends of OPEC," *Washington Times,* March 9, 2000.

121. Joe Knollenberg, "Common Sense Needed on Global Warming," *The Hill,* April 21, 1999.

122. Quoted in Press Release, "U.S. PIRG Report Distorts Science of Global Warming," Competitive Enterprise Institute, April 6, 2000.

123. Peter Huber, "Al Gore Is No Match to Teddy Roosevelt as Environmentalist," *Bridge News,* January 24, 2000.

CHAPTER FOURTEEN

1. "Remarks Commemorating the First Anniversary of the Brady Law and an Exchange with Reporters," *Public Papers of the Presidents,* February 28, 1995, p. 326.

2. *Staples v. United States,* 511 U.S. 600 (1994).

3. "Teleconference on the Passage of the Brady Bill and an Exchange With Reporters," *Public Papers of the Presidents,* November 24, 1993, p. 2459

4. "Remarks Accepting the Presidential Nomination at the Democratic National Convention in Chicago," *Public Papers of the Presidents,* August 29, 1996, p. 1439.

5. "Remarks on Concluding a Whistlestop Tour in Michigan City, Indiana," *Public Papers of the Presidents,* August 28, 1996, p. 1571.

6. Author interview with Mary Ellen Glynn, September 15, 1996. Also, James Bovard, "Clinton's Gun Hoax," *Wall Street Journal,* September 16, 1996.

7. Author interview with Gerald Arenberg, executive director of the National Association of Chiefs of Police, September 10, 1996.

8. General Accounting Office, "Gun Control: Implementation of the Brady Handgun Violence Prevention Act," January 1996.

9. Ibid.

10. Ibid.

11. Ibid.

12. "Brady Bill May Mean Rise in Crime, More Work for Understaffed, Overworked Police," PR Newswire, December 2, 1993.

13. General Accounting Office, "Gun Control: implementation of the Brady Handgun Violence Prevention Act," January 1996.

14. Ibid.

15. Ibid.

16. "DOJ Defends Brady Bill Law," Associated Press Online, March 22, 1994.

17. Michael Sniffen, " Brady Law Checks Blocked 69,000 Handgun Sales Last Year," Associated Press, June 21, 1998.

18. "Clinton Statement on Justice Dept. Report on the Brady Law," U.S. Newswire, June 21, 1998.

19. Author interview with Nanda Chitre, June 24, 1998. Also, James Bovard, "Truth Is the Casualty as Clinton Takes Aim at Guns," *Wall Street Journal,* June 25, 1998.

20. Meghan Hoyer, "Brady Act Benefits Overstated in Indiana," *Indianapolis Star,* June 24, 1998.

21. "Interview with Katie Couric of the National Broadcasting Corporation," *Public Papers of the Presidents,* April 29, 1999, p. 763.

22. "Remarks at a Democratic National Committee Luncheon in Aspen," *Public Papers of the Presidents,* July 24, 1999, p. 1486.

23. "Address before a Joint Session of Congress on the State of the Union," *Public Papers of the Presidents,* January 27, 2000, p. 160.

24. Chris Mondics, "Feds' Failure to Enforce Law Gives Gun-Control Foes a New Argument," *San Diego Union-Tribune,* September 7, 1999.

25. Gary Fields, "Checks Yield 29 Federal Convictions," *USA Today,* December 1, 1999.

26. "Prepared Testimony of Susan B. Long, Co-Director, Transactional Records Access Clearing House, Syracuse University, and Associate Professor of Quantitative Methods, School of Management, Syracuse University, Before the House Committee on Government Reform, Subcommittee on Criminal Justice, Drug Policy and Human Resources, Subject: 'Measuring Enforcement of Weapons Laws by the Bureau of Alcohol, Tobacco and Firearms'," Federal News Service, November 4, 1999.

27. Quoted in James Bovard, "Truth Is the Casualty as Clinton Takes Aim at Guns," *Wall Street Journal,* June 25, 1998.

28. Orrin Hatch, "The Brady Handgun Prevention Act and The Community Protection Initiative: Legislative Responses to the Second Amendment?" *Brigham Young University Law Review,* vol. 1998, no. 1, p. 103.

29. Author interview with Paul Blackman, June 25, 1994.

30. "Clinton Adviser Rahm Emanuel and NRA President Charlton Heston Discuss the Ken Starr Investigation and Gun Control Policy," NBC News Transcripts, *Meet the Press,* June 14, 1998.

31. Author interview with Nandra Chitre, June 24, 1998.

32. "The President's Radio Address," *Public Papers of the Presidents,* December 5, 1998, p. 2432.

33. "Clinton Eyes Handgun Waiting Period," Associated Press, December 5, 1998.

34. Philip Heymann, "The Limits to Federal Crime-Fighting," *Washington Post,* January 5, 1997.

35. Orrin Hatch, "The Brady Handgun Prevention Act and The Community Protection Initiative: Legislative Responses to the Second Amendment?" *Brigham Young University Law Review,* vol. 1998, no. 1, p. 103.

36. John Lott, *More Guns, Less Crime* (Chicago: University of Chicago Press, 1998), p. 91.

37. "Remarks in a Telephone Conversation with the Space Shuttle Endeavor Astronauts and an Exchange with Reporters," *Public Papers of the Presidents,* December 10, 1993, p. 2555.

38. "Remarks at the Creative Artists Agency Reception in Beverly Hills, California," *Public Papers of the Presidents,* December 4, 1993, p. 2530.

39. "Remarks on Legislation to Ban Assault Weapons," *Public Papers of the Presidents,* May 2, 1994, p. 957.

40. "Remarks on Legislation to Ban Assault Weapons and an Exchange with Reporters," *Public Papers of the Presidents,* May 5, 1994, p. 991.

41. Joseph P. Tartaro, " Violent Crime Control and Law Enforcement Act of 1994: The Great Assault Weapon Hoax," *Dayton Law Review,* vol. 20, Winter 1995, p. 619.

42. Ibid.

43. Ibid.

44. "Remarks on Legislation to Ban Assault Weapons," *Public Papers of the Presidents,* May 2, 1994, p. 957.

45. "Remarks on Gun Control Legislation and an Exchange with Reporters in Paris," *Public Papers of the Presidents,* June 17, 1999, p. 1128.

46. Jeff Brazil and Steve Berry, "Clinton Urged to Tighten Gun Import Law," *Los Angeles Times,* October 23, 1997.

47. Jeff Brazil and Steve Berry, "Clinton Imposes Import Ban on Assault Guns," *Los Angeles Times,* November 15, 1997.

48. Elizabeth Shogren, Jeff Brazil, and Steve Berry, "Clinton Moves to Limit Import of Assault Guns," *Los Angeles Times,* October 22, 1997.

49. "Remarks at a Democratic National Committee Dinner in Portola Valley, California," *Public Papers of the Presidents,* May 14, 1999, p. 901.

50. "Interview With Katie Couric of the National Broadcasting Corporation," *Public Papers of the Presidents,* April 29, 1999, p. 763.

51. "Remarks on Legislation to Ban Assault Weapons and an Exchange with Reporters," *Public Papers of the Presidents,* May 5, 1994, p. 991.

52. "Remarks and a Question-and-Answer Session at the Adult Learning Center in New Brunswick, New Jersey," *Public Papers of the Presidents,* March 1, 1993, p. 332.

53. Frank Murray, "Clinton Aides Back Away from Gun-Ban Statement," *Washington Times,* March 14, 1994.

54. "Interview With Charles Gibson, Diane Sawyer, and a Discussion with Students on *Good Morning America*," *Public Papers of the Presidents,* June 4, 1999, p. 1033.
55. "Remarks on Receiving the Abraham Lincoln Courage Award in Chicago," *Public Papers of the Presidents,* June 30, 1995, p. 1171.
56. Carl M. Cannon, "First Posturing, Then Honest Talk," *National Journal,* June 5, 1999.
57. "Remarks to the American Federation of Teachers," *Public Papers of the Presidents,* July 28, 1995, p. 1321.
58. "Remarks in Marrero, Louisiana," *Public Papers of the Presidents,* October 24, 1996, p. 2169.
59. Peter Baker, "Clinton Cites Officer's Car Death in Opposing 'Cop-Killer Bullets'", *Washington Post,* October 26, 1996.
60. "Remarks on Signing the Memorandum on Child Safety Lock Devices for Handguns and an Exchange With Reporters," *Public Papers of the Presidents,* March 5, 1997, p. 284.
61. Department of Treasury, Bureau of Alcohol, Tobacco and Firearms, "Antiterrorism and Effective Death Penalty Act of 1996: Report Responding to Section 809: Assessing and Reducing the Threat to Law Enforcement Officers from the Criminal Use of Firearms and Ammunition," April 1997 (draft).
62. Ibid.
63. Tom Barry, "Cop-Killer' Bullet Study a Mystery," *Austin American-Statesman,* September 2, 1997.
64. "Prepared Statement of Chairman Bill McCollum before the House Committee on Judiciary," Federal News Service, March 25, 1998.
65. Bruce Blum, "Biting the Bullets," letter to the editor, *Washington Post,* January 14, 1995.
66. "Remarks by President Bill Clinton and First Lady Hillary Rodham Clinton and Other Speakers, Subject: Gun-Related Provisions of Omnibus Crime Bill," Federal News Service, April 27, 1999.
67. Carl M. Cannon, "First Posturing, Then Honest Talk," *National Journal,* June 5, 1999.
68. "Opening Remarks at a Roundtable Discussion on Increasing Trust between Communities and Law Enforcement," *Public Papers of the Presidents,* June 9, 1999, p. 1065.
69. "Opening Remarks at a Roundtable Discussion on Increasing Trust Between Communities and Law Enforcement," *Public Papers of the Presidents,* June 9, 1999, p. 1065.
70. "Attorney General Pledges Long-Term Support from Nation," Associated Press, April 22, 1999.
71. "President Clinton's Weekly Radio Address," Federal News Service, April 24, 1999.
72. Kevin Vaughan, "Police Dispute Charges They Were Too Slow," *Denver Rocky Mountain News,* April 22, 1999.
73. "New Developments in the Investigation into Columbine High School Shooting," NBC News Transcripts, *Dateline NBC,* April 26, 1999.
74. Nancy Gibbs and Timothy Roche, "The Columbine Tapes," *Time,* December 20, 1999.
75. Ted Anthony, "A Moment of Surprise, Then Hours of Terror," Associated Press, April 23, 1999.
76. Barbara Vobejda, "Response In Littleton Was Swift, but Unsure," *Washington Post,* May 12, 1999.
77. David Olinger, "Columbine Rescuers in the Dark; Officers in School Were Unaware of Dying Teacher," *Denver Post,* May 30, 1999.
78. Sam Howe Verhovek, "Terror in Littleton: The Overview," *New York Times,* April 24, 1999.
79. James Brooke, "Terror in Littleton: The Details; Attack at School Planned A Year, Authorities Say," *New York Times,* April 25, 1999.

80. Richard A. Serrano, "Tragedy in Colorado; Police Begin Removal of 15 Dead at School," *Los Angeles Times,* April 22, 1999

81. Ted Anthony, "Police Defend Response to Massacre," *Des Moines Register,* April 23, 1999.

82. Author interview with Colorado law enforcement expert who wished to remain anonymous, June 7, 1999.

83. Nancy Gibbs and Timothy Roche, "The Columbine Tapes," *Time,* December 20, 1999.

84. Author interview with Stephen Davis, June 1, 1999.

85. Author interview with Jack Beam, June 15, 1999.

86. Kevin Vaughan, "Judge Unseals Autopsy Report on Eric Harris," *Denver Rocky Mountain News,* June 25, 1999.

87. John Lott, "Perspectives on Gun Control," *Los Angeles Times,* March 19, 2000.

88. Sheryl Gay Stolberg, "By the Numbers; Science Looks at Littleton, and Shrugs," *New York Times,* May 9, 1999.

89. Lawrence Southwick, "An Economic Analysis of Murder and Accident Risks for Police in the United States," *Applied Economics,* vol. 30, May 1998, p. 593.

90. Ibid.

91. "Brief of Petitioner," *Staples v. U.S.,* no. 92-1441, July 7, 1993.

92. Ibid.

93. Author interview with Stephen Halbrook, August 2, 1994.

94. "Brief for the United States," *Staples v. U.S.,* no. 92-1441, August 9, 1993.

95. *Staples v. United States,* 511 U.S. 600 (1994).

96. Quoted in "Testimony of Eric M. Larson, Collectors Arms Dealers Association, House Appropriations, Treasury, Postal Service and General Government, FY 97 Treasury, Postal Service Appropriations," Federal Document Clearing House, April 30, 1996

97. Ibid.

98. Eric Larson, "Violating the Rule of Law: The Bureau of Alcohol, Tobacco and Firearms Has Not Corrected Errors in the National Firearms Registration and Transfer Record, Which Unjustly Subjects Law-Abiding Citizens to Imprisonment, Fines, and Confiscation of Their Historic Firearms," Testimony presented to the Subcommittee on Treasury, Postal Service and General Government of the Committee on Appropriations, House of Representatives, March 31, 1999.

99. Ibid.

100. James Bovard, "Disarming Those Who Need Guns Most," *Wall Street Journal,* December 23, 1996.

101. Author interview with University of Maryland professor Lawrence Sherman, December 16, 1996.

102. Letter from Peter Proctor to author, December 4, 1996.

103. Leef Smith, "Increasingly, Abuse Shows Female Side; More Women Accused of Domestic Violence," *Washington Post,* November 18, 1996.

104. Email from Sarah Thompson, December 7, 1996.

105. *U.S. v. Lopez,* 514 U.S. 549 (1995).

106. "President's Radio Address," *Public Papers of the Presidents,* September 11, 1999, p. 1725.

107. Daniel Ruth, "Zero Tolerance for Zero Tolerance," *Tampa Tribune,* June 7, 1999.

108. Dennis Cauchon, "Schools Struggling To Balance 'Zero Tolerance,' Common Sense," *USA Today,* April 13, 1999.

109. Charles Babington, "White House Draws a Bead on Guns," *Washington Post,* December 15, 1999.

110. "Transcript of Remarks by President Clinton at Rally for Gun Legislation," U.S. Newswire, March 15, 2000.

111. Quoted in Neal Boortz, "A Look Into the Mind of an Anti-Gunner," *www.boortz.com,* March 13, 2000. Clinton made the comment during an interview on Cable News Network.

112. Marc Lacey, "In Gun Control, Clinton and Gore Have Found a Common, Constant Theme," *New York Times,* March 15, 2000.

113. Daniel LeDuc, "NRA Finds A Surprise Pitchman; Anti-Gun-Lock TV Ad Features Glendening," *Washington Post,* March 30, 2000.

114. Sam Skolnik, "DOJ Reined in Cuomo on Gun Litigation," *Legal Times,* December 13, 1999.

115. Eric Lichtblau and Ricardo Alonso-Zaldivar, "Smith and Wesson Agrees to Key Safety Reforms," *Los Angeles Times,* March 18, 2000.

116. "Press Conference with Secretary Andrew Cuomo, Department of Housing and Housing and Urban Development, Senator Charles Schumer (D-NY), Representative Carolyn McCarthy (D-NY) and Others, Subject: Gun Agreement with Smith and Wesson," Federal News Service, March 22, 2000.

117. "Agreement between Smith and Wesson and the Departments of the Treasury and Housing and Urban Development, Local Governments and States; Summary of Terms," HUD Website, March 17, 2000.

118. Ibid.

119. Ibid.

120. Ibid.

121. Ibid.

122. Ibid.

123. "Remarks Commemorating the First Anniversary of the Brady Law and an Exchange with Reporters," *Public Papers of the Presidents,* February 28, 1995, p. 326.

124. Morgan O. Reynolds and W. W. Caruth III, "Myths about Gun Control," National Center for Policy Analysis Report no. 176, December 1992, p. 10.

125. "Clinton Eyes Handgun Waiting Period," Associated Press, December 5, 1998.

126. "Interview With Charles Gibson, Diane Sawyer, and a Discussion With Students on "Good Morning America", *Public Papers of the Presidents,* June 4, 1999, p. 1033.

127. Eric Schmitt, "Clinton Unveils Program to Buy Back Guns from Private Owners," *New York Times,* September 10, 1999.

128. National Rifle Association, Institute for Legislative Action, "Clinton-Gore Gun Surrender Scheme: Political Gimmickery at its Worst," Fax Alert no. 3, September 10, 1999.

129. Carla Crowder, "Critics: Gun Buybacks a PR 'Gimmick'; Research Shows Programs Fail to Reduce Violence," *Denver Rocky Mountain News,* September 16, 1999.

130. Barbara Vobejda, David Ottaway, and Sarah Cohen, "Recycled D.C. Police Guns Tied to Crimes," *Washington Post,* November 12, 1999.

131. John Lott, "Guns and Crime and Traditional Myths," letter to the editor, *Wall Street Journal,* May 25, 1999.

132. Lott, *More Guns, Less Crime,* p. 137.

133. "Remarks on Action by the House of Representatives on Assault Weapons and an Exchange with Reporters," *Public Papers of the Presidents,* May 5, 1994, p. 994.

134. *U.S. v. Emerson,* 46 f. Supp 2d 598(1999).

135. Ibid.

136. Ibid.

137. Reply Brief For Appellant (U.S. Government), *U.S. v. Timothy Joe Emerson,* No. 99-10331, U.S. Court of Appeals for the Fifth Circuit, submitted January 27, 2000.

138. Tony Mauro, "Scholar's Views on Arms Rights Anger Liberals," *USA Today,* August 27, 1999.

CHAPTER FIFTEEN

1. "Transcript of President Clinton's Press Conference," U.S. Newswire, April 23, 1993.
2. House of Representatives, Investigation into the Activities of Federal Law Enforcement Agencies toward the Branch Davidians, House Report 104-749, August 2, 1996.
3. Ibid.
4. Bureau of Alcohol, Tobacco and Firearms: "Synopsis of Surveillance—February 19, 1993," internal memo from Davy Aguilera, approved by Phillip J. Chojnacki, February 24, 1993. This report was uncovered in 1999 by a FOIA request by David Hardy, an Arizona investigator.
5. House, Investigation into the Activities.
6. Ibid.
7. Scott Parks, "Military Role in Davidian Siege Cloudy," *Dallas Morning News,* September 26, 1999.
8. House, Investigation into the Activities.
9. "Charges of Sexual and Ethnic Harassment within Alcohol, Tobacco, Firearms," CBS News Transcripts, *60 Minutes,* January 10, 1993.
10. "Alcohol, Tobacco, Firearms and Harassment; Female ATF Agents Say Sexual Harassment within the Agency is Rampant and Unchecked," CBS News Transcripts, *60 Minutes,* May 23, 1993.
11. "Joint Hearing of the Crime Subcommittee of the House Judiciary Committee and the National Security, International Affairs and Criminal Justice Subcommittee of the House Government Reform and Oversight Committee, Subject: Review of Siege of Branch Davidians' Compound in Waco, Texas," Federal News Service, July 24, 1995.
12. House, Investigation into the Activities.
13. Quoted in "Hearing of the Senate Judiciary Committee Subject: Federal Raid at Waco," Federal News Service, November 1, 1995.
14. Jennifer Autrey, "Critics of Raid Demand Inquiry into Helicopters," *Fort Worth Star Telegram,* September 25, 1999.
15. Lee Hancock, "Agent Acknowledges Changing Story on Raid," *Dallas Morning News,* January 19, 1994,
16. Stephen Labaton, "Hedging Earlier Defense, Agency Chief Admits Waco Raid May Have Been Flawed," *New York Times,* April 3, 1993.
17. Tim Weiner, "Agent Says His Warnings over Waco Were Ignored," *New York Times,* July 25, 1995.
18. "Hearing of the Crime Subcommittee of the House Judiciary Committee and the National Security, International Affairs and Criminal Justice Subcommittee of the House Government Reform and Oversight Committee, Subject: Review of Siege of Branch Davidians' Compound in Waco, Texas," Federal News Service, July 21, 1995.
19. "Joint Hearing of the Crime Subcommittee of the House Judiciary Committee and the National Security International Affairs and Criminal Justice Subcommittee of the House Government Reform and Oversight Committee, Subject: Review of Siege of Branch Davidians' Compound in Waco, Texas," Federal News Service, July 20, 1995.
20. Treasury Department, interoffice memorandum from Robert McNamara to John Simpson et al., "Preliminary Investigative Plan," April 14, 1993. This memo, which became public

during the 1995 congressional Waco hearings, was stamped, "Close Hold—Some Information Is Law Enforcement Sensitive."

21. "Joint Hearing of the Crime Subcommittee of the House Judiciary Committee and the National Security, International Affairs and Criminal Justice Subcommittee of the House Government Reform and Oversight Committee, Subject: Review of Siege of Branch Davidians' Compound in Waco, Texas," Federal News Service, July 25, 1995.

22. Laurie Kellman, "Fire Agents, Lawmakers Say; Davidian Details 'Hell' During Siege," *Washington Times,* July 29, 1995.

23. David Vise and Lorraine Adams, "FBI Produces New Waco Documents; Logs Detail Aggressive Federal Tactics," *Washington Post,* October 8, 1999.

24. "President Bill Clinton News Conference White House Rose Garden," Federal News Service, April 20, 1993.

25. Lee Hancock, "FBI Missteps Doomed Siege Talks, Memos Say," *Dallas Morning News,* December 30, 1999.

26. "Reno on Waco: 'I Would Not Do It Again'; Purpose of Assault Was to Save Lives, She Says," *Washington Post,* May 15, 1995.

27. Laurie Kellman, "Koresh Agreed to Give Up, Panel Told; Lawyers Say 'Bureaucrat' Rejected Deal," *Washington Times,* July 26, 1995.

28. Memo quoted in "Joint Hearing of the Crime Subcommittee of the House Judiciary Committee and the National Security, International Affairs and Criminal Justice Subcommittee of the House Government Reform and Oversight Committee, Subject: Review of Siege of Branch Davidians' Compound in Waco, Texas," Federal News Service, July 31, 1995.

29. "Joint Hearing of the Crime Subcommittee of the House Judiciary Committee and the National Security, International Affairs and Criminal Justice Subcommittee of the House Government Reform and Oversight Committee, Subject: Review of Siege of Branch Davidians' Compound in Waco, Texas," Federal News Service, July 31, 1995.

30. "Day Nine of Hearing into Actions of Federal Agents at Waco, Texas," Federal Documents Clearinghouse, July 31, 1995.

31. "Afternoon Proceedings—Koresh Compound Hearings," Transcript no. 189—15, CNN News, April 28, 1993.

32. Edward Walsh and Richard Leiby, "Reno Says FBI Misled Her about Waco Arms," *Washington Post,* August 27, 1999.

33. Ellen Cantarow, "Not Tears Alone: Toxic Effects of CS, or O-chlorobenzylidene Malonitrile, a Tear Gas," *Technology Review,* October, 1988. The controversy was also in the mainstream press: Glenn Frankel, "Israel's Use of Tear Gas Scrutinized," *Washington Post,* May 31, 1988.

34. Jerry Seper, "FBI Used Chemical Banned for War," *Washington Times,* April 22, 1993.

35. Failure Analysis Associates, Inc., "Investigation of the April 19, 1993, Assault on the Mt. Carmel Center, Waco, Texas," Menlo Park, Cal., July 1995. Report prepared for the National Rifle Association.

36. Laurie Kellman, "Gas Hit Children Hardest, Panel Told," *Washington Times,* July 27, 1995.

37. Ibid.

38. "Transcript of White House Press Briefing by George Stephanopoulos," U.S. Newswire, April 22, 1993.

39. "Afternoon Proceedings—Koresh Compound Hearings," CNN News, Transcript no. 189-7, April 28, 1993.

40. Dick J. Reavis, "What Really Happened at Waco," *Texas Monthly,* July 1995.

41. "Hearing of the Crime Subcommittee of the House Judiciary Committee and the National Security, International Affairs and Criminal Justice Subcommittee of the House Government

Reform and Oversight Committee, Subject: Review of Siege of Branch Davidians' Compound in Waco, Texas," Federal News Service, July 31, 1995. The presentation of Rep. John Shadegg highlighted the extent of the damage done by the FBI prior to the fire.

42. Ibid.

43. Lee Hancock, "Tank Action at '93 Siege Draws Criticism," *Dallas Morning News*, February 6, 2000.

44. Ibid.

45. Author interview with Alan Stone, April 13, 1995

46. See http://www.indirect.com/www/dhardy/waco.html. Hardy's four-year long battle with federal agencies to comply with the Freedom of Information Act law and provide documents on Waco was detailed in Jim Yardley, "Tenacity of 2 Played a Role In Reviving Inquiry on Waco," *New York Times*, September 2, 1999. Filmmaker Mike McNulty was also profiled in this article.

47. http://www.indirect.com/www/dhardy/waco.html.

48. Ibid.

49. This information is from the website of Waco investigator David Hardy at http://www.indirect.com/www/dhardy/waco.html.

50. Lee Hancock, "FBI Didn't Plan to Fight Waco Fire," *Dallas Morning News*, March 2, 2000.

51. Peter B. Nugent, "Police Endorse Flash-Bang Devices; Worcester Captain Says Distraction Grenades Should Be Used Sparingly," *Worcester Telegram and Gazette*, December 18, 1996.

52. "Prepared Statement of the Federal Bureau of Investigation Submitted by Larry A. Potts, Before the House Committee on Government Reform and Oversight, Subcommittee on International Affairs and Criminal Justice, and the Committee on the Judiciary, Subcommittee on Crime," Federal News Service, July 26, 1995.

53. Lee Hancock, "Delta Force Had Active Role in Raid, Ex-CIA Officer Told," *Dallas Morning News*, August 27, 1999.

54. Jim Yardley, "Tenacity of 2 Played a Role in Reviving Inquiry on Waco," *New York Times*, September 2, 1999.

55. David Jackson and Lee Hancock, "Task Force for Waco Is Scrapped; Senate Subcommittee to Review Handling of Siege, Other Cases," *Dallas Morning News*, October 15, 1999.

56. Leah Quin and Mike Ward, "Military Secrets in Report on Waco," *Austin American-Statesman*, September 11, 1999.

57. David Kopel and Paul Blackman, *No More Wacos: What's Wrong with Federal Law Enforcement and How to Fix It* (Amherst, NY: Prometheus Books, 1997), p. 227.

58. Ibid., pp. 226-27.

59. Ibid., p. 227.

60. Stepher Labaron, "Death in Waco: The Government's Plan," *New York Times*, April 21, 1993.

61. Michelle Mittelstadt, "FBI Wanted to Reward Waco Team," Associated Press, October 8, 1999.

62. "Waco: What Went Wrong?" Transcript, ABC News, *Nightline*, April 19, 1993. (emphasis added).

63. Ibid. (emphasis added)

64. "President Bill Clinton News Conference White House Rose Garden," Federal News Service, April 20, 1993.

65. Ibid.

66. Ibid.

67. Fred Barnes, "How Serious is Filegate?" *Weekly Standard*, July 8, 1996.

68. Jim McGee and Brian Duffy, *Main Justice: The Men and Women Who Enforce the Nation's Criminal Laws and Guard Its Liberties* (New York: Simon & Schuster, 1996).

69. Mickey Kaus, "Local Hero—Janet Reno," *New Republic,* May 24, 1993.

70. Ibid.

71. "President Bill Clinton, News Conference, White House Rose Garden," Federal News Service, April 20, 1993.

72. Stephen Labaton, "Reno Contradicted in New Report on Decision to Attack Waco Cult," *New York Times,* October 9, 1993.

73. Stephen Labaton, "Inquiry Won't Look at Final Waco Raid," *New York Times,* May 16, 1993.

74. For instance, see editorial, "The Waco Whitewash," *New York Times,* October 12, 1993.

75. Jerry Seper, "Tragedy Blamed on Cult," *Washington Times,* October 9, 1993.

76. Michael Isikoff, "FBI Clashed over Waco, Report Says; Attack on Davidians Draws No Criticism," *Washington Post,* October 9, 1993.

77. Department of the Treasury, *Report of the Department of the Treasury on the Bureau of Alcohol, Tobacco and Firearms Investigation of Vernon Wayne Howell, also known as David Koresh* (Washington, D.C.: Government Printing Office, 1993).

78. Robert Jackson and Lianne Hart, "Trial Begins for 11 Davidians Charged in Waco Murder Conspiracy," *Los Angeles Times,* January 10, 1994.

79. Ibid.

80. Kathy Fair and Wendy Benjaminson, "Profile: Walter S. Smith Jr.: Judge in Cult Trial Rules with Iron Fist," *Houston Chronicle,* January 16, 1994.

81. Hugh Aynesworth, "Waco Judge: 'Smart' and 'Vindictive'," *Washington Times,* January 30, 1994.

82. Kathy Fair and Wendy Benjaminson, "Profile: Walter S. Smith Jr.: Judge in Cult Trial Rules with Iron Fist," *Houston Chronicle,* January 16, 1994.

83. Ibid.

84. Sue Anne Pressley, "An Opportunity for the Branch Davidians," *Washington Post,* January 9, 1994.;

85. Lee Hancock, "Judge Cautions Cult Lawyers about Self-Defense Claims," *Dallas Morning News,* January 11, 1994.

86. Kopel and Blackman, *No More Wacos,* p. 238.

87. Ibid., p. 242.

88. Ibid., p. 241.

89. Department of Justice, Office of Inspector General, "The FBI Laboratory: An Investigation into Laboratory Practices and Alleged Misconduct in Explosives-Related and Other Cases," April 1997.

90. Mark Smith, "5 Davidians Get Maximum Prison Terms," *Houston Chronicle,* June 18, 1994.

91. Lee Hancock, "No-Nonsense Style Defines Waco Judge," *Dallas Morning News,* October 25, 1999.

92. Sam Howe Verhovek, "11 in Texas Sect Are Acquitted of Key Charges," *New York Times,* February 27, 1994.

93. Ibid.

94. Robert Jackson and Lianne Hart, "11 Waco Cultists Are Acquitted of Murder Charges; Trial: Outcome Indicates Jurors Placed Most Blame on the Government," *Los Angeles Times,* February 27, 1994.

95. See Reavis, *Ashes of Waco,* pp. 297-99, and Kopel and Blackman, *No More Wacos,* pp. 243-44.

96. John Parker, "Reno to Ricks in 1994: No One Cares about Waco," *Oklahoma City Daily Oklahoman,* September 4, 1999.

97. "Joint Hearing of the Crime Subcommittee of the House Judiciary Committee and the National Security, International Affairs and Criminal Justice Subcommittee of the House Government Reform and Oversight Committee, Subject: Review of Siege of Branch Davidians' Compound in Waco, Texas," Federal News Service, July 24, 1995.

98. "Transcript of President Clinton's Remarks on *60 Minutes*," U.S. Newswire, April 24, 1995.

99. Janet Reno, Speech to Federal Law Enforcement Agents, Jersey City, New Jersey, May 5, 1995. (Speech text provided by Justice Department press office).

100. Ibid.

101. James Bovard, "Not So Wacko," *New Republic,* May 15, 1995.

102. David E. Sanger, "White House Chief of Staff Calls Attention to Waco a 'Diversion,'" *New York Times,* May 15, 1995.

103. Editorial, "'Callous Disregard,'" *Washington Times,* July 17, 1995.

104. "President Bill Clinton's Remarks to Directors of Federal Law Enforcement Agencies," Federal News Service, July 20, 1995.

105. Christopher Connell, "Treasury Secretary Defends ATF, Voices Concerns about Hearings," Associated Press, July 5, 1995.

106. "Prepared Statement of the Federal Bureau of Investigation Submitted by Larry A. Potts, Before the House Committee on Government Reform and Oversight Subcommittee on International Affairs and Criminal Justice, and the Committee on the Judiciary, Subcommittee on Crime," Federal News Service, July 26, 1995. (emphasis added)

107. "Joint Hearing of the Crime Subcommittee of the House Judiciary Committee and the National Security, International Affairs and Criminal Justice Subcommittee of the House Government Reform and Oversight Committee, Subject: Review of Siege of Branch Davidians' Compound in Waco, Texas," Federal News Service, August 1, 1995.

108. Ibid.

109. Ibid.

110. Ibid.

111. Ibid.

112. "Joint Hearing of the Crime Subcommittee of the House Judiciary Committee and the National Security, International Affairs and Criminal Justice Subcommittee of the House Government Reform and Oversight Committee, Subject: Review of Siege of Branch Davidians' Compound in Waco, Texas," Federal News Service, July 20, 1995.

113. Editorial, "Janet Reno, Torchbearer," *Washington Times,* May 1, 1997.

114. Richard Leiby, "Trial Set in Suit over Davidians' Fiery End," *Washington Post,* July 14, 1999.

115. Michael Sniffen, "Reno Vows to 'Get to the Truth' on Waco," Associated Press, August 27, 1999.

116. Edward Walsh and Richard Leiby, "Reno Says FBI Misled Her about Waco Arms; Thorough Probe Vowed on Use of 'Pyrotechnic' Gas," *Washington Post,* August 27, 1999.

117. Melinda Hennenberger, "As Pressure Builds, Reno Appears Calm," *New York Times,* September 4, 1999,

118. Lee Hancock, "FBI Cameras Encircled Compound, Files Show," *Dallas Morning News,* October 14, 1999.

119. Daniel Klaidman and Michael Isikoff, "A Fire That Won't Die," Newsweek, September 20, 1999.

120. Keith White, "Danforth Breaks with NRA over Ban of Some Assault Weapons, Gannett News Service, November 12, 1993.

121. Letter from John Lott to the author, October 2, 1999.

122. See Jerry Seper, "Deputy in Waco Probe Is Target, Too; Dowd Investigation Focuses on Lobbying," *Washington Times,* September 21, 1999; also, Jerry Seper, "Justice Clears

Ex-U.S. Attorney of Interfering in Referendum, " *Washington Times,* September 24, 1999.

123. Jerry Seper, "Bond Says Report Omits Taxpayer Cost to Target's Campaign," *Washington Times,* October 2, 1999.

124. Jennifer Harper, "McCurry Has Final Words as Top Clinton Spokesman," *Washington Times,* October 2, 1998.

125. Lee Hancock and David Leeson, "Danforth Visits Site of Davidian Siege," *Dallas Morning News,* September 21, 1999.

126. William H. Freivogel and Terry Ganey, "Government's Chief Lawyer in Waco Suit Has Critics among FBI and Davidians," *St. Louis Post-Dispatch,* January 14, 2000.

127. Laurie Kellman, "Waco Probe Stalls in Congress," Associated Press, October 8, 1999.

128. Lee Hancock, "ATF, Military Deny Shots in Final Waco Siege," *Dallas Morning News,* January 26, 2000.

129. Lee Hancock, "Waco Video Analyzed," *Dallas Morning News,* May 11, 2000.

130. Cindy Loose, "Waco Siege Investigator Found Dead In His Home," *Washington Post,* April 29, 2000.

131. See http://www.indirect.com/www/dhardy/Carlos.html.

132. Sarah Foster, "FLIR Expert Had 'Heart Attack'" World Net Daily, May 17, 2000.

133. Tommy Witherspoon, "Justice Department Seeks to Limit Reno Testimony," Cox News Service, March 23, 2000.

134. Lee Hancock, "Reno Testimony Used in Bid to Halt Part of Waco Suit," *Dallas Morning News,* April 6, 2000

135. Ibid.

136. Ibid.

CHAPTER SIXTEEN

1. "Remarks on the Assault Weapons Ban," *Public Papers of the Presidents,* April 6, 1998, p. 582.

2. Senate Committee on the Judiciary, "Ruby Ridge Report of the Subcommittee on Terrorism, Technology and Government Information," Report 95-S522-4, December 1995.

3. "Department of Justice Report Regarding Internal Investigation of Shootings at Ruby Ridge, Idaho, During Arrest of Randy Weaver," Released through Lexis Counsel Connect/American Lawyer Media, June 1995.

4. Ibid.

5. Ibid.

6. Associated Press, "FBI Admits Photos of Idaho Shootout Scenes Were Staged," *Los Angeles Times,* May 28, 1993.

7. Jim Fisher, "Weaver Case: More Comeuppance for the FBI," *Lewiston (Idaho) Morning Tribune,* November 1, 1993.

8. "Department of Justice Report Regarding Internal Investigation of Shootings at Ruby Ridge, Idaho During Arrest of Randy Weaver," Released through Lexis Counsel Connect/American Lawyer Media, June 1995.

9. David Johnston, "U.S. Won't Charge FBI's Sniper in Siege," *New York Times,* December 8, 1994.

10. Author interview with investigative journalist Greg Rushford, November 7, 1999. Rushford wrote about a number of OPR cover-ups while working for *Legal Times* from 1986 to 1994. See also, U.S. General Accounting Office, "Department of Justice: Office of Professional Responsibility's Case-Handling Procedures," March 1995.

11. David Johnston, "U.S. Won't Charge F.B.I.'s Sniper in Siege," *New York Times,* December 8, 1994.

12. Federal Bureau of Investigation National Press Office, "FBI Director Disciplines FBI Employees in Connection with Ruby Ridge Incident," U.S. Newswire, January 6, 1995.
13. Ibid.
14. Ibid.
15. David Johnson, "FBI Chief Reprimands Officials on Their Role in a 1992 Idaho Raid," *New York Times,* January 7, 1995.
16. Jerry Seper, "Freeh Again Clears FBI of Misconduct in Siege," *Washington Times,* February 15, 1995.
17. Federal Bureau of Investigation National Press Office, "FBI Director Disciplines FBI Employees in Connection with Ruby Ridge Incident," U.S. Newswire, January 6, 1995.
18. Frank Scafidi, "Don't Blame the FBI," *Washington Post,* May 15, 1995. Scafidi wrote: "The sniper fired another shot at this suspect and struck him again, but the bullet passed through him and through the open door of the cabin, striking Vicki Weaver who was standing on the other side of the door and out of the sniper's sight." There is no evidence anywhere in the trial record or various federal investigations to support this version of events.
19. Federal Bureau of Investigation National Press Office, "FBI Director Disciplines FBI Employees in Connection with Ruby Ridge Incident," U.S. Newswire, January 6, 1995.
20. Author interview with Chuck Peterson, January 9, 1995.
21. Author interview with Dean Miller, January 9, 1995.
22. James Bovard, "No Accountability at the FBI," *Wall Street Journal,* January 10, 1995; Louis J. Freeh, letter to editor, *Wall Street Journal,* January 26, 1995; and James Bovard, letter to editor, *Wall Street Journal,* February 27, 1995. For an excellent analysis of the government's actions and cover-up, see Alan Bock, *Ambush at Ruby Ridge: How Government Agents Set Randy Weaver Up and Took His Family Down* (Irvine, Cal.: Dickens Press, 1995).
23. *Ruby Ridge,* Senate Judiciary Committee, Senate Report 95-S522-4, December 1995.
24. Michael Sniffen, "FBI's No. 2 Official among 12 Disciplined in Idaho Shootout," Associated Press, January 6, 1995.
25. Ibid.
26. Editorial, "Ruby Ridge and Waco," *Washington Post,* January 9, 1995.
27. Editorial, "The Guns of Waco and Ruby Ridge," *New York Times,* July 14, 1995.
28. James Bovard, "I Hear No Evil," *American Spectator,* January, 1996.
29. "Department of Justice Report Regarding Internal Investigation of Shootings at Ruby Ridge, Idaho During Arrest of Randy Weaver," Released through Lexis Counsel Connect/American Lawyer Media, June 1995.
30. Ibid.
31. Pierre Thomas and Serge F. Kovaleski, "Justice Dept. Pledges Thorough Probe of FBI Conduct in 1992 Idaho Siege," *Washington Post,* July 14, 1995.
32. Ronald Ostrow, "Freeh Suspends 4 FBI Officials in Siege Probe," *Los Angeles Times,* August 12, 1995.
33. George Lardner and Pierre Thomas, "U.S. to Pay Family in FBI Idaho Raid; Weaver, Children to Receive $3.1 Million," *Washington Post,* August 16, 1995.
34. Department of Justice, press release, "Civil Suits Settled in Ruby Ridge Case," August 15, 1995.
35. Ronald J. Ostrow, "FBI Hailed Amid Howls over Ruby Ridge," *Los Angeles Times,* August 18, 1995.
36. "Hearing of the Terrorism, Technology and Government Information Subcommittee of the Senate Judiciary Committee, Subject: Ruby Ridge," Federal News Service, September 7, 1995.

37. "Senate Judiciary Committee, Terrorism, Technology and Government Information Sub-committee, Subject: Federal Raid in Ruby Ridge, Idaho," Federal News Service, September 9, 1995.

38. "Director Freeh Testifies at Hearing into Action of Federal Agents at Ruby Ridge, Idaho; Washington D.C.," Federal Document Clearing House, October 19, 1995,

39. Ibid.

40. "Hearing of the Terrorism, Technology and Government Information Subcommittee of the Senate Judiciary Committee, Subject: Federal Raid at Ruby Ridge," Federal News Service, October 18, 1995.

41. "Hearing of the Senate Judiciary Committee, Terrorism, Technology and Government Information Subcommittee, Subject: Incident at Ruby Ridge," Federal News Service, October 13, 1995,

42. Senate Judiciary Committee, *Ruby Ridge,* Senate Report 95-S522-4, December 1995.

43. John Hanchette, "Ruby Ridge Hearings Underscore FBI's Internal Turmoil," Gannett News Service, September 22, 1995.

44. "Ruby Ridge: Report of the Subcommittee on Terrorism, Technology and Government Information of the Senate Committee on the Judiciary," Senate Report 95- S522-4, December 1995.

45. Ibid.

46. Author interview with David Nevin, November 22, 1995.

47. James Bovard, "They Call This Valor?" *Wall Street Journal,* March 13, 1996.

48. "Five Deputies in Weaver Siege Win Bravery Awards" *Seattle Post-Intelligencer,* March 2, 1996. See also, Transcript, United States Marshals Service—Director's Honorary Awards Ceremony, U.S. Marshals Service Aircraft hangar, Oklahoma City, Oklahoma, March 1, 1996.

49. "Department of Justice Report Regarding Internal Investigation of Shootings at Ruby Ridge, Idaho, During Arrest of Randy Weaver," Released through Lexis Counsel Connect/American Lawyer Media, June 1995.

50. "Ruby Ridge: Report of the Subcommittee on Terrorism, Technology and Government Information of the Senate Committee on the Judiciary," Senate Report 95-S522-4, December 1995.

51. "Department of Justice Report Regarding Internal Investigation of Shootings at Ruby Ridge, Idaho, During Arrest of Randy Weaver," Released through Lexis Counsel Connect/American Lawyer Media, June 1995.

52. "Ruby Ridge," Report of the Subcommittee on Terrorism, Technology and Government Information of the Senate Committee on the Judiciary, December 1995, p 49-50.

53. *Kevin Harris v. Arthur Roderick, Lon T. Horiuch, et at.,* 126 F. 3d 1189 (1997).

54. Ibid.

55. Jerry Seper, "FBI Agent Gets Full Pension in Plea Deal," *Washington Times,* November 1, 1996.

56. James Bovard, "Another Justice Cover-Up: Ruby Ridge Goes the Way of the Fundraising Scandals," *American Spectator,* December 1997.

57. *Harris v. Roderick et al.,* 126 F. 3d 1189 (1997).

58. Daniel Klaidman, "The Standoff Never Ends," *Newsweek,* September 1, 1997.

59. Daniel Klaidman and Michael Isikoff, "Facing More Fire at the FBI," *Newsweek,* October 18, 1999.

60. Jerry Seper, "Ruby Ridge Charges Brought," *Washington Times,* August 22, 1997.

61. George Lardner, "U.S. Argues Idaho Can't Prosecute FBI Sniper," *Washington Post,* March 14, 1998.

62. *State of Idaho v. Lon Horiuchi,* Case no. CR 97-097-N-EJL, May 14, 1998.

CHAPTER SEVENTEEN

1. Kim Eisler, "Reno Seems Ready to Leave Justice to Be Law School Dean," *Washingtonian,* August, 1999.
2. Janet Reno, Speech to Federal Law Enforcement Officers, Jersey City, New Jersey, May 5, 1995.
3. "Criminal Law Symposium: Lifetime Achievement Award Presented to Attorney General Janet Reno," *St. Thomas Law Review,* vol. 9, Spring 1997, p. 483.
4. Rory Little, "Who Should Regulate the Ethics of Federal Prosecutors?" *Fordham Law Review,* vol. 65, October 1996, p. 355.
5. Heather Mactavish, "Janet Reno's Approach to Criminal Justice," *UCLA Women's Law Journal,* vol. 4, 1993, p. 113.
6. Allen Beck and Christopher Mumola, *Prisoners in 1998,* U.S. Department of Justice, Bureau of Justice Statistics, August 1999.
7. Melinda Beck with Bob Cohn, "Reno's Darkest Hour," *Newsweek,* July 31, 1995.
8. "Hearing of the Senate Commerce, Science and Transportation Committee, Subject: TV Violence," Federal News Service, October 20, 1993.
9. Ellen Edwards, "Reno: End TV Violence," *Washington Post,* October 21, 1993.
10. Peter H. Lewis, "Judges Turn Back Law to Regulate Internet Decency," *New York Times,* June 13, 1996.
11. "Weekly Press Availability with Attorney General Janet Reno," Federal News Service, March 13, 1997.
12. "ACLU Says Justice Dept. Seeks to Criminalize Internet Speech," Newsbytes, January 23, 1997.
13. Ibid.
14. Jeff Jacoby, "Microsoft's Real Crime: Success," *Boston Globe,* October 22, 1998.
15. "Justice Department News Conference, Subject: Judge's Findings of Fact in Microsoft Antitrust Case," Federal News Service, November 5, 1999.
16. For a good analysis of the flawed nature of the government's case, see Stan Liebowitz and Stephen Margolis, *Winners, Losers, and Microsoft* (Oakland, Cal: Independent Institute, 1998).
17. Editorial, "Where There Is Smoke," *Washington Times,* September 27, 1999.
18. Laura Mansnerus, "Tobacco on Trial: Making a Case for Death," *New York Times,* May 5, 1996.
19. Editorial, "Lighten Up," *Investor's Business Daily,* March 31, 1994.
20. "Clinton Terrorists' Gun Law Violations," *American Rifleman,* November/December 1999.
21. Neil Lewis, "Records Show Puerto Ricans Got U.S. Help with Clemency," *New York Times,* October 21, 1999.
22. Robert Mott, "Clemency for Terrorists Raises Valid Questions," *Sacramento Bee,* October 26, 1999.
23. "Clinton Increased Threat of FALN," *State Journal-Register* (Springfield, IL), October 26, 1999.
24. Ibid.
25. Jerry Seper, "Babbitt and Rubin 'Fined' $625,000 for Their 'Misdeeds,'" *Washington Times,* August 11, 1999.

26. Jerry Seper, "Treasury Shredded Indian-Trust Documents," *Washington Times,* December 7, 1999.
27. Ibid.
28. Ibid.
29. William Rempel and Alan Miller, "Funds Probe Unfairly Spared White House, '98 Report Says," *Los Angeles Times,* March 10, 2000.
30. Editorial, "Justice Delayed and Derailed," *New York Times,* July 15, 1998.
31. Jerry Seper, "Justice Official Ordered Halt to Probe of Gore," *Washington Times,* March 14, 2000.
32. Richard Berke and Katharine Seelye, "Gore to Embrace Campaign Finance as Central Theme," *New York Times,* March 12, 2000.
33. "Hearing of the Senate Governmental Affairs Committee, Subject: Independent Reauthorization," Federal News Service, May 14, 1993.
34. "Weekly Media Briefing with Attorney General Janet Reno, Justice Department, Washington, D.C.," Federal News Service, June 24, 1999.
35. "Clinton Asks for Hate-Law Expansion," Associated Press, April 6, 1999.
36. "Remarks at an Access Now for Gay and Lesbian Equality Dinner in Beverly Hills, California," *Public Papers of the Presidents,* October 2, 1999 , p. 1901.
37. "Remarks to the Voices Against Violence Conference," *Public Papers of the Presidents,* October 19, 1999, p. 2083.
38. See http://www.usdoj.gov/kidspage/bias-k-5/index.htm.
39. Ibid.
40. Nat Hentoff, "Unjust Criticism from Justice," *Washington Post,* May 30, 1998.
41. Quoted in editorial, "Hate Crimes, Thought Police?" *Investor's Business Daily,* November 23, 1998.
42. Quoted in Richard Dooling, "Punish Crime, Not Hate," *Wall Street Journal,* July 20, 1998.
43. Ibid.
44. "Remarks Announcing Community Policing Grants," *Public Papers of the Presidents,* October 12, 1994, p. 1992.
45. "The President's Radio Address," *Public Papers of the Presidents,* February 11, 1995, p. 231.
46. "Speeches by Vice President Al Gore and Tipper Gore Following the Super Tuesday Primaries," Federal News Service, March 7, 2000.
47. Ian Trontz, "Money for Additional Police Officers Fails to Add Up," *Palm Beach Post,* August 17, 1998.
48. "Police Grants Don't Always Mean New Officers or Long-term Employees," Associated Press, August 16, 1999.
49. Matt Kelley, "Funding for Computers Calculated as Officers," *Omaha World-Herald,* May 16, 1999.
50. Michael Berens and Gary Marx, "Phantom Force," *Chicago Tribune,* May 16, 1999.
51. Matt Kelley, "Audit Faults Grants for New Officers Justice Department Findings," *Omaha World-Herald,* May 16, 1999.
52. U.S. Department of Justice, Office of Inspector General, "Management and Administration of the Community Oriented Policing Services Grant Program," Audit No. 99-21, July 1999.
53. Ibid.
54. Ibid.
55. Matt Kelley, "Audit Faults Grants For New Officers Justice Department Findings," *Omaha World-Herald,* May 16, 1999.
56. Michael Berens and Gary Marx, "Phantom Force," *Chicago Tribune,* May 16, 1999.
57. Ibid.

58. Ibid.

59. Ibid.

60. "Remarks by Louis Freeh, Director, Federal Bureau of Investigation, at the 106th Annual Commencement Ceremonies, The Catholic University of America, Washington, D.C., May 13, 1995" (distributed by FBI Press Office).

61. Louis Freeh, "Ensuring Public Safety and National Security under the Rule of Law: A Report to the American People on the Work of the FBI, 1993-1998," Federal Bureau of Investigation, 1998.

62. Ibid.

63. The case against Sessions was weaker than it was portrayed by most of the media. For an analysis of the shakiness of some of the criticism of Sessions, see Greg Rushford, "Sessions' Trials and Errors," *Legal Times,* February 8, 1993.

64. Scott Tyson, "Turf Wars Ensnare Plain-Talking FBI Chief," *Christian Science Monitor,* October 1, 1999.

65. Daniel Klaidman, "Pushing the FBI into the 21st Century," *American Lawyer,* October 1994.

66. Louis Freeh, "Ensuring Public Safety and National Security under the Rule of Law: A Report to the American People on the Work of the FBI, 1993-1998," Federal Bureau of Investigation, 1998.

67. Ronald Ostrow, "Budget Cuts Left FBI Short on Ammo, Freeh Says," *Los Angeles Times,* November 18, 1994.

68. Al Kamen, "The Bureau Branches Out," *Washington Post,* July 11, 1994.

69. Roberto Suro, "Law Enforcement Ethics: A New Code for Agents," *Washington Post,* August 21, 1997.

70. Jeff Taylor, "FBI: Incompetent or Political?" *Investor's Business Daily,* September 30, 1997.

71. Jerry Seper, "Senator Raps FBI Report on Jewell Interrogation," *Washington Times,* July 29, 1997.

72. Jerry Seper, "Panel to Hear of FBI's Jewell Queries," *Washington Times,* July 28, 1997.

73. "The President's News Conference with Prime Minister Howard in Canberra," *Public Papers of the Presidents,* November 20, 1996, p. 2408.

74. Editorial, "John Huang's Tale," *Washington Times,* December 20, 1999.

75. Quoted in Doug Bandow, "Victim-in-Chief," *Washington Times,* November 30, 1999.

76. Daniel Klaidman and Evan Thomas, "The Victim of His Virtues," *Newsweek,* April 14, 1997.

77. "Clinton Defends Purposes of FBI Clearance List," CNN, Transcript #1251-1, June 9, 1996.

78. Ibid.

79. Editorial, "Filegate: The Invisible Scandal," *Investor's Business Daily,* June 20, 1997.

80. George Lardner, "Many Notified After FBI 'Heads-Up'," *Washington Post,* August 2, 1996.

81. U.S. House of Representatives, "Investigation into the White House and Department of Justice on Security of FBI Background Investigation Files," House Rpt. 104-862, September 28, 1996.

82. Ibid.

83. Ibid.

84. William Safire, "Air the Facts on 'Filegate,'" *Denver Post,* July 24, 1998.

85. William F. Clinger, "White House, FBI Both at Fault in 'Filegate'," *The Hill,* July 31, 1996.

86. "Investigation into the White House and Department of Justice on Security of FBI Background Investigation Files," House Rpt. 104-862, U.S. House of Representatives, September 28, 1996.

87. Charles V. Zehren, "FBI Counsel Rapped," *Newsday,* March 29, 1997.

88. "FBI Counsel Shapiro Leaving," Associated Press, May 22, 1997.

89. Office of Inspector General, "The FBI Laboratory: An Investigation into Laboratory Practices and Alleged Misconduct in Explosives-Related and Other Cases," U.S. Department of Justice, April, 1997.

90. Ibid.

91. Ibid.

92. Kim Weissman, "Congress Action," May 18, 1997.

93. David Burnham, "Bumblers in the Bureau," review of *Tainting Evidence,* by John F. Kelly and Phillip K. Wearne, *Washington Post,* June 21, 1998.

94. Stuart Taylor, "Watching the Detectives," *American Lawyer,* October 1997.

95. Jerry Seper, "Freeh Misled Congress, IG Says,*" Washington Times,* March 18, 1997.

96. Ibid.

97. "FBI to Pay Whistleblower $1.16M," Associated Press, February 26, 1998.

98. Michael Grunwald, "'Minimal' Punishment Meted in FBI Lab Flap; Critics Call Justice Dept. Report Whitewash," *Washington Post,* August 6, 1998.

99. Michael Sniffen, "Justice Censures FBI Lab Workers," Associated Press, August 7, 1998.

100. "Hearing of the Senate Judiciary Committee, Subject: Federal Bureau of Investigation Operations," Federal News Service, June 4, 1997.

101. Christopher Kerr, "Flawed Process That Led FBI's Ruby Ridge Inquiry Astray," *Washington Times,* September 15, 1995.

102. David Burnham, "The F.B.I.," *Nation,* August 11, 1997.

103. Ibid.

104. Ibid.

105. David Vise and Lorraine Adams, "FBI Chief Wants Job in Private Sector; Facing Financial Pressure, Freeh Seeks to Leave This Year," *Washington Post,* April 4, 2000.

CHAPTER EIGHTEEN

1. "Remarks to the 54th Session of the United Nations General Assembly in New York City," *Public Papers of the Presidents,* September 21, 1999, p. 1779.

2. David Binder, "In Yugoslavia, Rising Ethnic Strife Brings Fears of Worse Civil Conflict," *New York Times,* November 1, 1987.

3. Ibid.

4. "Address to the Nation on the Military-Technical Agreement on Kosovo," *Public Papers of the Presidents,* June 10, 1999, p. 1074.

5. Doug Bandow, "NATO's Hypocritical Humanitarianism," in Ted Carpenter, editor, *NATO's Empty Victory,* (Washington, D.C.: Cato Institute, 2000), p. 38.

6. Boris Johnson, "Cold War Warrior Scorns 'New Morality,'" *The Daily Telegraph* (London), June 28, 1999.

7. Quoted in Wlady Pleszczynski, "To Lie for Kosovo," American Spectator Online, March 27, 2000.

8. "Remarks Announcing Airstrikes against Serbian Targets in the Federal Republic of Yugoslavia (Serbia and Montenegro)," *Public Papers of the Presidents,* March 24, 1999, p. 513.

9. John Pilger, "Revealed: The Amazing NATO Plan, Tabled at Rambouillet, To Occupy Yugoslavia," *New Statesman,* May 17, 1999.

10. Boris Johnson, "Cold War Warrior Scorns 'New Morality,'" *The Daily Telegraph* (London), June 28, 1999.

11. George Kenney, "Rolling Thunder: The Rerun," *Nation,* June 14, 1999.

12. Alexander Cockburn, "Hillary Clinton-Style Social-Worker Liberalism Has Some Dark Areas," *Los Angeles Times,* August 19, 1999.
13. "Author Gail Sheehy Discusses her New Book, *Hillary's Choice,"* CNBC News Transcripts, *Hardball with Chris Matthews,* December 27, 1999.
14. Alexander Cockburn, "Hillary Clinton-Style Social-Worker Liberalism Has Some Dark Areas," *Los Angeles Times,* August 19, 1999.
15. "The President's Radio Address," *Public Papers of the Presidents,* March 27, 1999, p. 531.
16. "Clinton Remarks at Memorial Day Service," U.S. Newswire, May 31, 1999.
17. "Remarks to the Veterans of Foreign Wars of the United States at Fort McNair," *Public Papers of the Presidents,* May 13, 1999, p. 879.
18. Lee Hockstader, "Holocaust Memories Contribute to Israeli Ambivalence on Kosovo," *Washington Post,* April 1, 1999.
19. AP, "Ariel Sharon Fears Refugee 'Terrorists,'" *New York Times,* April 7, 1999.
20. Ivo H. Daalder, "What Holbrooke Wrought," *Weekly Standard,* June 28, 1999.
21. Francis X. Clines and Steven Lee Myers, "Conflict in the Balkans: The Overview," *New York Times,* March 27, 1999.
22. "Videotape Address to the Serbian People," *Public Papers of the Presidents,* March 25, 1999, p. 520.
23. Richard Boudreaux, "Civilian Deaths in Airstrikes Erode NATO Credibility," *Los Angeles Times,* May 31, 1999.
24. "Civilian Deaths in the NATO Air Campaign," Human Rights Watch, February 7, 2000.
25. Richard Norton-Taylor, "NATO Cluster Bombs Kill 15 in Hospital and Crowded Market and Hospital," *The Manchester Guardian,* May 8, 1999.
26. W. F. Deedes, "NATO's Deadly Legacy Will Cause Years of Suffering," *Daily Telegraph,* September 13, 1999.
27. "William Cohen Holds Defense Department Briefing," *Federal Document Clearinghouse Political Transcripts,* April 7, 1999.
28. George Will, "Plan for Kosovo shows Clinton Administration's Bewilderment," *Seattle Post-Intelligencer,* April 29, 1999.
29. Daniel Pearl, "War in Kosovo Was Cruel, Bitter, Savage; Genocide It Wasn't," *Wall Street Journal,* December 31, 1999. The article also noted: "Ethnic-Albanian militants, humanitarian organizations, NATO and the news media fed off each other to give genocide rumors credibility."
30. "President William J. Clinton Delivers Remarks on Kosovo; Fort McNair, President William J. Clinton," Federal Document Clearing House, Political Transcripts, May 13, 1999.
31. Ibid.
32. "Remarks by Secretary of Defense William Cohen at Commencement of Graduating Class, U.S. Naval Academy," Federal News Service, MAY 26, 1999.
33. Brian Mitchell, "Body Count So Far Doesn't Support Charges of 'Genocide,'" *Investor's Business Daily,* November 17, 1999.
34. Ibid.
35. Arianna Huffington, "Clinton Plays into Milosevic's Hand," *Chicago Sun-Times,* April 11, 1999.
36. Robert Salladay, "Attack on Yugoslavia," *San Francisco Examiner,* April 16, 1999.
37. Bradley Graham, "Pentagon's Doses of Data May Obscure Air War Effect," *Washington Post,* May 24, 1999.
38. Ibid.
39. James Kitfield, "Command and Control the Messenger," *National Journal,* September 11, 1999.

40. Ibid.

41. Anne Pandolfi, "Study Finds Much TV Coverage of Kosovo Supported Clinton," Associated Press, July 19, 1999.

42. "NATO Briefing Regarding the Situation in Kosovo, Briefer: Gen. Wesley Clark, NATO Supreme Commander," *Federal News Service,* April 13, 1999.

43. "NATO Accused over Misleading Videos," Associated Press, January 6, 2000.

44. Patrick J. Sloyan, "Wrong Pilot Blamed for Convoy Attack; 'A Deliberate Misrepresentation,'" *Newsday,* April 18, 1999.

45. Ibid.

46. Ibid.

47. Paul Richter, "Milosevic Not Home as NATO Bombs One of his residences," *Los Angeles Times,* April 23, 1999.

48. John F. Harris, "Clinton Asks Public to Be Patient with NATO Bombing Campaign," Washington Post, April 25, 1999.

49. Ibid.

50. Lara Marlowe, "'They'll Hit Bakeries Next, Since Soldiers Eat Bread!,'" *Irish Times,* April 26, 1999.

51. "War Powers Act Case Dismissed," *National Law Journal,* June 21, 1999.

52. Robert Novak , "NATO Commander's Belligerency Showing," *Houston Chronicle,* May 6, 1999.

53. John F. Harris, "In Handling of Crisis, a Different President; Aides Note Clinton's Calm, Steady Focus," *Washington Post,* June 8, 1999.

54. Ibid.

55. Ibid.

56. "Address to the Nation on the Military Technical Agreement on Kosovo," *Public Papers of the Presidents,* June 10, 1999, p. 1074.

57. Alan Kuperman, " Kosovo Deal Represents 'Botched Diplomacy," letter to editor, *USA Today,* June 14, 1999.

58. Robert Fisk, "The Trojan Horse That 'Started' a 79-Day War," *Independent* (London), November 26, 1999.

59. "Remarks at Whiteman Air Force Base in Knob Noster, Missouri," *Public Papers of the Presidents,* June 11, 1999, p. 1085.

60. John Barry and Evan Thomas, "The Kosovo Cover-Up," *Newsweek,* May 15, 2000.

61. Ibid.

62. Nicholas Rufford, "Cook Accused of Misleading Public on Kosovo Massacres," *Sunday Times* (London), October 31, 1999.

63. "Videotape Address to the Serbian People," *Public Papers of the Presidents,* March 25, 1999, p. 520.

64. "Transcript of Clinton Remarks to the Troops and Officers of U.S. Task Force Falcon, Including 1st Infantry Troops," U.S. Newswire, November 23, 1999.

65. Ibid.

66. Editorial, "The Wreck of Kosovo," *Boston Globe,* November 27, 1999.

67. Peter Finn, "NATO Losing Kosovo Battle, *Washington Post,* August 4, 1999.

68. Robert Fisk, "Serbs Murdered by the Hundred Since 'Liberation,'" *Independent* (London), November 24, 1999.

69. Michael Kelly, "Kosovo's Killers," *Washington Post,* December 8, 1999.

70. Eve-Ann Prentice, "Kosovo's Bleak Midwinter," *Times* (London), January 3, 2000.

71. Paul Watson and Scott Martelle, "Kosovo: Army Accuses NATO of Violating Peace Agreement," *Los Angeles Times,* September 12, 1999.

72. Paul Watson, "Christian Sites Being Decimated in Kosovo," *Los Angeles Times*, September 22, 1999.

73. Robert Fisk, "Was it Rescue or Revenge?" *Independent* (London), June 21, 1999.

74. "Transcript of Clinton Remarks to the Troops and Officers of U.S. Task Force Falcon, Including 1st Infantry Troops," U.S. Newswire, November 23, 1999.

75. Paul Watson, "Extremist Albanians Target Moderates in Kosovo Strife," *Los Angeles Times*, November 20, 1999.

76. Steven Lee Myers, "Clinton Opposes a Plan by Allies to Give Serbs Aid," *New York Times*, October 11, 1999.

77. Ibid.

78. Ibid.

79. Steven Erlanger, "Serbs Reject U.S. Plan Linking End of Sanctions to Free Vote," *New York Times*, November 6, 1999

80. "Transcript of Clinton Remarks to U.S. Troops following the Thanksgiving Week Meal," U.S. Newswire, November 23, 1999.

81. "The President's News Conference," *Public Papers of the Presidents*, December 8, 1999, p. 2537.

82. "Remarks at the Opening of the Organization for Security and Cooperation in Europe Summit in Istanbul," *Public Papers of the Presidents*, November 18, 1999, p. 2395.

83. "Clinton Hails Yeltsin," Associated Press, January 2, 2000.

84. Jeremy Rabkin, "World-Wide Scofflaw: The War on Yugoslavia Is an International Crime," *American Spectator*, May 1999.

85. Henry A. Kissinger, "New World Disorder," *Newsweek*, May 31, 1999

86. "Interview with Wolf Blitzer of Cable News Network's 'Late Edition,'" *Public Papers of the Presidents*, June 20, 1999, p. 1143.

87. Edward Cody, "Out of Work and Hope, Serbs Evacuate Kosovo," *Washington Post*, February 17, 2000.

88. William Pfaff, "The News From The Kosovo-Serbia Border Is Bad," *International Herald Tribune*, March 9, 2000.

89. Naomi Koppel, "Ground Troops Urged for Yugoslavia," Associated Press, March 29, 2000.

90. Jane Perlez, "Spiral of Violence in Kosovo Divides U.S. and Its Allies," *New York Times*, March 12, 2000.

CHAPTER NINETEEN

1. Elizabeth Shogren, "Clinton to Bypass Congress in Blitz of Executive Orders," *Los Angeles Times*, July 4, 1998.

2. James Bennet, "True to Form, Clinton Shifts Energies Back to U.S. Focus," *New York Times*, July 5, 1998.

3. "Executive Order 13083—Federalism," *Public Papers of the Presidents*, May 14, 1998, p. 866.

4. John Godfrey and Paul Bedard, "Conservatives Blast Executive Order," *Washington Times*, July 29, 1998.

5. "Clinton Suspends Executive Order on Federalism," Associated Press, August 6, 1998.

6. Frank Swaboda and Kirstin Downey Grimsley, "OSHA Covers At-Home Workers," *Washington Post*, January 4, 2000.

7. Ibid.

8. Cindy Skrzycki, "The Regulators: Lawmakers Examine 'Guidance,'" *Washington Post*, January 14, 2000.

9. Declan McCullagh, "The Seedy Side of the FCC," *Wired News*, September 28, 1999.
10. Ibid.
11. "CBS News Unveiled Its Compassion for Janet Reno, Fidel Castro, and Photographed INS Gunman," Media Research Center, April 24, 2000.
12. "Janet Reno Holds News Conference on the Retrieval of Elian Gonzalez," Federal Document Clearing House, April 22, 2000.
13. Ibid.
14. "Joe Lockhart Holds News Conference on the INS Raid to Retrieve Elian Gonzalez," Federal Document Clearing House, April 22, 2000.
15. "President William J. Clinton Delivers Remarks on the INS Retrieval of Elian Gonzalez," Federal Document Clearing House, April 22, 2000.
16. Laurence Tribe, "Justice Taken Too Far," *New York Times,* April 25, 2000.
17. "CBS News Unveiled Its Compassion for Janet Reno, Fidel Castro, and Photographed INS Gunman," Media Research Center, April 24, 2000.
18. Howard Kurtz, "Media Tilt Towards One Photo," *Washington Post,* April 24, 2000.
19. David Vise, "Reno Allowed Photos During Elian Siege," *Washington Post,* April 25, 2000.
20. The *New York Times* reported that "the newspaper's top editors believed that the photo of the agent with the assault rifle needed to be put in context, because it was not clear where the gun was pointed and whether the agent's finger was on the trigger. The editors decided to run that photo with an article by one of the newspaper's media critics about the photos and how they were used." Melody Petersen, "Deciding Which Photograph Best Captured Day's Events," *New York Times,* April 24, 2000.
21. Thomas Friedman, "Reno for President," *New York Times,* April 25, 2000.
22. Garry Wills, "Conjuring Evil," *New York Times,* April 25, 2000.
23. Clinton's final five-year budget proposal would result in a net tax cut of only $4.4 billion; in contrast, spending would increase $343 billion. Daniel Mitchell, "Clinton Proposal Would Make U.S. Tax Code Even Worse," *Bridge News,* February 10, 2000; "Roth Statement at Finance Hearing on Clinton Fiscal 2001 Budget," *Tax Notes Today,* February 9, 2000.
24. Jonathan Peterson, "Gore Defends Fund-raising Efforts As Legal," *Los Angeles Times*, March 4, 1997.
25. "Remarks by President Bill Clinton at National Prayer Breakfast," Federal News Service, February 4, 1999.
26. Bruce R. Dold, "GOP Foolishness Overshadows Clinton's Errors," *Chicago Tribune,* July 25, 1997.
27. "Remarks at a Democratic National Committee Dinner," *Public Papers of the Presidents*, August 2, 1999, p. 1544.
28. Paul Light, "The True Size of Government," *Government Executive,* January 1999.
29. Robert J. Samuelson, "Our Growing Government," *Washington Post,* February 16, 2000.
30. For a detailed analysis of attention deficit democracy, see James Bovard, *Freedom in Chains* (New York: St. Martin's Press, 1999), pp. 97-139.

Index